CELEBRATING
50 YEARS

Texas A&M University Press
publishing since 1974

THE LOST WAR FOR TEXAS

Vistas, Sponsored by Texas A&M University–San Antonio

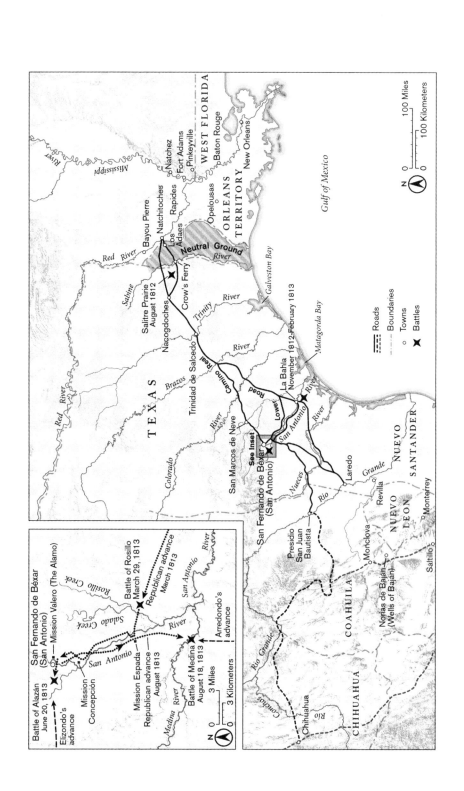

THE LOST WAR FOR TEXAS

Mexican Rebels, American Burrites, and the Texas Revolution of 1811

James Aalan Bernsen

TEXAS A&M UNIVERSITY PRESS | College Station

Copyright © 2024 by James A. Bernsen
All rights reserved

First edition

∞ This paper meets the requirements of ANSI/NISO Z39.48–1992 (Permanence of Paper). Binding materials have been chosen for durability.

Library of Congress Cataloging-in-Publication Data

Names: Bernsen, James Aalan, 1971– author.
Title: The lost war for Texas: Mexican rebels, American Burrites, and the Texas Revolution of 1811 / James Aalan Bernsen.
Other titles: Vistas (Series: College Station, Tex.)
Description: First edition. | College Station: Texas A&M University Press, [2024] | Series: Vistas, sponsored by Texas A & University San Antonio | Includes bibliographical references and index.
Identifiers: LCCN 2023058501 (print) | LCCN 2023058502 (ebook) | ISBN 9781648431739 (cloth) | ISBN 9781648431746 (ebook)
Subjects: LCSH: Gutiérrez-Magee Expedition, 1812–1813. | Burr Conspiracy, 1805-1807. | Filibusters—Texas—Biography. | Revolutionaries—Texas—Biography. | Texas—History—1810–1821. | Mexico—History—Wars of Independence, 1810-1821. | BISAC: HISTORY / United States / State & Local / Southwest (AZ, NM, OK, TX) | HISTORY / United States / State & Local / General
Classification: LCC F389 .B37 2024 (print) | LCC F389 (ebook) | DDC 976.4/02—dc23/eng/20240108
LC record available at https://lccn.loc.gov/2023058501
LC ebook record available at https://lccn.loc.gov/2023058502

To Stephanie and Diego

Contents

Key Characters ix
Acknowledgments xi

Introduction *1*
Chapter 1. The Great Conspiracy *12*
Chapter 2. The Edge of Empire *32*
Chapter 3. Romantics and Rogues *48*
Chapter 4. West Florida and Texas *64*
Chapter 5. The Secret Agent *74*
Chapter 6. The Tejano Revolt *88*
Chapter 7. Intrigue on the Frontier *105*
Chapter 8. Rebels in Exile *120*
Chapter 9. Encounter in New Orleans *132*
Chapter 10. The Expedition Forms *144*
Chapter 11. Racing toward War *159*
Chapter 12. The Rebels Strike *173*
Chapter 13. The Republican Army of the North *186*
Chapter 14. Trinidad to La Bahía *204*
Chapter 15. Toledo's Band *215*
Chapter 16. The Siege *222*
Chapter 17. Rebels Victorious *233*
Chapter 18. Murder on the Salado *246*
Chapter 19. Royalist Resurgence *260*
Chapter 20. The Fate of Texas *275*
Chapter 21. The Battle of Medina *294*
Chapter 22. Rebels Never Quit *316*

Chapter 23. The Return to Texas   *330*
Chapter 24. Epilogue   *347*

Appendix A: *List of Mexican/Tejano Rebels*   *361*
Appendix B: *List of Foreign Volunteers in the Republican Army of the North*   *363*
Notes   *367*
Bibliography   *457*
Index   *471*

Key Characters

Rebels

Augustus Magee	US Army Lieutenant who resigns to lead the Republican Army
José Bernardo Gutiérrez de Lara	Mexican revolutionary who organizes and leads the filibuster into Texas
José Álvarez de Toledo	Cuban revolutionary who succeeded Gutiérrez as political leader in Texas
Samuel Kemper	Second Commander of the Republican Army
Reuben Ross	Third Commander of the Republican Army
Henry Perry	Fourth Commander of the Republican Army. Leads later filibusters in Mexico.
Miguel Menchaca	Mexican Captain in the Republican Army of the North
José Menchaca	Former Spanish officer who led a brief filibuster in 1811 before switching sides and abandoning his army
Antonio Delgado	Mexican Captain in the Republican Army of the North, responsible for the execution of royalist officers
Juan Bautista de las Casas	Leads the Casas Revolt in San Antonio, January 1811

Spaniards

Joaquín de Arredondo	Spanish General who campaigns against rebels in Northern Mexico and defeated the republicans at the Battle of Medina, 1813

Ignacio Elizondo	Spanish Lieutenant Colonel from Nuevo Leon who changed to the rebel side before switching back and joining forces with Gen. Joaquín Arredondo to reconquer Texas
Nemesio de Salcedo	Spanish Commandant General of the Interior Provinces
Manuel de Salcedo	Spanish Governor of Texas
Simón de Herrera	Spanish Governor of Nuevo Leon, ordered to Texas as military commander
Juan José Manuel Zambrano	Leads coup against the revolutionary Casas regime, March 1811

Americans

William Shaler	US Special Agent to the Cuban and Mexican provinces
John H. Robinson	US Special Agent to the Spanish Commandant General of the Interior Provinces
Robert Smith	US Secretary of State, 1809–11
James Monroe	US Secretary of State, 1811–17
W. C. C. Claiborne	Governor of the Orleans Territory
Daniel Clark	New Orleans businessman/politician. Leads opposition to Governor Claiborne, affiliated with the Mexican Association.
James Workman	President of the Mexican Association
Lewis Kerr	Key leader of the Mexican Association
James Wilkinson	General in the US Army. Supports and then betrays the Burr conspiracy.

Acknowledgments

There are many people who deserve sincere thanks for helping me along the road that led to this book, starting with my parents, who taught me that learning takes a lifetime and never ends. I was also blessed to work with two great mentors, the late Dr. Arnold Krammer of Texas A&M University, who inspired my love of history, and Dr. Jesús "Frank" de la Teja of Texas State University. Frank gave freely of his time, wisdom, and unparalleled insight into late Spanish colonial history in Texas, even after he allegedly retired. If any of my work appears to be that of more than an amateur historian, it is due to his insight, patience, and his irreplaceable role as a sounding board for ideas and theories.

Several other gifted historians assisted me in reviewing the manuscript and providing insights into the time period: Dr. Bradley Folsom, Dr. Stephen Hardin, Dr. William C. Davis, and Dr. David Carlson. I also benefitted greatly from the insights of gifted amateurs. Tom Green, one of the pillars of the small group of Battle of Medina enthusiasts in Atascosa County, Texas, kindly shared his layman's research. Brian Stauffer of the Texas General Land Office graciously helped with translating a number of crucial documents. Dr. Daniel Degges provided his insight into the Mexican Association. Rick Detwiller of Boston, Massachusetts, provided me with his own research, which helped me expand on the background of Augustus Magee. Scott McMahon of the Presidio La Bahía helped me visualize how the siege took place. David McKenzie, a reader of my blog, stumbled upon a trove of heretofore undiscovered—and invaluable—documents in the National Archives and shared them with me. There were many others whose passion has helped me on my journey: Ben Pease, Brian Hendrix, Lawrence L'Herrison, Martha Fleitas, Ricardo Rodriguez, Jody Edward Ginn, Michael Cage, and Brandon Seale.

I'd like to thank the staffs of the Briscoe Center for American History and the Benson Latin American Collection, both at the University of Texas at Austin; the Texas State Archives; East Texas Research Center; the Historical Society of Pennsylvania; the Beinecke Rare Book and Manuscript Library at Yale University; the

Houghton Library at Harvard University; the Gilder Lehrman Collection in New York; the Lindenwood (Missouri) University archives; the Clements Library at the University of Michigan; the archives of Northwestern State University; and the United States National Archives.

Lastly, I want to thank the two most important people in my life: my wife Stephanie Torralva Bernsen and my son Diego. I wrote the first draft of this book while on a military deployment to Afghanistan, cranking out pages deep into the night about a two hundred-year-old insurgency, then getting up for my twelve-hour, seven-day-a-week shift countering a modern insurgency. As a consequence, our family video chats were often cut far shorter than I would have preferred. Their patience and love helped me get through a period of my life that was both extremely difficult and rewarding at the same time, and they have been there for me throughout this process.

THE LOST WAR FOR TEXAS

Introduction

"When the almost superhuman exploits of that little band shall be properly set forth, it will form one of the most thrilling and spirit-stirring episodes in the history of Texas. Perhaps there is nothing comparable in modern chivalry, to their unflagging valor, lofty daring and astounding triumphs."[1]
—*Mirabeau Buonaparte Lamar*

"The majority of people to this day do not realize the role that . . . Texas played in liberating her glorious patria. Nevertheless, a few of her [most notable deeds] can be salvaged. . . . Let us get to the work then, and let the people know the truth."[2]
—*Anonymous Tejano*

IN AUGUST 1812, an army of American frontiersmen, hunters, and adventurers crossed into Texas from Louisiana, not to fight in their own country's newly declared war against Great Britain, but to make common cause with Mexican rebels in their struggle with Spain. Mexican Texans, or *Tejanos*, had launched a revolt the year before, but a conservative reaction restored monarchical rule after only two months. Now, this private invasion by Anglo Americans—a *filibuster* in nineteenth-century parlance—aimed to restart the aborted revolution and open a supply line to rebels in the Mexican heartland, inaugurating a year of bloody conflict that changed Texas forever.

As the *Republican Army of the North*, which the force was called, pushed deeper into Texas, it gained new recruits from the Tejano and Native American populations until it became a truly heterogenous force with a unified goal of freeing all of Mexico from the Spanish Empire and opening up trade to the United States. After a series of stunning victories that shattered royalist power in the province and led to Texas' first Declaration of Independence and constitution—as a *Mexican* state—the rebels were routed by a Spanish relief army in the largest battle ever fought in Texas, the bloody Battle of Medina, on August 18, 1813. The victory for Spain was complete but pyrrhic: the violent year in Texas would devastate the province and set in motion a chain of events over the next three decades that doomed the hopes of Hispanic dominance of the Southwest.

This first *Texas Revolution of 1811*, which took place a quarter century before the far more well-known *second* revolution of 1836, was longer and bloodier than that later conflict. There were more engagements, a siege more than seven times as long as that of the Alamo, and three pitched battles with more participants than San Jacinto. The human toll of this first war was also far greater. While violence against civilians in 1836 was minimal, it was not so in 1813.

When Spanish general Joaquín de Arredondo defeated the republicans, he unleashed a reign of terror straight out of the dark ages. How many tourists who stroll today along the San Antonio Riverwalk, or glide by on sightseeing barges, are aware that at this very location, *hundreds* of rebels and others merely suspected of being disloyal were brutally killed—in some cases even drawn and quartered—their bodies left to rot where they lay for months afterward? Or that a nightmare of brutality, forced labor, and rape was meted out to rebels' wives, while their starving children begged for food in the streets? On a per capita basis, the war was likely the bloodiest ever fought in North America. One-third of the civilian population of Texas was killed or exiled in a space of two weeks; the resulting demographic collapse could only be reversed nine years later by the dangerous expedient of importing foreign settlers—with profound consequences for the Spaniards' Mexican heirs.

Most people today are unaware that this first revolution even took place. The Texas Revolution of 1811—more commonly called the *Gutiérrez-Magee Expedition*, or more obscurely, the *Gachupín War*—is forgotten even in the land in which it was waged.[3] Until 2018, the revolution was not even mentioned in the Texas Education Agency's *Texas Essential Knowledge and Skills* criteria for the seventh grade, where Texas history is taught. While people across the Lone Star State and far beyond know the names of Houston, Crockett, Travis, and Seguín, who knows the names of Gutiérrez, Magee, Kemper, or Despallier? Who remembers Reuben Ross and his courage at Rosillo? Who knows Miguel Menchaca, with his heroics at the siege of La Bahía and his vow to never retreat at Medina? Who knows Juan Savías, the dark-skinned Mexican fighter who overcame the racism of his comrades with a timely act of bravery that saved the rebel army and won the admiration of all? Who knows of Joséfa Nuñes de Arocha, the mother of seven who courageously defied a tyrant at the risk of her life?[4]

Most Texans, Americans, and Mexicans alike would be astonished to know that this first revolution contains stories and conflict, passion, and drama as deep and as powerful as its made-for-Hollywood successor. If one seeks heroes or villains, there are plenty to be had on both sides. Men who fought bravely for their king died valiantly alongside men who fought for a republic. Those who proclaimed liberty perpetuated atrocities equal to those committed by the forces of authoritarianism. The conflict produced profound moments of idealism and intrigue, loyalty and betrayal, heroism and cowardice, humanity and barbarism.

The Lost War

There are several reasons why this conflict remains obscure. In the first place, it never fit into the nineteenth-century narrative that became the Texas myth, defined as it was by a six-month revolution containing requisite storylines of heroism, martyrdom, and good versus evil, with the latter often framed (incorrectly) along ethnic lines. Neither does it properly fit the expansion-of-slavery narrative added by twentieth-century historians who retroactively imagined all events before 1860 as a mere prelude to the Civil War. While contemporaneous with the War of 1812 and the wider Napoleonic struggle, its relationship to both has been overlooked. Nor has the fight in Texas been fully appreciated in light of its pivotal role in the Mexican War of Independence, even though the failure of the republican cause in Texas cut off Mexican rebels from foreign aid, directly resulted in the death of Father Hidalgo, and prolonged the revolution by nearly a decade. Sadly, as the anonymous Tejano quoted above was painfully aware, Mexican historians too had already dismissed Texas' role in the revolution even in the early days of their nation's independence. This disinterest was deepened by the legacy of 1836 and the Mexican–American War of ten years later. As one writer noted, for historians south of the Rio Grande, "Texas serves as a bitter memory of conquest, and Mexican historians have long ignored the formative experience of Texas in Mexican history."[5]

Put simply, there was no room for the 1811–13 revolution in either the Mexican myth of tragic victimhood or in American triumphalist Manifest Destiny. From opposite poles, both nations reached a consensus of disinterest. It is, furthermore, the very fact that historians self-segregate into thematic and geographical research boxes that obscures an event that crosses over such boundaries liberally, is steeped in all of them, and cannot be interpreted solely based on discrete schools. As historian David Narrett has written of such events, "The motif of multiple 'entangled' histories is . . . a dominant theme of borderlands-frontier history." And the Texas Revolution of 1811 is nothing if not entangled.[6]

Texas historians, who most of all should be interested in this conflict, treat this war as a mere footnote because of their peculiar fault: *Alamo blindness*, the inability to see beyond the brilliant glare of 1836. They may, on occasion, write of the bloody Battle of Medina which concluded the war, but in a cursory, disembodied way, as if it were an isolated event with no context, rather than a culmination of two years of revolutionary strife and the harbinger of conflict to come. As a failed revolution, the 1811 war has been seen, when noticed at all, as a flash-in-the-pan event with no bearing on later Texas. *The revolution of 1836 changed everything*, so the thinking goes. *That of 1811 did not.*

This book will challenge that paradigm. Here I will argue for a continual narrative from the events preceding the first revolution right up to and beyond the second. The Texas Revolution of 1811 was not a *separate play* in the drama of Texas history but the *first act*, which laid the groundwork for subsequent ones, including Anglo settlement in the 1820s, the 1836 Revolution, and the Mexican–American War that followed. In a few cases, the same characters—Anglo, Tejano, and Mexican—are present in both major acts of the drama. Two rebel officers who were on hand at the signing of the first Texas Declaration of Independence in April 1813, Tejano José Francisco Ruiz and American James Taylor Gaines, were reunited two decades later among the fifty-six delegates who put their signatures on the second. More commonly, the rebels of 1811–13 were the fathers of those of 1836. One family featured three generations of rebels fighting for Texas liberty: Luís Grande and his son-in-law Bernard Martin Despallier served in the first conflict, and two grandsons fought in the second, including Charles Despallier, who died at the Alamo. Albert Sydney Johnston, who served the Republic of Texas, fought in the Mexican–American War and the US Civil War, had not one but *two* older brothers who fought in 1811–13, and a third who was a key organizer of the rebel army.[7]

Texas also had a forgotten but robust colony of foreigners—mostly French but also Anglo-Americans—in East Texas when future empresario Stephen F. Austin was a child. They lived, built farms, and had children in the days before this first revolution, and this diversity was a casualty of these years of conflict. Many would serve in the war and return after Mexico finally won its independence. In fact, at least two dozen of the earliest Texas colonists in the Austin era are verifiable veterans of the 1811 revolution, and there were no doubt more among the many names lost to history. Far from being the pathfinder in the wilderness leading the innocents, it was *Austin* who was the babe in the woods compared to "Old 300" settlers who were Texas veterans like Aylett "Strap" Buckner, Martin Allen, and A. W. McClain. These men knew these forests and fields far better than Austin. They had marched in them, fought in them, and seen their friends die in them when the Father of Texas was a mere child.

At least two of them, Edmund Quirk and John McFarlan, lived in Texas in the 1790s, fought there in the 1810s, and returned to settle in the 1820s. The editor of the first newspaper of Austin's Anglo-American colony was Godwin Brown Cotten, the same man who sixteen years before had helped print the propaganda broadside of the Mexican revolution in the north. Cotten had survived the brutal and merciless Battle of Medina, in which no quarter was given to the rebels by the victor. In the 1830s, he printed his newspaper next door to the office of a young lawyer named William Barret Travis, who no doubt recalled his neighbor's chilling tales of that

INTRODUCTION 5

battle near San Antonio as he drafted his appeal to the world under startlingly similar circumstances inside the Alamo. His fellow defender of that fort, James Bowie, grew up surrounded by many 1811–13 veterans, and counted two of them among his closest friends.[8]

At the same time, Tejano veterans spent months, years—or in the case of Ruiz nearly a decade—as exiles in Louisiana with a bounty on their heads. This forgotten Mexican-Texan diaspora in the United States profoundly shaped the way this population viewed liberty, trade, and their American neighbors, helping forge a Tejano identity that was, for the elites in particular, significantly different than the broader Mexican one. This population, sadly relegated by the traditional narrative to mere scenery in the epic of revolution that swept their native land, were in fact key players, organizers, and active agents of change in their own right. This first revolution, despite the presence of a large Anglo volunteer force, was fundamentally *their* revolt. The Tejanos' birth as republicans is indeed the true origin of liberty in Texas, and in the words of their foremost leader, "Noble citizens of Béxar sacrificed their lives and property, performing heroic deeds of valor" that were equal to their neighbors of the north. In this struggle, the alliance between Tejano and Anglo-American forged in 1812–13 would pave the way for a similar coalition two decades later.[9]

Furthermore, the revolution provides resonating parallels to 1836. After being routed by republicans, the Spanish army returned in greater force, far sooner than the rebels expected, defeated them in a battle of terrible carnage near San Antonio with no quarter given, and chased the survivors toward the American border. If these scenarios of 1813 and 1836 sound similar, it is not a coincidence. Among the Spanish officers in the first war was a nineteen-year-old lieutenant and understudy to General Arredondo. This young officer, Antonio Lopez de Santa Anna, would return to Texas twenty-three years later and repeat those lessons, almost as if he had scripted it that way, which he probably did.

The men who witnessed the rebellion firsthand interpreted it through a broader context than would future historians—as a global struggle of republicanism versus monarchy that united battlefields in Texas with those in Baltimore, Venezuela, and even the frozen fields around Moscow. One of the men in this story had visited Europe in the midst of the Napoleonic wars and returned to America eager to volunteer in an ideological crusade. Another took his experience fighting for Spanish-American liberty in Texas and made it his passion—sailing to Venezuela to become the chief physician for *El Liberador*, Simón Bolívar. In December 1813, with the bodies from the fateful final battle in Texas still unburied, a young Louisiana district attorney wrote to the American special agent who had been a key observer on the scene, proposing a history of the event: "The Revolution of Texas is one of those occurrences, over the theater of the world, which merits the attention of the historian, as well when we consider the instructive and interesting incidents to which it has given view, as its connection with that mighty struggle, in which the whole of

America is at the present moment engaged, in throwing off the dominion of Europe, and in establishing their independence."[10]

But this account was never written, nor indeed was any detailed history attempted for more than 120 years. Since then, there has been only one scholarly book-length treatment of the war, Julia Kathryn Garrett's *Green Flag over Texas* (1939), along with four books covering it in depth as part of a broader narrative: Harris Gaylord Warren's *The Sword Was Their Passport* (1943), Ted Schwartz's *Forgotten Battlefield of the First Texas Revolution* (1985), J. C. A. Stagg's *Borderlines in Borderlands* (2009), and Ed Bradley's *We Never Retreat* (2015). Several books and scholarly articles have also interpreted various aspects of the conflict. While these generally get the major events right, they misinterpret the expedition's origins, fail to connect it to later events and people, and perpetuate falsehoods and assumptions, long circulated in a historical echo chamber, ossifying into a dogmatic, erroneous interpretation.[11]

In defense of these authors, their works have been hindered by a paucity of original source materials: half a dozen authentic accounts, seemingly contradictory, most of which were written decades later by biased survivors. When I started this journey, I had little expectation that I would find more than this. I was a veteran of Iraq and Afghanistan using my GI Bill for graduate school in history. Finding the same wall of inscrutability, I employed several tools to break it down. The first was my training as a military intelligence officer, which gave me insight into the origins, mechanics, functioning, and support nodes of foreign-supported and facilitated insurgencies—of which Texas in 1812 was as clear an example as were the modern conflicts in which I had served. Equally valuable were internet-based genealogical and digital resources that were exploding on the landscape in the second decade of the twenty-first century. Supplementing traditional archival-based research, these allowed me to approach the story from a new perspective, drawing back the veil on relationships and connections never before uncovered. I also dug deeper into many of the primary source documents, particularly the papers of US Special Agent William Shaler, shining new light on the conflict's greatest controversy.

The Role of the Madison Administration

Of greatest interest to historians is the degree to which official or covert US government support may have been provided to the revolutionaries in Texas, specifically the role of President James Madison and Secretary of State James Monroe. The consensus of the existing historiography of the Gutiérrez-Magee filibuster falls squarely in the camp of US support. This view, however, is based on little more than conjecture and extrapolation from sources taken out of context. In this book, I will demonstrate that this consensus can no longer be sustained.

This *interventionist* view was cemented early on by the work of two of the historians noted above: Julia Kathryn Garrett (1939) and Harris Gaylord Warren (1943).

INTRODUCTION 7

These authors undertook extensive research, finding many sources that were previously unknown. Considering the era in which they worked and the vacant landscape before them, these were extraordinary achievements to which all subsequent historians owe a debt of gratitude. But they also made a great and fatal error: a rush to judgment on this key point, which the evidence not only fails to support but, properly understood, explicitly refutes.[12]

Garrett and Warren both concluded that the filibuster was materially organized, supported, and conducted with the approbation and facilitation of Monroe, and that the on-the-ground representative who did the coordination on his behalf was Special Agent Shaler. This became the sole evidence behind the administration support thesis as perpetuated by other interventionists, such as Richard Gronet (1969) and, more recently, Owsley and Smith in their book *Filibusters and Expansionists* (1997).

In this interpretation, William Shaler is the indispensable man. This is both by explicit statement and by necessity, since there is no other person with the authority, power, and proximity to the conflict who could be its guiding hand. This entire chain of logic, however, can be invalidated. Below are some key points never acknowledged in interventionist accounts, and which will be expounded upon in detail in this book.[13]

In the first place, Shaler was neither hired by nor had ever met James Monroe. Shaler was inherited by Monroe in March 1811 after the Virginian replaced Secretary of State Robert Smith. Smith, who actually appointed Shaler, was not only very different from Monroe in outlook and temperament, but was a disruptive, alienated person within the administration, forced on Madison by the Senate and greatly distrusted by the president. Shaler's very circumscribed mission—as outlined by Smith, *not Monroe*—was absolutely not to support or encourage a filibuster, as his own instructions clearly indicate. This instruction letter, the single most important document related to the filibuster (essentially the smoking gun disproving interventionism), was unused by and likely unknown to Garrett, Warren, or even modern historians with the same thesis.[14]

Shaler was furthermore sent on a mission in tandem with two other agents dispatched to different areas of the collapsing Spanish Empire, all with identical instructions, none of which contemplated active engagement in revolution. Neither was Shaler supposed to go to the Louisiana-Texas border at all, but was to first visit Cuba, then Mexico (specifically through *Veracruz*). That he ended up in New Orleans was mere chance after he had been expelled from Cuba, and that he later met the Mexican rebel José Bernardo Gutiérrez de Lara and ventured with him to the border was also an accident, the result of a delay in the departing of a barge. They had been introduced by the governor of the Orleans Territory not in a conspiracy to launch a filibuster, as the interventionists assume, but because of the governor's paranoia *against* such an adventure by intriguers *outside of government control*. Eschewing the governor's voluminous correspondence to focus on a cherry-picked letter or two out of context and ignoring hugely important documents—including Shaler's crucial instructions—Garrett and Warren seized upon this rendezvous and infused it with undue nefariousness.[15]

The fact is, Shaler could not have worked with Monroe on any secret plan to invade Texas. He had no orders from the secretary, nor indeed any communication whatsoever from him or anyone in the state department *for a year prior to the expedition's launch*. He did not even know he still had a job, much less have reason to feel empowered to lead a revolution alongside a man he had never met, and about whom he had received no guidance. The agent received his first letter ever from Monroe only a month before the filibuster began and the only advice it provided was "proceed to Mexico"—meaning Veracruz. Garrett and Warren, focusing on letters in which Shaler expressed sympathy for the rebel cause—as indeed almost all Americans of any political stripe did—transformed that sympathy into support of a filibuster by presumption, overlooking key letters disputing their thesis, and downplaying as a deception Monroe's explicit statement after the fact that the agent should disavow the enterprise.

Once on the frontier, Shaler did not materially support Gutiérrez's efforts in any way besides assisting in drafting propaganda themes, lecturing him on democratic institutions, and providing petty cash to pay his room and board. He never raised troops, provided any substantial monetary resources (as was alleged), nor did he approve of Gutiérrez's activities along these lines. Through most of July 1812, when Gutiérrez was organizing his filibuster, in which William Shaler was supposedly the indispensable motive force, the agent was in fact bedridden with illness. Upon recovering, he wrote a letter specifically asserting that Gutiérrez was acting behind his back, which Garrett and Warren ignored. Nor was this an obfuscation or ruse on the part of Shaler. A crucial letter to the president, in which the agent painfully and insubordinately charged the secretary of state with negligence, disproves any possible subterfuge or secret correspondence.

Garrett's errors were ones of overeager assumptions feeding a preconceived narrative. Warren's were greater. He asserted, "When Shaler and Gutiérrez arrived at Natchitoches on April 27 or 28, they began immediately to prepare for the invasion of Texas," and cites as a source, Gutiérrez's diary, which says nothing of the sort. Shortly thereafter, he states, "Everything seemed to point to the possibility of organizing a strong expedition.... William Shaler apparently believed that the Secretary of State was fully cognizant of the activities ... a dispatch from Monroe dated May 2, 1812, contained the significant statement that the President approved of Shaler's course." This passage is deceptively constructed. The May 2 letter was actually a response to Shaler's letter of March 9—a two-month lag the author ignores, but which is vital in understanding what the administration knew and when.[16]

Furthermore, in stating "the president approved of Shaler's course," Warren makes it appear that the administration supported a filibuster. But the secretary's actual wording was "I have the pleasure to communicate the president's approbation of your conduct *while in Cuba*, and of the motives which induced you to leave that island, by New Orleans for Mexico" (emphasis added). Shaler's instructions and further letters clarify that by "for Mexico," Monroe meant to go to Veracruz to find the rebels in Mexico proper, not proceed to the land border with New Spain. A trip to Texas was never considered or advocated by the administration and was only approved after the fact for intelligence-gathering purposes.

These points, which I will lay out in this book, will show that the administration's direct or tacit support of the filibuster was simply not possible. That Madison and Monroe were expansionists and may have had some shady dealings of this sort in *other areas*, such as West and East Florida, is entirely another matter. That many adventurers took the president's anti-Spanish statements and interpreted Shaler's presence on the frontier as evidence of covert support is indeed likely. But his journey being accidental, this cannot confer agency on the administration. In point of fact, in the spring and summer of 1812, with America about to go to war with the most powerful empire in the world and policy makers far more eager to invade Canada than Mexico, the administration made no such effort to support a filibuster into Texas. Mexico had the administration's sympathies but not its attention. Not only was a filibuster never enabled, but every communication sent by the administration or their territorial governor on the topic was unequivocally opposed to such a venture *outside of a declaration of war with Spain*, which never in the end materialized.

The Burr Connection

This brings us to who actually *did* launch the filibuster: the restless and revolutionary men of the West. Some modern writers have dismissed these men as "nameless frontiersmen or adventurers seeking new lands" who were unwitting tools of expansionist presidents. But while these men supported expansionism generally, they were nonetheless independent of—and among key players in this drama, *actually hostile to*—the government specifically. When they came face to face with another administration agent, John Robinson, they threatened to lynch him *for carrying an American flag* in their revolutionary republic and presumably, spying upon them. This was no mere posturing but in deadly earnest. These men were not pawns, but willing players within a conspiracy far broader, populist, and independent than previously understood.[17]

A further problem with the above characterization is that the men who invaded Texas are in fact *not* "nameless." Indeed, we have learned a great many of their names. Garrett and Warren, seeing the forest but ignoring the trees, cite fewer than two dozen, and never delve deep into their backgrounds. Henry Walker in the 1960s, in his annotation to the recently rediscovered first-person narrative of William McLane (which Garrett and Warren, writing three decades before, had never read), put together a list containing 63 names of known Anglo and French participants, alongside very rudimentary sketches of their backgrounds. In my research, I have increased this number to 204 men, from American newspapers, diaries, letters, archival, and genealogical sources. On the Tejano side, the Spanish kept extensive lists of rebels whose property was seized for participation in the rebellion.[18]

While archives are still the best fount of information, the internet has opened up wide swaths of the archival landscape to review and has made finding such documents easier and, in many cases, text searchable. Web-based genealogy has been a quiet revolution with vast implications for historical research that have been underappreciated. Not only did this allow me to find new sources; it enhanced and validated older ones and provided new clues for archival research, creating an ongoing feedback loop. In one case, a seemingly insignificant name found in a family history written in 1897 was the clue to validate the partial authenticity of an account of the expedition which some historians have questioned.[19]

Finding these names was just the first step; the next was turning them into biographies and then into patterns, insights, cues for research, and conclusions. Indeed, this backdoor approach helped shine light on the only plausible alternative to the interventionist narrative. This is truly the gorilla in the room, which previous histories have entirely overlooked in their rush to prove interventionism: The origins of the 1812 Gutiérrez-Magee expedition lie not in the State Department but in an external source: the Aaron Burr conspiracy.

Six years before the eventual invasion of Texas, former US vice president Aaron Burr, disgraced for his killing of Alexander Hamilton in a duel, conceived of a plan to invade Spanish lands at the head of a mercenary army and create a new nation. Histories of that fascinating plot invariably become mere biographies of its colorful namesake, and far too often, it is presumed that once Burr leaves the stage, his footprints vanish with him. On the contrary, as historian Julius Pratt noted, "Burr, in his ill-starred enterprise . . . merely attempted to do what the whole Southwest dreamed of, and after his failure, the border was still peopled by men of like mind." It was these men—and the Mexican rebels who embraced such convenient allies—who were the authors of the invasion of Texas in 1812.[20]

As noted, the interventionist narrative is built entirely on flawed secondary sources nearly one hundred years old. To maintain it requires assumptions, leaps of logic, and a conspiracy so deep and well-concealed that every single documentary source supporting it has vanished while numerous ones to the contrary have survived. The alternative, the *Burr hypothesis*, comports with Occam's razor, the principle that the simplest interpretation is the one most likely to be true. And that is this: In 1806, a coalition of Western adventurers, New Orleans mercantile leaders, and Mexican revolutionaries conceived a plan to invade Spanish territory and liberate it for their own personal gain, not that of the American government. And in 1812, as I will argue, the same actors conceived *and actually implemented* nearly the exact scheme.

But this thesis is not based on mere conjecture; there is strong evidence to support it, which I present here for the first time. First, three of the top five deputies of filibuster leader Augustus Magee were key recruits to the 1806 conspiracy, including the man most closely connected to him, William Murray. Second, the man chosen by Gutiérrez and his conspirators to lead the expedition, John Adair, had been tapped for the same role under Burr. Third, Gutiérrez in his own diary notes that upon entering the United States, he was bombarded by offers of independent support outside of government auspices. Fourth, in the trials of some of the more obscure Burrite figures, we find plans for an invasion developed in 1806 that line up well with what was actually attempted in 1812. Finally, the organization behind these plans was the *Mexican Association* of New Orleans, a covert group of mercantile and society leaders in that city committed to the independence of Mexico, under its spiritual guru, Daniel Clark. Many of its members—individually and as a class—have connections to the filibuster, and Clark is explicitly identified by one source as closely connected to the invasion. His history is absolutely clear on one point: he wanted nothing to do with any official expedition.[21]

These forces allied with a preexisting league of banditti in the so-called Neutral Ground, with its own Burrite connections and already in contact with revolutionary elements within the Texas population. Indeed, what emerges is a filibuster far more organic in its origins than has ever been recognized: most of the facilitating players in the drama called the Gutiérrez-Magee expedition were already at work long before Bernardo Gutiérrez, Augustus Magee, or William Shaler ever arrived on the frontier.

Furthermore, the true beginnings of the conflict lie not in the filibuster of 1812, but in the *native Tejano rebellion* of 1811, a fact which has long been veiled by the filibuster-centric narrative. The interventionist line also, by denying agency to Mexican Texans in launching their own revolt, unintentionally whitewashes the key truth that Americans *joined* but did not *create* this revolution.

The Lost War for Texas brings together this human story of the conflict's origins with a new and more comprehensive examination of the battles and controversies, intrigues and tragedies of this forgotten struggle, and an analysis of its legacy to the more well-known revolution and republic which succeeded it. Although there are great historical movements involved—American proto Manifest Destiny and the Napoleonic Wars loom large in this tale—the bulk of the history revolves around the individuals who made it up. With apologies to Hegel, it is not the impersonal, fate-driven movement of history that makes a revolution; it is the man on the ground, musket in hand, willing to risk his life and fight for a cause, his family, lust for riches, or just adventure. This is the story of those men: Mexican rebels, the Anglo-American *Burrites* who joined with them, and the revolution they fought together.

1

The Great Conspiracy

ON A TORRID, muggy day in mid-June 1804, a group of men rode along the banks of Bayou Sara—a tributary of the Mississippi upstream from Baton Rouge—past bald cypress trees, pecans with limbs groaning with their bounty, and live oaks dripping their curtain of moss nearly to the ground. This was the Spanish province of West Florida, they were militia, and their arms readied for a desperate fight. The captain of the riders reined in his mount and slowed to a trot before a log-hewn home with a broad porch. The doors and shutters of the house were closed fast. They were expected.[1]

The man atop the lead horse was an alcalde, or local magistrate, of the Spanish government, but he had the very non-Spanish name of Alexander Stirling. That was not unusual in this strange, isolated geographical absurdity. West Florida comprised what is today eastern Louisiana and the coastal lands of Mississippi and Alabama. It was called "West" to distinguish it from *East* Florida—roughly corresponding to the modern state of that name. Parts of it had variously been French, British, and now Spanish, and these groups, as well as American immigrants from the neighboring lands, had left their mark. "A more heterogeneous mass of good and evil was never before met in the same extent of territory," the new American governor of the nearby Orleans Territory described it.[2]

As the riders halted before the house, a man holding a rifle stepped out of the door and demanded to know the militia's business. Stirling announced that he was here to evict the Kemper brothers. Scarcely were the words out of the alcalde's mouth when four more men, all armed, stepped out of the house. More, perhaps a dozen, remained inside, gun barrels peeking out of the windows.[3]

The oldest of the three Kemper brothers, the notorious Reuben Kemper, was away in New Orleans, and perhaps Stirling had thought here was an opportunity to make his move. But at this moment, a large man, more than six feet tall, stepped out of the door, rifle in hand, and the alcalde must have realized that he had misjudged the situation. For it was the youngest brother who was proudest and most defiant.

Twenty-eight-year-old Samuel Kemper was courageous, bordering on reckless. He had been born in the revolutionary year of 1776, an heir to a proud tradition of resistance to authority. The Kempers were descendants of German indentured servants who had settled in Fauquier County, Virginia. Known as a "free state" for its tradition of opposition to the coast, the county fostered an independent streak that would cling tenaciously in later generations. In no one was this rogue spirit stronger than in Samuel Kemper.[4]

Before the Louisiana Purchase, the Spanish empire had stretched in a continuous arc from Florida to the Strait of Magellan at the tip of South America. When Napoleon Bonaparte sold Louisiana to the Americans, the transaction left an isolated section of Spanish land cut off from the rest of the empire except by sea, the *Floridas*. What was worse for the Spanish was that the French treaty with the United States left a nebulous boundary, which the American government was prepared to interpret liberally, and according to President Thomas Jefferson, the purchase included West Florida. The land itself was of marginal value; America mostly wanted the region for its rivers, which were crucial to inland trade.[5]

For the moment, Jefferson was willing to leave the issue to diplomacy and time, convinced that demographic expansion would one day render the controversy moot. The United States, with a burgeoning population, low crop yields and lands quickly exhausted by primitive farming methods, was straining toward the Spanish frontier. It was a nation always on the move, its people ever hungry for new land. In the two decades since the Revolutionary War, settlers had poured into the trans-Appalachian West. The population of Kentucky alone would soar from 12,000 in 1783 to 410,000 by 1810.[6]

The population also spilled over into West Florida, but there, the Spanish authorities thought they could manage this growth by luring American settlers to the nearly empty and unprofitable lands, which they would transform to the benefit of the Spanish crown. It was not as improbable a hope as it seems, tapping as it did into the universal desire of the men of the West: land. While land within the United States required significant investment, it could still be had for virtually nothing in the Spanish dominions, where the government was benevolently indulgent and taxes nonexistent. Spanish leaders hoped that these Americans, not yet cemented in nationalism for their still infant republic, might repay this generosity with their sympathies (or at least acceptance) once they mixed with the polyglot population of Spanish, French, and former British loyalists, and their hopes were not entirely unfounded.[7]

To develop the province, Spain wanted settlers, not speculators, and required all land deeded to foreigners to be occupied. This did not deter clever Americans who gobbled up the free land, which, should America ever gain West Florida, might make a fortune for a far-sighted man. One of these investors was Senator John Smith of Ohio, who hired Reuben Kemper, the son of a prominent Cincinnati minister, to live on the land as his agent and had even sponsored the young man in a mercantile venture there. Reuben in time was joined by his younger brothers Nathan and Samuel, who settled in the house Reuben had built on Bayou Sara. When the store failed, however, Smith secured a judgment to oust his tenants, and Stirling was attempting to enforce the order.[8]

On the porch, Samuel Kemper shouted back that he would rather fight than comply, and the alcalde saw he was in deadly earnest. Stirling rode with his men out of rifle range, where they took up positions and set up a watch on the house until reinforcements could arrive. That evening, however, the "boys in the house" escaped and made their way the short distance north to Mississippi, on the American side of the border. But if the "Spanish" thought they were done with the Kemper gang, they were sorely disappointed. Though the brothers' feud was personal, there were others for whom the men represented an opportunity.[9]

The Restless and Revolutionary West

In the early days of the United States, the mystic cords which would one day bind the embryo nation together were but fragile threads. The nation had weathered the Shays's and Whiskey rebellions, when marginalized western settlers in the latter had seen their grievances trampled by the menace of federal armies. The rebels had been defeated, but their underlying economic alienation endured. As long as the West remained aggrieved, true national unity remained elusive, as the nation's first president, himself a western land speculator, well knew. "There is nothing which binds one country or one state to another but interest," George Washington had written. "Without this cement, the western inhabitants can have no predilection for us."[10]

Now these westerners were expanding, pushing beyond the frontier, spreading the line of settlement—with or without government support. No one called it *Manifest Destiny* yet, precisely because the nature of the destiny they were shaping was ambiguous. A continental empire was the vision of but a handful of dreamers; most contemporary theorists thought there was a geographical limit to the size of a republic. As the nation grew, they feared, the fledgling constitutional order would sunder against the tyranny of distance and the lack, as Washington had put it, of common interest. While the nation's first president was frightened by this prospect, the third took a more casual view of the issue. "If they see their interests in separation," Thomas Jefferson wrote, "why should we take sides with our Atlantic rather than our Mississippi descendants? . . . God bless them both, and keep them in union, if it be for their good, but separate them, if it be better."[11]

Modern Americans see sectionalism, in hindsight, as North versus South, but in the first decade of the nineteenth century, the powerful divide with the potential to split the nation was East versus West. "Westerners, quite simply, saw the world differently from their eastern brethren," one historian wrote, and many of them "had come to consider that their fate was in their own hands rather than that of the distant federal government."[12]

The migrants to the frontier wanted land, economic opportunity, and a democracy more expansive than the elites of the East would allow. As another historian put it, "Government was all right in some sort of self-sustaining way to fight off other nations and chastise the Indians, but beyond those functions, it was not only superfluous, it was an exasperating nuisance." Here, there was no border, only a frontier, where sovereignty was not fixed, but "open to competition and challenge." In such circumstances, the people themselves "may seek to establish alternative political organizations and centers and ultimately alternative politics through mitigation and secession." America was still an experiment, a gambler's wager, and the westerners, a side bet. National feeling was "a sentiment more frequently thin and volatile than hard and fixed."[13]

"The West was another name for opportunity," wrote Frederick Jackson Turner, the region's most famous historian. "Here were mines to be seized; fertile valleys to be pre-empted, all the natural resources open to the shrewdest and the boldest." But these resources were in the hands of others. As they pushed west, settlers displaced Native Americans, who frequently fought back in bitter raids. Even peaceful tribes were often dispossessed by these predatory individualists. But the one spot on the continent that these westerners coveted above all others was in the hands of a European power. It was New Orleans, and that power was Spain.[14]

At a time when shipment of goods by land was prohibitively expensive, the Mississippi River was the continent's great highway for trade, and it was this waterway that could make the western lands and their people rich or—if denied to them—doom them to enduring poverty. As this highway flowed through Spanish territory, keeping it open had been the overwhelming demand of the West, and closure, their worst nightmare. In October 1802, the Spanish Intendent of Louisiana made this fear a reality when he briefly suspended the right of deposit for goods in New Orleans, effectively blocking all trade. Western outrage for a time boiled into a war frenzy. "The whole country was in commotion," Henry Clay later wrote, "and at the nod of the government, would have fallen on [Spanish] Baton Rouge and New Orleans."[15]

Many western settlers nursed a festering antipathy toward Spain, a potent cocktail of generations of English-Spanish conflict: fear of Catholicism, belief in the "black legend" of Spanish cruelty, and a newly discovered zeal to evangelize the new republican creed to the "oppressed" lands of Spanish America. New Orleans was an open wound and a pretext to vent this hostility, and westerners were willing to act *with or without* their government's consent to obtain it. A Kentuckian writing under the pen name "Cariolanus," in the December 27, 1802 (Frankfort) *Morning Chronicle*, declared, "Kentucky has the advantage of invasion, and will no doubt use it. If unsupported by the Union, she moves alone to the combat; she is situated on the waters rapidly descending to the point of attack; she will overwhelm [New] Orleans and West Florida with promptitude and ease."[16]

The plots envisioned operating *outside* of government auspices. Not only did the planners keep the government out of these schemes; they even turned to foreign powers to effect them. In 1791, John O'Fallon hatched a scheme to invade Spanish Louisiana under the French flag and signed up three to five thousand men (and even offered bounties for women as well) for his own private army. President Washington vigorously suppressed the enterprise, and used the example to pass the Neutrality Act of 1794, which proscribed attacks against nations with which America was at peace. This did not deter another attempt three years later, when William Blount, the sitting US Senator from the frontier state of Tennessee organized a conspiracy to aid Britain in seizing New Orleans and Spanish Florida in exchange for free access to the Mississippi River for American merchants. The conspiracy unraveled and Blount was impeached, but the popularity of the idea was demonstrated to all when the Senator, disgraced back East, was given a hero's welcome upon returning home.[17]

Into this turbulent scene strode James Wilkinson in 1784. He had served as the youngest American general in the Revolutionary War, then retired with ambitions to make his fortune in land and trade. In 1788, he brazenly sailed a cargo of goods to New Orleans and won the astonishment and admiration of the West by negotiating an exclusive export deal with the Spanish authorities. Of course, there was a good reason the Spanish had given him such a deal, which no one but he knew: Wilkinson had by this point become Spain's paid spy. Working through him, the Spanish sought to satisfy the western desires by enticing the region to secede and *join* their empire.[18]

George Washington had always distrusted Wilkinson but saw him as just the tool he needed, shrewdly reasoning that if he could not create an "interest" for the people of the West, he could at least create one for the men whom the people followed. In 1797, knowing nothing of Wilkinson's treason, Washington made him a general once more and with seniority—the top officer in the entire army. Washington hoped the West would not move without him, and so long as he drew pay from Philadelphia, Wilkinson had a reason to hesitate before launching any illegal venture. Nonetheless, the general continued to plot with a boldness unparalleled in American history: He concocted simultaneous schemes against the country that paid his salary and the one which paid his bribes. While he served the Spanish, he told fellow Americans in confidence that he "looked forward to the Subversion of the Mexican Kingdoms, it is a noble theater—I shall ascertain every devious as well as direct route." Thus he fed secret information to the Spanish authorities while simultaneously betraying them, even sending a young "horse trader" named Philip Nolan into Texas, presumably to scout the area for future invasion while corralling mustangs. The Spanish governor of Louisiana, like Washington, distrusted the American general but paid him anyway, afraid of "the mischief that might arise from vexing him."[19]

That western schemes were still popular after Blount's downfall was clear to all, and even more worrying was the affection of these turbulent men for revolutionary France, where the terror had turned radical. Indeed, even the infamous ambassador from that government, Citizen Genêt, following the lead of O'Fallon and Blount, had conceived a similar plan to invade New Spain. He reportedly enrolled and even partly armed more than two thousand men in his scheme. The United States ordered him sent home for this and other offenses.[20]

Federalist presidents feared this growing discontent, along with the rise of Thomas Jefferson's new Republican party, a movement sympathetic with the French, antimonarchical and *anti-Federalist*. As Washington's successor, John Adams, fought a Quasi-War with republican France on the high seas, Republicans chafed on the frontier. When Jefferson defeated Adams for the presidency in 1800, he concluded a peace with France and turned his attention to the western problem. After Spain retroceded New Orleans to France, Jefferson secured the astounding triumph of the Louisiana Purchase. But for some westerners, this only whetted their appetite.

That Jefferson had even known about the secret treaty returning Louisiana to France was attributable to an outsider who had settled in New Orleans, integrated himself into Creole society, and risen to prominence. Daniel Clark Jr. was an Irish immigrant who had moved to Louisiana in 1786. Establishing himself in New Orleans, the twenty-year-old quickly became fluent in Spanish and French and immersed himself in business, shipping, land schemes, and the selling of slaves. He was soon rubbing elbows with all the leading men in the community and became for a time the secretary to the Spanish governor, Esteban Rodríguez Miró, the man paying Wilkinson's bribes.[21]

Clark, however, had no love for the Spanish Empire. For starters, he believed in free trade through the port, while Spain limited trade first only with other Spanish ports, then with foreign ones under many restrictions. After Clark left the Spanish service, he became a tireless advocate for Americans upstream. Being intimately connected to the Spaniards also allowed him to negotiate the appropriate bribes for his American clients to gain market entry. He quickly became close with the entire American mercantile community and entered into a venture with Wilkinson to import food from the Ohio Valley to the bustling urban community.[22]

Recognizing his utility, President Jefferson appointed Clark as consul and used him as his personal eyes and ears in the territory. This paid off handsomely when Clark learned of the secret treaty retroceding Louisiana to France and urged Jefferson to purchase the territory. When this was accomplished, Clark even established an ad hoc private militia to assist in the handover, which served as the city's sole constabulary force for a full three weeks.[23]

Clark was ambitious for himself and the province. He reveled in his new role as the lead American in the city and thought of himself as the certain appointee for the governorship of the new Territory of Orleans. Everyone in the city knew the prominent role he had played in the drama. As one friend wrote, with only slight exaggeration, "The United States owe the acquisition of Louisiana to Daniel Clark." But other reports made their way to Washington, painting Clark in a far less flattering light. Wilkinson wrote that the Irishman "possesses capacities to do more good or harm than any other individual in the province—He pants for power, and is mortified by disappointment." The president, therefore, bypassed the Irishman and advanced the youthful territorial governor of Mississippi, William Charles Cole Claiborne, to the Orleans post. It was a severe blow to Clark, who soon became the governor's most intractable foe—they would even fight an inconclusive duel.[24]

Claiborne was an outsider, arriving in the territory with a disdainful attitude toward the French Creoles, which heightened their discontent. The Orleans Territory was a region unlike any the United States had absorbed before in its short history of expansion. New Orleans, at the purchase, was instantly the sixth largest US city, with a population of 8,000 permanent residents. This included 3,500 whites but also 3,100 slaves and 1,500 free people of color—a situation unique in the young republic. Almost everyone spoke French. In the hinterland of the territory, furthermore, were Spanish and even German residents.[25]

Claiborne's impossible task was to bind these in affection to the American government. The French and Spanish in the community were disaffected and nearly rebellious. As a mere territory, Orleans' population was without a political voice and, even worse, subject to restrictions on the importation of new slaves. Americans moving in could bring them, but the Creoles could not, which fell especially hard on those fleeing the revolution in Haiti. They were furthermore forced to pay taxes and prove their land titles, something never required under the Spanish.[26]

Clark took up the cause of the Creoles, and that of the eager westerners flocking into the territory as well. This prospect properly terrified Claiborne, who complained of "adventurers who are daily coming into the Territory from every quarter, possess revolutionary principles and restless, turbulent dispositions." These were the heirs of Whiskey and Shays, of O'Fallon and Blount, and of "Cariolanus." Claiborne nervously warned Jefferson that they were fodder for "a few designing, intriguing men [who] may easily excite some inquietude in the public mind." He was referring to Daniel Clark and a growing group of malcontents who clustered around him, with an agenda far more expansive than territorial politics.[27]

The Mexican Association of New Orleans

Clark and his allies began building a secret society from among the key business and civic leaders of New Orleans. The *Mexican Association*, as it was known, kept its affairs closely guarded. Its defenders dismissed it as "an innocuous political club dedicated only to acquiring information about Latin American affairs." Others feared it was a paramilitary force aimed at invading America's neighbors. Indeed, it was a little of both. As a member of the group, New Orleans Mayor John Watkins wrote, "It had for its object collecting information relative to the population of New Spain, which in the event of war, might be useful to the United States."[28]

The group optimistically made plans to recruit eight thousand militia from Louisiana, ten thousand from Kentucky, and join them with regular troops and five thousand slaves who would be offered their freedom to launch a crusade against New Spain. They would not wait for the Stars and Stripes to waive over the enterprise—indeed, they did not wish for it. Clark "would have nothing to do with such an undertaking *if headed by the government*" (emphasis added). The organization's president, James Workman, "appeared disgusted with the tardy operations of our government, and expressed his wish to form a military association for the purpose of outstripping them" as an "independent corps." That this revolutionary association would join forces with the growing influx of radical westerners who shared Clark's "hunger for Spanish land and silver, as well as his disdain for the American government" was inevitable.[29]

The cause for which "turbulent" westerners and New Orleans' mercantile community could be united was West Florida. Its strategic importance was well-known to all parties. As Spanish governor Vicente Folch had put it, "West Florida must be considered an object of greatest importance to Spain, just as the American government is certain to eventually endeavor to acquire it at almost any cost or risk."[30]

Daniel Clark had first met Reuben Kemper in 1803, when the latter had served in his volunteer militia, and did business with the Kempers through an associate, Edward Randolph. Following the Kempers' expulsion from their Bayou Sara home, Randolph (it remains unclear whether he consulted Clark) saw opportunity in their misfortune. He goaded Nathan and Samuel Kemper into a rash and foolish scheme to get their land back. Thus, on August 7, 1804, with about twenty to thirty men, mostly in their teens and early twenties, the Kempers rode south below "the line," the latitude that marked the border. Once there, they unfurled a flag with a single star—the first *Lone Star* flag—and read a proclamation hastily drafted by Randolph calling for rebellion from Spain.[31]

As revolutions go, it had dramatic potential but turned to farce. Their compatriots, initially told their mission was a rescue of captured friends, balked at the enlarged plan. Most American settlers, rather than flock to the Kempers' cause, remained loyal to Spain. Even those on the American side of the border were hesitant to join up, guessing correctly that this was a private feud wearing the clothes of revolution. The force penetrated deep into Spanish territory, aiming to surprise the small garrison at Baton Rouge, but it had been alerted. The Kempers retreated to Mississippi to become mere raiders, occasionally slipping into Spanish territory over the next few months, stealing cattle and causing mayhem, but drawing no new adherents, as their bullying tactics created enmity and bitterness. When everyone is a land speculator, those who disturb public order win few friends. President Jefferson, hoping to negotiate a bloodless settlement on the border, ordered Claiborne and his counterpart in Mississippi to suppress any future uprisings of the sort.[32]

And there the issue might have ended, but for an event originating on the Spanish side, which would inflame the frontier. On September 2, 1805, about two dozen Spanish subjects, mostly Americans but also former British loyalists, slipped across the border into the US territory of Mississippi. With them were several African American slaves, armed. The white men also blackened their faces. Because of these disguises, the shock of what would follow would be doubly offensive to the race-conscious (and paranoid) citizens of the region.[33]

The mob broke into the Kempers' homes and seized the men violently. When Nathan's wife shrieked piteously from the bedroom, her husband, on the verge of blacking out, heard a man call back to his fellows in the house: "If the bitch utters another word, put her to death." Then they clubbed her unconscious and left her and Nathan's three-year-old son, William Peter, behind. Samuel, who had defied the alcalde so forcefully, was pulled from his bed and struck on the head by a double-barreled shotgun. In the street, his assailants tossed him to the ground and tied a rope around his neck, dragging him along for about one hundred yards behind a horse. Reuben Kemper, seized from another house nearby, was beaten until witnesses feared he would die.[34]

The Kempers were then taken south of the line where a Spanish patrol happened to show up at the exact spot in the dark night where the vigilantes had abandoned the captives before fleeing. The Spanish militiamen at least did not continue the beatings, but they had fugitives from the law in their possession, so they took them to a nearby Mississippi River landing, hog-tied them, and put them into boats to float down to Baton Rouge. While on the journey, the Kempers managed to shout to a friend on the American side of the river, who alerted the authorities. An ad hoc posse of soldiers intercepted the Spaniards and freed the Kempers.[35]

The vigilantes were arrested and tried, but ultimately released in an apparent effort by a local judge to defuse the situation. The judge also made the Kempers promise to commit no reprisals, which they promptly violated, assaulting the men as they left the courthouse, Reuben even cutting one man's ears with a dull knife. The American threat to Baton Rouge was over for now, but the bitterness remained. The Kemper brothers' motives once they turned the feud into a revolt have long divided historians. They have been treated variously as heroes—Mississippi named a county after Reuben—and as something far from it. Historian Isaac Cox said the "revolution" was "nothing more than random thuggery in response to an unfortunate lawsuit."[36]

Nonetheless, for a brief time, these men of little wealth or status became famous throughout the country. Thomas Jefferson read about them and, garbling the accounts, which invariably turned them into models of patriotism, mentioned them in a letter to Congress. Word of the assault spread in the Southwest and further encouraged American anger against the Spanish. The *National Intelligencer*, the leading Jeffersonian newspaper, reported the account under the headline "Daring Outrage!" The attackers were deceptively described as Spaniards, with no mention that they were, in fact, Anglo-Americans. Some accounts did note the participation of slaves, which was shocking to Mississippi and Orleans Territory plantation owners, who lived in constant fear of a slave revolt. An American militia colonel threatened to capture and burn every Spanish vessel he came across on the rivers and throw the crew overboard. Washington County, Mississippi, passed a resolution stating that anyone trading with the Spanish was "an enemy to his country." The state's governor, Robert Williams, sent a letter of outrage to his Spanish counterpart in West Florida, decrying the "inhuman manner" in which the Kempers were treated, and made sure it found its way into the press.[37]

Enter Aaron Burr

On June 5, 1805, a few months before the attack on the Kempers, a middle-aged, balding man arrived in New Orleans, delivered to the city in a government barge arranged by General Wilkinson, bearing a letter from him to Daniel Clark. "This will be delivered to you by Colonel Burr, whose worth you know well how to estimate," it began. "To him I refer you for many things improper to letter, and which he will not say to any other."[38]

The former vice president of the United States, Aaron Burr, had fled to the West to escape the fallout from his killing of Alexander Hamilton in a duel. Here he found a breath of fresh air—and new opportunity. He had begun scheming with Wilkinson even while vice president. In fact, it had been Burr's influence that secured the general the dual role of civil *and* military commander of upper Louisiana (portions of the purchase north of modern Louisiana), which placed him in the ideal seat to launch a conspiracy. Now, inspired by the general's visions of a new field for glorious achievement, Aaron Burr had gone to the frontier to investigate the pulse of the people.[39]

Like Blount, Burr was received with rapturous applause everywhere he went, stroking his ego and holding out the promise of redemption through some great enterprise. His alleged plans—for there were several iterations of the scheme—included alternatively launching an expedition to invade New Spain, or in a very unlikely scenario, severing the territories of Upper Louisiana and Orleans from the Union to create a new empire. What these schemes had in common was an attack on Spanish territory. In case of an American war with Spain, the attack would be legitimized and merged with the national effort, but if war did not come, it would be a private invasion of the kind Clark preferred.[40]

Wilkinson played both options and prepared the army to take part. Writing to the secretary of war, he remarked that if war came, "These dispositions [of mine] with judicious and rapid movements, attended by the Cross for your Banner, and a Band of Irish Priests who have been educated in Spain, (of whom I know a dozen) and we should take possession of the Northern Provinces without opposition, after which we might increase our force according to our means and at our discretion."[41]

Wilkinson's fanciful plan to march under a cross and Catholic priests with an army of protestants was cynical and unrealistic. After all, anti-Catholicism was one of the key factors in American hatred of Spain. For those who sought ideological kinsmen to the south, the implicit contradiction they faced was solved by imputing the Spanish Americans' impoverishment and degradation to a "priest-ridden" condition. Put simply, they were *victims* of their own religion. In addition to this bigotry, Americans generally had a stereotypical view of Spanish territory, particularly Mexico, as the land of gold and galleons—and it certainly was no myth. At the time, Mexico's silver mines produced two-thirds of all the world's output of that precious metal. Spreading republicanism might attract a man to contemplate a revolution, but adding the allure of wealth (and land, invariably) was enough to arm him with the courage to undertake it.[42]

In Kentucky, Burr recruited the state's foremost political player, John Adair, into the conspiracy. A former Revolutionary War militia officer from South Carolina, who like Wilkinson had moved west and prospered, Adair served a decade in his state's House of Representatives, rising to the speakership. Even as he was being courted by Burr, Adair was appointed US senator in 1805. He was also, crucially, brigadier general of the Kentucky Militia. As a leading man in politics and military in his important western state, he was a key convert to the cause. Adair would later claim he had been misled: Burr and Wilkinson, so he asserted, had suggested that the expedition was government sanctioned. However, given his zeal for the cause both before and after, the defense sounds dubious; Adair knew what he was doing. He wrote to Wilkinson that the men of Kentucky were as "greedy after plunder as ever the old Romans were." He added, "Mexico glitters in our eyes—the word is all we wait for." While Adair was using the Romans as a metaphor, Wilkinson was envisioning their enemies. Still playing both sides, he warned the Spanish of the plot he himself had coauthored, revealing to them "an army of adventurers similar to the ancient Goths and Vandals" would descend on Mexico. It seems clear that Wilkinson thought Spain too weak to heed his warning, but perhaps if they paid him more money, he implied, he could defeat the scheme.[43]

In New Orleans, Daniel Clark held a sumptuous dinner for the former vice president and his supporters in the city. Although the attendees at the dinner and their conversation were closely held secrets, it seems from later testimony that this was the moment when Burr and the Mexican Association joined together. The forces gathering against Spain were diverse indeed. In addition to American businessmen and adventurers, they included the Catholic leaders in New Orleans and beyond: Burr, echoing Wilkinson, claimed that more than two thousand Roman Catholic priests in New Spain were sympathetic to the conspiracy. This was certainly an exaggeration, but he did have the support of the bishop of New Orleans, who had traveled to Mexico "and knew the discomfort of the masses and the clergy." Much of this dissent came from the suppression of the Jesuits. This order was a source of power *independent* of the Spanish crown, had built schools and other institutions, and was greatly revered in Mexico. This alone made the order and its members suspect in the eyes of the monarchy, but after a series of riots and plots within Spain in the 1760s, the king expelled the Jesuits from the empire. Burr now supposedly designated three unnamed members of the order to act as agents of the conspiracy.[44]

Madame Theresa de St. Xavier Farjon, the mother superior of the Ursuline convent, hosted Burr as well, and was in on the perilously expanding secret. Burr had told her and others that people in Mexico were ready to join the cause as soon as their liberators arrived, as long as the invaders "protect their religion and will not subject them to a foreign power." This included the American government as well, another reason Clark was so keen to exclude it.[45]

Not long after this event, Daniel Clark took one of several suspicious commercial voyages to Veracruz, meeting with Spanish officials and bringing back intelligence on Spain's military dispositions. "I have been twice, since I last wrote you to the *Land of Promise*," Clark told a friend. "I have made some money and acquired more knowledge of the country." He thought Mexico could be invaded successfully, but as a historian put it, "wanted the expedition to be carried out by private individuals who would establish a new empire of their own."[46]

Burr, having arrived courtesy of Wilkinson, left mounted on one of Clark's horses. After two weeks in the city sowing seeds, he then traveled through West Florida, then back upriver, leaving his new friends with vague plans by which he would recruit an army in Ohio and sail down in the latter part of 1806 for an invasion of Mexico. The association, for its part, was more interested in starting the assault on Spain through West Florida, probably because its members had investments there. The isolated province was also weak and ripe for the plucking. The associates had clearly followed the Kemper brothers' failed revolt and raids; then came the bombshell news of their kidnapping and beating.

Recruits for Conspiracy

In March 1806, as Samuel Kemper, newly arrived in New Orleans, strolled along a street, he was approached by a well-to-do man in elegant clothes whom he had never met before, who invited the tavernkeeper to a dinner. Word of Samuel's arrival in the crescent city had evidently preceded him, and people had taken notice—important people. Such were the times that powerful men sought out tavernkeepers and adventurous spirits and seduced them with praise, promises, and potential riches—to do the things of which the wealthy man dreamed but only the bold man with nothing to lose could dare.[47]

The story of the Kempers' brutal capture and torment at the hands of the "Spanish" had excited the members of the shadowy Mexican Association. At a dinner shortly after the attack, the prospect of war with Spain was the talk of the hour.

As one attendee, John Prevost, would recall, "when the glass began to circulate, every American spoke freely their opinions of the approaching conflict.... In the unguarded hour of social intercourse, we were all gay, and all of us with the spirit of Americans ... declared our readiness to offer our services against the enemies, should events render them necessary." The mood was jovial, and it was said, "every man became a conqueror, or an emperor."[48]

Daniel Clark, in his opposition to the governor, may have been the originator of the association, but its two guiding members were two fellow Irishmen, James Workman and Lewis Kerr. The former had proposed a conquest of Spanish America in 1799 while still a British subject. After settling in New Orleans in 1804, he clung to the idea. "Mexico may be our own," Workman told a friend, "provided we act like men." He found a ready compatriot in Kerr, a lawyer who had worked in Ireland and India, who had now sought opportunity in New Orleans.[49]

Their vision was preached openly in the *Orleans Gazette*, whose editor, J. M. Bradford, was also a likely member of the association. In May 1805, the paper declared that in any war with the United States, Spain would have everything to lose: the Floridas and New Mexico "with all its wealth." But that would only be the beginning; they would push on to Mexico proper, where "the soldiers of liberty, animated by the Spirit of '76 and the genius of their Washington would go off to the field, not with a hope of plunder, but to avenge the cause of their country and to give freedoms to a new world." Eighteen months, he said, was all it would take to liberate two continents and place them under "the dominion of laws."[50]

Two days after being intercepted on the street by a member of the association, Samuel brought along his older brother Reuben to the home of Kerr. In a well-appointed parlor, where windows were closed and curtains drawn to conceal the interview from prying eyes and ears, amid cigars, laughter, and copious wine, Kerr became serious. The Kempers were asked to take an oath of secrecy, which they did after being assured—as they later claimed in testimony—that the plan had the president's support. "Mr. Kerr stated that we Americans were forming a society for the purpose of taking Baton Rouge, and the Floridas, that he knew we should have no objections to an enterprise of that kind—that our fate had been hard among the Spaniards, that country would be a great acquisition to ours; that in fact our country must have it," Reuben recalled.[51]

Kerr said the association had spies at Mobile, Pensacola, and other places, and he thought that the government would ultimately extend its interests beyond the Floridas, perhaps to Mexico. Then he got to the point: He wanted Reuben and Samuel to recruit a private army from among the people of Tennessee, Kentucky, and their home state of Ohio. Reuben objected that he and Samuel were not qualified for such an appointment and were too poor to undertake such an extensive endeavor. "He said that was all nothing," Reuben wrote, "*that they had money at will*; we should not be furnished if we went to either place with less than five thousand dollars each, and power to draw for any sum—one hundred thousand dollars at least."[52]

Eventually the word "millions" was tossed out. It was the sort of sum in which only governments dealt. This was heady stuff for the tavernkeeper and his brother, but Reuben claimed he began to sniff out inconsistencies in the story. If the expedition were indeed authorized, why would there be difficulty in recruiting men? Certainly, they would flock to the flag. "[Kerr] said there must be forts built and a force sufficient to support the country from an enemy until everything could be arranged." This implied the men would be moving *in advance* of government approval. Reuben said furthermore that volunteers for a fight were easy enough to find, but volunteers to build earthworks were not. Kerr suggested impounding slaves from nearby plantations. The more the brothers heard (or so they would one day claim), the less they believed the plan was actually sanctioned by Jefferson. Leaving without making any commitment, the Kempers returned to the City Hotel, where a few days later, Reuben was approached by Workman, who continued the pitch.[53]

Workman, who identified himself as the president of the association, said that most of the key civilian and military officials in New Orleans were members and that "some of the latter named gentlemen were more employed in the promotion and carrying into effect our great and important views already, than they were in their professed service." Indeed, Workman claimed they were stockpiling cartridges daily. They could provide all the resources, but they needed men.[54]

Reuben's account, taken in a deposition intended to show his innocence after Burr's arrest, paints the brothers as skeptical. But despite their alleged reticence, Reuben and Samuel Kemper continued to meet with the association in the ensuing days, and the organizers, who took extreme measures to preserve security, began treating the brothers as if hired already, which they probably were. They dined at Judge Workman's house, where the guests toasted Burr, and met an unnamed young Mexican exile who told them of his country and the prospects for revolution there.[55]

The Kempers were tasked to raise recruits and for this purpose were given a cypher and code words to use in their letters. "Bees-wax" meant muskets, "coffee" was powder, and "live hogs" were men. Upon returning to his home in Mississippi, Reuben was visited by several envoys to see how the "bees-wax" and "live hogs" were coming. One of these was a man whom the Kemper brothers knew well, Josiah Taylor, a US Army officer, who came to visit the Kempers in April, likely to follow up on their progress.[56]

Taylor was a key member of the conspiracy, possibly its linchpin. As the assistant military agent in New Orleans, he was in charge of the procurement of supplies and disbursement of cash on behalf of the army and was therefore perfectly positioned to assist in obtaining any additional supplies for the enterprise under the cover of his day job. He had been recruited before the Kempers and was being used as a go-between to seduce additional army officers. Soon after Reuben and Samuel were propositioned, he brought along a young artillery officer named William Murray, based at Fort Adams, near Baton Rouge, to meet with the association.[57]

Murray was an obvious choice for the venture. His father of the same name had been a trader and a land speculator in Illinois and Kentucky, where he had been among General Wilkinson's associates in the Spanish conspiracy. Now, the army officer son accompanied Taylor to a private dinner with Workman. After the meal, when the tablecloth was removed, Lewis Kerr, the same man who had propositioned the Kempers, joined them. After pleasantries were exchanged, Kerr turned to Taylor and asked, "Is Murray one of us?" Murray took this to refer to a secret fraternal society. "I answered I was no freemason and knew nothing of the science," he later recalled.[58]

"Yes, by God, he is one of us!" Taylor interjected, vouching for his fellow officer. Kerr then steered the conversation toward the Spanish territories generally, but particularly the means of taking Baton Rouge. Murray had seen the Spanish defenses personally and was contemptuous of them. "I observed that if the United States would make me a colonel," Murray later testified, "I would take it with five and twenty men or forfeit my head."[59]

"After a number of inquiries about Baton Rouge and the Red River country," Murray later recalled, "[Kerr] proceeded to lay open their plan of seizing upon the money in the banks at New Orleans, impressing the shipping, taking Baton Rouge, and joining [Venezuelan Revolutionary Francisco] Miranda by way of Mexico." The young officer would state after the fact that "I had never been expressly informed that the government of the United States authorized the expedition, nor had I particularly inquired; but when I found that the expedition was seriously contemplated, I took up the undoubting impression that it was secretly authorized by the government."[60]

But the artillery officer began to grow nervous (or retroactively claimed so) when he inquired about logistics. He asked "how they were to be furnished with the necessary supplies[,] whether by the government or by individual contribution." Kerr explained that the money seized from the banks would suffice, and the conspirators would then "return it in the case they were ultimately successful in the enterprise." Murray found the prospect of robbing banks incredible. If the government was in on the conspiracy, he told Kerr, certainly such an extremity was unnecessary. He left this first meeting wary and called on the only friend he had in New Orleans except Taylor. It was his father's former business associate, Daniel Clark. Murray was unaware, or so he claimed, that Clark himself was connected to the Mexican Association.[61]

"When I told Mr. Clark that I was calculated on as the officer to attack Baton Rouge, he advised me by all means to do it," Murray later recalled. Clark, who had recently been elected as the Orleans territorial representative in Congress, promised that he would do everything he could in Washington to aid Murray's venture. He let slip a statement suggesting the US government might take a more hostile view of the attack than what Kerr had averred. "It would require a large force to retake it" from Murray's armed force, Clark allegedly told the officer, adding that, "if the government should be disposed to trouble me [Murray], before they could send off a sufficient force, [I] should be in a situation to take care of myself."[62]

Murray was clearly in, though he too would later testify otherwise. In fact, when the crisis erupted in November 1806, a Spanish spy would write to his government that Murray had received numerous Burr-related letters which he refused to show to his commanding officer, but "he has only permitted two of his friends, officers, to read one paragraph in which he was offered an important position."[63]

Murray was not Taylor's only recruit. The officer had previously brought in Capt. William Cooper and Lt. William Platt, according to the testimony of another convert, militia Lt. Thomas W. Small. Kerr told Small "that the officers of the army are generally concerned with us," and that the plan was "to seize Baton Rouge, erect the ancient Mexican standard" and under the guise of this revolutionary army, collect forces. The Mexican Association's mercenary army would then seize Spanish Mobile, where they expected to find $200,000 in cash. "Afterwards they would push on for the province of Taxos [sic]." Workman, later speaking to Small, made the same proposal to seize New Orleans' banks. The judge even had an assistant, a Mr. John J. Connoly, translating the laws of Mexico for use when the conspirators entered that country. Small met with Connoly, who said, "Burr is coming down, which side will you take, Small?" The lieutenant took the Burr side and swore an oath that demonstrated the Mexican Association's lofty ambitions: *"To use all means and to aid and assist in effecting the emancipation of Mexico and Peru."*[64]

The Kempers, Taylor, Murray, Small, and likely others had been brought into the great conspiracy, though they would all claim they had been deceived. As Small would testify, "During all these communications and transactions, the idea was ever held up, of the private sanction of the government, which I have ever since I returned to Orleans suspected strongly to be a mere catch to ensnaring the thoughtless and unreflecting into acts of infamy." Yet there was no such sanction, and the fates of all these conspirators—the great and the Small alike—were ultimately in the hands of just one man, upon whom everything in Burr's great conspiracy depended for success. And that man was not Aaron Burr.[65]

Spain Moves First

The conspiracy was soon the worst kept secret on the frontier, in large part because of Aaron Burr's lack of discretion in speaking so frequently of his plans. On Louisiana's nebulous western border, still in dispute from the purchase, American and Spanish forces had been poised at knife's edge for three years. The Spaniards, well aware of the Burr rumors through reports like those about Murray, finally stirred to action. In Chihuahua, Nemesio Salcedo, the Spanish Commandant General of the Internal Provinces, whose domain included Texas, ordered a dramatic reinforcement of the garrison in this border province, dispatching six hundred troops, doubling the imperial force in the territory. To command them, he sent Lt. Col. Simón Herrera, the governor of Nuevo León, a competent commander who had led a successful expedition against the Comanche and Apache. But Herrera was also clever and diplomatic—and unlike most Spanish officers, he well understood the United States and its political climate. He was fluent in his neighbors' language, having married an English woman, and had at one point personally met George Washington. In 1805, he took his force to the frontier.[66]

While the United States argued for the Sabine River as the border of Louisiana, the Spanish asserted it was the Arroyo Hondo, just west of Natchitoches, Louisiana, and about thirty miles further east of the Americans' preferred line. Herrera approached this line, then crossed it, stationing outposts in October 1805 at Bayou Pierre and La Naña. Spanish troops came within seven miles of Natchitoches. As they patrolled inside what America believed to be its own territory, Wilkinson belatedly moved his troops to the frontier. The tension on the border gripped the nation. As one writer noted, "On the Forth of July [1806], there were not a thousand persons in the United States who did not think war with Spain inevitable, impending, begun!" With war imminent, and with two armies in close proximity, any spark could start it, and Wilkinson, the master schemer, was the man with the firebrand in his hand.[67]

In October, while the general was meeting with his aides planning the American response, a young man arrived at Wilkinson's advanced headquarters, announcing himself as a new volunteer for the American army. He entered the tent with Wilkinson, and when the latter's aide left the room, his demeanor changed. He identified himself as Samuel Swartwout, an agent of Burr. He produced an urgent letter and handed it to the general, who took it into his private room and opened it. On the parchment, he beheld a series of strange symbols: circles, numbers, squares with dots inside them or positioned in quarters around them, and various additional hieroglyphics. The general retrieved his hidden cipher key and began translating its revolutionary contents.[68]

"Yours postmarked 13th May is received," the author wrote. "I have obtained funds and have actually commenced the enterprise." Wilkinson was to be "second to Burr only" and had authority to dictate the ranks of his officers. The invasion was, according to Burr, welcomed by many in New Spain: "The people of the country to which we are going are prepared to receive us—their agents now with Burr say that if we will protect their religion, and will not subject them to a foreign power, that in three weeks all will be settled." The general was asked to "send a list of all persons known to Wilkinson west of the mountains, who could be useful, with a note delineating their characters." He certainly had such a list, if not on paper, at least in his mind. Clark, Workman, Kerr, and others had theirs too, including Taylor, Murray, and the Kempers with their "live hogs." The time was at hand to launch Burr's long-anticipated invasion of New Spain. But it was not to be.[69]

Had the letter come just a few weeks earlier, it would have been welcomed enthusiastically. In early 1806, Wilkinson had possibly used his connections to betray a scientific expedition under Thomas Freeman and Peter Custis to the Spaniards, perhaps hoping to trigger a war. The Spaniards dutifully confronted the expedition, but the war never materialized. In June, the general launched his own expedition under Lt. Zebulon Pike, ostensibly to explore and contact the Indians, but almost certainly to scout the way to Santa Fe. Pike and his men were captured, but Wilkinson did not know it when the momentous letter arrived.[70]

As late as September 8, Wilkinson had written to Adair, the Kentucky Senator and militia commander. "The time looked for by many and wished for by more has now arrived for subverting the Spanish government in Mexico," Wilkinson wrote. "Be you ready and join me; we will want little more than light-armed troops... 5,000 men will give us the [Rio Grande], 10,000 Monterey... 30,000 men to conquer the whole province of Mexico. We cannot fail of success."[71]

At the time, Wilkinson had believed war was certain within a week, but since then, the circumstances had changed significantly, and James Wilkinson, the shameless intriguer, uncharacteristically blinked. He had not heard from Burr in months, and before receiving the letter, he possibly thought the attempt was abandoned. When the messenger delivered the communication, it was a shocking three months old. But there was more to Wilkinson's reticence. It may have been the rumors of his previous treason that were beginning to spread, the dubiousness of the probable success of the Burr scheme, or even fear about the dangerous exposure for his family from the risky venture. It likely had something to do with another payout from Spain as well.[72]

Whatever the cause, James Wilkinson decided to abort the plan and cut his losses. In the end, the general embraced a path that had always worked for him before: when in doubt, *betray someone*. In November 1806, Wilkinson fired off a preemptive note to Jefferson, warning him of the conspiracy and feigning innocence. He then turned to the border and negotiated an agreement with Lieutenant Colonel Herrera to create a *Neutral Ground*, in which neither side would send military forces to avoid any unfortunate accidental clashes. It was a spur-of-the-moment decision with momentous consequences for the future.[73]

With his back thus secured, Wilkinson marched his troops to New Orleans to cover up his involvement in the scheme. He appealed to Governor Claiborne to give him authority "to repress the seditious and arrest the disaffected." Though Burr's army was at this point little more than a myth, Wilkinson inflated the danger to the already paranoid governor: "You could not for a moment withstand the desperation and numbers opposed to you," he wrote. He invoked Clark and *even more frightening dangers* to stir the governor to action: "And the brigands, provoked by the opposition, might resort to the dreadful expedient of exciting a revolt of the negroes. If we divide our forces, we shall be beaten in detail!"[74]

When Claiborne balked, Wilkinson went around him and exercised de facto martial law anyway, swiftly rounding up anyone who could implicate him to keep them silent. The general seized Burr's agent, Peter V. Ogden, and several others and had them imprisoned aboard the USS *Aetna*, a bomb ketch anchored in the Mississippi. From thence, they would have been transported to Washington, out of reach of his enemies, if not for the intervention of Kerr, who was hired as a lawyer for one of the accused and brought a writ of habeus corpus before Judge Workman. The latter approved it and had Ogden released.[75]

The lawyer and judge were now the greatest threats to Wilkinson. Indeed, Kerr, who had a commission as a colonel in the militia, had been given "nearly a thousand stands of arms" and Wilkinson feared that the next target of arrest might be himself. An excuse to move preemptively came on January 14, 1807. General Adair, who had left Burr in Nashville in December unaware that the plan had been betrayed, had just arrived in New Orleans. A rumor had him coming from the mouth of the Cumberland with an army, but in fact, he came only with two domestic servants. Wilkinson nonetheless saw his chance. The Kentuckian was dragged from his dinner by armed troops. At the same time, Kerr was sitting after dinner at a friend's home when "a party of dragoons suddenly entered the room," arrested him, and had him hauled before the general, along with Workman, who was similarly ambushed. The intervention of a local judge preserved the Mexican Association's members in New Orleans, but Wilkinson successfully spirited away Adair, locked in the hold of the schooner *Thatcher*. He was transported to a military prison at Fort McHenry in Baltimore. No charges were filed against him, but by the time he secured his release, a month had passed, and the fictitious narrative which Wilkinson had crafted, placing himself as the hero destroying the secret cabal, had taken hold in the public mind.[76]

At the trial of Workman and Kerr, the veil of secrecy around the Mexican Association was finally pierced—at least partially. Murray and Small were deposed, though the Kempers' connection remained unknown until later. Far from denying their association, the defendants admitted it. The organization, they said, was conceived at a time "when we believed ourselves exposed to the hostilities" of Spain. Kerr said that he and Workman, "in conjunction with many other characters of respectability, or influence, and of enterprise in this territory," developed the association's plans for protection but also for "its ultimate object intended to provide for the permanent safety, to advance the best interests, and to promote the real glory and honor of our country."[77]

This was done, "with a view, in case of war, of proposing to our government an expedition against those colonies, to be carried on from the resources to be provided and supplied by the members of that association, and by such other persons whom they might be able to engage in their enterprise." Anticipating a lack of interest among politicians, among other reasons because of the cost, the defendant's counsel added, "the expedition contemplated by [Kerr] and his associates was therefore a private one, dependent, principally upon the resources and exertions of individuals, both in the United States and Mexico." The organization's secrecy, they explained, was not due to treasonous intent, but to shield the plans from Spanish spies and protect the conspirators' economic interests in Mexico. Asked why they had not even informed Governor Claiborne, Kerr explained that it was due to the governor's nature of "amiable indiscretion." The project, they insisted, had already been abandoned before Wilkinson's arrests.[78]

The Mexican Association members were all acquitted of violating the Neutrality Act, based on lack of evidence that the plan was actually implemented. No proof, furthermore, was presented showing leaders of the Mexican Association anticipated secession of the Orleans territory as part of their plans; this aspect of the scheme came out in Aaron Burr's own separate trial. This was probably never a realistic plan, possibly it was even a diversion to fool the Spanish. But with Wilkinson's clever manipulation, it would be cemented in the mind of Claiborne. It would become the governor's motivating fear, and any future machinations would be seen in light of it, with serious consequences for 1812.

The Mexican Association members suffered in various degrees. Mayor Watkins of New Orleans lost his job. Kerr was bankrupted and frozen from the governor's inner circle. James Workman, on the other hand, survived relatively unscathed. Daniel Clark, who had taken his congressional seat as the Orleans representative in Congress shortly before, fought to save his reputation by attacking Wilkinson in print, exposing the Spanish payments to his former associate, of which he well knew. The general dismissed the accusations, defending the cash as mere compensation for goods his businesses had sold. He further attacked his accusers in court: "The attempt was worthy of the authors—worthy of the cause it was destined to abet," he testified. "It deserves all the merit which is due to the desperation."[79]

In the Orleans Territory, a bitter peace evolved in the wake of the affair: Wilkinson and Claiborne in a lopsided alliance, while Clark, who had some popular support among the people, hated them both and they hated him. But behind the backs of the governor and the general, the old Burr conspirators, Clark, Workman, and Adair, had not given up the dream of a new Western Empire. Neither would the conspiracy's lesser figures, like the Kempers, Taylor, and Murray. Wilkinson and Burr's scheme had "prodded and aroused many of their fellow countrymen, hungry for land, starving for trade and Papist-hating, to feverish awareness of what beckoned resolute men in the land of Texas and the halls of Montezuma." Within five years, these men would once again unite in the same cause and begin the march to the southwest. For them, and many others on the frontier, Mexico still "glittered in their eyes."[80]

2

The Edge of Empire

ON SEPTEMBER 3, 1808, a pair of stagecoaches arrived at the Red River across from Natchitoches, Louisiana, and were ferried across to the town. In the wagons were a small party of travelers easily discernable amid the hunters, Indian traders, and settlers looking to start a new life on the fringes of America's newest territory: a distinguished-looking thirty-two-year-old Spaniard, his well-dressed wife, his young daughter, a chaplain, and a handful of servants. The muddy streets onto which they stepped would have been crowded by a bustle of traders in animal skins and hawkers selling cattle, goat, pigs, and more. The town was far more crowded than the Spaniard remembered. Natchitoches—pronounced *Nack-uh-tish*—had doubled in size since he had last been in Louisiana. It now boasted more than a thousand souls: a mix of French Creoles, Spaniards, Anglo-Americans, slaves, and a few resident Indians. But this traveler was just passing through. Don Manuel María de Salcedo y Quiroga, for this was his name, was en route to the nearby Spanish province of Texas, where he was to be the new governor.[1]

As they made their way through the town, Salcedo and his retinue would have been struck by the presence of a large fort, built on a pine hill two streets to the west of the river, two city blocks long surrounded by a wooden palisade. Above it flew a flag of fifteen red and white stripes, with a field of blue containing the same number of stars. Fort Claiborne—named after the Orleans territorial governor—had seemingly sprung up overnight, in August 1804, little more than a year after the United States gained the province. It was large, well-stocked with arms, and its defenses all pointed west—toward Salcedo's new province.[2]

The Spaniard probably noted all these changes in the frontier outpost with a touch of bitterness. Five years before, Louisiana had been Spanish territory and Salcedo was a member of the province's elite. A twenty-five-year-old military officer with pedigree and position, Manuel had arrived in 1801, along with his father, Juan Manuel de Salcedo. The latter had been appointed governor of the restless Spanish province with a mostly French population, but his rule was destined to be short. On

November 30, 1803, the governor had to endure the spectacle of the lowering of the Spanish flag and raising in its place the tricolor of republican France, which true lovers of monarchy such as himself loathed. Barely a month later, the equally reviled American flag would supplant it in turn.³

For the Salcedos, Spanish colonial administration was the family business. Young Manuel had attended the Royal Academy at Ocaña at age seven and the Royal Seminary of Nobles until his seventeenth birthday. Upon graduation, he became a lieutenant serving under his father, who commanded the infantry battalion of the Canary Islands at Tenerife, before the elder Salcedo received the orders which took him to Louisiana. As his father's aide in that province, Manuel held among other roles the position of boundary commissioner for the transfer, a job that almost certainly took him to Natchitoches. In Louisiana, he married María Guadalupe Prietto y la Ronde, a native Louisianan of mixed Spanish and French blood. After three years back in Spain, Manuel was headed once more across the ocean, not to Louisiana, but to the top provincial post in Texas.⁴

The job had come open upon the death of Governor Juan Bautista de Elguézabel in 1805. In this nepotism-driven bureaucracy, Manuel would serve under the Commandant General of the Internal Provinces of New Spain, his uncle Don Nemesio Salcedo. Manuel Salcedo's seat of government would be San Fernando de Béxar—today's San Antonio—a small, dusty outpost of mostly adobe houses and crumbling missions far from the coast, distant from all trade and subjected to the occasional Comanche raid. Making matters worse, Manuel would have to submit to micromanagement and abuse by his stern, uncompromising, and domineering uncle, the absolute authority for four of the northernmost provinces of New Spain, answerable at that time only to the king. Still, for Manuel, the new assignment must have seemed a glorious opportunity for distinction. Texas, small as it was, had become the lynchpin of the defense of all New Spain.⁵

His first problem was how to get there. Compelled to side with Napoleon, Spain was drawn into war with the world's largest naval power, Britain. After the Franco/Spanish fleet was devastated at the Battle of Trafalgar on October 1, 1805, Don Manuel could not risk the sea route to Veracruz. Instead, he chose to travel to the United States and proceed overland. The party sailed, likely on a neutral American ship, to Bedford, Massachusetts, by water to New York, by stage to Philadelphia, then on to Pittsburgh. From thence they came down the Ohio and Mississippi Rivers to Natchez, then overland to Natchitoches. The journey of 5,200 miles was a grueling one for the young family. From the time he received his appointment to the time he arrived in Texas, a full year and a half had passed.⁶

The circuitous route was eye-opening for Don Manuel. It was, after all, the same route Aaron Burr was to have taken, and along the way, Salcedo dined with many former Burr conspirators and sympathizers like the governor of Kentucky, Christopher Greenup. Although these Westerners no doubt veiled their passions in his presence, more than a few of them caused Salcedo some unease with their fervor for republicanism and hostility to the monarchy he so revered. By 1808, many Americans in the East thought the Burr matter was over, but Salcedo was left with the impression that the conspiracy was still very much alive.[7]

The changes the Spaniards had seen in the Orleans Territory were even more disconcerting. The new American territory now boasted more than seventy thousand people—*double* the population it had held when he had left it just five years before. Next door, poor Texas had scarcely four thousand non-Indian residents and soldiers, and was the weakest province in all of New Spain. Neighboring New Mexico and Coahuila had six times and ten times as many people, respectively. With an empire stretching from Texas to Tierra del Fuego, Spain simply could not populate it all.[8]

The Iberian nation had always had difficulty recruiting settlers for this remote province, with its frequent droughts, lack of exploitable mineral resources, and hostile Indian population. Consequently, it remained little more than a buffer. "Born of imperial strategic needs, Texas remained a bastion against intruders, Indian and European, throughout the colonial period," wrote historian Jesús F. de la Teja. But following the Americans' arrival on their borders, it became apparent that Texas would not even fit that bill without a large influx of Spaniards. Salcedo's predecessor, Elguézabal, had sounded the alarm in January 1804, soon after the Americans had occupied Louisiana. "Pending the arrival of a sufficient number of settlers from other provinces," he wrote, "it will not be possible to stop entirely, or even to check effectually, the entry, invasion or the execution of any other schemes the aforesaid Anglo-Americans may have in mind or wish to carry out."[9]

Spain heeded the warning and responded with an uncharacteristic burst of action. King Charles IV ordered a massive infusion of Spaniards—as many as five thousand civilians—to Texas. The would-be settlers had gone so far as to sell their homes and assemble in the Port of Cádiz, while massive amounts of supplies were built up and the ships were prepared. All came to naught when on December 4, England declared war on Spain for siding with Bonaparte. Then came Trafalgar and the blockade of the Spanish fleet the next year. The colonization expedition was abandoned, the settlers returned to their homes or found new ones, and the last hope of a demographic bulwark of European Spaniards in Texas vanished.[10]

But the chaos of the Spanish Empire had only just begun. The king's son and heir apparent Ferdinand stoked public resentment against his father's prime minister, causing a major riot. In consequence, in March 1808, Charles IV abdicated, and his son took the throne as Ferdinand VII. Offering to mediate the dispute, Napoleon invited both to a conference, where he abruptly imprisoned them, forcing Ferdinand to abdicate in turn in May. Napoleon then placed his own brother, Joseph Bonaparte, on the Spanish throne. The subsequent French takeover of Peninsular Spain was to be extended to the entire empire. All of this happened during Manuel Salcedo's long journey to Texas, and colonial officials from San Antonio to Buenos Aires now faced a difficult decision: submit to Bonaparte, support Spanish monarchists in exile rallying behind the cause of the imprisoned King Ferdinand VII, or choose independence.

French Intrigues in Texas

Salcedo first became aware of the dire threat to his mission while stopping in Philadelphia, where an American told him of the passage through that town of a shadowy Frenchman who claimed to be Bonaparte's envoy to New Spain. Gen. Octaviano D'Alvimar carried with him plans to entirely remake the colony, appointing top Bonapartists to positions of power. The Frenchman, with a head start and no family to slow his progress, would beat Salcedo by a month. Fortunately for the Spaniard, when Napoleon's representative arrived in impoverished Nacogdoches, Texas, on August 5, 1808, audaciously wearing a full French cavalry uniform and declaring himself the lawful authority of the king, the garrison commander promptly detained him.[11]

Even if Salcedo had wanted to push straight on into Texas in September, his family was likely at the end of their endurance upon reaching Natchitoches, so the governor paused at the home of one of the more influential residents of the town, Dr. John Sibley. The Spaniard may have previously met Sibley, who had immigrated to Louisiana when the region still belonged to the Catholic monarchy. Sibley was a physician who had moved to Spanish territory a year before the handover, when he applied for and was awarded the crucial post of US Indian Agent.[12]

The Indian problem was equally central to internal politics and foreign affairs of both Anglo and Spanish North America. Eastern Indians displaced by American settlement streamed west, first into French and Spanish Louisiana but ultimately into Texas as well. Texas tribes like the Caddo and Wichita were soon beset by waves of these migrating outsiders. They traded and intermarried with these newcomers but came into conflict as well. The native Caddo villages on the Red River were frequently raided by the Choctaws. The great Caddo chief Dehahuit persuaded the Spanish to arrange a peace, which they did, but much to his consternation the Spanish then allowed these interlopers, along with Chickasaws and other tribes, to settle in Texas.[13]

With the sale of Louisiana to the United States, this already tenuous relationship became more fraught. With the Stars and Stripes now waving from Natchitoches, the doorway to Texas was no longer in Spanish control. Indians were a key source of proxy power and influence on the frontier, and the man most responsible for implementing Indian policy for the United States in the region was Sibley. His task was to maintain friendly ties, or at least prevent hostility, with tribes on the frontier, which he did primarily by providing them with goods from the government. The doctor frequently gifted supplies, firearms, and even American flags to Indians in Texas as far south as Matagorda Bay, buying them off to secure peace for America at the expense of Spain.[14]

Salcedo stayed with Sibley for four days, and the two likely had many conversations. Sibley reported that Salcedo was "a modest unassuming man and appears to have sense enough to govern such people." On the topic of D'Alvimar, Salcedo informed his American host that on his arrival, "He shall send every Frenchman out of the province and shall begin with Delvimere [sic] if he finds him." Sibley certainly would have agreed to the sentiment because he saw the French as much of a threat to America as to Spain. Though Napoleon had sold the province in a moment of crisis, the little general was notoriously opportunistic and deceitful, as the Spanish had lately learned. He might exploit any opportunity to restart his American empire. In a letter to US Secretary of War Henry Dearborn, Sibley warned that many Frenchmen of Louisiana possessed "spirits . . . much exhilarated with what they believe so fair a prospect of being united to the French government."[15]

Although D'Alvimar had been detained in Texas, the Spanish authorities had not yet arrested him, waiting instead for someone in higher authority to guide them. All the more reason for Sibley to urge Salcedo, a legitimate symbol of the exiled monarchy, to hurry to his province. Sibley was skeptical about the future of New Spain: it must either attempt independence or seek the protection of England, he believed, and it was this latter course that Americans feared the most. Still, Sibley wrote that he had initiated "a very friendly intercourse" with his Spanish guest and "the heart of the new Governor Salcedo is entirely with us."[16]

Don Manuel clearly concealed his true feelings. For him, the French may be the immediate threat, but Sibley's nation was the long-term one. He had seen the population boom and witnessed the Burrite sentiment throughout the West. When Burr's scheme failed in 1806, Natchez had become a place of settlement for many of his followers. Two years on, they were still there, longing for Mexico and poised at the head of the Natchez and Texas trail, an overland route that bypassed the main American garrisons and deposited its travelers in Natchitoches, at the gateway to Mexico.[17]

Salcedo certainly would have pressed his interlocutor for more information about the American frontier and politics. Loosened by enough stiff drink, Sibley might have railed on a subject about which he would write to Secretary of War Henry Dearborn days later: the faults of Governor Claiborne. Like Daniel Clark, Sibley was no friend of the young, naïve governor, who to Sibley's annoyance, had appointed foreigners to positions of importance in the territory. "I do not believe that all the acts of Governor Claiborne put together, since he has been [governor] of this territory has, or ever will compensate for the mischief he has done to this . . . district by his appointing an Irishman judge," he wrote. The Irishman in question was District Judge John C. Carr. Salcedo probably heard both points of view on the matter—at some point in his stay in Natchitoches, he likely spoke directly with Carr as well. Little did Salcedo realize, the judge's intrigues or incapacities would, in no small way, decide his own earthly fate.[18]

Salcedo could not even take comfort in his neighbors' fierce divisions. As it would continue to surprise the Spaniards for the next three years, the very internal strife that would have paralyzed a monarchy *had the exact opposite effect* in a republic, as Burr had nearly demonstrated. Salcedo realized that the American government need not be involved for American citizens to threaten his province. It would only take "some adventurous rebels, licensed by the liberty of their laws."[19]

"The Anglo-American is naturally industrious," he wrote to another governor, "and if he were not so he would not like to live in wildernesses, where his subsistence depends upon his industry; this same kind of life hardens them, and necessarily makes them to be soldiers." He pointed to the rapid development of Kentucky, Tennessee, and Ohio, unchecked by the law. "Consequently, it has resulted that when the decrees and governmental provisions have not been agreeable to them, whether they may be from Congress or from territorial channels, they have not obeyed them, or at least they have attempted not to obey them."[20]

American armies were nimble, with smaller trains than the ponderous equipage of a Spanish force. The troops survived off the land, and their provisions were "corn alone, and whiskey, which they give for a daily ration to the soldier." Americans' small field artillery, Salcedo reported, could be moved by horseback. But there were disadvantages too. The officers were generally not professionally trained as Spanish officers were, and desertion was common. Still, noting how open and exposed Texas was, Salcedo concluded that the province "is not only penetrable, but advantageous to getting into it."[21]

With brooding thoughts like these on his mind, Salcedo set off for Texas. To get there, he had to cross the Neutral Ground which Wilkinson and Herrera had established two years before. The pact the two officers had signed had held, contrary to all expectations. It was, however, a mixed blessing: While it had prevented conflict between the two nations, it created an ungoverned land that became the home to squatters, deserters, runaway slaves, and thieves. It would be, like so many of the legacies that Manuel Salcedo would find in his new province, a bedeviling, festering wound. As the Spaniard mounted a fresh horse and pushed westward, he faced an immense challenge. In the end, he would risk everything he had—including his life—to save the monarchy's most fragile province.[22]

"The Continental Key to America"

Salcedo's new home of Texas was in the words of one of the governor's colleagues, "the continental key to America," a vital but poor province at the northern extremity of an empire that stretched to the Strait of Magellan. Unlike the Anglo-American colonies, the Spanish New World Empire was peopled by a relatively small colonial population living alongside variously Hispanicized native tribes and, increasingly in Mexico proper, people of mixed Spanish, Indian, and African blood known as *castas*.[23]

In the northeast of Texas lived settled but independent native tribes like the Caddo, who were generally peaceful. But in the west, Spain faced a number of nomadic tribes, unbowed and often hostile, particularly the Comanche and Lipan Apache. A treaty after 1785 brought some hope that the province could be further developed, but the fragile peace was punctuated by occasional raids and spontaneous outbursts of violence. Securing this peace depended entirely on the efforts of the overstretched Spanish royalist garrison. Unlike other Mexican provinces, where a class of rich, powerful miners and semi-autonomous captains of industry could hire private mercenaries, Texas had only this weak, ill-equipped, and under-strength royal force, which had to guard the gateway from America as well as the frontier.[24]

This insecurity was an existential threat to the principal industry of the province—the grazing of cattle, horses, sheep, and goats. Often pastured far from settlements, these herds were always endangered, as was the populace who depended on them. The latter complained to royal authorities that "the enemy Indians have pursued and harassed us, for which reason we have not been able to raise our heads above water." Ranchers faced internal challenges as well, in the form of competition from their own church, and its mission ranches. These enjoyed better funding, access to cheap Indian convert labor, and legal perquisites from the viceroy. To this was added force and intimidation. When two San Antonio residents, Vicente Álvarez Travieso and Francisco José de Arocha, were awarded the right to graze on the banks of the Guadalupe River, the missions blocked them by moving their own herds onto the tracts.[25]

After ranching, Texans also raised crops like corn, beans, and some sugar cane, but these were mostly for subsistence. Governor Elguézabal had complained that the Spanish Texans, or *Tejanos*, had not yet learned to manufacture textiles or rope, raise cotton, build flower mills, or conduct any industry at all. The governor would never admit it, but the fault lay with Spanish policy, which greatly circumscribed trade. Even cattle raising, nominally a major industry, was barely at subsistence levels. The locals "suffer a damaging shortage of good cattle for which reason the scarcity of meat is almost continual," Elguézabal wrote in 1803, "and it is true that if the hunters did not find buffalo annually between the months of May and October to supply the need in part, the greater portion of the families would perish in misery."[26]

The population of Spanish Texas on Salcedo's arrival was 2,933 citizens and about 1,000 soldiers. The bulk of the latter were the reinforcements Herrera had brought up in 1805. The civilian population was divided between five towns. The largest by far was the capital, San Fernando de Béxar, in the southwest extremity of the province, consisting of about 1,700 citizens, plus most of the province's soldiers. It was originally built as a presidio to defend several missions. This was merely a collection of adobe buildings gathered around a central plaza, rather than a real fortress with walls, though the closest mission, San Antonio de Valero, was at least somewhat fortified. It had been secularized and by 1808 was the headquarters of the Spanish garrison. When a force of soldiers called the *Alamo de Parras* company took up residence, the fortress became known thenceforth as the Alamo. In time, the town, while never abandoning its official name of San Fernando, took its name from the mission and was called by its modern appellation, San Antonio.[27]

Downriver from the capital and near the coast was La Bahía, situated around a mission and a presidio, with a population of 405. It was the only town not on the main *Camino Real* (King's Highway), which ran northwest towards Louisiana. This latter was the main artery for Spanish Texas, more of a corridor rather than a single road, pieced together over the centuries from Indian paths and patrol routes, primarily linking sources of water. Along this, moving upward from San Antonio were two small towns, both established within the previous two years. The first was the small settlement of San Marcos de Neve on the river of the same name, with eighty-two residents. Next was the town of Trinidad de Salcedo, with about ninety-one persons, along the modern Trinity River. But the most important town to the defense of Texas lay at the far end of this highway, after "160 leagues of wilderness, which gives rise to grave risks in their transit." This was Nacogdoches, with about 655 souls.[28]

Town on the Edge of Empire

Nacogdoches, Texas, and Natchitoches, Louisiana, stood about ninety miles apart, astride the disputed border. Their names were both derived from related Indian tribes, but there the similarities ended. While Natchitoches was bustling, rapidly changing, and dynamic since the American takeover, Nacogdoches was a poor town that had seen much change but little growth. The ideological boundary was just as stark: America (novel, expanding, and republican) butted up against New Spain (traditional, monarchical, and fiercely closed to outside influences). One was protestant, embracing the Enlightenment, and the other was Catholic, rejecting most elements of it. The viceregal government of New Spain was particularly hostile to any new ideas that hinted at revolution. In late 1803, shortly after the Louisiana Purchase brought America and its ideals up to the very edges of Texas, the call went out to scour the province for anything subversive. The commander in Nacogdoches reported to the governor: "In order to comply with the letter which the Commandant General sent you under date of the 1st of November . . . I have tried with the utmost diligence to see if there are in this village copies of the impious writings with the title *Contrat Social* by Jean Jacques Rousseau, and *La Bororquia, or Victim of the Inquisition*. However, none have been found."[29]

While it is doubtful that many of the impoverished and mostly illiterate residents of Nacogdoches would have known what to do with the works of the famous Swiss philosopher or an obscure anticlerical Spaniard even if they had them, the fear Spanish leaders held for subversion was genuine. With their homeland under threat from French republicanism and their provinces challenged by Jefferson's "Empire of Liberty," the only way they knew to fight back was to close the door to the outside world, particularly after it became clear that no new convoy of Spanish settlers was forthcoming.

Of course, for New Spain, and particularly Texas, closed doors were nothing new. The empire embraced the mercantilist system in which most civilian trade outside of a tightly held monopoly was barred from access to foreign markets. Spain's governing economic law, the *Casa de Contración* built up exhaustive and elaborate rules for trade, and the colonies' interests were effectively subordinated to the powerful merchants in Cádiz. Colonies themselves were structured along similar exploitative lines, so that the further one went toward the periphery, trade became next to impossible. On the frontier, these restrictions ran to absurdity: citizens of Texas were prohibited from trading with neighboring Louisiana, even when that province was also Spanish. Thus the people of Nacogdoches were banned under severe penalty from commerce with nearby Natchitoches and were instead forced to route all their trade through Mexico. Manufactured goods imported from there, in turn, cost as much as four times their original price after transportation costs were factored in.[30]

All trade, therefore, was oriented to the south, and the sole external output for Texas goods—and for imports as well—was the annual fair held in September in Saltillo. For those Tejanos who might dream of shipping their wares abroad, the nearest port was Veracruz. These were, respectively, 350 and 650 miles distant from San Antonio. It was difficult for Tejanos to ship their products such a distance in oxcarts. Ferries were rare, bridges nonexistent, floods frequent, and Indian attacks through long stretches of vacant wilderness were serious. This trade they nonetheless attempted, mostly bringing products of the cattle industry: live animals, but also jerked meat, candle tallow, hides, and some finished leather. The profits were never great, and by the 1790s, even the vast herds of feral cattle in Texas were diminishing.[31]

While this outlet provided some economic connection between interior Mexico and San Antonio, the route from thence to Nacogdoches crossed a further 450 miles and 8 rivers. Thus the furthest town in Texas was nearly twice as distant as San Antonio to the Mexican market, making it almost impossible for residents of the frontier to trade. For these, even trading within Texas was extremely difficult, and most residents of the town practiced only subsistence agriculture. With no way to sell their surpluses, the excess in good years simply rotted. In lean years, citizens lacked the cash or opportunity to make up for failed crops.[32]

Want was endemic and starvation always threatened, but the Spanish government held firm to its anti-trade policies for ordinary citizens while granting special dispensation to select government officials to circumvent the ban. The province's Indian agent, ironically an Irish-American (now Spanish subject) named William Barr, was allowed to travel to Natchitoches to buy gifts for native tribes but was mostly *prohibited* from selling any of the articles to Spaniards. One can only imagine

The Edge of Empire   41

the bitterness of the dutiful Spanish subjects dressed in ancient rags, upon seeing Indian chiefs contentedly leaving town with newly imported fabrics. Piling absurdity on absurdity, the commander of the garrison charged with preventing smuggling was on occasion allowed to cross the border to buy clothes for his troops. Outfitted in Louisiana cloth, these soldiers scoured the countryside hunting citizens who might be smuggling, among other items, Louisiana cloth. Even this exception for the troops was restricted to emergency needs, and the rebuke for violation could be stern. Commandant General Nemesio Salcedo wrote to the Nacogdoches Adjutant Inspector Francisco Viana in July 1806, berating him for purchasing in Natchitoches the very paper upon which he wrote his reports.[33]

Citizens on the border, but inland as well, were subject to spies reporting on possible nefarious activities, as in the case of one Nacogdoches resident named Nieves Peres. As the garrison commander reported to the governor, "It was said that they did introduce goods, and that in the month of December, Nieves's wife was known to be making at home some skirts of fine India lawn [woven textile], with small green flowers and other colors."[34]

Given such dire want, smuggling was endemic. When the Americans took over Louisiana, the profits to gain became very attractive. "The temptation to violate the law was obviously great," historian Mattie Austin Hatcher notes. "The people had no inducement to devote themselves to agriculture . . . and it's not surprising that many of them fell in with the plans of [Anglo] intruders." This trade took place on small covert roads or "Contraband Traces" that paralleled the Camino Real. With no cash to pay for smuggled goods, wild stock became the currency of purchase, and Texas authorities admitted that sometimes as many as a thousand head of cattle were illicitly shipped across the border to Louisiana in a single month.[35]

Spanish commanders in Nacogdoches charged with enforcing the ban on trade were hardly brutal or uncaring. They recognized the inhumane and impossible orders they were required to enforce, and while professing loyalty to the king, on occasion would push back, writing to authorities for relief for their starving *paisanos* (countrymen). Viana, the adjutant inspector, wrote in 1808, just six months before Manuel Salcedo would arrive, "The poverty which this post of Nacogdoches has always suffered is well known. The loss of this year's crop and the inability to provide for itself from [San Antonio] because of like scarcity there," he wrote, made starvation a real threat. Viana also appealed to his superiors to allow him to journey to a small Spanish town orphaned on the wrong side of the border. "[Residents] are begging me to go to Bayou Pierre because there [they have] corn and flour, so they may bring some for their sustenance. Should I permit them, or should I see them suffer . . . ?" It was not just trade at stake. Viana mentioned a priest who wanted to go to the Neutral Ground to exhume and repatriate a captain of the militia who had died there on patrol. A settler from Bayou Pierre had come to visit relatives in

Nacogdoches. "Am I to receive him . . . or expel him?" Viana wrote. "These are the matters that come up and which nobody believes I have orders from a government as mild and Catholic as the Spanish, to prohibit."[36]

But he did have such orders. All requests for leniency were routed to the governor in Béxar, who passed them on to the Commandant General in Chihuahua. Governors might sympathize, but the Commandant General was the supreme authority and Nemesio Salcedo was strict on this point. At times, local commanders seem to have turned a blind eye to limited, local smuggling and quite possibly engaged in it themselves. Their troops certainly did. It was one manifestation of the Spanish American tradition of "obedezco pero no cumplo [I obey, but I do not comply]." Still, authorities sent out a steady succession of commanders to Nacogdoches, each of whom was sacked and replaced for various offenses, of which complicity in smuggling was always an undertone. Many were outsiders and left little permanent mark on the community, but one commander was enduring.[37]

A Frontier Commander Battling Smugglers

Alferez (Lieutenant) José María Guadiana was a perennial second fiddle of sorts. Almost always second in command, he rose to the top job and was stripped of it at least four times. It seemed he was never quite good enough, highly ranked enough, or in possession of the requisite family connections to win the job outright; but whenever a commander was cashiered, Guadiana invariably was the man on the scene brought in to clean up the mess until a replacement could arrive. In 1799, he had prosecuted the town's founder, Don Antonio Gil Ibarbo, for smuggling, among other offenses. Ibarbo was found guilty and expelled, but his relatives launched attacks on Guadiana, charging him with scandalous behavior, including intoxication, licentiousness, and "a continuous contraband, with goods of commerce." Guadiana was also removed, and a replacement commander was sent up from another command. In time, Guadiana was cleared of the charges and returned, once again as second in command.[38]

On another occasion, the plucky officer was transferred away but sent back on orders of the Commandant General after it was clear a later commander, José Joaquín Ugarte, did not know enough about the Texas frontier and needed help. In 1804, this latter officer made an ill-advised trip to Natchitoches to witness the handover of Louisiana, fraternizing with the American and French commissioners on the scene. This was too much for the Commandant General, for whom no crime was worse than contact with foreigners. Ugarte just could not win: Salcedo further faulted him for not at least using the occasion to spy on the construction of Fort Claiborne. He sacked Ugarte and once again placed Guadiana in charge. And so it continued. Over the years, this resourceful officer—like a bad penny—would always turn up, rotating between the two top jobs for over a decade, but never going away, his experience and knowledge remaining invaluable.[39]

Guadiana ultimately became the garrison's point man for suppressing the smuggling trade and tracked every major illicit ring from 1800 onward. It was a full-time job. Smuggling was endemic on the frontier, but even some respectable citizens from San Antonio participated. While the commanders in Nacogdoches may have at times turned a blind eye to small-scale smuggling by Spanish residents, which in the case of Nacogdoches often kept them from starving, they could be aggressive where it counted: large-scale smuggling conducted by non-Spaniards. Guadiana was particularly assertive, and it was perhaps this trait that kept him in favor regardless of whatever failings he had. When Governor Manuel Salcedo rode into his new province in October 1808, he only needed to talk to Guadiana, who could easily lay out the whole history of contraband for the new governor. And it was a long history.[40]

The first major external smuggler was Phillip Nolan, who, as we have seen, was the protégé of the American general and Spanish spy James Wilkinson. His story is too complex for a full treatment here, but in summary, he entered Texas legally in 1791 through Wilkinson's connections with the Spaniards and was given a license to export horses. He then began to exceed his quota while conducting illegal surveying work, eventually drawing the ire of—and banishment by—Spanish officials. Not only was he close to Wilkinson; he had extensive dealings with *Daniel Clark*. This raises questions as to how early the conspiracy against Spain began. Did it launch Nolan's nefarious reconnaissance or did his maps launch the conspiracy? Mapping, trade, conspiracy, and rebellion boiled in an amorphous soup of intrigue, and the Spanish, ignorant of the details but suspicious by nature, distrusted everyone.[41]

Guadiana's endless patrols were the fruit of this skepticism, and in 1799, it was he who launched the investigation of Nolan. Two years later, a Spanish expedition hunted him down, and in a sharp engagement, Nolan was killed and more than twenty of his accomplices were captured. Nolan's second-in-command Robert Ashley then raised a new group of fifty "vagabonds" in late 1803 bent on a smuggling raid, but the US takeover of Louisiana encouraged Ashley's men to desert to join the ongoing rush for new land.[42]

The next shadowy smuggler whom authorities chased but never caught was a mulatto named Dionisio Dennis, who was particularly worrisome to the Spaniards because he had bypassed the hard work of rounding up mustangs and was instead buying tamed horses from accomplices among the Spanish population as far south as Béxar. There were Spanish smugglers too. A man named de la Rosa was investigated in 1806 and found to have exported horses and imported goods. The next year, José Antonio de León was charged with stealing horses and selling them in Louisiana. The Spanish hunted smugglers like these for the better part of a decade. Guadiana was conspicuously active, tracking bandits along the Sabine and on the coastal road that runs from La Bahía to Louisiana.[43]

The Introduction of Foreigners

Another revelation for the new governor was that foreigners, including Anglo-Americans, had *already* penetrated his domain. In fact, Anglo-Americans had been settling in Texas in the 1780s, before future empresario Stephen F. Austin was even born. By 1801, the census of Nacogdoches, which only listed male heads of households, identified sixteen Americans, as well as eight Englishmen and Irishmen, not counting ten others of those nations listed as "deserters." These joined the same number of Frenchmen, and even a few Italians and Germans living in the town. Foreigners made up at least 10 percent of the town's population, likely more when wives and children are considered. Most of these men hide in plain sight in the Spanish archive under Hispanicized names like Guillermo Suel (William Sewell), Miguel Cro (Michael Crow), or Josué Ris (Joshua Reese).[44]

They were no spies or advanced harbingers of a secret plan of conquest, just settlers from that generation not yet cemented in their American nationalism, who came to live their lives on cheap land. As the Spanish themselves attested, most were unquestioned in their loyalty to Spain and were Catholic, either by birth (many were of Irish ancestry) or by conversion. Almost all had settled in Nacogdoches. An exception was a Daniel Boone (not the famous frontiersman, but possibly a relative), who settled in San Antonio, where he was employed as a blacksmith and experienced armorer, upon whom Spanish officials relied. Others moved deeper into Mexico and would surface in Texas as members of the Spanish military, such as Don Carlos Morrison, a Nacogdoches interpreter and Capt. Don Francisco Adams, a skilled soldier who was identified as a former instructor at a Spanish military school and was probably English, not American.[45]

In Nacogdoches, two men stood above the rest. William Barr was the Indian agent mentioned previously. He was born in Londonderry, Ireland, but immigrated with his parents to Pennsylvania at age twelve. He settled in Louisiana in 1786, becoming a Spanish subject, before continuing to Texas, where he became a merchant, and in 1800, the Spanish Indian agent. As such, he was the exact counterpart of the American Indian trader John Sibley. The next year, Barr joined with three other men to form the trading house that would eventually be known as Barr and Davenport. His chief partner, Samuel Davenport also claimed Irish heritage, possibly to win acceptance by the Spanish, but was in fact of English stock. He too had immigrated to Louisiana in 1780, settling in Natchitoches and working in trade, before joining Barr, four years his senior, in Texas.[46]

Barr was authorized to trade in Louisiana to procure Indian goods, but he evidently found other legal (and possibly illegal) ways to bring in additional merchandise. At some point, the Spanish governor authorized the firm to export horses as a legal exception to smuggling rules, possibly in lieu of payment for Barr's role as Indian agent and to allow him to earn the cash with which to buy his trade goods. Barr and Davenport grew wealthy and established large ranches with hundreds of heads of various livestock. Being almost the only commercial enterprise in town, the two men became the chief citizens and financiers in Nacogdoches, even lending cash to the Spanish garrison commander to pay his soldiers when the money sent from San Antonio was delayed or when unexpected expenses arose. A Catholic priest reported that the two "greatly benefit the settlers of this town not only because they always employ a considerable number of them in their business, but also because they assist them in every way they can, so that these men are looked upon as leaders of this town."[47]

Then there were the Frenchmen, the largest group of non-Spaniards in Texas. When Spain took control of Louisiana in 1763, the French population was gradually absorbed into the empire and a number of them began spreading from New Orleans. Like the Anglo-Americans, these Frenchmen—and assorted other Europeans who had mixed with them—began immigrating to Texas in the late 1780s and early 1790s. By 1801, thirty-two French heads of household were listed in the Nacogdoches census. Like their fellow foreigners, they took Hispanicized names like Estevan Goguet and Juan Sarnac. After the Louisiana Purchase, their numbers would swell significantly, when many fled as refugees to Catholic Texas from protestant America.[48]

Even the Spaniards in the town were unlike their cousins to the south, a product of distance and their unique history. They had originally settled in a town called Los Adaes, located east of the Sabine, which had been the original capital of Texas. But when Spain absorbed Louisiana, this town was abandoned and the capital moved to San Antonio. The settlers prevailed on Spanish authorities to let them build the new town, Nacogdoches, closer to their old lands—and old friends. For these frontier Spaniards, neighboring Louisiana was a familiar, not a foreign land, and the outsiders who now settled among them were hardly alien. This concerned Spanish officials, who saw daily interactions with foreigners to be as disruptive as actual smuggling. One day in May 1787, on the Rancho de la Botija just outside of Nacogdoches, a ranch worker stepped into a corral and saw a rancher named Luís Grande playing a guitar, singing a *décima*—a lyric song—about an Italian trader well loved by locals (and mistrusted by Spanish authorities) named Vicente Micheli:[49]

> Vizente como hombre rico y tiene unto de castor
> tiene la dama en su casa y para este no hay prision.
> *Vicente is a rich man and he has beaver oil*
> *He has a woman in his house, and for him there is no prison.*[50]

Even to joke that Texas was a prison, along with the allusion to smuggling and luxury goods was no laughing matter to Spanish authorities. Guadiana ultimately had Grande and fifteen *vecinos* (subjects) arrested for writing or performing "scandalous couplets, insulting and directed towards altering the public tranquility," in a sedition inquiry that lasted a month. Spanish authorities and locals alike were well aware of the recent American and French revolutions. Grande and others were not advocating revolt, but as one historian has suggested, these were nonetheless "the first rumblings of revolutionary activity" that linked Texas to the worldwide republican tide. It is hardly an idle notion, as we shall see, for the singer, Luís Grande, would play a key role in Texas' first revolution, and two of his grandchildren would be center stage at the most important event of the second, inside an abandoned mission in San Antonio, fifty-five years after he had sung his rebellious song.[51]

D'Alvimar Arrives in Texas

This, then, was the Nacogdoches which in August 1808 saw the arrival of French general Octaviano D'Alvimar on his mission to bring Texas into the French orbit. Captured by a Spanish patrol, he was presented to Guadiana, who was once again nominally the garrison commander. The lieutenant demanded the Frenchman's passport and D'Alvimar assumed a haughty air, only reluctantly surrendering it to the much junior officer. It was not even in Spanish, was signed "In the Name of Napoleon I, Emperor of the French," and it demanded that the lieutenant "give free passage to Mr. Octaviano D'Alvimar ... into the Spanish Colonies." Guadiana was flustered, and somewhat in awe of this polished, urbane officer, fluent in seven languages. And there was his "flamboyant" uniform, so starkly at odds with Guadiana's own well-worn one. As one observer would note in San Antonio, "Covered with insignia and brilliant crosses it challenged the genial sun." To imprison him would be impossible—after all, he claimed to be the emissary of the king, although a pretender to the crown—but to set him free to continue on his path could be equally disastrous.[52]

So, for a few days, D'Alvimar was detained in Nacogdoches but given the liberty of the town. It was inevitable that the resident French Creoles would seek him out. The man who did so was Bernard D'Ortolant, a native of Bordeaux, who had arrived in Louisiana in the 1760s, served as a Spanish militia captain and Indian interpreter in Natchitoches, and moved to Texas in 1793. By 1808, he lived with his two sons and seven slaves on a ranch west of town and was the most important French Creole in the community. The fifty-nine-year-old D'Ortolant had always been loyal to the king, but according to a confidential report sent to the governor, he "conversed with [D'Alvimar] much, and besides at unaccustomed hours, and propositions were heard of him that indicated pleasure that the French would conquer the Spaniards." Even for those who were not French, here was a real live symbol of the perilous weakness of the Spanish empire. Before long, Guadiana received word from higher authorities to send D'Alvimar on to San Antonio, which he did, and with this dangerous man gone, D'Ortolant went back to acting as an outwardly loyal Spaniard, Guadiana praising him in his reports. But the Spanish leadership grew increasingly skeptical of all foreigners.[53]

For all the diligence of the royal officials who had fought to keep out Rousseau, suppress seditious music, and detain D'Alvimar, they continued to ignore the real source of brewing discontent in frontier Nacogdoches. This was the human need for trade suppressed by the indifferent mercantilist policies of the Spanish crown. A revolutionary spirit was stirring not from a passion for democracy but from more materialistic motives. The currency of insurrection was the need for corn and flour, and the flower patterns of Señora Peres's India lawn. It was tableware, tools, pots, and whiskey. It was all these things—and the horses that would generate the capital to pay for them—which ultimately were to prove just as revolutionary as the *Contrat Social* or the seditious *décimas* could ever be.

3

Romantics and Rogues

SIXTEEN HUNDRED MILES away at nearly the same time that Manuel Salcedo was entering Texas, a young graduate of Harvard University just a few days past his twentieth birthday delivered his first literary production to the publishing house of Oliver and Monroe at No. 70, State Street, in Boston. Henry Adams Bullard was brilliant, having simultaneously earned both his bachelor's and master's degrees from the university the year before. Unlike many of his classmates, Bullard came not from the Boston elite; he was raised in the backwater of Pepperell, in far northern Massachusetts, and while most of his class moved on to professional jobs or the clergy, he remained at the university, working as an employee for two extra years to pay off his tuition. Bookish, with a passion for languages, he held romantic visions of travel, adventure, and revolution.[1]

Burr's aborted attempt at private war making two years before was not an isolated event. The *filibuster*, a private military expedition seeking to foment rebellion or conquest, was rooted in English tradition, where adventurers like Sir Walter Raleigh and Sir Francis Drake "forced a trade with the [Spanish] inhabitants . . . [and] sometimes plundered the Spanish governors." With the Spanish monarchy tottering, Americans felt the pull of this inheritance alongside the tug of their republican heartstrings. They turned to spreading the gospel of republicanism with all the fervor of religion and ideology cooked into one dish, garnished with a hearty side course of personal self-aggrandizement. Indeed, principle and self-interest were often inextricably interwoven, the former providing moral zealotry and the latter motivation for personal risk.[2]

There was a third factor: nationalism, but in the early days of the American nation, this was almost indistinguishable from republicanism itself. Thus liberating Spanish America on the one hand and possibly incorporating its lands into "America" on the other were not inconsistent notions. Few considered that the newly freed populations might not want to be part of the America of the north. But, then, what was "America?" A union, federation, something more nebulous? Thomas Jefferson's Empire of

Liberty, as he conceived it, was a confederation of republics, nearly autonomous, with free trade and liberty.

For the filibusters, it was all the same. It was an age in which grand undertakings involving mortal danger were engaged, with a cavalier attitude toward complicating, inconvenient philosophical abstractions. Expansionism was the impulse; westerners eyed Spanish Florida and Texas, northerners eyed Canada, and even Americans of the middle states caught the fever. A few months before Burr would turn his attention to Mexico, a private expedition organized in New York targeted a battlefield even further distant—Venezuela, the heartland of Spanish American rebellion.[3]

In the first decade of the nineteenth century, no one alive save Napoleon himself was a greater figure of romance and revolution than the Venezuelan, Francisco de Miranda. He had fought in the army of Spain during the American War of Independence and won glory at the Siege of Pensacola. Embracing republicanism, he rose to the rank of general in the French army before turning to the cause of his homeland. He had sought aid from President Jefferson and Secretary of State James Madison, and while they gave him no official support, they did little to stop him.[4]

Miranda turned to private financiers and volunteers for an attack on the Spanish Empire at the same time as Burr, recruiting a force of two hundred men, mostly in New York. Miranda, the very picture of a Latin American Napoleon, attracted the powerful and poor alike, "a motley mix of university-educated men, military officers, doctors, printers, coopers, butchers, unemployed tradesmen, and . . . one hundred sailors." They ran the gamut from William Stephens Smith, the son-in-law of former president John Adams, to an eighteen-year-old New Jersey boy of no great family name with a flair for adventure named David G. Burnet, who three decades later, during another revolution, would become the interim president of the Republic of Texas. Another teenager about the same age would have gladly joined the expedition if he could: Henry Adams Bullard. This was exactly the sort of romantic adventure of which the young Harvard University student dreamed.[5]

Apostle of the Filibuster

In hindsight, it was fortunate for young Bullard that he missed his first chance at revolution. After stopping off in Haiti to train, the rebels took an oath to "the army of Columbia" and then sailed to South America. The Spanish were waiting for them, capturing two of the three vessels and sixty members of the expedition. Ten were tried as pirates, hung, beheaded, and quartered. Miranda and others (including Smith and Burnet) escaped. The shock of Americans so mutilated in a foreign war, followed soon after by reports of the Burr escapade, brought new scrutiny to the whole affair. Put on trial for violating the Neutrality Act, Smith claimed he had been acting under President Jefferson's secret orders. It was a plausible story—Jefferson's antipathy toward the Spanish Empire was barely concealed—but the charges rang hollow in his particular case. Smith, after all, was the son-in-law of Jefferson's chief political rival, Adams.⁶

As the trials neared, the defenders of Smith and other filibusters needed to make their case in the court of public opinion, and in typical early republic fashion, their chosen vehicle was an anonymous book arguing for the filibuster in sympathetic terms. They chose as their writer the young Bullard. Passionate about the cause and mustering all the literary genius of his nineteen years, the Harvard graduate penned a three hundred–page tome titled *The History of Don Francisco de Miranda's Attempt to Effect a Revolution in South America, in a Series of Letters*. Its title page bore a quote from Shakespeare which well summarized Miranda's life—and Bullard's too in due course—"Thoughts tending to ambition, they do plot unlikely wonders."⁷

The "letters" consisted of twenty-eight epistles written by Bullard under the guise of an American in the expedition, describing and justifying the effort at private war making. In an early letter in the book, the "correspondent," writing to an unknown friend from aboard ship, explains the reasons the filibusters signed up. After claiming that the destination was unknown, he added: "Generally, I can say that we are engaged in an expedition to some part of the Spanish dominions, probably in South America, with a view to assist the inhabitants in throwing off the oppressive yoke of the parent country; and establishing a government for themselves, upon which we are told by our general they have resolved; and for which he says that they are entirely disposed and prepared."⁸

Why would Americans risk their lives in a foreign revolution (and one that certainly contained no prospects of American territorial aggrandizement) on such limited information from their secretive commander? "Perhaps it is a matter of indifference to many of the volunteers in what cause they act, if it do but promise them an opportunity of distinguishing themselves by martial achievements and afford a chance of acquiring some portion of the riches, supposed to be in the hands of unworthy possessors in the south."⁹

It was possible to "liberate" the oppressed of the southern continent while simultaneously seizing riches because the "unworthy possessors" were the native-born Spaniards, and as they were an elite class that would be expelled, the rebels could dispossess them, much as their fathers had done to American loyalists, while leaving the Creoles perhaps no richer but no poorer either. Taking up the same theme as Smith in his trial (and to influence the jury), Bullard claimed the authority of President Jefferson was secretly behind the expedition.¹⁰

"We are encouraged in the belief that our government has given its implied sanction to this expedition," Bullard wrote. He referenced the "official language" of Jefferson and his party, and just like the Kempers a thousand miles away in West Florida, took it as sanctioning the act, preliminary to a certain declaration of war. "Under such impressions, we think we shall not be called to account as violating the pacifick [sic] relations of the United States." These sentiments, it must be noted, were designed to deflect guilt in the trial. Nonetheless, something very much like them was clearly a motivating factor for Miranda's men and others. Who dare restrain them? Man, as they believed, was autonomous and could leave the country of his own free will, and that included doing so in an armed fashion.[11]

Bullard's arguments would also foreshadow others that would be aired in the years to come, as American citizens, self-empowered through revolutionary zeal, would *anticipate* their political leaders' will—or use it to justify their actions—and become the instruments of republicanism, whether authorized or intended, or not. To Bullard, and many like him, the spreading of liberty allowed such license and excused any means employed for the glorious ends. "We flatter ourselves it is honorable and humane to be thus engaged," he wrote. "Still, I am sensible that nothing short of complete success will ensure such a design the approbation of the mass of mankind. If we succeed, our fame will take care of itself."[12]

Orator of Republicanism

On the Fourth of July 1808, as Henry Adams Bullard was preparing his tome, another Massachusetts-born lawyer was standing before a packed crowd in Reverend John Giles's Meeting House in Newburyport, Connecticut. Nathaniel Cogswell, thirty-five, was a smart, ambitious lawyer from nearby Haverhill, with hopes of making a political splash. The audience for his speech was much larger than merely the local citizens in the room because Cogswell's oration—and others across the country that day—would ultimately be reprinted in pamphlet form and distributed across the nation. In the early 1800s, with the revolution fresh in memory and veterans everywhere, the Fourth of July was akin to a high holy day of the Republic. The annual addresses given on that date were sober, important affairs, but also partisan events where orators wrapped themselves in the mantle of revolution, claiming their side to be the true inheritors of the Spirit of '76, and disparaging their opponents as enemies of it.[13]

Cogswell was a zealot for republicanism and grew up with the revolution, in a very real sense, all around him. His grandfather, also named Nathaniel, demonstrated his patriotism during the war by loaning funds to the cause which he never recouped, and donating various equipment to New England soldiers. Eight of his sons joined the Continental Army, including Thomas Cogswell, who left his wife and two-year-old Nathaniel to join the troops surrounding Boston in 1775. Thomas led a company at Bunker Hill and was promoted successively throughout the war, from captain to major to lieutenant colonel, ultimately becoming wagonmaster general, the army's senior supply officer. He and his brother had been present at Washington's famous Newburgh Address and were charter members of the Society of the Cincinnati, the revolutionary veterans' organization.[14]

At age eleven, Nathaniel was sent to the prestigious Phillips-Exeter Academy in nearby Exeter, New Hampshire. From there, he continued to Dartmouth College, where he earned his master's degree in 1794. Cogswell chose to enter the legal profession and read law under another revolutionary veteran. In 1805 Nathaniel began his own practice in Gilmanton, New Hampshire. At age thirty-two, he was among the most highly educated young men of his generation, well-connected and comfortable enough financially to take a tour of Europe during a lull in the Napoleonic Wars. As a family history relates, "His fine person, genial nature, and attractive manners made him a favorite in [London] society." He was young, good-looking, and single—a man eager after distinction.[15]

The first decade of the century was among the most partisan of times in American history. The *Revolution of 1800*, which had seen Thomas Jefferson and the Republican Party triumph over the Federalist John Adams, had ripped open a political scar in American society. The split was popular versus elitist, rural versus urban, agrarian versus mercantile, pro-French versus pro-English. Though Cogswell's family by social status should have been Federalists, they were nonetheless Republicans, and now Nathaniel, freshly invigorated by his recent trip to Europe, stepped up to the podium in Newburyport to give his July 4th speech.[16] He began: "We, my friends, are this day assembled to commemorate the anniversary of our national existence. This event is the most illustrious and splendid epocha in the annals of the world. The wide, the extended range of the history of nations . . . does not furnish a single parallel. Other nations of the earth have arisen by slow degrees . . . to the rank of great and powerful empires. But America was born in a day!"[17]

Cogswell gave a tribute to revolutionary soldiers who, like his relatives, had endured "with undaunted fortitude and patience, the numerous privations and hardships which they were doomed to suffer." He noted veterans in the crowd and, echoing Washington at Newburgh, praised those who had become "old and grey in the cause of freedom." The revolution was an ongoing crusade; the burden now fell to his generation, who were "just entering upon the theater of action." Cogswell sounded popular republican themes and cheered America, "the first and only independent nation on the fourth quarter of the globe." Before three years would pass, Cogswell, along with Bullard, would endeavor to change that.[18]

Although the partisan gathering in Giles' Meeting House was no doubt enthusiastic, the response was far less pleasant when the Federalist writers weighed in. The *Monthly Anthology and Boston Review* savaged the speech. "Gentle Reader, for mercy's sake, and as you dread the twitching torturing pains of a side-ache—hold your sides—for here comes. . . . Nathaniel Cogswell, Esq. *plenum sed*, with his silk gown, satin breeches, open clock'd stockings and all, with his oration in one hand and with the other hand extended, and brandishing in fierce gesticulation . . . here he comes and hark! He begins." The *Anthology* compared Republicans like Cogswell to "idolators"—a biting attack in such a religious age—and its criticism of his speech left nothing unsaid: "The oration is remarkable for its language; which, being unnaturally compounded and jumbled wildly together from the two most abhorrent things in nature, rumbling bombast and the tamest and most drowsy strain of narration, we decidedly think . . . the worst and the flattest—the very flattest that ever was, or ever will, may, can, shall, would, might, could or should be spoken or written by any man, woman, child, monkey, baboon, magpie, parrot, flounder, porpoise and so downwards, or upward, if you please."[19]

Cogswell, neither deterred by such attacks nor shy about self-promotion, penned identical letters to President Thomas Jefferson and Secretary of State James Madison, enclosing copies of his speech for their reading, wishfully suggesting that the town, recently a haven of the *Essex Junto*, would convert to Republicanism. His speech had perhaps earned him a small part of the respect, which so many ambitious men of the age craved, but only a hint. Like Bullard, Cogswell dreamed of being more than just a narrator of the epoch-defining events occurring around him. To an heir of republican war heroes in the Napoleonic Age, the idea of dramatically reshaping the world on behalf of liberty must have seemed too good for him to sit on the sidelines. Before long, Cogswell would drift to Philadelphia, where he would meet his fellow Bay Colony native, Bullard, and join him on the road to Texas.[20]

The Lieutenant

The third young man from Massachusetts who would play a role in the coming conflict in Texas took a quite different path. In mid-June 1808, this youth from Boston landed at a bend on the Hudson River along a valley still mostly filled with virgin, wooded hillsides, and made his way up the bluff to a rather modest set of buildings that served as the nascent US military academy. West Point, as it was known, was at the time little more than these structures, a dozen cadets and one officer. That it had even survived was remarkable.[21]

In 1801, when Jefferson became president, many feared for its fate. The Virginian's hostility to the army was both principled and political. He had a "low estimate of, or rather contempt for, the military character," as Winfield Scott would later put it, and furthermore, the army's elitist officer corps was overwhelmingly Federalist. Upon winning the presidency, Jefferson began a crusade against the army that ranged from the serious to the petty: he sought to break up the Federalist monopoly of the officer ranks but also went so far as to ban the small, ceremonial pigtail that officers wore in their hair as a mark of their profession. But he kept West Point. Failures in frontier warfare had demonstrated the need for experienced soldiers, and Jefferson wanted a national university to focus on science and engineering for peacetime purposes. West Point fit the bill for both.[22]

Jefferson's skepticism of a class of professional officers was also tempered by the hope that he could "shape" them, endeavoring to fill the ranks with officers who were Republicans or "without any political creed." He went so far as to personally interview one candidate for appointment. "To which of the political creeds to you adhere?" he asked the young man. After the latter mentioned that his family were Federalists, Jefferson responded, "There are many men of high talent and integrity in that party, but it is not the rising party." The young man was admitted, but the intimidation was taken in earnest.[23]

Although the youth in the above anecdote was not the nineteen-year-old Boston native who presented himself at the school on June 15, 1808, he might as well have been. Augustus William Magee was no working-class Republican, and he certainly was not a Jeffersonian noble tiller of the soil. Magee was from one of the wealthiest families in Boston, with a strong connections to the Federalists. He was just the sort of officer about whom Jefferson would have been wary, but who managed to fill the ranks of the army despite the best efforts of the president.[24]

Magee was "very tall, very robust, of a handsome person and countenance." Although no known portraits of him exist, contemporary images of his parents and two older brothers show strong genes that young Augustus probably shared. He had light brown hair framing a long face with a prominent vertical nose. Like his brothers, he may have sported long sideburns down to the edge of his jaw. Though his family had wealth, it had been earned by hard work, and no Magee would have lived off his inheritance. That was the legacy of Augustus' late father, who had risen from Irish obscurity to Massachusetts elite through a mix of hard work and a fortuitous chain of marriages.[25]

James Magee was a Presbyterian, born in County Down, Ireland, in 1750. He went to sea as a mere boy and became a ship's captain while still in his twenties. He may have immigrated to America as early as 1768. When the Revolution broke out, the skilled sea captain offered his nautical experience to the cause, sailing as a privateer. He commanded four vessels during the war before being captured in 1781. After the revolution, Magee prospered as a trader and married Margaret Elliot of Boston, the daughter of a successful tobacco dealer.[26]

James Magee's real springboard into the Bay State elite came after his wife's niece married Thomas Handasyd Perkins, son of one of Boston's great mercantile families. The two in-laws soon formed a partnership and a friendship. They were a perfect team: Magee, the master mariner, and Perkins, fourteen years his junior, a superb businessman. They became the foremost American merchants in the burgeoning and lucrative China trade.[27]

Shortly before his third son, Augustus, was born in 1789, James Magee and T. H. Perkins sailed on what would be their final voyage together, aboard a newly built ship named for Magee's wife, the *Margaret*. Augustus Magee was already four years old when he first laid eyes on his returning father. Though the family had been well-to-do before, they were now truly rich. James Magee retired and purchased a palatial home on thirty-three acres of sculpted English gardens in Roxbury, then a wealthy Boston suburb. In fact, under former Royal Governor William Shirley, the house had served as the colony of Massachusetts' executive mansion. Young Augustus, who would in time seek fortune and glory in the wilderness of Texas, grew up in this luxurious, idyllic landscape.[28]

In 1801, when Augustus was only twelve, his father died of a lingering illness. To compound the family tragedy, James's brother Bernard, also a sea captain, was killed by natives in the Pacific Northwest. For Augustus Magee, the death of his father and uncle left him with only one male guardian—his uncle-in-law T. H. Perkins. Although Augustus' two older brothers were serving on Perkins' ships, the uncle-turned-patron may have envisioned a different role, possibly as clerk or ship's sales agent (known as a "supercargo") for the young boy, and this meant education at an elite, private school. The year after his father's death, Augustus was enrolled in Phillips Exeter Academy in Exeter, New Hampshire, about fifty miles from Boston, the same school which Nathaniel Cogswell had attended a few years before. Phillips Exeter was then, as it remains today, one of the most elite institutions of learning in America. Of the school, it would be said in 1859 that "such a galaxy of names as appear upon the catalogue of this institution will not, perhaps, be found in connection with any other academy on this continent."[29]

Presumably, after four years, Augustus earned a bachelor of arts degree (A.B., in Latin). While most graduates went into business, the clergy, or frequently continued on to Harvard University, Magee pursued a markedly different course: the US Military Academy. If Perkins had plans to bring young Augustus into the family business, these were wrecked by politics. In 1807, President Jefferson's Embargo Act brought foreign trade to a standstill, and there was little employment available for an overeducated young relative. On the other hand, a military career promised an alternative for talented young men. On April 12, 1808, Congress authorized an increase of the army to 3,358 men, including 8 regiments. This then was an opportunity for Augustus Magee.[30]

Magee completed the short but rigorous course at the academy in seven months, average for the time, and graduated on January 24, 1809, qualifying as an artillerist. He was assigned to the Atlantic coast forts, which were being expanded amid a war scare with England. He did not stay more than a few months, because General James Wilkinson needed more troops in Louisiana, as he was rapidly bolstering the defenses of New Orleans and building up his forces near Spanish West Florida. As the young officer packed his trunk for Fort Adams in the Mississippi Territory, he left the East behind for good. No one could have predicted the height to which he would rise, or the role he would play in history, in the next three years.[31]

Smugglers of Horses

On October 15, 1808, only about a week after Manuel Salcedo had passed through the region on his way to Nacogdoches to assume the governorship of Texas, a Spanish patrol was scouting the Louisiana/Texas borderlands between the Angelina and

Neches Rivers near a place called Las Plasetas, searching for runaway slaves and contraband, when it came across the tracks of a large herd of horses. The eight soldiers and one civilian were led by Sergeant Pedro de la Garza Falcón. It was only the third day of the patrol, and their mounts were relatively fresh. Those of any smugglers exiting the province, Falcón knew, would not be. Surveying the tracks with his experienced eye, he assessed them as being about five days old, but guessed that the smugglers were still nearby. His men soon spotted a large herd of horses in the distance. Falcón could make out five men watching the horses. He ordered his men to prepare their weapons; then they rode forward.[32]

As soon as they saw the approaching Spanish *soldados*, the smugglers, unarmed but all mounted, bolted for their camp. One man whom Falcón recognized as "the foreigner Juanito"—"Little John"—McFarlan, stopped and gave up without a fight. A soldier and the civilian, Joaquín Montes de Oca, were left with him while the rest of the Spaniards took up the chase. The remaining smugglers reached the camp and proceeded to retrieve their arms. Three of them stood their ground at their tents and aimed their weapons towards the Spaniards, but the last one, who Falcón recognized as Edward Popejoy (*Pop Yoel* to the Spaniards), jumped on the back of a honey-colored horse and galloped away as fast as the animal would go. Two of Falcón's men spurred their mounts and, after a dramatic chase, shot the man from his horse, killing him.[33]

Back at the smuggler's camp, Falcón recognized the men, for although they were Anglo-Americans, they were—like McFarlan—all Spanish residents: Henry Quirk, Joseph Magee, and Joseph Brenton. Falcón eased the standoff by suggesting he might take a bribe. When the foreigners lowered their vigilance, his men seized them by force. The Spanish collected ninety-nine horses, twelve fillies and colts, and assorted mules and jackasses. It was clear, however, that even the horses were no mustangs obtained on the frontier. Almost all had brands; around seventy of them were from one ranch. Most of them had been bought from citizens of Texas and paid for with smuggled merchandise from Louisiana.[34]

The prisoners were marched to Nacogdoches and delivered to Lieutenant Guadiana, who placed them in the town's small jail. It was the biggest capture of smugglers since Phillip Nolan, and the criminal enterprise that was broken up by Falcón on that day would turn out to be extensive—and *not foreign*. Although Popejoy and Brenton appear to have had minor roles in the escapade, Magee, Quirk, and McFarlan were well-known to authorities. Joseph Magee, a native of Ireland (no relation to Augustus Magee), had come with his brother John to Texas, probably through Louisiana. John Magee was one of the first settlers and principal merchants of Trinidad de Salcedo, where he lived with his wife, Harriet Burgess, and ran a small mill made of iron. When Spanish officials later searched his home, they found a chest full of contraband goods and notebooks implicating more Anglo settlers, as well as Tejanos, in the smuggling scheme.[35]

The smuggler that Falcón identified as "Little John" was John McFarlan, age forty-three. He was a native of Virginia, but was far more Irish than American, and had settled in Texas before 1801. He was well known to Spanish authorities under various Hispanicized names—Juan McFarel, Mafallen, and even Macfarzon. He lived in the vicinity of Nacogdoches with his wife, Sarah Sanders, and his father-in-law. His occupation was listed as a farmer, but he was also known to travel as a hunter, frequently ranging far from his farm east of Nacogdoches to the frontier. In July 1802, Lieutenant Guadiana, returning from a trading visit to friendly Indian tribes, came across McFarlan and two of his servants on the way back from a buffalo hunt on the plains, but the group was clearly catching a few mustangs as well. The next year, he was again capturing horses, ostensibly delivering them to locals, so the Spaniards did not suspect him.[36]

Horses were McFarlan's specialty, but long before he was arrested as a smuggler, the foreigner was a *legal* trader in them. Little John, along with an Anglo-American resident, Juan Pedro Walker, was employed by the government from 1803 to 1804 in constructing a new church in Nacogdoches, hiring several native Tejanos for the project. But supplies for the construction being impossible to find in Nacogdoches, McFarlan and Walker were authorized by local officials to purchase the necessities in Natchitoches and to legally export horses in lieu of cash payments. Commandant General Nemesio Salcedo, however, rejected the deal. The Nacogdoches garrison commander, Miguel Músquiz, proposed a compromise: continue to pay McFarlan and Walker in horses, but instead of exporting them, the men would "keep the same here for their benefit." It was a clumsy solution and practically begged for the legitimate trade to be resumed as criminal. Whether or not "Little John" had broken the law before, he was a smuggler henceforth.[37]

If McFarlan's turn toward crime was surprising to authorities, that of his co-conspirator was not. Indeed, at the time Sergeant Falcón captured Henry Quirk, he was the most wanted fugitive in Texas. Known to the Spaniards as Enrique Querque or Kuerke, he was a forty-seven-year-old native of Virginia, who had come to Texas in 1798 and was living on the large ranch of his elder brother Edmund. In March 1808, Guadiana had been on the trail of smugglers, and the clues had led him to the Quirk Ranch near the Sabine. "There is no doubt that Henry Quirk, brother to Edmund Quirk, Sr. is the one who exported this livestock," Guadiana determined. Both brothers became fugitives. After his capture, Henry confessed to the crime of smuggling, but Edmund remained on the loose.[38]

Edmund Quirk Sr. (*Reimundo Kuerke* to the Spaniards) fought in the American Revolution in his twenties before moving to Kentucky like so many veterans. He first became a Spanish subject as a settler in Louisiana, but by 1797 had moved to Texas, and eleven years later he owned large holdings of land. His ranch, with its proximity to the Sabine, had long worried Spanish authorities, who distrusted—rightfully so in this case—foreigners living so close to the border. With Henry imprisoned, Edmund

Quirk now became Spanish authorities' most wanted fugitive. "Quirk's conduct has always seemed suspicious to the government," wrote Spanish commander Francisco Viana. "In my time, he has been punished, rebuked and summoned before the judge . . . several times for sheltering foreigners without passports, and several times because stolen stock was found on his ranch."[39]

The breakup of the ring had consequences that would continue to escalate—and implicate. The Spanish confiscated incriminating papers, including Magee's account book. In it, a few residents, mostly foreigners, but also Tejanos, were listed alongside the goods Magee had sold them. The men's property was confiscated, while their families begged to keep enough to maintain themselves. Another Irish-American settler in Trinidad, Miguel Quinn, who like McFarlan had a license from the governor to deal in horses *within* Texas, was implicated as having sold the stock to the deceased Popejoy to export. Both Quinn in his testimony and Magee in his letters indicated the purchaser was William Owens, a merchant in Natchitoches. Quinn was in fact deeply involved in Quirk and Magee's smuggling rings.[40]

A month after the enterprise was broken up, a party of Americans in the Neutral Ground seized the Spanish trader Samuel Davenport and his muleteers. Governor Salcedo suspected it was retaliation, reporting rumors that a party of Americans without government authority was assembling in the Neutral Ground "for the purpose of extricating the smugglers that you are holding for such crime." The Spanish increased their own vigilance, bolstering the frontier with 150 men sent to strategic crossings. The would-be rescuers of the four smugglers were deterred, but the *banditti* in the Neutral Ground would endure. It was, as Salcedo had suspected, closely tied to the same smuggling rings that the Spanish had suppressed, having been organized by Miguel Quinn, who had been implicated in the ring, and using Edmund Quirk as its secret messenger into and out of Texas.[41]

The French Creole

Quinn's home village of Trinidad de Salcedo was a new town, settled only in the last five years, and named after the Trinity River, along whose banks it lay, and Commandant General Nemesio Salcedo. From the beginning, Trinidad was intended to host the growing numbers of immigrants Spain began accepting after the Louisiana Purchase. Spanish officials wanted a place to put them that was *not* on the border, to deter smuggling. Additionally, a town on the Trinity would facilitate trade up and down the Camino Real and would be a useful post for a garrison of troops to defend against Indians and smugglers. It was the ideal place, so thought the Spaniards, to settle the newcomers.[42]

One of these was Bernard Martin Despallier. Born either in Haiti or Louisiana, he was the son of a French officer from lower Normandy, France. He was well-traveled and had lived for a time in Baltimore and New York, where he became a mason. His family had a plantation in Haiti, but after the revolution there, Bernard Despallier returned to Louisiana and settled in Rapides Parish, near modern-day Alexandria, Louisiana. Here he became an officer, like his father, but in the Spanish service, where he rose to become the captain of dragoons in what was basically a militia unit.[43]

While most Frenchmen in Louisiana rejoiced when news came of the handover of the province to France, not so Despallier. He claimed to have remained loyal to Spain even during its recent war with France and now sought refuge in Texas. In 1806, interim governor Manuel Antonio Cordero appointed him second-in-command of the military garrison at Orcoquisac, a former mission site in coastal East Texas. This appointment of a foreigner—though a Spanish subject most of his life—enraged the hardline Commandant General. Cordero responded by praising Despallier's experience in Louisiana, and his extensive knowledge of the Indians who had recently settled in East Texas—the Alabamas and Choctaws—which included a near fluency in their language. Salcedo ordered him discharged anyway, and Despallier settled in Trinidad as a civilian.[44]

In touch with creoles in Louisiana who he claimed hated the new American rule of their province, Despallier saw an opportunity to bring them to Texas as part of a new colony, which he hoped to lead. Along with a Carmelite Priest, Father John Brady, Despallier wrote to Spanish authorities, promising more than one thousand families, one-fifth of them Spanish, the rest French. These refugees, he said, wanted to live in a Catholic country, remain Spanish vassals, and "shed our blood" for Spain if need be. The petition was forwarded to Madrid and the "good and kind" king approved Despallier and Brady's petition not long after his own hoped-for relief of Spanish settlers failed. But the settlement foundered on practical grounds. It required, among other things, the construction of a port on Galveston Bay. The viceroy in New Spain had neither the cash to build such a port, nor the interest, since it was a danger to the mercantilist system.[45]

With his settlement idea in shambles, Despallier sought opportunities to engage in legal trade at every occasion, but began to chafe under Spanish policy, just like the Tejanos, with whose grievances he was well-acquainted. Even before he had immigrated to Texas, Despallier, a widower in his late twenties, had married a Tejana, the nineteen-year-old María Candida Grande. She was the child of the very same Luís Grande who had been arrested as a young man for singing a seditious song about a foreigner. Now his daughter had married one, and predictably Despallier, like his father-in-law, soon ran afoul of Spanish authorities. Though the nature of the suspicions against him is obscure, he was likely working with fellow Trinidad resident Joseph Magee to illegally import luxury goods. He fled back to Louisiana, where in time he would be joined by Edmund Quirk and a growing number of foreign Texan refugees, who longed to return under more favorable circumstances.[46]

Explorers, Traders, and the Rogue of Missouri

The case of the smugglers captured by Falcón and his men would wind on through the slow-moving Spanish justice system for two years. Hidden among the mountains of evidence was a note suggesting a broader contraband network with ominous ties. Among Magee's papers was a letter in which a correspondent said he owed the smuggler forty-five pesos, asking a third party to pay Magee who "has done for me a particular favor." The author, Joseph A. McLanahan, had been a squatter in the Neutral Ground. Spanish Lieutenant Guadiana's sources indicate that two months before the smugglers were arrested, he and a party of four traveled by boat from New Orleans to explore the area, making maps of the territory and its crossings, for smuggling purposes—or perhaps something bigger. Guadiana, writing to the Spanish governor of West Florida, added, "I have also learned that neither the voyage nor the purpose of the afore-mentioned foreigners is authorized by their government." Guadiana's suspicions were correct. McLanahan may have been allied to Joseph Magee, Quirk, and other smugglers, but his work was likely destined for a more nefarious frontier schemer, former Burr conspirator and prospective filibuster organizer from Missouri named John Smith T.[47]

The curiously named Smith T—the T stood for "Tennessee" and was appended to his name to distinguish him from the many other John Smiths on the frontier—was an ambitious mining and land speculator from Missouri. He was an eccentric: always impeccably dressed, with very correct manners, a very sensitive face with soft blue eyes—yet surprisingly prone to anger and violence. He had been among the early settlers of Tennessee and then moved to Missouri in 1797 when that territory was still Spanish. He was an opportunistic, ruthless entrepreneur. As a biographer put it, "virtually every economic aspect of Smith T's life revolved around greed and exploitation." His stock-in-trade was land grabbing, claims jumping, and speculation. Despite having no technical background, he moved into mining, particularly of lead. Here he ran into competition with the man who would be his nemesis: a fellow American also recently arrived in Spanish territory, Moses Austin.[48]

The feud between Smith T and Austin characterized the early days of Missouri. The two men employed small private armies and fought proxy battles for control of lucrative mining claims. While Austin aligned himself with the new American settlers, Smith T sided with Spanish and French Creoles. Austin stood for at least a modicum of law and order while Smith T—who was said to have killed fifteen men in duels—was far less scrupulous on the subject. When frontier magistrates sought to arrest him, he threatened to kill them. With a family connection to General Wilkinson, who not only served as the senior military officer in upper Louisiana but was simultaneously the governor of Missouri, Smith T was essentially above the law. Wilkinson protected him and for many years allowed the rogue to profit from an illegal mine on US government land.[49]

Figure 1. John Smith T. Courtesy of Alamy Photos.

Smith T had dreams of a filibuster long before the Burr affair—he had possibly been planning a takeover of Missouri before the Louisiana Purchase brought that territory into the United States. He had joined the Burr conspiracy, likely at the urging of Wilkinson, who needed his relative's expertise in mining. Wilkinson's true objective had always been wealthy Santa Fe, and Texas and the other territories between him and that goal were a means to an end. Early in 1806, at the height of his Burr plotting, the general had dispatched an expedition to New Mexico under Lieutenant Zebulon Pike, one of his own army subordinates. The young officer thought his mission above board, but Wilkinson was using him for his own purposes. "Lt. Pike himself was as yet ignorant of the nature of his journey," Wilkinson wrote a fellow conspirator. The general was building up maps which were ostensibly for the nation's use but were really for his and Burr's. But at Santa Fe, Pike was captured by the Spanish along with his entire party.[50]

When the general abruptly betrayed the conspiracy, Smith T was abandoned like so many others. Still, he seems to have taken up the mantle that Wilkinson left, even resorting to the general's preferred method of espionage by expedition. It was likely he who had sent McLanahan to the Neutral Ground in 1808, for when the latter returned to Missouri, he was immediately employed by Smith T in another expedition dispatched in the wake of Pike. This one would be sent under the guise of a trading venture to New Mexico. The man chosen to lead the expedition was the mining baron's younger brother and right-hand man, Reuben Smith.[51]

On December 20, 1809—an odd time of year to launch a purported trading mission—the younger Smith, McLanahan, and James Patterson set a course westward from Missouri. An article in the *Louisiana Gazette* revealed the secret of the expedition to the public—and the Spanish too. "About the 20th . . . Capt. R. Smith, Mr. M'Lanehan and a Mr. Patterson set out from the district of St. Genevieve upon a journey to St. a Fee. . . . We presume their objects are mercantile; the enterprise must be toilsome and perilous . . . altogether through a wilderness heretofore unexplored."[52]

Expanding trade was not just a cover for the expedition; it was an end in itself as important as any other. The trade war with European powers and the subsequent embargo gave a new impetus to developing new markets. For citizens of the United States, who had begun to visit South America with increasing frequency in the 1790s, free trade was part and parcel of their republican revolution against the old world. As the Napoleonic War had exposed the dangers of dependence on Europe, new markets free of such mercantilist vicissitudes were enticing. But there could be no free trade with an insular, monarchical nation. What Smith T, Daniel Clark, the Mexican Association, and possibly even small-time smugglers like Henry Quirk realized was that extending trade to the Spanish empire *implicitly required* separating that empire from European control. Thus trade to Spanish lands, whether they be in Venezuela, Nacogdoches, or Santa Fe, was an inherently revolutionary act.[53]

McLanahan would later explain the ostensible motivations for the expedition in a letter to Missouri Governor Benjamin Howard. The three had undertaken the journey, "indulging in common with our fellow citizens of the United States a portion of that spirit of enterprize [sic] which has with unparalleled rapidity advanced our country in the scale of prosperity and happiness." McLanahan admitted to the governor that he was well aware of Spain's mercantilist history, but "it is well known to your excellency that a new era has taken place." The Spanish monarchy in Europe had been "shaken to its centre" by the Napoleonic takeover, and a wave of "consequent amelioration had pervaded many of the glooms on the continent of America." He then concluded, "In the spirit of these considerations, and under the genius of our liberal institutions our tour was commenced." But his hopes were premature. Although the citizens of Santa Fe seemed happy to see the traders when they arrived, the governor of New Mexico—who also reported to the uncompromising Commandant General Nemesio Salcedo—immediately clasped them in irons and sent them to his superior in Chihuahua. Unlike Pike, who had been treated with courtesy by his fellow officers among the Spanish military, the three traders' fates would be hard.[54]

4

West Florida and Texas

WEAK AS SPAIN'S position was before, it collapsed in the wake of the Napoleonic invasion of 1808. Ferdinand VII's forced abdication was followed by his imprisonment, sparking a popular uprising in Spain itself. Rebel successes on the battlefield encouraged a junta to form and declare Ferdinand king again, setting up a government-in-exile in his name in Cádiz. The War of Spanish Independence that followed pitted partisans of Ferdinand against many of the Spanish elite, who supported Joseph Bonaparte. With two competing governments vying for authority over the world's largest empire, the United States chose to stay neutral. Jefferson would recognize neither Luis de Onís, the envoy of Ferdinand, nor the ambassador representing Bonaparte. Diplomatically, as far as the American government was concerned, Spain had ceased to exist. This ambivalence was not lost on Westerners.

For President Jefferson and his secretary of state and soon-to-be successor James Madison, the most troubling development was the Spanish junta's surprising conclusion of an alliance with England, its ancient protestant nemesis. This raised a new and terrifying specter for America: British intervention in Spain's new world possessions. When Britain and Spain had still been at war two years before, the British had occupied Buenos Aires and Montevideo in a clear demonstration of Spanish weakness in the face of British sea power. What might they now demand as the price of their alliance? When it came to the neighboring Spanish territories, Jefferson had long counseled patience. To him, the empire's collapse was inevitable, and until that happened, the neighboring provinces were better off in the hands of a weak power than a strong one. But should England seize portions of the empire, even to hold it in trust and safeguard it from French agents like D'Alvimar, America would face the worst of all possible outcomes: a hostile England, already entrenched in Canada, could establish itself in Florida and Texas. The United States would be surrounded.

Adair's Warning

On January 9, 1809, following Madison's victory in the presidential race, John Adair, the Kentucky general and former Burr conspirator, took pen to paper and wrote a letter to the new president. Adair had been seventeen years old at the outbreak of the American Revolution. He fought first as a volunteer, then as an officer, rising to the rank of major by the end of the war. Moving west, he came to the attention of General Wilkinson while serving in an expedition against the Miami Indians in the Ohio Territory in 1791. Under the latter's tutelage, he rose to the rank of brigadier general in various campaigns over the next decade and was elected to the US Senate from Kentucky. It was natural that Wilkinson had recruited him into the conspiracy.[1]

But the collapse of that venture and Wilkinson's betrayal had shattered Adair's political career. Although he had beaten charges of treason, he was wrecked as far as public office was concerned. Western opinion was changing, as states like Kentucky and Tennessee grew more settled. The days of Blount, where men could openly flirt with secession and be cheered for it, were fading. In the wake of Burr, a newspaper could proclaim, "the universal execration in which the conspiracy and its author are held in the state of Tennessee. The same sentiment exists, and we feel the pride of an American in being able to say so, throughout the whole extent of the western country."[2]

That this had to be stated so forcefully to Eastern readers suggests just how tenuous it really was. Furthermore, what had sullied the conspiracy for many was the association with western *secession*. When it came to an attack on *Spanish* lands, however, the conspiracy still had widespread support. Still, poor adventurers could dream all they wanted, but men of substance with much at stake, like Adair—with his large family and his plantation, White Hall—had to be much more circumspect. Since 1808, Adair had spent much of his time in the Mississippi and Orleans Territories, as well as Spanish West Florida, where he constantly eluded "the creatures of Wilkinson." But even as he traveled, other adventurous spirits he met proved to him that the dream of 1806 was not dead.[3]

These men looked up to Adair, he said, "principally from the circumstance of my having suffered & been denounced as an enemy to my country." Though he continued to profess his innocence, the general claimed this lingering suspicion had given him entre into the confidence of many who would never share their true thoughts with the administration. Now, Adair offered a warning to the president that all was not quiet in the West. "I can assure you sir," he wrote, "that the govt. of the US has many enemies, and but few warm friends here."[4]

The French of Orleans, he said, had not accepted the United States, "Bonaparte is their God; they are Frenchmen at heart, ready to join any power, who will attempt to make them a dependency of France," he wrote. There was also a British party which, though few in number, was made up of talented men and spread across the region.

In Mississippi, Federalists predominated who were hostile to the administration, particularly over its embargo and their inability to sell their cotton because of it. Even the Republicans were "restless under the territorial restrictions," and unless the Orleans Territory was made a state, nothing would satisfy them. "Deny them this and the Atlantick [sic] States at once becomes to them a tyrant, withholding their dearest rights; for the purposes of oppression." Adair opined that three years since the Burr episode, circumstances had gotten worse, not better. "Few, very few of either class are warmly attached to the union of the East & Western states," he wrote. Then he came to the key issue at stake: West Florida. He described the people there "as ripe fruit; waiting the hand that dares to pluck them; and with them all Florida." If America did not do the plucking, someone else—the British—would. "The proper management of these people is, at this moment, all important to the union."[5]

The Fall of Spanish West Florida

For many Americans, the failure of the Louisiana Purchase treaty to add West Florida was a shocking oversight, and some were even willing to trade Upper Louisiana—today's Arkansas and Missouri—for it. The idea had several appeals: it would open the river trade routes south from the United States, round out the country's borders, and remove a path of invasion or point of constraint for foreign powers. The Jefferson administration wanted nothing to do with an exchange of territory. The president first sought legal means to obtain the province, but these failing, reverted to aggressive assertions that West Florida was part of the purchase, though it clearly was not.[6]

Unlike Texas, West Florida was cut off from almost any contact with Spanish lands except through a very tenuous sea lane to Cuba. Chronically short of troops and incapable of paying them, the Spanish governors saw their position more and more vulnerable both to outside nation-states and filibusters. The Kempers' target in 1804 had been Baton Rouge, on the province's western flank, but on the eastern side, the port of Mobile remained a key link in the Spanish defenses. In 1810, an organization calling itself the "Mobile Society" began agitating near that port. It is unclear whether the group was independent or an affiliate of the Mexican Association, but it seems to have been motivated by the same impulse and functioned in an equally secretive manner. One of its leaders, firebrand lawyer Joseph Pulaski Kennedy, declared that since the president did not recognize the ambassador from the Spanish junta, "the province of Florida *could not be considered as belonging to any foreign prince or state*, and consequently an expedition against that province, would not come within the provisions of the act of congress" (emphasis added). Spain, he was asserting, was a failed state, so attacking it was no crime.[7]

West Florida had two governors, one at Mobile and another at Baton Rouge. Wilkinson sought to sway the former, Vicente Folch, who had been nearly abandoned by Spain, to join the United States rather than be gobbled up by Napoleon's agents or the British. The governor in Baton Rouge, Charles DeHault Delassus, a Dutch-descended Spanish officer, faced a similar problem. With a Bonapartist pretender on the Spanish throne, the same Anglo-Americans who had six years earlier refused to follow the Kempers' call for rebellion began to stir, though in a much more procedural manner. As autonomous juntas spread across the Spanish Empire in reaction to the Napoleonic takeover, West Floridians embraced this idea as well, and called a series of conventions in the summer of 1810.[8]

This was far from a plot in common cause with the Kempers. The first meeting was held at the farm of Alexander Stirling, the very alcalde who had driven Samuel and Nathan Kemper from their home. Indeed, it was fear of the Kempers and lawlessness, as much as anything, which drove the West Floridians to act. Nor was the move initially revolutionary: These "conventionalists" even corresponded with Governor Delassus, who *endorsed* the self-appointed legislative body. Precisely because this second effort was more orderly and peaceful than the Kempers' assault, it gained adherents rapidly. The meetings were open to all, and a pro-American influence was present, led by Fulwar Skipwith, a former US diplomat who had moved to West Florida. Some of these Anglo-Americans began to make the case that annexation to the United States would open the territory to increased settlements, which would cause land values to rise, enriching all. But others among the more recent American arrivals, the so-called Caintucks, hoped a US takeover would invalidate British and Spanish land claims, in favor of those Americans who had helped secure the territory, meaning themselves.[9]

This of course terrified the long-term residents. There were many in West Florida—possibly even a majority in some parishes—who had no interest in becoming part of the United States. Some were loyal to Spain, including "merchants, traders, river boat operators and others who enjoyed the lax regulations and available market," but also more humble men, including "piney woods farmers in the uplands and Creole French, along with a smattering of [Spanish] Isleños." While there was still hope for Spain, these people showed surprising loyalty, and "without the backing of many Anglo-Americans, British, French and Spanish residents in the Parishes, the Iberian presence would have collapsed much sooner." But, now, Spain was becoming less and less a viable option.[10]

A third group of "independents," as historian Samuel C. Hyde Jr. referred to them, "cautiously flirted with the possibilities that could arise from the creation of an independent nation." The Kempers were among this group, who "had issues with the Spanish but likewise remained suspicious of the Americans." Some of the more rogue spirits "openly feared and opposed annexation by any government that represented enhanced authority," Hyde notes. "If viable, an independent nation could offer abundant land and political possibilities while also serving as a bargaining chip in negotiations with foreign powers."[11]

All of these elements were present in the convention, and the peaceful nature of the movement's beginning days broke down. Up to this point, the governor, De Lassus, had cautiously supported the convention, hoping to steer it in a direction amenable to Spain, and the legislative body, in turn, recognized his authority. But this farcical relationship between Spanish power and rebel amateurs broke down after the governor called for reinforcements to put down the embryo legislature. On September 23, 1810—only a week after the call for revolution in Mexico inspired by the same erosion of Spanish authority—a small group of convention-affiliated rebels seized Fort San Carlos at Baton Rouge, the fort Samuel Kemper had been unable to take several years before. They arrested De Lassus and raised the same blue flag with a white star that the Kempers had carried with them. It was soon hoisted at Mobile as well by Kennedy and his supporters. The convention then declared a new Republic of West Florida. What had started as an ostensibly loyalist revolt for Ferdinand VII had evolved into an independence movement, precisely as was happening throughout Spanish America.[12]

On November 7, the convention elected Skipwith as governor. But at this point, just as Madison feared, the movement got out of control. Rather than move toward America, Skipwith moved *away from it*. The former American diplomat, now the nominal president of his own country and aware of the potential power he wielded, suddenly grew hostile to the United States. The governors of the Mississippi and Orleans Territories were scheming to take over the region and had made a deal to that effect without contacting him. Now, Skipwith pushed back, arguing that America had failed to enforce its claim to West Florida, and consequently had lost the right to the territory. He was not alone. Secretary of State Robert Smith received reports indicating "a shift of power in the West Florida government," historian Cody Scallions has written. "Previously, the convention members openly sought incorporation by the US Government . . . but now many favored remaining an independent state."[13]

Skipwith's actions were more than just pique at being left out of discussions. Though he was by nature in the pro-American group, he was well aware of the diversity of sentiments in the province. He and others in the convention knew what they had in their newly founded micro republic: they could either remain independent or, if annexed, do so for profit. The province was the ultimate bargaining chip, and the convention was not going to simply turn it over without a deal. Annexation had to include recognition of land claims, separate statehood from Louisiana, and pardons for the many American deserters among their ranks. Skipwith and others in the convention now attempted to raise troops to resist. The rebel leader and American authorities negotiated for several weeks, inconclusively. "Mr. Skipwith would be respected," Governor Claiborne wrote, "but I could not recognize him as Governor and Commander in Chief of Florida, nor enter into correspondence with him." For his part, after expressing his desire to become part of the United States, Skipwith nonetheless said that rather "than surrender the country unconditionally and without terms, he would with twenty men only . . . surround the flag-staff and die in its defense."[14]

It was a bluff, and Claiborne called him on it. With a proclamation in hand from President Madison stating that the United States would seize West Florida under its Louisiana Purchase claim, he marched in at the head of three hundred men from Fort Adams. "I had reason to apprehend opposition & was prepared to meet it," Claiborne wrote to former president Jefferson. The Senate of the new republic, hearing of his advance, passed a resolution decrying that "the honor and independence of this state is threatened by a neighboring power, in violation of the laws of nations," but it too backed down in the end. At St. Francisville, Claiborne met with local militia, gathered around the West Florida flag. Claiborne addressed them, then ordered the flag to be taken down and replaced with the Stars and Stripes. The militia gave in without resistance. In Baton Rouge, Skipwith refused to comply but told his men not to resist. A "peaceful protest" was staged, but soon the American troops, bolstered by gunboats in the river, hauled down the lone star flag. After seventy-four days, the West Florida Republic had ceased to be.[15]

The Orleans Territorial governor had brushed aside Skipwith and the convention, never recognizing them as a legal government of anything. The only consideration they received was that Claiborne did not immediately arrest the many deserters and criminals in their ranks. Meanwhile, in Mobile, Governor Folch was beginning to break down. He wrote to his superiors in Cuba that if they did not send forces to help him defend the province, he would turn it over to the Americans on January 1. But weeks before that deadline came, Claiborne marched over from Fort Adams and the point was moot.[16]

Far from becoming heroes to the government, the leaders of the West Florida revolt were treated as little better than criminals in the aftermath. "It is no wonder that those who had expected to profit by the transaction resented the loss of their petty advantage," historian Isaac Cox wrote. For most Americans, the back-and-forth was unseen and unappreciated, and in time, the episode would melt into the growing myth of Manifest Destiny, obscuring just how complex it was. But, as another historian asserted, "West Florida was indeed an independent nation progressing to the status of a viable republic rather than a mere transitional stage in continental development." For the men of the West, who had poured their hearts, souls, and in some cases their fortunes into the project, the annexation of West Florida was no national triumph; it was a betrayal. Governor Claiborne was well aware that many remained bitter and disaffected. "The late change in affairs gave no satisfaction to some individuals; a state of revolution and commotion, was better suited to their views than a state of government and just laws."[17]

Frederick Kimball, a bitter, skeptical West Floridian lamented, "What is intended to be done with us . . . it appears [Americans] wish us to be given to Spain again after decoying us to an unlimited surrender and then robbing us of all the means of defense we had taken from Spain. All I can say is that I wish I had command of the fort when Claiborne arrived and that I had known as much as I do now, I certainly would have blown him out of the river and then he must take his own course either to heaven or to hell." Claiborne and the US government had won the day, but bitterness like this would endure and resurface in the memories of veterans like Samuel Kemper and others who would one day be in a position similar to the conventionalists when they marched into Texas as part of a filibuster army.[18]

Four Governors in Texas

Watching from a distance as Americans absorbed a nearby province of the empire, the new governor of Texas, Manuel Salcedo could only guess that his would be next. The only question was whether the blow came from an authorized invasion or a private one. Either way, he was wary of the Americans, whose government, he said, "looks at the matter coldly and in malicious expectation" of a successful revolution in Mexico. Texas, he said, was the *antemural* or "outer works" of the defense of New Spain. The governor had known no peace since the day he had set foot inside his province, where, as he put it to his uncle, "the cares and resulting business have been multiplying daily." He complained that he worked entirely alone, with no legal adviser, secretary, scribe, or any other employee to help him with his burdensome work. But this description is only part of the story. By April of 1809, Spain had dispatched no less than *four* governors to Texas, and they were still there.[19]

The first had been Coahuila Governor Manuel Antonio Cordero, who had been sent to Texas as acting governor on the death of Governor Elguézabal in 1805. Then came Nuevo León Governor Simón de Herrera, who was tasked with securing the frontier in the crisis of 1806 and had signed the Neutral Ground agreement. Both stayed on and in their way had shaped Texas. If two extra governors superior to himself did not trigger Manuel Salcedo's insecurity, his uncle piled on one more: Governor Bernardo Bonavía of Durango. He was ostensibly sent to Texas to replace Cordero, who was needed back in Coahuila. But the latter remained for a time, and the province continued with four governors and not a single secretary. Bonavía, however, saw this multiplicity as an advantage. On April 19, 1809, he and Manuel Salcedo drafted a request for the other two governors, seeking their input on a combined plan of action for Texas. They may have hoped that a unified front could penetrate Commandant General Nemesio Salcedo's intransigence and hostility to innovation.[20]

Cordero, who had supported the French creole Bernard Despallier's settlement plan four years before, recommended efforts to reinforce Nacogdoches with immigrants and settlers, despite the fact that the commandant general was not pleased with the settlers Cordero had let in so far. Herrera, with three years' experience in East Texas, also endorsed this plan and called for a significant increase in the army.

In order to support these troops, he proposed opening a new port at Matagorda. East Texas should on no account be abandoned, as to do so would be interpreted by the United States as an acceptance of its inflated Louisiana Purchase claims. For his own part, Manuel Salcedo warned of the danger that came from American citizens acting on their own initiative, based on his experience spending time with Burrites like Governor Greenup. He too called for aggressive settlement. Bonavía, who was senior (he was a brigadier general), capped off this series of letters with his own passionate call for more open trade and a port at Matagorda. The general also disagreed with his superior's handling of smuggling. Though he thought the arrest of illegal traders such as the Joseph Magee and Henry Quirk groups showed diligence and loyalty among the soldiers, Bonavía pointed out that smuggling was conducted not from strictly criminal motives but from necessity. His solution to prevent smuggling was to allow a legal alternative and recommended the opening of free trade for useful goods, particularly farm implements, tools, and machinery. Exports, furthermore, should be duty-free. Bonavía argued that, given the poverty on the frontier, "there is no army or measure capable of stopping contraband trade."[21]

But their hopes of swaying the inflexible heart of Commandant General Nemesio Salcedo were sorely disappointed. To this official, New Spain's frontier province was not a territory to be improved but a buffer zone that existed solely for the needs of the Spanish Crown. All decisions were based on that principle; hence his puritanical defense of the mercantilist system even at the expense of the people. The danger of the seductive commerce of ideas overrode the necessity of the commerce of goods. Texas' residents, to the commandant general, were mere tools to an end. Their wants and desires were subject to his veto; they were forced to settle not where they could prosper, but near a military garrison, in order to provide for it. A month before the meeting of the four governors, Nemesio Salcedo even declined a request by his nephew to repair the royal road or *Camino Real*. As young Manuel explained to Cordero, isolated in Nacogdoches, "[The Commandant General] . . . declares that the road from here to Nacogdoches has to remain in the condition in which it is, without making bridges, foot-paths nor other work that may facilitate its transit." Governor Manuel Salcedo thought the best defense for *Texas* was to develop it. His uncle thought the best defense for *New Spain* was to keep Texas an impoverished buffer. When the Commandant General received the letters of the four governors, he dismissed all of their suggestions and ordered Bonavía to stick to the status quo.[22]

And what was that? A province with fewer than three thousand non-Indian residents and more than a thousand soldiers. These latter, unfortunately, were dispersed almost to uselessness in the towns and smaller outposts. Manuel Salcedo put the number of troops actually needed for proper defense at four thousand—which would have meant a ratio of four soldiers to every three citizens. It was simply not affordable under the best of systems, and the Spanish mercantilist economy was not that. It was a moot point since the Commandant General had no such troops to spare. Another plan of the younger Salcedo to train and equip a militia in Texas was discouraged by his uncle, partly for fear that arming the populace might encourage them to rebel.[23]

If Governor Salcedo's troop request sounds paranoid, it nonetheless was based on a real danger. He had traveled through America and met its people firsthand, particularly the Westerners of Ohio, Kentucky, and Tennessee—the same people who were confiding in John Adair. "The idea that some have that we ought to hold the Americans in contempt is an error," he wrote in a memorandum for the Spanish court. "In the first place . . . they are not to be underestimated as enemies. Second, the Anglo-Americans are naturally industrious." These Westerners, he tried to explain to Spanish authorities, did not act like good subjects, precisely because they were *republicans* and had been conditioned by habit to behave differently on the frontier "where settlement in such spacious areas makes complete and immediate submission to law difficult even if their laws are strict and wise. Consequently, it has happened that when the laws and governmental measures, be they of the congress or the territorial judges, have not suited the settlers, they have not obeyed them or at least they have tried not to," he concluded. Though Americans like Sibley had been cordial to him personally, the hostility to his empire in the West was universal.[24]

Just how bad the situation was in Texas came to light in the spring and summer of 1810, when Governor Salcedo on the orders of his uncle, mounted an inspection tour. He traveled from Béxar to Trinidad to Nacogdoches, then back again. Repeatedly, on the march, the governor's diary records soldiers' weapons, long stored in the armory, malfunctioning amid field conditions. On April 20 alone, eight muskets were noted as having broken.[25]

The governors continued to argue with the Commandant General. Bonavía persisted, to the point of severe reprimands from his superior, to call for more immigrants. To the Commandant General's suggestion that nearly all of the Louisiana immigrants had been smugglers, fugitives, atheists, and other sundry bad people, Bonavía responded that, with the exception of smuggling, which was a response to something akin to government-mandated impoverishment, most of these residents were good Spanish subjects. And there were many more in Louisiana who could be brought in quickly. He pointed to the large number of Canary Islanders in that province, who would gladly move to Texas, where the city of San Antonio had been founded by fellow Isleños.[26]

Again, these pleas fell on deaf ears, and the Commandant General moved forward with a plan he had been nursing for some time to expel most foreigners. In Nacogdoches, while on his inspection tour, Governor Salcedo followed up on orders from his uncle to review the status of all foreigners living in the province. He ordered Lieutenant Guadiana to take depositions from dozens of them in Nacogdoches. The canvass showed a robust population of Anglo Americans and Frenchmen, increased since 1801, living with wives and families. The governor saw the Americans as generally little threat, though he admitted concerns about the Frenchmen. But even before this report reached the Commandant General, the latter had made his decision. On March 13, in a confidential letter to his subordinates, he gave the final order to expel most foreigners.[27]

Nemesio Salcedo, who had only briefly visited Texas, was also certain he knew better than all four governors on the scene about how to defend the province against invasion. His plan involved bolstering Trinidad as a base of operations and the fortification of San Antonio as a rallying point. The plan was to move the fight closer to reinforcements and lengthen the invaders' supply lines—hence his otherwise baffling decision to block the improvement of Texas' roads and river crossings. San Antonio was expected to hold out until a relief force could arrive from the interior. La Bahía was to serve as a base for defense along the coast. Although he had rejected a port for commercial reasons, he did consider building one for military ends, although it too was impractical, and could also be used by an invading force.

As for making a stand at Nacogdoches, this was impossible. The town's defenses were little more than a stockade of pickets and a half dozen cannon, all but one or two of which were unserviceable. Guadiana and others had shown interest in strengthening the town, but there was no money to pay for fortifying it. Sickness and poor food supplies were additional complaints of the garrison. Commandant General Salcedo, moreover, believed that the town was too distant and too exposed to save against any organized foe. He also likely suspected its loyalty given the history of smuggling and other connections to its sister city of Natchitoches. In this, he was to be proven correct.[28]

5

The Secret Agent

IN MAY 1810, a letter arrived at the residence of a New York merchant sea captain and trader, William Shaler, bearing the name of Robert Smith, the US secretary of state. It was a correspondence not particularly unexpected. Smith was a former merchant well versed in maritime law, who had served eight years as President Jefferson's secretary of the navy, so he and the New York mariner were well-known to each other. The navy was small and relied on merchant captains to be the nation's eyes and ears on the high seas. They were usually the first to bring news of worldwide troubles, and William Shaler had performed this role often. Shaler was already awaiting a letter from Smith; he had written to him just six months before to propose a new system of signaling flags for American vessels. The British had developed a system eleven years before, but Shaler suggested a homegrown version, which would be useful given the increasing likelihood the two nations might go to war. Shaler likely expected this message was a response to his proposal. Opening the letter, he found it was about an entirely different matter. "Sir," wrote Smith, "should you have declined going to Europe, it is the wish of the President that you would repair to this place [Washington, D.C.] as soon as you conveniently can, as he is desirous of availing the public of your services in an important and confidential employment." Perhaps Shaler had previously discussed some sort of sensitive work before with Smith, or Madison, with whom he was acquainted. If so, Shaler was the perfect man for the job: He had comfortable wealth, but no wife or children, and was therefore available for a spur-of-the-moment assignment serving his country.[1]

Shaler made haste to Washington, arriving five days later, settling in at the urbane boarding house of Mr. John Doyne, located at Ninth and D. Streets, a block from Pennsylvania Avenue. The next day, May 30, 1810, at 11:00 a.m., Shaler walked up the steps of a plain brick edifice 150 feet long, situated just west of the White House. It had a corridor running the length of the building, with rooms on either side, housing the Navy Department, Postal Service, Patent Office, and office of the surveyor of Washington. Shaler took the stairs to the second floor, where the Department of State was housed in a series of four rooms. The sea captain, who had a long face, clean-shaven except for deep sideburns and curly auburn hair on a receding forehead, was ushered into the secretary's reception room, which was modest, as was the man who occupied it, a portly fellow with a round face, deep-set eyes and Roman nose.[2]

Though the position of secretary of state had been the springboard to the presidency for the two most recent executives, Robert Smith was no titan of the republic. Just over a year before, James Madison had occupied these rooms, and when he assumed the presidency, he had every intention of filling the role of secretary of state himself, promoting the Swiss-born Albert Gallatin, Jefferson's secretary of the treasury, to the nominal head of the department. But Gallatin had many enemies, including Senator Samuel Smith of Maryland, who rejected him and foisted his brother Robert upon the president. From the first it was a calamity: Madison sought to rid himself of Smith, who then undermined him. The president "did not trust Smith's competence in the position and redrafted many of Smith's diplomatic notes." He did not relax his mistrust after Smith's failure to negotiate a trade agreement with British Minister David M. Erskine—which might have avoided the War of 1812. Smith, therefore, was a disruptive, discordant spirit in the administration, on a very short leash, neither empowered by Madison to enact his own vision nor trusted to fully share the innermost confidences of the president. Robert Smith handled the details, but the president still handled the larger strategy. But one subject on which Madison and Smith could agree was the importance to America of the worldwide meltdown of the Spanish Empire.[3]

As we have seen, the year before, the Spanish envoy, Luis de Onís, had arrived in America but was never recognized by the administration. The new American president was unsure just who was the legitimate ruler of Spain. It was not an academic question: To embrace Onís was to court war with France, to recognize his Napoleonic rival, conflict with England. This same confusion was spreading across Spanish America, and battle lines were forming. The Spanish response to occupation had been to create a junta as a government-in-exile in Cádiz. Drawing on centuries of Spanish political theory, the colonies did the same. In Venezuela, where Miranda had failed four years before, a junta had recently been established, pledging loyalty to the imprisoned Ferdinand. As Smith and Shaler were meeting, New Granada and Argentina were establishing juntas of their own. West Florida was next, though neither man knew it at the time. Though these juntas invariably pledged loyalty to the king, it was clear to all that the longer the crisis continued, the more likely independence would become. All of these potential new nations were important to the United States, but what Smith was particularly worried about that day were Cuba and Mexico.[4]

Governor Claiborne in New Orleans the year before had written Smith to describe a conversation with two Spanish officers who had secretly paid him a visit. The officers told Claiborne that Spain was at the mercy of Bonaparte, but the Spanish American possessions would not submit to French rule and would prefer independence instead. "I was told that the independence of Mexico was agreed upon and would be declared the moment the fall of old Spain was officially announced, and that the friendship and support of Great Britain and the United States would be earnestly solicited," the governor wrote, then added, "I was asked whether a minister from Mexico would be received by the American government. . . . I was then told that a Minister from Mexico to the U. States was already talked of."[5]

As the news grew darker for the Spanish Empire throughout 1809 and the first half of 1810, Madison and Smith knew it was only a matter of time until these whispers of rebellion would become facts on the ground. If Spanish America were to revolt, it was imperative that the United States move decisively to establish relations with the new countries stretching from Mexico to Peru. With mercantilism the rule across much of the globe, there was no prize for second place. America had to beat the British to the punch or see the hemisphere fall into London's sphere of influence. The failed British invasion of Buenos Aires in 1806 and the occupation of Montevideo in 1807 were cautionary tales. Just as importantly, this could be the opportunity to establish a hemispheric alliance of republicanism and free trade that would inoculate America from European shocks like the Napoleonic wars. To that end, Smith had called the New York sea captain to this meeting.

Merchant Captain and Republican Evangelist

William Shaler was born in 1773 to a respectable Connecticut family but lost both his parents as a child. Swindled by a trustee of the estate, the young William, his two younger brothers, and a sister were left penniless. Shaler, only thirteen, took a job with the New York trading firm of Ingraham, Phoenix, and Nixsen, where he soon learned accounting and other skills. Intelligent and intensely focused on self-improvement, he rose quickly and by twenty-one was employed as a commercial agent on a ship bound for Europe. He learned French, Greek, Latin, and modern languages in his free time. Shaler's commercial voyages took him across the world through many adventures—once being stranded on the island of Mauritius, off the coast of Africa, when pirates had captured one of his ships.[6]

In 1799, rocked by the early shocks of the Napoleonic wars, Spain briefly opened her ports to foreign trade. Shaler and his partner, Richard J. Cleveland, took advantage of this unexpected boon, and sailed for Montevideo and Buenos Aires on board their ship *The Friends*. The pair then sailed to France and found themselves interned during the Quasi-War between that nation and America. Shaler and Cleveland, while waiting for the conflict to blow over, contemplated what they had discovered in the short first venture into Spanish lands. They were young men, both twenty-six years

The Secret Agent

Figure 2. Portrait of William Shaler. Collection of the New York Historical Society, gift of Daniel P. Ingraham, 1874.

old, and ambitious. The partners now planned their next voyage: a sail to South America, followed by passage into the Pacific and a continuance to Asia.[7]

Shaler was fired by passion for republicanism, both from patriotism as an American and from his love of literature. As he immersed himself in French-language philosophy, Shaler undoubtedly studied the man who was the great inspiration for revolution, Jean Jacques Rousseau, the same Swiss writer who so terrified Commandant General Nemesio Salcedo and his governors on the Texas frontier. Shaler, who was developing a profound interest in the Spanish world, was also prepared to take personal risks to evangelize Spanish America. Among the items he mixed with his

European cargo for this proposed journey were Spanish translations of the Declaration of Independence and American federal and state constitutions.[8]

In Hamburg in the fall of 1801, Shaler and Cleveland purchased and fitted out a brig of 175 tons, the *Lelia Bird*, and sailed for the New World. In Valparaiso, Chile, they were allowed to trade only necessary supplies before the authorities thought even this too risky and arbitrarily interned them. Although prohibited from leaving the port, they were at liberty in the city. Shaler, who had also brought books on the Spanish language and was trying to teach it to himself, practiced his shaky Castilian with many of the Creole families in the city and discovered, as he had hoped, fertile ground for the spreading of revolutionary messages. These Creoles wanted trade and were curious about freedom. Wherever he could, Shaler spread the twin gospel of liberty and of the wealth that would come from free trade. Somehow smuggling his pamphlets ashore, he passed these copies of the American founding documents to eager and interested Creoles. Upon release, he and Cleveland did the same thing at San Blas, Mexico.[9]

At San Diego, Spanish officials refused them landing rights, but they smuggled goods ashore at night to willing purchasers in the town. When lurking Spanish patrols captured one of their boats, Shaler responded boldly. Landing a party, he rescued his men by force and sailed out of port under a hail of cannonballs from the shore batteries. He returned fire with two broadsides from his well-armed merchantman. Cleveland, his partner, wrote that no civilized people in the world were more degraded than the Spanish Creoles, nor more sensitive of the fact. "Hence," he wrote, "we lost no opportunity of confirming the advocates of free government, and convincing the wavering of the self-evident proposition, that governments were instituted for the happiness of the people, and not exclusively for that of the rulers." Returning to the United States, Shaler published his diary as "Journal of a Voyage Between China and the North-Western Coast of America," which brought him renown among his countrymen. Along with his newfound wealth from his journeys, this brought him into elite circles, where he met Madison and befriended Smith. His experiences of his voyage were no doubt material for his conversations with such men.[10]

He was one of the first Americans to visit California and described how the locals eagerly traded with American merchantmen: "The government have used all their endeavors to prevent this intercourse, but without effect, and the consequence has been a great increase of wealth and industry among the inhabitants." At Guaymas, on the coast of Sonora, the story was the same. Shaler reported the people in utter material want, but "from the great abundance of gold and silver in it, [goods] are no where in greater demand." Treated better here than he had been in California, he dined cordially with Spanish officers aboard his ship but refused their invitation to come ashore, suspecting he would be detained.[11]

The Secret Agent

William Shaler had stumbled upon the same truth, which the smugglers on the Texas frontier and the Santa Fe traders had confirmed: The people of the Spanish colonies were eager for the benefits of trade and were willing to take extraordinary risks—even revolution—to get them. Republican idealism and the opportunity to make a personal fortune were not competitors; for eager Americans now enlightened by the prospects for trade, they blended together with perfect harmony.[12]

Shaler's Instructions

As the Spanish Empire to the south rapidly approached what in modern parlance would be called a failed state, President Madison decided to dispatch a series of special agents to Spanish New World colonies. Three agents were sent simultaneously. In addition to Shaler, who was appointed special agent to Cuba and Mexico on June 18, 1810, Robert K. Lowry was appointed agent to Caracas on June 26 and Joel Roberts Poinsett to Buenos Aires on June 28. Their instructions, minus geographic particulars, were identical: they were to seek out rebel regimes when and wherever they were to appear and open relations in anticipation of recognition and trade negotiations. Shaler's instructions began:[13]

> **Department of State June 18th 1810**
>
> Sir,
>
> As a crisis is approaching which must produce great changes in the situation of Spanish America, and may dissolve altogether its Colonial relations to Europe, and as the Geographical portion of the United States and other obvious considerations give them an intimate interest in whatever may affect the destiny of that part of the American Continent, it is our duty to turn our attention to this important subject, and to take such steps, not incompatible with the neutral character and honest policy of the United States, as the occasion renders proper.[14]

Shaler was ordered "to proceed without delay first to . . . Havana and thence by way of Vera Cruz, or of any other port to Mexico." He was given the following charges: (1) to "diffuse the impression" of US goodwill toward the people of Spanish America; (2) in the event of an independence movement to establish contact and open lines of communication with rebels; (3) learn local sentiment toward the US and report it; and (4) report on the population, characteristics, and wealth of the territories.[15]

Shaler's instructions contained a paragraph not included in the instructions to other agents, designed to smooth over sentiment over the United States' aggressive assertion of its West Florida "rights" (Claiborne had not yet seized the province).

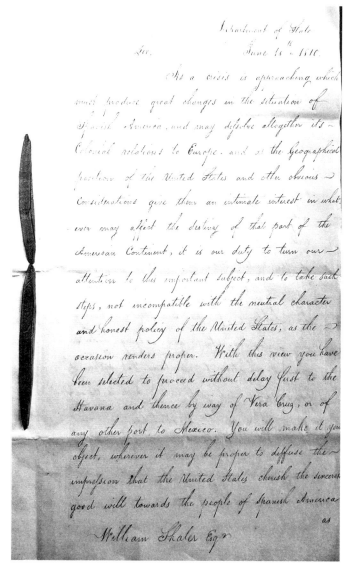

Figure 3. William Shaler's instruction letter.
Historical Society of Pennsylvania.

Shaler was to "bring into view the peculiar relation of the United States to the Floridas and the considerations which ought to reconcile the other parts of Spanish America to an eventual incorporation of [the Floridas] into our Union."[16]

The president considered the island of Cuba to be the most precarious of the territories because it would always be at the mercy of the Royal Navy, which had actually captured Havana in 1762, only trading it back to Spain at the negotiating table. It was also valuable for trade because of its sugar industry. Smith instructed Shaler to feel the pulse of the island, and if that pulse was favorable to incorporation with America, to report it. At this point, Madison certainly was not planning to dismember Mexico, or so Smith informed his agent. Though he thought it probable America's Louisiana Purchase included Texas, he was content to leave that problem to another day. If rebels succeeded in winning independence in the land of Montezuma,[17] he felt sure the outcome would be positive: "If your conversations at Mexico should be drawn to the Southwestern boundary of Louisiana, it will be sufficient for you to let it be understood that the United States will carry into that discussion, particularly in the case that it should take place with a neighboring instead of a foreign authority, a spirit of amity and equity, which with a like spirit on the other side, forbids any unfavorable anticipations."[18]

The agents were given commissions in order to negotiate with any new independent or autonomous regimes they might discover. Since their mission might be problematic should they need to deal with royal governments upon arrival, they were also provided fallback credentials, in Shaler's case as Agent for Seamen and Commerce.[19]

On June 21, 1810, as Shaler was making his final preparations to depart for Cuba, he received another note from Smith's aide John Graham, specifically addressing the question of Texas. Graham explicitly informed the agent that in dealings with rebels in New Spain "the many considerations induce me to believe that there is no wish here to insist on the Río Del Norte [Rio Grande] as one of the Boundaries." With this, the State Department made it clear to its agent that the United States had no intention to press a claim on Texas and his mission should be conducted accordingly. Much ink has been spent by historians seeking to read more "duplicity," to Shaler's mission, given the course of events that followed, but as far as Robert Smith was concerned, the instructions were clear and Shaler was not to deviate from them. As events proved, however, at a distance from Washington the agent encountered circumstances never envisioned and had to adapt and interpret his instructions to meet them. And although his orders never contemplated him traveling to Texas, events pushed him there and would link him inextricably with its fate.[20]

The Neutral Ground

In 1809, most of the small US Army was deployed to the western frontier where its peacetime mission was not war in its strict sense, but rather "overawing whites and Indians on the frontier." This force was organized under General Wilkinson, the schemer who had joined—then betrayed—the Burr conspiracy. His forces in the Louisiana Purchase lands were divided between Upper Louisiana (today's Arkansas and Missouri), and Orleans Territory (modern Louisiana). He had brought 2,000 troops to New Orleans in the wake of the Burr Conspiracy, and 3 years later had

2,772 (half the strength of the entire US Army) in the Mississippi River region. He left a garrison in the city, and posted a small force at Fort Claiborne, another at Fort Stoddart above Mobile, and the remainder at Fort Adams. This latter post was situated south of Natchez, Mississippi, just above the Spanish post of Baton Rouge. In the brutal heat and swampy climate, disease devastated the force, taking 800 lives, with a further 160 men deserting. In a period of two years, Wilkinson had lost half of his entire army. The shocking mortality was noted by one officer, who stated that in March 1810, he saw "the shallow graves of American soldiers on the Spanish shore, who died during that mortality, who were food for crows."[21]

Wilkinson had belatedly moved the bulk of the troops to higher, healthier ground east of Natchez near the town of Washington, where conditions were primitive and miserable, but at least the deaths abated. Cantonment Washington, as this temporary camp was called, was thus anything but a glorious posting for one young officer who arrived sometime in late 1809 or early 1810. Augustus Magee had graduated from West Point in January 1809 and had been appointed to the artillery and assigned to the Atlantic coastal forts, to assist in updating the fortresses to accommodate more advanced cannon. In this capacity, he possibly served on the islands of Ellis and Bedlow—today's *Liberty Island*—which at the time guarded the approaches to New York City.[22]

Now, he had been shipped off to the frontier, probably in the immediate aftermath of the move to the new site, and certainly aware that he was replacing the men lost in the frightful illnesses of the previous two years. This was probably not the last disappointment on the frontier for the young Bostonian. As historian Samuel Watson notes, officers like Magee, with his ties to elite and Federalist traditions, were generally more disposed to see in the frontier "societal entropy and disorder." Even his professional status within the army was diminished. He was assigned to a new light artillery company but in name only, being essentially used as infantry. This company was incorporated into a consolidated regiment of all combat arms under Lt. Col. Zebulon Pike, who had returned from Spanish captivity and had become a national hero due to his exploits in his Santa Fe mission, including the discovery of the peak that would bear his name. The famous officer would soon choose Magee for increasingly difficult tasks on the frontier.[23]

In October 1809, Wilkinson was recalled to Washington to face a second court martial over the deaths under his command. The scheming general would beat these charges too, but in the meantime would be gone from the frontier for a crucial span of nearly three years. In his absence, dissension was rife and feuds among officers were common and severe. A dispute at the highest levels between Brig. Gen. Wade Hampton and Col. Thomas Cushing led to the latter's court-martial. Similarly, the commander at Fort Claiborne in Natchitoches, Lt. Col. Constant Freeman, filed charges against one of his officers, Capt. Joseph Cross, who then turned around and swore out charges against Freeman and a junior lieutenant, which resulted in dueling courts-martial of all three men.[24]

It was to this troubled fort on the frontier—the same that Manuel Salcedo had visited—that Augustus Magee was detached in the spring of 1810. At Fort Claiborne, Magee served under Capt. Charles Wollstonecraft, who commanded the First United States Artillery and, since Freeman's court-martial, the post as well. Wollstonecraft also came from a privileged background, but a quite different one from the Bostonian. He was nineteen years older than Magee and came from a liberal English family that had embraced the American revolutionary cause wholeheartedly, along with other radical issues. (He was the younger and favorite brother of the famous British feminist Mary Wollstonecraft. His niece, Mary Wollstonecraft Shelly, would achieve fame as the author of the novel *Frankenstein*.) Charles Wollstonecraft had failed in law in England, then moved to the United States and joined the American Army at the late age of thirty.[25]

In the three and a half years since Wilkinson and Herrera had signed the Neutral Ground accord, the United States and Spain had both scrupulously adhered to it. No troops of either side had entered the territory between the Sabine and the Arroyo Hondo. But in April 1810, Governor Salcedo began to receive reports from his licensed trader, Samuel Davenport, of American settlers setting up homesites near the abandoned Spanish town of Los Adaes. Salcedo, then in Nacogdoches as part of his tour, sent word to Captain Wollstonecraft that he intended to march into the territory to expel them. This would violate the agreement and could spark a new confrontation between the two nations. But while many Americans on the frontier would have welcomed a conflict, Wollstonecraft pleaded with Salcedo to delay his march while he wrote his superiors for guidance.

The officer, as an outsider to the western expansionist sentiment, could see the fault was not that of the Spanish; indeed, he suspected these settlers had been encouraged in their brazen act by those within his own community at Natchitoches. In July 1810, he would write that "I have been able fully to ascertain that Doctor Sibley the Indian Agent has been the adviser and promoter of the settlement complained of by the Spaniards." Sibley, he told his superiors, had lands surveyed in the Neutral Ground and crops planted in partnership with his former overseer, a Mr. Petit. "All the settlers have advised with him," Wollstonecraft wrote. "This man endeavors to create a disturbance & opposition to the order of the government, as well as to interrupt the good understanding between the two nations by secret council to the men who have settled on the public lands of a most pernicious nature."[26]

The Englishman-turned-proud-American made it clear what he thought of Sibley: "If required, I can fully unmask this pretender to patriotism." It is likely that Sibley was setting up squatters to stake a claim prior to—as he expected—America gaining the Sabine as its border. He certainly saw these settlers as a peaceful alternative to the banditti who had made their home in the Neutral Ground, but the Spanish (and Wollstonecraft) did not see the distinction. Although there is no evidence that Sibley had a deeper purpose to subvert New Spain itself, Commandant General Nemesio Salcedo was convinced he had revolutionary intent. Now his nephew, Governor

Manuel Salcedo had to deal with the settlers urged on by Sibley, who had so generously hosted him and his family two years before. And at the same time, the governor was busy enforcing the order from his uncle to expel most foreigners from Texas. The Spanish treated these issues as separate, and they had begun so. But some of those expelled, bitter and vengeful over their treatment, would soon make common cause with the squatters and adventurers now setting up in the Neutral Ground.[27]

Salcedo had suggested he might march in unilaterally, but the Spanish did not want conflict between the two nations any more than Wollstonecraft did. Governor Bonavía, still in San Antonio, was the first to suggest a compromise—a joint patrol. Wollstonecraft passed the suggestion up the chain of command. His superior, Colonel Cushing, saw at once the heart of the problem: "I have no doubt but the intruders who are the subject of the communication, have taken their present position in full confidence that neither nation can remove them without a breach of the agreement." In May, Secretary of War William Eustis agreed to the plan. Salcedo, patiently waiting on the Americans, wrote to Wollstonecraft he was eager to cooperate "in order to convince you of the good faith, equity, and true harmony with which I desire to operate in an affair so necessary for the preservation of the peace which happily exists on that frontier."[28]

By 1810, the Americans recognized that more than just peaceful settlers had entered the Neutral Ground, and a portion of them were deliberately targeting Spanish caravans. "They have threatened Messrs. Davenport & Barr," Wollstonecraft observed, "whom they suspect of having informed against them, and I was told by one of the men, that some time ago, it was in contemplation to stop Mr. Davenport's carts, which were carrying merchandise from this post to Nacogdoches."[29]

This danger had forced the Spaniards in early summer 1810 to request American assistance to pass through the Neutral Ground. Wollstonecraft gave the job to the newly arrived young officer, Augustus Magee, who commanded an escort of ten American soldiers. At a creek just west of the old Spanish capital of Los Adaes, the party was ambushed by bandits, who waited until Magee and the bulk of the escort had passed before robbing the Spaniards. Magee saw this was happening but feared that firing on the bandits might endanger the Spaniards. Instead, he and the escort retreated to the fort to get reinforcements. By the time they returned, the bandits had abandoned their captives and fled with their loot. Magee later recognized two of them entering Natchitoches and had them arrested.[30]

While there is no doubt that a hardened criminal element existed among the banditti of the Neutral Ground, the evidence suggests that the more organized core of men operating there was politically motivated. As historian Eric Hobsbawm has shown, the line between crime, revenge, reform, and revolution among such groups is frequently blurry. The Spanish believed some old Burr conspirators had sought shelter there. They also became convinced, as part of their investigation, that the banditti had in fact evolved out of the efforts to rescue the smugglers Quirk, McFarlan, Brenton, and Magee. It was not lost on them that the chief victim of their depredations, the firm of Barr and Davenport, had the exclusive royal right to trade with Louisiana, and they believed the bandits were targeting their traders in retaliation.[31]

As noted, the Missouri mining magnate and filibuster supporter John Smith T had sent a trading expedition into New Mexico. Through Joseph McLanahan, he was tangentially connected to the banditti in Texas as well, and though there is no proof that he was their patron in 1809, he would become so in time. Thus what appears to be random raids on caravans was likely a deliberate effort, parallel to at least, but possibly in coordination with the Santa Fe push. There are three ways of interpreting the banditti's actions, which are not mutually exclusive: On the one hand, being tied to the smugglers, the rogues who attacked Spanish caravans were targeting the competition. Also, by interdicting trade goods destined for the Indians, their predations had the effect of wrecking Spanish efforts to buy off the peaceful dispositions of otherwise hostile tribes. But, most importantly, their activity effectively amounted to an economic blockade of Texas. Whether they realized it or not, these banditti had already become a revolutionary force on the border. And the evidence strongly suggests that they indeed *did* know what they were doing.

In June, Wollstonecraft received authority for the joint patrol, and now had to contact Spanish authorities across this turbulent ground. "I feared sending a soldier alone as an express," he wrote, "lest he should be waylaid or seduced from his duty by the intruders," who had been making hostile threats. For this dangerous task, Wollstonecraft again turned to Magee. On June 9, the young officer escorted an express into the Neutral Ground. Once it was safely in Spanish territory, he turned back. But before returning, he passed on a warning to those people he encountered. It was imperative to demonstrate that Spain and America were in accord, Wollstonecraft noted, "as [the banditti] have threatened to attack the Spanish troops should they cross the Sabine." The residents of the Neutral Ground were warned that the United States and Spain had agreed to a joint patrol and that they would be expelled if they did not leave immediately. Their homes and crops would be burned to discourage their return. Some settlers complained bitterly to Magee; they had already planted crops and wanted a delay until harvest time to avoid complete ruin. They would not get it.[32]

The Joint Patrol

On August 1, 1810, the military forces of the United States and Spain met on Neutral Ground at Bayou Piedra in an unprecedented collaboration of arms. The two contingents were by design equal: the Spanish consisted of one officer, one sergeant, three corporals, and fifteen soldiers. The American numbers were the same, but less two of the corporals. The Spanish had also brought along Samuel Davenport to serve as a translator. The two officers met, exchanged greetings through Davenport, and sized each other up.[33]

The American commander was, of course, Lt. Augustus Magee. His Spanish counterpart, whom he met for the first time, was the perennial second-in-command in Nacogdoches, Lt. José María Guadiana. Other than rank, the two officers had almost nothing in common. Magee had grown up in an opulent mansion, Guadiana in the impoverished northern provinces of New Spain. They also stood athwart a generational divide. Guadiana had been in the Spanish service since 1788, before the young American across from him was even born. The Spanish lieutenant had served on campaigns in the west under the competent commander Don Juan de Ugalde, who then served in La Bahía for a time before transferring to Nacogdoches. Administratively a member of the Second Flying Company of San Carlos de Parras in San Antonio, Guadiana had served in the garrison on the frontier for most of the last fifteen years. In his career, he had fought the Apache, chased Philip Nolan, imprisoned smugglers, and in all that time had only been promoted twice. In contrast, Augustus Magee was still a young officer of twenty-two and had already made first lieutenant. He was ambitious and expected to make captain soon.[34]

After meeting up, the two forces settled into a routine. On the first morning, the Americans made breakfast for all, and presumably, they set an alternating schedule for the next two weeks. That day, the troops rose at five thirty and began their journey at a slow pace since most of the men were on foot. At one in the afternoon, they arrived at the home of Miguel Crow along the Sabine River. Crow was an Anglo-American and Spanish subject whose residence predated the Neutral Ground agreement and therefore grandfathered him to occupy the ranch. He was authorized by his government to reside in the territory to operate a ferry. From Crow, the patrol learned that an American had built a home not far away and went to it. Finding it vacant, they burned the house. Of course, the owner was nowhere nearby, for this was the home of Joseph McLanahan, the same man who had been mapping the Texas frontier and had departed with the Missouri traders Reuben Smith and James Patterson, bound for Santa Fe. As the Spanish/American party was burning his home, McLanahan and his associates were imprisoned by the Spanish in Chihuahua.[35]

Where unauthorized settlers were encountered by the joint patrol, they were ordered to leave immediately with whatever they could carry, or by the next morning if it was late in the day. Their homes would be burned and the troop would continue on. Likely in response to the pleas of the settlers regarding their crops, Magee, in his report, explained that "although the houses were destroyed, the corn was left standing and the cattle undisturbed on the promise of their being driven off when they could be collected." He also allowed the settlers time to carry away their belongings and furniture. On August 3, they burned the home of James Cunningham. The next day, the same fate was meted out to Louis Latham, who had his family with him. Then it was "the foreigner Fennimore" who was expelled, and three other dwellings were destroyed. As the party moved onward, more and more homes were found already empty as news of their mission spread.[36]

The unit sometimes split up into smaller parties to cover more ground, always mixing nationalities. On August 6th, Guadiana and Magee were in one such group with about half of the troop, when they came upon the home of the Frenchman Pierre Bolin, who begged to be given eight days to gather his widely scattered cattle. The request was granted, but the group seized his home, spent the night in it, and burned it the next morning. Like Crow, some settlers were grandfathered. Discovering one house which the group thought might qualify, Magee left the party for four days to travel to Natchitoches to investigate the matter. His soldiers continued to work under their own sergeant, but with Guadiana as the only officer for that time. There were no conflicts reported between the parties, but during the night of the 9th, one of Magee's soldiers deserted, possibly upset at the mission or "seduced," as Wollstonecraft had feared.[37]

The patrol had been a model of bilateral military cooperation: neither Magee's nor Guadiana's reports mentioned any dissension, strife, or disagreement between the two parties. The two frontier commanders and their troops had, despite all odds, formed a comradery. On the 12th, they held a farewell breakfast of sorts. The Americans roasted a cow that Magee had confiscated, and the Spanish roasted a young bull. Then they proceeded on a last round of enforcement, ousting the family of Benjamin Caller. His case shows how compromised local American officials were and how much Wollstonecraft—the dutiful enforcer of the laws—was stepping on toes. Caller was identified as a dependent of the American Lt. Col. Constant Freeman, Wollstonecraft's court-martialed predecessor, and also had ties to the Indian agent Sibley. In all, thirty-four persons were expelled, two families were Spanish, and the rest were American or French. What the party did *not* find much evidence of was the much-feared banditti. It seems the more mobile adventurers fled in advance of the troops' arrival, leaving only the settlers with homes and crops behind to face the punishment.[38]

Wollstonecraft was pleased with Magee's performance; the officer had "executed his orders in perfect harmony with the Spanish Commander; conducting himself with humanity towards the settlers." The raid had been a shock to the small Neutral Ground community, but within a few months, new people would move back in. Some would return to their burned homes, but a growing number would be the very banditti whom the Americans and Spanish had sought to expel. In the absence of a peaceful civil population of farmers and families, these bandits would thrive. As for Guadiana and Magee, as well as their go-between, Samuel Davenport, the friendly relations built up over the two-week patrol would have long-term consequences. In two years' time, the crusty, middle-aged Spanish officer with a penchant for alcohol and women and the Anglo-American Spanish trader Davenport would find themselves serving side-by-side under the youthful New Englander's command—this time as soldiers of a revolution. Some of the very men they had expelled would serve under them as well.[39]

6

The Tejano Revolt

THE LONG-ANTICIPATED revolution in Mexico began on September 16, 1810, when Miguel Hidalgo y Costilla, a parish priest in Dolores, issued his *Grito*. Word of the rebellion quickly spread to the United States, where John Sibley, the Indian Agent and Neutral Ground land speculator, learned the news from an American, Jonathan Hale Platts, who had been imprisoned in San Antonio for five months before being released and making his way to Nacogdoches. Platts informed Sibley "that ... Mexico is in a state of revolution, the parties opposed to each other are the [Creoles] against the Europeans, the former are for complete independence from all the world on republican principles, the latter are for Ferdinand the Seventh and monarchy."[1]

Reaction in the United States was mixed. Federalists feared the spread of French and radical democratic influence, but the republican press took up the cause with alacrity. Leading the charge to bolster support of the rebels were two of the most influential newspapers in the country, the *National Intelligencer* and *Niles' Weekly Register*. Hezekiah Niles, the editor of the latter, lashed out at the Federalists. To him, this was a continuation of the struggle of 1776, and he (inaccurately) placed the parties in convenient terms for his readers: Spanish rebels were "Whigs" and royalists were "Tories."[2]

Federalists, Niles complained, were praiseworthy of the European Spaniards fighting against Napoleon but were oddly silent regarding the *American Spaniards*. "Ought we not to feel more interested in such events, occurring, as it were at our own doors, than in the choice of *masters* in Europe?" he wrote. "Like naturally seeks its like, and if truly attached to the *republic* of North America, ought we to be indifferent as to the establishment of a *republic* in the southern continent, a sister, of whom we may entertain the happiest anticipations?" Niles called on Americans to embrace the cause wholeheartedly. "If ever a people were justified by the laws of nature and nature's God, in dissolving the political bonds that held them to another, it is the people of what is called '*Spanish America*'—What outrages, indignities and insults have not been heaped upon the heads of these colonists!"[3]

Burr's claims in 1806 to have an underground network of priests throughout Mexico who would rally to his cause were probably overstated, but not entirely fanciful. Mexican rebels, clergy and lay alike, were well aware of the Burr adventure and of American sentiment, and sought to leverage it. While events of subsequent years would sew mistrust among Mexicans toward inviting such men into their country, Mexican rebels in the first decades of the century believed that Americans—whether backed by their government or simply mercenaries—were valuable allies and an open lifeline to the United States was indispensable. Zebulon Pike, who had spent months among the Mexicans, had judged their mood and promised his countrymen that these people "turned their eyes towards the United States, as brethren of the same soil."[4]

For both sides, a far stronger inducement than brotherhood was something more material. The Mexican Association of New Orleans had its eyes on commerce. For the rebels' part, a pathway to the northern republic could allow them to trade the gold and silver specie, which they had in abundance, and of which Americans before 1849 were chronically short. In exchange, the rebels could obtain what the United States had but Mexico desperately needed: food, supplies, weapons of war, and the men proficient in their use. With no navy, the rebels could only get these resources overland, and the path to the United States lay through Texas. Thus, despite its relative insignificance in terms of population, the frontier province assumed an elevated importance in revolutionary strategy.

There, the first sign of the revolution was the departure of two of the four governors in Béxar, Antonio Cordero and Bernardo Bonavía. With their own provinces endangered, the two governors were ordered home late in 1810. Nonetheless, Gov. Manuel Salcedo still had an able partner by his side in the one remaining governor, Simón Herrera, an effective military commander with five years' experience in Texas under his belt. Although there is reason to suspect Herrera may have harbored some sympathy with the rebel cause, in the end, the two governors would stay loyal to Spain and would share the same fate.[5]

On October 24, 1810, Commandant General Salcedo issued a proclamation to the people of Texas, warning them against sympathizing with the rebellion. He blamed the Hidalgo revolt on antireligious Napoleonic agents like D'Alvimar and encouraged Texas leaders to strengthen their efforts and vigilance. He did not provide his nephew with more resources, only threats that he and Herrera could pass along to the populace: those who supported the rebels or succored French agents would be put to death.[6]

Up to now, the greatest concern of Texas officials had been the frontier town of Nacogdoches with its mixed population of Spaniards and foreigners, addiction to smuggling, and proximity to the United States. This fear seemed to be justified in May 1810 when two Spanish women in Nacogdoches claimed to have overheard William Barr, the Indian agent, speaking of a secret plan to revolutionize Mexico.

Despite the fact that even the women admitted Barr had expressed disapproval of such a plan, the Irishman instantly fell under suspicion. Barr had profited so much in the service of Spain, and by all accounts was the most loyal foreigner in the province. His own stone building was at that moment being rented by the Spanish garrison of Nacogdoches. Despite all of this, he was arrested. Although the Spanish would later drop the charges for lack of evidence, the damage was done. Upon his release, Barr, suffering from a "mortal illness" that was not helped by his confinement, traveled to Natchitoches for treatment. He died there at the home of one of his agents, Juan Cortés, on September 9—two weeks before the *Grito* he had predicted so presciently. His affairs and his position as Indian Agent were inherited by his partner, Samuel Davenport, the same trader who had been the go-between during the Spanish-American joint patrol a month before.[7]

San Antonio de Béxar

When the fire of revolution burst forth in Texas, it would not be on the frontier or instigated by foreigners; it would come from the residents of the capital. San Antonio had been little more than a village around the mission until the arrival on March 9, 1731, of fifty-six settlers from the Canary Islands. Eighty years later, their descendants, known as *Isleños*, were still among the foremost civic leaders of the community. These included the Arocha, Delgado, Leal, and Travieso families, all closely tied by bonds of blood, marriage, and business. Also among the city's chief citizens were military officers and their descendants, particularly the Seguín, Flores, and Menchaca families. The majority of the settled population, however, were poorer settlers, active and retired soldiers, and Hispanicized Indians.[8]

The economy of Texas was almost entirely agricultural and heavily oriented to ranching. "Their principal employment is to rear horses, mules, cows, and sheep," wrote a French traveler in Texas in the 1760s. As noted previously, hostile Indians and even their own missions competed for the best lands. What was left was nearly all monopolized by the Isleño elites, jealous of other residents seeking to join their class. Irrigation too was increasingly concentrated in their hands, and as a result, most of the common families could only practice subsistence agriculture on small plots within or just outside of the town. But even the elites were still mere Creoles—purebred Spaniards but born in the New World—a second-class status that no amount of wealth could ever remove. They were always beneath the *peninsulares*, the native-born Spaniards, and would never be able to match the social standing and in some cases rights of their European-born countrymen. The most discontented Creoles referred to these Europeans with a unique pejorative that combined haughtiness, deceit, injustice, and brutality into one word: *gachupín*.[9]

Alongside this resentment, there grew up in San Antonio a feeling of identity increasingly alien from that of Spain itself, or even of much of Mexico. "During the five decades after Béxar's founding, the inhabitants developed a sense of belonging to the region," wrote historian Gerald Poyo. These residents "increasingly shared aspirations and goals that did not always conform to the Crown's strategic objectives." Texas was always envisioned by the Spanish authorities as a buffer, but to the citizens living there, it was home. During the years of benign neglect, this tension was modest, but during the late 1700s, Spanish royal officials began asserting more authority within Texas, particularly over the province's cattle resources. Like their Anglo-American counterparts in the thirteen colonies, the people initially confined their discontent to petitions.[10]

When rebellion did break out in Mexico after the *Grito*, Spanish leaders in Texas saw no evidence to suggest that propaganda had penetrated deeply into the populace. But Tejanos were ignorant neither of the outside world nor of the calamity facing their empire. They had, after all, been asked the year before by their leaders to contribute to a fund for the defense of Spain. That the largest empire in the world would beg the settlers of one of its most impoverished outposts for a few pesos likely impressed them, and not in a good way. The turmoil—and the revolution—could not be hidden from them.[11]

José Antonio Menchaca, then just a young boy, recalled, "Secret letters were received here from parties who were desirous to throw off the Spanish yoke in Mexico." Tejanos answered these letters, saying the revolutionists "could rely upon help from here, that there were a great many here who would willingly enter into the plot." Mexican revolutionaries in late 1810 sent two agents from neighboring Nuevo Santander into Texas—Francisco Ignacio Escamilla and Antonio Sáenz—to stir up the ill-paid and poorly clothed troops of the Béxar garrison. This they attempted by word of mouth and through propaganda pamphlets. These came from a Mexican revolutionary in that province named José Bernardo Gutiérrez de Lara, who was working with his rebel priest brother, Father Jóse Antonio Gutiérrez, to spread revolution in the Rio Grande Valley. The rebel agents were discovered, clasped in irons and placed—since the city had no formal prison—in cells within the Alamo mission. With the capture of the rebels, Governor Salcedo now knew the danger was real. On November 21 he wrote, "I am ready to make the sacrifice of my person . . . defending the rights of our Catholic monarch, Don Ferdinand VII to the last breath."[12]

What had spurred the governor to such histrionics was the spread of the revolution on the Rio Grande, only a few hundred miles away. Under the influence of José Antonio Gutiérrez, communities there were rapidly falling to the insurrectionists. The governor of supposedly safe Nuevo Santander fled his province and declared to the viceroy that "revolution and terror range in the settlements along the Rio Grande." This was too close for comfort for Salcedo, and certainly for Herrera, whose own province was now exposed. Rather than wait for the contagion to spread to Texas, Manuel Salcedo chose to take the danger head on and announced plans to take his small force south to crush it. It was a fateful decision. The garrison of San

Antonio, small as it was, was the only defense against Indian raids, and stripping the town of its soldiers would leave the city exposed to an opportunistic attack by Lipan Apaches or Comanches. Knowing this, Salcedo ordered city officials to raise a citizen guard, but his uncle the commandant general's attempts to suppress the formation of a militia meant that there was no sufficiently trained or equipped core of men to undertake it.[13]

The job of enlisting a new militia from scratch fell to the alcalde, Francisco Travieso, and he thought it was little more than a death sentence for his town. Travieso was the grandson of Don Vicente Álvarez Travieso, a Canary Islander from Tenerife. Don Vicente had been among the city leaders in the 1750s, when they complained about draining the garrison in the face of a similar threat. Now, as his grandfather had done, Francisco Travieso took a stand, once again citing the safety of his city. Furthermore, the garrison had become an existential part of the town's identity. "Soldiers with families built their homes near the post," historian Jesús F. de la Teja has written, "and when they left military service, continued to reside in them." Indeed, by the early nineteenth century, not only were most of the garrison troops locals; some were third- or fourth-generation soldiers of their companies. Travieso's stand drew widespread support.[14]

The Casas Revolt

Having issued threats, Governor Salcedo now tried appeals. On January 6th, he posted a proclamation calling for loyalty, denouncing Hidalgo, and "putting forth arguments to prove the good faith of the Europeans." But on the night of January 15, 1811, Sáenz escaped from his heavily guarded prison cell in the Alamo. He and a group of conspirators then schemed to seize Salcedo and declare Texas for the insurgents. The plan was compromised and Sáenz was rearrested. Salcedo, realizing his proposed march to the Rio Grande had fueled the enterprise, now cancelled it. But a week later, on the afternoon of January 21st, he announced that he was taking the troops out of town on military exercises to the Guadalupe River. Universally, it was thought to be a ruse. That evening, Ensign Vicente Flores visited Travieso at his home and told him the soldiers of the garrison were with him and would refuse to march. They just needed a leader.[15]

They found him in the person of Juan Bautista de las Casas, a retired captain of the Villa de Croix frontier defenses of Nuevo Santander, who had recently moved to San Antonio. The rebels evidently knew something about Casas and his revolutionary leanings that the Spanish authorities did not, suggesting a whisper campaign, if not a full-fledged underground resistance, was already active in San Antonio. It counted many prominent soldiers of the garrison, including several officers: Flores, noted previously, and Captains Vicente Tarín and Pedro de la Garza Falcón. The latter, who had been promoted to the ranks of officers in the intervening years, was the same soldier who had captured the smugglers Quirk, McFarlan, Brenton, and Magee two and a half years before. To this conspiracy were added the sergeants Miguel de Reyna, Blas José Perales, Patricio Rodríguez, and Trinidad Pérez, whose support would be invaluable in persuading the common soldiers to join. Travieso and Flores then proceeded to Casas's home, where he readily agreed to the revolt. The conspirators worked on their plan until well past midnight. Sleeping little, Travieso awoke before dawn to start the coup in motion.[16]

As the last notes of the bugle call sounded on the morning of January 22nd, Travieso and Flores, wrapped in long cloaks to hide their identity, along with Casas and three or four soldiers, approached the Alamo, where the soldiers were gathering for morning muster. Travieso pulled a musket from under his cloak and took up a position outside the door of the captain of the guard. Casas entered and told Capt. Nicolás Benites he was seizing the city on behalf of the revolution. The captain refused to surrender but was overpowered. Casas came out to the soldiers, still in formation from the drum call, and they received him enthusiastically.[17]

Salcedo and Herrera, sensing something was afoot, rushed across the river to the Alamo, where they met Casas, with Travieso and Flores flanking him. The governors demanded to know the meaning of their appearance. Casas spoke: It was revolution, and the governors were to be imprisoned. Salcedo had expected this, but now that the moment had come, his will broke down. Pathetically, he volunteered to demote himself and become just an ordinary soldier in the ranks. He even asked a nearby *soldado* to give him his musket so that he could shoulder arms like the rest of the men. The soldier, not sure how to take this suggestion from the officer who for three years had been his commander, started to hand him the weapon. Casas stepped between them and said it was too late. The governor would be a prisoner, and there was no way to prevent it. Salcedo, Herrera, and several officers with them then gave up, and after nearly a century, royal authority in San Antonio ceased. Still, old habits die hard: As the two governors were marched past the troops for what most thought to be the last time, the soldiers snapped to attention and presented arms, just as they had always done.[18]

Good Governance or Independence?

What were Casas, Travieso, and the conspirators fighting for? At this point, it was not independence. For Travieso, it was probably little more than saving his town and people from the Indians. Casas may have wanted to command. One of those watching the scene was a youth a month shy of sixteen. Though he would one day be a future leader in the Republic of Texas, José Antonio Navarro stayed out of the conflict. He would later recall the event as "a spontaneous eruption of pent-up disorganized rage lacking any clear purpose other than retribution and a settling of scores."[19]

Most supporters of Casas simply wanted better, more accountable government, and in this they were little different from popular revolutions throughout New Spain, which often began with the cry, "Long live the king! Death to bad government!" For years, the people of San Antonio had seen misguided policy ruining Spanish Texas. Salcedo, given the choice, might even have agreed with them, but was powerless to do anything without the approval of his uncle the Commandant General, the epitome of the haughty, European-born Spaniard or *gachupín*. Some Tejanos may even have dreamed of a Mexican republic, but for most who joined the cause, it was not so ideologically black and white. It was just another step on the road they had unwittingly traveled since the day Joseph Bonaparte had seized the throne of their kingdom. Like their revolutionary counterparts in Massachusetts decades before, for Mexican Texans, rebellion came first; republicanism would come later. [20]

The first tentative steps toward that goal came that evening when Casas promptly released the revolutionary agents Escamilla and Sáenz, who had been scheduled to be executed. Also released was one Francisco Arocha—of one of the most important San Antonio families—who had likely been among those involved in freeing the two agents the week before. When news of the coup reached the revolutionary leaders in Coahuila, they promptly conferred upon Casas the title of interim governor.[21]

With Salcedo and Herrera in irons, other royalists in Texas were unable to offer significant resistance. At La Bahía, the garrison commander, Luciano Garcia, was summoned to Béxar but, being loyal, fled to Coahuila instead. Another officer, Agabo de Ayala, took over command in the name of Casas, but found opposition from the presidio chaplain, Father Miguel Martinez, and some of the leading citizens of the town.[22]

For the towns along the Camino Real northward toward Louisiana, Casas sent a trio of rebel emissaries to negotiate surrender. For this mission he chose Sáenz, Travieso, and Gavino Delgado, a San Antonio alcalde sympathetic to the revolution. They arrived in Trinidad on January 28th, and the town immediately declared its support for the rebellion. The rebel agents' aim was to arrest and dispossess all European-born *gachupines*, regardless of their station. This included priest Francisco Maynes, as well as Trinidad resident Antonio Castaño, who was old and impoverished, but still Spanish-born and thus an enemy of the revolution. Sáenz, the outsider, thought his Tejano compatriots greedy in these doings, writing that they had come "with the sole idea of pillage." Still, he did nothing to stop them. Moving on to Nacogdoches, the party arrived at noon on February 1st with about eighty cavalry or mounted infantry. The garrison commander, Don Cristóbal Domínguez, learning of their mission, commanded that no resistance be given as he was taken into custody. Sáenz had intended to seize his property, but the citizens of the town demurred, saying Domínguez "had been a father of all." Bowing to this sentiment, Sáenz simply inventoried his property for future action. Another man, called "*El Gachupín*" by fellow residents, protested he was actually a native of the Valley of Santiago in Mexico and should be spared.[23]

With Domínguez arrested, the rebels reinstalled the Mexico-born Guadiana as Nacogdoches' commander. The same officer who had been possibly complicit in Philip Nolan's smuggling in the 1790s, then captured him in 1801, and who had cleared the Neutral Ground alongside Augustus Magee in 1810, was now hunting royalists and stripping them of their duties, property, and liberty. In one example, he wrote to Casas that the postmaster had his goods seized, as he was "suspected of being a European."[24]

Sáenz seized the archives and the treasury and set himself up in the most substantial home in the village, Samuel Davenport's stone house. He declared that as the authentic representative of the Hidalgo Revolt, he was in authority, but the Tejanos with him resented this outsider's pretensions and began to squabble again over the seizure of goods. At last, Travieso burst into the house and the two began an argument which led to a scuffle. At one point, the slight Davenport stepped between the arguing Mexicans, but Travieso continued to lambaste the rebel agent "with the most indecorous words" and appeared to be growing violent. Finally, Sáenz called the guard, who arrested the very Tejano who had begun the coup which had freed Texas.[25]

When word of the revolt in Texas spread to the United States; John Sibley immediately informed the secretary of war. Sibley and others heard of the changes in Nacogdoches almost immediately after they happened, courtesy of Edmund Quirk, a former Nacogdoches resident who was still on the lam after his brother and his associates had been captured for smuggling two years before. Quirk had been sneaking into Texas, as a courier between revolutionary residents and sympathetic exiles and Americans. Further reports allowed Sibley to draw a detailed picture of the revolution.[26]

Sibley reported full rebel control throughout Mexico, but in fact, they would be engaged in a back-and-forth with the royalists for the next decade. Most importantly for Americans, the new government in Texas had opened free trade with Louisiana. "There was a general rejoicing amongst the people [of Nacogdoches] on the occasion." Sibley wrote, adding a note of caution, "Three million of a hardy warlike people, our neighbors, having changed their government, between us and them there are no fixed boundaries, commercial nor any other regulations, through whose country our revenue and laws prohibiting the introduction of slaves may be infringed will no doubt be subject of consideration of our government." The Madison administration had anticipated the revolt, which was why it had named William Shaler as its agent and tasked him to venture to Veracruz. But Shaler was still in Cuba, waiting for the revolution that would never happen there.[27]

The *National Intelligencer*, upon learning of the revolution in Texas, opined, "God grant them success." Nacogdoches was weak, it noted, with no more than 50 or 60 soldiers "under the command of Lieut. Godiano [sic]; this officer was there in command under the royal authority, but he is an American and has renounced his former master; he is therefore left in command—although at present everything is quiet and amicable on our frontier." The paper sounded a note of caution that was prophetic: "Yet the revolution may change men and things."²⁸

Men and things were indeed changing in San Antonio. On February 9, 1811, Casas issued a proclamation to the people of the town, reminding them that they were to have been abandoned by Salcedo and Herrera, the very same men who were honor bound to defend "your homeland, religion and sovereign." This, he explained to the people, would have been a disaster. To this sentiment, his listeners no doubt agreed, but then Casas, in his vanity, went further: "You were afflicted by all these considerations when the omnipotent God inspired me to take up your defense which I did with my whole soul at a time of dire need and misfortune," he wrote. His fellow conspirators must have scoffed at being left out. The people of San Antonio should consider themselves fortunate, he added. "As far as you can be impelled by your patriotic sentiment, raise your prayers to the Almighty in thanks for the leisure you have obtained through the sacrifices of your leaders."²⁹

Alongside this hubristic polemic, Casas announced that he had been vested "with all the powers that my judgment merits." Though he may have been the right man to lead the coup, it was apparent Casas was the wrong one to govern, alienating nearly everyone. Delgado and Saenz, returning from Nacogdoches, thought they had performed very well in seizing the second-largest town in the province, but they received no appreciative welcome, perhaps due to Travieso's complaints. Rather than praise, Saenz was greeted with arrest, accused of pocketing some of the confiscated wealth. The charges were soon dropped, but the damage was done. The rebel governor continued to assert himself like a bull in a china shop, even threatening the priest of La Bahía when he protested the summary confiscations. The people of Texas had gotten freedom from the gachupines, but they had not gained good government. Adding to the problems they faced, the Indian situation on the frontier was also rapidly deteriorating. Though the Comanches had a treaty with the Spanish, rebellious warriors from the Kotsoteka band under an influential chief known as El Sordo (the Deaf), in league with warriors from the Wichita tribe, raided Spanish ranches near San Antonio.³⁰

The Zambrano Coup

The struggle for independence in Mexico was never as ideologically consistent as the American Revolution of thirty years before, a result of traditions: Whereas Anglo-Americans revolted for the *restoration* of "English liberties," Spanish-Americans had no such legacy on which to build. Indeed, to group the sides in terms of "royalist" and "republican" at this stage is problematic. Even Hidalgo's movement was "a premature and improvised call for revolt that did not, in fact, aspire to independence from the Spanish crown but only autonomy within the family of Catholic principalities that made up the quickly disintegrating empire." Tejanos were even more ambivalent. While the citizens of Nacogdoches were hobbled by decades of oppression, the Béxareños in the capital were simply ornery and independent, resistant of government control, as Salcedo had learned over the previous three years. Increasingly, they were frustrated and resentful, and responding to vague impulses *for* good government and *against* arbitrary autocracy. Since the nominally republican Casas offered nothing truly liberating, for Spanish Texans it amounted to little more than lining up in parties in an ongoing struggle for ascendancy. This accounts for the fluid nature of such groupings, in which a particular individual would switch back and forth from one "side" to another—something that would later strike unsympathetic Anglo Americans as duplicity.[31]

In general, elites in Texas, like those in Mexico, formed the revolutionary core, but some Creoles in high positions often had Spanish royal patronage to thank for having been raised above the masses. Even some Spanish *peninsulares* with liberal leanings were not royalists, and the common people were not always rebels. There were "multitudes of individuals of all ranks, origins, functions and degrees of sophistication, who were disaffected with both sides of the war, and who found themselves alienated from insurgent as well as royalist objectives."[32]

Casas's incompetence and arrogance had alienated two key groups in the community: old, established officers and the city's political elite: Canary Island descendants, some of whom had been among the earliest supporters of his coup. As a reactionary movement began to form, it was wide-based and crossed boundaries of politics and association. It united people like Sáenz and Travieso, who had almost come to blows in Nacogdoches. They began to work the populace and the army separately. Casas did nothing to stop them. "Blinded with revolutionary illusions, the government were overconfident in their security," wrote one historian. "Either through stupidity or leniency, the enemy was permitted to work." While Travieso was appealing to the influential citizens, Sáenz recruited soldiers, including five militia lieutenants, some of whom had been among Casas' initial supporters: Francisco Flores, Juan Veramendi, José Francisco Ruiz, Ángel Navarro, and Juan Caso, as well as some sergeants and corporals. To lead what was becoming the second coup in two months, the conspirators chose thirty-eight-year-old Juan Manuel Zambrano.[33]

Zambrano had enjoyed a colorful career. Born in San Antonio, he then moved to Monterrey, where he became a military officer. At twenty-one, he returned to his hometown and established himself on a small piece of property. In 1805, he was elected city steward of San Antonio. He was also a subdeacon (lay minister) of the Catholic Church, but he was hardly an ideal man of God: he was a gambler and womanizer, so notorious that in 1803, the people of the town had petitioned the governor to act against him. He stood out among his fellow Spaniards with long, blonde hair, and frequently wore his shirt with an open collar and his sleeves rolled up to his elbows, cavalry sword strapped to his waist, as if he were ready to brawl with the first person he met.[34]

Zambrano had a house in the town, but also a large rancho called La Laguna de las Ánimas (All Soul's Lake) just outside, near Mission Concepción. He maintained a large flock of 77,000 sheep, as well as nearly 800 head of cattle, 100 horses, and other additional livestock. The property boasted a flour mill and no less than 32 servants and 2 slaves. When he clashed with the authorities in San Antonio, which was frequent, it was to this property he retreated. Now, a delegation of anti-Casas citizens persuaded Zambrano's two brothers to travel to this ranch, where they encouraged him to come into town to lead a revolt. He took up the charge, and showing a cleverness to match his courage, told his listeners exactly what they wanted to hear so that royalists and rebels alike embraced him.[35]

One afternoon in late February, an event occurred which hastened the end for Casas. At a time of day when many people would normally be taking siestas, an unusual caravan arrived in the town from the south, attracting much attention. At the head of the party was a man resplendent in a beautiful military uniform. None like it had been seen since D'Alvimar had passed through three years earlier, and the French being feared by all parties, the association was unfortunate. The uniform was in fact that of the embryonic Mexican Republic, and its wearer was Gen. Ignacio Aldama, a Guanajuato-based insurgent, lawyer, and brother of noted revolutionary Juan Aldama. Ignacio and his retinue had been dispatched at the first word of the Casas revolt on a mission to the United States to gain support for the rebels. With him was a Franciscan friar, Juan Salazar, who had been commissioned to ask the United States for "six, eight or ten thousand men of all arms, offering them a million pesos for every thousand individuals." The rebel envoys had brought with them a substantial amount of money—in excess of one hundred silver bars—intended to be used to purchase weapons in the United States. But this only fueled rumors among the skeptical Béxareños.[36]

Soon after the party arrived, the outsiders were approached by Zambrano and others and asked to replace Casas. They refused to get involved in the local dispute and prepared to continue on to the United States. Zambrano chose this as the time to make his move. He stirred up some of the populace with a rumor that Aldama was a secret French agent and, to entice others, pointed to the cash he carried with him with a hint at plundering it. At 8:30 p.m. on the evening of March 1st, a shadow group of plotters met and decided to move on Casas. In the early morning hours of March 2nd, the captain of the militia of Béxar, Don Mariano Rodríguez, delivered the city guard over to the coup.

"Gentlemen, if you are willing to agree with me," Zambrano told them, "I will suggest the mode and form of government we ought to have." He then outlined the convention he planned to establish, and a quick election was held among the conspirators setting the membership, all of them promising not to obey "any authority besides those holding their office by virtue of a commission emanating from our Catholic Sovereign Ferdinand the VII."[37]

At daylight on March 2nd, Zambrano, this new *junta,* and some assembled troops marched to the government house where Casas was staying. Hearing the commotion, citizens of San Antonio turned out. The rebel governor, roused from sleep, came out of the house, partly dressed. Casas "was immediately notified by the President in the name of the whole armed force, to surrender his office and to exhibit all the papers and orders he had received from the chiefs of the rebellion against our King and lawful sovereign." Casas protested. He was then ordered to comply or "suffer the penalty of his crime, on the spot." He submitted, merely asking for a moment to return and dress fully. He was allowed to do so, but as he did not immediately return, Zambrano ordered his officers to enter the building, where they found Casas burning documents. He was seized and placed under arrest.[38]

José Antonio Navarro thought the coup deplorable, especially the participation of some who had so lately been supporters of Casas. These men "imbued with the false honor of being faithful to the most detestable tyrant of Europe, made an ostentatious show of plunging the fratricidal dagger in to the heart of their Mexican brother," he wrote decades later. "Thus they hammered the rivets of their own chains, condemning themselves to trudge sorrowfully behind the plodding Spanish ox to earn their daily bread." But these are reminiscences with the aid of hindsight. Zambrano's true intent may indeed have been to reestablish the monarchy, but he cleverly avoided "tearing off entirely the veil" of his full plan until the conspirators were secure. The people of Béxar would learn soon enough.[39]

Good governance was virtually the only position that could ensure broad support, and Zambrano acted quickly to show his commitment to it. His junta worked deep into the night of March 2nd, ordering an election of a new town council. It would include, among others, some of the leaders of the initial Casas revolt, as well as the marginalized elites. This was not the death-to-traitors promise that Salcedo had made. This election completed, the junta and council marched toward the church of San Fernando to solemnize the results.[40]

But even this show of unity did not quell some rebellious spirits in town. The next day, around sunset, the junta was informed that the Mexican rebel envoy, Father Juan Salazar, was at that very moment speaking in the street, urging a group of fifty to sixty locals to rise up and join the revolutionary party. It says something about the tenuous position of Zambrano that he did not immediately take action. He was weak, having detached some of his most loyal troops to distant outposts to bring them in line with his counterrevolution, and he may have been wary of the dependability of the remaining troops in San Antonio. The junta decided to wait to detain Salazar until the next morning, when a patrol would return. Evidently, the Franciscan Salazar tried to move on the junta that night but was overpowered with the troops at hand.[41]

Zambrano then turned his attention to the rebel agent Aldama, who was still at liberty in one of the government buildings. Zambrano charged him with being an agent of Napoleon. He pointed out that Aldama's elaborate uniform included the insignia of the Legion d'honneur, a French medal. Aldama, affecting indignation, cut it off his own chest with a knife and denounced Napoleon. Zambrano now demanded Aldama surrender his knife. When he refused, the burly Zambrano overpowered him and tossed the weapon aside. Aldama was arrested, and with him went the last overt opposition. Zambrano sent envoys to Nacogdoches and recalled the fugitive former commander, Domínguez, with orders to return and take over from Guadiana.[42]

Zambrano ordered the Europeans released and their property restored, returning as nearly as possible to the status quo before the Casas Revolt. But while that affair had outwardly become a failure, it had changed things in Texas in subtle ways. When Zambrano published a list of new members of his ruling junta who had taken an oath to King Ferdinand, a large crowd gathered, and it was read to them. They responded with a petition to question Zambrano's motives. Was he trying to establish "a model republic, to guarantee frequent meetings of the junta, and make public all measures of the government?" An oath to the exiled King, they were saying, was not incompatible with reform.[43]

Zambrano responded to this citizen petition—a rare event in Spanish Texas—with assurances that he would be fair, open, and honest. Community leaders were not imprisoned, and as long as the garrison remained in the town, the proximate cause of the first revolt was moot. This leniency did not extend to Casas. The insurgent leader was sent to Monclova, where he was tried, and found guilty. He was shot in the Zapopan neighborhood on the edge of the city on August 3, 1811. His head was returned to San Antonio, where Zambrano placed it on a stake in the center of the city for all to see. By then, he had consolidated his power.[44]

Texas was greatly dependent on trade from the south, so the Béxar junta sought to reestablish contact with the Commandant General. For this task, the junta appointed two soldiers to sneak through rebel lines: Capt. José Muñoz of the militia of Nuevo León, who had been serving in San Antonio, and Capt. Luis Galán. The junta gave them two separate commissions, one to show to rebels, and another for royalists. But, recognizing the new spirit of public inclusion in San Antonio, Zambrano presented the men to the assembled people, read out the commissions, and sent them on their way on March 8th amid an almost festival-like atmosphere of well-wishing.[45]

Betrayal at Baján, Unrest in San Antonio

Texas governor Manuel Salcedo's arrest at the hands of rebels had been a complete humiliation. "I was disobeyed, surprised and arrested by the troops," he complained bitterly. "On that day, the banner of the rebellion was raised [in Béxar], I was clumsily slandered . . . and after 22 days in prison, I was sent to Coahuila with a pair of shackles, mocked and despised by the drivers. . . . The cares, shame and anguish caused in such a terrible event, we all suffered."[46]

But once he arrived in Coahuila, things turned out quite different than he expected. Within a month, his "prison" was a hacienda fourteen miles outside of Monclova. There were no chains, he and his party had the freedom to move about the house, and the guards were friendly. It was a minor miracle that he was alive at all—the Mexican War of Independence was not characterized by acts of mercy—and indeed he had nearly been shot upon arrival. Gachupines like Salcedo and Herrera were as reviled by true rebels as ever was the French nobility by the Jacobins. Casas did not have the stomach for the deed himself and had shipped the prisoners south just to get them out of San Antonio, where they were a possible magnet for counterrevolution. In the end, the counterrevolution did just fine without them.

Had the rebels shipped their captives to Saltillo, as originally planned, they would surely have been killed. But fervor in Coahuila was not deep, and closet royalists were everywhere. When the governors and their fellow captives had arrived, two ranch owners, brothers José Melchor Sánchez and Miguel Sánchez, who did not even know Salcedo or Herrera, approached the rebel governor and offered to take the party of royalists and imprison them at their ranch near Santa Rosa. The governor agreed. The Sánchez brothers even sent friends who were respected by the rebels to argue to authorities in Saltillo to delay the forwarding of the captives onto that place. One of these envoys was a Dutch immigrant to New Spain who styled himself the Baron de Bastrop, who would, years later, play a large role in Texas history.[47]

Meanwhile, the two envoys from Zambrano's Texas, Captains Muñoz and Galán, rode into the Presidio of the Rio Grande, carrying their dual instructions. Brought into the home of the local postmaster and surrounded by notables of the town, they guessed the mood and presented royalist credentials. To their relief, they had chosen correctly. Now under a protective guard, they continued, eventually arriving at the home of Lt. Col. Ignacio Elizondo, a rebel commander who was in theory Salcedo's jailer, but who in fact had recently defected to the royalists. Elizondo was an opportunist. He was "of tall stature and robust, good looking, of a swarthy florid color." At forty-five, he had a history of financial troubles that had caused friction with Nuevo León's interim governor, Pedro de Herrera, brother of his "captive" Simón de Herrera. As a result, the officer's career was in tatters. When the rebellion came, joining it seemed a good way to restore his position. Now, with the rebels on the run in Saltillo and Zambrano having ousted them in Texas, that decision looked like a bad bet. Undoubtedly, Salcedo and the elder Herrero sensed this and offered him a pardon. In taking it, Elizondo, a relatively unknown officer, would restart his royalist career with an act of deceit.[48]

After the *Grito*, Father Hidalgo had built up a massive army of eighty thousand, mostly peasants, but also committed revolutionaries, adventurers, impressed Indians, and "still others because it afforded them opportunities for crime, corruption and mayhem." But this cumbersome force was ill-trained; few of the infantry were armed with muskets; many had only spears, slingshots, or bows and arrows. Even Hidalgo had a difficult time restraining them; they sacked Guanajuato with terrible slaughter. With this cautionary tale on their minds, Spanish forces and some elite creoles rallied and, defending key points, inflicted a series of defeats on the rebels. At the Battle of Calderon Bridge, the rebels were crushed and the army retreated northward, shedding deserters until it was a mere seven thousand men. Dispirited by these reverses, rebel leaders ousted Hidalgo, replacing him with Juan Aldama, the brother of the agent whose arrival in Texas had triggered Zambrano's counterrevolution. The retreating rebels also carried with them over two million dollars in gold and silver. The plan was to link up with other rebel forces in Coahuila and dispatch the funds to the United States for the purchase of weapons through Texas, which they still thought to be in rebel hands. Manuel Salcedo's spies, including Bastrop, had given him wind of the plans, and he sensed an opportunity, if only he had troops at his disposal.[49]

It was Elizondo who provided the men. Pretending loyalty to the rebel cause he had abandoned, he invited Aldama and Hidalgo to join him at a place called the Wells of Baján in Coahuila, the only spot in the desert between Saltillo and Monclova where water could be found. Humiliated in battle and convinced at last that only weapons from America could turn the tide, the rebels accepted the offer. They expected that Elizondo in Coahuila and Casas in Texas would assist them, and still ignorant of events happening in the north, probably assumed that the first shipment of funds to America had already gotten through. Before long, the rebels expected, their gold and silver would bring not only weapons but a flood of American volunteers. Retreating further north—they were prepared to continue to Texas if need be—would shorten their supply lines and lengthen those of the royalists. Despite their string of defeats, it was probably with a tinge of optimism that the rebel leadership approached the wells.[50]

Elizondo sprang into action. In Monclova, he led a successful coup, seized the nominal head of the rebel army there, and proclaimed the city in favor of the royalists. Simón de Herrera, released from his prison, was reinstalled in the governorship. Then Elizondo mustered his forces and rode out to meet the oncoming rebel army at Baján. Arriving before the rebels, Elizondo deployed his 342 men in the best position for an ambush in a plan conceived by Texas governor Salcedo. Elizondo, with no qualms about treachery, sent envoys ahead to the rebels, telling them in friendly terms that he awaited their arrival. Meanwhile, he had Indian scouts track every move of the oncoming army.[51]

On March 21, 1811, the rebel army, exhausted from their journey, straggled into the trap. At the head were the leaders with a small guard, followed by a long baggage train. The bulk of the army, a thousand men, was well behind them. As they passed Elizondo, the troops saluted him, continuing eagerly to the refreshing water that lay in wait for them. After they had neared the wells, Elizondo surrounded the advanced contingent, which gave up without resistance. When Gen. Ignacio Allende protested and called Elizondo treasonous, Allende's son was shot down.[52]

The Tejano Revolt

The haul was staggering. Two dozen key rebel leaders were captured—along with their vast trove of gold and silver—and eight hundred soldiers disarmed. The sheer number of prisoners was overwhelming—almost three for every captor. There were still rebels in the area, and the danger of a counterattack was strong, but Manuel Salcedo arrived soon after with a division of troops. Added to Elizondo's force, this secured the complete victory. In one fell swoop, Elizondo and Salcedo had crushed the remnants of the army that had once threatened Mexico City. Four months later, Hidalgo would die a martyr's death before a firing squad. Though there were still Mexican rebel armies in the field, it seemed to many that Spain had turned a corner and was now winning the war.[53]

For Governor Manuel Salcedo, the reversal in fortune from humiliated, deposed governor to savior of the empire was complete, if not fully acknowledged by his uncle the commandant general, who simply ordered him—without a word of thanks—back to his old job in Texas. That province was still as weak as ever, and as long as rebels remained anywhere in Mexico, Texas was an object of their schemes. Before the success at the wells, Salcedo had revived his old plan to use his own troops to put down the revolt and ordered Zambrano to prepare every available man to join him in Coahuila.[54]

It had been just such a march that had precipitated the first revolt. Now, as Zambrano prepared to move south with a force of five hundred men, there came another attempted coup. On March 25th, a priest, Father Arocha, and a chaplain named Garza organized some followers with a plan to seize the city's artillery, housed at the Alamo. Spies uncovered the plot and Zambrano, moving at one o'clock in the morning, seized the ringleaders. A few days later, a final uprising emanated from within the prison of the Alamo, where Father Juan Salazar and General Aldama bribed their guards, also with the intent of seizing the artillery and leading a rebellion. Unfortunately, one of the soldiers they sought to enlist betrayed the cause.[55]

But these were futile, last gasps of the revolt, and it was clear that if change was coming, it could not come from within Béxar. The populace simply had no weapons with which to challenge the garrison. Zambrano could now fully reassert control over other areas of Texas, especially Nacogdoches, which had been enjoying its free trade with the United States. On May 1st, he at last ordered Guadiana to return to San Antonio "to answer to the charges due to the fault that he has committed with this noble council." The lieutenant found some reason to delay his journey. After a contingent of Texas troops had defeated rebels in Coahuila, Zambrano felt comfortable enough to send 150 men of his garrison to assert royal control in the rebellious town. He also purged his force of key rebels, including several sergeants, corporals, and soldiers. Among the officers summarily cashiered was Ensign Don Pedro de la Garza Falcón, who had broken up the smuggling rings of Quirk and Magee before joining the revolt. Meanwhile, the head of Casas had made its return and had been elevated atop a pike for all to see. It would be joined by others.[56]

The six months of rebellion and counterrebellion in Texas had been a disaster for the rebels but had been no great victory for the royalists either. The province's inherent weaknesses remained, alongside new ones birthed in the chaos. No commander could be sure of his troops' loyalty ever again. Should rebellion come, they might defect on principle, or just to the side they thought was winning. More importantly for observers on the other side of the border like Sibley, Claiborne—and more nefarious men—the Casas revolt had opened an intriguing window into revolutionary sentiment in Texas.

Spanish leaders had their hands full over the next year trying to rebuild their province politically, but it was clear to all that a Rubicon had been crossed. Tejanos had taken sides and it would not be forgotten. A reckoning for Travieso, Guadiana, and the other rebels was coming, unless another rebellion came first. The people of Nacogdoches, their appetite whetted with six months of open trade, had more reason than ever to defy Spanish authority. With Tejanos pulling for revolution on the one hand and Americans pushing for it on the other, it was no longer a question of if there would be an invasion, but when—and who would lead it.

7

Intrigue on the Frontier

GOV. WILLIAM CHARLES COLE CLAIBORNE of the Orleans Territory had one of the most difficult jobs in America in the first decade of the nineteenth century. The precocious Claiborne had been slated for distinction early on. By the time he was thirty, he had served on the Tennessee Supreme Court, the US House of Representatives, and had been appointed governor of the Mississippi Territory. Two years into that job, the United States purchased Louisiana and President Jefferson moved the up-and-coming young man a few hundred miles to the southwest to take the job as the first governor of the Orleans Territory, the part of the vast domain generally corresponding to the modern state of Louisiana. Claiborne's rise came despite a signal lack of charisma. Historian Peter Kastor describes him as "a rather thin-skinned individual of modest talents and ambitions."[1]

As we have seen, when Claiborne won the governorship over the businessman Daniel Clark, the latter formed an enmity toward the governor that never abated, and "had a great deal to gain by impeding Claiborne's successful administration." Clark had the electoral support—he won a seat as the territory's delegate in Congress—but Claiborne, who was appointed, had the administration's patronage. Should Louisiana become a state, the two were clearly headed on a collision course. In Washington, the irascible Irishman Clark found ways to needle the prickly governor, and in 1807, Claiborne, offended by a remark that Clark had made in Congress, challenged his nemesis to a duel. A ball from Clark's pistol struck the governor in the right thigh. The wound healed, but the rivalry festered.[2]

The Burr affair loomed large over this strained relationship. Clark and all involved escaped conviction for treason, and many thought the power of the conspirators was broken. But not Claiborne—the Burr conspiracy was ever in his thoughts; the Mexican Association consumed him with paranoia. Historian Andy Doolen has written, "In the aftermath of the panic [1806], the Mexican Association remained a subversive transnational organization in the eyes of federal officials." The organization was likely fractured, perhaps decimated, but it certainly had not vanished;

evidence indicates it was alive for at least a decade after the Burr affair. From 1808 on, Claiborne was endlessly sounding the alarm over the actions of a hostile cabal with revolutionary intent. This was more than lone fear: some of his correspondents shared similar reports and concerns, and one who also saw the secret society's shadow in the borderlands was Claiborne's counterpart in Texas. Spanish governor Manuel Salcedo, who had passed through Natchez on his way to Texas, wrote,[3] "The partisans of Colonel Burr insist on their designs against the Internal Provinces of Mexico.... They are to float down the Ohio and Mississippi in flatboats—some will ascend the Arkansas and move on to New Mexico; others will cross Texas ... Some of them are actually on the Washita lands, where there are many in Natchez who entertain suspicious projects."[4]

As the Spanish crisis deepened that year, Claiborne reported, "The Burrites have become the most flaming Spanish patriots and are laboring to excite against the Government & its friends, all the vengeance of the enthusiastic Spaniards [of Louisiana]." The Spanish consul in New Orleans, Louis de Clovet, thought the danger was immediate: "From what I can hear and penetrate it seems that the project of Burr is coming to life." If the Spanish and American officials are to be believed, conspirators began putting the pieces of Burr's shattered dream back together as soon as the prosecutions for the affair ended. The Mexican Association possibly played a part in the renewed agitation in West Florida in 1810 that precipitated the final American occupation of Baton Rouge, and the bitterness of the more extreme Burrites at the outcome in West Florida would prove palpable.[5]

Claiborne could only generally guess at the organization's intent and its leading actors, whom he described in letters as "base men in New Orleans, who would not be unwilling to raise their arms against the U. States." The governor was constantly trying to ferret out the group's plans, and especially after the Burr affair, sent numerous warnings to then-Secretary of State James Madison.[6]

"A very honest man immediately from the Mississippi Territory informs me, that ____ with at least 30 of his adherents, are now at Natchez," he wrote in September 1808, "and that they do not conceal their hostility to the American government." The unnamed man was possibly Reuben Kemper, and behind him, Clark. The group was even casting its eyes on Cuba as well. A strong European power in possession of it, they feared, would wreck Western commerce in the event of a war, and "may induce the Western citizens to pursue their best interest, which was to form a separate government."[7]

It is doubtful the group was still conspiring for secession if they ever had been. But the idea stalked Claiborne, and he was accordingly attuned to any rumblings of a western plot. In early 1809, as Madison was preparing to assume the presidency, the governor fired off another warning: "You are not uninformed Sir, of the very heterogeneous mass of which society in New Orleans is composed; England has her partisans; Ferdinand the Seventh some faithful subjects; Bonaparte his admirers; &

there is a fourth description of men, commonly called Burrites, who would join any standard, which would promise rapine and plunder."[8]

The governor hoped to build a legal case against the association's leaders to finally break its power—and with it, presumably, political opposition to himself—but all he had to work with were rumors. Upon hearing that a group of Americans arrested in Campeche in Mexico's Yucatán Peninsula were being charged with actions hostile to the Spanish government, Claiborne wrote to Don Benito Pérez, the governor of that province, asking if he had any knowledge about who in New Orleans might be supporting the men, but the captives, who professed their ignorance, gave up no information.[9]

The group even had two newspapers, the *Orleans Gazette*, which Claiborne noted was used for mostly domestic political agitation against him, and a secret paper called *la Lanterne Magique*, "The Magic Lantern," which expressed more openly Burrite ideas. Claiborne did have a spy in the organization, and one must assume based on the man's reports that the governor was not just chasing phantoms. But the spy refused to put anything in writing for fear of his life, so the governor in November 1809 turned to the adjutant general of the territorial militia, Col. Henry Hopkins, to investigate.[10]

"Information has reached me which justifies a suspicion, that certain persons in this Territory are associating and confederating together with designs hostile to the Interest and Laws of the U. States," Claiborne wrote. "My information is not of such a nature, as to enable me to decide with certainty as to the existence of the association or the real view of the associates, but the primary object is supposed to be the rendering of Mexico and the Interior provinces independent of Spain, nor is it thought improbable, but it may also be in contemplation to attempt the severing from the United States of... Louisiana." Claiborne ordered Hopkins to communicate anything he learned about the group.[11]

But the officer found nothing, or was himself involved, since the association, through Clark and Kerr, had deep ties with the militia. Much of the military structure of the territory was sympathetic to the organization's goals, if not complicit in them, a legacy of General Wilkinson. The general's personal involvement after 1807, however, is doubtful given the recriminations between him and Clark, and at all events by 1810 he was out of the territory facing his court martial. Nonetheless, he and others had been planting seeds of Western adventurism for so long that it only required natural fertilizer—and perhaps the slightest watering—to cause them to germinate.

In November 1809, the governor personally investigated a soldier at Fort Claiborne for allegedly writing two letters in which he revealed a plot among American army officers to revolutionize Mexico. Captain Francis Newman was married to a Spanish woman from Texas, and allegedly wrote the letters in French to her uncle, Joseph Solís of New Orleans, with details—though vague—of the conspiracy. They were intercepted and given to Claiborne. The letters aroused concern at the highest levels, and copies were shown to President Madison. Secretary Smith wrote to Claiborne, "To judge from some expressions in Newman's Letters, this is probably the Revival of Burr's plans, under different Circumstances. It therefore becomes important that we should be upon our guard and the president charges you immediately on receipt of this letter ... to take every legal and proper measure to arrest and bring to Justice as well those who may be about to attack the territories of a friendly nation as those who may be preparing to attack our own."[12]

Although some in the government assessed the letters to be forgeries, Claiborne believed them authentic. He ordered Lt. Col. Constant Freeman, the commander of the fort, to send the captain to New Orleans to be interviewed. Though the governor specifically told Freeman to only say to Newman that he was to deliver a letter to the governor, Freeman disobeyed orders and informed the suspected officer of the real purpose of the trip. Thus fortified, the young captain had plenty of time to prepare his story when confronted with the incriminating letters. Claiborne interrogated the officer personally:

> **Question**—Have you any knowledge of a correspondence between Governor Salcedo, of the province of Techas [sic], and certain persons in New Orleans?
>
> **Answer**—I have no knowledge of a correspondence between Governor Salcedo and any person whatsoever.
>
> **Question**—Have you any knowledge of a plan for the revolutionizing of the Spanish provinces?
>
> **Answer**—None whatever.
>
> **Question**—Did you ever learn that it had been proposed to any one or more officers of the army to unite in a project to effect the independence of Mexico?
>
> **Answer**—Never.[13]

Claiborne was not sure what to make of the case and, without truly damning evidence, sent the young officer back to his command. "At all times, the *utmost vigilance* on the part of the officers of the government in this territory is essential," he wrote to Secretary of State Smith, "but it is particularly so at the present period, when foreigners and *strangers* are daily arriving among us; *of whom* many are of doubtful character and desperate fortunes, and may (probably) become willing instruments in the hands of those unprincipled, intriguing individuals, who would wish to disturb the *peace, and Union* of the American States." He added, "That there are such individuals in this territory, I have long since known, and I have no reason to believe that their hostility to the interest of the U. States has in the least abated." A month later, Claiborne added a foreboding note in another letter to the secretary, "I have taken Sir, such means as were in my power to ascertain the truth of the various reports which were afloat, that certain persons in the territory had combined together for the purpose of effecting a revolution in the Spanish provinces." The governor found "no satisfactory proof upon the subject," but his gut told him there was something to the rumors.[14]

His instinct was right; three years after Burr, the conspiracy still infected the frontier army. At Newman's post, Fort Claiborne, there was a split in the garrison, which had resulted in the courts-martial that had divided the post: Freeman and Newman on the one side, and Captains Charles Wollstonecraft and Joseph Cross on the other. This controversy appears to have been deeper than that of a senior officer and his favorite lining up against midlevel officers, for the two sides show clear predilections for and against clandestine operations against New Spain. On the former side was Freeman, who had settled squatters on lands he illegally claimed in the Neutral Ground, and Lt. Newman, married to a Spanish woman and likely working with her family to revolutionize the province. On the other side were Captains Cross and Wollstonecraft, who at every step supported the letter of the law and were a threat to revolutionaries. Indeed, it was not until Freeman was removed and Wollstonecraft took interim command in Natchitoches that any American officer began to take steps against the Neutral Ground's illegal inhabitants.[15]

The Banditti Return

To call the frontier between the United States and New Spain a border is a great exaggeration. Guadiana and other commanders were assiduous in enforcing Spain's sovereignty, but their men were dispersed to uselessness. From 1809 to 1811, there were numerous reports, rumors, and speculations about penetrations of Anglo-Americans gathering horses on the Sabine or searching for mines further west along the Brazos. An Apache chief, Cordero, even reported Americans living with tribes as far west as New Mexico.[16]

The Spanish did not have the men to chase all these phantoms, and the priority was the Neutral Ground. The Spanish-American patrol of 1810 cleared out the zone for a time, but the chaos in Texas as a result of the Casas Revolt relaxed the pressure and the squatters returned. John Sibley, the American Indian Agent in Natchitoches, said the lawlessness was worse than before: "That belt of country between this town & the River Sabine called Neutral Ground, has become a harbor for thieves, robbers and murderers to an alarming degree. I was yesterday out with a coroner's inquest on the body of a man a citizen of the U. S. who was found dead, who had been robbed and murdered by them, a few miles from this town." Sibley, who like Freeman had secretly sponsored his own group of settlers in the strip only to see them removed, added, "That this would be the case was foreseen since that *honest industrious* settlement of people at the Adaize [los Adaes] was broken up by order of our own & the Spanish government last summer" (emphasis added).[17]

While there were certainly true desperadoes amongst the banditti, the largest group (about fifteen in number) was the same band of mercenaries affiliated with the exiled Anglo-Spanish Texas smugglers. They had been first organized with ambitions to liberate Henry Quirk, under the auspices of his brother Edmund, who had been forced to flee Texas and leave his family behind. In 1808, after the Quirk/Joseph Magee smuggling ring had been broken up, this party of bandits had captured and detained the Spanish Indian agent Davenport and contemplated an armed attack to free Quirk. By 1811, they were under the patronage of a Quirk ally, Miguel Quinn, the Trinidad resident who had been implicated as an associate of Edward Popejoy, the dead smuggler from the 1808 episode. Quinn was arrested by the Spanish in December of that year but escaped in 1810, leaving his shackles in a river as he fled. He was declared a fugitive and his property—mostly horses with a value of 439 pesos—was auctioned off early the next year. Now Quinn, exiled to Louisiana, was patronizing this small band under the leadership of a thirty-year-old American named Thomas McKinnon.[18]

That the banditti's ultimate goal was revolutionary there can be no doubt. The practical effect of their depredations was to establish an economic blockade of Texas, not just of government supplies, but also Davenport's supply of Indian trade goods. This included various kinds of cloth, finished clothing, jewelry, pipes, tools, mirrors, knives, axes, and more. Restricting Spanish access to these items made it more difficult for royal officials to secure peace. The Indians naturally would have seen any diminution of their supply of goods as a sign of Spanish weakness at best and bad faith at worst. In the war to come, the Spanish would be facing more enemies than just republican revolutionaries.[19]

Quinn and his associates were primarily motivated by their vendetta, but Spanish sources confirmed that they were coordinating their operations with an American the Spanish only knew as "Smith," who was seeking to aid the Mexican Revolution through a filibuster. This was the Missouri mining baron and former Burr conspirator John Smith T, the same deadly duelist with his own private militia who had funded the trading expedition to Santa Fe. His likely patronage of Joseph McLanahan's activities on the Texas frontier suggests that he was equally committed to exploring both a northern and southern route into Spanish lands, exactly as his relative Wilkinson had proposed years before.[20]

It had been two years since his brother Reuben Smith, McLanahan, and a small party of traders had vanished into the wild on the road to Santa Fe, and since then, nothing had been heard of them. When news finally arrived, it came not from the west but from a Philadelphia newspaper, which reprinted a Spanish account of the capture of "spies or emissaries of Bonaparte." The Spanish source promised "justice should not be delayed in order to purge the Spanish soil of such vermin." The subsequent outrage on the frontier was swift, turning the three traders into heroes and victims much as had been the case for the Kemper brothers in West Florida six years earlier. An editorialist in the *Louisiana Gazette,* passing along these incendiary remarks, reminded readers of its earlier announcement of the allegedly peaceful mission:[21] "Messrs. Smith, M'Clanahan and Patterson, strangers to the policy of Mexico and the monkish barbarism of the natives, conceived they would visit white men clothed with the Christian name; unhappy credulity! They would have found more generosity in the breast of an Arab, more hospitality in the den of a Hiena. [*sic*]—The assassins of Mexico have ere this butchered three respectable inhabitants of Louisiana!!"[22]

Even before this news, Smith T had been exploring options to obtain the release of Reuben and his compatriots. A story retold in Missouri lore has him venturing deep into Mexico to free his brother personally, which is doubtful, though he may have ventured into Texas during the Casas revolt. At any rate, he recognized that the uprising in San Antonio had provided him with the perfect opportunity for a filibuster. An American volunteer force, securing Texas alongside Tejano rebels, could penetrate the outer ring of Spanish defenders and join up with rebels deep within Mexico, or as he likely preferred, open up a route to Santa Fe.[23]

In March 1811, Smith T, burning with fraternal loyalty, a deep hatred for Spanish authorities, and his customary dreams of loot to be won, began to put together a filibuster army of three hundred men, who were to rendezvous at the junction of the Canadian and Arkansas Rivers, near modern Fort Smith, Arkansas. Their mission was "to effect the release of the men and to bring back what gold they could conveniently seize." If they could not release the traders, they would push through and join the revolutionaries in Mexico.[24]

Smith T and the "Fat Father"

With Casas's revolt, the people of impoverished Nacogdoches had achieved the long-sought dream to establish legal trade with the United States, only to see it snuffed out by Zambrano's counterrevolution. Natchitoches, on the Louisiana side of the border, became a conduit of information in both directions. Spanish republicans got their news of the progress of the revolution in Mexico and communicated with Americans sympathetic to their cause through Edmund Quirk. Quirk at this time was apparently coordinating his efforts with Nacogdoches commandant Guadiana, who had yet to be removed and tried for his role in the Casas revolt. Also conspiring with the exiles was the Nacogdoches resident and French Creole Bernardo D'Ortolant (who had placed so much hope in D'Alvimar three years before) and a man identified through interrogations as "The Fat Father." This was Father José María Huerta, the Nacogdoches parish priest. When Spanish authorities reoccupied the town, this group went underground and, through the medium of Quirk, retained a line of communication with the Americans.[25]

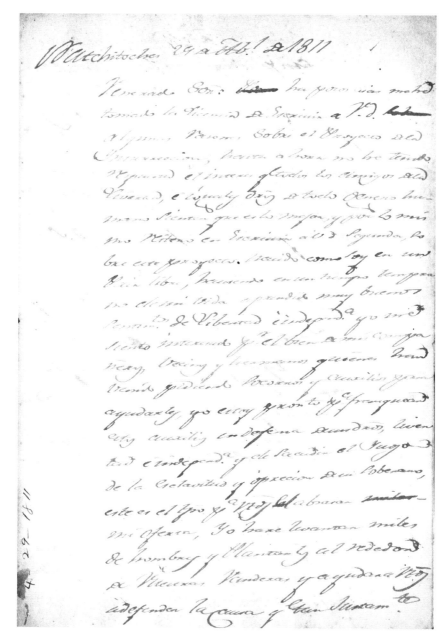

Figure 4. Letter from John Smith T to Father Huerta Offering Aid for Revolutionaries in Texas. Béxar Archives.

Smith T, in his proposed Santa Fe expedition, had conspired with an Irish Catholic priest named James Maxwell. Turning to Texas, he again resorted to the clergy, writing on April 29, 1811, from Natchitoches to Huerta. He obviously benefitted from inside knowledge from Maxwell or Quirk because he assumed the priest was sympathetic to the rebel cause. Saying nothing about his captured brother, he made it clear he was ready to cast his lot with the forces of Hidalgo:

> Venerable Sir:
> A few days ago, I had taken the liberty of writing to you some explanations regarding the project of insurrection. Up to now I have not received a reply, and the interests of all of the enemies of liberty and equal rights of all humankind believe that that is for the best; and for this reason I will reiterate [the explanations] to you in a second [letter], regarding this project.[26]

As an American, Smith T told Huerta he had been born in a free country, and raised in liberty and independence, "I feel interest for the good of my compatriots, neighbors, and brothers, who have come asking for relief and assistance." To aid Huerta and other supporters of the revolution, Smith T was willing to assist the Mexicans "in defense of their rights, liberty, and independence, and to throw off the yoke of slavery and oppression of their sovereign." Father Huerta had but to embrace his offer and the men would come.[27]

> I will lead thousands of men in an uprising and place them around your banners and help you to defend the cause that so justly you have begun to defend. The gods wish to protect you until victory is won, [but] you must with the utmost promptness abandon your King, who is undignified to rule your [people], because he has surrendered his sovereignty to the tyrant Napoleon, having caused the spilling of so much blood in the heart of his Kingdom. No. No, it is not possible! Your conscience and the laws of nature demand justice.[28]

Huerta as a "father and protector of the people" could lead them and they would follow. Smith T paraphrased the Declaration of Independence, telling the priest that the Mexican people had the right to abolish a government that had become oppressive and to enact laws that "are in favor of humankind." "If you so desire, you will count on me regarding this project, and you will inform me . . . about how things are in the Kingdom, since here there are a considerable number of men ready to march to your aid and defense; and if it were necessary to send more, more would come with the utmost brevity to unite with us."[29]

The "thousands of men" echoed the optimistic, unrealized assumptions of the Burr conspirators six years before. Though the filibuster sentiment was popular throughout the West, the fact of the matter is no one knew how many men they could raise until the actual event. The Miranda expedition of 1806 had been pitifully small. The numbers who had participated in West Florida had been minimal, and when the Kemper Brothers had initially waved their Lone Star flag, few men rallied to it. But men of the West were more passionate for the Mexican idea—and what they could gain from supporting it—and as Quinn and Smith T seemed to think, the numbers did not *have to be* that large. Spanish weakness was known to all, and the knowledge that a population of fifth columnists resided in Nacogdoches, with a key commander like Guadiana and a Catholic priest among them, must have encouraged the Americans. While Smith T began to raise his forces for a filibuster, the banditti held an advanced position on the frontier.

So deep was Smith T's collaboration with Mexican rebels that word even filtered to the rebel commandant general of the northern provinces, José Mariano Jiménez, who spread a rumor that the filibuster army, 1,200 strong, had already entered Texas in late 1810 and captured Nacogdoches. He expressed satisfaction with "the arrival of the advance of the Anglo-American auxiliary army to our borders" and used the "news" as a rallying cry to his fellow Mexicans who had not yet taken up arms. "Selfish [Spanish] Americans, indolent patriots, lukewarm spectators of our risks and combat, will you not yet declare yourself? You still do not shake that shameful apathy? Do you want to participate alone in glory, not dangers?" The report was premature but illustrates the depths to which Mexican rebels longed for such aid and suggests the sort of welcome for which Smith T and the Burrites of the American frontier were hoping when the march for Mexico finally began in earnest.[30]

A Royalist Victory and the "Ghost" of Burr

As Manuel Salcedo resumed his duties as governor of Texas, he saw his province assailed on all sides, "to the east by a troop of American bandits . . . to the North by the Indian nations . . . and in its capital by the fire of the finished insurrection." He expected the latter would be reborn "because part of the principal impulses of it and the minions of the wicked Casas are walking through the streets." Texas was also bankrupt and starving from the "scarce entrances of foodstuffs from other provinces," occasioned by the banditti blockade on the north and rebels in the south.[31]

In June 1811, before the governor could return, Lt. Col. Juan Manuel Zambrano attempted to break this stranglehold. He arrived in Nacogdoches, where he reasserted royal authority, reinstalled Col. Cristobal Dominguez and removed Guadiana. His true goal was to reopen royal trade at the head of a caravan, which was to be the first resupply of Texas in months. Zambrano personally guided the mule train to Natchitoches because it carried $20,000 in cash, almost certainly the seized silver that the rebel Aldama had brought up from Mexico. It was just the sort of target for which the banditti had been waiting. With orders from Quinn and Smith T, they stalked the blonde royalist and his men "for taking away from [them] their equipment and bind[ing] them, dead or alive." The purpose was not to kill him, but to detain him and stop his trade, as it had been before with Davenport. Zambrano made it safely through to Natchitoches, but on his return the banditti caught up to him and, after a brief shootout, captured the Spaniard alive.[32]

The infamous leader of the countercoup in Béxar, "Sam Brannon" as the Americans called him, was now in the banditti's grasp. They bound him and took him a short distance to the home of the ferryman, Miguel Crow. But word having reached Nacogdoches, Dominguez sent a relief party which completely surprised the bandits. "Several discharges between them [and] the result was, the Spaniards retook all their Goods & what property belonging to the robbers, consisting of twenty mules, some money, goods, saddles, value-less clothing etc. & returned to Nacogdoches with the whole," Sibley wrote. The Spanish had also captured McKinnon, the leader of the bandits and a John Weiss of Virginia. Sibley reported one of the banditti killed and added that the Spaniards "wounded another by the name of Taylor from Georgia." This was not just an ordinary frontier adventurer, but in fact one of the most important players in the 1806 Burr conspiracy, who had now returned—as if from the dead—for the showdown with Spain that had been denied him six years before.[33]

As noted in chapter 1, US Army lieutenant Josiah Taylor was a key member—perhaps the lynchpin—of the Burr Conspiracy in New Orleans. It was he who had recruited William Murray and Ensign Small and had been a liaison with the Kemper Brothers and their "live hogs." As the US Army purchasing agent in New Orleans, he was James Wilkinson's righthand man for all things logistical. But in the crucial weeks when the conspiracy was poised to launch, something extraordinary happened: On July 3, 1806, a few weeks after recruiting Murray and the Kempers, Taylor was reported by Lt. Col. Constant Freeman, via Col. Thomas Cushing, to have died "after a violent fever of only four days."[34]

There are compelling grounds to dispute the news of his death. Freeman, the sole reporter of the story, was the same officer who had tipped off Lieutenant Newman of Claiborne's suspicions, which along with his sponsoring of Neutral Ground settlers suggests he too was sympathetic and possibly himself involved in the plot. Cushing, too, had once been described as "violently opposed" to the Jefferson administration. Lt. William Swan, who assumed Taylor's role as purchasing agent, was also a Burrite—indeed, he would play a supporting role in the coming filibuster in 1812. Furthermore, the Burr trials uncovered some questionable expenditures and accounting irregularities by Taylor, including purchases of unjustified extra rations, which Wilkinson requested, along with "considerable sums of public money unaccounted for," which included a $3,000 payment to the general. That Taylor was abusing his official position to serve as the conspiracy's quartermaster seems likely; he was possibly also laundering money for Wilkinson to hide his Spanish pension.[35]

"Wilkinson was always known to have lived extravagantly," with nowhere near the salary to support it, Daniel Clark pointed out in his post-conspiracy polemic against the general. Governor Claiborne, Clark asserted, had also been suspicious, "until he found means to remove his doubts by an assurance that the money was received by Lieutenant Taylor, the military agent at New Orleans." But this was a false faith, Clark said, built on the silence of a *dead* man:[36]

> [Wilkinson] has by his own admission, reduced [his innocence] to this point . . . it must have been received from either lieutenant Taylor *for the general's drafts on the treasury for extra services*—or it must have been received from some other person for a purpose which he is ashamed to avow. Now if received from Mr. Taylor, nothing would have been more easy than to have silenced his accusers by producing his accounts. . . . [Wilkinson] has hung up his defence on that point, and unless he shows it to have been received from Taylor, there will be no doubt that the *Mexican* dollars in the *Mexican* bags, were received from [Spanish consul] Marquis de Casa Calvo.[37]

According to Daniel Clark, this was the smoking gun that could have secured the conviction—*and possibly execution*—of Gen. James Wilkinson, the senior officer in the entire US Army, for treason. Indeed, as the broader case makes clear, Josiah Taylor was the sole man whose testimony could have convicted the entire leadership of the conspiracy, since he was the one man who connected Wilkinson and his conspirators in the Army and Upper Louisiana with the Mexican Association in New Orleans. In the trial of Workman and Kerr, prosecutor James Brown noted that "the deceased Lieutenant Taylor, it would appear, was a favorite of those associates for the conquest of Mexico."[38]

His supposed death guaranteed the trials would fail and led to not-guilty verdicts all around. However, several months after this *military* Taylor died, a *civilian* Josiah Taylor appeared six hundred miles away in Clarke County, Georgia. This person, if independent of the *military* Taylor, appears in no other records prior, including census data. These two Josiah Taylors were of identical age, the *military* Taylor gaining his initial commission as an ensign in 1802, when the purportedly *civilian* Taylor would have been twenty-one years old.[39]

Furthermore, this *civilian* Josiah Taylor from Georgia—if he *was* a separate man—who otherwise had no connection to the frontier "came to Texas in 1811 on an exploring expedition" in one euphemistic family account, where he instantly joined with Smith and Quinn's Neutral Ground banditti, leading to his wounding by the Spanish. Recovering, Taylor would join the coming filibuster as a senior officer from the very beginning, find success as a battlefield leader of great skill, and ultimately command half the army in combat—all this despite having *no military background*. In contrast, the allegedly deceased *military* Josiah Taylor had experience as an infantry, artillery, and staff officer perfectly suiting him for this role. The *civilian* Taylor, in joining the expedition, would ultimately work to revolutionize Mexico—the same

Intrigue on the Frontier   117

passionate goal of the "deceased" *military* Taylor—in close association with William Murray and Samuel Kemper, both of whom the *military* one intimately cooperated with in an identical scheme six years before.⁴⁰

As extraordinary as it sounds, the evidence suggests Josiah Taylor, in collusion with Lieutenant Colonel Freeman and possibly others in Wilkinson's frontier army, faked his own death in order to take some key role in the proposed Burr expedition, removed to Georgia to lay low after it collapsed, and returned in 1811 to participate in the filibuster. In any other context, this theory would be absurd. Given the nature of the conspiracy and the life-and-death stakes involved—notably in his last meeting with Kemper just prior to his "death," Josiah Taylor said he was in the conspiracy "at all hazards"—it seems more plausible that there was only one Josiah Taylor, rather than that two separate men with the exact same name and similar biographical backgrounds existed in Louisiana in 1806 and 1811, respectively. And now Taylor, like a growing number of other adventurers, had made his way to the frontier to confront the Spanish.⁴¹

The Capture of Quirk

The banditti had been beaten this time, but they would not give in, and they were growing. "The robbers I believe have a camp or place of rendezvous at some place . . . between the Rio Honda & Sabine," Sibley reported. "And I believe they are sending emissaries to Rapides, Oppolousas [sic] & to this town [Natchitoches] to engage Recruits, for some other outrage."⁴²

The Spaniards' biggest catch was apprehended separately from the engagement on the Sabine. This was Edmund Quirk, the former Spanish resident, now a bandit courier and rebel spy. He and other prisoners and witnesses rounded up in the subsequent dragnet were an intelligence bonanza, allowing the Spanish to outline the nature of the conspiracy that had been building on their borders for years.⁴³

Although Edmund Quirk claimed in his interrogation he had been on personal business when he was caught, the Spanish did not believe him. He was, they suspected, "going with advice to Smith." The Spanish, who by now were aware of the letters to Huerta, asked if "the said Smith, or others of his party had been invited by some of this village, in order that with their factions, they will aid them in upholding the intruder government [Casas]?" Then they demanded, "What are their names and ranks?" Quirk claimed ignorance but was certainly lying. Interrogating Miguel Crow, the Anglo-American who operated the ferry where the attack had taken place, the Spanish put similar questions to him. He was more talkative.⁴⁴

> Asked: If he knows what purpose the said Smith was [engaged in], and if perhaps he has heard said that he would have some interest toward seizing Zambrano, and what he was attempting with his person?

> [Crow] . . . I say Smith was attempting to seize Zambrano in order to raise a revolution in this village; that he has heard it said.
> Asked: If he has heard said or if he knows how Smith was attempting to raise that revolution, and with whom was he depending for this?
> [Crow]: That he does not know how Smith was thinking of raising the revolution, nor yet on whom he was relying; that this revolution was for commercial purposes.[45]

Crow, a poorly educated man who claimed he had only been intimidated into working with the bandits, passed along snippets of conversations to help the Spanish outline the conspiracy in depth. Commerce had always been the heart of the scheme. Like Clark in New Orleans, Smith T was an aggressive capitalist always looking to broaden his ventures. But the drive for trade was equally strong among the people of Nacogdoches. At the same time that Americans were pushing towards Texas, Tejanos were pulling their neighbors towards them. During the Casas revolt, Crow testified, Father Huerta and Lieutenant Guadiana had conspired to seize the latter's superior officer, Commander Don Christóbal Domínguez, which they ultimately did. Crow explained the plan had been a joint one between Mexican rebels and Americans, who targeted Domínguez "because if he came to command at this village, he would not allow them to trade."[46]

Quinn and Smith T were "gathering up people of various parts of the government of the United States for raising the revolution and taking steps for attaining commerce." The "Fat Father" in Nacogdoches had an understanding with Quinn, the ferryman told his interrogators. "Quinn, who is in Natchitoches, was the one who was supplying them what these American bandits were needing," he said, but "Father Huerta had to pay it to Quinn," since the money had to be raised in Spanish territory "for total payment of what the matter will cost." Other sources claim Huerta only promised credit: he agreed that the Americans, upon entering Nacogdoches, would be paid by seizing the public coffers and government property. Crow informed his interrogators that the purpose of this cabal was "for raising a revolution and gaining this place, for afterwards insinuating themselves in the kingdom." The Spanish interrogators scoffed at the idea that only a dozen or so men could lead a revolution. Crow said the Americans "understood that people would come from the interior to aid them; and that from Kentucky he knows that three hundred men are going through Santa Fe with the same end."[47]

Those of the banditti who had escaped made their way back to Natchitoches, where they began to talk of a rescue attempt. "I am informed that some of the scoundrels have declared since their return from the Sabine, that they will raise a force of 2 or 300 men and take Nacogdoches," wrote John C. Carr, the parish judge in Natchitoches, to Governor Claiborne. "This they will find rather difficult; I shall be on the alert, and their first movement will be the *signal* of *their capture*."[48]

Smith T was already well advanced towards raising the force that Crow and Carr referenced, but in his preparations, he had been too vocal, his plans too public. Sibley wrote, "It is no doubt true, that in this town, at Rapides and Opelousas some efforts have been made to engage men pretendedly for that service, and that a correspondence in writing has been carried on upon that subject between persons here & leading characters of the revolutionary party in the Spanish country." Partly on the basis of accounts such as this, government officials threatened all who were involved with arrest. With his patron Wilkinson no longer available to protect him, Smith T could not hold his men together and his army dissolved. His plans were in shambles, and for revolution to be revived in Texas, it would need a new approach and new leaders. The hopes of the American conspirators, and of their now imprisoned allies in Nacogdoches, would depend on events in Mexico.[49]

8

Rebels in Exile

THE SMALL TOWN of Revilla in northern Mexico was about as removed from the chaos and ferment of the worldwide conflict as any place in September 1810. Revilla—which today lies beneath Falcon Lake on the US-Mexico border—was a tiny outpost along the comparative oasis of the Rio Grande in the western portion of the Tamaulipan brushlands. It was a poor town, but had a few notable men of substance and reputation, to whom the people looked for leadership in this strongly paternalistic society. Among these were two brothers, José Bernardo and José Antonio Gutiérrez de Lara. In 1786, their father, Santiago Gutiérrez, was a senior member of the town council and owned seven thousand acres on the southern bank of the Rio Grande. While his oldest son José Antonio was trained in the law and the clergy, José Bernardo and another brother were trained to run the estate. When the father died, Bernardo (as he was commonly called) inherited the land and the associated place in society. Nuevo Santander had been established by a Spanish empresario named José de Escandón, and his particular fiefdom was ruled by military and wealthy elites. "Authority was so heavy-handed that permission was needed for even the most minor of activities," writes one historian. An up-and-coming Creole like Bernardo Gutiérrez, who was wealthy and well educated, was thus destined to a second-class status. His relative wealth could never mean leisure. In addition to running this vast estate, Gutiérrez made a living as a blacksmith and merchant.[1]

Bernardo Gutiérrez may indeed have been at his forge when news of the *Grito* arrived in Revilla. Close on the heels of this news would have come a proclamation from the governor of Nuevo Santander province, Col. Manuel de Iturbe, warning residents against supporting the revolt in stark terms. But after news arrived that rebel Lt. Gen. José Mariano Jiménez had taken San Luis Potosí, Iturbe's own soldiers deserted him and he fled. Around December 1810, the Gutiérrez brothers joined the revolution, not at first drawn to the cause from a desire for republicanism, but rather a feeling of betrayal from the corrupt governance of the gachupines, who they viewed as traitors to their own nation and king. Though they were rebels, the brothers saw themselves as the true loyalists to their king and the Catholic faith.[2]

It was José Antonio, the priest, who first embraced the revolution. This was of course a revolt spearheaded by the Catholic clergy, who were more well-versed in enlightenment ideas than is often assumed. They had even pioneered ideas of popular sovereignty and saw divine right—a key tenet of Martin Luther—as anathema. José Antonio made up a list of everything he could offer the revolution: "a shotgun, pistol, rifle, five pounds of gunpowder . . . [cash and] two hundred pesos in books, and a half-built house." But the greatest thing he had to contribute was himself, and he soon became a leading member of the revolutionary cause in the province. His brother Bernardo, for his part, could easily have remained neutral in the conflict, but he also offered his services to the rebel cause.[3]

"At this time," he would write years later, "I who anxiously desired to see the four provinces free from the ignominious Spanish yoke, could not be indifferent when I saw the insuperable difficulties which presented themselves, but the desire of overcoming them led me to consider the proper means of disorganizing the royalist forces." But what skills did he have? None but his reputation, which even his enemies would later admit was one of respect throughout the province. "Among the various ideas which occurred to me, I chose that of making a great number of proclamations and of paying some couriers generously to get them into the canton of Aguallo," he wrote.[4]

When the beleaguered royalists fled Nuevo Santander, the Gutiérrez brothers and other rebels turned to neighboring Coahuila, where Governor Cordero, recently returned from his extended stay in Texas, was fighting to keep his province in royalist hands. Cordero marched south to challenge Jiménez, and the two armies met on January 6, 1811. But the rebellion in Mexico was spreading faster than even Cordero knew, and a successful plot of pro-rebel officers in his ranks led to the dramatic defection of virtually all of his army, which made the governor a prisoner.[5]

The royalists counterattacked, and a string of victories by an up-and-coming commander, Joaquín de Arredondo, recovered most of Nuevo Santander. At the same time, the army of Jiménez, Juan Aldama, and Hidalgo suffered the defeat at the Calderón Bridge and began the retreat which would end in disaster at the Wells of Baján. In a conflict in which various personalities frequently changed sides based on who was winning, the Gutiérrez brothers remained faithful to the revolutionary cause. On March 16, 1811, with the insurgent army in retreat and its fortunes at a low ebb in the north, Bernardo Gutiérrez appeared before the rebel chiefs at the Hacienda de Santa María outside Saltillo and gave an emotional appeal to the gathered rebel leaders, offering to dedicate his life to the revolution. He was appointed lieutenant colonel in the rebel army and was ordered to raise recruits along the Rio Grande. But at this crucial moment, news arrived from San Antonio that Casas had been overthrown and Ignacio Aldama—with his load of silver bars—was captured. The mission to the United States was the rebels' greater priority. Gutiérrez offered to take his place. As he would later recall,[6] "Seeing the very great importance of executing this plan, principally because of the great resources which we should expect from the immense advantage of communication with a powerful nation . . . and being impelled by the desire of executing the adopted plan and of sacrificing myself in the service of my country, I could do no less in this case than offer myself to my superiors for the purpose of overcoming all obstacles and entering the United States where I could do much."[7]

With the revolution in the north of Mexico collapsing, his prospects were grim. General Arredondo was rapidly subduing the province, brutally suppressing revolt and rolling up the towns along the Rio Grande, including Revilla. Bernardo was forced into hiding "like the miserable mole among the leaves," he wrote in his diary. But there was still hope. His brother Antonio, now near Mexico City, wrote that sixty thousand rebels were in possession of the passes between the capital and the port of Veracruz, and that the country around the capital was mostly in rebel hands, with thousands of men flocking to the revolutionary cause. Linking these forces to the outside world could save the rebellion, if only Gutiérrez could find a way across royalist Texas to the United States.[8]

By chance he came into contact with an exiled Tejano who offered hope. José Menchaca was a royalist officer descended from San Antonio's presidial elite. He had aided Zambrano's men in finding Governor Salcedo, but now, perhaps implicated in the rebellion, he was fleeing "on account of the persecution of the Commanding-General Salcedo, who was seeking to take his life." The native Texan offered to guide the rebel envoy through his home province. Together with twelve men gathered in Revilla, they set out in the last week of July 1811, "with arms, munitions, money, and pack animals." This included a large amount of gold and silver. One of the men in the party estimated the funds at fifteen million dollars.[9]

Menchaca's aid was essential, for he was able to avoid the main Spanish road by taking a circuitous route around San Antonio and passing through Indian villages to the northwest of the settled parts of Texas. Along the way, Gutiérrez promised the Indians he would return and offered them guns if they would join the cause against the Spanish. On several occasions, the men were attacked by hostile tribes, but they scattered them and continued on their way. The Spanish were not ignorant of Gutiérrez's plans and sent out patrols to intercept the rebel party. These failed to find their quarry, but one of their number, a Frenchman named John Garniere, somehow did. Impressed into Spanish service as an artillerist, he was a reluctant royalist and eager to join the revolutionaries. Slipping away from his patrol, he found and joined the rebel band. The group continued "by the most secret and unfrequented route" and reached the Sabine near an Indian village, where they crossed on September 16th—the one-year anniversary of the revolution.[10]

Then their luck ran out. A patrol of fifty Spaniards surprised the rebels at the home of a Frenchman where they had stopped to eat. In a running battle, Gutiérrez and

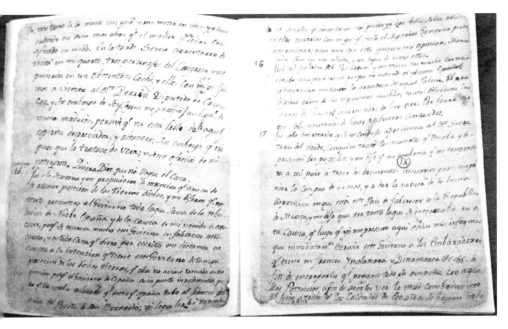

Figure 5. Diary of José Bernardo Gutiérrez de Lara. Courtesy of Texas State Archives.

eleven of his men escaped into the woods, "with arms in hand," Gutiérrez wrote in his diary, "losing everything we carried, and most important of all, the papers and dispatches which proved my commission in a positive manner." Also lost was the money. Learning of the attack in Natchitoches, a small party of only fifteen American "volunteers" was put together from among the civilians and rode west, ready to do battle with the Spaniards. They discovered Gutiérrez and his men, exhausted and huddled just inside American territory along the Arroyo Hondo, having made their escape.[11]

Gutiérrez at this moment was a castaway. He represented a rebellion with armies in the field but with fragmented leadership. The insurgent's mission was to make his way to Washington, somehow secure American support, and to do so with no money, contacts, or means at his disposal. But luck now smiled on the rebel. Natchitoches welcomed the refugees with open arms and gave them food and shelter. Here they met sympathetic Spanish exiles like the Curate Sosa and the former Spanish officer and trader, Juan Cortés, whose connections stretched from Barr and Davenport in Texas to leading merchants in New Orleans. Meanwhile, Americans like Sibley, the Indian Agent, gave him letters of introduction to important people in the United States. Army Capt. W. H. Overton at Fort Claiborne wrote letters introducing the Mexican to his brother, Gen. Thomas Overton in Tennessee and Secretary of War Eustis in Washington.[12]

Gutiérrez's mission was to establish official relations with the United States, but this would take time, and the rebellion could not wait. He realized that there was opportunity here in Natchitoches. He first sought to negotiate with local merchants to send muskets to the Rio Grande, where a cache of money supposedly existed. Though the deal did not come through, he knew that if he could establish a beachhead in Texas, Americans would be sure to aid him. He therefore deputized José Menchaca to build up a force of filibusters from among the eager Americans, with the mission to secure a foothold for the revolution in Texas. Although he does not mention them in his diary, it is likely that he or Menchaca met with Quinn or other Americans affiliated with the previous group of banditti or who had recently been expelled from the Neutral Ground.[13]

Gutiérrez for his part would proceed to Washington in accordance with his instructions, to try to win official support from the Madison administration. On September 27, 1811, the rebel wrote a letter to Secretary of State Monroe asking for arms, money, and men for the cause, which would be reimbursed by a grateful Mexican nation, whereupon "treaties advantageous to both nations should be drawn up." He sent this note by the fastest courier, and then started out for Washington to deliver the same message in person. In a letter to the Mexican congress written decades later, Gutiérrez described his journey:[14] "The first place I reached was Natchez, capital of the Mississippi territory. There was a Spaniard there who had been consul for the King of Spain in New Orleans, and this grand rascal paid two assassins to kill me on the road. They followed me for six days, during which time I suspected nothing. At the end of the sixth day they attacked me, but as I did not carry my arms to play with, I put a quietus on them and continued without this danger."[15]

The bravado in the statement may have been exaggeration, but such dangers were real and the incident plausible. Gutiérrez continued, traveling overland through the West, speaking to governors, generals, and merchants, laying out his needs in terms of funds and arms for the revolution. "I found them all attentive to our just cause. They made me many offers and aided me to reach their government." But there were others who insisted on bypassing official channels. After all, Gutiérrez was crossing the very heartland of the Burrites. Quite a few of the men he met with had been implicated with the former vice president, and some were clearly still adherents. As Gutiérrez recorded,[16] "The rest of the people, principally in Kentucky and Tennessee . . . did not even want me to proceed, wishing me to remain there, and saying that they would make up a considerable army of volunteers, with which, under my command, we would invade the provinces of Mexico and sweep before us all the oppressors of our liberty."[17]

Gutiérrez, however, stuck to his mission and continued to Washington. He was aided on his way by more letters of introduction, which he gathered along the route. A former US Senator from Tennessee recommended him to Madison as "a true American." His journey through the United States in the fall of 1811 was eye-opening for the

Mexican. In addition to eager Burrites, he found opulence that was inconceivable for someone from Northern Mexico, even a relatively wealthy resident such as himself. Nashville, with its "multi-storied buildings," fascinated the man who had never even been to Mexico City. At one point, he stayed with a Native American family living in a home just like the Americans and dining on fine China with silverware. Another Indian he visited, who lived along the Tennessee River, had a large house with windows and even owned slaves.[18]

He passed caravans of settlers moving south to settle in West Florida, even in the dead of winter. The Mexican rebel seems not to have connected this event with the recent removal of Spanish authority from that province. He had no fear at all of American immigrants flooding the territories he hoped to liberate—in fact, he would encourage it.[19]

The letters written by friends in Natchitoches aided him greatly, opening doors all along the way. When he showed up at the home of Gen. Thomas Overton bearing the letter from the latter's brother, the general gave the Mexican every courtesy he could: "He was very cordial; he exchanged compliments with me like a well-bred person of the first rank. This gentleman is one of the generals who fought against the British arms; he took part in thirty battles; his whole body is full of signs of the wounds which he received in these battles until the [Americans] achieved their independence. It is a pleasure to see the decoration of this gentleman's house, upstairs and down. They entertained us with an ostentatious table and sumptuous beds."[20]

The general gave Gutiérrez further letters to ease his way to Washington, recommended hosts with whom he could stay, and accompanied him on horseback for three leagues. At "Cragfont," the plantation of Gen. James Winchester, another Revolutionary War veteran, Gutiérrez was received like family. He stayed in the general's large Georgian/Federal-style home, with its broad porches and elaborate interior woodworking. He played with the general's children, teaching them Spanish words late into the night until Winchester scolded his children for tiring out the guest. "Day broke without any unusual happening except that I was buried in a luxurious feather bed," Gutiérrez recorded in his diary. When friends of generals and politicians were not available, he stayed with private citizens. Most had never met a Mexican before. Traveling through the snowy landscape, he frequently filled his journal with invectives about greedy and rude innkeepers, but also flirtatious landladies as well.[21]

Arriving in Knoxville on November 26, 1811, Gutiérrez's contacts introduced him to Governor William Blount, the same man who twenty-five years before had lost his US Senate seat after he conspired for Western secession. Blount immediately invited the traveler to a dinner that night with himself and other men of distinction. The governor and the Mexican revolutionary became close, with Gutiérrez teaching Spanish words to the man who had once dreamed of joining his territory to Spain. Although by now the glow was fading on Western secession, the idea of establishing a new republic in the Spanish lands was as strong as ever. As he traveled, word of Gutiérrez's journey and of the Mexican revolutionary prospects spread, as did his pleas for support. By the time Gutiérrez left Knoxville, he had introductions to congressmen, Speaker of the House Henry Clay (himself a Westerner and friend of Spanish-American independence), and most importantly, President Madison.[22]

But while he had been traveling across the United States, a calamity befell the revolutionary cause in Texas. After Gutiérrez's departure, his associate Menchaca, who had been left to organize a filibuster, raised two hundred to three hundred volunteers, mostly Americans and French, but probably including some Spanish residents of Orleans Territory as well. That he came up with such numbers so rapidly suggests this force was built from the remnants of John Smith T's aborted filibuster from six months before. He promised his recruits plunder, land, and $1 a day. Setting out for Nacogdoches, "in high spirits, flushed with the love of liberty, and panting for glory," the Menchaca force entered Texas on October 15th.[23]

It was a fiasco. Accounts are sketchy, but it appears a large Spanish patrol surprised them. Menchaca either lost his nerve or, as Gutiérrez believed, was bribed to betray his army and joined the royalists. The Americans, thus abandoned, were fortunate to escape across the Sabine without losing a single man. Menchaca was brought back to San Antonio and pardoned. Royal authority was strengthened, and all hope for freeing Texas was gone for 1811.[24]

Mexican Envoy in Washington

At 11:00 a.m. on December 11, 1811, Gutiérrez stepped into the office of the secretary of war, William Eustis, which was located in the same building William Shaler had visited a year before. It was particularly good timing, and he was well received. The day before, the House of Representatives had passed a resolution expressing its support for the establishment of independent republics in Spanish America, holding out the promise of quick recognition and trade with any that became free. Gutiérrez met for two hours with Eustis on the next day. The secretary of war had at his side an employee borrowed from the State Department for the meeting, the talented John Graham, who had served as minister to Madrid and as Claiborne's secretary in Louisiana, and who was among the few in official Washington fluent in Spanish.[25]

What were William Eustis's thoughts on the revolution in Mexico? He had received most of his news from the Indian Agent John Sibley, who reported excitedly on the progress of the revolution, and the inflated hopes he harbored for it. But there was another opinion from a source with a different viewpoint altogether. It was one of the army's newest heroes, who had traveled through Mexico and knew it better than probably any living American, Lt. Col. Zebulon Pike. The officer/explorer wrote to the secretary "that Mexico proper and the Internal provinces will ultimately declare their independence, no person possessing the least knowledge of the history of mankind will attempt doubt for one moment." But here, he tempered his own enthusiasm with concern. The Mexican Revolution, he cautioned, was far more like the French one than the American. The Europeans had sown an "inveterate hatred" in the breasts of the Creoles, Mestizos, and Indians, and in "the just explosion of their Revolutionary principles" they would drive the Europeans out or exterminate them. The rebels, he admitted, were poorly equipped and at a disadvantage against the professional Spanish military. "But should a man of zeal [and] patriotic views who could see in the parties no distinction but that which is informed by vice or virtue put himself at the head of a strong force and declare his intention of making the country independent," then the rebels could prevail. This, however, might not be as positive of an outcome as most Americans assumed.[26] "When this period arrives, they will instantly become the rival of the United States. Prophesizing a population quite equal, far exceeding [America] in riches—and from their despotic habits of government being enabled to raise large bodies of troops on the conscription plan and them of the best cavalry (or equal to any in the world) They will always be able to threaten our southwest frontier with a formidable force."[27]

Sent in October, the letter arrived at the War Department eighteen days before the Mexican rebel did, so these dire musings had to be on the mind of William Eustis when Gutiérrez walked in his door. Official American policy treated Texas as a lawful part of the Louisiana Purchase, and with sentiments like Pike's on his mind, Eustis was all the more convinced of the necessity of maintaining a buffer to the west of New Orleans. He began the discussions with Gutiérrez by asking if it would be possible for the United States to enter Texas to seize land that it claimed under the Louisiana Purchase. This force, he suggested, could then provide covert aid to the rebels. Gutiérrez said that would not be possible, to which Eustis replied there was no other way to aid the Mexicans, since America and Spain were still at peace. "I told him that the aid I asked should be given in such a way as would benefit both Americas," Gutiérrez wrote. "My way of thinking did not displease the government; he gratified me by saying that our cause was favored by all this nation; that they would aid me to defend it." But as Gutiérrez would learn, there was a big difference between sympathy and direct support.[28]

Nor in diplomacy did anything ever come free, even among friends. A few days later, Eustis clarified that the United States wanted possession of all the lands it felt rightfully belonged to it from the Louisiana Purchase and this included Texas. Gutiérrez was taken aback. The novice envoy had not been prepared for conditions on American aid. "My reply to them was that I could not vote upon these things, nor could they treat of them with me; that only the Supreme Government could decide them," he wrote. Even so, Eustis kept pushing. What, he asked, was Gutiérrez's opinion? Was such a deal possible? "María Santisima, help me and rescue me from these men!" the frustrated rebel wrote in his diary. He supposedly learned to swear in English for the first time after these meetings.[29]

On December 16th, the Mexican was given a brief audience with President Madison, but since Graham was not present to translate, there were no formal talks.

He had to content himself with a tour of the White House and marveled once again: "The grandeur of this palace aroused my admiration," he wrote. "The perfect order of its very rich furniture; so many different lamps of crystal ornamented with fine gold. Outside, it has only windows of fine glass—one hundred and two of them." The White House, with its windows and lamps, as with the other public buildings Gutiérrez saw and praised in Washington, would be burned by the British in two and a half years.[30]

The next day, Gutiérrez was conducted to the secretary of state's office to meet with James Monroe, who had recently replaced the disruptive Robert Smith. Translating for the meeting again was Graham. The secretary of state began with a more positive message: He laid out the steps America was taking diplomatically to pave the way for Mexican Independence with European leaders. But to Gutiérrez's plea for arms and supplies, Monroe was emphatic: The rebel needed to return to Mexico to regain the credentials he had lost in the flight. Letters of recommendation from westerners could earn a meeting, but only credentials from the rebel leaders themselves could earn America's trust on such a sensitive matter.[31]

Still, Monroe told the Mexican that if England and America went to war, which he expected at any time, it would almost certainly trigger war with Spain as well. In that event, America could immediately place an army of fifty thousand men in New Spain to aid the independence movement. The numbers, as Gutiérrez reported them, were unrealistic. This was ten times the size of the army as it existed on the day the two men met, and even after the mobilization for war a year later, it would amount to one quarter of the forces America had available. They would have been deployed at an excessive distance from the centers of power in a conflict in which control of the sea would belong to Britain, and they were in addition to the forces needed to protect the coast and those slated for the more important invasion of Canada. The suggestion was merely a trial balloon, and predictably, when Gutiérrez asked for the proposal in writing, Monroe balked.[32]

Although he was making little progress, Gutiérrez was enjoying Washington. He went sightseeing throughout the town, visited the navy yard, and practiced his English by listening to the congressional debates over the growing controversy with England. He spent Christmas in the home of a French couple who spoke his language, and he met a blur of officials, representatives, as well as several fellow exiles from Spanish America. But none of these would be as fateful as the meeting that followed a day in late December, when the Mexican opened the pages of the *National Gazette*, published in Philadelphia, and saw, to his surprise, a long article written in his own language.[33]

The Cuban Rebel

The letter was so compelling that he copied it verbatim into his diary. It was from a former member of the Spanish Cortes, or parliament, from Cuba who had abandoned the body and fled to America. After describing his reasons for coming to the United States, the author wrote that while he loved "good European Spaniards, I detest the wicked ones, and above all the tyrants." Even the Cádiz government-in-exile was little better than the French, and for that reason, he had concluded the only course for the New World was "the liberty and absolute independence of all the continent and islands of the hemisphere." He concluded, with words that struck happiness in the heart of Gutiérrez:

> I am an American, and I shall with joy pour out my blood to contribute to this happy and glorious regeneration. These are the sentiments of my soul, and the great ideas which fill my imagination. I am your humble and obedient servant,
> JOSÉ ÁLVAREZ DE TOLEDO[34]

Gutiérrez was even more overjoyed four days later when the author himself arrived from Philadelphia. On December 30th, the Mexican rebel met the Cuban for the first time and took stock of him. Toledo was slightly shorter than Gutiérrez, but "well formed and of beautiful countenance." He was certainly more socially polished than the Mexican. Gutiérrez was impressed, even a bit starstruck. Toledo was "a man of great talents, and passionately devoted to the cause of the liberty of Mexico," Gutiérrez wrote. "The discourses of this gentleman are admirably great and just."[35]

They took a walk to the capitol and toured the House and Senate Chambers, as well as the Supreme Court, then also housed in the building. As the two American Spaniards dreaming of revolution strolled through the streets of Washington, they built a rapport. The new year of 1812 would dawn in two days, and they must have thought a great deal about the future, new beginnings, and their dreams to transform their native lands into places with freedom and "good government" that would allow them to match all the wonders they had seen in the United States.[36]

Gutiérrez almost certainly learned something of Toledo's background during their talks. He was the son of Don Luís de Toledo y Liche, a native of Seville, who had come to Cuba in the Spanish navy, and was currently serving as the captain of the Port of Havana. Young José Alvarez had studied at the Escuela Naval de Cádiz and served in the navy from 1806 to 1807. After fighting with the Army of Galicia against the French, he was evacuated with British forces to London in 1808. At the time, he had been a staunch royalist, and had devised a plan to rescue Ferdinand VII, but nothing came of it. Toledo likely *did not* share with his new acquaintance his affiliation with the secret *Logia de los Caballeros Racionales*, a quasi-Masonic revolutionary society of Spanish liberals, as Gutiérrez had a more traditional Catholic view of Masons.[37]

In 1810, Toledo had been appointed to the Spanish Cortes, which was then meeting as part of the government-in-exile in Cádiz. There, even though he was a son of a native Spaniard and had studied in the parent country, he saw firsthand how shamefully he and his fellow American delegates were treated by the arrogant Peninsular

Spaniards, who were ignorant in the extreme about the New World. "Those who led the majority at the congress expressed themselves in the most stagnant and humiliating terms," Toledo wrote. One, a lawyer, stated "that he still did not know to what animal class the Americans belonged." Toledo concluded that they saw Americans only as "beasts, incapable of leaving slavery." The Cuban delegate responded with a letter to his constituents denouncing the government-in-exile as a farce, but in June 1811, the letter was intercepted, and he was forced to flee. Before he left, he was armed with a commission by fellow American delegates to revolutionize Cuba.[38]

Toledo had arrived with passion, energy, and a way with words, just at the right moment. Spanish Consul Onís had just dispatched the latest thorn in his side, a Portuguese native who was spreading pro-liberty propaganda. In his case, it was a simple matter of bribes. But scarcely had Onís solved this problem than his place was taken by Toledo, who showed up ready to fight a propaganda war in the newspapers. At the same time that he had written his letter announcing his reasons for coming to America, he had published a pamphlet that was now circulating among the Spanish exiles and interested Americans who had followed Spanish revolutionary news since Miranda.[39]

The *Manifesto or Satisfaction in a Point of Honor* laid out his vision of the conflict and was intended as the keystone of a broader propaganda effort, which is why Toledo had been meticulous enough to place his letter in several papers. In addition to the *Gazette* that Gutiérrez had read, it was published in William Duane's *Aurora*, the paper of choice of the more partisan Republicans. Duane, an early proponent of the infant doctrine that would eventually come to be known as Manifest Destiny, saw the West as "territory to be liberated from European corruption." Before the doctrine would evolve into one that dispossessed Hispanics, it was embraced by Americans who thought liberating their southern neighbors was simply the complementary outgrowth to their own struggle.[40]

While many New World Spaniards continued to support a connection to peninsular Spain in principle, Toledo suggested that corruption in the motherland might be more endemic and irredeemable. His experience at the Cortes had been eye-opening. "One believed one saw the ancient Emperors of Constantinople, enclosed with the Clergy in their palace, consuming entire days and nights in arguments over theology, while the formidable nations of the north invaded and dominated the best provinces of the Empire." He called for independence: "Sixteen million inhabitants occupying this delicious Continent are never represented in the eyes of the Government and Rulers in Europe, except as a horde of miserable slaves who must blindly obey whatever they are ordered to, and in profound silence kiss those same chains that they have dragged since the time of Cortez and Pizarro."[41]

Toledo wrote in an eloquent style that Gutiérrez, who fancied himself a propagandist, could not match, as he called for a new beginning for Spanish America: "Hear my voices, breathed across the fertile and pacific banks of the beautiful Delaware, exalted by the holy love of humanity, and generous fervor for the *Patria*. Work to make the Peoples of the New World happy, and to be the admiration and sweet envy of the proud and tyrannized Europe." Speaking to his fellow Cubans, he told them, "Remember that you are free according to the law of nature and the eternal law of the Almighty, and according to the price itself of the blood that you have spilled with so much heroism." America was a model, but not a perfect one. Perhaps referring to slavery, he wrote, "In the Constitution of the United States you can find beautiful things: select the good and avoid what may be deadly for America some day."[42]

Toledo had come to Washington, much as Gutiérrez, to negotiate with the administration for help for the forces of rebellion in Cuba. Indeed, possessing credentials, which Gutiérrez did not, he was strongly encouraged and given a letter of introduction to the administration's agent, New York sea captain William Shaler, who was still in Havana. At this point, freeing Cuba was likely the sole plan of José Alvarez de Toledo, but between his talks with Gutiérrez and letters from the island that informed him of the poor prospects of rebellion there, he began to realize that the best hope for freedom for his homeland was through the success of the revolution in Mexico.

The two Spanish creoles traveled from Washington to Philadelphia, where Toledo introduced Gutiérrez to the many Spanish exiles there. At this time, such men gathered together in small discussion groups known as *tertulias*, often affiliated with secret societies, where they networked, raised funds in the United States and abroad, and continued to plot revolution in their home countries from the shadow of Independence Hall. Gutiérrez and Toledo were soon intriguing as well.[43]

Gutiérrez's original plan had been to win support of the administration for aid for the revolution while Menchaca led a filibuster into Texas and seized enough territory to declare a government that could send Gutiérrez credentials for further negotiation. Menchaca's betrayal had wrecked this scheme. The Cuban and the Mexican, learning of this failure, now conceived of an alternative. Gutiérrez, fortified with his many contacts in the American West, would return to the frontier and assume the abandoned role as leader of a revolutionary army. Toledo, in turn, would remain in the United States and take up Gutiérrez's old post, raising aid and sending it to Texas. The plan was drawn up entirely by the two Creoles, but they did expect assistance from individual American filibusters, and possibly—if the expected war with Great Britain and Spain came to pass—some version of Monroe's suggested American intervention. Each of them carried a small amount of money—two hundred dollars in Gutiérrez's case—that had been given to them by Monroe in their meeting. It was little more than a humanitarian gesture that aided the impoverished revolutionaries with travel expenses, but it was pregnant with meaning that Onís and other Spaniards knew well: the United States, though neutral, definitively favored the side of the revolutionists. How much aid the country would ultimately give, neither of them knew as Gutiérrez bid adiós to his new collaborator in early 1812 and booked passage on a ship bound for New Orleans.[44]

9

Encounter in New Orleans

ON DECEMBER 21, 1811, US Special Agent William Shaler stepped off the gangway of a ship newly arrived from Havana at the port of New Orleans. The town was dreary, humid, and gritty, certainly not the enchanting place it would one day become. "The general appearance of the city is not pleasing to the traveler," another visitor could write even two decades later. "There are no domes or towers or columns, nor any handsome buildings of exquisite architecture . . . [but] at the approach of the levee rises a jungle of masts." A merchant seaman himself, Shaler was at home on the ocean and may have even found his voyage invigorating. In his career, he had entered many ports from Marseille to Hamburg, to Canton, to Hawaii. Each one had its own variation of sights, smells, babble, and bustle.[1]

The clamor in the crescent city this day, as was reported in the *Louisiana Gazette and Daily Advertiser*, was the first report of a momentous natural disaster, a massive earthquake that had been felt upriver in Natchez a week before, the greatest seismic event ever recorded east of the Rocky Mountains. The quake, with aftershocks continuing for as long as a year, centered around the town of New Madrid, in what is today Arkansas. But the real upheaval that was on the mind of William Shaler that day was the one whose epicenter was at *another* Madrid, some 4,700 miles away. The collapse of the Spanish empire, he wrote, could "menace" the peace and rights of all independent nations, and America should be wary of the aftershocks to come.[2] "The consequences of the establishment of a number of independent republics on this continent in the whole space comprehended between Louisiana and Patagonia, where the same language will be spoken, and the same laws govern, seem to defy the grasp of the human mind: I confess that I cannot pretend to estimate their extent."[3]

Already, several provinces in the New World had declared autonomy or opened rebellion. Shaler, dispatched in late 1810 as a special agent for Cuba and Mexico, had started his journey in the former, as instructed. He settled into his position as Commissioner for Seamen and Commerce and awaited events. At first, he received his further instructions from the State Department, as had been arranged, through his former business partner, Nathaniel Ingraham. With the American takeover of West Florida, Secretary Smith wrote him of the official government position that America "could not remain an unconcerned Spectator of the occurrences of such important events in our own immediate neighborhood."[4]

As long as US territory was not threatened, the administration was just observing, but West Florida was a warning of the "uncontrolled current of a revolutionary impulse." In response, Madison had been forced to occupy it, and to Shaler fell the mortifying task of informing the Spanish governor and captain-general of the island, the Marqués de Someruelos. The agent did so by copying Smith's language verbatim, indicating a hesitance to stick out his neck on such a delicate topic. It was an impossible sell, and if Shaler had expected the diplomatic gates to open and welcome him before, they certainly would not now do so after the president's duplicitous act. The Spanish, through distrust and indifference, gave him little attention and no information. And they *absolutely* would not give him a passport to travel onward to Mexico.[5]

Shaler, mostly confined to Havana and its outskirts, busied himself the best he could, navigating his way through Spanish elite society; making connections where possible; and writing long essays on the island's economy, its crops, and leading persons. But all was quiet on the Caribbean island. As outside news filtered past the Spanish censors, it must have seemed that this was the only place in Spain's empire that was *not* in revolt. Governor Claiborne in Orleans Territory learned of Shaler's presence through the state department and began writing him about a series of issues related to his consul position that included Haitian Creole refugees, interned sailors, and most importantly, several American prisoners in Cuba who had been captured by the Spanish for filibustering in West Florida.[6]

In June 1811, Shaler was approached by revolutionary members of the Creole elite, who contacted him through his Spanish translator. He had several meetings with them to no great success, as they were still wary of making a move against royal authority, and he had nothing to offer them but sympathy. The Spanish officials may or may not have known of these meetings, but when Shaler made an unauthorized trip out of Havana, he was hauled before Someruelos and asked to explain himself. The American agent, whose Spanish was rudimentary, defended his conduct in an interrogation that lasted forty-five minutes, speaking entirely in French, which the captain-general, for his part, could understand, but only speak with difficulty. Using the indiscretion as an excuse to finally rid himself of the suspicious American, the captain-general ordered Shaler off the island.[7]

The blow was a blessing in disguise. It had been a dispiriting year in Cuba, where he had practiced his meager Spanish but accomplished little else. His meeting with the Creoles had convinced him their prospects were dim. In October he had received a letter from Claiborne, telling him much that the Spanish authorities kept secret from the people, and it concerned the *other half* of his instructions: "Accounts from the western frontier of this territory, represent that the interior provinces of Mexico are again in a state of revolution, and that the revolutionists have gained many advantages." Expelled from Cuba, and with Veracruz still closed to him, Shaler decided to get as near as he could to the action and booked passage to New Orleans.[8]

Upon his arrival, Shaler met with Claiborne several times. It is clear from the governor's letters that the secret agent kept him in the dark about his ultimate purpose. While they discussed Mexico at length, Shaler no more told Claiborne about his mission as an envoy to revolutionaries than he did the man on the street. "Mr. Shaler was introduced to me by the former Secretary of State Mr. Smith, and I have taken it for granted, that he is still in the confidence and service of the Government," Claiborne wrote his former secretary, John Graham, a deputy in the state department. "His conduct in this city has been marked with great circumspection."[9]

Shaler was not quite sure he *was* still in the confidence of the government. He had been hired in June 1810 by Smith, serving a president who in turn was, in the words of the State Department Historian, "poised to undermine [Smith's] authority and seek his ouster." Push had finally come to shove in March 1811, when the president at last asked his secretary to resign, offering the post of ambassador to Russia—the most out-of-the-way exile to which he could send him. "Smith refused the mission and retaliated in a published address, hoping to topple the Madison Administration," the official history reads. He finally resigned on April 1, and Madison replaced the disgruntled diplomat with James Monroe, the governor of Virginia and former Louisiana Purchase negotiator.[10]

This was not auspicious for Shaler, who was Smith's man. These battles occurred midway through the agent's stay in Cuba, and he never received official word of any kind on the matter. The agent's correspondence was mostly one-sided, probably by design, since he was operating in foreign—and if his instructions had been known, hostile—territory. The result was isolation and ignorance.

Shaler had never previously met his new boss, Monroe. The agent dutifully continued his robust reporting to the department, informing Monroe of any information he gained, outlining his plans and seeking approval for them. Shaler had received no new orders countermanding or amending his original instructions from Smith. Having failed in Cuba, his guiding document clarified his next steps were to proceed "to some port in Mexico as a passenger in private vessels, and that you lose no time in repairing to that place where the local authority of Mexico may reside." This being impossible, he now waited in vain for news in the crescent city. In January 1812, he wrote to Monroe, "Since I had the honor to address you by the last mail, no intelligence has reached this place from either Mexico or Cuba. I have conversed with a Spaniard lately from Natchitoches. . . . He informs me that nothing is known there of the operations in New Spain, and that all is apparently quiet on the frontiers."[11]

In February, he sent more hopeful news and rumors of happenings in Mexico. A brig had arrived from Jamaica on the 13th of the month. From its captain, Shaler learned that "the communication between Mexico [City] and Vera Cruz was absolutely cut off, that the insurgents were in very great form, improving in discipline by a regular system of partisan warfare, and daily gaining ground." There had been a battle near Xalapa, and though it was a royalist victory, the merchant reported to Shaler that the Spanish had suffered heavy losses. "In the opinion of the best-informed men he conversed with there, nothing could check the torrent of revolution and save Mexico but a powerful reinforcement from Europe."[12]

Despite all these letters to Monroe, the agent received nothing in reply, week after interminable week. Impatient, he sent several political essays to stimulate the debate within the executive, and perhaps to display his erudition and win over the stranger who was now his boss. One of these laid out the demographics of Mexico, the nature of the people, and warned of the dangers of leaving the revolution to run its own course, which might result in the worst possible outcome for America: a takeover by the British—"a government who has subjugated India"—under the guise of helping their Spanish allies:[13] "The revolution in Mexico has come too far for mediation. Consequently, British bayonets must be employed to reduce and disarm the insurgents; and when that insurrection is thus quelled, *who will be the real masters of that country*? Will any man in his right senses pretend that the imbecile government of Spain will then have any authority there? No; a British Chief will dictate laws to, and control the policy of, Mexico."[14]

If this were the case, Shaler warned, "to suppose that the resources of New Spain will not be turned against the U. S. is extravagant." The gold and silver of Mexico indeed loomed large in American thinking, imbuing that land with an exaggerated sense of potential power. The agent, therefore, urged action to forestall a British takeover. The Mexicans were "unanimous for independence," but at a severe disadvantage without arms and organization. Only America could aid them, he suggested, through a mix of regular troops, volunteers, and fifty thousand stands of arms for the ill-equipped masses of Hidalgo's army. Once the revolution was achieved and a friendly government was in power,[15] "Then would [a] free and independent Mexico be our friends from the strongest of all considerations. Gratitude and a common interest; then should we be amply remunerated for our generous efforts by the goodwill of a people become free through us and by the advantages of an extensive, a peaceful, and a mutually beneficial commerce."[16]

The Agent's Plea

For all of this voluminous correspondence, Shaler received not a letter in return—no orders, nor even confirmation that his own letters had been received. First in Havana, and now in New Orleans, the agent increasingly felt abandoned as the gap in the department's correspondence would ultimately stretch to nine months. Though mail service was excruciatingly slow, even that could not explain the silence from Washington. At his wit's end, Shaler, after much handwringing, wrote directly to his onetime acquaintance, Pres. James Madison, to find out where he stood. Jumping the chain of command in this way was a bold and risky step, tantamount to insubordination against Monroe.

> Sir,
>
> Many circumstances of my errant life having led me to an acquaintance with the Spanish American provinces, and to a tolerable knowledge of their language, manner and character of their inhabitants, they actually became long since the favorable object of my reflections. I therefore believed that I possessed a complete show of the qualifications requisite for the mission you did me the honor to appoint me to, notwithstanding the defects of my education; and feeling a strong desire to serve my country under an administration that all who know me, know full well my firm, undeviating and disinterested attachment to, I accepted that honor with pleasure [and] enthusiasm.[17]

After noting some business failures that had wiped out much of his fortune, Shaler said he was nonetheless pleased to be in his position and his instructions "offer the greatest importance: the hope of being useful." However, he considered himself "as standing alone in the world, without an ancient friend and being but very slightly known to any person in the government except yourself." He now came to his real point,[18] "I have long hesitated in the propriety of this step, and I beg you to believe, Sir, that nothing but my very precarious situation, apparently rendered more so by the late total silence of the Department of State would induce me to take it. I [have] confidence that the reasons will be regarded by you, Sir, as sufficient excuse for this reluctant intrusion."[19]

Shaler posted the letter and waited, uncertain if his venturesome action would break the logjam or precipitate his recall. At long last, on May 2nd, two months after this despairing cry for help, and after a total of a *dozen* letters to the secretary of state with no answer, Monroe finally sent a response to Shaler, which did not even mention his most recent letter to the secretary, much less the one to Madison.

> Sir,
>
> I have had the honor to receive your several letters bearing date on the 13 and 25 Nov. 6, 8 & 27 Dec. 4 & 15 February last.
>
> I have the pleasure to communicate the President's approbation of your conduct while in Cuba, and of the motives which induced you to leave that Island, by New Orleans, for Mexico. I should have written to you at New Orleans sooner, had I known your stay there would have afforded sufficient time for the purpose. From the early departure of the mail, however, I can only add the President's wish that you should proceed immediately to Mexico in fulfilment of your original instructions.

> I have the honor to be very respectfully, Sir,
> Your Obt. Svt.
> Jas. Monroe[20]

Shaler, though relieved, would have been mystified by the letter. "Proceed immediately to Mexico?" How exactly could he? Had Monroe not read his letters saying that the port of Veracruz was closed? The Casas revolt and Hidalgo's northern army had both been crushed, so there was no land route either. The administration was simply too distant to respond in any meaningful way to developments on the frontier. It was the nature of diplomacy in the age of sail, barge, and horse, when instructions would often be overtaken by events and become irrelevant before they were even written, much less implemented. Diplomats far from Washington had to adjust on the fly and frequently interpret the intent of their orders against changed circumstances. It was trying enough for an experienced hand; Shaler was a novice thrust into this important role. His frustration was shared by all who served at distant points from authority. Gen. Wade Hampton, upriver at Baton Rouge, wrote around the same time, "all officers commanding at so great a distance ought to have . . . a distinct understanding of the views and wishes of this government, and that without it, his own embarrassment and mortification is not all he has to lament. The public interest must suffer, and he will find himself charged with faults which nothing, but a spirit of divination, would have guarded against."[21]

Shaler, with no such "distinct understanding" of the views of the negligent Monroe, had to rely on the divination and act accordingly. Even before the secretary's letter arrived, he would depart for Natchitoches. It was the closest point to the action where real intelligence could be gained. Furthermore, the slim hope of the rebels opening up Texas again was still better than the impossibility of them gaining Veracruz, with its large garrison, port, and stone fortifications. In March, Shaler had booked passage on a barge headed upriver to the frontier town, but the boat's departure was postponed, and in the sultry New Orleans heat, Shaler stewed. The delay, as it turns out, was to have important consequences.[22]

The End of the Banditti

After the robbery of Zambrano's caravan, officials on both sides of the border began to revisit the question of the Neutral Ground. The men whom Wollstonecraft had captured would stand trial in Rapides, successfully arguing that the government had no jurisdiction in the Neutral Ground and hence they could not be prosecuted. This would change with Congress's impending approval of the new boundaries of the State of Louisiana, but that act came too late and the men walked free. In June 1811, Claiborne wrote to the Natchitoches district judge, John C. Carr, reminding him of the United States government's policy on filibusters.[23]

"As regards the project of attacking Nacogdoches, it is advisable that you cause to be arrested, and bound over to their good behavior all persons engaged in the same, or against whom any well-grounded suspicions exist," he wrote, reminding the judge of the Neutrality Act. The governor ordered Carr to work with the forces at Fort Claiborne and the local militia to suppress the enterprise. At the same time, he wrote to the area's military commanders, Orleans militia Colonel Shaumberg and Captain Wollstonecraft at Fort Claiborne. In addition to the governor's letter, Carr also received one from Simón Herrera in Texas, asking for American assistance in another joint expedition. The judge responded to Herrera politely, but informed him of Congress's approval of Louisiana statehood, which set the border as the banks of the Sabine. Carr took this to mean that the Neutral Ground agreement was now at an end, and since US sovereignty covered the area in dispute, there would be no more joint expeditions.[24]

Although Carr, the civil authority in Natchitoches, took this position, the US military did not, with General Hampton explaining that the law "was merely conditional." Hampton, who had complained of the difficulties of interpreting policy at such a distance, wrote to Claiborne, "It is unquestionably more proper for the president of the U.S. to determine a point of so much political delicacy, than that a military commander should take upon himself that authority." As an end-run around this impasse, Carr could call upon Colonel Shaumberg of the militia, but the latter, with very few men and possibly sympathetic to the Mexican rebels, was never pressed on the issue. Amid this inaction, the banditti had quickly reformed within the Neutral Ground and probably joined the forces of José Menchaca. Their aborted invasion came and failed with Menchaca's defection, but Judge Carr, who had taken no action to stop it, was curiously slow to inform Claiborne. The bewildered governor wrote to Monroe, "No official information has reached me upon the subject and indeed [even] after very positive orders, which I had given to the Parish Judge of Natchitoches, and to the Commanding Officer of the Militia, to put down any enterprise of that nature, and the request I made of the Commanding Officer of the Troops of the U. States at Natchitoches to aid the Civil Authority, if called upon."[25]

When the outlaws robbed a caravan, killing an American, Carr forwarded to Claiborne a petition from the merchants of the city asking that "measures be taken to put an end to a system of brigandage, which is calculated to destroy all friendly intercourse, between the citizens of this territory and the inhabitants of the neighboring Spanish provinces." Still, Carr, the same Irishman that the Indian agent Sibley had described three years before as Claiborne's worst appointment, took no legal action. He was overwhelmed in his mission, possibly intimidated by the banditti and its supporters, and would complain that the civilian justice system was "wholly inadequate" to the task. Claiborne forwarded the news to General Hampton with a request for another military intervention. At last, the general responded, on February 6, 1812, ordering Pike to take a force to Natchitoches, and to "remove the intruders and banditti from the strip of Neutral Ground lying between the Aroya [sic] Hondo, and the Sabine."²⁶

Pike set out from Fort Adams, once again bringing with him Lt. Augustus Magee, who had apparently returned to that post some time in the preceding year. Upon arrival at Fort Claiborne, Pike sent an emissary, Lt. William King of the 5th United States Infantry Regiment, to Lt. Col. Bernardino Montero, who had at last replaced Guadiana, slated to stand trial for his role in the Casas revolt. Unlike the civilian Carr, Pike was not opposed to a joint raid but made it clear he would not wait for the Spanish army bureaucracy—as slow as his own—to make up its mind. "I have to inform you that should you decline a co-operation, I shall proceed with the United States troops alone to effect the object," the officer wrote. "This has become necessary and is due to the respect which my government owe to her laws and moral character, as we are informed that the principal part of the persons in question are subjects from our territories." The Spanish would belatedly agree to joint action, but by that point, the American patrol had been completed.²⁷

Pike once again placed Magee in command of the mission, to be joined in the Neutral Ground by another party under Lieutenant Elijah Montgomery, to be junior to Magee. "You will remove every person who may be within the aforesaid territory who was not settled on said land previous to the date of the convention entered into between General Wilkinson and Colonel Herrera in 1806," he wrote Magee, authorizing him to burn their houses and arrest anyone who had "the least suspicion of their having been concerned in the late murders and outrages." Unlike 1810, this time there would be no warning.²⁸

Magee led his troops into the Neutral Ground on March 4, 1812. He stopped first at a Coushatta Indian village, but finding no trace of the bandits there, proceeded to the abandoned Spanish fort of Los Adaes, where he rendezvoused with Montgomery on the following day, when they began their work in earnest. "That evening I marched from the Addayes [sic] on the road to the Sabine river, burnt a house that a man by the name of Sharp had improperly erected," Magee reported. "Took him prisoner and ordered his family to leave the ground." On the road, Magee next came across one Frederick Stockman, and finding four or five men at his home, detained him.²⁹

Stockman's case was particularly unfortunate. The sixty-four-year-old German had been a settler in Louisiana before the Americans purchased the province, and moved to Trinidad de Salcedo in Texas sometime before 1806, along with his American wife Catalina Bonte and their six children. Five of these were born in Spanish Louisiana, but another, six years old in 1812, had been born in Texas and given the Spanish name José Antonio Stockman. Two months before Magee's raid, as part of the Spanish plan to expel foreigners, the settler was ordered by Trinidad Commandant Felipe de la Garza "that without delay he go to the country from whence he came." To what country was a German who had been a Spanish subject for decades, married to an American, with a toddler born in Texas, to go?³⁰

Magee found the first of the actual banditti at Stockman's house, though it is unclear whether he was hosting them by choice or compulsion. The officer arrested a man named White, who had in his possession a rifle, horse, and two hundred dollars in cash, as well as merchandise that he claimed was his own, but which was probably stolen. Magee then burnt poor Stockman's home and now arrested the ill-starred German. Continuing, he reached the Sabine and surprised the ferryman Crow, whom the Spanish had previously detained as a witness to the attack on Zambrano. Magee arrested two men, named McWilliams and Buckner. Aylett Buckner, the latter, would one day return and join his onetime captor in entirely different circumstances on the road to Texas. Magee then apprehended a man by the name of Sutton, who informed the American officer of the presence of a nearby camp of banditti. Taking McWilliams with him as a guide, Magee crept up on the camp at night. He reported:[31] "When within sight of their fire I left Mr. McWilliams in [the] charge of two men, made two detachments in order to flank and surround them, but the night being very dark, and the ground unknown to me, I could not get to thence, without being discovered. On my entering their camp they fired one or two guns at my party and fled. I fired at them as they ran and gave orders to disperse and hunt them."[32]

Magee then set up an "ambuscade" and waited for the men to return, but they did not. "Some of them must have felt my shot," he informed Pike. On the 9th, he bagged the biggest trophy of the hunt: Miguel Quinn, the former Texas smuggler, Spanish prisoner, and now the patron of the banditti, although Magee likely did not realize this. Magee continued his patrol, once again attempting but failing to surprise a group of men, catching a few more, and burning all the houses he found. He had captured thirteen "robbers"—presumably exclusive of civilians like Stockman—burned nine homes and returned to Natchitoches on March 17th. Magee's report, however, was not the full story. Captives like McWilliams did not simply inform on their fellow banditti of their own free will. A far more damning account of the raid was supplied by Sibley, who wrote to a friend.[33]

"Col. Pike came here about two months ago and sent out lieutenants Magee and Montgomery with about 40 men who patrolled the country as far as the Sabine, laying everything waste. One would have thought they had read General Tauro's [sic] expedition to la Vendee & were endeavoring to imitate his recorded exploits amongst women and children," Sibley wrote, referencing an infamous French Revolutionary general. Magee had his prisoners "stripped, tied to trees, whipt and burnt with chunks of fire . . . to make them confess." Sibley made it clear he thought a "strict enquiry" should be conducted into Magee's behavior. None ever was.[34]

The next month, despite Carr's statement that the Neutral Ground was now American sovereign territory, the Spanish finally mustered a force to raid the region on their own. Capt. Isidro de la Garza took a sergeant, two corporals, and seventeen soldiers, and Samuel Davenport, again as interpreter, into the Neutral Ground and burned houses. The two raids together were enough to break the back of any criminal gang, but the Neutral Ground banditti were more than that. They were an insurgency with revolutionary intent taking advantage of a lawless border region and would keep coming back in dogged pursuit of their agenda: the overthrow of Spanish authority in Texas or, at a minimum, the reestablishment of illegal trade. As history has repeatedly shown, such a force is rarely deterred by mere transitory raids. They would return, and the young, ambitious American lieutenant Augustus Magee would not stop them the next time. He would lead them.[35]

The Rebel Returns

José Bernardo Gutiérrez de Lara had seen his whole view of the world transformed by his experience in the United States. He had been received in the halls of the government in Washington and met with ambassadors of Europe. In Philadelphia, he had seen portraits of Bonaparte and all of the crowned heads of Europe—even, for the first time in his life, that of his own Spanish king. He had marveled at the industry of Virginia and Maryland, saw his first steamship, and had even toured a prison so humane that a Spaniard from Majorca had exclaimed to him in response, "Friend, in the world over which I have travelled, I have not seen a government which is wiser than this and which contributes more to the general happiness."[36]

He had been overwhelmed by the interest and general outpouring of support for the Mexican rebel cause. "I have noted also the great desire which many of them have, to go to Mexico, and many of them have put themselves to school to a teacher whom they have paid to teach them the Spanish language," he wrote in his diary. One "very beautiful young woman of an illustrious family of Baltimore" took this passion to even greater heights. At a dinner, Gutiérrez described General Rayón's crusade, which seized the woman with such romantic visions that she begged Gutiérrez to take her to meet the general. "Only from hearing me refer to the great virtues with which he is endowed and being enamored of his virtues she has shown an extravagant love for him; she has many toasts drunk in fine wines to his health. She asked me if I could safely take her with me; I replied that it was not possible. She said that if woman's dress made it difficult, she would take with her men's clothing to use when it was advisable."[37]

But Gutiérrez was returning to fight a revolution, not to conduct a transnational dating service. He sailed on February 12th in the company of another Mexican republican exile, Tadeo Ortiz de Ayala, and after a voyage that included treacherous ice, storms, and even a French pirate corvette that stalked the ship, he arrived at the mouth of the Mississippi on March 16th, and in New Orleans a week later. He went straightaway to Claiborne's residence and presented the governor with a letter of introduction from John Graham.[38]

Claiborne was confused. He had received no correspondence, as he would have expected, from Monroe himself mentioning Gutiérrez. "I have been somewhat at a loss, as to the degree of countenance proper to show him," the governor wrote to

Graham. What concerned Claiborne was his persistent fear of various conspirators in the city, and the utility they might find for a lightning rod such as this blacksmith from Revilla. Delayed for any period of time in New Orleans, the Mexican revolutionary would be a magnet for French, Spanish, and British agents, as well as Claiborne's bitter enemy, Daniel Clark and his allies, the band of schemers who called themselves the Mexican Association.[39] "This stranger has already given me to understand that he is wholly destitute of funds and that some advances from me are calculated on. I presume I shall not do wrong in soliciting Captain Shaler to advance such sum as may be necessary to make his voyage to Natchitoches comfortable. Were I not to do so, his return to Mexico would be greatly retarded, unless he should fall into the hands of some of the Intrigues (foreign or domestic) which this city abounds."[40]

Indeed, no sooner had Gutiérrez arrived than several such men had made approaches to him, which the Mexican claimed he had rebuffed. He was almost certainly deceiving the governor. His whole goal in going to New Orleans, he would later admit, was to obtain support for a filibuster *outside* of American governmental control. "I established my residence in New Orleans," he wrote fifteen years after the fact, "in order to obtain, by private negotiation, and quickly, the help that was denied by the [government]."[41]

It was to prevent this that the governor wanted the Mexican out of town quickly. The same day that he arrived, Gutiérrez was given an appointment for a formal meeting at 4:00 p.m. When he returned, Gutiérrez found Claiborne had invited another guest to their meeting—Shaler, who was still in town awaiting the long-delayed barge. The president and secretary of state had never intended to connect Gutiérrez and Shaler; when they had met with the Mexican in December, they still thought their agent was in Cuba. Gutiérrez's unexpected arrival had greatly troubled Governor Claiborne, harried as he was, and pawning him off on Shaler seemed to be a convenient way to kill two birds with one stone. The New Yorker, Claiborne thought, could be a protector of the Mexican, and as he turned the rebel over to his care, the governor suggested that Shaler transport him to the frontier, then turn him loose, since "it would not be proper to show any further countenance to this stranger."[42]

Claiborne was certainly sympathetic to Gutiérrez's cause, and was not curt or dismissive to the Mexican. As Shaler and Gutiérrez would linger in New Orleans awaiting an opportunity to go upriver, the governor would host them both several times, particularly Gutiérrez, who he sought to influence to his view of republicanism. Like Shaler and all other supporters of the Republican presidents, Claiborne was a friend of Mexican independence. "The late events in the interior of Mexico, excite much solicitude," he had written in 1811. "The Revolution will I hope assume a proper direction." By this, he meant a pro-American republic, open to trade, not something on the French model, or open to foreign subversion.[43]

To speed the two away from the snares of New Orleans schemers, Claiborne prevailed upon a friend, Benjamin Morgan, who had business interests and an agent in Natchitoches, to assist them along their journey. Morgan arranged passage for the two men on another barge, the *Marcelette*, belonging to his agent, Juan Cortés. Cortés was the former Spanish officer who had fled Texas after being implicated in smuggling—he had been an associate of Philip Nolan—and in whose home the Spanish trader William Barr had died. He of course knew Gutiérrez already, for he had been one of the Natchitoches residents who had helped the Mexican refugee get back on his feet after narrowly escaping Spanish capture the previous year. His affairs brought him into contact with both pro-Spanish and revolutionary circles. After Gutiérrez had left the frontier for Washington in 1811, Cortés had remained in Natchitoches and would have well known the ferment that the rebel's visit had created, as well as the frustration at the failure of Menchaca's filibuster. He was an associate of Morgan, who himself had ties to the Mexican Association, and given his connection to Nolan, indubitably connected to Clark as well. Over the next ten days as they made their way upriver toward the frontier outpost, Cortés had plenty of time to discuss with his countryman the prospects for revolution outside of Shaler's hearing.[44]

Governor Claiborne provided one last service, writing letters to Sibley the Indian Agent, Judge Carr, Colonel Shaumberg of the Militia, and to his cousin, Judge Richard Claiborne, introducing Shaler *but not Gutiérrez*. After turning them over to Morgan and Cortés, Claiborne could turn his full attention to something more important: the upcoming statehood of Louisiana and his own campaign for elected governor. As for the Mexican rebel, Claiborne thought he had washed his hands of him. Shaler would see him over the border and that would be the end of it. Instead, the governor had pushed him out of the arms of one group of conspirators into the waiting embrace of another.

The frontier rebels had been rocked by successive setbacks: the failure of the Menchaca filibuster, the arrest of Lieutenant Guadiana and the silencing of Father Huerta, the Spanish capture of Edmund Quirk, and the American capture of Miguel Quinn. But now at this low ebb, they would be revived by a revolutionary stimulus: a leader with credibility among the Mexicans and support among the legions of western adventurers to start an invasion of Texas. As a correspondent wrote to the *Natchez Chronicle*, the return of the Mexican rebel had fanned excitement on the frontier. "The present moment is pregnant with important events—a few weeks will unfold them."[45]

10

The Expedition Forms

IN THE LAST WEEK OF April 1812, three bedraggled Americans entered Natchitoches from Spanish Texas. It was the traders, Reuben Smith, James Patterson, and Joseph McLanahan, who had set out to Santa Fe with the avowed goal of opening up trade, but who were likely in the more nefarious service of Reuben's brother, the Missouri mining magnate and schemer John Smith T. It had been a year since the *Louisiana Gazette* had feared the men had been "butchered," but here they were, alive. Once again, it was a tale to stir outrage on the frontier.[1]

The three Americans, with one Spaniard and two slaves, had been captured on March 18, 1810. Spanish spies had read the news of their departure, and the troops in New Mexico were waiting for them. Taken to Santa Fe, they were brought into the house of the interim governor, Don Francisco Xavier de Lizana. Their papers were examined, and they were interrogated. Reuben Smith told the Spanish their goal was to settle in the territory to trade, but the Spaniards doubted them. "The sustained vain character of the first one, his air and military bearing ... makes me suspect that, far from being merchants or what they pretended to be, they are military men, subjects of great consideration, commissioned by the Congress to make some discoveries."[2]

They were certainly not commissioned by Congress, but independent and mercenary. The men were transported to Chihuahua and placed in a prison, where Patterson allegedly witnessed the execution of Father Hidalgo in July 1811. They were forced for a time to work in a mine, like convicts. Eventually released, they were required to stay in the city, where they were reduced to begging in the streets until Smith, a gunsmith, was able to find some work. An article about their capture appeared in a Veracruz newspaper and somehow made it to the United States, where Patterson's father saw it and alerted the US government, which filed a protest. They were released and made their way through Texas, arriving in Natchitoches like a bombshell amid the already fervent hostility toward the Spanish regime.[3]

When word had first leaked out about their treatment, there was talk on the frontier of an expedition to liberate them, but as we have seen, this filibuster was first suppressed, then collapsed with the desertion of José Menchaca. Now, after riling up Natchitoches with their harrowing tale on their return, the men traveled back to Missouri, seeding their story everywhere they went, arriving in June 1812 as heroes. McLanahan declared that the people of New Spain "ardently desired" free and reciprocal trade with America and "our return under more auspicious circumstances and with whatever views would be hailed by them with joy and exultation." That was exactly the news that adventurers in the West wanted to hear, and it aligned with the reports that Father Huerta had been smuggling out of Nacogdoches with the help of Edmund Quirk. The traders, upon their arrival in St. Louis, immediately began recruiting men for an expedition, likely from among those who had contemplated rescuing them before. Although the new expedition was supposedly secret, McLanahan referred to it obliquely in his letter to the governor of the territory:[4]

> The reasons Sir, which suggested to us the laudable nature of our first enterprise operate now upon us with double force. Although blindfolded as it were by tyranny we have yet seen enough to awaken enquiry and stimulate exertion . . . We think we can calculate the amount of opposition, we feel that we can justly appreciate the glowing reception we shall meet from the unfortunate, the imbruted American Spaniards . . . *The enterprise, Sir, which we contemplate undertaking* may as you will readily perceive, be attended with difficulty and danger. (emphasis added)[5]

Sentiment for a filibuster was strong and was aided by enthusiasm for settlement. These mysterious Spanish provinces were just then beginning to be known to Americans, through reports from Pike and other travelers. Texas, as one account of the era stated, "appears, from all accounts, to be really a kind of paradise," the soil "so luxuriant that it requires little or no cultivation and is enameled with the most beautiful flowers and shrubs." The author concluded that "the beauties and enjoyments of the place inspire the soul with the most delightful emotions." If all this is true, a newspaperman opined, "who would not wish to inhabit such a spot?" He answered: "Those *paper* soldiers [militia], or men similar to them, supported the fatigues and privations of a seven years war, humbled the pride of Britain, and established the independence of their country, nor have they degenerated."[6]

With McLanahan, Smith, and Patterson making a triumphant return through the West, the souls of the militia began to stir with the same fervor that had once stimulated Burr, Wilkinson, and Adair's dreams of western adventure. While it remains unclear if any of the three traders themselves returned to Texas to fight, it seems likely many of their recruits did.[7]

CHAPTER 10

Shaler and Gutiérrez Arrive

By coincidence, on the same day that the three traders left Natchitoches—April 28, 1812—William Shaler and Bernardo Gutiérrez de Lara arrived in the town on horseback, having quit the barge at Rapides, the furthest point where the river was navigable. It had been a twenty-day journey up rivers and overland, filled with more sights and adventures for the Mexican, who survived an attack by a panther and a close call with alligators while swimming across a stream.[8]

Shaler and Gutiérrez arrived at 10:00 a.m., narrowly missing the traders who had departed that morning. Natchitoches was abuzz. The men had talked openly of a filibuster, saying a mere five hundred men would suffice to create "a complete revolution." The Spanish garrison in Texas was larger than that, but the traders expected many would desert to the republican cause, as their lengthy detention in Spanish territory had exposed a restless, revolutionary spirit they claimed was pervasive there. Shaler informed Monroe about the men's arrival. "From the information I have of the character of those gentlemen, and from what I hear of their conversations here," Shaler wrote, "I should not be surprised to hear of their again entering that country, and in arms."[9]

Shaler had never considered a filibuster and was not sure how to take the idea: "If such speculations should be contrary to the policy of the U.S. it is probably time that measures should be taken to prevent them," he wrote, "for it appears that the banditti assembled on the Sabine would have succeeded if they had not been deserted by their leader, Menchaca. Such at least is the opinion here and the practicability of such a scheme is the general topic of consideration." But not everyone Shaler met thought such an enterprise could succeed or wanted it to. The merchants who had signed the proclamation to Claiborne complaining of the banditti were wary of any gathering of "desperate men." They were likely influenced by Samuel Davenport, who after all had once been a merchant of the frontier town before taking Spanish citizenship. The American Spaniard trader was in Natchitoches that day, and to Shaler, he gave the royalist perspective, reporting rebel losses in central Mexico and freshly arrived troops from Spain. "He accordingly supposes that the communications with la Vera Cruz will soon be opened again, and he speaks with confidence of quelling the insurrection entirely in the course of the ensuing summer," Shaler reported. Davenport, despite the ferment in Nacogdoches, the Casas revolt, the failed attack of Menchaca, and even the death of his partner, Barr, was still loyal, likely because the return of Spanish authority to Nacogdoches had restored the trade monopoly—and placed it back in his hands.[10]

There were, however, many within the town decidedly for the rebels. They claimed the rumors of Rayón's defeat were exaggerated, "and reported for the sole purpose of depressing the people in the internal provinces," Shaler indicated. The rebels, they asserted, had three complete armies in the field, under Rayón, Morelos, and Villagrán, as well as numerous guerillas operating against Spanish lines of communications.

They were growing in strength, this party asserted. "The royal troops are disaffected and continually deserting . . . at the distant points they are neither paid nor clothed, and the chiefs are robbing and realizing the resources of the country for their own account," Shaler wrote. Then he added what was the unspoken truth behind the American excitement: "If arms would by any means be found the revolution would be consummated in a short time."[11]

Arriving when they did, Shaler and Gutiérrez attracted immense attention. "All the leading men began to visit us with the greatest deference," Gutiérrez noted in his diary. The American agent continued to conceal his true mission, since revealing it would render impossible any transit across royalist territory in the future. Still, the men of Natchitoches suspected his purpose, and his connection to Gutiérrez was interpreted as covert support for an expedition. The president had recently sent a message to Congress that, while not calling for direct American participation in the Spanish rebellion, hinted at support of the rebels. Just as with William Stephens Smith's testimony after the Miranda expedition, this suggested a "nod-and-wink" attitude. Gutiérrez for his part likely said nothing to contradict the convenient rumor.[12]

Shaler's own activities have long been grounds for speculation among historians. There is no doubt that all Americans except the most partisan Federalists were united in support of the rebels, but what *form* that support took was another matter entirely. Monroe, in his meetings with Gutiérrez, as well as Sibley, Shaler, and Claiborne in their letters, had proposed overt support. This, along with Claiborne's intense interest in Gutiérrez and Shaler's aid in taking him to the frontier, has been frequently misinterpreted as an *intent* to enable an expedition. But that support was always contingent either on war with Spain, or in the case of Monroe's proposal (if it was even serious), on an agreement with the rebels which was never consummated.

The existing documents, including Shaler's instructions and letters to and from the frontier, show no hint of a plan to support a filibuster. Any secret conspiracy between the administration, Claiborne, and Shaler is impossible given the circumstances. Shaler was still unaware he even had a job anymore—Monroe's May 2nd letter was still months away from arriving. Shaler's insubordinate letter to Madison puts to lie any possible separate correspondence. In all of Shaler's movements since Cuba, the agent was groping his way in the darkness without orders, most of that time with the administration unaware he was even on the mainland. This precludes any possibility of coordination.[13]

As the official and private letters of all participants plainly state with no exception, the administration only supported *legitimate* government involvement under the right circumstances—war with Spain—but was strongly opposed to independent action outside of its control. Shaler asked the government for clarification. "If, as I conceive it to be the case, it does not comport with either the policy or dignity of the government of the U.S. to tolerate such private military expeditions, this point certainly requires their immediate attentions." But this attention did not come. Shaler's letter was written in May. It would be two months before he received anything from his superiors, and this letter merely responded to one he had written in *January* announcing his arrival in New Orleans. By the time Washington caught up to the reality of the filibuster, it would be far too late to stop it. Shaler himself had no civil authority to do so and would have broken his cover if he had tried.[14]

The frontiersmen rallying to the calls of Mexican rebels, the banditti, the exiled foreigners from Texas and the Missouri traders recently returned with vengeance on their mind needed no government stimulus to launch their attack. Although an expedition was still illegal, these adventurers were nonetheless emboldened. War with Spain's ally England was expected at any moment, and the declaration would surely include Spain anyway. This would clean up the legal technicality of the Neutrality Act and turn conspirators into patriots in due course. In the meantime, these men interpreted the ambiguous signs from the administration in ways convenient to their purpose. McLanahan, writing his governor, referenced Madison's message as "the admonition of our patriotic President." He had concluded in his letter, in a line almost identical from Bullard's fictitious Miranda survivor six years earlier, "we cannot permit ourselves to apprehend that the countenance and approbation of our venerated government will be withheld from an expedition."[15]

Shaler meanwhile began to meet with people in the community with an eye to obtain real intelligence on the situation in Mexico. At the same time, he endeavored to keep his ward, Gutiérrez, away from intriguers. Since Shaler moved in as a guest of Capt. Walter H. Overton at Fort Claiborne, while Gutiérrez stayed in boarding houses, this proved to be impossible. Within a few weeks of their arrival, a Frenchman, Jean Jacques Paillette, who had come to the territory in 1803 and owned a plantation two leagues downriver from Natchitoches, approached the Mexican and offered, in the name of the French government, to raise and equip four hundred men and provide $100,000 for arms and supplies to invade New Spain. It was a princely sum; Shaler at the time was debating loaning his impoverished rebel friend another $100 for expenses. The American, growing uneasy, said he was not sure if Paillette was a French agent, a Spanish one, or "a mere joke." He advised the Mexican to listen carefully to any proposals and inform him of the contents. It would not be the last outreach to Gutiérrez. Shaler, mindful of Claiborne's fears, was wary of anyone who might court the Mexican, but especially those connected with the French.[16]

Other than what he read in Gutiérrez's letter of introduction from John Graham, Shaler knew very little about the Mexican with whom he was entrusted. He no doubt learned the story of Gutiérrez's escape the year before from people he met in Natchitoches, but he quizzed the Spanish loyalist Davenport as well. The latter knew of Gutiérrez through Governor Herrera and reported that the Mexican, though a rebel, was "a person of very respectable family, character and fortune in his own country." But he was impoverished by his journey and vulnerable. Claiborne had told Shaler to abandon him at the border, but now that it came to it, the agent thought that would just empower people like Paillette. "It appeared necessary that this gentleman should

The Expedition Forms   149

be taken care of," Shaler wrote to Monroe, "for had he been left to his own resources in Orleans he must from necessity have fallen into the hands of persons who might have engaged him in views very different from those of the president." [17]

There was no doubt that Gutiérrez would one day return to the revolution, and would certainly influence Rayón and other rebel leaders, so Shaler began his diplomacy in Natchitoches, by educating Gutiérrez on American policy. He explained the views and interests of the various European countries in the Napoleonic struggle, their relations with the United States, and "the only system of policy likely to procure the untrammeled honorable independence of his country with the elevation of his own character." Shaler prided himself that he was gaining Gutiérrez's full confidence, but one suspects the Mexican—provincial but not stupid—tired of being patronized. Shaler added hopefully, "I think he will not engage in any plan whatever without my approbation."[18]

But the agent could not keep the Mexican a prisoner, and Gutiérrez, upon learning the news from Mexico, found the counseled patience difficult to follow. In early May he received word that Spanish general Joaquín de Arredondo had ordered Gutiérrez's rebel brother—as well as their mother—imprisoned. "Col. Bernard Gutiérrez is here and very uneasy," John Sibley wrote. "He is not disposed to take any steps that would meet the disapprobation of the government of the U.S. but every account from his country informs him that the blood of his friends is flowing, and he, not able to assist them in the manner he approves." Shaler reported Gutiérrez had several "very zealous friends" from his previous visit the year before, "who assure him that he is anxiously expected in the provinces, and that if he has anything favorable to communicate, the whole country will rise and open a communication with the armies." The rebel's arrival also caught the attention of the enemy. In the next week, the Spanish agents in the town sent three couriers back to Texas to report on his activities. Soon, even the commandant general in Chihuahua was anxious about the "traitor Bernardo Gutiérrez" and his "perverse ideas ... directed toward revolutionizing the kingdom." Even mere propaganda, Nemesio Salcedo warned, "would have the most fatal consequences." Gutiérrez planned exactly such a campaign, but was beginning to consider much, much more.[19]

In addition to the French proposal, the "zealous friends" included a group that sometime in early May offered five hundred men under "a leader of military skill" with two pieces of artillery and ample funds, to assemble by the Sabine and march against San Antonio. Shaler demanded to know who they were, but Gutiérrez told the agent he had given his word of honor not to betray their identities. Nonetheless, he assured Shaler that the men were Americans and "respectable." This group was likely the old Mexican Association, or some of its adherents, because the leader they would eventually choose was the Kentucky militia general, John Adair. Furthermore, Shaler would later report to Monroe that a correspondent from New Orleans had informed him that "Daniel Clark is reported to be connected with Adair." Shaler was wary, but without Claiborne's years of experience with the association—and corresponding fear of it—was merely relieved that the group was not French. As always, he wrote to Monroe for advice and waited in vain for a reply.[20]

Meanwhile, the Spanish and American attempts to dislodge the banditti in the Neutral Ground had met with only temporary success. Arresting men was one thing, successfully trying them for banditry was another. Only two of the men Magee had captured were sentenced to prison; the rest were released after denying in court what they had told the lieutenant under "punishments and threats." In June 1812, Governor Salcedo wrote to Wollstonecraft that the danger was returning. The release of the bandits meant that "peace will be altered again on the frontier, principally by the suggestions and intrigues of some fugitive revolutionists that [fled] from this quarter and others, who I am told have in object to revolutionize this country." But frightful as an attempted revolution was, Salcedo's first goal was to merely avoid economic strangulation. He thus asked the Americans to provide an escort for a legal Spanish trader, an associate of Davenport named Apolinaris de Masmela. The banditti were back and once again enforcing an economic blockade of Texas.[21]

They were also clandestinely entering the province, likely to facilitate their couriers to sympathizers in Texas. The Spanish learned of these activities through a spy: a former officer in their service now retired as a farmer, Pedro Antonio Sáenz. Having learned of the rebels' presence, Saenz slipped out of his house, telling his wife he was going hunting for food, and walked four leagues on foot to deliver a warning to Nacogdoches. He was either spotted or betrayed, because when he returned home, the rogues were waiting for him. "The bandits came to suspect that he was our agent," the Nacogdoches commander wrote. "They came to surround him in his house, and threatened him with death, which they did not commit because of the many tears and supplications of his wife."[22]

A Warning to the President

The hotbed of recruiting for the coming attack was a triangle roughly linking two Louisiana towns, Rapides and Opelousas, with Natchez, Mississippi. Natchez was the old Burr rendezvous point, perched along the river and astride a convenient road that led westward overland to Natchitoches. This made it, as it would have been for Burr, the ideal route for men coming from Mississippi, Missouri, Tennessee, or Kentucky. They could easily slip past any but the most aggressive patrols from Fort Adams, as well as avoid Baton Rouge entirely.[23]

But here, rumors of a filibuster began to spread, and it was inevitable that they would reach curious ears. A young apprentice doctor, Orramel Johnston, overheard talk of the endeavor about the same time the conspirators had approached Gutiérrez. His initial instinct was to suspect in the expedition the hallmarks of another Burr-style plot, which as a passionate supporter of Madison and the Republican Party, he opposed. He was a mere youth of nineteen, but feeling the weight of this intelligence, took pen to paper, writing to an unknown correspondent in Washington, asking him to forward a letter to the president. "It contains something of a very serious nature; the faster it is forwarded the better it is for him," he wrote. The letter he forwarded is lost, but after a visit to Natchitoches, he saw even more evidence of the conspiracy and followed up on June 12th with his own warning to Monroe. Saying that his only motive in writing was "a duty that I owe to my God and to my country," he outlined what he had heard. Johnston found suspicious both Shaler and Gutiérrez, who he said went by the title of "Spanish Ambassador," and although it was known that they had lately arrived from Washington, he wrote, "no one knows their business."[24]

"On the other hand," Johnston added (correctly guessing that the two events were connected), "there is a Gen. John Adair, a Major Welsh and a captain Glass who are now in the counties of Opelousas and Rapides busy in levying volunteers to revolutionize Mexico. They have levied to the amount of five hundred men and there is a very great prospect of their raising as many more."[25]

Johnston, a good Republican voluntarily spying in the service of his president, was torn. On the one hand, he was afraid of a new Burr expedition and what it might portend. But on the other, aware of Gutiérrez's visit to Washington, he could not rule out the notion of a secret *government* plan in the works. Was this conspiracy he had uncovered a case of treason or of patriotism? "My suspicions are tolerable strong as it relates to Bernardo and Shaler, perhaps Bernardo has obtained assistance from the United States. If he has, everything will terminate well enough in one point. But in the other point, how will it terminate? Nobody knows their designs, what they are going to do."[26]

Johnston warned the secretary of state that if this was a real threat to the country, the frontier was effectively defenseless. There was no militia available and only one hundred men at Fort Claiborne under Captains Wollstonecraft of the artillery and Overton of the infantry. Rumors of large troop movements abounded: Wilkinson coming with regular troops or an independent army forming. Most concerning to Johnston was that Captain Overton seems to have not been in on the secret, whatever it was, and was making it known that if any force came without government support, he would oppose it. Overton's ignorance suggested that "it is a very excentrick [sic] movement contrary to the orders of government." Rumor met counterrumor. Another report spreading was a story that Spain had opened up a new port in Texas for the British. If war was imminent, this then was proof of hostile intent, and the West was open to invasion. "What is to retard [the English] from marching an army to this Country and . . . [taking] possession of all Louisiana?" Was this conspiracy in fact the government's preemptive response, Johnston wondered?[27]

The sketch that emerges from the young doctor's speculations and other information makes it clear that Adair, the old Burr conspirator who had admitted to Madison that he was still in the confidence of many Burrites, was at this stage raising a private force for a filibuster, using networks of sympathetic current and former army officers, to rendezvous with the existing group of adventurers put together in Natchitoches and the Neutral Ground by the Texas exiles. They would be joined by any volunteers coming south from Missouri, where the Santa Fe traders—and likely John Smith T—were promoting the cause. Adair traveled to Opelousas and coordinated with Capt. William Swan, a deputy quartermaster general. He was the same officer who had taken over Josiah Taylor's role when he allegedly died, and who likely helped conceal the subterfuge. Another man, a Mr. Ward, was ascending the Red River with two large barges loaded with arms.[28]

Stopping individual recruits was impossible, but there were official efforts to frustrate the filibuster. Captain Wollstonecraft, who was being replaced by Overton, was scheduled to depart the fort in August. When he did, he took with him to New Orleans all but two of Fort Claiborne's cannon and nearly six hundred small arms. "Indeed, I fear for this garrison from these men . . . [who] may probably attempt to supply themselves with what it contains," Wollstonecraft wrote. "[It] is principally from that fear" that he had moved the cannon away.[29]

Orramel Johnston's letters of warning were far too late, and they could change nothing, even if they were ever read expeditiously, which it is doubtful they were. He was a nineteen-year-old unknown, and writing to the president and secretary of state was presumptuous to say the least. But whereas he had been eager to inform on the expedition, Orramel had an older brother with an entirely different outlook. Josiah Stoddard Johnston *was* a somebody—he had served as a member of the Orleans Territorial Legislature from 1805 to 1807. He was far more politically experienced and savvy. While Orramel had been a mere teenager in the Burr affair, Josiah knew many of its participants well. As the legislator representing Rapides Parish for seven years, he was the most influential person in a community in which the second was Reuben Kemper.[30]

Josiah Stoddard Johnston was in fact personally involved in the very secret machinations that had so concerned his younger brother. He had become General Adair's chief deputy, organizing things in Rapides while Adair did so in Natchez and Swan did likewise in Opelousas. Josiah likely calmed his naïve brother by revealing his own role, and this had a powerful influence on him. The skeptic Orramel would ultimately join the expedition he had so feared, alongside another brother, Darius. Thus did pro-Madison Republicans join forces to fight side by side with Burrite forces hostile to the administration, marching alongside the rogue banditti, who would serve under a man who had persecuted and even tortured them. Indeed, the men who would make up this little filibuster army were nothing if not diverse in background and outlook. Whatever cause for which they thought they were marching, Orramel and Darius Johnston, like so many men on the frontier, would be swept up in a growing wave toward Mexico.[31]

Gutiérrez Recruits

William Shaler's attempts to keep Gutiérrez away from intriguers were ultimately doomed, but the American agent could not abandon him, since the blacksmith from Revilla was the only representative of Mexican rebel forces in the United States. In June 1812, Shaler drafted notes for a letter from Gutiérrez to the Mexican rebel commander Rayón, which he hoped to send through Bernardo's network in northern Mexico. It was a risky move to involve himself directly, and the letter was probably never sent for that reason, but its contents show the American agent's outlook toward the revolution. Shaler regaled Rayón with accounts of American military stores and the ability to "maintain a foreign war." Most importantly, the people were eagerly behind the Mexican cause. Shaler wrote, in words penned for Gutiérrez, "Amongst all classes I observe a great enthusiasm for our cause, which they call their own, and only wait the signal of their government to fly to our aid. They say that we should unite and expel all European domination from the American Continent."[32]

Shaler, like nearly everyone in America, expected that war with England would necessarily involve Spain as well and open up the dam of enthusiastic volunteers for a Mexican expedition. For this reason, he had counseled Gutiérrez to be patient. Better to await an opportunity for a legal invasion than launch a preemptive—and *illegal*—one. This is not what the Mexican wanted to hear. Despite telling Shaler he would follow his counsel and do nothing that was contrary to US interests, by June, he was in league with Adair and others in a conspiracy to organize a filibuster into Texas. Gutiérrez tried to conceal his machinations from the agent, but Natchitoches was a small town, and within a month of their arrival, Shaler had learned that the talk of an invasion of Spanish territory was far from idle. As he wrote to Washington, "I [am convinced] that there are three different expeditions forming to enter the neighboring provinces. The first will consist of all the idlers on this frontier in number from 300 to 500 men; 2 some adventurers in the Mississippi Territory have formed the same plan, their form will be more respectable in its composition and will consist of about 500 persons. 3 in Upper Louisiana [Missouri] I am informed that still more respectable in composition and numbers will be raised under the auspices of the 3 gentlemen lately returned through here from Chihuahua."[33]

His numbers were inflated, but his suspicions were correct and corresponded to the three groups generally promoting the expedition: the first being the conspiracy in Natchitoches that had been built up by the Texas exiles Quinn and Quirk, and which had supported the banditti; the second being the Mexican Association remnants and the adherents that Adair and Reuben Kemper were recruiting in Natchez and Rapides; and the third being the recently returned Santa Fe traders aligned with John Smith T. Shaler thought that the three groups, with common goals, would combine once they arrived in the Neutral Ground. He informed Monroe that a man from

Tennessee had arrived from Natchez on June 7th and had met with Gutiérrez for some hours, returning the next day. It was Captain Swan, but tellingly, Shaler was unaware of his rank, suggesting he traveled as a civilian.[34]

The agent feared he was losing control of Bernardo. "I have reason to believe that the arrangement is made for him to join the expedition after they are assembled on the other side of the Sabine," he wrote to Washington. Gutiérrez was in fact already sending couriers into Texas, but he told Shaler these were merely to establish contact with the rebel armies deep within Mexico, and the agent even agreed to submit notes for the rebels to assure them of America's goodwill, in keeping with his instructions.[35]

The Mexican was playing a double game with Shaler, meeting behind his back, possibly even exploiting a period of prolonged illness experienced by the agent. Many on the frontier suspected that Shaler was a representative of the government in some manner related to New Spain, but with what orders, they knew not. Still, he made his hostility to an American filibuster known, and as a result, he wrote Monroe, "All such information is carefully kept from me." Shaler, realizing his ward had gone rogue, now discovered a "weakness of mind" in the Mexican, who sometimes indulged himself "in the most ridiculous flights of vanity." Gutiérrez at one point had Shaler draw up for him a plan for a provisional government, as if he were to be the ruler of all Mexico, and when he heard that General Rayón had set up his own, Shaler wrote, "Nothing can exceed the mortification he expresses. . . . He declares that it cannot be true." Gutiérrez was still demanding money too, which Shaler continued to provide from his own funds, hoping that he might one day be reimbursed. In truth, the agent could not turn him loose, for fear of losing what little sway he still had. "I have not however altered my conduct towards him in the least," Shaler wrote, "and I even intend to suffer myself to be deceived so far as to advance him a small sum of money if he requires it."[36]

Gutiérrez was now the nominal head of the filibuster, though he was not its mastermind. It was an organic thing with many fathers and attracted men to it by magnetism. The Mexican rebel, however, gave the effort something around which to coalesce and imbued it with legitimacy. Through him, the conspiracy had a political leader, if not yet a military one. It was gaining men and even several pieces of small artillery, which arrived in Natchitoches from New Orleans in early July. It is unclear from whence these came, but they were almost certainly forwarded by the Mexican Association, possibly through militia connections.[37]

Rebel Exile and Loyalist Commander

Gutiérrez also won an important ally in the French Creole exile from Spanish Texas, Bernard Despallier. Upon hearing of the Mexican revolutionary's arrival, the man who had briefly been second in command of a Texas frontier post, married the daughter of a rebellious Tejano, and dreamed of a colony of French Creoles on Spanish soil became a partner in rebellion. Fluent in French, Spanish, and English, and a long-standing resident of Rapides, he was the perfect recruiter of the many adventurers on the frontier and could likewise tap connections deep within Texas as well. Though Gutiérrez had a sliver of legitimacy from the revolution within Nuevo Santander, he was poorly known in Texas. Despallier knew civilians and soldiers alike in Nacogdoches and Trinidad, and now, to aid Gutiérrez, he wrote a series of letters arguing for revolution and for the people of Nacogdoches to rally around the cause.[38]

One of these—possibly smuggled into Texas via his contacts among the Indian tribes—was addressed to the captain of the first company of the detachment of Nacogdoches, but which was really meant for the people of Texas. It outlined twelve reasons why the Creoles of the town should follow Gutiérrez, who had "sacrificed everything for the benefit of the grandest and most just cause in the Hemisphere of Columbus." Despallier claimed aid had been promised from both the United States and nations of Europe and that an American declaration of war against Spain was imminent. The men of the United States who would march with Gutiérrez would do so with no ulterior motive but to help their fellow men achieve their freedom. Gutiérrez contributed pamphlets of his own to the effort.[39]

Far surpassing either of these letters, however, were the words of Gutiérrez's partner in Philadelphia, José Alvarez de Toledo. He had given to his colleague a message to the people of Mexico called "The Friend of Man." This powerful message of revolution called on the "Sons of Montezuma" to "shake off the barbarous and ignominious yoke." He included a Catholicized version of American revolutionary doctrine: man had been given liberty by God, and reason to use it; therefore the people should create their own government. These pamphlets were not intended to be sent merely in small groups. On May 25th, Gutiérrez noted in his diary that he visited a print shop "to see printed a thousand copies of the proclamation." It was likely funded by the Frenchman Paillet.[40]

The Spanish were aware of much of this from spies in Natchitoches. Masmela, Davenport's associate, reported that as soon as any newcomer came to Natchitoches, Despallier "tries to seduce him with stories and lies" on behalf of Gutiérrez. "It seems they bring seductive proclamations printed in the North, and I know for a fact that they are going about recruiting individuals to secretly conduct letters" to Texas, he wrote. "This news should cause you to be very vigilant with those traveling from here in order to intercept anything they might bring, watching particularly for the relatives of Espallier's [sic] wife, his friends, and the Indians who come from here."[41]

The man to whom this letter was addressed was a Spanish officer who had been placed in the key position of garrison commander of Nacogdoches after the Spanish reasserted their authority there in mid-1811. Lt. Col. Bernardino Montero was a loyalist through and through. Informed about Gutiérrez and Despallier's efforts, he set his watch. "For my part, I have taken as many precautions as I have been capable of to prevent the circulation of seditious papers," he wrote to Salcedo, vowing to stop these efforts to "disturb our repose with the depraved goal of placing us in a state of revolution." Montero was contemptuous of republics. Revolution, he declared, would make Spaniards "enslaved to a nation without government or religion, like that of America." He may even have employed a ruse suggested by Masmela: sending double agents to Natchitoches pretending to support the rebellion while seeking to undermine it. The spy cautioned not to send men from pro-trade Nacogdoches, "because of the little confidence that can be placed in them."[42]

Thus Montero was waiting like a spider when Gutiérrez and Despallier's agent, a Spanish deserter named José Francisco Banegas, slipped into Nacogdoches. Banegas hid out in the home of a former comrade in the garrison and began to distribute the propaganda secretly around the town. But on June 27th, he was captured by three of Montero's soldiers with dozens of booklets and pamphlets, including "The Friend of Man." He was condemned to die, and the remaining pamphlets were publicly burned. In San Antonio, Governor Salcedo responded to these incursions by reminding the people of their duty. In an address prepared for "The Veteran Troops on Duty in this Province," he reminded the people that they had once rebelled in support of Casas and had been pardoned for it by royal decree. Their penance was to fight against revolutionary intrigues. The soldiers who had captured Banegas had shown the example and were each given a medal.[43]

Some propaganda still got through, both into Texas and Nuevo Santander. In the latter province, one of Gutiérrez's agents traveled in the guise of an Indian innocently grazing his sheep, but wherever he went, he spread the pamphlets. Salcedo's first news of these revolutionary incursions was a report from another Spanish officer, Captain Bustamante, who informed him that the otherwise poorly educated Indians of the Rio Grande Valley were "questioning the right of the King over the people, and asserting the right of self-government, and protesting love of liberty and freedom."[44]

Finding a Commander

On May 7th, a "magnificent banquet" was held at Fort Claiborne in honor of Gutiérrez. The garrison included many men sympathetic to the Burrite cause of revolutionizing Mexico with American arms. Among them was Capt. Francis Newman, the same soldier married to a young woman from Texas who had been interrogated by Claiborne about his letters to his Spanish uncle. But other officers, including certainly Captain Wollstonecraft and possibly his replacement Overton, were opposed to any illegal enterprise should war not be declared on Spain. Nonetheless, an expedition was beginning to coalesce, and as Bernardo Gutiérrez spoke of his hopes for revolution and called to mind the parallels between the

Mexican struggle and the one of 1776, Lt. Augustus Magee, if he was in attendance, no doubt listened with profound interest.[45]

The two may have first met a week before, when Gutiérrez was introduced to the officers of the garrison, and over the next few weeks, they became better acquainted. William Shaler met Magee too, and would later write of him as being of "a very commanding appearance as an officer, and of prepossessing manners. He passes for one of the best-informed officers of his age in the American army."[46]

The conspiracy that would become known as the *Gutiérrez-Magee Expedition* had, as we have seen, predated the arrival of either Gutiérrez or Magee on the frontier. But the collection of adventurers that was gathering could not succeed without leaders. Men from Natchitoches to Knoxville had begged Gutiérrez to launch an invasion the year before. Now he was back and embracing the gathering armed force that providence itself seemed to be placing in his hands. His propaganda was also introducing him to long-suffering Tejano rebels looking for a savior to help them reenter the revolutionary fray.[47]

But the American frontiersmen would never consent to being led by him in battle, especially after the Menchaca fiasco. He had no martial experience and could speak little English. To attract an army of Americans, Gutiérrez needed to find an American commander: a military man, someone who could organize, train, and manage an army in the field. The first choice of everyone on the frontier had been General Adair and he was an early convert—Orramel Johnston's warning to the president places Adair well-established in the conspiracy within a month of Gutiérrez's return to Natchitoches in the spring of 1812.

Gutiérrez, who had almost certainly met Adair during his sojourn through the West the year before, reached out to the general through a seemingly unusual intermediary to visit with the slave-owning Adair: a free Frenchman of color named Pedro Girard. But Girard was a possible veteran of the Burr conspiracy, had been at one point in the employ of General Wilkinson, and possibly knew Adair. In July, Girard traveled to Rapides to meet with the Kentuckian. The town was the latest home of the Kemper brothers, with whom Adair was probably already discussing the expedition. But the general was absent when the man arrived. Gun shy of any action that could once again land him in legal troubles, he was returning from a trip to Natchez "in order to know what the disposition of [the United States] Government [was] for our republic," according to Girard. In his stead, Adair's aide, Col. Josiah Stoddard Johnston, posed six questions for Girard to forward to Gutiérrez. They centered on Adair's standing vis-à-vis Gutiérrez and his government, and how many troops would be required. On this last point, the Americans made it clear they would not go small.[48]

"The intent of the General and of Colonel Johnson [sic] are that he wishes to enter with a respectable force, or that he will not take any command; that he expects to have 2,000 men enlisted here at the beginning of November," Girard wrote. "Colonel Johnson is of the opinion that Your Excellency does not begin his operations before the return of the General from Natchez." Then in a blow to Gutiérrez's pride, Girard informed the Mexican, "Colonel Johnson said to me that in the General taking the command that Your Excellency would not have anything to do with it; that the General would name his agents to supply his troops, as also he would name the people necessary for the offices."[49]

These conditions were too much and would have insulted any Mexican with half the pride Gutiérrez possessed. Adair's troop numbers were consistent with previous variants of the Burr conspiracy and were commonly accepted on the frontier. But they were fanciful without overt US government backing, especially with the prospect of war against England looming and all men needed. But from Gutiérrez's perspective, the invasion did not *need* thousands. The prospects might look daunting in Natchez, but on the frontier, Spain never looked weaker. The thousand Spanish soldiers in Texas were reportedly rife with rebel sentiment, many of them having supported the Casas coup, and now holding Gutiérrez's propaganda in their hands. The clock was ticking, and at a much faster speed than Adair's conservative timetable. Four months was too long to wait—a commander was needed immediately.

Fortunately, one had already been recruited. Adair envisioned this officer would organize things on the frontier with the Mexican before the general, with his force, would march down from Rapides. Though Gutiérrez would never cut off Adair entirely, should his promise of a vast host materialize, he now decided to move forward with the man at hand: the American lieutenant and scourge of the Neutral Ground, Augustus Magee.

11

Racing toward War

BY THE SUMMER OF 1812, Augustus Magee had served in the army for three years, but the only enemies he had fought had been his fellow Americans. He had been ambushed and humiliated by the banditti, then sent to suppress them on two successive occasions. While at Fort Adams, he was in the reserve behind the force that had occupied West Florida, snatching it away from the rebels there. More and more, it became apparent that the role of a soldier on the frontier in times of peace was more constabulary than martial. The appalling and unhealthy camps and the poor pay likely added to his disenchantment. Still, there was hope for those in the profession of arms. Before the summer was over, the United States would initiate conflict with Great Britain, the nation Magee's father had fought as a privateer thirty years before. This was a road to martial glory, and for Magee, a rare and valuable West Pointer in the midst of a dramatic expansion of the military, it seemed to bode well for his future rise. But it was not to be.[1]

In May 1811, General Wilkinson had recommended Magee for promotion, stating that his "conduct promised to do honor to his profession." The general had barely met Magee, if at all; he likely endorsed the promotion solely on the word of his trusted subordinate Pike, who had praised the young officer in dispatches. Given this support, Magee's chances must have seemed good. But in early 1812, he learned that his promotion had been unexpectedly rejected by Secretary of War William Eustis.[2]

The evidence strongly suggests *politics* as the most likely reason for Magee's rejection. Augustus Magee himself was not overtly political, but was no doubt found guilty by association. His late father was almost certainly a Federalist by virtue of wealth and mercantile profession, but it was Magee's relative and patron, T. H. Perkins, who waved the banner of Federal opposition to the Jeffersonian Republicans frequently, defiantly, and obnoxiously. While Augustus Magee was studying at West Point in 1808, Perkins worked conspicuously against Madison's election, and he antagonized the new president in 1810 when he led the official escort through Boston for the British minister whom Madison had spurned.[3]

On March 31, 1811, Perkins led a meeting in Boston's Faneuil Hall that adopted resolutions denouncing the Republicans. "You are soon to have no commerce but on land; no fisheries but in your rivers and ponds," the document stated. "You now obey the commands of the enemy of the human race, Bonapart; these commands are sent to you through the proud tyrannical, slave holding PLANTERS of your Southern States." Madison was not mentioned by name, but the allusion could not be missed. The Republican response shouted, "Treason Detected!" and it was obvious to whom the crime was attributable: Perkins, as the moderator of the meeting, was the only person listed by name on the Federalist broadside. All of this transpired a month and a half before Magee's promotion was forwarded to Washington, where it sat on the desk of William Eustis, Madison's new secretary of war, a fellow Bostonian, and a political enemy of Perkins. The merchant prince had become for his nephew-in-law more albatross than patron.[4]

Magee's "sole object . . . as far as I am able to judge is military fame," Shaler would write. No doubt he looked with admiration at his mentor, Pike, who at a young age had written his name into the eternal lore of his nation. "The field of action is the sphere for young men," Pike once wrote in a sentiment he had doubtless shared with Magee, "where they hope and at least aspire to gather laurels of renown, to smooth the decline of age; or a glorious death."[5]

Rejected by America, Magee would seek fame and fortune elsewhere. He was giving up a lot; by all accounts, he was a competent and capable officer, and not only part of the moneyed elite of the new nation, but also of the intellectual one, courtesy of his time at Phillips Exeter. Though there was hope of redemption in the war to come, it was not enough to hold the young lieutenant with injured pride—at least not when he had an alternative pathway to martial glory calling to him from the south, the Mexican Revolutionary Army.

The Youth Becomes a Rebel

That Magee ultimately took such a course is extraordinary. He was the only *serving* officer of the US Army who joined a filibustering expedition during the first part of the nineteenth century. The details of how the expedition recruited the young lieutenant from a wealthy Boston family to join as its commander remain obscure, but there was no shortage of pro-filibuster influences to seduce Augustus Magee. Burrite elements were present in spades in Forts Adams and Claiborne. In 1808, John Ellis, a West Florida associate of the Kempers, had reportedly stated, "That he usually visited the American officers [at Fort Adams] and that their conversations usually were concerning the taking of the fort at Baton Rouge." After that fort had fallen two years later, officers on the frontier still had visions of other Spanish conquests, as was shown by the case of Captain Newman at Fort Claiborne, who was likely plotting with the family of his Tejana wife to revolutionize her homeland in November 1809.[6]

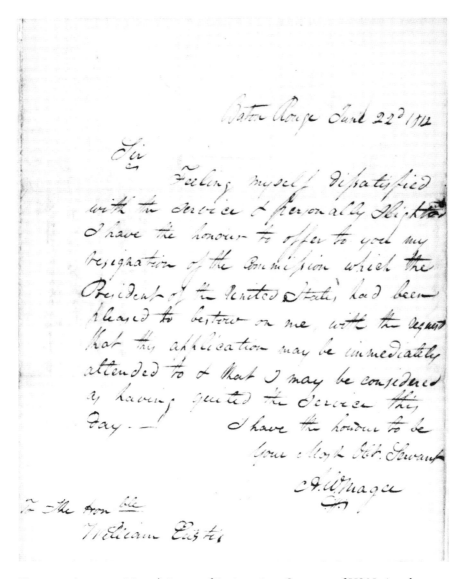

Figure 6. Augustus Magee's Letter of Resignation. Courtesy of US National Archives.

The most likely source of Magee's recruitment was a fellow officer he had served alongside in the Fort Adams artillery regiment, William Murray. It was he who had been brought in early 1806 to meet with Lewis Kerr of the Mexican Association, who had asked, "Is Murray one of us?" "Yes, by God, he is one of us!" had been the reply of Josiah Taylor, who had purportedly died but was now alive and well, prowling the frontier with the banditti, and who was no doubt tapping his old connections, including the artillery officer he had brought to Kerr six years before. Murray, of course, had been more than just any Burr recruit. An anonymous Spanish spy had reported, "Lieutenant Murray has received letters on [Burr's plans], which he does not wish to communicate to any person, although Colonel Cushing has requested him to do so. He has only permitted two of his friends, officers, to read one paragraph in which he was offered an important position." Coming eight months after his meetings with the Mexican Association, it is likely that these letters came from Kerr.[7]

After his recruitment into the nefarious organization became public, Murray had been transported to Washington, DC, to stand trial for his role in the affair. Like Adair, he avoided conviction, and despite his promotion a year after the trial, he resigned from the army in October 1809, took up the legal profession, and settled in Natchitoches. It is unknown exactly when Magee arrived, but the officer likely served alongside him for a short time in the fall of that year. At any rate, Magee's duties took him to Fort Claiborne in Natchitoches frequently enough, giving him ample occasion to visit and strengthen his relationship with his fellow artillerist. That they were close is clear: Murray ultimately gave what was the nearest expression of friendship one man could give another in the early nineteenth century—he served as Magee's second in a duel. When a quarrel with a Frenchman led to a contest of honor, Magee chose Murray to stand by his side. In the fight, Magee lost his pinky finger but killed the other man with "a heavy blow of his sword." Murray had stood by Magee then, so it is natural the older man would have heavily influenced the young lieutenant.[8]

The secretive nature of the Mexican Association precludes a full understanding of how it operated after the Burr affair. Did it remain fully intact, functioning as it had in 1806, or break into a loose affiliation of men merely joined by a common cause and infrequent but powerful personal ties like Murray, Taylor, and the Kempers? Some structure did support rebels in West Florida, and the Mobile Society is another clue, but these are tantalizing hints, not proof of the organization's tentacles. A court would never convict based on such evidence—which was precisely the point. These traces, both circumstantial and documented, do suggest there was an organized hand promoting filibuster efforts, and that the attack on Texas was coordinated, planned, and directed by men independent of the US government.

In the first place, the strategic vision, as described in 1806 to the Kempers, Murray, and Ensign Small, and recorded by them (in separate testimonies given in ignorance of each other) was consistent with the goals of the later expedition: the filibuster was never designed to merely invade and detach Texas, but to use that province as a springboard for future invasions into Mexico. As Murray's testimony and the West Florida experience showed, neither was annexation to the United States desired, unless it came at a steep price which amply rewarded the men who had hazarded their lives and fortunes in the enterprise. The Mexican Association wanted to open Mexico for trade on terms favorable to its commercial leaders. Merely extending

American title to Texas simply pushed the wall of mercantilism further south—it did not eliminate it and it certainly offered no *exclusivity* to the men who funded the effort. The volunteer with the musket may have desired Texas land, but the Mexican Association wanted Mexican *silver*, which they knew was unavailable in Texas. Pushing forth beyond the Rio Grande was a requirement of the invasion.[9]

In the second place, the roster of the expedition which was lining up behind Augustus Magee and Bernardo Gutiérrez would include 1806 recruits—Murray, Taylor, and Samuel Kemper—as well as tangentially connected men like Samuel D. Forsyth. These, along with two other men, would be the senior officers of the filibuster to come. Adair, reprising the role he had been promised by Wilkinson in 1806, was to be the overall commander for the venture, and though he never came to the battlefield himself in the end, the Kentuckian established a sort of base of operations in Natchez, the old Burrite mecca, alongside Reuben Kemper. Crucially, there is no evidence the Kentuckian Adair and Mississippian Kemper had even met during the original Burr affair, further suggesting their joining of efforts was encouraged by a third party who knew them both—Clark being the most likely candidate, since Shaler's sources connected him to Adair.[10]

The Kentucky militia general had probably never met young Augustus Magee either, but through Murray or some other intermediary had assented to his taking the initial command of the gathering forces. The lieutenant, having led two incursions into the Neutral Ground and established a working rapport with the pro-revolutionary Nacogdoches officer, José Maria Guadiana, must have seemed the perfect addition to the expedition, and the ideal interim commander—at least until Adair finally descended from Mount Olympus to lead the venture.

Magee, then still attached to Fort Claiborne, went behind his commander Wollstonecraft's back, and while at Fort Adams on June 22, 1812, he sat down and took up a pen and paper to write out his letter of resignation from the US Army. With his brothers engaged in distant voyages in Perkins's ships, his mother and sisters in far-away Boston, and he himself in a miserable outpost with little hope of advancement in the US Army, Magee was going to plot a new course for himself that no politician in Washington could derail. "Feeling myself dissatisfied with the service and personally slighted," he wrote, "I have the honor to offer to you my resignation of the commission which the President of the United States had been so pleased to bestow upon me."[11]

In this act, Magee deceived his superiors. The resignation was submitted not through any officer in his own chain of command but through Col. Joseph Constant, who was neither from Magee's permanent post (Fort Adams) nor his temporary post (Fort Claiborne); nor was he even in the same combat arm as Magee (he was the newly appointed Commander of the 3rd Regiment of Infantry, whereas Magee was an artillerist). By the time Captain Wollstonecraft would learn Magee had resigned, the young lieutenant was already outside the United States at the head of a rebel army. The English-born officer was apoplectic: "Magee, my lieutenant at present as I learn is the leader [of the expedition]," he wrote in a letter that would announce to the war department the first news of the filibuster entering Texas. He added as a postscript: "If this young man's [resignation] has not been accepted it would be well that you should proclaim [him] a deserter." Then, knowing nothing of Constant's intervention, he testily asked, "Who gave him his furlough?"[12]

Magee had already been covertly working on his scheme even before his resignation. A month before he put pen to paper, he had met with representatives of the Neutral Ground banditti. These were men he had suppressed—and in some cases even tortured—and it must have been a tense and eventful gathering where these former enemies buried the hatchet and agreed to unite their causes. Recruits were told to meet on June 14th at a specific rendezvous point in the Neutral Ground: Crow's ferry, where the banditti had captured Zambrano. This allowed the army to filter past Natchitoches in small groups, only concentrating once they were outside the grasp of US authority, a trick probably learned from the failure of Smith T's filibuster.[13] As one government official put it, "Notwithstanding the officers of the United States were vigilant in preventing troops from marching from Louisiana to make war in Mexico, yet the affair was so well managed, that although it was known that the enterprise was on foot, it was extraordinary to see two of those engaged in it together at any one time."[14]

After completing this task, Magee ventured to New Orleans to procure supplies and enlist "a number of young men, mostly dare-devil fellows who could be easily induced into any kind of adventure," and these recruits were given the rendezvous location. He likely also arranged supplies on this trip. If Murray indeed recruited the disgruntled officer, it seems plausible he also traveled with him and introduced him to the Mexican Association and its mercantile backers. The dream of 1806, "to use all means and to aid and assist in effecting the emancipation of Mexico and Peru," was at last coming to fruition.[15]

The General Returns

While Magee recruited, the great schemer, Gen. James Wilkinson, was at last nearing Orleans Territory on his return from Washington. The court-martial had found him not guilty in the appalling deaths of his troops from disease. Congress had at last declared war on England on June 18th, and Wilkinson was urgently needed in New Orleans to prepare the city for war. As the filibusters began making their way to Texas, the general was sailing slowly up the Mississippi River from its mouth to the city.

Wilkinson's first inclination upon hearing of the filibuster was to exploit it, not by joining it but by following it up, possibly seizing Texas from the filibusters after they had expelled the Spanish, just as had happened in West Florida. He asked the secretary of war if this was not the chance "if we should not have too much work on our hands, [to] give us a fair opportunity to extend our occupancies to our western limits the Rio Grande?" However, receiving no encouragement from the administration, he would soon think better of the idea. Not long afterward, a representative of Gutiérrez arrived seeking to lure the scheming general into the venture. Perhaps the Mexican rebel hoped that Wilkinson could undertake what he had failed to do in 1806. Reaching out to him was dangerous, however, if it incited the general to decisive action to suppress the filibuster. Gutiérrez evidently judged the risk worth taking and once again dispatched his trusted agent, Girard. The free Frenchman of color was known to the general, having been in Wilkinson's cryptic words one of "my ancient 'employees.'" Finding the general's ship becalmed on the Mississippi below the city, Girard boarded and handed him a letter from Gutiérrez, which read:[16]

> Natchitoches 16 July 1812
> Although I have not the honor of a personal acquaintance with you, yet I know by reputation the noble, great & high qualities of your great soul, the greatness of which have made you for a long time past favorable to our glorious and just independence.
> This encourages me to address you, believing that you will contribute with all your influence and power to favor the most just & greatest of causes which ever have been given rise to in this hemisphere, being interested in it the most sacred rights of humanity and the greatest interests of civilized nations.[17]

Gutiérrez revealed the full plans for a filibuster into Texas, giving Wilkinson information he had never shared with Shaler and requesting support. There was no hiding anymore. The rebel was asking Wilkinson to adopt a variant of the policy Monroe had once suggested, but without Monroe's hint of territory in exchange. Wilkinson reported this to the secretary of war. "In sum," the general wrote, "Mr. B. wishes to learn from me the disposition of the government and also my own dispositions & purposes, with respect to the Mexican conflicts. He wishes to get them and ammunition from me. He wishes to know what might be the feelings of the government in relation to the expedition they are projecting."[18]

Girard told the general that the Mexican had a small force already organized, and expected two thousand more men from Kentucky, Tennessee, and Orleans Territory. Wilkinson dismissed this as fantasy: "I have no clear evidence that they have as yet embodied two hundred," he said, accurately assessing the filibuster's strength. Girard admitted the conspirators had consulted Adair about taking command, but in Wilkinson's words, the Kentuckian "was undetermined and it appeared [is] waiting events." The general now possessed the information he needed to stop the filibuster. That he did not do so was not because he wanted it to succeed. Rather, he was dismissive of the whole affair and said additional information from Girard was "scarcely worth the repetitions because [it is] not quite creditable." He thought the force too small to be worth his time to suppress, but he did state his opposition. His answer must have been a blow to the surprised Girard.[19]

"I did not hesitate to reply, that . . . the expedition [was] not only unauthorized by, but in opposition to the dispositions of the government," Wilkinson wrote, "that whatever might be the governmental or national sympathy, a scale of discretion and justice governed the conduct of the executive departments; and that no illegal assembly of the citizens of the U.S." would be tolerated. As a sop, Wilkinson gave a message for Girard to pass to Gutiérrez: "Tell him to have patience, to wait the maturation of the fruit, to trust in the justice of God, to believe in my devotion to the liberty of mankind, and to merit the friendship and protection of my country, by respecting its government and supporting its laws."[20]

That the rebel was making proposals to the senior US general in opposition to the advice of both the US special agent on the scene and the Orleans Territorial governor suggests two possibilities: either he hoped the administration had grown warmer to the cause in light of the conflict with England or he hoped Wilkinson would aid it himself despite official neutrality. Perhaps this approach was proposed by Girard or others who had known Wilkinson from the Burr days, but the old schemer was more pragmatic, cautious, and—after two courts-martial—on a much shorter leash than he had been on back then.

Wilkinson thought the raid Quixotic but promised to Washington that he would take tough action to stop it: "It is my intention to instruct Captain Overton who is, I understand a good officer and an excellent man to put an end to the trouble in that quarter by laying hold of and putting in custody Lt. Magee & the leaders of the meditated enterprise, and a singular demonstration of the disposition of the government." But Wilkinson was already too late. Even before his meeting with Girard, Magee's force had crossed the border into Texas.[21]

A Gathering of Adventurers

Rogues and the respectable alike came to the frontier from all quarters. One of them, Warren D. C. Hall, would recall nearly forty years later, "Many of the most respectable men joined the expedition from a spirit of chivalry & conceiving in so doing they were embracing the interest of humanity in aiding an oppressed people who had long groaned under the yoke of Spanish tiranny [sic] in their struggles for liberty." A fictional account, but based on a detailed firsthand manuscript of the author's father, preserves the spirit of the moment, when adventurers with little understanding of what they were signing up for rushed to the Neutral Ground with a cavalier attitude toward the perils that they faced:[22] "We left New Orleans . . . a band of jolly adventurers with rainbow hues of good times, and frolic luring us on, and we kept our spirits up with joke, *repartee,* tricks and games playing . . . until wearying with them, we settled down to soberness of thought, and then began to ask ourselves whither our journey tended."[23]

Certainly not all recruits to the cause were such innocent youths. On the night of August 5, 1812, a group of about twenty to twenty-five "desperadoes" were passing four miles above Baton Rouge on their way to Natchitoches. They were led by "Little John" McFarlan, the former resident of Spanish Nacogdoches who had been captured among the smugglers in 1808. He had apparently been sentenced to death by the Spaniards but was pardoned and exiled to the United States, where he appears in the 1810 census of Natchitoches. He traveled, possibly to Natchez to collect recruits, and was hurrying to join in the filibuster.[24]

The group had crossed the Mississippi, onto the lands of a Colonel Haverey on the west bank, where they stole some corn. Confronted by the landowner's son, the intruders "threatened him and said they would have a supply of fowls [too]," Captain Wollstonecraft would report. After an argument, one of the men pulled a weapon and shot the young man in the head. They then beat the wounded man and fled with their stolen food. At last report, the youth was not expected to survive. Captain Wollstonecraft, now at Fort Adams, sent out soldiers who ran into the returning militia. "The report just now is that the militia have fallen in with them and had an engagement, that 8 are kill'd and several wounded, also two of the militia wounded," he wrote. McFarlan and the rest escaped and continued on their journey to the Neutral Ground.[25]

In Natchitoches in mid-July, William Shaler finally received his long-awaited reply from Monroe, forwarded from New Orleans. It had been written in May and the last letter of his own that Monroe referenced was from February 4th. This five-month lag in their correspondence obliterated any hope of effectively coordinating a coherent government policy toward the filibuster. Since he had first heard of the conspiracy, Shaler had been writing Monroe, reporting every detail he learned, seeking guidance in vain. This was his first response from the government since before he had left Cuba, and the last news it responded to was from before Shaler had even met Gutiérrez.[26]

Monroe, in Washington, was getting hints of a conspiracy from Sibley and Claiborne as well, but the latter had been writing similar letters since the Burr expedition six years before, and his latest accounts contained nothing more definitive. Shaler's initial letters had been similarly vague, but upon receiving the May 2nd letter the agent wrote another, giving more information of the plan. Though the conspirators were deliberately hiding information from him, Shaler gave what details he could, adding with a note of resignation to the inevitable: "Sir, it appears to me obvious that if it is not stopped here (which does not at present seem likely) it is desirable that its sweep beyond the Sabine should be complete and which in my judgment can hardly fail if it is conducted with common prudence and address. *I shall therefore endeavor to profit by its consequences*, and proceed to my destination as soon as there appears to be a shadow of safety" (emphasis added).[27]

Monroe received the letter and this time replied immediately, on September 1st. He reminded Shaler that the conspiracy was a violation of the Neutrality Act, but recognizing that his agent had no legal standing to stop it, simply told him, "It will be proper for you to discountenance the measure." Then he promised to write Shaler in more detail on the subject. He never did, and in fact did not send another letter to his agent for two more months. It would have availed nothing if he had, for even this first letter would arrive three months *after* the expedition had already started.[28]

Shaler continued firing off letters to Monroe, who for his part was much more focused on his own government's plans to invade Canada than he was on those of some of its citizens to invade Mexico. Until the delayed letters would arrive, the agent was paralyzed by indecision. While frontiersmen organizing the expedition might claim to interpret the president's wishes from his messages to Congress, Shaler had to know what the president *really* wanted. If Madison secretly supported a filibuster, Shaler would be frustrating the president by trying to stop it. If the president *did* oppose it, how was Shaler to intervene? Reveal his secret commission as an agent to Mexico and wave it at the conspirators?

"By one party I am believed to be the cunning director of those plans, while the other regards me as a spy upon their actions," the agent lamented, "so that I am deprived of a full certain information of what is going forward, and I have also the mortification to find that they have so far gained upon the mind of Bernardo as to destroy all his confidence in me." To reveal his mission would break his cover and could prematurely end any hope of him ever completing his journey, if and when the Mexican rebels established a base within reach. Second, a man who tried to thwart the rebels would be the *last* person they would want as an envoy. And even if Shaler *had* been disposed to intervene, circumstances prevented it. At this crucial moment, the agent was "confined with a fever" from July 12th to August 18th—the period when the expedition fell into place and moved into Texas.[29]

The Governor's Response

One person who *was* trying to stop the filibuster was Governor Claiborne in New Orleans. In July 1811, when he had first heard rumors that the banditti in the Neutral Ground were making common cause with the rebels in Mexico, he had sent word to Judge Carr in Natchitoches to stop them. "As regards the project of attacking Nacogdoches," he wrote Carr, "it is advisable that you cause to be arrested and bound over to their good behavior all persons engaged in the same, or against whom any well-grounded suspicions exist." Carr at least claimed to be supportive, promising the governor, "I shall be on the alert, and their first movement will be the *signal* of *their capture*." Writing to his friend in Texas, Colonel Herrera, who had returned after the failure of the Casas revolt, Carr said that he had "no other desire than the preservation of the good harmony that exists in our respective governments." [30]

To enforce Claiborne's orders, Carr could call on the militia under Colonel Shaumberg, but this was a pitiful force, as Sibley informed the governor. Shaler, too, had said of them they had "neither the arms nor organization or disposition to do anything useful." Moreover, the conspirators were very careful to confine their activities to the Neutral Ground, where there was arguably no legal authority. The only alternative was to call on the hundred or so federal troops at Fort Claiborne. Carr, as a civil official, believed he had no authority over them. To act, especially as it required entering the Neutral Ground, they needed orders from senior leadership, and this had taken an agonizingly long time in the case of the suppression of the banditti.[31]

Shortly after that episode, however, Pike had given Captain Overton essentially carte blanche to repeat it, should it be necessary. He told him that in his situation, "where the civil authority has been and is daily openly put at defiance," he should assist the authorities, but added, "on these subjects you must act as the circumstances direct." This, however, assumed that the civil authorities would ask for assistance. Overton had no instruction to do anything until such a request was received, and the call never came.[32]

In Rapides Parish, from whence many of the army's recruits originated, the governor initially had the perfect ally to stop any filibuster: his older cousin, Justice of the Peace Richard Claiborne. It was likely this Claiborne who had suppressed the 1811 recruitment in Rapides, but he had made enemies in the process. In November of that year, he wrote of "a party unfriendly to the administration of the United States, and of course unfriendly to every Republican character, who might be appointed." One of these was even an old Whiskey Rebellion fugitive. This group of malcontents had, in Judge Claiborne's words, "early began with their malevolence against me." They had tried to get him dismissed and, when this failed, had the judge indicted by a grand jury for "oppression, extortion and altering and mutilating records." The justice was acquitted, but within a month of writing the above letter, he resigned his position and fled town. In December 1811, two new justices of the peace were appointed. Both were likely supporters of the filibuster, and one, Samuel D. Forsyth, would even join it.[33]

There simply was no strong interest on the frontier to stop an invasion. "Constrained by American constitutionalism and the national culture of individual mobility," historian Samuel Watson wrote, few in authority would move against any such effort unless it was a clearly organized armed force on American soil. Dispersed with legally protective cover stories as hunters, the members of the filibuster were essentially untouchable. "As long as they maintained a veneer of deniability—however implausible to anyone but sympathetic local magistrates and juries of their peers," Watson wrote, "filibusters were usually free to cross the border individually, if armed, or in groups if not."[34]

Although the imminent filibuster became common knowledge in Rapides and Natchez, it took time for the full import to filter downriver, since the recruits generally bypassed more settled areas along an old Indian road called the Natchez and Texas Trail. The state of the mail within Louisiana at the time was also in great confusion. What reports the governor did receive sounded like a rehash of the same vague rumors that had circulated for six years, and the only action he felt necessary was to reiterate his orders to Judge Carr.[35]

The governor, moreover, was a very preoccupied man. Orleans Territory had recently become—thanks to an act of Congress—the *State of Louisiana*, and the governor was focused on politics. In late June, just as Augustus Magee was resigning his commission and joining the conspirators, Claiborne resigned as governor of the Orleans Territory and prepared for what he expected to be a contentious campaign for governor of the new state. To his surprise, he would win with 70 percent of the vote over several hapless opponents, frustrating his antagonist, Daniel Clark. Still, it took a further two weeks to count ballots, and then the governor had to surmount his "enemies" in the state senate, which dragged their feet in confirming his election. During this time, Claiborne was still in limbo. Having resigned, he was technically governor of nothing until the election was certified and he was sworn in as the chief executive of the new state, which was not completed until July 30th. It was during this "political storm to which I have been exposed," as he called it, that the narrow window to stop the filibuster came—and went.[36]

In early July, the news of the declaration of war against England reached Louisiana. To those who thought such a conflict would invariably result in war with Spain, this was the news for which they had been waiting, and the filibusters stepped up their preparations. About the same time, Claiborne received a letter from Shaler warning him about the expedition brewing on the frontier. The next day, a visitor handed the governor a copy of "Articles of Association" secretly circulating in Rapides Parish for an expedition. Although his source told him that nothing would be done unless Washington approved the filibuster—Adair's position—Claiborne did not believe it. He at last realized there was more to the proposed venture than the eternal rumors he had seen for years. Still, as he informed Monroe, he had the issue in hand—or so he thought:[37] "The advice which on a late occasion I gave to the Civil Authority at Natchitoches [Carr], to bring the Law to bear against any person or persons engaged in setting on foot ... a military expedition or enterprise against the dominions of a foreign prince or state, at peace with the U. States, and my instructions to the officer commanding the Militia to give all necessary aid to the Civil Magistrate, supersede *for the present*, the necessity of further interference on my part."[38]

Two days later, he wrote to Carr and Colonel Shaumberg to send a detachment of militia to provide escort to a Spanish caravan that Governor Salcedo had requested. That seemed to suffice for now. If more were needed, they could call on the army leadership. But Overton was not inclined to act, and higher leadership was still driven by discord as a result of the distracting court-martial of Colonel Cushing by

General Hampton. Finally receiving news that General Wilkinson had arrived in the Mississippi and was "momently expected," Claiborne chose to wait for the man who outranked both of them. But movement upriver in the days of sail was a tricky thing, and days dragged on. Wilkinson, who never moved fast in a crisis unless it suited his own interests, would not reach New Orleans for another two weeks. Time was slipping away, and the military would get no new orders. The only real hope was the civilian authority, where the single point of failure for any effort to stop the filibuster was Judge Carr.[39]

Claiborne finally assumed his new governorship on July 30th and focused his energies on preparing for the war with England, in which New Orleans was sure to play an important role. But in the first week of August came a bombshell letter across his desk. Judge Carr—the Irishman whom Sibley had warned four years before was Claiborne's greatest mistake—had resigned his office! A thunderstruck Claiborne now suspected (correctly, as it turns out) that the judge had done almost nothing to comply with his orders given a year before. Whether Carr acted out of sympathy for the expedition or fear of enforcing an unpopular act against an armed multitude, it is probable that Claiborne's orders to stop the filibuster had precipitated his resignation.

The governor dispatched another letter to him immediately. "I cannot without considerable inconvenience to the public interest, accept for the present, your resignation as Judge of the Parish of Natchitoches & I request you to continue in the functions of that office," he wrote the judge. "Having understood that a project to invade the Spanish Province of Tehus [sic] was still in agitation by a number of individuals at or near Natchitoches, I must solicit your attention to my letter of instruction under the date of 30th of July 1811 & must again request your vigilance in the maintenance of Law and good order." With Carr having quit his job and Wilkinson leisurely sailing up the river, freezing the Army command structure, Claiborne did the only thing he could do on his own as governor—issue a proclamation:[40]

> WHEREAS I have received information that a number of persons are combining in a project to invade the Dominions of Spain, a State in amity with the United States, and for that purpose assembling at or near Natchitoches, within the limits & Jurisdiction of Louisiana, it becomes my duty to issue this my Proclamation, hereby solemnly cautioning the Citizens of this State against entering into, or in any manner countenancing the project aforesaid, and that no one may remain unadvised of the Consequences, which await the parties concerned . . .
>
> And I do enjoin and require all officers Civil and Military of the State to be vigilant in the maintenance of order and the preservation of the Laws.[41]

Claiborne did not even have a seal for his new state, so he issued it under his own private seal on August 11, 1812. But it was too late. The motley filibuster army now had two commanders—one political and one military. The Mexican rebel now had his chance for revenge, leading a revolution for the country to whose cause he had committed his life and fortune. The American lieutenant, denied promotion to captain, was now raised to *colonel* by Gutiérrez and at last had his opportunity for glory—and perhaps some revenge of his own against the Republicans in Washington. The *Gutiérrez-Magee Expedition* was on the move. It would not wait for Adair, and certainly not for Claiborne. On August 7, 1812, four days before the governor's proclamation was written—and weeks before it would arrive on the frontier—the advanced party of the rebel army had left the Neutral Ground and entered Texas.[42]

12

The Rebels Strike

THE INVASION OF August 1812 was not a new war but a continuation of the revolution in Texas, which had been snuffed out by Zambrano a year before. It was simply the logical continuation of two impulses that merged with the peculiar symbiosis of the moment: the Mexican rebellions of 1810–11 and Western Burrite adventurism. Rarely was a war launched with such ambivalence and disregard of the odds. The conquest of Texas, like the simultaneous American invasion of Canada, was boldly assumed to be "a mere matter of marching." In both cases, the assumption would be proven wrong in dramatic—and deadly—fashion.[1]

The *Republican Army of the North*, as the force would soon be called (to distinguish it from the Mexican armies further south under Rayón), was initially only about 130–50 men armed mostly with hunting rifles, well-supplied with ammunition and other stores, gathered in the Neutral Ground in late July 1812. Sibley reported that a European Frenchman "of smart appearance" who had resided in Mexico had brought a barge load of goods, arms, and ammunition up from New Orleans, which he gave to Gutiérrez to augment his supplies. The army's agents in Natchitoches claimed that they would be five to six hundred strong in ten days and had three pieces of artillery but expected six more soon. They were not going to wait. "'Tis said they will proceed to Nacogdoches in five or six days," Sibley wrote, "where most of the inhabitants as well as the soldiers they expect to join them. Some useful articles will at that place fall into their hands; but no cannon."[2]

General Adair was still holding to a November invasion timeline, but the filibuster leaders were impatient. All signs pointed to the moment being at hand: the distress of Gutiérrez's family, the Santa Fe traders' call for vengeance, the impatience of the Texas exiles as the Spanish dragnet closed in on their Tejano allies, the Spanish arrest of Quirk, and the impossibility of keeping the motley army too long at idleness. Spanish deserters had been making their way to Natchitoches since May, and the latest group of them arriving in July included the surgeon of the Nacogdoches garrison. They reported that "the whole country beyond the Rio Grande is in a state of insurrection," that the Republicans were in possession of Monclova, and that a force entering now would meet no resistance at either Nacogdoches or San Antonio. At nearly the same time came the stunning news of the American declaration of war on England. Magee and Gutiérrez judged the time was right to make their move, and they would do so with or without Adair, who could catch up to them with a large reinforcement.³

It was a fateful decision. Had they waited just two or three weeks, Claiborne's proclamation might have sapped enthusiasm for the expedition. Indeed, Adair, responding to it, issued a statement clarifying that his force was only going to join the filibusters if war was declared on Spain. It was not, he did not march, and his hesitance would solidify into paralysis. Still, there would be men enough at least to start a revolution, and the rebels hoped success would be all the recruitment they needed. Magee published an order, approved by Gutiérrez, promising his men forty dollars a month—eight times what an American private was paid—and a league of land in Texas. He admonished them they were going to a Catholic country and must respect that religion. Any who did not want to march on these terms were free to quit. As far as is known, none did. Thus the Republican Army of the North "raised the standard of Mexican Independence and pushed forward into the interior of Texas."⁴

A Caravan, a Deception, and a Rash Commander

Another factor that pushed Magee into attacking—possibly prematurely—was the opportunity to catch a particularly valuable quarry: Zambrano. By the summer of 1812, Texas was once again in desperate need of resupply, and a goods caravan waiting for the perilous crossing needed an armed escort. In early July, Zambrano returned to Nacogdoches with a significant reinforcement. The forty-year-old now escorted a valuable load of wool—around a hundred thousand worth, mostly from Zambrano's own ranch—and a number of mules destined for Natchitoches.⁵

"Sam Brannon" tried to get good intelligence before he started out on his mission, and to that end had written to Judge Carr in Natchitoches to enquire about the possibility of crossing unmolested. Carr wrote back that there was nothing to fear, as "any depredation or breach of the laws that may be committed east of [the Sabine], and within the limits of [Louisiana] will be rigorously punished by this government." Carr had to know this was untrue, which suggests the judge too was by this point in collusion with the enterprise. This might account for his sudden decision to resign his post rather than enforce the law and suppress the filibuster, and for the rebel force's precise intelligence about Zambrano's movements.⁶

The Spanish actually learned of the presence of the rebel force before they received Carr's letter saying all was quiet on the frontier. Davenport's associate, Masmela, had written to the Nacogdoches Commandant Bernardino Montero with the news. "A considerable number of Americans are assembling in the neutral territory as volunteers for the purpose of coming to attack us and going to the assistance of the insurgents," Montero reported to Governor Salcedo.[7]

The Spanish officer now canceled existing orders for two companies to return to San Antonio and ordered the captain of militia "to assemble the citizens who have arms and are capable of handling them." He had no intention to wait for the American assault. He had at his disposal around one hundred troops of the garrison, eighty-five men who had arrived with Zambrano, and the militia. Leaving the caravan of goods in Nacogdoches, Montero and Zambrano would march forth and ambush the invaders as they entered Spanish territory. "In two or three days I will take the field and encamp at the hill where the old pens were, so that, in case (the Americans) dare to attack us, they shall be well received with our balls."[8]

Montero moved to an advanced position closer to the Sabine, where on July 27th, he learned from a French Creole who lived on the river that 365 Americans with 6 cannons were waiting at Miguel Crow's ferry crossing, on the American side. The American numbers were half that, with possibly two small swivel guns. The Spanish sent out scouts to seek out the enemy. Nine days later, one of these spotted three "Englishmen" on the opposite bank of the river, acting as sentinels. As soon as they saw the Spaniards, the Americans retreated back into the forest and hid. Two small Spanish parties sent to investigate fords on the river near a place called "los hayes" promptly vanished. "At this I wished to attack them to prevent worse damage which I expected," Montero would later report. "I moved with my train as far as the Arroyo las Borregas, there I made a feint." The move, he informed his superior, possibly coloring his account with hindsight, was more to test his own men than the enemy. He was being bold because he thought his troops suspect. "For those who were with me I made it appear that my determination was to reach the Sabine and reconnoiter the enemy's force."[9]

On August 7, the invasion of Texas began, as an advanced party of the Republican Army of the North crossed the river near the road "de Ormigas" and entered Texas for the first time. For all his bluster, Montero immediately turned back to Nacogdoches. With about two hundred men, the Spaniard probably outnumbered the Americans, though he did not know it. Magee had about 130 men, with only half across the river. He himself would ford the next day with the rest. American sources claim the enemy's main body was discovered on August 8th by four scouts concealed in trees. As these men observed the advanced guard of "Zambrano's" force (it was actually Montero's) approaching them on horseback, they waited until they came within fifty yards and fired. Two Spaniards fell from their horses—one killed, one wounded. Before they could reload, the spies saw the full Spanish force come into view, and the Americans beat a hasty retreat. The Spanish sources tell a different tale—their force was tiny; the man killed was a mere muleteer. This was the first blood spilled in the invasion and likely occurred somewhere east of today's Milam, Texas.[10]

Eighty of Magee's men quickly formed up and marched out to meet the Spaniards, but by the time they arrived at the site, the Spanish had retreated. Montero's main force never found the enemy, for he had tested his men and decided they would not stand. He left a party of twenty men under the command of Ensign Vicente Gonzales at a place called Attoyac, and with the rest of his men returned to Nacogdoches. Even as they did, about a dozen of Montero's troops slipped out of formation and deserted to the rebels.[11]

Salitre Prairie and the Fall of Nacogdoches

Magee seems to have remained at the Sabine to supervise the crossing of his force, but he nonetheless sent a detachment to strike the enemy where he could find them. The man he chose for the task was someone who knew the Spanish well: the Burr conspirator and West Florida veteran Samuel Kemper. The tall, rough tavern keeper turned revolutionary had made his way to the frontier from Rapides and had been appointed second-in-command by Magee. It was likely a political choice: His brother Reuben was working closely with Adair, recruiting for the expedition.[12]

Samuel Kemper had no regular military background, and he and his brother had utterly failed in their first action at Baton Rouge. But in the later campaigns around Mobile, he had gained some more experience moving larger numbers of men. He himself had disparaged his own military abilities six years before when he was recruited into the Burr conspiracy. Yet he would be a quick learner and, now on the ground in Texas, would evolve into a commander of intelligence, courage, and boldness.

The Spanish detachment Montero had left behind was encamped at a place called Salitre Prairie, on land owned by Edmund Quirk. The smuggler turned spy was himself still in Spanish custody, but Miguel Quinn and others in the army—possibly including one of Quirk's sons—knew the land well. Thus, even though they were in enemy territory, the republicans probably knew the ground better than did the Spaniards. After locating the royalist camp, the rebels approached undetected until nearly upon the enemy.[13]

The Spanish troops had risen for the morning and were reciting their customary Ave Marias. At that moment, their advanced sentinel, Juan Galván, cried out, "Holy Mary, companions, there is only to take arms and you are lost." His fellow soldiers, seeing the enemy upon them and being unable to resist, surrendered. Only Galván, the scout, was able to find a horse tied up and escape. He mounted it bareback and, with his musket in hand, rode away and reported the ambush to Montero. The Spaniards lost two men killed and fourteen captured—all of whom quickly joined the rebels and were sworn in by the republican Antonio Flores.[14]

While the skirmish was tiny, the so-called Battle of Salitre Prairie wreaked a powerful toll on the morale of the Spanish regulars. Zambrano had spread horror stories about the invading banditti, but a young soldado named Pedro Prado wrote to his mother, "It is a lie." The first encounter with the Americans was a revelation, he said. "About the fifth day of August, the English [sic] captured me on the Sabine River," Prado wrote, "and my dismay was gone when they caused me to see the just cause and the point it defends, and they soon calmed me and my companions."[15]

When the attack came, Montero and Zambrano, who had retreated to Nacogdoches, were already struggling to hold their force together. Many of their men were only recent arrivals to the town, a mix of troops from northern Mexico and other parts of Texas who had spent most of the last few years in garrison. Many had defected from the Spanish army once before during the Casas revolt and had only been pardoned because Salcedo could not spare the men. Their loyalty to their leaders was threadbare enough. The militia's was even worse.[16]

Montero, upon receiving the report of the defeat, ordered the drummer to beat to arms for the citizens to turn out, but none did. He ordered the drums to sound a second, then a third time. "The citizens did not turn out, but my eyes were opened when . . . the few who presented themselves told me to be gone with my companion Zambrano, for we will be assassinated," Montero recalled. He still hoped to make a stand with just the regular soldiers but found the people were unafraid of the oncoming enemy. They were calm, even *rejoicing* at the news. It seems the efforts of Father Huerta, Edmund Quirk, and Gutiérrez's propaganda had been effective. As for Montero's own troops, they were "lukewarm." He ordered them to mount and offered horses to several citizens to accompany him. None did, and instead urged Montero to depart now. Zambrano had evidently become separated from the Spanish forces, and now arrived in some woods near the town with a mere eight men and sent a message to Montero. That he did not enter personally suggests he knew the tenor of the people.[17]

Montero thought it would be useless to try to defend the villa "with such small force" as he had, and would be worse to leave a rear guard. He announced his intention to abandon the entire town and take his forces with him on the retreat toward San Antonio. *All of them*, regulars and militia. This shocking announcement caused consternation among those assembled. The regular soldiers would be returning to their permanent home in San Antonio, but for the militia, most of whom had lived in the town for decades, even their entire lives, retreat meant the abandonment of their wives and children to the mysterious foe that had appeared on their border. It was unthinkable. A young officer spoke up and asked how Montero could possibly give such a shameful order in the face of the enemy. Montero supposedly shouted him down. He was not to question the order, merely to obey. When the militia was called out, only one man turned out with his musket in hand. The militiaman, Pedro Procela, told Montero "that he was a Spaniard, a servant of the King, and . . . that I should order what will appear to me proper." Montero's last act as commandant was to appoint Procela to remain "in command of the citizens."[18]

The Americans would later report a variation of the story that must have been told to them by deserters. As the garrison grudgingly marched out of town, it had scarcely gone one hundred yards when a captain of the militia suddenly and without authority gave command for the force to halt. He rode up to Montero and once again demanded that the officer explain to him why they were fleeing, and exactly what was this mystery army from which they were running. Montero, or the hot-tempered Zambrano (in the American version), raged at him and demanded that the men obey without question. When more soldiers began to align with the militia captain, Montero or Zambrano supposedly declared that he would go to San Antonio, raise a new force, and come back to Nacogdoches, where he would erect gallows and hang every one of them. Still the captain defied him, and when the soldiers made their decision, the entire force of militia, plus about sixty of the eighty regulars, deserted and went back into town, leaving the two lieutenant colonels Zambrano and Montero and their pitiful remnant of a force to march on alone.[19]

The remaining Spanish troops and three hundred of the townspeople marched out to meet Magee's army, which was about twenty miles away and closing. The two groups met, and Magee spoke with the Spaniards. The translator he brought with him was the former Texas resident Despallier, well-known to the Tejanos. The townspeople were prepared to open the city to the army, provided Magee's forces did not harm anyone and protected private property. Magee assured that his force came with the intention of doing damage, "neither to the religion nor to the interests of the citizens." A messenger from the townspeople raced back to Nacogdoches and delivered the report to the rest of the citizens, who prepared for the army's arrival. The two forces, Spanish and American, then proceeded together the rest of the way to Nacogdoches, and the town was surrendered without a fight.[20]

The entire villa turned out and the entry took the form of a parade. "The volunteers entered Nacogdoches in triumph on the [11th] and were joyfully received by the inhabitants, who immediately joined them to the number of 240 among which are about 50 regulars," a stunned William Shaler reported when the dramatic news arrived in Natchitoches a week later. "They have secured a considerable quantity of arms, military stores, provisions and booty of public property." The town was secured, and the jails were open. One of the prisoners freed was the former commandant turned rebel José María Guadiana, still awaiting transport to San Antonio for trial. Montero had probably only left him behind to avoid causing even more dissension in his ranks. The plucky officer who had been demoted and promoted so many times before, once again assumed his old position—now as a rebel commander. What became of Father Huerta, however, is unknown.[21]

The festive, cordial mood in the city endured in a general goodwill between the Americans and the Spaniards for the next few weeks. Spanish residents with contacts in Natchitoches soon wrote to their friends there with high praise for the army; any fears of plunder or oppression of the citizens were dissipated. The force seems to have behaved with extraordinary restraint, which to the merchants and citizens of Natchitoches, long fearful of the "banditti," was just as surprising as the dramatic victory. Shaler gave credit to Magee, who had instilled discipline in his force in the short time he had been with it.[22]

The American officer had also added to his army "a number of young men of respectable character and education." This group, so at variance with the banditti, was another reason for the good behavior of the army, Shaler insinuated. These included Kemper's recruits, who joined the frontier hunters and Spanish exiles, and some doctors and lawyers (such as the brothers Darius and Orramel Johnston), who added a more middle-class aspect to the force. For those who expected plunder, there was plenty of government booty to go around without troubling the locals. This included Zambrano's hastily abandoned caravan of wool and donkeys. This was turned over to the rebel army's new quartermaster, a key and very recent convert.[23]

Winning over Davenport

As late as July 21st, Samuel Davenport was still sending warnings to the Spanish authorities, but by early August, he was secretly communicating with citizens of Nacogdoches and encouraging them to welcome the rebels. What drove him to such a radical step? He had been surprisingly loyal, even when the Casas revolt had rocked Texas. A Spanish investigation two years before had declared that Davenport and his partner, Barr, were "faithful vassals of His catholic Majesty." Still, Commandant General Nemesio Salcedo had said they "do not have nor can have other characterization than that of foreigners tolerated until now through necessity."[24]

Barr's subsequent arrest, detention, and death from illness may have felt like a betrayal to Davenport. Another event that possibly swayed him—or removed a restraint on rebellion—was the untimely death of his twenty-six-year-old wife, María Luisa Cañon. Early in 1812, she began to suffer from a "disease of the chest" and the sole doctor in Nacogdoches could do nothing for her. Davenport begged Governor Salcedo to allow him to bring a doctor from Natchitoches, despite an official ban on such activity. "Her life is extremely important to me and her small children," Davenport wrote. "I can do nothing, and I am desperate." The unusual request was approved, but it was too late; she died in late February. The deaths of the two people closest to him—in both cases likely hastened by Spain's paranoid policies—no doubt affected Davenport. Still, he only joined the rebellion once it was inevitable. It is even possible that he was compelled to do so.[25]

Given the title of quartermaster, he would oversee the expedition's primitive but vital network of supply. Now he took up his task and sorted through the goods which Zambrano had abandoned. In addition to the wool, which he estimated as eighty thousand pounds, he discovered stores of flour, gunpowder, munitions, and even silver bars. Davenport arranged to take the abandoned goods caravan to Natchez, where it would be sold for cash to buy much-needed supplies. Meanwhile, Colonel Magee paused his army to consolidate his position and wait for Gutiérrez to catch up with reinforcements. But he did not lessen his pressure on the routed Spaniards, dispatching Captain Despallier in pursuit. The former Spanish officer's chase was so relentless that the royalists began to abandon what little military stores they had with them in order to lighten their load.[26]

At this time, there appear to have been at least two groups of soldiers fleeing southward. In addition to the column of Zambrano and Montero, Sgt. Pedro José de Aldape led a section of men, which may have been a frontier detachment isolated from the main force. As Aldape's column worked its way south over the next few days, it left a trail of exhausted horses—and deserters—as it went. On August 12th, he wrote, "On going out from there, two soldiers from La Punta, Teodoro Sahis [Sáiz] and Trinidad Gonzales, deserted me; in company with them one of the militia auxiliaries of New Santander, Don Juan Savas [Savías]." The latter must have been a bitter blow indeed, for just the day before, Aldape had praised Savías as "the distinguished soldier," a mark of high praise. Savías, an apparent humble, ordinary soldier, would return to Nacogdoches and join the rebels, where he would indeed distinguish himself in time.[27]

On the 16th, Aldape, who had picked up some stragglers to replace some of the deserters, merged his force with Montero's, then moved on to Trinidad. There, Montero collected a total of eighty-five soldiers, including eighteen of the remaining escort of Zambrano and the bulk of the Trinidad garrison. It was better than the ten to twenty with whom he had so ignobly fled from Nacogdoches, but was still too small to offer effective resistance. He bitterly put pen to paper, his account no doubt deflecting blame from himself, but nonetheless painting a portrait of a battle that was lost long before the first rebel had crossed into Texas.[28] "The fact is that these [Spanish] troops and people manifested a turning before the time for attacking the enemy, for when the occasion presented itself to them they cowardly sought the means of living ever in dishonor. . . . I am of the opinion subject to yours, that Nacogdoches for the present should be abandoned as well as [Trinidad] and the Atascocito."[29]

Montero's superiors agreed, and indeed had already planned to give up the town. "Whenever the fate of those inhabitants will be considered exposed and destitute," Nemesio Salcedo had written two months before, "it will be best to abandon the establishment, and gather together those same inhabitants in [San Antonio]."[30]

Back in that capital, Manuel Salcedo fumed. He confirmed the order to pull back, adding that Trinidad was small and its inhabitants were "almost all foreigners." Salcedo did not blame his army for the debacle, although he must have been shocked by the wholesale desertion of nearly the entire garrison of Nacogdoches. He instead complained, with perhaps a begrudging admiration for their boldness, that the Americans, who "suffer at this time various political convulsions," were nonetheless "able to be resolved to entertain themselves with the hope of possessing . . . the treasures of this kingdom." He blamed "unworthy Spaniards" who were encouraging "the ambition of a new nation, whose republican government is a friend of all rogues."[31]

The chief villains in the governor's eyes were the two Bernardos, Gutiérrez and Despallier, the latter "a Frenchman, fugitive for three years from this province on account of offenses and knaveries." It was their propaganda that had enticed so many of the citizens and soldiers of Nacogdoches to go over to the rebels. From Salcedo's perspective, Magee's claim that he was "not coming to offend the natives" was a story he had seen before. "But, ha!," he wrote, "Incautious towns having agreed to that with the same treachery, the French entered into Spain."[32]

Nacogdoches he wrote off as seduced by a naïve desire for trade. But San Antonio was better than that, "since it contains good natives, and they know the perversity and ambitious ideas of our neighbors." It was here that he would regroup his forces and plan his next move. Salcedo informed the viceroy of the disaster and appealed for a portion of a newly arrived force of Spanish regulars. He also asked for aid from governors and commanders in neighboring provinces. Only Antonio Cordero, the governor of Coahuila, who had served alongside him in Texas, could spare the men, saying that he would send his best company of troops.[33]

To the people of his province, Salcedo declared, "I vow before the Almighty to die before allowing that his sacred temples and divine images are subjected to the scorn and derision of the Lutherans, sacrilegious, and other heretics and protestants who try to undermine our happiness and Catholicism." All good Spaniards should take the same vow. Recalling his impressions of the Burrites he had met, he told his people, "Let the coward and traitor flee from us, and go join the heretical mob, which comes solely to satiate its desire for the silver and gold of this kingdom. Live among them without law or fear of God; surrender to all manner of vice; but afterwards prepare for the inescapable lash of the Almighty, to die in complete misery, desperation, and the scorn of heaven and earth." He challenged the populace to "fight and cover ourselves in glory," and to "earn the title of defenders of the Mexican kingdom."[34]

The insurgent paper of Oaxaca, the *Correo Americano del Sur*, in reporting Salcedo's proclamation, said the governor's words proved he was "a barbarian, as are all [who] belong to his party." As for the Mexicans' new protestant allies, the paper noted that the gachupines had first allied with the European English, becoming "their dearest and intimate allies," so Salcedo's criticism was hollow. Magee's volunteers, the writer opined, were worth the risk. "If the generous Anglo American, lover and protector of independence, did not come to aid us out of good faith for our heroic efforts but, in disregard of their fundamental constitution, trample even our most inviolable rights and have their perfidious sights on subjugating us, we would nevertheless celebrate our luck, counting ourselves free of the outrageous cruelty of Spanish despotism."[35]

The American Volunteers

So what *did* motivate the army that had gathered in the Neutral Ground? It was, in fact, a motley collection of individuals with a variety of backgrounds and a diversity of motives. It was, as Shaler had predicted, several groups consolidating into one on the frontier. There were the Texas exiles—Quinn, McFarlan, and Despallier. This group included Anthony Dubois, a French Creole who lived in East Texas as a farmer with his wife, four sons, and one daughter as late as 1809 before he was likely expelled. Another former Spanish resident was Antonio Pared (whose real name was Parish or Parrot), a native North Carolinian who had been living near Nacogdoches since 1798, working as a carpenter. French Creoles Pierre Dolet and Jean Baptist Prudhomme had been expelled to the Neutral Ground. Some of these men had lost everything when Spain forced them out, and hoped for a restoration of their property, alongside the free trade of which they had long dreamed.[36]

Closely aligned with these were the so-called banditti of the Neutral Ground. There were indeed some rough, murderous men in the group. The man who "commanded the border ruffians" was James McKim, a veteran of the American Revolution who had fought with George Rogers Clark. Moving west after the revolution, he became a Spanish subject in 1786, settling first in Louisiana before moving to the Neutral Ground, where he lived near Edmund Quirk. He had been branded as punishment for some offense in North Carolina and would keep a journal (since lost) of the expedition, and reportedly entertained his fellow soldiers by reading from it. One member of the expedition would describe McKim decades later as a "fit associate of the robbers along the Sabine." But there were more peaceful Neutral Grounders too. Among this group was at least one man whose house Magee had burned, Louis Latham, and possibly others. "McGee on entering the service found that many of the men whom he had driven off the Neutral Ground were now marshalled under his command," Capt. James Gaines would write, "and as he had been very tyrannical in the execution of his task of expelling them; he expected to be assassinated by them; they were never fully reconciled to him."[37]

One of the more colorful Neutral Ground recruits was a fearless fighter named Aylett Buckner, a notably strong and physical Scots-Irish redhead, nicknamed "Strap" for his size and strength. Much of his history has come down in the manner of tall tales and frontier exaggeration. Buckner, so the stories said, "hunted the strongest game with no other weapon than his bare fist; and the wildcat, the wolf, and bear soon became scarce." Behind the myth, the known details of "Strap" Buckner's life indicate a kernel of truth: he was young, hot-headed, querulous, and courageous.[38]

The expedition also included respectable men from Natchitoches, both the banditti's victims and their customers. William Owens, a Natchitoches merchant originally from Baltimore, had done business with Joseph Magee, Henry Quirk, and other Texas smugglers. Owens also had a grudge against the Spanish, who he said had harbored some of his escaped slaves. Most merchants, however, supported the status quo and only came to embrace the revolution from a fear of being cut out of a new monopoly. Another group was the recruits from Louisiana and Mississippi. These were the Burr diaspora—the Mexican Association's recruits. This included, as we have seen, Kemper, Murray, and Taylor. The latter according to one family account, organized a small company of men, "with two important requirements in mind; they had to be well-mounted and proven marksmen with the rifle."[39]

Other recruits forwarded by Adair included men of property like Joseph Carr (no relation to the judge), a man of substance from Mississippi; Reuben Ross of Virginia; and Henry Perry. The latter two would both rise rapidly in the Republican ranks. A few of the filibusters were veterans of the American Revolution, including sixty-two-year-old Peter Sides and sixty-six-year-old Benjamin Allen, who brought with him two sons and a grandson. David Phelps, forty-six, was the son of revolutionary war general Noah Phelps, who had helped capture Fort Ticonderoga. He had himself been a young soldier in that war, later becoming a physician before moving west to Kentucky. Thomas Hussey Luckett Jr., who would command the Republican Army's artillery, was the son of Thomas Hussey Luckett Sr., a major of the "Maryland Line," a regular-army regiment mostly drawn from that state, and a charter member of the Society of the Cincinnati.[40]

The expedition attracted professional men caught up in nineteenth-century romantic notions of martial glory. In an era in which a few months' service could bestow upon a man a lifetime of being addressed by the honorific "Major" or "Colonel," even the slightest conflict was an opportunity for distinction, and professional men flocked to the cause. Gutiérrez, who praised these men in his contemporary diary, would claim in a later and more bitter age that the whole force was "mostly doctors and lawyers gifted in all matters, especially in the matter of rascality."[41]

Among the lawyers were Magee's friend Murray, who brought with him Warren D. C. Hall, a young man who had been studying the law under Murray's father. Joining Hall in turn were two men who were likely his brothers, John "Jack" Hall and Darlington Hall, all originally from the Carolinas. Another lawyer was Darius Johnston, who joined his doctor brother Orramel, the author of the skeptical letter about the expedition.[42]

In addition to Orramel, David Phelps, noted above, was also a doctor. But the preeminent physician in the army was Samuel D. Forsyth. He had been appointed a surgeon's mate in the US Army in April 1807 and was assigned to the Second Regiment of Infantry at Fort Adams. He resigned a year later, possibly enticed by the opportunity of the frontier, and entered private practice as a doctor in Rapides. Here, as was noted before, he became a Justice of the Peace, where he appears to have done nothing to suppress the filibuster that he would ultimately join.[43]

There was fear on the frontier that serving army soldiers might follow Magee into the expedition, but none did. Even so, there were plenty of former soldiers eager to participate. These included officers and enlisted as well. Samuel Barber, a native of Harpers Ferry, Virginia, had joined the army in 1801, enlisting for a period of five years and reenlisting again in 1806. He had been among the troops Wilkinson had brought to New Orleans to stop the Burr conspiracy and had deserted to Spanish West Florida not long after. Another recruit of low station was nineteen-year-old Henry Munson, a lifelong Spanish resident, having been born in Louisiana, whose family had participated in the West Florida rebellion alongside the Kempers. Of the possibly six hundred to eight hundred Americans and French Creoles who served in the expedition at one time or another, we can only definitively identify about two hundred of them (see appendix B). The remainder of the army likely consisted of men similar to the classes described previously.[44]

Wilkinson Sends a Spy

General Wilkinson had dreamed of invading Spanish lands for decades, but now that it was happening, he was none too pleased because the event held little opportunity for his own personal enrichment. In 1806, he had thrown in with the US government and now, having just survived his second court-martial in a decade, he was going on no adventures. On August 13th, he wrote to Captain Overton at Fort Claiborne: "No friend to the liberties of mankind, can . . . reflect on the past history and present circumstances of the poor [Spanish] Americans, without feeling a desire to see their condition ameliorated," he wrote, but added that the rebellion should be a native affair. As for the Americans who had boldly done what he had dreamed, but never consummated six years before, he predicted, "The enterprise of a band of adventurers, who professing to be moved by a love of liberty, take their first step in the violation of the laws of their own country, cannot serve the cause of the Mexicans, and must terminate in disgrace and ruin to those concerned."[45]

The general expressed the opinion that Claiborne's proclamation "will have the same effect in your quarter which it has produced here"—namely, drying up recruiting. He urged Overton to trust no one and be careful of whom he allowed inside Fort Claiborne. "Let your vigilance be unceasing, day and night," he wrote. Overton in his response sent greatly detailed information about the expedition, then explained why he knew so much. "Know then, sir, that the business has never been a secret!" he admitted. "The very atmosphere has been pregnant with the plans of this party for months," Overton said, "and the thing has become so public a topic that people were of the opinion that this government were not averse to it, the civil authority not interfering."[46]

Overton's admission is curious, because it had been he who had told Orramel Johnston that he knew nothing of the plan two months before when the young man had approached him. The likely explanation is that Overton, who secretly supported the filibuster, was deflecting suspicion, even blaming his predecessor, Captain

Wollstonecraft, who was himself opposed to the invasion. "Yet my communications would have been unceasing," Overton wrote, "had I not been superseded in this command by an older and more experienced officer than myself." Overton expressed personal support for the Mexican revolutionary cause but said that aid should not come while America was "repelling the common enemy."[47]

Wilkinson's letter was dispatched in the hands of a "Mr. Seay," who he said had served five years as a sergeant during the wars with the Indians. Seay, Wilkinson informed Overton, was to be allowed to cross the border, presumably disguised as a republican recruit, to spy on the expedition. In typical Wilkinson fashion, his mission was cloaked in intrigue. "His errand and his acquaintance with you must be concealed," Wilkinson wrote. After the spy had been employed to "procure all the information practicable of the situation, numbers, leaders and plans of the armament near you," this information was to be sent back to Wilkinson directly. "You must use much precaution respecting the bearer, or his life will be endangered. He will probably follow and join the armed body; you will furnish him a horse and whatever he may find necessary."[48]

Overton expressed concern with any further men leaving the country when it was at war, but was particularly bothered by *this particular* man, as he expressed to the general. "Believing it dangerous for this express to proceed to Nacogdoches, at this time, *should he be recognized*, and being possessed of the necessary information," Overton wrote. "I have advised his immediate return." The full identity of "Mr. Seay" remains unknown, but the secrecy suggests he was someone close to Wilkinson—possibly even one of his sons. It seems likely that Wilkinson, who would eventually be transferred to Canada and would play no role in the expedition himself, never really washed his hands of it completely.[49]

13

The Republican Army of the North

THREE WEEKS AFTER the rebels had marched into Nacogdoches, the news reached Alexandria, Louisiana, and was reprinted in the *National Intelligencer* in Washington on October 24, 1812. For Americans following the Mexican Revolution, this was the first they heard of a front in Texas, and the presence, much less dominance, of Americans in the army was not even noted. American editors placed considerable hopes in the leadership of Rayón and embraced this new front with enthusiasm. "It is supposed an attempt, if not already, will very soon be made on this last remaining prop of decayed monarchy in the west," the correspondent wrote. "Mexico taken, and the Republic triumphs!" The phrasing—in ignorance of American involvement—demonstrates how strongly the cause of republicanism was conflated with the national interest. For many Americans, the two were one and the same. News from Texas would travel southward as well, here too lathered with massive exaggeration. The *Correo Americano del Sur* reported that twenty thousand armed Americans were in Nacogdoches, heading for Mexico to "give us a hand in our glorious enterprise."[1]

The one man who was not with the rebel army was Bernardo Gutiérrez. The Republican Army's nominal leader was still in Natchitoches as late as August 10th, the day before his forces marched triumphantly into Nacogdoches. Shaler put it down to probable fear: "He seemed to be the only person who doubted of the success of his own enterprise." The agent had grown contemptuous of his protégé, who had circumvented and deceived him while he urged caution. Fear would be understandable, but the Mexican rebel had legitimate reasons for not being with his army. Gutiérrez may have been awaiting Girard's report of his appeal to Wilkinson, and Magee's invasion likely jumped the gun ahead of the planned march.[2]

Before Gutiérrez set out to join his army, he paid Shaler one last visit to smooth over their differences. He thanked the New Yorker for all of the kindness the American government had shown him and apologized for "his departure from the line of conduct he had pleased himself to follow on his arrival at this post." He had deceived the American but was not truly apologetic. Shaler thought that Gutiérrez made a "humiliating" figure, and vowed to Monroe, "not to give him any further countenance."[3]

"Parties of men are constantly arriving here from Natchez and different parts of the Miss. Territory," Shaler wrote, "so that I [think it] probable that the forces of the volunteers will in a short time amount to 500 Americans." No one was stopping them, neither Judge Carr nor Captain Overton. Claiborne's proclamation would not arrive on the frontier for another two weeks. Gutiérrez gathered these new arrivals and followed his colonel across the Sabine.[4]

The entire citizenry of Natchitoches, even those who had been "the most violently opposed to the Mexican revolution," were now jumping on the bandwagon. The merchants, who initially had feared the loss of trade from the Spanish government, now hoped to make up the difference with the rebels, even offering credit to the same rogues they had so recently disparaged. Some even sent supplies to the army free of charge. In early September, the confiscated caravan of Zambrano's wool arrived in Natchitoches, where a portion was sold, with an additional 40,000 pounds forwarded to Natchez, where it was put up at the public sale for 12½ cents a pound for the rebel coffers.[5]

Inflated stories of the prospects of the revolutionaries circulated broadly, becoming a much-needed recruiting aid to counteract Claiborne's proclamation. "There is a great deal of money at St. Antonio, and the property of the royalists collected there is immense," read one letter, sent by a rebel in Nacogdoches. It was divorced from reality, but the imaginary plunder fueled authentic greed. The tale was reprinted in American newspapers under the words *"CASH! For those who will fight for it."* The article even included a route for men seeking to join the army. In Opelousas on September 1st, a party "composed of the most abandoned characters" passed through, prepared to do just that.[6]

An Extraordinary Little Army

The Republican Army of the North included such "abandoned characters" but also respectable men, idealists, and professionals as well. It left no muster rolls or indeed archives of any kind, and the details we know are mostly from scraps of documents, letters sent out from Texas, and from a half dozen short firsthand accounts written decades later. The author of one of these was William McLane, a Pennsylvania native who was about twenty-five at the time he heeded the call and went west to join the filibuster. Arriving in Nacogdoches on August 20th, the new recruit was directed to the stone house that was Davenport's home, which had become the temporary headquarters of the expedition. "I found Bernardo Garteres [sic], Magee, Kemper, [Reuben] Ross, [Henry] Perry, [Thomas] Slocum, and Dr. [Samuel] Forsyth, [and] Col. Davenport," McLane would write. "They comprised the regimental officers, staff of the expedition." Anglo-Americans still greatly predominated in the army and monopolized senior command. No one, even Gutiérrez, contemplated pushing Magee aside. The arrangement suited all for the time being.[7]

In addition to the members of the army staff noted by McLane, the two Burr conspirators, Capt. William Murray and Capt. Josiah Taylor would later be promoted to Major. Another officer with a likely Burr connection was Capt. Thomas Luckett, who would ultimately command the rebel artillery. The senior officers seem to have represented some of the interests present in the campaign, with the rest likely elected, as was customary. Three unnamed captains paid their own men out of their pockets. Joining the American officers was the American-Spaniard Davenport, who added a second title as company captain to his quartermaster job when he persuaded about thirty Spaniards of Nacogdoches (probably his employees and other dependents) to join the cause and serve under him.[8]

Another recent arrival, who would serve as co-commander in Nacogdoches alongside Lieutenant Guadiana, was James Gaines, who had served as a soldier at Fort Stoddert in Mississippi. Born in 1776 in Culpepper County, Virginia, he was a cousin of Gen. Edmund Pendleton Gaines, who ironically had been a key figure in the arrest and prosecution of Burr. James Gaines had worked alongside his cousin as a surveyor along the Natchez Trace after the Louisiana Purchase and served for a time as a sheriff of a Louisiana parish.[9]

The army was mostly Anglo-American, but also included a number of French Creoles. Despite Shaler's warning against Gutiérrez having any association with Frenchmen, the Mexican rebel seems to have taken all comers to his cause. The most prominent of these was Despallier, who was joined in Nacogdoches by several other former French residents of Texas, including Dolet and Prudhomme mentioned previously, along with another Neutral Ground resident, Alexander Germieul. They would ultimately be joined by at least a half dozen other Frenchmen, two of whom Gutiérrez would use as secretaries: Louis Massicott and Francis J. Menepier. Also joining was Bernard D'Ortolant, the same former officer and Nacogdoches resident who had spoken at such length to the French general Octaviano D'Alvimar in 1808.[10]

Gutiérrez was impressed and praiseworthy of the army's initial success, issuing a proclamation "To the Republican Volunteers at Nacogdoches," in which he addressed them. "I desire you to receive from me the tribute of my private feelings, and also as the agent of my Mexican brethren," he wrote. He thanked them, but subtly reminded them—should any Americans forget—that they were "volunteers in the Mexican Cause," not in some other which they might imagine. They had shown "activity, zeal, promptitude and courage" in obeying the orders of their officers, who of course were acting under his command. Their conduct, he hoped, would be continued "to *the discomfiture of tyrants*, to the *emancipation of the Mexicans*, and to the complete success of the enterprise you have undertaken, which will crown your exertions with glory, honor and fortune."[11]

Pouring on the praise to the recruits (and perhaps to undermine Claiborne's proclamation), he proclaimed that "the spark which lighted the flame of independence in the northern part of America is not extinct in the bosoms of the descendants of those who fought, bled, and prevailed over tyrants." Gutiérrez believed, as many Americans also did, that Texas was already won and that Salcedo would retreat in panic beyond the Rio Grande: "You are now, fellow-soldiers, in peaceable possession of one of the out-posts established by European tyranny, the more effectually to enslave the oppressed Mexicans. This possession has been obtained without bloodshed on your part, from the consciousness in the minds of the cowardly instruments of tyranny, that they can [never] prevail in arms against the brave, free, and independent citizens of the United States of America."[12]

He assured his volunteers, possibly unfavorably impressed with the squalor of Nacogdoches, that once the army's numbers increased, they would move against the enemy "in their strongholds." When this was done, "you are to look for the reward of your toils, dangers, sufferings and difficulties, in the enjoyment of all the rights of honored citizens of the Mexican republic." This meant the right to cultivate lands "which I pledge myself will be assigned to every individual among you." It also meant the right to work any gold, silver, or other mines they might discover and to tame wild horses. They would be paid forty dollars a month, from surplus property seized from royalists.[13]

Gutiérrez's proclamation was reprinted on October 17th in Washington. "It would appear from the foregoing," an editor's note appended, "as if the army were chiefly composed of the citizens of the United States—to prevent which the proper authority has issued a proclamation." For most Americans, this was a surprise. But among the Republican press, the ominous news was drowned out in a wave of hopeful and exaggerated reporting. "St. Antonio is virtually in the possession of the United States, and ... the American Eagle is displayed as far west as that post!" the Red River Herald raved. "This event will secure effectually the independence of Texas—and will, no doubt, be the harbinger of liberty to the whole Mexican province." This admixture of American success and Mexican liberty was hardly discordant to the writers' ears, though such language would have disturbed Gutiérrez.[14]

Among the Federalist press, however, this was further proof of Republican duplicity. An army of Americans was taking possession of a foreign country "to convince the Spaniards *how much we respect the rights of nations*!" Federalists lamented that some of the men in the expedition were likely drafted militia abandoning their service. "It is hoped," their Boston party paper, the New England Palladium noted sarcastically, "the Spaniards will not be so *barbarous* as to set the Indians on these armed *friends*, who come only to give them liberty, conquer and govern them!"[15]

Certainly, New England's most notable Federalist, Thomas Handasyd Perkins, would have agreed wholeheartedly with this cynical viewpoint, at least until the stunning revelation that came just a few short weeks later, when the local *Independent Chronicle* reported that the leader of this force was none other than the youth whom he had raised virtually as his own son. "Gen. Magee (an enterprising and brave officer, a native of Boston)," Perkins learned from the paper, was with his army, "on their way to St. Antonio, where they would make only a short stay, but would proceed on over the river Grand, to aid the Spanish revolutionary patriots." Southern Federalists from the beginning were much more favorable towards the expedition and provided the young widow Margaret Magee a noble—if not entirely true—last impression of the son whom she would never see again:[16] "There is something singular in the beginning and progress of this enterprise. A young Lieutenant, scarcely twenty-four, starting at the head of a company of forty, or fifty, of whom he had severely chastised a short time before, and forming of these the nucleus of an army to fight in the cause of the Patriots!—It certainly evinces a bold and romantic genius."[17]

General Wilkinson remained contemptuous of the rebel force "composed of the refuse of society," and vowed to stop it, but once it crossed the border, it ceased to be a priority. He had other battles to fight, and not all of them against enemies and bureaucracy. In the midst of his preparations against potential British attacks, his forces suffered from a powerful hurricane, which struck Fort St. Philip at the Southeast Coast of Louisiana. While Claiborne urgently awaited Wilkinson in New Orleans to stop the filibuster, he had turned back downstream and sailed in the other direction to inspect his devastated fortress.[18]

Mexican Republicans

With Nacogdoches in its possession, the Republican Army of the North now had a sizeable Spanish contingent recruited from the town. Lieutenant Colonel Montero, even in the midst of his flight, put pen to paper and tried to account for as many of his men as he could. The soldiers who deserted to join the republicans included three from the regular company of Béxar, four from the Alamo de Parras company, six from the company of Nuevo León, and seven from that of Nuevo Santander. Those who were captured from August 3 to 11 included troops from Béxar (two), Alamo (nine), Nuevo León (eleven), and Nuevo Santander (seven). The total, 49, matches Shaler's estimate (50), suggesting that his number of the combined force (240) is probably accurate as well. Most of the militia likely chose to "serve" in Nacogdoches, close to their families. Still, this was a sizeable contingent of Spanish, or Mexican (as they would eventually begin to think of themselves), rebels. Spanish spies reported these new recruits mostly enthusiastic for the cause. "All the Spaniards were pleased, and all were rendering service" one wrote. But another spy told of *alferez* (second lieutenant) Gonzales, who "is found very sad" at the revolutionary turn.[19]

The sudden influx of these Spanish speakers into a predominately English-speaking army necessitated leaders fluent in their own language, with Despallier and Davenport as their initial officers, but the republicans absorbed trained men from among the former Spanish officers as well. Lieutenant Guadiana, as we have seen, was restored as garrison commander. He was joined by a forty-six-year-old for-

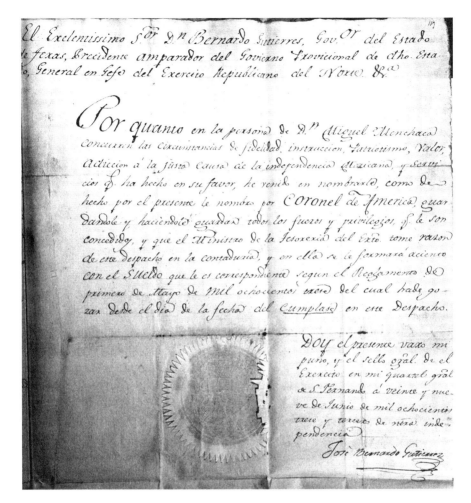

Figure 7. Col. Miguel Menchaca's Commission in the Republican Army of the North. Courtesy of William L. Clements Library, University of Michigan.

mer soldier who had been in exile. Miguel Menchaca was "a rough, uneducated, but strong-minded Mexican of Texas," dark-complected, tall and thin, somewhat stooped, with a pitted face. Unlike his relative José, who abandoned his filibuster in 1811, Miguel Menchaca would remain faithful to the rebel cause. The republicans made him a second lieutenant; he would later rise to captain and would in time become the senior Mexican/Tejano officer in the army. Among the captured Spaniards who defected was 2nd Lieutenant Vicente Tarín, a lancer and member of the Alamo de Parras company, which gave the fortress in San Antonio its name. His record shows the complexity of the rebellion: He had once been charged with smuggling and buying foreign goods with Texas horses, but on March 2, 1811, had led the troops who had rallied to Zambrano to overthrow Casas.[20]

Other Mexican rebel officers were Don Vicente Gonzales, José Peñelas, and a Spanish noncommissioned officer, Sgt. Esmeregildo Guillen. Even Pedro Procela, the supposedly loyal militia officer whom Montero had left in command, was in the end an easy convert. He joined the rebel army and became a captain. Additional men from San Antonio, who had stolen away from that town on the news of the invasion, arrived to join the army, including Antonio Martinez, Gavino Delgado, and Vicente Flores, the officer who had brought over the Béxar garrison to the Casas revolt a year before.[21]

Arms, Logistics, and Organization

Having received word from Despallier that Trinidad had been abandoned, Magee sent two companies to secure the town. In the meantime, he trained and equipped his motley force. Shaler speaks of volunteers who "went out either singly or in small bands usually armed as hunters," sneaking past Natchitoches to join the army, which would suggest men who brought along their rifles, as opposed to men bearing muskets. A rifle, such as the popular Kentucky or long rifle, is far more accurate than smooth-bore muskets, but this comes at a sacrifice of rate of fire. For this reason, a musket—to which a bayonet could also be affixed—was the preferred weapon for military operations. It allowed a mass of men to concentrate fire and, if disciplined, keep this "well-regulated" fire up for sustained periods.[22]

A core of specialized sharpshooters with rifles is evident in the expedition's operations. Nonetheless, Spanish sources and the history of subsequent battles—which in some cases lasted several hours—suggest many, perhaps the majority of, men were equipped with muskets, although most without bayonets. Magee even experimented with issuing his men a large number of lances which he had found in Nacogdoches, but there is no evidence they were used in battle. To train, Magee and his captains appointed corporals and sergeants who drilled the American volunteers in the morning and again in the evening each day. The Spanish rebels were not asked to drill, nor did they voluntarily do so. The republicans had very few cavalry—perhaps thirty men, armed not with traditional cavalry sabers, but with rifles and muskets, which meant they had to dismount to fire. Unit organization was no doubt primitive in these early days, but as the army would grow from new recruits, it would develop additional companies and, eventually, two separate battalions, with additional officers.[23]

In addition to their pay, which despite promises, would be infrequent, the men were given two pounds of flour per day, and a pound and a half of meat, some of which came from sixty of Samuel Davenport's cattle. A force of hundreds of men also required a supporting cast of teamsters, cooks, and other people necessary to supply the army's needs. It can be presumed that the supplies were transported by Davenport's network of Mexican teamsters. There were also African slaves who accompanied the army, including Josiah Taylor's servant Thomas—who fought in the army as a combatant—and two slaves owned by Magee. One was an unnamed Spanish slave who belonged to Nacogdoches resident José María Mora, in whose home Magee had been quartered. Mora sold him to the Bostonian for a thousand pesos to act as an interpreter. There were likely many others who served in support roles. For cooks, the army likely included male and female slaves, but possibly also some Anglo-American and Mexican women accompanied the army.[24]

After praising his Anglo allies, Gutiérrez now focused on his own people. If the reception that Nacogdoches had afforded the army was any indication, then the importance of reaching out to the populace in San Antonio was immense—far more so than Magee's experiment with lances. To that end, Gutiérrez sat down on September 1st to draft a series of propaganda documents. It would be his chief contribution to the war effort.[25]

In the first of these, Gutiérrez explained how he had spoken with America's "supreme government" and "conferenced with all the ministers and ambassadors of the kings of Europe." He informed the Tejanos that "almost all educated nations have been declared in favor of our independence by offering me . . . the most powerful and liberal offerings, so that we can destroy the tyrants who have oppressed us."[26]

Another letter was to the troops of Texas. "Many of our friends and countrymen have died unjustly under the sword of these tyrants," Gutiérrez wrote them, "their blood asks us for a just vengeance from the grave, their spirits are before the throne of God clamoring . . . for our victories." He was marching "with a force of American volunteers who have left their homes and families to undertake our cause and fight for our freedom, [who] as brothers and inhabitants of the same continent with great will [have] unsheathed their swords in defense of the cause of humanity and to reject the oppressors, the Europeans."[27]

A third letter was to the people of Mexico generally and sounded many of the same themes but placed additional emphasis on his commitment to Catholicism and Mexico's special role as a place "favored by the protection of great God" and the Virgin of Guadalupe. In addition to his initial band of American volunteers, Gutiérrez said he had additional thousands who might join by land and sea. And what was his aim? "To put this, our kingdom, under a total and free independence from all . . . European government . . . and make use of that free right that nature has given them in establishing the laws by which they are to be governed."[28]

These were soaring themes, which played well to the audiences Gutiérrez had chosen. The challenge was how to get the documents into San Antonio. For this task, Gutiérrez chose a civilian, Despallier's father-in-law, the seditious lyricist, Luís Grande. He was accompanied by a deserter from the presidial troop of San Antonio named Ancelmo Bergara. Grande was given a sealed document containing a dozen proclamations, which he was to smuggle into San Antonio and see "that they are thrown into the doors of the houses of the most trustworthy." This method would allow the rebels "to communicate the truth to each other and avoid many misfortunes."[29]

Taking the job was risky. Grande's family had been specifically identified by the Spanish as a threat, and he himself had suffered for his son-in-law's exile. At one point he had been imprisoned in Nacogdoches for over a year before being expelled from Texas himself. Knowing the risks, he took the job anyway. Having served as a mail carrier, and accompanied by the well-traveled deserter Bergara, he was well-acquainted with the Camino Real and all its side paths.[30]

Grande bore a passport Gutiérrez had given him, which included an image of the Virgin of Guadalupe, stamped in sealing wax. This would not only guide him past American scouts, but also protect him among the Nacogdochito, Tawakani, and Bidais Indians who supposedly had an order from rebel emissaries to kill anyone who did not present such a document. Deep into their journey, Grande and Bergara came across two men coming from Béxar, who identified themselves as recent deserters, and hearing of the propaganda plan agreed to join them. But it was a setup. The "deserters" were actually Spanish spies, who departed the camp near the Colorado River, pretending to go north, but then doubled back to San Antonio and informed royalist authorities.[31]

Grande and Bergara were captured on September 16th—the second anniversary of the Grito—and given a swift trial. The verdict was "that they may be shot as criminals without giving them more time than that very necessary for getting themselves ready to die Christianly." Another emissary of Gutiérrez was also captured on the way to the Mexican rebel's hometown of Revilla, but there is a good chance that others made it through. Gutiérrez had written twelve documents in all, not counting copies, and the Spanish records include only three that were captured.[32]

Meanwhile, Magee was preparing to advance on Trinidad. His army would shortly grow to between 450 and 600 men. He had arranged to leave Capt. James Gaines alongside Guadiana in Nacogdoches, to protect it from Indian attacks, secure it as a logistics hub, and from it forward along new recruits who were arriving in small bands. Magee had at least two, possibly as many as six small cannon he had brought with him, but those that he found in Nacogdoches were worthless. He also had to wait for the arrival of carts full of "bomb-shells and other instruments of war."[33]

Resupply, reorganization, and weather too would delay Magee's advance for nearly a month. The delay was also useful to allow for Gutiérrez's proclamations to pave the way for the army, which was vital, since Magee expected the people to embrace their liberators and large numbers of Spanish deserters to rally to their flag. On September 13th, he decided the Republican Army of the North was ready and marched south.[34]

The Second Agent

Ninety miles away, American Special Agent William Shaler waited in the hot, humid climate of Natchitoches. The last letter that he had received from Monroe—the sole one, in fact—was dated May 2nd. The only useful piece of advice it provided was "You should proceed immediately to Mexico in fulfilment of your original instructions." Since that date, Shaler had fired off ten letters to the secretary of state informing him of any details he could learn of the growing expedition. The silence, once again, caused Shaler to wax philosophically. In his letterbook, where he recorded copies of all his correspondence, he penned an essay titled "Reflections on the means of restoring the political balance and preserving a general peace to the world." He wrote at length about England, France, the political balance in Europe, and his most favorite topic, the fate of the rebellious nations in the Western Hemisphere. Spanish and Portuguese colonies, with "their soil, climate, and coasts, bays and harbors, seem to mark them as destined by nature to favor the greatest development of human industry, if they were freed from the shackles of barbarism, and ignorance, and under the influence of wise and patriotic governments."[35]

Shaler never sent the essay to the secretary of state, but even if he had, he might as well have been lecturing the moon, for all the response he was getting. It had been two years and ten months since he had been given the mission of establishing relations with Cuba and Mexico. When he had left then-Secretary of State Robert Smith's office, revolutionary success had seemed imminent, but Cuba had been a complete bust, and Mexico's complex war was impossible to predict. The apparent failure of his own mission must have been depressing for the agent, as is suggested by an otherwise minor detail. Inside his letter book, he glued a newspaper clipping dated Santiago, Chile, February 24, 1812. It was there every time he opened the book, and he must have read it over and over in frustration. It was a newspaper clipping describing the glorious reception of his colleague, Joel Roberts Poinsett:

> The Consul took his seat, and the President, addressing himself to him, said: "Chile, Mr. Consul, by its government and its corporations, recognizes in you the Consul General of the United States of North America. That power attracts all our attentions and our attachment. You may safely assure it of the sincerity of our friendly sentiments. Its commerce will be attended to, and your representations directed to its prosperity will not be without effect. This is the universal sentiment of this people, in whose name I address you."[36]

This then, was what success looked like. Poinsett, one of the two special agents Smith had sent out in addition to Shaler, had struck diplomatic gold. The contrast with Shaler's own failure must have been galling for a man who by all accounts had a strong sense of vanity. If this was not enough, his younger brother and fellow sea captain Nathaniel Shaler, master and commander of the privateer *Anaconda*, was gaining fame—and with a captain's share in the booty, a fortune too—capturing British ships. William Shaler's only hope for distinction now lay with the very same private invasion that he had opposed just weeks before.[37]

Shaler had expected disaster, but Gutiérrez and Magee had triumphed. Now, despite his reservations, he began to see this unlikely event as fated to open his road to the Halls of Montezuma, where he too could be received rapturously like Poinsett. But at this moment, he was suddenly struck on August 25th by Claiborne's proclamation, which arrived after a two-week trip up the Mississippi. After complete government inaction to stop the filibuster, the senior official on the frontier was now declaring it illegal! Shaler, ignorant of Carr's disobeyed orders, was dumbfounded. It seemed to him like closing the barn door after the horses had run out. He wrote to the governor:[38]

> I have this moment received your favor of the 12th enclosing your proclamations against the Sabine expedition. I regret very much that it had not appeared a month sooner, as then that expedition would have been put down before anything was done, and no person of character would have been injuriously committed. For my part notwithstanding that all my feelings are enlisted in the cause of the Mexican patriots, and that it is of moment to me to have the road opened, I have from the beginning reprobated such an expedition as contrary to laws, and good policy, and all my communications have been in that spirit.[39]

But Shaler did not want to lose this opportunity now that he had it, and he tried to win Claiborne over to his new way of thinking. "I confess to you in this confidence of friendship, that since it has been suffered to proceed this far, and with such success, that I regret to see it fail now," he wrote. "I think it would be injurious to the public interest." While professing obedience to Claiborne's proclamation, he suggested to the government that "some communications made to you from this place have been exaggerated." Magee, he tried to assure the governor, was "a man of honor; his sole object is military fame." Neither the Bostonian nor anyone else in his command was harming the United States. "His conduct thus far has been praiseworthy." Shaler argued for his own innocence in the matter of the filibuster. He had stated clearly to Gutiérrez that, despite his hope for Mexican success, the administration "would never approve of such unauthorized proceedings *by men unknown, not under their control, and in no manner possessing their confidence*" (emphasis added).[40]

"I have not entered into this review, Sir," he told the governor, "from any apprehensions that you suspect me of connivance, but in order to enable you to do complete justice to my character if it should be called into question which from exaggerated accounts that I hear have reached Orleans may be the case."[41]

Shaler now wrote to Monroe to possibly head off an ill-timed intervention that would doom the Mexican Revolution in Texas upon which his mission vitally depended. Although everyone's preference was for a fully Mexican face to the revolution, Shaler admitted, it was a good thing to have Augustus Magee and *a few* Americans with him. He argued that Magee served a purpose "to prevent Don Bernardo from running into the extravagance of revolutionary injustice and tyranny," which he had begun to fear after some of Gutiérrez's more delusional flights of rhetorical fancy. But the same week he was writing this, a thousand miles away in Washington, Shaler's first letters about the enterprise were finally arriving on the desk of James Monroe. At long last, the secretary of state was awake to the danger and wrote Shaler in precisely the language his agent had wanted *before*, but which he now feared: "As the parties who are said to have combined for the purpose of assisting the patriots in Mexico are acting in opposition to a Law of the United States, it will be proper for you to discountenance the measure, so far as the expression of your opinion may avail. I shall write to you soon more fully on this Subject."[42]

Of course, it would be nearly sixty days before Shaler would receive these instructions to "discountenance" an invasion that was by then already three months old. Long before then, Shaler would be struck by an even greater shock. On October 5th, a well-dressed, refined young man named John Hamilton Robinson entered Natchitoches and called on Shaler. When the two were alone, Robinson produced a document for Shaler to read. It was his instructions from Secretary of State James Monroe. Robinson was appointed as a special agent and envoy *to the Spanish government*.[43]

The man who showed up at Shaler's doorstep in October 1812 had been to Mexico before. He was a young physician who had accompanied Pike on his expedition in 1806. Even before then, he had established a reputation as a wanderer of great pretension and ambition, but questionable character. In one case in 1803, he appeared at a slave auction in Virginia with bulging saddlebags and outbid the competition, but when it came time to pay, asked to do so on credit. The bags, so the story went, were filled with stones. Not long after this incident, Robinson, who had been a schoolmaster in Virginia, moved west and began to practice medicine, despite having only "commenced the study of physic" a few months before.[44]

In Missouri, he came to the attention of Wilkinson and was personally selected by the general to accompany Pike. During the expedition, he behaved in a mercenary manner, as befitting his own history and that of the scheming general. After they were captured, Pike's party was treated much more humanely than the Santa Fe traders mentioned in this book, and Robinson got to see as much or more of the conditions inside New Spain than they had.[45]

Robinson was one of the few Americans to have had a personal audience with Commandant General Nemesio Salcedo in Chihuahua, and on his return trip through Texas, he had made friends with Simón Herrera. It was this experience and his innate ability to endear himself to powerful men which undoubtedly drove

Monroe to choose him for a mission to the Spanish now. But why send a new envoy when Shaler was already on the edge of the territory? And why keep Shaler in the dark about it? Robinson was appointed in July, but Shaler was not even informed until the September 1st letter, which did not even arrive before Robinson himself did.[46]

Shaler, of course, was not supposed to *be* on the border, but in Veracruz. Monroe never sanctioned the Natchitoches trip until after the fact, then tolerated it as a temporary expedient. He always intended Shaler to move on to find the Mexican rebels and he had no expectation of Shaler making the 1,500-mile trip by land. The secretary of state had nonetheless sent Robinson along with a letter for Shaler in the event their paths crossed. In it, he informed Shaler that Robinson's "employment will not interfere with yours, but cooperate with it, in cultivating a good understanding between the United States and the Governments and people of the Provinces to which you are *respectively* sent" (emphasis added). Shaler was the agent to the *Mexican* revolution, wherever its seat of government was to be found. Robinson was the agent to the *Spanish* Commandant General of the Interior Provinces. Monroe did not know who would win the war in New Spain and was covering his bases.[47]

Robinson's mission—already obsolete by the time he arrived—was to find a solution to the problem of the banditti in the Neutral Ground and to assure the commandant general of the US goodwill. Monroe seems to have been ignorant about the character of the gruff, uncompromising commandant general, and possibly Robinson oversold his connection to this man. Given his ignorance, it is not impossible that Monroe hoped that Nemesio Salcedo might follow the precedent of West Florida governor Folch, who had almost turned his province over to America out of desperation when faced with his own empire's spiral into chaos.[48]

When Robinson was dispatched, neither he nor Monroe had known about the filibuster, only the banditti. This not only made the mission obsolete, but insofar as the Spanish suspected the US government's involvement, it gave Robinson's embassy the appearance of duplicity. For Nemesio Salcedo, who did not even tolerate dissent from his nephew, the idea of citizens acting contrary to their government's direct orders was an alien concept. For the Spaniard, the role of government was to *control* its subjects, so Washington was responsible whether the Americans ordered the attack or merely let it happen.

As far as Shaler was concerned, the second agent "marches too far in the rear of events." The filibuster was now the only issue, and the agent thought the republican wave pushing across Texas was unstoppable. "The volunteer expedition from the most insignificant beginning is growing into an irresistible torrent that will sweep the crazy remains of Spanish government from the internal provinces," he wrote. This would open Mexico "to the political influence of the U. S. and to the talents and enterprize of our citizens." Only a force from Great Britain could prevent the fall of Mexico.[49]

Robinson would not be dissuaded. He was an ambitious young man, nine years younger than Shaler, impressed with a powerful belief in his own potential for greatness. Zebulon Pike, no stranger himself to pride, had written of Robinson, "His soul could conceive great actions, and his hand was ready to achieve them; in short, it may truly be said that nothing was above his genius." Wasting no time in Natchitoches, Robinson set out for Texas, where he expected, no doubt, to prove that genius.[50]

Robinson was hardly the only person with delusions of grandeur, and on this point, Shaler was far more concerned about Bernardo Gutiérrez. The event that now caused him to seriously question Gutiérrez was a dispute over Bayou Pierre, a town founded by Spain but marooned east of the Sabine. With the approval of Louisiana statehood, the town was now definitively within the boundaries of the new American state. Thus, in early October, when Shaler heard rumors that Gutiérrez was conscripting residents of the community into the Republican Army, he was appalled. Shaler dashed off a letter to his former ward with harsh words for the Mexican. "It appears to me sir of the most signal impolicy; that you should gratuitously attempt to shock the American authorities in a point of great delicacy, which is evidently not within your competency, at a time when so many Americans are crowding by your standards and when you are drawing your very existence from these states," he wrote. "It seems like attempting to wound the hand that administers relief to you. To imprison an American citizen Sir without his having infringed any of your laws, is a violation of the law of nations and an insult to our government."[51]

Shaler rode to Bayou Pierre to investigate, bringing along with him Captain Overton from Fort Claiborne and several soldiers. Though he had never exercised any authority on the government's behalf before, Shaler did so now, he claimed, only out of extreme necessity: With Judge Carr having resigned, no one else would. Arriving in the small community, he interviewed Don Marcello de Soto, the town's administrative official. Soto clarified that the order had indeed been sent to him but explained that he had ignored it. Shaler, with no one to arrest, rode back to Natchitoches.[52]

When word of his concerns reached Gutiérrez, the latter wrote an apologetic letter claiming innocence and suggesting the "overzealous" Pedro Procela, who had written the order, had been the culprit, not him. Nonetheless, Shaler remained suspicious of Gutiérrez's actions, and had a nagging feeling that the Mexican would do something reckless. "I do not however mean to insinuate anything against the intentions of Bernardo," he wrote Monroe. "On the contrary I believe he means well, but his ignorance of mankind, and total political incapacity, together with his weakness and preposterous vanity, render him a just object of dread if he should come into the possession of uncontrolled power." Shaler's words would prove to be prophetic.[53]

Confrontation in Trinidad

Magee's strength by September was at a minimum three hundred Anglos and one hundred Mexican rebels. In Natchez, Adair was still recruiting. "The business of volunteering for New Spain has become a perfect mania," Shaler wrote. "I hear of parties proceeding thither from all quarters, and they are constantly passing through this village from Natchez. Several young gentlemen of respectable characters and acquirements have gone on." The numbers would start to trail off in November, following the widespread news of Claiborne's proclamation, but they would never cease entirely. Shaler would later find it difficult to track the numbers and at one point said he did not know how many there were in the republican force within three hundred men.[54]

Magee departed Nacogdoches on September 13th, heading south on the Spanish royal road. During the march, the Bostonian was forced to deal with widespread insubordination. Like the Texas rebels of 1836, these were citizen soldiers to whom obedience to authority was deemed optional. The Republican Army was mostly on foot. In 1812, horses were still a luxury for most Americans, and though Spanish Texas had them aplenty, East Texas did not. For the duration of the campaign, oxen would be the main beasts of burden for the army. The men carried most of what they needed on their backs; they had no uniforms and almost no extra clothing of any kind. The fictional account of Hiram McLane, based on his father's actual remembrances, preserves a story in which an expedition recruit packed a trunk filled to overflowing with genteel clothing including "elaborately ruffled shirts," soap, handkerchiefs, slippers, and more—all of which he was ultimately forced to jettison upon entering Texas "first because we have no sort of use for them, and second because we have no way of transporting them, if we did need them." The Republican Army would be characterized by poverty and want in all things. But the silver lining was that in consequence of its lack of supply wagons and baggage, it was highly mobile.[55]

Magee's army had with them at least three four-pounder cannons and one of an unknown, smaller size. These were small cannon for their day, but more portable, and easier to get across the numerous streams the army would encounter. The army arrived at Trinidad de Salcedo in a few days, establishing itself near the mostly abandoned town. The republicans called the place Camp Tranquitas. Here they paused to await reinforcements and better weather before moving on.[56]

This was a Mexican Revolutionary Army made up of mostly Anglo-Americans, fighting for a vague ideal of liberty. They carried no Mexican flag—Hidalgo's forces had carried a banner with the Virgin of Guadalupe on it, and the tricolor we know today as Mexico's standard would not exist for nearly a decade. Still, they needed some ensign, and it appears to be Gutiérrez in a moment of rare unselfishness, who proposed an emerald green banner in tribute to Magee's Irish roots. It was a flag representing the army, not a political entity, and for this purpose it probably did not matter what it was, so long as it stood out amid the smoke and chaos of the field. The proposal was accepted, and the army marched under these colors, as far as is known, without any adornment. It is notable that despite the presence of West Florida veterans like Samuel Kemper, who had raised the first lone star flag, no one in the army seems to have suggested a similar adornment for this Texas invasion. The use of the star, an American symbol, would have been inconsistent with the aims of Gutiérrez or Magee.[57]

Flags were pregnant with meaning, as was demonstrated on October 15th, when a great convulsion broke through the camp. When Magee investigated, he saw his men leading John Robinson, the American agent, who had been captured a short distance away. Magee was alarmed, particularly because Robinson carried with him the stars and stripes. Magee was at minimum a pragmatist concerned with keeping a Mexican face on the enterprise. Perhaps his hostility was even deeper. He had bitterly resigned his commission, almost certainly over the politicized snubbing of his promotion. He was from a family of New England Federalists violently hostile to President Madison. Indeed, his great patron T. H. Perkins would in two years be a representative of the antiwar—its enemies would say secessionist—Hartford Convention.[58]

But Magee was not the only one in camp offended; the outcry was general. West Floridians like Kemper remembered bitterly how they had fought to liberate the territory only to see the United States sweep in and claim it, suppressing the West Floridian assembly and denying all land claims of those who had fought. In their minds, the political takeover was a betrayal. Magee demanded to know Robinson's business with the flag, inside what he evidently referred to as a "republic."[59]

Robinson was taken aback. "I answered that I had been sent by the President of the United States to the Captain General of Mexico on public business, and that I bore the flag of my country for my personal protection," he wrote later. He added that his government knew nothing about any republic in Texas. Then the agent tried to show his passport. Magee dismissed it as worthless. "He observed," Robinson wrote, "that the general opinion in the camp was, that I was sent to take possession of the country in the name of the United States, an act, which he and all who were with him would oppose. That the Florida business was still fresh in their memories, and that he would not answer for my life if I attempted to proceed, his men having sworn they would murder me, and that he had not power sufficient to restrain them etc. etc."[60]

Robinson was surprised by the violence of the rebels' hostility. He was placed in confinement and the next day brought before a council of war. It seems to have been more mob than formal trial. Charges were hurled at the agent, including the allegation that he had bribed a Spaniard with one thousand dollars to convey him around the rebel camp. Robinson asked for evidence, and when the crowd looked for the man who made the charge, he had slipped away.[61]

"[The accuser's] object, as appeared afterwards, was to excite the troops to rise and take my life before I could have an opportunity of being heard, and had actually succeeded so far, as to raise a party of ten Americans, who had sworn to effect it," Robinson wrote. But there would be no lynching on this day. When the lack of evidence was admitted, the rebels began to calm, some even apologizing to Robinson for their hasty assumption of his guilt. Finally, after two days of debate, a representative of the council delivered the verdict, which showed an army deeply imbued with Burrite sentiment.[62] As Robinson reported the decision: "We find ourselves competent to make war against either the United States or New Spain separately, but not against both those powers combined, and as we are at war with the latter, good policy dictates that we should not draw on ourselves the enmity of the former, we will therefore suffer her agent Doc. John H. Robinson to pass to his point of destination, so far as it is within our control, on the following conditions."[63]

Robinson was required to leave his flag behind, take a passport of Gutiérrez's "republic," pledge his honor not to disclose to the Spanish the republican position or strength, and proceed alone, leaving behind his servant. The agent agreed to the conditions and signed a document that pledged "his honor to the commander of the American and Mexican troops, that he will not reveal or disclose anything relative to their position, strength or intentions, which may accidentally have come to his knowledge during his detention in said camp, the same having been required of him."[64]

Robinson in San Antonio

The agent continued down the Camino Real toward San Antonio, swimming the Trinity and several other rivers over the next four hundred miles. The Spanish had established pickets on the Guadalupe River under Capt. Don José de Jesús Rodríguez, to watch the four likeliest crossing points. Rodríguez's orders were to "absolutely prevent the crossing through the said line of any individual, be it of whatever class and condition" in either direction. On October 30th, Robinson reached this first outpost, where he was captured, taken to San Antonio, and brought before Manuel Salcedo.[65]

The governor received him cordially with "a suavity of manner, uncommon in the character of a Spanish officer." Then Herrera entered the room. Recognizing the companion of Zebulon Pike immediately, he embraced Robinson. Turning to his fellow governor, he replied with warmth, "This then is the prisoner of whom we have heard so much since last night, let me tell you, I rejoice to see him once more, he is my particular friend, and I beg leave to introduce him to you as such." This began a relaxed, friendly conversation. Robinson claimed a good understanding of Spanish, although Samuel Davenport thought it poor. Nonetheless, Herrera, with an English wife, spoke Robinson's language well. Robinson pleased Herrera by delivering a personal letter from his old friend Pike, whom he had visited in Baton Rouge on his way to Texas.[66]

"[The Spaniards] were very much pleased when I informed them that the President of the United States was friendly disposed towards them and that he desired to establish friendly relations with [Spain]," Robinson reported. The Spanish officers all reciprocated these sentiments and congratulated Robinson on his safe arrival. Herrera and Salcedo sped him on his way. On November 2nd, the two governors, along with an honor guard of about twenty officers, rode with him two leagues further down the Camino Real, then parting with him, returned to San Antonio while he rode onward toward Monclova.[67]

Despite Robinson's promise to the filibusters, it appears that he did indeed betray their location (deliberately or otherwise) on the Trinity and their intentions. The Spaniards of course were already aware of Magee's movements from their spies and were considering the option of marching out in force to meet him. But what Robinson gave to the two Spaniards that was far more powerful was a propaganda coup. Rumors of the invasion were impossible to suppress in San Antonio, and many of its citizens and soldiers thought surely if the United States was on the rebels' side, the revolution would succeed.[68]

But Robinson's mere presence disproved this: the United States, they learned, had not authorized the invasion, and the Spanish commanders publicly proclaimed this to their people. America, Salcedo and Herrera explained, was friendly toward Spain, and the army of Gutiérrez and Magee was "a band of vagabonds, that has no other object in view, but to plunder and ravage your country, and even take from you your wives and daughters." The Spanish authorities even enlisted priests to share this message with their flock. Robinson, though sympathetic to the revolution, had done great injury to the rebel cause simply by showing up. His presence momentarily stopped the hemorrhaging of royalist support, bolstered Salcedo and Herrera, and shifted the momentum back to the royal side.[69]

14

Trinidad to La Bahía

"ON MY ARRIVAL at this place . . . I was very much surprised to find the country in the situation that it then was," read a private letter from Rapides, Louisiana, reprinted in the October 12, 1812, *National Intelligencer*. "All the laboring men & mechanics had left it; a number of the drafted militia from the Mississippi territory were and are daily going to join Col. Magee and Don Bernardo." Another article dated two weeks later added, "From accounts, there will be no opposition at St. Antonio. Letters from Col. M'Gee state, that they will make but a short stay at St. Antonio, but proceed on over the River Grand, where it is reported a division of Gen. Rayon's army have arrived."[1]

The tidings from America's southwestern frontier could not have been in more stark contrast to news elsewhere. A month before Magee had launched his attack on New Spain, an American invasion of Canada had failed; the British had then taken Detroit, a calamity that shocked the nation. Magee's little band of volunteers (still greatly outnumbering the native Mexican rebels in their ranks) were the only force of Americans on the continent who were having military success.

President Madison and Secretary of State Monroe probably paid little attention to Texas; they had bigger concerns. In addition to the Canada fiasco, there were antiwar riots in Baltimore that summer, and the defeat of Napoleon in Russia no doubt meant Britain could turn greater attention to America. But for the men of the West, reading about the success of the Republican Army, the outlook was hopeful. Those who flocked to Texas routed through Natchez and Rapides, where Adair and Reuben Kemper were aiding in the organization and logistical support of the Republican Army. Sibley and Claiborne both reported Adair was to take the leadership of the army, but Shaler soon clarified that the general was organizing a *separate* force that would only enter with government approval. It was likely just a cover story, but if the sanctioned war *did* materialize, Adair could march south in glory, push Magee aside, and win fame and redemption as the man who opened up the road to Mexico City.[2]

Magee Resumes the March

The army continued to add men as it made its way deeper into Texas. Arriving around this time were a Captain Scott and the smuggler "Little John" McFarlan, who had escaped the American militia that had attacked his band of recruits. He too was made a captain in charge of rebel scouts. Magee added a second West Pointer, Samuel Noah of the Class of 1807, who was actually the academy's first Jewish graduate. Appointed to the infantry arm, he had been stationed at Fort Adams, Mississippi, where he met then-captain Winfield Scott, Pike, and probably Magee as well. He was forced to resign in 1811 for unknown reasons and subsequently joined the filibuster, in the words of a family historian, "allured by visions of a golden future."[3]

The day after the American agent John Robinson left the camp, the Republican Army packed up and moved south, crossing the Trinity River probably near modern Midway, Texas. Magee continued to march along the Camino Real because of the necessity of moving the wagons and other baggage. From accounts reaching Natchitoches, the army was in good spirits and eager to march on San Antonio. There, Robinson's arrival had convinced Gov. Manuel Salcedo of what he was facing: "Vagabonds led by the traitor Gutiérrez, one Frenchman from Louisiana [Despallier], and an American officer retired from service." In response, he consolidated his troops and called for reinforcements from across the neighboring provinces—the latter with little success. "Unfortunately . . . it appears that in each province another King is served," Salcedo despaired, "and we do not realize that we are all Spaniards."[4]

With information gleaned from Robinson, Salcedo took the initiative: He ordered Capt. Félix Ceballos and José de Jesús Rodriguez to guard six fords of the Guadalupe River near present-day New Braunfels. Should the enemy appear, these captains were to oppose or delay them. Magee, at that time moving south on the Camino Real, sent out scouts before him to reconnoiter the territory, and one of these, arriving at the crossing of the Colorado River near modern Bastrop, came across a friendly Mexican who warned that the Spanish were planning an ambush on the Guadalupe, only sixty miles away.[5]

Magee was unnerved. This was not the routed force that he had driven from Nacogdoches, and which was rumored to be all but ready to quit Texas. Salcedo likely outnumbered him now and had more and larger cannons than the four small ones Magee possessed. Magee's army only numbered around 450 men. Three quarters or so were Americans, well-armed and skilled with their weapons, but individualists to a fault and ill-disciplined. The Mexican rebels under Davenport and Despallier's command were mostly Spanish defectors and some militia, their arms inconsistent. Magee certainly doubted their worth. It would be a week or more before he could reach the Guadalupe, and Salcedo could fortify in the meantime. Cutting across country to try to slip across the river to the east or west was also out of the question.

His army needed to stick to roads and dependable fords, and Salcedo blocked the path.[6]

From the Mexican informant, Magee learned that Salcedo had stripped the garrison from the presidio of La Bahía. This important point to his southeast was a small village further down the San Antonio River, straddling the coastal road that paralleled the Camino Real. It was very much out of the way, but once reached, there was a good road northwest to San Antonio that could put Magee *behind* Salcedo, and with no large rivers between him and the capital. Furthermore, the presidio at La Bahía was the best-constructed fort in all of Texas, stouter by far than the Alamo. If he had to shift to the defense, La Bahía was the place to be. Though it was not as close to the sea as its name implies—it was indeed nearly thirty-five miles from "the bay"—it was nonetheless well placed to await reinforcements or resupply by sea. There was a small branch of the road between the San Marcos and Neches Rivers, and Magee selected this alternative route. Upon reaching the Guadalupe well southeast of Salcedo's force, he crossed it safely and proceeded to La Bahía in the first week of November.[7]

The Presidio

"We arrived at La Bahía without opposition or even being discovered until in possession of that garrison," Davenport later wrote. Magee sent scouts into town and, upon their favorable report, entered with the full army later that night. The inhabitants were friendly but surprised at the smallness of the force that had so easily taken Nacogdoches. That town, so far from Mexico and so close to the allure of American trade, had always longed for change. Trinity, with its mixed population, had a natural inclination to rebel. La Bahía, on the other hand, was entirely Spanish and more closely aligned with San Antonio. Gutiérrez nonetheless found the citizens desirous "to shake off the oppressive yoke" and supportive of his plans to establish a government and a republican constitution. They wanted Creole commanders, relief from Spanish mercantilism, and their religion and property respected.[8]

The Republican Army occupied the presidio, finding plenty of corn, and according to Hall, several houses full of salt for preserving meat, which would become very useful in the weeks ahead. Additionally, a box of cash was discovered, and the soldiers received what was for most of them their first pay, ten dollars. Most importantly, the republicans found in the fortress a single nine-pounder cannon to add to the shorter-range carronades they had. The republicans, tired no doubt from two weeks of marching, settled down in their new home, safe behind their walls. In the town, which they also occupied, they erected defensive wooden walls across the ends of the streets.[9]

The precautions were just in time. Friendly Indians had told the rebels that the Spanish had retreated to San Antonio, but they were wrong. The governor instead had cut overland in pursuit of his enemies. If he could not ambush the republicans, he would besiege them. Magee, upon arrival, had sent a scouting party up the San Antonio road under Capt. Josiah Taylor, but Taylor and the five men who rode with him mysteriously disappeared. Unbeknownst to Magee, they had been captured by a Spanish patrol. Shackled together in pairs, they were marched back to San Antonio to be imprisoned in the Alamo. Another party, reconnoitering southward toward the Nueces River, was led by McFarlan. In this case, it was the royalists who were surprised: McFarlan's party captured a Spanish sergeant and twenty-five men. But riding back to La Bahía, they were surprised to see the fortress surrounded.[10]

On November 13th, six days after the republicans took the town, Salcedo had arrived in force. The rebels, caught off guard, quickly manned the walls, firing their nine-pounder at the approaching enemy. A ball took the head of a Spanish soldier clean off, stopping the army in its tracks. Salcedo, who had rushed cross-country to catch the enemy, had no comparable artillery and pulled back to a safe distance. McFarlan, arriving a short time later, observed the enemy's camp, puzzled as to how to get through to the fortress with his prisoners. He waited until nightfall and slipped past the Spanish. His prisoners had previously expressed a desire to join the rebels, but upon seeing the small size of the republican force, now refused, and were instead locked inside a prison cell within the fortress.[11]

The presidio which the Republican Army occupied was a square stone-walled fortress about one hundred yards long, with two bastions. It contained a stone chapel, a barracks probably built into one of the walls, and a guard house. It was located south of the town. Soon after taking it, the Republican Army began fortifying. "They erected a bastion of earth on each side of the fort," writes Henderson Yoakum, citing McKim's diary, "on which they mounted the guns they found in the fort, and also the three six pounders they had brought with them."[12]

The Spanish took up positions around the fortress. Herrera occupied the old Espiritu Santo mission, about a thousand yards away on the north side of the river, within a bend of the San Antonio where it curved closest to the presidio. Salcedo assumed a position astride the Béxar Road, just outside of cannon range. Another force under Cristóbal Domínguez, the former Nacogdoches garrison commander ousted by the Casas Revolt, encamped south of the outpost. The river curved into another bend to the northeast of the fortress, where low-lying areas were prone to flooding. Though it was not a perfect encirclement, the disposition prevented any easy escape of the republican army.[13]

The Spanish had around 1,000 men, to the rebel force, anywhere from 450 to 800. Still, the fortress was stout, and Herrera and Salcedo were not confident enough in their men to attempt a frontal assault. Magee decided on a quick action with the intent to draw the enemy into a fight close to the walls, where the nine-pound cannon, on a bastion facing the main Spanish force, was his ace card. On the very evening that the Spanish arrived, the American sent out a force of 18 men on horseback under Capt. Thomas Slocum to attack a force of about 150 Spaniards on the mission side. The battle was short, and about seven or eight royalists were killed. The rebels then pulled back to the fort as planned, but disaster struck when one of the men fell from his horse and a mounted Spaniard lassoed him. William McLane recalled, "The enemy, being so elated with their first exploit, galloped over the prairie for hours, dragging their captive by the neck, yelling like savages. Having exhausted their horses, they returned to their quarters and cut off the head of their captive and raised [it in] view" of the presidio.[14]

For the classically educated Magee, this ghastly spectacle must have brought to mind Achilles's dragging of Hector before the gates of Troy. "They are a rascally set of treacherous cowards," he wrote to Shaler. "God never made greater villains." With night coming on, both sides retired to their camps, and the incident "dampened the ardor" of those in the fort. The republican troops were brought to quarters at every minor alarm, often in the dead of night and "paraded for hours in mud half leg deep, produced from the rains and tramping of the stock." Mud and excrement too, for the livestock had been brought inside the fortress, making it a cramped and sickly place.[15]

Health was indeed on the mind of Augustus Magee, who since Trinidad had become increasingly afflicted by a pulmonary ailment, and he was doubtless not the only one. How to feed the livestock was another problem, as there was nothing inside the fort for them. There was ample grass outside the presidio, however, so Davenport as quartermaster sent the livestock out every day to pasture, guarded by a company under Captain Scott. The Spaniards made multiple attempts to seize this livestock, though the republicans' long gun discouraged them from getting too close. On one such attack, mounted royalists came out and "made quite a display in horsemanship, discharging their escopets [heavy cavalry carbines], poised on the left arm, at an elevation of forty degrees." This unusual ballistic fire was surprisingly effective. One of the balls penetrated the hip of one man, and another passed through Captain Scott's coat. "This so alarmed the Captain that he resigned his commission and procured a horse and guide and took 'French leave' [went AWOL] in the night."[16]

Davenport replaced Scott with a Mexican, a former soldier from Béxar named Juan Galván. He was the same Spaniard who, at Salitre Prairie, had ridden through his army's camp in panic when Kemper had surprised them. Captured, he became like so many others, an involuntary rebel. He now drove the livestock too far beyond the walls and was attacked. The Spaniards killed the only Anglo-American in the escort and captured the Mexicans. Galván was almost certainly deserting, for he soon appeared among the enemy's camp, once again in the Spanish service. In addition to the men lost, he had taken with him two hundred horses and mules. Some citizens of the town apparently defected to the Spanish as well, including one man who buried several thousand dollars in the ground before fleeing.[17]

"This gave rise to much discontent for the moment among our officers & men," wrote Davenport, "and after some deliberation Colonel Magee thought it expedient and did order a meeting of all the field officers and captains of companies to deliberate and determine on what manner we were to act." The Spanish were clearly not as enthusiastic for rebellion as he had been led to believe. They too could see the imbalance of the armies and had heard the same propaganda message that Salcedo had spread in San Antonio after Robinson's visit, dismissing the republicans as mere rogues. "Several of the inhabitants of La Bahía informed me of this," Davenport wrote. "Those that know the contrary told me that nothing had or could have operated so much against our cause as the unfortunate circumstance of that agent appearing at the moment he did."[18]

These defections were a serious blow to Anglo-Mexican unity. The Americans felt betrayed and suspicious of the remaining Mexicans. They had expected universal enthusiasm for their mission of liberation, and these ungrateful and deceitful people—as they saw it—were rejecting those gifts. What the Americans failed to appreciate was the complexity of a civil war. Raised on jingoistic stories of their own revolution, they had forgotten just how divided their own fathers' generation had been. Moreover, the citizens and soldiers of Spanish Texas did not have the luxury of principle that the outsiders enjoyed. Their lives—and, more importantly, the lives of their families—were at stake. If they backed the Spanish and the rebels prevailed, the consequences might be slight, but if they crossed Governor Salcedo and came out on the losing end, they would likely suffer a traitor's death. In the end, and as a practical matter, the Americans had somewhere to run to if they failed. The people of Spanish Texas did not.

Magee, blind to this, lashed out. "We are differently received in this country to what we expected & indeed you have no conception of the treachery of these people," he wrote to Shaler. "I have nothing to depend on but my Americans, and that is but a bad one." The Massachusetts-born officer, who had wrecked his career in a moment of pique and tied his fate to this foreign adventure, now despaired. "My hopes of effecting a revolution in this country, with the means I now hold, are entirely blasted, but still I am strong enough to open my road, whatever course I choose to go."[19]

Magee Parlays

Magee no doubt knew what Napoleon thought of fortifications—that a force that remained in them was already beaten. He felt trapped by his enemies and deceived by his allies, but in truth he had no one to blame but himself. He had been as much a prisoner of illusions as anyone. War is more than evicting squatters from cabins. This was a real war, a civil war—the most barbarous kind—and a foreign one he could not understand.

Magee called a council of his officers to deliberate, evidently excluding the Mexicans for lack of trust. The Americans unanimously agreed to Magee's plan to send a parlay to Salcedo and Herrera. The deal Magee was to propose was "for our retiring from the government, alleging that we had been treacherously deceived by the inhabitants of the province as to their wishes." Magee sent over a flag of truce, followed by the passage of several letters back and forth. With the ground rules for the meeting set, Magee set out for the mission, along with his closest confidant, Maj. William Murray. On the Spanish side, Salcedo, Herrera, and Lieutenant Colonel Arcos met the Americans.[20]

Manuel Salcedo and Augustus Magee had much in common; they were both men of privilege who commanded forces of much humbler stock than themselves. Salcedo had even traveled through Magee's home state of Massachusetts about the same time Magee was leaving it to go to West Point. But there was a deeper connection between them. They were both highly insecure, troubled, and dispirited at the downward trajectory of their once brilliant careers. In November 1811, after being humiliatingly ousted, imprisoned, and then released, Salcedo was ordered back to his post with no opportunity to defend his honor and prestige. "I find myself snubbed for lack of a public testimony with which to prove the injustice of how much my person, my honor, and my limited assets suffered," he had written his uncle the commandant general. Seven months later, Magee, whose own uncle had effectively poisoned his career with his rabid hostility to the president, penned a nearly identical sentiment in a letter to *his* superior. "Feeling myself dissatisfied with the service and personally slighted," he wrote the secretary of war. Two troubled, tragic, and insecure souls were meeting in search of redemption, and in this contest only one—possibly neither—could ever earn it.[21]

They chatted for several hours, with Herrera—fluent in English—likely translating. The Spaniards were not opposed to the Americans retiring, and agreed they could do so, provided they only took one weapon for every five men. The problem, however, was what to do with the Mexicans who had joined the rebels. As disgusted as Magee may have been with the defection of some of them, there were many—probably the majority—who had remained loyal and waited for word behind the walls of the presidio. Magee insisted that these men receive a full pardon and be permitted to return to their families without any punishment or loss of property, or to join the Americans on their march to the United States, as they desired.[22]

This Salcedo could not do. While the governor said he was authorized to grant them their lives, a full pardon was beyond his authority. He had spent four difficult years being second-guessed and browbeaten by his uncle. Even if he were inclined to be generous, he knew what the result of any such offer would be: Nemesio Salcedo would certainly order the execution of all traitors the moment Magee's Americans were clear of the colony. The Spanish rebels "must remain at the disposition of their government," he said, "to undergo such other punishment as might be found expedient to inflict on them for having rebelled against their lawful sovereign." Magee and Murray rode back to the presidio and the council of officers was reconvened. The Americans were universally contemptuous of the Spanish terms. Asked to shoulder arms to vote in favor, they instead pounded the butts of their rifles and muskets on the ground. "There was scarce a dissenting [voice] from a determination to die with their arms in their hands rather than deliver up a single individual of the government that had taken up arms with them, and such was the answer sent to Governor Salcedo and Colonel Herrera." One source claims Magee, humiliated by this display, stalked off to his tent, leaving the army on parade.[23]

The Spanish recommenced hostilities on the next day. They had only conducted skirmish attacks so far, in deference to the rebel nine-pounder, but had recently received nine brass cannons from San Antonio, capable of firing at longer ranges. Still, their shot had proven ineffective against the fort's walls. To move them closer, the Spaniards chose to occupy the town, which crept up to the very edges of the presidio. Around 9:00 a.m. on November 24, 1812, Salcedo and Herrera lined up their troops in their full strength, and with the cannon for support, they moved forward. "Sixty shot were fired to no effect except one ball which by accident took off the right hand of one of our volunteers," Davenport wrote. As the Spaniards moved toward the town to attack at two points, companies of republicans sallied out of the fortress to prevent them from seizing the houses. Small arms fire was exchanged during the cannon duel, but the forces stayed too far apart for the fire to be effective.[24]

Around three or four in the afternoon, two rifle companies of the republicans attacked the left wing of the Spaniards, which consisted of about two hundred mixed cavalry and infantry. It would be the first serious engagement of the war. The firing erupted and was intense for a time before the Spaniards, having lost an officer and five men killed, along with seven wounded, retreated. Only three of the Americans were slightly wounded. The disparity in skill with their weapons was telling. Davenport reported that many of the Spanish soldiers fired high, wasting their shots. "Nor could they, with three times the force, have injured us," he reported. The battle had a positive effect on the republican morale.[25] Gutiérrez wrote afterward: "The valiant Americans are determined to conquer or perish, and the deluded troops of the enemy do not care to fight, from what we learn, and from which we saw at their attack of yesterday, when their officers were forced to cudgel the soldiers into their ranks when they approached us, and we know that many have deserted and others have sent word to us that they did not desert to us as not knowing but the Americans would kill them for having fought with them."[26]

Gutiérrez admitted a few of his own Mexican forces had deserted to the enemy "from pure cowardice." But now things were changing. "After seeing the valor of the Americans, not even a woman will leave us, and as soon as we obtain something like a victory over them things will change entirely in our favor." It likely aided Mexican morale to know that the Anglo-Americans had been offered escape but chose not to betray them. Now they could also point to the heroism of their own.[27]

From the filibuster's outset, the Mexican rebels had been mere auxiliaries in their own revolution. Though they had been embraced by the Americans initially, the defection of Galván and Magee's bitterness toward them had soured the relationship. Then, at a moment when the garrison ran critically low on beef, a mission to scout out the countryside in search of cattle was proposed. The Spanish had grown wary of the republicans' nighttime forays and had placed outposts to intercept the rebels chosen for this increasingly dangerous job. It was at this moment that an obscure soldier from the Mexican ranks, "dark as an Indian" stepped up and volunteered for the perilous assignment.[28]

Juan Savías was a militia auxiliary from Gutiérrez's home of Nuevo Santander. He was the same "distinguished soldier" among the troops of Spanish Sgt. Pedro José de Aldape, who had deserted as they fled south from Nacogdoches. Joining the republicans, Savías had served faithfully but quietly ever since. Now, probably speaking through Despallier as a translator, he asked to be allowed to lead a small party to attempt to capture cattle and drive them back into the presidio. The Americans, stung by the desertion of Galván, were at first hesitant to trust this man, whose dark skin must have further given pause to some of them. But such was his plea that they eventually relented on the sole condition that some Americans accompany him. Savías, who thus became the first Mexican to lead forces in which Americans *were subordinate to him*, sallied out of the presidio on his mission. To the astonishment of all, he returned with his party several days later with fifty cattle, which he slipped through the Spanish defenses. The cattle were slaughtered, and the meat was dried and preserved. Savías, for his exploit, "was made a captain and proved to be a trusty man and good officer and was true and brave to the last," remembered fellow soldier John Villars.[29]

The decision to stand and fight and Savías's exploit raised republican spirits. The army now had sufficient stocks of beef, mutton, and corn; there was plenty of ammunition and the cannon were in working order. The Republican Army of the North included a number of mechanics and gunsmiths who worked day and night to repair the arms. In this, Gutiérrez found work as well. The blacksmith from Revilla put his nose to the grindstone to help maintain the weapons, leaving his forge, or so he claimed, to seize his gun whenever there was fighting. On the day after the skirmish, November 25, 1812, Gutiérrez and Magee sent a joint letter to the north for relief.[30]

They chose as their courier Samuel Davenport. Magee had given him orders, but these may have been merely to allow the former Spanish Indian Agent to save face. The republican quartermaster was not exactly the picture of the hardy, robust frontier soldier. He was of medium height, very slender, with small bones and sloping shoulders. Neither did he have the courage to compensate. Though morale was improving generally after the battle, the Indian trader had evidently been unnerved. What shook him was when his former subordinate, Galván, sent word back to the presidio that when the Spanish took the fortress, he would hunt down Davenport and have "the skin of his belly for a drum-head." Trying to stop the spooked Davenport would have been useless. By giving the fearful quartermaster orders, Magee took advantage of the man's skills. He was fluent in Spanish, knowledgeable of the terrain, and had deep connections both in Nacogdoches and its sister town in Louisiana. Sending him also spared Magee from losing a courier who was otherwise courageous and useful in battle.[31]

Davenport likely slipped through the Spanish defenses to the northeast, crossed the river, and skirted the town to reach the road from whence they had come three weeks before. Before the colonel parted with Davenport, he told him that he would attack again in a few days and, given the performance on the previous day, felt a revived confidence of success. This newfound optimism was likely for appearances, for in a letter Magee wrote that same day for his courier to take to Shaler, he continued to vent about the betrayal of some of the natives—"cowardly fools"—who would not join the rebellion but instead "kiss the hand that scourges them." Then Magee referenced a new development—a potentially watershed change in the mission of the rebellion. This new proposal he left for Gutiérrez to explain in detail.[32]

An Extraordinary Proposal

When Gutiérrez had met with James Monroe in the comfort of the State Department offices eleven months before, he had been taken aback by the secretary's assertion of a claim on Texas. When Monroe suggested an offer of aid contingent on handing the province over, Gutiérrez pushed back. In his diary, and in his later writings a decade later, he struck a determined and unwavering tone of national pride and fortitude in rejecting the offer. But in the muddy walls of the Presidio La Bahía, Gutiérrez's resolution—like Magee's—was breaking down, and he penned a letter of enormous significance to Shaler. He was prepared to accept Monroe's offer of aid on the same conditions it had been given. Texas was to be the price of American aid to Mexico. This proposal was not just the offer of one man, but of the *entire leadership* of the Mexican contingent. Speaking "on behalf of myself and the inhabitants of this province," Gutiérrez wrote that "the happiest day of my life will be that of the union of the two Americas, which we now desire." He urged Shaler to come to Texas with "a sufficient military force to secure what we have conquered from the enemy."[33] "On these terms we offer ourselves to the American government requiring again as the most interesting point that a military force for our security be immediately sent, and for the expanse of this province, and of the immense and further regions of which it is composed. We also pray that our families in Nacogdoches and in [Trinidad] may be protected, as the cruelty of [Salcedo] has his intention to put them to the sword."[34]

Gutiérrez and his officers pledged "with our hands the most solemn contract" to adhere to "whatever terms" the Americans would offer and begged of General Wilkinson that he communicate the wishes of the people of Texas to the government and "to all persons who may be able to secure us in the acquisition of our happiness." Gutiérrez signed as "Commander in Chief of the Republican Army encamped at La Bahía." Signing along with him were his secretary, Sabas Fuentes, Capt. Pedro Procela, Lt. Francisco Guerrero, Ens. Gregorio Ortega, and Sgt. Juan Garcia.[35]

Here was Texas offered to the United States all the way to the Nueces River for a minuscule price—cheaper than the Louisiana Purchase—twenty-three years before the Texas Revolution and thirty-six years before eventual annexation. If any evidence was ever needed to prove that special agent William Shaler was not on the border of Texas as part of a secret government plan hatched by the Madison Administration to seize Spanish Territory, it is proven by the agent's actions. He forwarded the letter to Monroe but did not even mention its dramatic proposal. "These papers speak for themselves and require few comments, as the letters speak the language of despair as to the object of the expedition," he wrote, dismissively. Shaler made no effort to enlist help from Wilkinson, General Gaines, or Governor Claiborne. He wrote, sadly, "The Spaniards evidently have the advantage in address and management, [and] there seems to be few chances of the success of that expedition." Then, he added, without much hope, "those are all in the results of a battle and must be known here very soon."[36]

15

Toledo's Band

NEWS OF THE EARLY successes of the Republican Army of the North reached Philadelphia in the fall of 1812, where it was eagerly received by Gutiérrez's co-conspirator José Alvarez de Toledo, who had remained as the revolution's advocate in the United States. In Philadelphia, he was encouraged by Americans like Ira Allen, an independence pioneer and brother of Ethan Allen, and William Duane, the prominent Republican publisher. There was also a considerable Spanish revolutionary diaspora, led by Manuel de Trujillo y Torres, who Duane called "the *Franklin* of the southern world." He had come to America as a man of means, but his resources had been whittled away, so he taught the Spanish language to the wealthy and interested, for extra cash.[1]

One of his likely students in Philadelphia was a young lawyer, newly arrived and eager to start his law practice in the booming city: Henry Adams Bullard. The youth, who in 1808 had written the history of Miranda's expedition in which he had so staunchly defended the filibusters fighting for Spanish American independence, was committed heart and soul to the cause—eager enough to learn the Spanish language. He inevitably gravitated to Trujillo's circle. And within this community, sometime in 1812, young idealistic Bullard met the rebel he had always longed to find: José Alvarez de Toledo. It was revolutionary love at first sight, as a later biographer would write: "We now find [Bullard], at that most critical period of his life, a young man of vigorous mind, with a liberal education . . . full of the high hopes and aspirations which the fame and example of such men would excite. . . . He was fascinated with the splendid pictures painted by the imaginative mind of the Spanish revolutionary soldier. Can we wonder what was his course?"[2]

Bullard soon became attached to Toledo, who tired of endless idleness in Philadelphia and began to plot an expedition of his own to join Gutiérrez. From April to December 1812, the Cuban organized his own parallel command staff for the Republican Army of the North, complete with exalted ranks given to young men with little experience beyond fervor to the cause. Bullard became his secretary. For his military deputy, Toledo in August 1812 chose another transplanted Massachusetts lawyer, about ten years older than Bullard with at least a modicum of martial experience: Nathaniel Cogswell. It was he who had given the passionate oration for republicanism in Newburyport four years before. Supplementing his passion for the cause was a family vendetta. His merchant grandfather and namesake had suffered a loss of more than eighty-five thousand dollars when one of his vessels was captured on the high seas by a Spanish man-o'-war.[3]

In addition to engaging Cogswell and Bullard, Toledo added a printer, Aaron Mower, perhaps recommended by Duane, to his retinue. Mower brought with him a small portable Portuguese printing press, with appropriate types for printing in Spanish. Joining him was Horatio Bigelow, a young printer from Boston, described as "a man of considerable intelligence and talents, and not destitute of merit, apart from his inveterate habits of intoxication." Along the way to Texas, the group would pick up two youthful apprentices for Mower, a shoe-store clerk named Samuel Alden and a twenty-two-year-old named Godwin Brown Cotten.[4]

Toledo added a veteran revolutionary, Don Juan Mariano Picornell. At fifty-three, "wrinkled with age, and yet full of zeal in the cause," the Spaniard was an experienced counterpoint to the little band of youthful idealists. Bullard would describe him as "an old Spaniard . . . who had been buried in the dungeons of the Inquisition; whose ankles had been rendered callous by chains." He had been in the same Miranda filibuster that Bullard had memorialized. Before he met Toledo, he had considered quitting the cause, but upon meeting the Cuban was reinvigorated in it. According to Spanish Minister Onís, Toledo brought him along as a pamphleteer. "Picornell was not able to resist the desire to become an important man, and therefore abandoned his plan of reconciliation in order to allow himself to be dragged away by the prospect of regenerating that beautiful country."[5]

Onís had been alarmed at the evident persuasiveness of Toledo's own pamphlets and had employed the Portuguese writer Don Miguel Cabral de Noroña, to respond in kind. It was likely he who attacked Toledo as "this spurious son of the Fatherland" and "like an ulcerated and pestiferous limb." He sarcastically called the Cuban "el marte-filósofo de Delaware"—the *Warrior Philosopher of Delaware*. But Toledo was not lightly dismissed, either as a propagandist or as a potential warrior. With the Republican Army in Texas showing early success beyond anyone's expectations, Onís feared that Toledo would help rally additional forces and resources to augment it.[6]

Onís decided that the sword was mightier than the pen and hired an assassin to target the pernicious Cuban. Diego Correa (alias Antonio Garbolán) had reportedly been hired by the junta in Cádiz to assassinate none other than Napoleon Bonaparte, and when the plan was abandoned, he threatened to murder anyone who knew his secret. A mulatto of low birth, a native of Tenerife in the Canary Islands, he arrived in late 1810 and roamed the Atlantic Seaboard of the American Republic doing jobs for Spain. Forty years old, over six feet tall, he perpetually carried "a short Spanish dagger, and also kept pistols, powder and balls . . . a box containing vitriol and other drugs." In February 1812, Correa attacked Toledo in print as a pretext, then challenged him to a duel, a convenient "legal" way to assassinate the troublesome Cuban. Toledo, tipped off to the plot, refused to take the bait, and after he warned American authorities, Onís abandoned the effort.[7]

Toledo, Cogswell and the Struggle for Northern Aid

Toledo and his followers continued to build support for the revolution and were having some success. Cogswell, well-connected in Republican circles from his family ties and vigorous self-promotion, was the chief go-between with northern businessmen seeking to obtain arms for the rebellion. "The want of pecuniary resources," he lamented, had upset the effort. But, in the fall of 1812, he was nearing a breakthrough, when the rug was pulled out from under the rebels. Cogswell explained in a letter to Gutiérrez:[8] "After having been unsuccessful in a number of negotiations, I was on the point of succeeding to the amount of a million of dollars when the proclamation of Governor Claiborne of New Orleans, which was published in all of the newspapers in the U. States, put a stop to the business. Gentlemen were fearful of advancing their money or engaging in a business, which had been denounced by the proclamation of the governor of a state."[9]

Still, the ever-zealous Cogswell was not willing to give in. He approached John Binns, the editor of the *Pennsylvania Democratic Press*, a leading Republican paper, who agreed to help. Binns published a counter to Claiborne's proclamation, written by Cogswell. In it, he noted a history of governors taking "a very great latitude" in their speeches and proclamations that did not match official US policy, insinuating that Claiborne had done so, and that a reasonable understanding of the current situation showed his error. "Enlightened men, both in this country and in Europe, have considered a declaration of war against Great Britain, as tantamount to a declaration of war against the party of Ferdinand the Seventh," Cogswell wrote. "The British Ambassador negotiated a treaty in 1808, with [Ferdinand], offensively and defensively pledging the parties in the strongest manner."[10]

Cogswell then reminded his readers of the gold and silver of Mexico, a far more fertile ground for the expansion of liberty than Canada. It would prevent Mexico from falling into hostile (English) hands and "strengthen our republican institutions." It would open free trade with one of the richest countries in the world and "give liberty and independence to six millions of people." Mexico, with all its wealth, could even repay America's generosity with a loan! The article was reprinted across the country and "obtained the name of the antidote to Governor Claiborne's proclamation," as Cogswell crowed hopefully. "I am told that it has had a great effect in smoothing the way and preparing the public mind to wish for the accomplishment of such an event.... I published, also, a number of other pieces in the newspapers on the same subject, and all tending to the same effect."[11]

Binns also gave Cogswell a lead on a possible source of weapons for the Republican Army. The printer was an aide-de-camp to Pennsylvania's war hawk Governor Simon Snyder and suggested that Cogswell might convince the governor to "loan" him ten pieces of four-pound brass cannon and other munitions. On the way to Harrisburg for the negotiations, Cogswell and Toledo stopped in Baltimore to conduct some other business. The day after their arrival at that port, a vessel arrived bringing stunning news. A counterrevolution had rocked Venezuela, and the beloved patriot Miranda—the Latin Napoleon—had *betrayed the cause*, joining the royalists.[12]

"The Patriots of Baltimore were thunder struck at the news, but I observed that Mr. Toledo and Mr. Orea the ambassador from Caracas did not appear to be effected [sic] by it," Cogswell wrote. "I thought it extraordinary ... knowing that both Mr. Toledo and Mr. Orea were the intimate friends and correspondents of Miranda, it excited my suspicions whether they were not connected with Miranda, and fully acquainted with his arrangements and his plots." Indeed, Toledo had very recently been in communication with Miranda and contemplated visiting him, as Cogswell recalled, "in order to make some arrangements."[13]

The two continued on to meet the governor but could not close the deal on the munitions. Returning to Philadelphia to rejoin Bullard and the rest of Toledo's party, Cogswell could not shake the memory of Toledo's reaction. He quietly approached some friends of the Mexican cause and told them the story. Some, like Bullard, thought he was overreacting. Others agreed Toledo's behavior was suspicious. But all of them, according to Cogswell, "advised me to keep a close eye upon his conduct, and if I found that he was acting a double or a traitorous part to acquaint [Gutiérrez] with it immediately." Cogswell now spied on his general every chance he could. He slipped into Toledo's room while he was out and examined the letters in his desk. Some of those he found concerned him greatly, particularly correspondence with a relative of Toledo's who was a member of the Spanish Cortes, another man who was a member of the regency, and "others, [among] the most inveterate foes of the Patriot cause."[14]

"Treason" in Philadelphia

Toledo really *was* playing a double game, though not the way Cogswell suspected. On October 5, 1812, probably shortly before the incident in Baltimore, the rebel had surprisingly shown up on the doorstep of Onís, the very ambassador who wanted him dead. Away from prying eyes, Toledo affected a conversion to the royalist camp, admitting to Onís that he had been in contact with American officials with the aim of promoting revolution. But Toledo, so he claimed, was really loyal to the king and offered Onís a stunning proposal: He would proceed to the frontier, take command of a force of two thousand men recruited to join the Republican Army of the North, take delivery of twelve thousand arms that the United States had allegedly promised, seize control of the revolution, then with the connivance of Salcedo, betray it, turning over his entire army and weaponry to the royalists in Texas.[15]

On its face, the plan appeared a betrayal of the rebels, but there is another possibility: The whole plan may have been a fraud. Toledo had long since burned through the paltry resources provided by the American government and was now, in the wake of Claiborne's proclamation, running out of angel donors in Philadelphia. The Cuban rebel was simply broke, and since the entire proposal was dependent on a cash payment from the Spanish ambassador, this was likely a desperate gamble to reverse his fortunes. There is evidence of duplicity in the offer. In the first place, Toledo deceived Onís on a number of points. He told the Spanish ambassador about Monroe's suggestion to arm Latin rebels, but he described it as a certainty, while it was always a mere hypothetical. No proposals had been made, much less arrangements for such a large number of weapons. Those discussions had in any case taken place nearly a year before, and Toledo had no contact from Monroe since then. Now that America was at war with England, it was doubtful Monroe would have let go of so many much-needed muskets, and Governor Snyder certainly did not have that many to spare. As for the two thousand men? They would likely not appear after Claiborne's proclamation. If General Adair had the wherewithal or intention to recruit that many additional troops, he would have marched with them as their commander, and would not have waited for Toledo, whom he had never met, and with whom he had never corresponded. Indeed, as events would prove, the hesitant American militia general and the scheming Cuban were on far from friendly terms.

It is likely that Toledo had hatched a plan to cynically take Onís's money and continue with rebellion anyway. Aaron Burr had tried the same trick six years earlier, and nearly convinced the Spanish to fund his attack against their own territory on the pretext that New Orleans alone was the target. The full extent of Toledo's plan will likely never be known, since the Spanish ambassador had no such money to give him. The best Onís could do was to offer to write to Salcedo in Texas and make the arrangements, promising payment in the future. This would not solve Toledo's immediate cash problem. Toledo nonetheless told the minister he would abandon his revolutionary activities henceforth, but upon departing, he immediately violated this promise.[16]

Onís had nonetheless credulously revealed some of his innermost thoughts to the Cuban, and Toledo in turn betrayed Onís to the Americans. Three days after the meeting, an acquaintance of Toledo's, William Duncan, wrote President Madison with information provided by the Cuban informing the president that Spain was considering a declaration of war against the United States for its actions in the Floridas. "How the foregoing information was obtained by Mr. Tolado [sic] I have not been informed, but whether it is authentic or not," it should be taken seriously, Duncan wrote. Whatever game Toledo was playing, he was coming dangerously close to provoking a war between the two powers.[17]

Toledo Goes South

In late November or early December 1812, Toledo and his staff journeyed to Pittsburgh, where they waited for the ice to clear on the Ohio River before continuing south for Natchez, where Adair had been organizing volunteers for the expedition. Toledo's group was fewer than a dozen, but perhaps he thought he could come to an agreement with Adair after he made his way down the Mississippi. "This little party embarked at Pittsburg [sic] for Natchez in the month of December on board a small flat-boat, which had been constructed for that purpose," Bullard would later write. "Nothing can be conceived more heterogeneous than this little party."[18]

There was the old Spaniard Picornell, a "Galician boy," and Alden, the shoe merchant, "who had advanced some funds for the enterprise, and who accompanied the general by way of collateral security." There were also two Frenchmen in the party. The first was a man from Marseille named Colonie, who Bullard says, in an attempt at humor, "boasted of having been a chef de brigade [brigadier] in the republican armies of France; but, such was his ardor in the cause, that he accepted the humble rank of chef de cuisine in the service of Toledo." The other Frenchman in the party was Arsène Lacarrière-Latour, a military architect who likely participated in the French Revolution before settling in New Orleans. In the end, Latour appears to have departed the group in northern Louisiana and returned home, where he would serve two years later on the staff of General Jackson at the Battle of New Orleans.[19]

Toledo's band was a mix of idealists and men of questionable motives. Possibly some were agents of European powers, including Colonie and Latour. Small they were, but fired with ambition and gifted with great talent, they could in fact exert a powerful influence on the ongoing revolution in Texas—provided they were not stopped beforehand. And there was indeed someone who wanted to stop Toledo, and it was not Onís. It was a man in his own ranks.

Cogswell's Crusade

Nathaniel Cogswell had been one of Toledo's earliest and most committed followers but had a dramatic falling out with the party during their final days in Pittsburgh. His detractors would later claim that he embezzled forty dollars from the printer Mower, who like Alden was also a financier of the expedition. Mower and the Massachusetts lawyer Bullard "both declared that they would not proceed to Mexico in consequence, with a villain of Cogswell's character." Toledo supposedly agreed. But Cogswell told a different and far more dangerous story, stemming from his concerns ever since Toledo's muted response to Miranda's betrayal. Although he was ignorant of Toledo's strange meeting with Onís, he increasingly began to believe that the Cuban was taking steps to sabotage the army.[20] "[Toledo] is, I think, the most passionate man I ever saw, and over which he has not the least control," Cogswell wrote. "I was two or three times, on the point of closing a bargain for some arms, when his hasty and ungovernable temper upset the whole. Whether it was done intentionally or not, on purpose to create a delay, I am not able to say; but be that as it may, he is the last person on earth that ought to receive the least countenance or confidence from the Patriots."[21]

As the deadline for their departure for Natchez approached, Cogswell finally made his decision. Two days before the party was to take up their journey, he broke the news that he was not continuing further. He apparently never explained why, leaving his friend Bullard in the lurch. But as Toledo's band headed southwest on a flatboat on the icy Ohio, Cogswell pulled out his pen once again. This letter was addressed to "Generals Bernardo Gutiérrez and Magee," who were at that moment suffering in the siege of La Bahía. He laid out at length his suspicions, then gave the men a warning. "I now pledge you my honor as a gentleman, and as an officer, and I call God to witness the truth of my assertion, that the object of Mr. Toledo is to play the same game with you as Miranda did in Caracas," he wrote. He suggested it was a wider plot of the Spaniards to sabotage the revolutions across the empire from within, using double agents believed to be patriots. "Such a man is Mr. Toledo. I pledge my life on the issue, for I know it to be the fact."[22]

> The object is to place himself at the head of the expedition. . . . He would then get rid of you and Magee as soon as possible, when he would manage everything in his own way, and as far forth as lay in his power to the utter ruin and subversion of the Patriotic cause. Rely upon what I now tell you. Toledo has not a single particle of Patriotism, his only object is by a great show of his interest, address, and effected [sic] patriotism to deceive you, and to get himself placed at the lead.[23]

Cogswell warned Gutiérrez to place no trust in Toledo, Picornell, and Latour, who he believed were all part of Miranda's plans. "I am willing to put my life on the issue, that if you allow either of them to step a foot into the territory over which you preside, or to have the least connection whatever, even as common soldiers, with your expedition, you will in the end rue it in tears of blood." It was a haunting warning, and as events would prove, prescient as well.[24]

16

The Siege

WHILE TOLEDO WAS making his way to Texas, the army he hoped to join was deep in its second month of siege. They had enough corn for six months, the beef from Juan Savías's raid, cash in their treasury, and Maj. Reuben Ross estimated that they could hold the position against a force three times their size. The flow of deserters had even begun to reverse: more Spaniards were now joining the rebels. But they were still surrounded and penned in a muddy fortress, living among livestock, poorly clothed, and frequently exposed to the elements.[1]

Republicans in small groups were able to slip out of the fortress almost at will. "Little John" McFarlan, the republicans' chief scout, hearing of Spanish officers hosting parties at an abandoned mission well behind the Spanish lines, where they "enjoyed the sparkling wine and the smiles of the women," decided to capture them. This was briefly accomplished, but while the captives played cordial hosts, the alarm was raised and it was McFarlan and his men who had to flee—minus their captives—passing through a Spanish ambush in which one man was captured or killed. "They entered the prairie in sight of the fort," recalled McLane, "exhibiting all the terror and alarm of Ichabod Crane, when fleeing from the headless horseman of Sleepy Hollow, their loose garments flying in the breeze and several of them minus a hat."[2]

A few days later, the republicans planned an ambush of their own. The enemy's envelopment of the presidio could never be complete with the force at hand, but the Spaniards sought to minimize the gaps through which republicans like Savías had snuck livestock. To this end, they dug a series of foxholes deep into the sandy soil, in which six to eight men were stationed. Each day, they sent out a guard on horseback to relieve the men at some of these outposts. The republicans, watching this, conceived a plan to ambush this force. One morning, about one hundred republicans had crept out to a point overlooking the path of the relieving troops and waited.[3]

"We were ordered when the last man passed the extreme right of our line, the man on the right was to fire," Hall recalled. "And by a well regulated and simultaneous fire the enemy was cut to pieces with the exception of one man taken prisoner and three

The Siege

or four escaped." McLane, however, remembered it differently: the fabled American marksmanship failed on that day, and every shot missed the Spaniards, who bolted. The two agreed on one thing: the single Spanish soldier captured. "He was brought in under great excitement, expecting every moment to be massacred," McLane recalled. "After tormenting the poor devil until he was almost paralyzed [they] turned him loose and dubbed him with the name of 'Christmas Gift.'"[4]

Christmas in La Bahía was otherwise a miserable affair for both armies. The republicans in the presidio were beset by "millions of lice—the earth seemed to be alive under and all around them." For the twenty-three-year-old Augustus Magee, La Bahía was an especially lonely place. Hall would describe Magee as "universally esteemed as a chivalrous, high-minded, and strictly honorable man of undoubted courage and intrepidity of character, possessing talents that eminently fitted him for a commander." But this praise sounds defensive and was doubtless the minority opinion. Indeed, Hall and William Murray were almost the only friends the young officer had. His Anglo-American contingent included many who would happily kill him and others prone to dangerous stunts like that of McFarlan. As for his Mexican contingent, he had refused to trust them since the defection of Galván. Of course, trust was a two-way street. The Bostonian still had a working relationship with Gutiérrez, but it was growing increasingly strained.[5]

For the filibuster commander, Christmas Eve had always been associated with a story of tragedy. His father, the privateer captain in the Revolutionary War, had been shipwrecked in Plymouth Harbor on December 24, 1778, and eighty-three of his crew died of exposure in the ice, wind, and waves that broke upon the ship. Every year in young Augustus's childhood, the survivors gathered at Magee's home on the anniversary. His father had endured this great calamity, yet faced with his own severe test, the son was now failing, and his gloom had spread to the United States. "It is now ascertained that Don Bernardo's expedition (the adventure headed by colonel Magee) ... has failed," the Alexandria (Virginia) *Daily Gazette* reported. Noting the parlay between Magee and Salcedo, the paper despaired, "No doubt is entertained of their ultimate capture."[6]

Magee's grim report baffled American agent William Shaler, who found the officer's talk of surrender hard to credit. The agent, stepping for the first time out of the role as a neutral observer, now began to counsel the young officer. "Pray did it not occur to you that your enemy would never have considered to exchange flags with you, and have agreed to meet you on a footing of equality but from a conviction of his weakness?" he wrote. "If you bring that enemy to a battle you must be victorious, when all partisans of the revolution will join you, and if they do not, you may then return with glory to your own country. [America] loves deeds of valor and would hail you with enthusiasm." Upon arriving in Natchitoches, Samuel Davenport had informed Shaler that Magee was contemplating an attack when the quartermaster had left the army. Shaler urged Magee to follow through. If it succeeded, "I doubt not but you will have as much cause of gratulation as you now seem to have of despair." Then the agent added a personal note: "No person has been more jealous of your fame than myself, and none desires so similarly that you should by your conduct in this expedition furnish to your friends and country an excuse for undertaking it."[7]

But there was a deeper cause to Magee's depression beyond desertions, stolen horses, even the Spanish shot that bounced off the walls of the presidio. Augustus William Magee, only twenty-three years old, was dying. It is unknown precisely when he realized this, but he had been sick possibly as far back as when the army was encamped at Trinidad. There the symptoms had evidently not prevented him from taking an active role in the army's management, but that was increasingly changing for the worse. In December, amid the squalor of his fortress, his health declined rapidly. Warren D. C. Hall and James Gaines claimed that the illness was consumption—modern tuberculosis. It was almost always fatal.[8]

In late December, despite an improved military situation, Magee decided to try to fight his way out. The army was mustered and given the orders, but on the morning of departure, the men were universally mutinous. They would stand and fight here. The men now proposed removing Magee from command. At this point, Magee's officers intervened. Pulling aside their friend, they talked him back from the cliff. Though the Bostonian was never officially replaced, his order was countermanded and the men went back to their positions. Augustus Magee, who had sacrificed his career for the expedition that bore his name, was now effectively deposed. Like Jim Bowie twenty-three years later in another Texas siege, Magee could only wait for the battle to come from his sickbed; he would not take part in it.[9]

Who would take over the expedition now? Gutiérrez could not command, for he had built up no trust with the Anglo-American contingent, which was three quarters of the force even before the Mexican defections. Instead, leadership in practice began increasingly to fall on the shoulders of Magee's second-in-command, the West Florida veteran Samuel Kemper. His history had been one of courage but little military skill. No one really knew how he would stand up in a real test. One would come soon enough.[10]

The White Cow

Just a month shy of six years from the day Samuel Kemper had sat in the plush New Orleans drawing room of Lewis Kerr and was recruited into the Mexican Association, the now thirty-six-year-old strapping tavern keeper had become the commander of an army in a momentous struggle for the destiny of an empire. Now he chose to send a second messenger north to follow up Davenport's mission. Word of their plight caused many who had been flocking to the standard from the United States to lose heart and turn back. To halt the collapse of the volunteer pipeline, form up a force, and bring them on with dispatch to relieve the garrison, Kemper needed a man of intelligence and courage. He chose thirty-year-old Maj. Reuben Ross, a former Washington County, Virginia, sheriff, who was in Gaines's words "of fair character, brave," and committed to the cause. He was ordered to proceed north and rally as many men as he could, sending word further onward to prevent the entire collapse of recruitment. Additionally, it was hoped that Ross could induce another ally to join the rebel movement—the many Indians of Northeast Texas. A second emissary either traveled with him or shortly thereafter on a similar mission, "Little John" McFarlan.[11]

There were skirmishes almost every day as the Siege of La Bahía rolled into its third month. The Spanish were too strong for the rebels to risk an attack, but too weak in turn to try to take on the stout walls, cannon, and accurate rifle fire of the Americans. When battle finally came, it did so in the most unexpected way. On January 24, 1813, the Spaniards at the mission were attempting to slaughter a cow when the animal escaped its corral and began running south toward the river. A company of the republicans, probably posted as the advanced guards inside the houses between the presidio and the river, spied the renegade animal, and a bevy of bovine banditti decided to seize the defecting animal.[12]

A company of men, probably without orders, crossed the river to intercept the oncoming cow, but the Spanish were also in chase, and the two sides exchanged musketry. The American company was led by Josiah Taylor. The former Burr conspirator, who had been captured at the beginning of the siege and imprisoned in San Antonio, had one day "brained one of the guards with a bench leg and made his escape." Returning to the army, Taylor had rejoined it and resumed his captaincy.[13]

At his side in battle was a man who would give one of the greatest examples of heroism in the history of the army, and he was not Spaniard, Mexican, French, or Anglo-American. It was Taylor's African American slave, Thomas, armed and fighting alongside his master. As Warren D. C. Hall recalled decades later, Thomas "was one of the best soldiers I ever saw, having been with him in several skirmishes I had an opportunity of observing his conduct." Thomas was in the thick of the fighting, where he was struck by Spanish musketry. Hall recalled, "After receiving a mortal wound, he still encouraged us to fight on."[14]

Reinforcements from both sides soon followed and the engagement became general. Despite all the fighting, Thomas Taylor was the only republican killed in the engagement, along with six wounded, probably because of the inaccuracy of Spanish musketry against dispersed troops. The American rifles, on the other hand, had wreaked frightening casualties on the enemy in this accidental engagement before they retreated back across the river as night approached. The Americans claimed two hundred Spaniards were killed or wounded (likely an exaggeration). After so much carnage, neither side bothered to record who got the cow.[15]

The republicans were still trapped in the fortress, many were sick, reducing those available to fight to merely three hundred men. The Spaniards had received reinforcements equal to that number. As Hall recalled, "Our situation now appeared far more desperate than formerly, our communication being entirely cut off from the country." Still, while few realized it at the time, the Battle of the White Cow had begun to turn the tide.[16]

The Third Power: Native Americans

In the meantime, Reuben Ross raced northward on his mission to bring back fresh volunteers. Arriving at Natchitoches on January 9th, he found few Americans passing through. These he sent on to Nacogdoches for Capt. James Gaines to assemble into a company. Then he turned his recruiting efforts to the Native Americans. He seems to have been tasked with recruiting the eastern tribes, while McFarlan possibly recruited the western.[17]

The tribal landscape of eastern Texas had been evolving for years as new tribes were pushed into Spanish lands by encroaching Anglo-Americans. These were sedentary, rather than nomadic tribes and included the Choctaws, Chicasaws, and an important tribe of Creeks known as the Alabamas and Coushattas. The Creeks were the dominant tribal group in the southwestern United States. While many Southern Creeks embraced England and saw a flood of trade goods and an evolution of Creek society *toward* the ways of the White Man, the northern Creeks recoiled against this assault on tradition. These tribes, the Alabamas and Coushattas, moved west, seeking to preserve their ancestral ways.[18]

In Texas, they established friendly relations with and fell under the powerful sway of another tribe, the Kadohadacho—known to Americans as Caddo—and their influential chief, Dehahuit, who led his people from the 1790s to 1833. He was a "very fine-looking man" and very shrewd, according to Sibley. "Nearly all the friendly nations recognize [him] as superior." Dehahuit could easily bring five hundred men into the field from his and allied tribes, but he was peace-loving. When the Spanish complained of his treaty with the Americans, he said, "He loved all men; if the Spaniards had come to fight they must not spill blood on his land, as it was the command of his forefathers that white blood should not be spilled on [Caddo] land."[19]

As the clouds of revolution gathered in July 1812, the Spanish had again sent an agent to Dehahuit, inviting him to join them. The chief traveled to Nacogdoches and received gifts but informed the Spanish once again he would remain neutral. Sibley had encouraged this. Though he was sympathetic to Gutiérrez's revolution, he took a firm line on Indian non-involvement. America had enough enemies without stirring trouble with the natives on the frontier.[20]

Major Ross and other backers of the Republican Army were not giving up so easily. Several "very influential characters" pressed Dehahuit to join the army with one hundred warriors of his own tribe and two to three hundred raised from other tribes. "Enticing offers were made to him," Sibley reported. "I did not interfere, though I knew all that was going on for I knew the Chief's firmness & that he would do nothing without consulting me." Dehahuit refused the republican advances and said that to join the war would be to violate his promise as well as take a step he had asked others not to take. He said that "nothing should induce him to act so inconsistent a part."[21]

Nonetheless, Ross did collect individual warriors from the Alabamas and Coushattas, Choctaws, and other small bands, but probably no more than one hundred, including about thirty Coushattas from a village on the Trinity, commanded by Chief Charles Rollins, a half-Indian son of an Anglo-American serving in the Republican Army. Better success was achieved by McFarlan, who was sent to recruit among the Lipan Apache and Tonkawas. Gaines, meanwhile, marched south with twenty-five or so Americans, plus some of the Alabama and Coushatta, who dubbed him "Captain Colorado," due to his striking red hair and ruddy face. In addition to these, Lieutenant Guadiana sent about 170 Mexicans to join the force as well. Reinforcements were at last coming to La Bahía, though in much smaller numbers than were hoped for.[22]

There was one tribe, however, with the size and strength to possibly tilt the balance of the revolution one way or another: the Comanches. These had an uneasy peace with the Spanish, but a grievance. When a chief named "El Sordo" came to San Antonio in August 1811 to atone for a raid he had conducted in violation of the peace, Herrera had seized him and sent him to Mexico in chains. "This shocking breach of diplomatic etiquette seriously damaged the already flimsy Spanish-Comanche alliance," wrote historian F. Todd Smith. At the same time, the Spanish peace with the Wichitas was collapsing as well. This all happened on the eve of the Republican Army of the North's invasion and might not have been a coincidence given republican overtures. Now that the Spanish were hard-pressed, all of these disaffected tribes began to assert themselves. On February 11th, a Comanche chief named Captain Cordero with a large number of warriors arrived at San Antonio and boldly asked for a "regalo" (gift) from the Spaniards. Local authorities had nothing to give him and suggested that he speak with the governor at La Bahía.[23]

There, Salcedo and Herrera received the delegation and tried to recruit them to their side. The Comanche chief said that he and his warriors "did not want to fight the Americans, that they were too brave and would kill too many of them." After Captain Cordero once again requested a gift, and was again refused, the Indians retaliated by seizing much of the Spanish livestock. The Comanches now effectively entered the war as a third combatant: Cordero's warriors returned to San Antonio, where they conducted a series of heavy raids, resulting in dozens of civilian deaths and the loss of large numbers of sheep, horses, and mules. It had been fear of being deserted that had led San Antonio's elites to launch the Casas Revolt. Now that their worst fears had come to pass, Spanish prestige in the city was broken and order collapsed. From the jails, several captured republicans, including the Anglo-Americans captured at the start of the siege, escaped or were released.²⁴

As many as one hundred Béxar citizens even traveled to La Bahía to join the rebels, alongside a growing number of Spanish deserters, who were hungry and ill-clothed even *before* the Comanches stole most of the army's food supplies. One of these was a corporal, Antonio Delgado, whose father had been executed by the Spanish. There were also two former American soldiers of Spanish ancestry, José María Mona and José Ignacio Ibarbo, who had themselves deserted from Fort Claiborne. The pair now fled back to the United States, where they turned themselves in to accept their punishment. Sibley saw this as the strongest proof of a collapse of Spanish morale.²⁵

The Twilight of the Siege

The shifting tides might have brightened the gloom of Augustus Magee, but on February 6, 1813, the long-suffering commander of the Republican Army of the North died. "When he was taken to the graveyard for burial," McLane wrote, "the enemy contributed their mite in honoring the dead, by discharging their cannon—rolling the balls around the graveyard." His replacement, Samuel Kemper, was now receiving daily reports from deserters about the poor condition of the enemy. The republicans were becoming better skirmishers too. Since the Christmas Day attack on the relieving force on the Spanish outpost, they had taken to conducting periodic night raids on these small, isolated pockets of Spaniards. Small groups of ten to fifteen men would creep up on a foxhole, rush it, and discharge their weapons into the pits, killing, wounding, harassing, and collecting deserters. Not for the first time in history had a siege become a trap for the besiegers; every day, the Spanish grew weaker and the republicans stronger, and both sides knew it.²⁶

Salcedo and Herrera had to act. On February 10th, in the predawn fog, they launched what would be, one way or another, the final battle for the presidio. The Spanish plan consisted of two main thrusts. One was to be a flanking movement overseen by Herrera to plant a cannon at the rear of the presidio, where it could be uncontested by the republicans' sole nine-pounder. The second was to be an assault on the town just outside the walls. To prepare for this, the Spanish broke up their southern camp two days before and, while pretending to abandon it entirely, kept a small force hidden throughout the next day in some woods between it and the western camp, where the bulk of their forces remained. The troops in the wood were to seize the town and put the presidio under fire while the main body followed.²⁷

But the republican scouts had spied on this advanced force. These Spaniards had camped in the wood during the day, but at nightfall, rather than stay in the cold brush, retreated back to their camp. Resurrecting the attack of Christmas Day, when they had tried to ambush the relief troops of the Southern outpost, the republicans thought to try their luck again. A force was assembled of fifty Mexicans led by Captain Miguel Menchaca, the senior native-born Tejano officer in the army, assisted by twenty Americans under William Francis. This group crept up during the night and endured the cold which the Spanish would not. In the early morning hours of February 10th, Menchaca placed his men in an ambuscade along the same path that the republican spies had observed the Spanish forces travel the day before.[28]

The republicans had expected this force to be about a hundred—not significantly larger than their own—but as the Spanish chose to use these men to lead a general assault, they had boosted it to about 160 "choice men." The morning was foggy; perhaps Salcedo had hoped this would conceal his assault. Instead, it cloaked Menchaca's ambush. As the dawn broke, the Tejano officer spied the Spanish troops coming forward and unleashed his surprise attack. The fire and smoke from the republican muskets cut through the mist and struck the Spanish with deadly effect. Caught in the open, unprepared for this shocking blow, they panicked and sought the first cover they could find—a deep gully from which there were only two exits. The joint Mexican/American contingent made several rushes on them to attack, and after a battle of four or five hours, succeeded in overrunning the position, capturing fifty-one Spaniards while the remainder fled—many throwing down their muskets as they did.[29]

As this battle went on, Salcedo waited for the fog to lift before he could commit his entire force of perhaps 1,200 men. He finally did so two hours after Menchaca's attack had begun, but he was ignorant of the full nature of his troops' defeat to the south. In fact, his plan was doubly compromised. Republican sharpshooters, with their rifles, had devastated the artillery unit Herrera had sent to flank the fortress and the gun never fired. The Spanish before the presidio pressed their attack nonetheless and were met by a contingent of republicans in the town. "Our men opened a warm fire on them and drove them back to the main army," Hall recalled. The republicans then fell back to a nearby ravine, unseen. At last, the entire Spanish force assembled and marched to attack the fortress. The republican troops in the ravine rose up and fired, causing confusion in the Spanish ranks. When the latter formed on a nearby hill, the republicans fell back to a picket post along the river.[30]

At the heart of the republican defense were the two Burr Conspirators recruited in 1806. "Col. Samuel Kemper & his aide de camp Major Wm Murray manifested during the whole engagement undaunted courage, chivalry, industry and perseverance," Hall recalled. They sent forward a contingent of thirty-six men under a Captain Gormley to take possession of a log house near the picket post. Meanwhile, the Spanish, arrayed in three divisions, resumed their attack, now on multiple sides of the fort. They drove Gormley's force back, but the captain regrouped his men and "made a resolute charge on the enemy who then occupied the log house and drove [the Spaniards] from their position with great slaughter" while no republicans were killed. The royalists charged the house again and retook the bastion, but at great expense; Gormley retired, again without any losses.[31]

The Spanish now placed a cannon to target the main gate of the presidio. The rebels, seeing this, rushed out of the fortress to reinforce Gormley's beleaguered company and "charged into the thickest ranks of the foe driving them back to the outskirts of the town, where they in turn were forced to fall back," as McLane recalled. The back-and-forth struggle now brought the Spanish to the walls of the presidio, where a few brave royalist soldiers even brought up scaling ladders. Once again, the rebels, "rallying, with renewed courage . . . forced the enemy back, pursuing as before." This was the third time the Spanish had pressed the rebels, but it was to be their last. As a republican reinforcement joined the brave band of troops outside the walls,[32] "Gormley again rallied his men and made a severe and desperate charge on the log house & drove the enemy from their position, and following up the rout, drove them in great confusion into the ravine near, where sixty-six men surrendered to him after sustaining great loss. At this point the warmest & most severe part of the engagement took place, our men stationed here having been repulsed from and [retaking] the log house."[33]

It was a hot fight, but after six hours, the republicans had not yet lost a man and had only four wounded. The firing and retreating with their longer-ranged hunting rifles had been devastating to the Spaniards. Finally, by 4:00 p.m., the royalists broke and fled back across the San Antonio River for the last time, at which point, in the words of McLane, "the rout then became general." The Spanish defeat was total—they lost two hundred or more men, including some of their "best and most distinguished officers." William Fisher, the Republican Army adjutant, exulted, "Several deserters also joined us on that day so that our victory may be understood as complete. Our loss in killed and some dead of their wounds since the beginning of the campaign is 15, while the loss of the enemy exceeds 200!!!" Gutiérrez wrote that the Republican Army "with astonishing bravery completely defeated the enemy." Hall added, "Our officers and men fought during the whole engagement like a brave and gallant band of heroes determined to conquer or die."[34]

That afternoon, it was Salcedo sending over a flag of truce. The Spanish commander wanted to bury his dead. While this was done, the governor assessed the situation. Continuing the siege was hopeless. It had been a brutal affair—by one account there were twenty-seven skirmishes or engagements during the course of nearly three months—and the Spanish lost nearly all of them. The army was almost out of powder, living on meat alone, had few clothes and no tobacco, and Salcedo had just received word from the viceroy that he had no more forces to spare for Texas. On February 19, Salcedo raised the siege and marched his army back to San Antonio.[35]

The glory on the battlefield had been won by Kemper, Murray, Menchaca, and Gormley, but a piece of the credit must also go to the Republican Army's fallen commander, Augustus Magee. "In the conduct of a difficult enterprise, he constantly supported the character of an intelligent soldier, and a man of pure honor and humanity," an anonymous account, likely written by a member of his army, reported. He had organized the force, trained it, even instilled discipline to the army, "which was composed of the most heterogenous materials." The last word on Magee was, in typical nineteenth-century style, a soaring, sappy poetic elegy, published in his hometown of Boston in May 1813. "Thine be the task, immortal fame! To enroll the youthful hero's name," the poem began. Magee had "in laurel plumage *Texas* trained," and "his martial skill gave order, force—and sketch'd the outline of a glorious course."[36]

> But tho' the wand of mystic pow'r
> Has roll'd for thee the eventful hour,
> And planted deep thy cold and lonely bed . . .
> 'Till fate in turn shall count us with the dead;
> Yet still, the monument of fame,
> Shall guard th' immortal glory of thy name[37]

But Augustus William Magee, left behind in a muddy grave in La Bahía as his army marched onward, was soon forgotten even by his own men, his grave lost, his name unrecalled by the province for which he had fought. The fortress which he and his compatriots had defended, in the town of La Bahía, would be the scene of even greater tragedy in Texas' second revolution. Renamed, it would instead bestow its "immortal glory" to a different cast of sacrificial victims during another revolution twenty-three years later in a place now known as *Goliad*.

Diplomacy in Chihuahua, Chaos in San Antonio

After leaving San Antonio in November 1812, John Robinson, the second agent sent by the US State Department, had traveled to Monclova and then to Chihuahua, where he arrived on December 11th. Commandant General Nemesio Salcedo, a man of average height with a stern countenance to match his authoritarian personality, greeted him. Possibly speaking in English, for he knew some of Robinson's language, he greeted the American. "I have waited with some impatience your arrival sir," he said. "I presume you have a letter from the President of the United States to me."[38]

But Robinson had no such letter, only flowery language. The president, he said, "regrets the many difficulties which have latterly given disquietude to these provinces," particularly those in Texas. He was talking about the old banditti, but all the commandant general wanted to hear about was the invasion. The American seemed to the incredulous Salcedo either an imbecile or a schemer and knowing of the doctor's previous affiliation with Pike's expedition, the commandant general greatly suspected the latter. Over the course of several weeks, the two held forth a lopsided diplomacy: patronizing verbosity disconnected from reality on the part of Robinson, and righteous indignation and outright hostility on the part of Salcedo. At last, the Spaniard "burst into the most violent paroxysms of anger." He raged at the American:[39] "You speak of national honor—a government formed by an unlawful act—and came into existence only yesterday—formed by people who can remain in no other governments—a government that has not power to restrain her subjects—see the conduct of your government towards Spain—and yet, you speak of national honor?"[40]

Robinson was at last dismissed and sent back to the United States. In Chihuahua, he had exhibited the antithesis of Midas's touch. He had accomplished nothing good for America with his mission and had nearly goaded the commandant general to violence against him personally. That such an event would have caused a war may be the only thing that prevented its occurrence.[41]

Returning to San Antonio within days after the Spanish retreat from La Bahía, Robinson was shocked at what he saw. "I found everything in confusion, every person alarmed for the security of his person and property," he wrote. The Indian raids and fear of a looming battle for their town had caused Bexareños to panic. "The citizens begged me to take of their property with me, such as horses mules and sheep, to a very considerable amount." Robinson said that as an agent of the US government, he could do nothing.[42]

The two royalist governors who had returned to their capital with their ragged force tried to put on a brave face, inviting the American to dine with them. It was a far cry from the happy dinner a few months before, when Salcedo and Herrera had welcomed Robinson as a harbinger of hope that the invasion by the rebel band could be turned back. Gloom now pervaded the city, and it was about to deepen. During the meal, a messenger came and delivered the news to Governor Salcedo that the Republican Army had left La Bahía and had already marched ten leagues—twenty-five miles—toward San Antonio.[43]

Robinson, no doubt wary of the reception he might get from the vengeful rebels, prepared to leave the city immediately. He went to see his friend Colonel Herrera for the last time. The Spaniard, who had fought alongside Bernardo de Gálvez, the great symbol of Spanish-American brotherhood, and had successfully defeated the Apaches and Comanches, was now trying to organize his forces to march out and meet the republicans in a final decisive battle. The amiable Spaniard who had been so kind to Robinson faced very long odds. It was likely he would never survive to again see his English-born wife, who waited for him in Monterrey. Robinson parted with sadness from his friend, then made his way up the Camino Real toward Natchitoches. On the way, he ran into an unusual traveling companion: the rebel Captain Bernardo Despallier, the Frenchman who had been the first commander of the Mexican contingent of the army. He was returning to Louisiana, possibly for health reasons or to rejoin his long-suffering family, having turned over his command to the able Tejano Miguel Menchaca. As they headed away from the war, the decisive battle for Texas loomed.[44]

17

Rebels Victorious

THE REPUBLICAN ARMY's new commander, Samuel Kemper, was tall, rough, and strong, far more salt-of-the-earth than his predecessor. He likely also shared his brother Reuben's penchant for "eloquent profanity." William Shaler categorized him as "a man of much courage and firmness, an excellent executive officer, but of no education and doubtful capacity for chief command." But courage and firmness, two qualities Augustus Magee had lacked, would do. Kemper was no tactician or skilled drillmaster like his predecessor, but he fit his army much better, and they him.[1]

On the day after the Battle of La Bahía, the republicans found the royalist camp deserted. The Spanish retreat was "a troublesome march, encumbered with wounded and dying men, disaffected troops and worn-down horses." As much as a third of the Spanish army deserted. The republicans, however, were in no condition to strike them. An unknown member of the expedition wrote to John Sibley that "all were badly prepared to pursue our victory; our horses were scarce and not in order for such expedition." Still, they knew that their perseverance was paying off. "A number of the principal republicans from San Antonio have come to us . . . rich staunch old friends, who have adhered to the cause from its commencement," Gutiérrez wrote. The citizens of the town, he added, would have risen up and seized the capital themselves if they only had weapons with which to do so.[2]

Though a pursuit was impossible, Kemper could still harass the fleeing enemy, and he chose for this vital assignment the company of Menchaca, augmented by Savías and the recent royalist deserter Antonio Delgado, alongside some Americans under a Captain Holmes. In using Mexicans in such a prominent role, Kemper demonstrated he was not Augustus Magee. The West Florida veteran was a hot-tempered man who had even shown his anger in a "violent quarrel" with a Mexican officer. Nonetheless, he was empowering these native soldiers in a way Magee had never done. It is notable that along with the creole Menchaca, the slave-owning Kemper also entrusted authority to the dark-complected Savías. This is not to say he was broad-minded, just more pragmatic. In the later stages of the siege, Kemper's Mexican officers had displayed skill, ingenuity, courage, and competence, and now he rewarded them with trust.³

He was not the only one to praise the Mexicans. "The citizens of San Antonio are chiefly in our favor, and generally throughout the province they are becoming Republicans thro' the incontrovertible argument of our American rifles," an anonymous member of the army wrote to Sibley. "Our army is considerably augmented by the Creoles and it is astonishing to see even prisoners lately taken and deserters lately come in acting with the bravery & fidelity of American volunteers." Some of Menchaca's men made their way into San Antonio, in advance of the royalist retreat, and had "effected the liberation of all our prisoners." Discovered by the Spanish, they escaped with thirteen freed comrades and even stole two hundred royalist horses.⁴

Kemper held back the rest of his force to recover their strength, with the exception of the ubiquitous scout, McFarlan, who led a raid on the Mission Nuestra Señora de Refugio about thirty miles to the south, capturing a small Spanish garrison there, including an "old Castilian officer" and sixteen men, who joined the rebels. At La Bahía, Kemper gathered food and livestock and waited for Major Ross, whom he knew to be approaching with his reinforcements. On February 24th, he and Gutiérrez dispatched Lieutenant George Orr to ride out and meet the Virginian. They included a note to be sent on to Louisiana to restart the flow of volunteers. "You will give information to the friends of the republican cause that the road is now completely open to this post and the province may be considered as our own," Gutiérrez wrote to Ross, then boldly proclaimed that the republicans would establish a port at Matagorda for supplies and troops. He asked the officer to purchase clothing, and ordered Ross to hurry any reinforcements forward, even if it was fewer than a hundred men, because any arrivals gave a positive morale boost to the army.⁵

The Spanish were reeling, and Salcedo and Herrera sought to parlay. The intermediary was Gavino Delgado, who had been one of Casas's agents to Nacogdoches, then joined Zambrano in his coup against the rebel leader. He had slipped out of San Antonio to join the Republican Army in Northeast Texas and now made his way back and negotiated with the Spanish commanders. The terms they discussed were unknown, but the Spaniards wrote directly to Captain Miguel Menchaca, offering their word of honor to "comply with what we have offered . . . as long as Menchaca for his part, does what Don Gavino has negotiated with us."⁶

Delgado was not the only one conversing across the lines. As the Spanish tumbled back toward San Antonio, the royalists were hemorrhaging support. Their failure in the siege, the inability to protect San Antonio, and the growing attractiveness of rebel ideas were wreaking their toll, both among the general public and the elites. One of the latter was a thirty-year-old militia commander named José Francisco Ruiz. He was the son of Jose Manuel Ruiz, a well-respected, though not particularly wealthy immigrant. José Francisco himself became the city's first public school teacher in 1803, before moving on to the legal profession. He served as the city attorney and on the ayuntamiento, or town council. In 1811, when Manuel Salcedo had seen the need to establish a militia, Ruiz was appointed as a lieutenant. A week later, the Casas revolt broke out. Though Ruiz was one of the most educated men in the city, he was no revolutionary—at least not yet. He was tied to many loyalists, including the two Zambrano brothers, by the family network known as *compadrazgo*. His late brother, José Antonio, had been a professional soldier serving on the frontier, who had captured the smuggler Henry Quirk. José Francisco's closest friend was another royalist soldier, José Ignacio Pérez.[7]

At the siege of La Bahía, José Francisco Ruiz was a lieutenant, and the second in command of Captain Mariano Rodriguez's militia cavalry company. At some point in the siege, he was wounded seriously enough to remove him from frontline service, but not from all duties, and he was assigned as Salcedo's quartermaster. He witnessed firsthand the collapse of the Spanish royalists' resources, and with the ignominious withdrawal, their will to fight as well. His politics underwent a dramatic shift, wrote historian Art Martinez de Vara, "as the social order and institutions that he had supported for his entire life dissolved around him." Seeking a political end to the conflict, he began a private correspondence to another old friend bound to him by family networks: the rebel captain Menchaca.[8]

Ruiz, learning of the attempt to parlay with Menchaca, warned his friend that the unknown contents of the deal were nothing new. This suggests that the Spanish did not offer a surrender, but perhaps an amnesty deal to split the Texas Mexicans from their American allies and from Gutiérrez, who was bypassed in the appeal to his subordinate. Ruiz told his friend that when the rebels came to San Antonio, "there will be many of us who have affection for our own." This, he said, was a crucial moment for the Tejanos. "As a friend I tell you that all harm to our countrymen that can be avoided will be to the good, as we should not think only of the present, but what is to come." The parlay, in the end, came to nothing, but Ruiz, while still in royal service, had become in his heart a rebel.[9]

The Battle of Rosillo

After Ross arrived with his reinforcements, Kemper and Gutiérrez departed La Bahía on March 18th. The force at this point consisted of three to four hundred Anglo-Americans, one to two hundred Mexicans, and about one hundred Indians. The army now faced a dilemma, perhaps discovered in some of the skirmishing before La Bahia, of distinguishing the Mexicans in the republican ranks from the royalists. This could be devastating in the fight to come. Samuel Noah, the West Point graduate, recalled, "An expedient, however, was soon presented and urgently recommended by a [Lipan Apache] Indian chief, which was simply to paint the faces of our Mexicans with rouge, the same with which they painted their own which at once relieved us from our dilemma."[10]

The army had no wagons left—perhaps they had been forced to burn those during the long siege—and had to leave their larger cannon behind. They brought their food along with them in the form of a herd of livestock. "The latter was very numerous and annoying," McLane recalled, "tormenting the poor tired soldier during the night, and if they failed to get an ample supply of food, they would nibble and bite him on the march—many of the men not having a second shirt, were eaten raw on the back and shoulders by these Mexican pests."[11]

When Simón Herrera heard the news of the republican advance, he marched out to meet them in a desperate, last-ditch effort to save royalist Texas. San Antonio was not defensible: the Alamo, which would gain fame twenty-three years later, was more ruin than fortress in 1813. Fighting in the city brought its own dangers; the people were disaffected and mutinous toward royalist authorities. The harried Spanish leaders, who had once been locked into cells in the Alamo by these same townspeople, may indeed have seen their capital city now as little more than enemy territory.[12]

Colonel Herrera's only hope was to catch the rebels in an ambush as he had planned several months previously—before Magee had bypassed it and moved to La Bahía. The royalists took the strongest position they could, below Salado Creek near its junction with the Rosillo Creek on the La Bahía road. The Spanish had been reinforced and were at least 850 men to the 600 or so rebels. It was about noon when the royalists opened up from "a beautiful place selected by them for the battleground," an open area between groves of trees. The Spanish "advanced in slow march, scattering their cannon balls around the Americans, tearing up the earth in their immediate vicinity, without hitting a single man." The Americans, however, quickly formed in line of battle, unfazed. The fact that the Spanish failed in their ambush is a sign of their chaos and poor organization, compounded by ineffective artillery.[13]

The republicans for their part had planned for such an attack, and they lay down on the ground to await orders. The cannons were placed on the Spanish left, and Kemper sent word to Ross, who was opposite, to take the guns, while the rest of the right wing supported him. "The signal was to be the [tap] of the drum, which by some mistake was not given," Ross later wrote Shaler. "This had like to have been of serious consequence. The Col. [was] waiting for [us to] rise, and I, for the signal." Some of the Indians of Ross' command had in fact attacked ahead of the signal and "were repulsed with the loss of their Prophet and main chief." The second-in-command, Charles Rollins, the mixed Anglo/Coushatta, led the charge. Ross, seeing them hard pressed, rose with his men and joined the attack.[14]

"The Americans rose to their feet and rushed to the very muzzle of their guns and discharged a volley of ball and shot into their ranks," McLane recalled, noting the use of buck-and-ball—a double charge of a solid ball and pellets to combine the power of a ball-loaded musket with the spreading pattern of a shotgun. James McKim said the men had been ordered to advance within thirty yards of the enemy, load and fire three times, and then load a fourth time and charge the entire line.

"The order was obeyed in silence, and with a coolness so remarkable, that it filled the Spaniards with terror."[15]

Ross, with his Indian and American troops, pursued the charge against the cannon on the Spanish left wing, while about one hundred Mexicans charged into their right, with the bulk of the Americans coming on in the center. Ross, charging headlong, outraced his men and found himself amid the enemy. In front of the Spanish cannon, he encountered the former royalist commandant of Nacogdoches, Bernardino Montero, standing his ground amid the onrush of the rebel army.[16]

It was an encounter that encapsulated the separate trajectories of Spaniards and republicans. On the one hand, the Spanish lieutenant colonel was a career officer who had risen to command the vital frontier post of Nacogdoches, was then pushed out by a rebel coup, regained his post months later, and then when the invasion came, had been deserted by all but ten of his soldiers as the rebels approached Nacogdoches. On the other side was an American former sheriff and amateur soldier from Virginia, fired by passion for revolution and dreams of a better life. Now they faced off in an unlikely individual duel amid the chaos of the battle.

"We marched so fast, I got among them when Lt. Col Montara [sic] marched on me for single combat at sword's point," Ross later recalled. "He lunged at me and we being very near (he touched my waistcoat) and as he passed I gave him a blow across the back of the neck." The wound was possibly not fatal, but as Montero passed by Ross, he was shot dead by a Natchitoches merchant, William Owens. But a moment later, the Baltimore-born Owens, who had traded with smugglers in Texas before joining the expedition, fell dead himself.[17]

Meanwhile, Ross engaged another Spanish officer with his pistol as that officer shot back with a musket. "His horse was killed, but I do not know that I killed him," Ross wrote. The republicans pushed their advantage. Dr. Samuel D. Forsyth, the former US Army surgeon's mate, fought in the battle and was so occupied with combat he "could hardly be prevailed upon to dress a wound while the action lasted." Captain Thomas Luckett, who commanded a select corps of riflemen who flanked the Spanish cannon on the right, would receive praise as "a Caesar in fight." Menchaca commanded a section of Mexicans and Indians.[18]

Bravery knew no flag. Montero died with such grace and dignity in charging the foe, despite the retreat of his men, that American newspapers would praise his courage. Nor was he alone. Maj. Henry Perry also dueled with a Spaniard, who "after several passes met the same fate as Montara [sic]." "In this engagement, the officers of the enemy behaved with the utmost gallantry," Hall recalled. "Some of them seeing they could not bring their men to fight, rushed forward sword in hand, determined to sell their lives as dearly as possible in single combat, and in consequence, a disproportionate number of officers was found among the dead." But the courage of these Spanish officers was not equaled by their commander. Herrera had fought bravely against the English, French, Comanches, and Apaches, but now displayed "the most unexplained act of military temerity ever attempted." At Rosillo, it was the officers who fought gallantly, while the men below them and the commander above failed in their courage.[19]

The fight was fiercer than any during the three-month siege which preceded it but was over in no more than fifteen to twenty minutes. Ross's men successfully took the Spanish cannon, and the royalist forces collapsed. "They exhibited the appearance of a flock of sheep scared by the wolves," McLane recalled. "Their own number and position precluding resistance or escape, numbers of their front rank threw down their arms and surrendered, taking position in the rear of the Americans as the safest place. They finally forced a passage to the rear, and broke ranks and run for dear life, leaving about four hundred dead on the field and a large number of prisoners."[20]

The Spanish Army in Texas, which had first established itself in this wild land in 1718 to protect the missions, and over the next century had endured privation, setbacks, and unfulfilled dreams, was no more. In addition to the dead, the Spanish lost seventy to three hundred captured, hundreds of horses and mules seized, several hundred muskets, and "a good supply of ammunition." The republican losses once again were slight—six killed and twenty-six wounded. The valiant Captain Miguel Menchaca was seriously wounded but would recover. Exhausted after the long march and sharp combat, but having captured plentiful provisions from the fleeing Spanish, the republicans spent the night on the grounds of Mission Espada, southeast of the city. Their numbers grew in the night, as residents from San Antonio flocked to join them.[21]

As they had done after La Bahía, the rebels followed up their victory with a raid on the enemy's horses, and in this case, they were spectacularly successful. A detachment of one hundred men under Captain Taylor, informed of the herd's location by deserters, surrounded the sixty or so Spanish guards and seized vast numbers of horses and mules. Hall put the number of horses and mules captured at three thousand, possibly an exaggeration, but in any event, it was enough to cripple the Spanish army. "During this interval," Hall recalled, "the soldiers of the enemy deserted to us in large numbers." The war was effectively over.[22]

The Capture of San Antonio

On April 1st, Kemper and Gutiérrez, advancing up the banks of the San Antonio River, made camp at Mission Concepción, only two miles from the city. From there, they advanced and formed in double columns just south of the town. Salcedo and Herrera had made futile attempts to fortify, but resistance was impossible. The rebels sent McFarlan under a flag of truce into the city to demand its surrender "stating that by ten o'clock the next day they wanted San Antonio's military plaza evacuated."[23]

Salcedo sent a delegation of three men from the city, including Juan Martin Veramendi, one of the foremost civic leaders. Already, a large number of Spanish troops and "a large number of the town's women" had fled San Antonio to join the Republican Army. Now Veramendi's delegation delivered a letter from the governor. Salcedo knew he was beaten and wanted to surrender while he still had something left of his army to get decent terms. He asked that the persons and property of San Antonio be respected, that the Catholic Church would be protected, that no taxes would be levied, and that the sick would be cared for. To these reasonable civil demands, however, he also asked that his soldiers be allowed to retire to the interior of Mexico with all their arms and their cannon.[24]

Gutiérrez sent a terse reply, rejecting the conditions. "The only way that exists to prevent the violent taking of the place [is] that we enter at discretion, advising that in this latter case we concur in the inclination to conduct ourselves with all courteousness that the customs of war may permit," he wrote. Gutiérrez and Kemper also informed Salcedo of their military titles—general and colonel—and demanded that these marks of respect be used in the future. He ended his note: "Our troops will be quartered within the Alamo."[25]

Salcedo, with no alternative, came out of the city. "On the 31st [sic] about noon, these commanders advanced towards Gutiérrez and his victorious army," a young José Antonio Navarro recalled years later. "They proceeded on foot, accompanied by their staff and other officers of rank. Brief, however, was the conference. The vanquished only asked a guarantee of their lives. The reply of Gutiérrez was evasive but conveyed an intimation that their request would be complied with."[26]

The governor offered his sword to Captain Taylor, who had only weeks before been his prisoner. Taylor refused and indicated that the sword be surrendered to his superior, Kemper. Kemper likewise refused since he was the military commander only. He told Salcedo to surrender his sword to Gutiérrez. Salcedo was a proud nobleman of Spain, and Gutiérrez was a Creole blacksmith from Revilla. This, then, was too much. The governor stopped short of Gutiérrez, and rather than giving the sword to him, stabbed it into the dirt before him and was taken prisoner.[27]

The rebels secured the prisoners with guards on either side. "Gutiérrez and his army crossed to the eastern side of the river," Navarro recalled, "compelling their prisoners to march in front to the sound of martial music, and they entered within the walls of the Alamo." Inside this fort, a few captives still remained imprisoned, including an American named Carlos Beltrán. Originally from Virginia, Beltrán claimed to have been among Burr's 1806 followers, and had proceeded on to Texas, where he was allowed to live in San Antonio—and had even risen in society because of his skill as a gunsmith. A youth when he had arrived, he was adopted by a Bexár widow and became thoroughly Mexicanized. When the expedition kicked off, he was imprisoned by the Spaniards. Since the battle, Beltrán had endured days of agonized waiting and hunger in the Alamo jail. The guards had failed to bring the prisoners food the day before. Then, as Beltrán recalled:[28] "Along about 3 o'clock we heard a great shout and tumultuous cheering, and we could no longer doubt the issue of the battle. There was no mistaking those cheers; no soldiers in all the world can surpass the American in the battle yell, or his exultant cheers over a victory. Then came a great commotion just outside our prison walls; the doors were thrown open, and seventeen of us—Americans—were led forth to freedom by our own brave countrymen!"[29]

The inmates were brought from their dark cells into the midday sun and freedom, passing the royalists marching to take their places in the same prison. As the Mexican contingent came up on the scene, they were led by Captain Antonio Delgado. He was the son of Manuel Martín Delgado, a republican who had been executed by Salcedo. In some accounts, during the execution, "the blood from the bleeding head of his father was sprinkled over his mother." As the rebels came into the town, the younger Delgado saw his father's head upon a pike at the Alamo crossing. Beltrán described the scene:[30] "When Captain Delgado saw this gruesome relic of the doting father, he burst into a fit of weeping, which soon changed to a paroxysm of uncontrollable fury. He hastened to the quarters, he found Salcedo with other Spanish officials, and with drawn sword forced his way past the guards and rushed upon Salcedo with the rage of a demon and would have slain him but for the interference of the Americans, who seized him and after a struggle bore him away."[31]

After the passion of the moment, the republicans focused their efforts on consolidation of the town. In Main Plaza, they posted the six cannon they had captured at Rosillo at the entrances to the streets. While some citizens were initially wary of this force, the republicans soon found "many warm friends for the revolutionary cause" among them. With the gachupín leaders imprisoned, the question was what to do with the remaining royalist soldiers. The republicans chose to disarm only those from the interior of Mexico who had not already defected to their side. The soldiers of the Alamo and La Bahía garrisons and the local militia were allowed to keep their weapons and return to their homes. These men, most of whom had once stood behind Casas, now became republicans once more, enrolled en masse into the rebel force.[32]

On April 6, 1813, former royalists took the oath to the Mexican Republic in the Plaza de Armas—among them a man who had grown up from his youth in this very plaza. José Francisco Ruiz was the Béxar militiaman who had corresponded with Miguel Menchaca after Rosillo. But the choice to become rebels divided families and friends. Ruiz's best friend and nephew, José Ignacio Perez, remained loyal. With a small group of royalist escapees, which included Zambrano, he now fled to the south. Still, Ruiz stood up for his absent friend, and as republicans expropriated property, he used his influence to protect Perez's home and ranch. The rebel leaders, Kemper, Gutiérrez, Ross, and others, now established themselves in the Alamo, where they "slept their first sleep of triumph."[33]

Neither Gutiérrez, nor the American volunteers, envisioned the war ending with the conquest of Texas. The Mexican rebel's plan from the beginning was to take advantage of the Burrite sentiment in America to open the door to Mexico.

Although native forces were intended to lead in the final push, Gutiérrez had neither the strength nor inclination to end his association with American volunteers. The Mexican Association's dream had envisioned the seizing of Texas to be the opening step, not the end of the campaign against New Spain. But the vast numbers of frontiersmen needed to push the battle beyond the Rio Grande had never come, due to Claiborne's proclamation, Adair's reticence, and the deepening of the War of 1812. Neither had the rebels discovered the rumored vast hoard of Spanish loot to purchase needed supplies. For the moment, at least, the army had taken Texas but could go no further.[34]

Gutiérrez had now accomplished what would have seemed a dream when he fled through Texas with a small band of followers just two years before. That it would not have been possible without his Anglo-American allies, he readily acknowledged. But this was a Mexican Revolution, not an American invasion, and after languishing in the shadows of the army, Gutiérrez now had a political capital in his possession and the influx of new Mexican troops was rebalancing the army. He therefore intended to take corresponding leadership of the movement, establishing a junta heavily filled with San Antonio's traditional leaders, with himself as president and Don Mariano Rodriguez as secretary. The Republican Army secured two spots on the council: the Anglo-American Nathan M. Hale, and a Frenchman, Louis Massicott. The latter, about thirty years old, was a recent arrival. He had an invaluable skill: fluent in English, Spanish, and French, he was appointed as the secretary of state, in charge of much of the day-to-day running of the government. Shaler knew him from Havana and described him as "a young man of talents and good character." Unknown to the American, Massicott was exactly the sort of influence Shaler feared; he was the on-site representative of the French agent Pedro Girard, about whom Shaler had warned Gutiérrez.[35]

The American agent, observing from distant Natchitoches, saw the unleashing of Gutiérrez as his own worst nightmare come true. Shaler had been disturbed by the rebel's delusions of grandeur and his intemperance, then came the incident at Bayou Pierre, in which Gutiérrez had allegedly attempted to conscript American citizens. Throughout the early stages of the campaign, the American agent had been reassured by the presence of Magee, who he thought could restrain the overzealous Mexican rebel and harness his energies in a more positive direction. But Magee was now dead, and Kemper showed no interest in taking on the role of chaperone. Would Gutiérrez now make Shaler's nightmares come true, or moderate his behavior and establish a government that would fulfill the needs of the American agent's commission?[36]

Gutiérrez himself was no Tejano but discovered in San Antonio a people yearning for change. The Casas experiment had schooled them in disappointment and the Zambrano coup made them wary of royal reform. What they wanted above all was peace and stability. "The expedition was no longer a movement from outside composed mostly of foreigners," notes Mexican historian Virginia Guedea. It had instead become "a clearly regional and identified movement for the objectives of the insurgents of New Spain, adopted by the inhabitants of the region." The Gutiérrez-Magee Expedition was over, and though Anglo-Americans were still vital players, a Tejano republic had taken its place.

Declaration of Independence

On April 6, 1813, the rebels drafted a declaration of independence. It was in fact, the first such declaration for what would soon be the new nation of Mexico, preceding by seven months to the day that of José María Morelos. The document was likely drafted with Kemper's input (it includes some language nearly identical to the West Florida declaration) but also shows the hands of Gutiérrez and even native Tejano crafters. Notably it ruled out an American takeover:[37] "We, the people of the province of Texas, calling on the Supreme Judge of the Universe to witness the rectitude of our intentions, declare, that the ties which held us under the domination of Spain and Europe, are forever dissolved; that we possess the right to establish a government for ourselves; that in future all legitimate authority shall emanate from the people to whom it rightfully belongs, and that henceforth all allegiance or subjection to any foreign power whatsoever, is entirely renounced."[38]

The declaration drew on the American one, but with a Mexican flavor. In a very Catholic note, it proclaimed, "Man is formed in the image of his Creator: he sins who submits to slavery." Under Spain, the people of Texas had been denied communication with other nations, prohibited from importing books; even thought was suppressed. "Our country was our prison," the declaration stated, echoing the long-forgotten song of rebel martyr Luís Grande. But the chief complaint of these native Tejanos was that which had first brought them into the alliance of convenience with their American and French neighbors. For them, this was fundamentally an *economic* revolution, and the enemy was the hated system of Spanish mercantilism, which was a particular Tejano grievance:[39] "In a province which nature has favored with uncommon prodigality, we were poor. We were prohibited from cultivating those articles which are suitable to our soil and climate, and of pressing necessity. The commerce of our country was sold to the favorites of the court; and merchandise was supplied under the enormous exactions of the monopolists. A barbarous and shameful inhospitality was manifested to strangers, even to our nearest neighbors. The product of our soil and of our country were alike denied exportation. Our trade consisted in a trifling system of smuggling."[40]

The king was never mentioned, though the document did complain that "some miserable wretches, styling themselves the rulers of Spain, have sold us to a foreign power [France]." The harshest words were for the captured governor Salcedo: "As a reward for our faithful services, a sanguinary vagrant, distinguished in his own country by no honorable action, is sent amongst us, and his government exhibited only acts of cruelty, insatiable avarice, and augmented oppression." The document was presented to the people of Texas. Samuel Kemper, hoping to draw more recruits, forwarded a copy to the editor of the *Daily National Intelligencer* in Washington, which declared "the fall of Santo Antonio may be considered as having decided the fate of that interesting country."[41]

A Constitution for Texas

But what was this new political entity? It would be eleven days later, April 17th, before Gutiérrez and his supporters would sign the first-ever constitution for Texas. It clearly answered the question: "The province of Texas shall henceforth be known only as the State of Texas, forming part of the Mexican Republic, to which it remains inviolably joined."[42]

Much has been said by later writers about the supposed disappointment of the Anglo-American volunteers at this, but they expressed no such sentiment at the time. Gutiérrez had been clear, and Magee, Kemper, and all the leaders of the expedition had agreed that this was a Mexican revolution, not an American takeover. It had been Gutiérrez, with no American prompting, who offered Texas to the United States, on specific terms which had been ignored, and the offer was now effectively rescinded.

If any Americans felt cheated, they had deceived themselves about the war for which they had signed up. In fact, none of them in any known document ever complained about this point. Most of the Anglos wanted *personal* aggrandizement. To the extent that they supported America's claim to Texas, they likely hoped that Mexico would sell all or part of the province. But if any transfer to the United States did not recognize their claims, then they would likely have shown the same hostility that Fulwar Skipwith had displayed in West Florida, exactly as they themselves had shown to Robinson. Gutiérrez likewise understood the materialistic key to the Americans' hearts, and no doubt believed it would override their nationalism. He was no xenophobe pushing foreigners away; on the contrary, he issued a call for "freemen of all nations" to come settle in Texas. Gutiérrez wanted new settlers and was not unwilling to exaggerate to attract them, writing that the newly liberated Texas was "as rich as Mexico in gold or silver."[43]

The new Tejano constitution further protected "our Holy Religion," which meant an established Catholic Church. This soothed the fears of locals, but for any Americans hoping to move to Texas, this was a greater impediment than the question of nationality. The document also protected personal property and gave some rights to the accused, with the very notable exception "during the time of the present war in the case of criminals of the republic, whose punishments will be decided by the Junta" with the approval of Gutiérrez.[44]

The document showed possible influences from the Constitution of the Spanish monarchy—that of the Cádiz exile government—and on this point, the constitution began to drift wide from republican principles, at least as the Americans understood them. The governor or "president protector" was to be selected by the junta, with no mention of popular sovereignty. Neither did the people have a vote for the top officials of the capital city. It was to be governed by two mayors and four district commissioners—the old Spanish system—all appointed by the unelected junta. The constitution simply replaced one unelected autocrat of Texas with a council of several of them.[45]

These were bitter pills indeed for some of the Anglo-American volunteers—and outsiders like Shaler—to swallow. This was not republicanism as they believed it to be, and their Mexican allies were *not* just like them. Of course, they *could not* be. The Americans' revolt against England had been a conservative, not a radical one. The Mexican rebellion as Gutiérrez and his junta saw it was also conservative, only *from a different starting point*. Each nation molded its revolution in logical clay from its own colonial legacy.

Spreading the Revolution

The goal of this new "State of Texas" was to serve as a launching pad for further efforts to liberate Mexico proper. Even though the army could not advance on its own, Texas could still aid the greater cause. To this task then, Gutiérrez also turned his attention. He began by issuing a proclamation to the people of Northern Mexico. "Most loyal Creoles, natives of this enchanting America," he wrote, "how you weep under the lethargic and oppressive weight of the European yoke. Awaken to the sound which gathers at your threshold.... Focus your attention on the events that have transpired since August of last year." Gutiérrez recalled the history of the Texas conflict: the Commandant at Nacogdoches fleeing from "our valiant Anglo American allies," the republicans seizing La Bahía and enduring a three-month siege, and the Battle of Rosillo on March 29th—"a memorable day for two generations to come." He appealed to the rest of Northern Mexico to join him:[46]

> Open your eyes and don't oppose strength. Follow the example of the patriotic city of San Fernando de Béxar [San Antonio], which without firing a single shot allowed the army free passage, thereby avoiding the bloodbath that would have ensued.... Accept the progress made in such a short time by that small number of men who began this glorious effort and who still have the strength to continue. Day by day their numbers grow, and soon they will grow to such a degree that their power shall overrule that of your oppressors.[47]

Signing this proclamation was the Nacogdoches officer who had now made his way to San Antonio, José María Guadiana (listed as the sergeant major) and Isidrio de la Garza, as "Commander of Volunteers," along with the senior militia officer,

José Manuel Prieto, and fifteen others whose names gave the rebels authority in Texas and beyond.[48]

Another proclamation began, "People of America, how long do you sleep in the deep sleep of indifference?" and urged the Mexicans to fight the gachupines. "They are the ones who have made the parents take up arms against the children, to one against the other, to brothers against brothers, and they are the ones who have originated a bloody internal war that has devoured the best talents of our homeland."[49]

Gutiérrez freely mixed warlike messages and peaceful metaphors, befitting a revolution where loyalties shifted dramatically, rapidly, and not at all permanently. They also reflected the divisions in Béxar, where "the thoughts and actions of the local population were cautious, complex, and aimed at preserving their interests," as one historian put it. This was not a rabidly republican community, and Gutiérrez had a modest base of support. His enemies today could be his allies tomorrow, and above all he had to win over these men.[50]

But not all was well in San Antonio, even in the midst of republican power. Among the Tejano leaders were some who were still sympathetic to the royal cause. Capt. José Nicolás Benítez had been a royalist before and had been one of the emissaries Salcedo and Herrera had sent prior to the surrender. Ostensibly embracing the revolution, he had been one of the signers of Gutiérrez's constitution, as well as several of his proclamations during April 1813. But in May, he fled the city, making his way south to rejoin the royal forces of Ignacio Elizondo. There, he told what he had learned about the rebel cause over the previous month. From him the royalists learned about Gutiérrez's plans, and even Comanche thefts of rebel horses. Why Benítez chose to return to the royal fold is unknown, but it may have been related to an event that had taken place during that crucial month, which was to shake the revolution to its core—far more than any constitution could—and sow division and dissent in the new republic, even at its moment of triumph.[51]

18

Murder on the Salado

GOVS. MANUEL SALCEDO and Simón Herrera were now prisoners of rebels for the second time in three years. To the Anglo-American volunteers, the royalists were an honorable enemy who had been vanquished on the battlefield, to be treated with all the civility that they themselves had shown to Magee. In fact, at the surrender, Salcedo had cheerfully singled out the former commander's aide, Maj. William Murray, and "observed to Mr. Murray that he met him then with more satisfaction than on a former occasion when they attempted to negotiate a capitulation at La Bahía." Colonel Kemper, Maj. Reuben Ross, and other American officers even dined with Salcedo at his home. But for the Mexican rebels, far too much blood had been spilt and oppression visited upon them to forget or forgive. Two years before, Casas had given mercy to these two men and his reward was to have his head dragged behind a cart and suspended atop a pole.[1]

One of the earliest Mexican historians to recount these events claimed the Junta was composed of "several of the most turbulent [men] in the village," bent on vengeance against the men they blamed for the deaths of Hidalgo and his companions. Along with this hatred lay a stark fact that the Mexicans knew all too well: as long as the royalist leaders remained in Texas, they would always be a magnet for counterrevolution. Indeed, as Salcedo had bought time in his negotiations following the Battle of Rosillo, a number of royalists had escaped south to the Rio Grande. Among them was the ever-elusive Juan Manuel Zambrano, who "was obliged to flee and make his way on foot, with incredible hardships, in company of four brothers, across a desert of more than eighty leagues."[2]

Gutiérrez's Tejano supporters now insisted the captured royalists be tried in military court. After Delgado's rage-filled attack on them, however, the Americans were wary the trial would be a sham. Kemper appointed a counsel to the royalists, choosing the Mississippi lawyer Darius Johnston, who had come to Texas along with his brother Orramel. But as the trial was convened, the Mexican judges neither allowed him to appear and offer a defense, nor to present any evidence on behalf of the accused. Gaines claims the judges were composed of the "family of the Monchacks [Menchaca] & their influenced." The result, given such circumstances, was predictable. Twelve royalists were found guilty and given the death penalty.[3]

The Americans felt this was a shameful dishonor for prisoners of war who deserved fair and honest trials. This was certainly hypocritical. Eight years before, Samuel Kemper attacked his former kidnappers after their trial, holding one of them down while his brother cut off his ear with a dull knife. But, now, he and his fellow Americans stood their ground for *justice* and "denounced the entire proceedings in the most scathing terms." They even hinted that carrying out the sentence would result in armed resistance, as Carlos Beltrán, the Mexicanized American recalled. "The excitement among the American troops was intense, and plans were set on foot for the arrest of Gutiérrez and his council," while their officers restrained their men. The revolution was one false move away from becoming a war between the Mexican and Anglo-American contingents of the Republican Army over the issue. On April 3rd, Gutiérrez called the army to the main plaza to announce his decision. Beltrán recalled:[4] "[He] announced that in consideration of the humane principles that govern the actions of all true patriots fighting for liberty and independence, and in deference to the wishes of the gallant Americans who had so nobly aided in the overthrow of the Spanish power in Texas, he had decided to commute the sentence of the council against the Spanish officials, to perpetual banishment."[5]

The general then surprised the gathered republicans with a piece of news. He had received reports that a vessel had recently arrived at a newly opened landing area in Matagorda Bay, where a small force of Mexicans was ready to open up trade. The ship, he explained, could transport the Spaniards to Cuba and exile. "This announcement was greeted with cheers on the part of the Americans," Beltrán wrote. The Mexicans, on the other hand, remained silent.[6]

In the meantime, Gutiérrez explained, keeping the royalists in San Antonio was impossible. He proposed instead to send them back to La Bahía, where a small rebel force remained. It was nearer the coast, and the presidio, as McLane recalled the argument, had "ample provisions, and a secure enclosure, within which they could have exercise during the day." The twelve officers would wait at the site of the former siege until the ship was ready to sail. The Americans "having no suspicion of their designs," assented to this, and though they still wanted the officers paroled on their honor, Gutiérrez placed them back in the Alamo prison, under a guard of Menchaca's men.[7]

Beltrán, the American who had lived so long amongst the Mexicans, had been chilled by his fellow Bexareños' stony silence upon hearing of the captives' reprieve. On the evening of April 3rd, he left the city to go visit José Sánchez, just outside of town. The latter, among the Tejano troops at Rosillo, had been severely wounded in the battle, and Beltrán and another friend, Pablo Rodríguez, spent the evening nursing their injured comrade. They returned just before dawn and were surprised to see a large body of Mexican cavalry waiting outside the Alamo. Out of curiosity, the two young men walked up to them and saw the prisoners being placed on horses for their journey. To their surprise, the men were bound securely with ropes to their horses. Ominously, the commander of the guard was the same Antonio Delgado who had threatened the royalists before.[8]

> I knew Captain Delgado quite well—we had always been on the most friendly terms—and, observing me closely watching his movements, he brusquely asked what I was doing there, and who had sent me to spy on his actions. I answered by saying that I was there on my own volition and that considering the high station held by these prisoners, I thought it a shameful humiliation to their dignity and manhood to tie them on their horses when there was absolutely no occasion for such brutal treatment, and that I would immediately report the matter to Colonel Kemper. This seemed to nettle the captain, and he ordered us away.[9]

Beltrán and Sánchez rushed over the river and entered the town, where they tracked down Kemper and Ross. The American commanders were appalled at what they heard. They had known of the transport—indeed, Kemper had even signed a letter authorizing it. But they had expected humane treatment and certainly would not have agreed to the troop being led by Delgado. Upon discovery that the party had already departed, Kemper and Ross "went straightway to the quarters of Gutiérrez and demanded the return of the prisoners without delay," Beltrán wrote. "They told Gutiérrez that they had pledged their honor, as American soldiers, for the safety of those men." Gutiérrez insisted that the Spaniards were safe, that Delgado was a reliable and honorable soldier, and if anything happened to the prisoners, Gutiérrez would have Delgado shot immediately upon his return.[10]

Delgado and his escort led the group of fourteen royalists, including nine native-born Spaniards and five Creoles, down the road toward La Bahía. It had been four and a half years since Manuel Salcedo had trekked across the United States, dined with Natchitoches Indian Agent John Sibley, then entered Texas on the heels of the French revolutionary Gen. Octaviano D'Alvimar. He had sought in that time to do his job dutifully to his king and country. His enemies, of course, would counter with charges of cruelty. Nonetheless, he had weathered storm after storm with few resources, while enduring the many slights and petty tyrannies of his uncle, the commandant general. During the Casas revolt, he had pathetically attempted to demote himself to ordinary soldier rather than go into captivity. Then, there was imprisonment, liberation, and the masterminding of the victory at the Wells of Baján, where he no doubt felt he had helped save the empire he loved so much.[11]

Simón de Herrera y Leyva was older than Salcedo by twenty years. He had been the governor of Nuevo León, fought bravely for his country in an expedition against the Portuguese in South America, helped besiege Gibraltar, then fought alongside Bernardo de Gálvez in the Spanish army in 1782–83. He even led a highly successful attack against a force of Apaches and Comanches. He had faced off with General Wilkinson in what had almost been an American–Spanish war in 1806, before the two had negotiated the Neutral Ground Agreement, preventing conflict, but ultimately fueling the insurgency that had now brought him to the very brink. With his good command of English and friendly disposition, he had won over the sympathy first of Dr. Robinson, then Augustus Magee, and finally Samuel Kemper. There are hints that Herrera may have even been a closet supporter of republicanism.[12]

Riding alongside him was his younger brother, Geronimo Herrera, and six fellow Spaniards. Three native-born but loyal Mexicans accompanied them: Capt. Miguel Arcos, who had been the judge who condemned Gutiérrez's messengers Bergara and Grande, was now bound along with his two sons. A civilian from San Antonio who had assisted in the arrest of the elder Delgado was also with them. Now this party was led by Delgado's son Antonio, and they were *not* going to La Bahia or Matagorda, and certainly not to Cuba. It is doubtful that the ship Gutiérrez had conjured up in his speech in the plaza in San Antonio had ever existed.[13]

A few miles southeast of San Antonio, and not far from the Rosillo battlefield, was a place called La Tablita. It lay near where the Salado Creek flowed into the San Antonio River, and here the party halted. The prisoners were untied from their horses and made to dismount. Their guards then proceeded to tie them to trees. The royalists begged their captors to at least delay the execution until a priest could be brought down from the city to give them last rites, but this was refused. "You sent my father into eternity, denying him the consolation of religion in his last extremity," Delgado allegedly sneered in Salcedo's face. One of the governors, probably Salcedo, was the third man to be tied up, and in Beltran's account called to one of the republicans, a Lieutenant Santos. He handed him his watch and his ring and asked that they be given to Dr. Orramel Johnston—the Anglo-American doctor and brother of their would-be lawyer—to be delivered on to his family.[14]

The rebels stripped the men of their clothing and then finished tying their victims. Lieutenant Colonel Herrera, according to Beltrán, "warned Delgado of the day of signal retribution and defied him to do his worst." Another account says of him, "It is said Herrera prayed earnestly to be shot instead of being butchered like a dog." A third account says it was Salcedo who made the request. It is unclear if this wish was granted, but given the level of brutality, one suspects it was not. According to one witness, the governor's tongue was cut out, ending these requests. José Antonio Navarro, who was not a witness but reported the event secondhand, said Delgado's men had no swords—only the dull knives they kept on their belts for camp use. "With inhuman irony, some of the assassins sharpened their knives on the soles of their shoes in the presence of their defenseless victims." They hurled insults at the prisoners and then cut their throats. When this was done, Delgado's men left them tied to the trees, where they drowned in their own frothing blood. After they expired, the bodies were cut down and tossed into the creek.[15]

The next day, Delgado rode up in front of the governor's mansion in San Antonio, where Gutiérrez had made his headquarters and walked in. Navarro, the youth who recalled the events decades later, had gathered with a number of other boys of the town and watched Delgado stride into the building. Taking off his hat as he stood before Gutiérrez, he stuttered and "uttered some words mingled with shame." He then handed the general a paper that held a list of those who had been executed. "I myself saw the blood-stained adornments that those tigers carried hanging from their saddle horns," Navarro recalled years later, "boasting publicly of their crime and having divided the spoils among themselves in shares." Navarro, himself a rebel in later years, would lament the stain of the murder. "O shame of the human race! O disgrace and affront upon the descendants of a Christian nation!" he would write. "Who can retain his composure and pass in silence these horrible [events], that they by their future conduct may wash out the foul stains that corrode our benign soil!"[16]

The murders may also have been used for terror purposes. An imprisoned royalist, Guillermo Navarro (no relation to Antonio), who had been an aide to Gerónimo Herrera, escaped and brought the news to royalist forces in Laredo. In his deposition, he stated that Delgado and his party of renegades bore with them some of the royalists' clothing, which were recognized by the victims' friends. His group then proceeded to arrest *more* royalists. Then the Spanish troops still in the city, who had by now been disarmed, "were gathered and given the option to join their [renegade] forces or be penalized by not having their firearms returned to them if they refused. Many, unwilling to forfeit their firearms, and already partial to the renegades, did join them."[17]

The Trial of Delgado

Anglo-American reaction was swift and furious. The men were near mutinous, and only Kemper and Ross' attempts to restrain their troops prevented them from attacking Gutiérrez. Instead, they arrested Delgado. It remains unclear whether Gutiérrez knew of the plan to execute the royalists, and he steadfastly maintained his innocence. The most charitable scenario is that Gutiérrez realized that Tejanos like Delgado were demanding vengeance, and he had to step aside and let them have it or face a mutiny of his own. Nonetheless, he had deliberately deceived the Americans and they believed blood was on his hands. Bringing the "president protector" of Texas to trial was impossible of course, but the Anglo-Americans had Delgado in their power. As a member of their army, he was subject to trial by court-martial, which the Americans promptly convened. But if they expected a brutish, simple villain on the stand, they were to be disappointed.[18]

Delgado defended himself, and Beltrán, one of the few Anglos who spoke Spanish, reported the speech of the accused, the memory of which stuck with him for decades afterward. He recalled his father, who had been a patriot, "one of the first to respond to liberty's call to her loyal sons." He had fought the gachupín and was betrayed by Salcedo, "by whom he was cruelly put to death and his venerable head—my father's head—was hoisted upon a pole—a horrible sight which all you gallant Americans witnessed when you entered the city." If the Anglo-Americans expected Antonio Delgado to beg for mercy, possibly implicating General Gutiérrez in an attempt to win their favor and save his own life, they were mistaken. On the contrary, Delgado asserted, he was under no orders and would prefer his jury to pin the entire blame for the murders on himself alone:[19]

> I am not a penitent. I have no regrets over the execution of the men who have been a scourge to my race and country. They have spared neither age nor sex, and it was the gachupín who set the precedent of death to all prisoners. Had these men been spared they would have been exchanged or released only to return and again deluge our unhappy country with the blood of my people. A gachupín never forgets, and no pledge, bond or parole entered into with a rebel is binding on his conscience. As a son, no less dutiful to his parent than loyal to his country, I have avenged the murder of my venerated father. If there is an American present who would have done less, let him rise up and pronounce me guilty.[20]

Delgado's passion, his filial dedication, and his courage to stare his jury down and boldly state his guilt supposedly won over the hardest hearts of the Anglo-Americans, and despite his guilty plea, he was found innocent. Gutiérrez in his own defense could simply point to Delgado's assumption of full responsibility, conveniently ignoring his promise to shoot his subordinate. The rebel in later years wrote an account in which he claimed the people of Béxar demanded the deaths; otherwise, "even the women and children would fall upon me and tear me to pieces." Gutiérrez wrote that he had been hesitant to comply, but this is not credible. Six months before, after the murder of his agents, Grande and Bergara, he had warned Salcedo that the result of any further death sentences against republicans would be that Salcedo and Zambrano "would be destroyed in the middle of the plaza."[21]

The Tejanos sought to soothe their American allies and prevent their wholesale abandonment of the cause by enlisting Capt. James Gaines to explain the royalist's crimes that justified their deaths: the seduction then betrayal and murder of José Menchaca and the capture and execution of Hidalgo. "This was the second & I deem all sufficient ground of the condemnation and execution of the above prisoners," Gaines wrote years later. For many, only the appeals of Miguel Menchaca and some of the principal Mexican officers convinced them to stay. Nonetheless, a bridge had been crossed, and the Americans, though they could reconcile with their fellow fighters, now completely lost faith in Gutiérrez, just as they had once lost faith in Magee. But there was no way to replace him, and he would continue to head the revolt in Texas, unless by some chance some other leader could be found.[22]

Toledo and His Nemesis

The news of the murders reached an astounded William Shaler in Natchitoches in early May. It had been just the sort of act of revolutionary excess that he had feared from his former protégé, though the magnitude of the crime was even greater than he had anticipated. "I am at a loss for language to express my sense of this black action," he wrote, forwarding the news to Monroe. Shortly after the murder, a party of Americans had gone to the site of the crime and buried the remains of the royalists. "The most lively indignation was expressed by all the Americans who regarded the army as dishonored by this act of treacherous cruelty," Shaler informed the secretary of state, "but it was generally applauded by the Mexicans as an act of just retribution, and no consequence followed."[23]

Shaler wrote with little expectation of guidance. Monroe was in another one of his silent periods. The secretary of state had not written his agent with any instructions since September, when he had told him to "discountenance" the expedition—after it had already commenced—and added, "I shall write to you soon more fully on this Subject." *Soon* had now stretched to eight months, and in the meantime, the only thing Shaler had received from Monroe was a new passport (which he had requested), a copy of the president's message to Congress, and copies of the *National Intelligencer*, for which Shaler had also asked. Deprived of meaningful orders, Shaler was forced to scour that newspaper—known to be a mouthpiece of the government—for anything useful to help him discern national policy. The secretary of state was understandably preoccupied with *America's* war, not the Mexican one. The office was too big for him, and James Monroe was not a delegator. Before the war would be over, he would even assume the job of secretary of war along with his own post.[24]

His agent to Mexico had been ordered not to be involved in the expedition, but there was now a *government* in San Antonio that claimed to represent the Mexican Republic. Although Shaler dismissed the recent constitution as "nothing more than an absurd revolutionary farce," the Béxar Junta was at least a quasilegal entity in possession of territory, which he interpreted, in the absence of orders, to meet the requirements of his instructions. There was just one problem: the government still had Gutiérrez at its head, and the murder of the royalists looked like revolutionary radicalism in the French style. For the Mexican cause to not lose the moral support of America, it needed to pull back from the brink, and the agent now found a new ally who could save the rebellion: José Álvarez de Toledo.[25]

The Cuban had arrived in Natchitoches in April, shortly after the news of Salcedo's defeat, explaining to Shaler that he was proceeding to take command of the Mexican armies in Texas, even though no one had invited him to do so. Toledo and his retinue had made their way west to Pittsburgh, then descended the Ohio and the Mississippi on a flatboat. Stopping in Natchez, they spent fifteen days talking with all the leading Burrites, including the infamous Harman Blennerhassett, on whose private island Burr had formed his own band of men to revolutionize Mexico.[26]

Toledo had believed he would be hailed with wild enthusiasm and an ever-growing train of new recruits to fight in Texas, but the backers of the rebellion were surprisingly wary. In Rapides, Toledo also found "the public mind unfavorably impressed towards him." Adair requested a meeting at his Natchez residence, but Toledo, sensing the ominous mood of the town, was suspicious. Not long after, he was in his lodgings at night when Reuben Kemper arrived and had Toledo arrested. The Cuban was soon released, but he had been "treated with a degree of indecency disgraceful to an American town." That Adair and the brother of Samuel Kemper would intervene so forcefully indicates how deeply involved these two still were in supporting and nurturing the invasion.[27]

The Burrites' fear of Toledo partly stemmed from a rumor campaign that had preceded him: that he was a French revolutionary agent. This suspicion would not have been helped by the company he kept. His cotraveler, Arsiné LaTour, was well-known in New Orleans, and suspected of being an agent of a mysterious French general, Jean Joseph Amable Humbert, a professional revolutionary who once led an invasion of Ireland and had arrived in New Orleans in 1810.[28]

But Shaler was not buying the fear of Toledo. He was "well acquainted with this gentleman's character." He certainly knew many of the same Cuban elite to which Toledo belonged, including, undoubtedly, his father, the Havana Port Commissioner, and they shared a mutual friend, Henry Breckenridge. As news from Texas shifted from excitement to horror, William Shaler, now emotionally invested in the little army in Texas, began to embrace Toledo and his little band as an alternative to Gutiérrez. While Adair and Reuben Kempers' counsels ruled back in Natchez and Rapides, the man to whom the people of Natchitoches increasingly looked was William Shaler. He now became the Cuban's open advocate:[29] "I have consequently by representing him in what I conceive to be his true character broken down the absurdity of his French agency, and he has obtained the sympathy and respect of all the inhabitants of this post. Every gentleman here who has any acquaintance in the Army has written such letters as will most certainly counteract the efforts of any unfavorable impressions attempted to be made there. He sent forward his attendant immediately on his arrival and proceeds himself tomorrow."[30]

As he had done with Gutiérrez, Shaler counseled Toledo to distance himself from French agents. Jean Jacques Paillet, who had approached Gutiérrez in June of the previous year, now made a pitch to Toledo, with the object to "draw him into an acknowledgment of his willingness to receive the aid of France, the amount, manner, and form of which was to be determined by ulterior instructions." Shaler discouraged Toledo's further association with Paillet. Toledo also abandoned the suspicious Latour. Around this time, Dr. John Robinson arrived from Texas. Now, angry at his hostile reception by Nemesio Salcedo and inspired by a secret meeting with Mexican revolutionaries in Chihuahua, Robinson was an undisguised convert to the republican cause and was on his way to preach the gospel to Monroe.[31]

Disaffection in San Antonio

On April 20th, about one hundred Americans in the Republican Army of the North left the force to return to America. Some quit in disgust over the murder of the royalists, others merely took furloughs, with every intention of returning. These included the young lawyer Warren D. C. Hall, who had risen to be a captain, and one of the army's first officers, Thomas Luckett, who had led a small company of riflemen that poured devastating fire on the royalists at Rosillo. Also quitting was West Point graduate Samuel Noah, who for the second time, found that army life was not for him. Joining the Americans in this exodus were most of the Coushatta Indians, who returned to their village.[32]

The worst loss, however, was the army's commander, Samuel Kemper, the West Florida veteran, although in his case the departure was not permanent. "It is understood that he is on furlough, and intends to return to the army of the republic as soon as he can arrange his affairs," a contemporary newspaper account reported. Kemper arrived back home in Rapides on May 26, 1813, where he praised the army to American audiences, hoping to entice new recruits—and possibly sway the American government to drop its hostility, as a newspaper editor noted:[33]

> The accounts which the colonel gives of the situation of things in the new republic are highly interesting. Taking everything into consideration, this will undoubtedly rank among the most extraordinary expeditions ever undertaken, that of Cortez not excepted. That a handful of men, five hundred miles in the interior of such a country as Mexico, should have been able to make a stand during six or eight months, and finally triumph, is truly a matter of wonder. There is little doubt but that a few thousand well appointed troops would march to any part of New Spain.[34]

This optimism was not matched in Texas, however. Coming amid widespread dissatisfaction, Kemper's furlough, which he essentially gave to himself, looked permanent. Gutiérrez could not go it alone; he still needed the Americans. Though the Mexican contingent was now a majority of the army, the foreigners were his best soldiers. Their rifles alone were superior to anything the Spanish army had, and they were more proficient with them than all but a few of the native Tejanos and deserters. The Mexicans' arms ranged from old, poorly maintained smooth-bore muskets to simple lances. Some of these troops had only deserted the Spanish under duress, and Gutiérrez would have been uneasy about them in a fight. Most importantly, with the Americans gone, Texas might lose its lifeline of supplies and support that the army needed to continue the revolution. Gutiérrez wanted more Americans, not fewer. A proclamation was issued to this effect "by the authority of the Junta of the state of Texas and Don José Bernardo Gutiérrez."[35]

> Freemen of all nations!
>
> The laws and government of the state of Texas, a member of the republic of Mexico, are such as to destroy the barbarous and perverse system which existed anterior to the establishment of the Republic by the Spanish patriots and their American co-adjutors in arms. They invite the emigration of freemen of all nations who are desirous of participating in the blessings which a republican form of government is calculated to extend to all men. . . . Such are the laws which now succeed the ancient tyranny which destroyed Texas.[36]

The Mexican revolutionary had already offered generous land bounties, and now he upped them, adding more land and two mules to replace each lost horse. American newspapers reported salaries for the army were "liberal beyond any thing I have ever seen." Majors were to be paid like American brigadier generals. At the same time, however, Gutiérrez made a plea for sole command of the Republican Army of the North. Since the beginning, he had been only the political leader; now he wanted full control. A proclamation made his case:[37]

> Soldiers, your chosen leader has abandoned you in the hour of triumph and without just cause; dissention is rife in your ranks, all of which is the work of the enemy. I appeal to your patriotism; banish insubordination, rally to the standard I erected on the Sabine and which has thus far led you to victory; follow my leadership, and with the recruits that will daily flock to your ranks, I will lead you to greater victories and the campaign so auspiciously begun shall close with your triumphal entry into the ancient city of Tenochtitlan.[38]

But this, the Americans would never accept. While they recognized the importance of having a Mexican at the head of affairs, they would never fight behind Gutiérrez in combat. It is tempting to ascribe racism to this reluctance. Certainly, it was not irrelevant, but Gutiérrez, as a white Creole, was hardly obnoxious to them on this account. As the case of the dark-skinned Juan Savías showed, the Americans did make exceptions to their prejudice after a native had proven his courage. Cultural differences, Gutiérrez's poor knowledge of English, and his lack of military experience all played a role, but weighing even above these in the Anglo reticence was their simmering furor over the murder of the royalists. Certainly, much of this handwringing was Anglo-American posturing of moral superiority, but the violent act fed into the existing Anglo bias against Spaniards—and of Spanish-Americans—as backward and cruel.

The American embrace of the Mexican revolution was predicated on the belief that the "priest-ridden," barbaric, and cruel Spaniards were oppressing the natives, and that the Mexicans, when freed from this oppression, would be just like the Anglos who liberated them. The more the Republican Army pushed into Texas, the more ambivalent the American volunteers would become about their allies, as they realized that the natives were culturally apart, proud rather than disdainful of their Catholicism, and unlikely to change upon liberation. Although future success would reinspire the Americans in the cause, it would never reconcile them to Gutiérrez. After his proclamation failed to win them over, the Mexican tried addressing them in person, to defend his conduct towards Salcedo and Herrera, "but his voice was drowned out in a storm of hoots and hisses."[39]

The Americans had a number of candidates eager to take the head of the army, but ultimately voted to give command to Capt. Reuben Ross. The thirty-year-old Ross had been a sheriff in Washington County, Virginia. Shaler describes him as a man of means, although other evidence points to his family's finances being rather precarious: the Rosses were, like so many of their class, land rich and cash poor. Ross had displayed dedication to the cause through his purchasing of supplies out of his own pocket and his dogged pursuit of volunteers in America—he may have traveled as far as Tennessee—while the army was in dire straits in La Bahía. Though he only gathered a small force, he still returned to the army and played a conspicuous role in the victory at Rosillo, when with his Coushatta Indians, he had charged the guns and gallantly dueled with Colonel Montero.[40]

Ross was better educated than Samuel Kemper but equally bold. He had stuck to the cause when many others left, but this was not only for military reasons. As the army settled down into life in San Antonio, nightly fandangos were staged, where the young Americans danced with exotic Tejana women. It was likely in one of these social gatherings that Reuben Ross met—and soon fell in love with—a young señorita named Gertrudis Barrera. Reuben and Gertrudis's blossoming romance was certainly not the only one between Americans and the women of Texas, but it would have immense implications.[41]

With Ross in command, the Anglo-American contingent stabilized. It had lost men but was still robust at nearly three hundred soldiers. There would eventually be new recruits too—the allure of further conquests, wealth and land was still powerful, and the Anglo-Americans even made peace with the murder of the royalists. Many in the American contingent still distrusted Gutiérrez, but what was the alternative? They had been promised money, land, and distinction. They would only get it if they stuck with the army.

Shaler's Rubicon

Up to this point, William Shaler had not been involved in organizing, coordinating, or otherwise aiding the expedition. But his hesitancy to play a role had been eroding over the months. He had in the end accepted that the expedition was the best hope to fulfill his instructions, and now that things had come this far, the little rebel army in Texas could not be allowed to fail. That would be calamitous. It would mean the end of republican expansion, refugees streaming into Louisiana, a resurgent Spain marching troops up to the border, and possibly the worst of all outcomes—Spain's ally England entering Texas to open a new front in the War of 1812, targeting New Orleans.

With the murders of the royalists, the temptation to intervene was too much for Shaler. When he had first met Samuel Davenport, the Spanish Indian agent had spied upon him, but now they supported a common cause. Davenport, along with Gutiérrez's former rebel mentor Juan Cortés, had begun "managing the affairs [of the rebellion] as a committee in Natchitoches," and Shaler fell in with them. With the arrival of Toledo and his staff, this committee had the perfect antidote to Gutiérrez. As he spent time with Toledo over the next few weeks, Shaler grew fonder of the Cuban, began to advise and guide him, and developed a personal attachment with Toledo that he had never truly shared with his accidental ward Gutiérrez.[42]

Toledo was more suave, urbane, and sophisticated than the Mexican rebel. Having fought alongside the British and lived for nearly two years in America, he knew some English, while Gutiérrez spoke none. Trusting Toledo, and certain that supporting an *ongoing* revolution rather than starting a new one was consistent with his vague instructions, the American agent took his first steps toward direct involvement. He started by quashing the rumors about the Cuban that had followed him from Natchez.[43]

In late April 1813, Toledo entered Texas, proceeding to Nacogdoches, where he and his little band would set up a temporary headquarters. One of his aids was the printer Aaron Mower, who had brought with him his small press. Bullard described him as "a man of singular versatility of talent, possessing a vast amount of practical knowledge, and at the same time brave, enthusiastic and enterprising." Mower would say of himself that he had "abandoned all of his interests and tranquility which he enjoyed in the bosom of his family in order to come to offer his services to the Mexican patriots." In early May 1813, Mower proceeded to set up the first printing press in the history of Texas. Its goal would be to print pro-republican—but more importantly pro-Toledo—propaganda.[44]

Later that month, William Shaler also entered Mexican territory for the first time. After a year of anxious waiting on the fringes of Texas, he came with high hopes. Perhaps wishing to match Poinsett's reception in Chile, Shaler wanted to look the part of a credentialed agent from the United States. On the 7th, he had written to

Robinson, who was on his way back east, asking his fellow agent to order for him a full-dress uniform for a US Navy captain, with epaulets, a gold eagle for a hat, and buttons for a waistcoat. Knowing this would take some time to arrive, Shaler purchased from Captain Wollstonecraft at Fort Claiborne some gold lace, presumably to add to a coat he already owned, and a cavalry saber. Dressed in this expedient uniform until his proper formal attire could arrive, Shaler rode into Nacogdoches, where Toledo and his retinue were already established.[45]

Shaler now received several letters from Gutiérrez, who stunningly dismissed the murder of the royalists, saying, "They have fallen by the hands of their own subjects." Blithely ignorant of the damage done to his relationship with the American agent, he waxed eloquently in a subsequent letter about revolution and destiny—all the things he and Shaler had discussed a dozen times before. He spoke of his own journey and marveled. "Who could avoid rejoicing to find himself so suddenly transported into his own enslaved country, raising in his land the all-sacred banner of liberty and independence, which his countrymen are now proved to venerate and defend!" His prospects had been gloomy but had turned around completely.[46] "Time and perseverance at length completed my wishes thus far, and my misfortunes have recoiled on my enemies. Aided by your brave countrymen, I have at length succeeded to throw in one promiscuous heap of ruin the work of tyrants, and in its stead, erect a venerable asylum for free men, by whose side our standard is unfurled to the winds of heaven."[47]

Gutiérrez, despite his faults, was nonetheless a first-rate visionary. He saw a future for Mexican Texas that reflected what he had seen in his eye-opening journey through the United States. "Industry and wisdom are now alone requisite to enable us to rank with the North," he wrote. "Our commerce would be extensive by sea and land. The soil and climate is suitable to all growths most common in your country. Yet more, its bosom contains the riches of Potosi in gold and silver . . . here will be the seat of comfort, wealth, union and harmony."[48]

Then he added an open invitation for Americans to come and settle in Texas: "It would please me much to see Americans removing from the Louisiana, Missouri, and other remote parts of your country less improved than this part of New Spain, to settle either on the frontiers or in the interior parts of this province." He asked Shaler to use his influence to make it happen. If ever William Shaler, or Madison, or Monroe had designs on Texas, here again was an opportunity. Gutiérrez had once before offered the whole province to the United States. Now he was offering the right to settle—which they must suspect would ultimately have the same result.[49]

Shaler again refused to take the bait. He was proceeding to San Antonio to establish his mission under a *new* commander of the revolution in Texas. Meanwhile, Toledo was busy organizing his growing band, disciplining them and gathering up supplies for a march to San Antonio to join the revolution—and then coopt it from the presumably unsuspecting Mexican rebel. He had even sent his old revolutionary veteran Picornell ahead to San Antonio to pave the way for his arrival.[50]

There things stood, "when, to the utter amazement of everybody," Bullard recalled, "an express arrived from Don Bernardo, with letters for Toledo, together with a formal and peremptory order to him to quit forthwith the territory of the republic." The stunning rebuke, Toledo's aide recorded, "was an enigma which none could explain at the time." William Shaler had been mystified by the hostility towards Toledo that had spread like wildfire through the West: first Adair and Reuben Kemper had threatened him and then came Gutiérrez's letter. Now, as the agent opened the correspondence that had been forwarded along with Gutiérrez's order, he finally learned the author of these suspicions. It was Toledo's disaffected former subordinate, Nathaniel Cogswell. The Massachusetts lawyer had written his letter to Gutiérrez on December 12th, informing the rebel of his suspicions of Toledo. Gutiérrez replied, forwarding this letter to Shaler. "You can scarcely form an idea how much I feel indebted to you for the detection of Toledo," Gutiérrez had written Cogswell, "whose conduct whilst with you, in every respect goes to show he is inimical to the cause of the patriots. . . . The assertions you have made on the subject of his mission to this country perfectly proves and convinces me, his object is treachery."[51]

Still a stranger in a province controlled by Gutiérrez, Toledo had no choice but to comply with the order and retired across the Sabine. But Gutiérrez's order had made no mention of Toledo's compatriots, so his staff remained in Texas, organized themselves into a company of forty well-armed men in uniform, under the command of Bullard, and took up the march for San Antonio.[52]

19

Royalist Resurgence

WITH THE INITIAL success of the Casas Revolt, the viceroy of New Spain, Félix María Calleja, became alarmed at the possibility of a rebel land route to the United States. In January 1811, he ordered a five hundred–man expedition to Texas to suppress the revolt. The man whom the viceroy chose to take the lead in quelling rebellion in Northern Mexico was Col. José Joaquín de Arredondo, a Spaniard of noble birth whose family business was military command.

His father, Nicolás Arredondo, made his name fighting rebels in the Río de la Plata region of South America, where he was cruel and uncompromising. Joaquín entered the service in 1787 as a twelve-year-old cadet and, upon completion of his training, joined the Royal Guard, where service included a requirement of officers to have *limpieza de sangre*—purity of blood. With Celtic ancestry that gave him light skin and fair hair, young Joaquín fit the racial bill. To those in Mexico where he would ultimately serve, he would be the most gachupín of gachupines.[1]

He served in the War of the Pyrenees against France in 1793 and participated in an invasion of Portugal in 1801. Arriving in New Spain the next year, Arredondo was assigned to Veracruz, where he was placed in command of a vital weapons depot. In 1810, he was promoted to colonel and took the leadership of one of the most important commands in New Spain, the Veracruz infantry regiment. When he was ordered to Texas in 1811, he sailed with only two hundred men and four officers; among the latter was a young cadet, a Creole named Antonio Lopez de Santa Anna, who would serve under him throughout the campaign and into Texas.[2]

That province by then had reverted to royalist control, but Arredondo found plenty of work fighting rebels in Nuevo Santander, where he was clever and aggressive, traits often lacking in his class. Learning that insurgents were seeking to lure him into an ambush in the town of Aguayo, he set a trap of his own. Knowing of spies in his midst, he informed his men that he would take a day to rest before proceeding to the town. Then, to their surprise, he ordered a snap night march on

April 11, 1811, and seized the town without a shot. He showed that he had brutality to match that of his father: He tortured and hanged the rebel leaders and publicly whipped deserters. Then he shrewdly pardoned them on the condition that they fight to regain their honor. For his success, Arredondo was promoted to the governorship of Nuevo Santander.[3]

These excesses did not occur in isolation, and cruelty was practiced on both sides. The revolution in Mexico was stark and brutal, and Joaquín de Arredondo was of the perfect temperament to fight it. He also learned from close cooperation with his superior and mentor, Calleja, who frequently burned villages and executed prisoners en masse. Alongside these tactics, Arredondo would add his own innovation: psychological warfare. His soldiers once imprisoned locals on false charges, torturing them for several days before Arredondo arrived, freed the prisoners, and told them it was merely a practical joke.[4]

Some of the general's worst abuses were against women, who were frequently compelled into service cooking for his troops and beaten for the slightest infractions, or for merely not producing food to his soldiers' liking. He tolerated wholesale rape by his troops, and even neighboring royalist commanders allowed their soldiers to leave to protect their wives from the depravity. Brutality, in this case, worked. The revolution in Nuevo Santander was effectively crushed in 1811–12, never resurfacing again under Arredondo's watch. The lessons of his father had been validated, and Joaquín would never depart from them.[5]

By the time Arredondo learned about Gutiérrez and Magee's expedition, the contending armies in Texas were into their third month of the siege of La Bahía. Salcedo, pressed as he was, had sent messages to Coahuila for help, but not to Arredondo, who was at that time campaigning in the southern part of Nuevo Santander. The governor of Texas had thought a relief from such a distance was not feasible, and unlikely to be approved by higher authorities.[6]

And perhaps it would have been so for an ordinary Spanish commander. But Arredondo was not ordinary. Though he was in the middle of a bitter fight against rebels in his province, he at once turned his eyes northward. Arredondo had likely mulled over the strategic situation of Texas long and hard when he had first been tasked to go there, and evidently convinced himself that the distant, unpopulated frontier province was the linchpin for all New Spain. Assertive to the point of insubordination, he wrote his superior, the viceroy, that he was disobeying his orders, turning away from the rebels at his front, and marching on Texas. For a Spanish commander to take this step was unheard of. The viceroy, as *vice king*, was the ultimate authority in New Spain, subservient to the sovereign alone. It was a bold move, but it paid off. Viceroy Francisco Vanegas was indeed angered but was soon to be replaced by Arredondo's friend and mentor, Calleja. The latter retroactively approved the move and unleashed his aggressive commander.[7]

Propaganda and Purgatory

Arredondo was supremely practical and knew that marching to Texas required extensive planning, building up of his forces and supplies, to which he turned his attention in spring 1813. He also knew the importance of propaganda, had seen it firsthand in the war with France, and now turned to it with alacrity. Gutiérrez, he announced in flyers spread throughout the province where he was recruiting, was a Napoleonic stooge whose intention was to turn Texas over to the United States. The Americans in turn would turn the Spaniards into slaves and destroy the Catholic faith. To this he added a stark warning: Any town embracing the rebellion would "be put to fire and sword and nothing will remain of it but ruins to serve as a lesson for the future." Arredondo was bringing a holocaust to Texas, but no one could say that he had not warned them.[8]

The Spanish commander found a powerful ally in the Bishop of Monterrey, who besides his belief in the Spanish monarchy, also had a grievance against the rebellion. The silver that the envoys Aldama and Salazar had delivered to Casas to purchase arms in the United States had been expropriated from his own cathedral. Calling upon the divine mysteries of Catholicism—and the credulity of his flock—to rally men to the army, the prelate offered indulgences to those who would fight for Arredondo. For those who did not, he decreed punishment in the afterlife: for every month of the campaign in which any man refused to fight, he would suffer one thousand years in purgatory.[9]

With the afterlife covered, Arredondo focused on the practical: money, arms, and artillery. Though many local authorities balked at his demands, news of the fall of San Antonio and the murders of Salcedo, Herrera, and their officers finally convinced them to support the assertive general, who seemed to be the only royalist official in Northern Mexico who appreciated the full danger threatened by the loss of Texas.[10]

Arredondo put the rebels on notice. He sent out a force of sixty men to Revilla, ostensibly to intimidate restless Indians there, but also to capture Gutiérrez's wife and children. The officer in charge reported the narrow escape of "the evil woman and family on foot," who successfully made their way to San Antonio to join the rebel leader. On April 6, 1813, Arredondo, not waiting for reinforcements or supplies, marched to an advanced post at Laredo on the Rio Grande, armed with a new decree from the viceroy, which declared that the people of the territories in rebellion were not to be treated as Spaniards and subjects of the king. Arredondo was authorized to impose laws as if he were a conqueror of foreigners.[11]

Since the capture of San Antonio, Gutiérrez had focused on rebuilding government and policing the city and neighboring areas. Even as some Lipan Apaches were allied to the republican cause, another group of the same tribe raided the ranches outside of San Antonio and were driven off "with some loss." Republican commander Reuben Ross commissioned a force to guard against this new threat, choosing

Carlos Beltrán, the Hispanicized American, who had served in a similar role under the Spanish, to lead it.[12]

Gutiérrez, with so many problems, could not move his army beyond Texas, at least not without the Anglo-Americans, and they would not move without reinforcements. Nor were they so inclined to resume their march. After months of living in the mud of La Bahía, teeming as it was with lice, they were in a city, with real houses, beds, food, drink, and for some, señoritas. "The American troops gave themselves up largely to every form of dissipation—cards, horses, wine and women," wrote Beltrán. Having lived for so long among the Spaniards, Beltrán became reacquainted with his own countrymen—and not always pleasantly. "I must say that probably no other like body of adventurers was ever assembled in the broad domains of America," he said of the volunteers. "There were apostate preachers, and I believe I might be justified in stating that three-fourths of the privates and many of the officers in the army never cared to discuss their antecedents in the presence of honest, respectable company." They were from a broad swath of America, representing almost all states, as well as Englishmen, Irishmen, Scots, Frenchmen, and Louisiana Creoles. He continued:[13]

> They were brave, hardy determined men, they had been trained to use the rifle from childhood; those from Tennessee, Kentucky and other sections of the Mississippi Valley had been raised on the border and were schooled in all the arts of Indian warfare. Discipline they regarded as being [necessary] only for their own safety and final success, and this sentiment was all that held the army together. There were exceptions, especially among the officers, most of whom were impelled by lofty motives. They foresaw the wane and decadence of the Spanish power in America. They were disciples of Aaron Burr, whom they regarded as a political prophet.[14]

Indeed, in the presence of officers, Beltrán claimed he heard many of these "lofty" discussions firsthand. Though Gen. James Wilkinson had inspired a generation of Westerners to adventures beyond their borders, the general was frequently a source of scorn in their company, as "the lure of Spanish Gold" had caused him to betray their idol, Burr. These discussions were conducted openly, even though one of their numbers would ultimately include at least one of the general's own sons, who himself was "most vehement in the denunciation of Burr's treatment."[15]

Though "lofty motives" seemed to have inspired some, many of these abandoned the enterprise after the massacre of the Spaniards. Claiborne's proclamation had been the first filter, and the atrocity was the second, a sieve through which men of principle were strained off, and those who remained were more often like Gaines, who could reconcile themselves with the crime. These, Beltrán wrote, were Burrites through and through, seeking to establish a new republic, independent of Mexico *and* the United States. In their view, "Gutiérrez and his Mexican compatriots were convenient tools." Marching on Monclova or other points to the south was for the

Burrites a necessity to secure both booty and security. "An invasion in that direction would further weaken the Spanish power and establish on a firmer basis the western borders of the new republic," Beltrán wrote. Now these Burrites sought to increase their numbers. They sent men to Natchitoches and beyond, hoping to counteract any negative reports that had spread about the army and raise new recruits. Such new men, replacing those who had quit, "arrived in small squads almost weekly during the month of May and these brought reports of other and larger bodies that would arrive in June."[16]

The Mexican contingent may have been growing weary of their shotgun wedding with the Anglo-Americans, and these newer arrivals probably did not help. Beltrán reported that Gutiérrez, while still proclaiming gratitude to the Yankee volunteers, spread hostility to them among the Mexican contingent. He had likely heard of the Burrite talk—and possibly some of Arredondo's propaganda along those lines—and used it to stoke resentment. These foreigners seemed to do little more than drink, play cards, and dance with *Mexican* women. Beltrán, bilingual and intimately connected within the local population, reported that Gutiérrez and Delgado asserted among their allies, "If they succeed in this, the Mexicans will be reduced to slavery, and you will see your children auctioned off on the block, as they sell negro slaves in Virginia,"[17] argued Delgado. "Witness the supreme contempt these adventurers entertain for our people, argued Delgado, and the oppression and ill-treatment they mete out to the citizens of Béxar. They seize our property, they invade our homes, debauch our women, they take whatever suits their lecherous and depraved fancy, and give nothing in return."[18]

Beltrán claims Delgado went even further, proposing that the Mexicans turn on the Anglos. "Destroy these adventurers first, then as a united people, we will turn our arms against the Spaniard and drive him into the ocean." In this account, Delgado supposedly—one must recall Beltrán's hostility to him for context—found adherents and began to organize a conspiracy to destroy all of the Anglos in San Antonio. But there were other Mexicans who fought against such division. Principal among these was Capt. Miguel Menchaca, who had fought bravely alongside the Americans from the start, was trusted by them, and felt no conflict between his loyalty to Mexican Texas and the Republican Army of the North. It was likely he who first tipped off the Americans to the threat, and he urged Colonel Ross to take strong actions, even to go so far as arrest Gutiérrez and Delgado and "send them in irons to Nacogdoches." Ross, however, demurred. Delgado could talk, but the Americans were still the more powerful force and could defend themselves. More Mexicans were likely with them than against them, and to arrest the conspirators would needlessly create the very conflict, if not outright war between the two camps.[19]

While the republican contingents passed their days in an internal cold war, events were moving forward on the fringes of Texas. "They had frequent intelligence that there were great exertions made in the interior to organize an army to invade their repose," McLane recalled. "But the Mexican scouts came in frequently and reported everything quiet and solitary between San Antonio and the Rio Grande." The Spanish, however, were not as distant as the republicans believed. The normally reliable Irishman McFarlan and his team of scouts rode out to patrol the Laredo road, but after a long and fruitless search, he found nothing. McFarlan then steered the patrol along the Nueces River instead. In doing so, the scout had narrowly missed a discovery of momentous importance: the arrival of a new Spanish army in Texas.[20]

Elizondo Steals a March on Béxar

Lt. Col. Ignacio Elizondo had been one of the earliest converts to the republican cause in 1810, but had switched to the royalist side and had captured Hidalgo. When Gutiérrez and Magee had invaded Texas, he possibly even considered changing his allegiance again. When John Robinson had passed through Coahuila on his return to the United States, he had diverted to visit Elizondo on his ranch, where the Spaniard was deathly ill. The American agent, also a doctor, had attended Elizondo and probably saved his life. "I have always been known to be friendly to the revolution," Elizondo had told the American, saying he had taken the side of Spain, but added, "If the President of your Government will extend to us his hand, even his countenance, we shall be free."[21]

But by healing Elizondo, Robinson had not saved a friend of the revolution. The opportunist had at last chosen a side, and that side was the king. When Gutiérrez had reached out to him to join the rebels, Elizondo responded with venom. "Were you to hide in hell itself as the last refuge, from there I will drag you by the hair, cast you into the flames, and when you are burnt to ashes, scatter your remains to the four winds." It was passion such as this that had won over Arredondo, who now made Elizondo his second-in-command for the reconquest of Texas.[22]

When Arredondo first reached the Rio Grande at Laredo, he arrived with only a small, advanced force consisting of a portion of his Veracruz Regiment. He was met there by the Spanish survivors of the Battle of Rosillo, including Juan Zambrano. Elizondo soon arrived at Laredo with a credible force of seven hundred men. Arredondo, in mid-June, ordered his new deputy to enter Texas in a reconnaissance in force, which he did, gathering an additional 300 militia, plus assorted regulars to form a total force of 1,100. Alongside this considerable force, as was always the case during that time, there marched as many as five hundred camp followers: teamsters attending the pack animals and women. The latter were wives and girlfriends of the soldiers, who in some cases even brought along their children. Spanish generals tolerated the women's presence because they could cook for the army, and it made recruiting their husbands easier.[23]

Arredondo sent Elizondo north because he had expected the Republican Army was on its way to him. He was to advance to the Frio River, a clear, aqua-blue stream that cuts in a wide arc at a nearly consistent sixty miles from west to southeast of

San Antonio. From this point of good water and safety, Elizondo was instructed to obtain intelligence, disrupt enemy spies, and most importantly *keep his army intact.* He was not to engage the enemy and not enter the capital, or even come near it. Arredondo wanted to await further reinforcements from the viceroy before taking on the still-undefeated rebels. He made this point clear in a letter to Elizondo, and at several meetings at his house in Laredo with his staff. But the general had inserted one caveat in his orders: If the Republican Army, on the march, attempted to flee back to the capital with their artillery, they should be "pursued and annihilated" before they could return to San Antonio. At the Frio, probably near modern Dilley, Texas, Elizondo learned the Republican Army was still in the capital. From reports of spies, he learned about the dissension in the rebel ranks, saw an opportunity, and violated his orders. He sent word to Arredondo that he was crossing the river and, not awaiting approval, pushed forward in a rapid advance.[24]

The republicans sent their livestock out to pasture each day, and since lands west of town were at threat from Indians, the horses were instead taken to graze south of the city. There, on June 11th, Elizondo's cavalry caught a rebel outpost by surprise, capturing nine men and forty horses. The same day, at a place called Puerto del Salado, he surprised another group of seventeen Mexican rebels and six Americans. The Mexicans immediately surrendered while the Americans fired back, "but they were immediately raised up on [Spanish] lances," as Elizondo put it. Three of the Americans were killed, and the rest taken into custody along with the Mexican rebels, with another three hundrded more horses captured.[25]

Beltrán, in command of Tejano scouts, claimed it was his men who first discovered Elizondo's presence, after a tip from a group of Indians known to his lieutenant. The rebel scouts crawled across the chaparral alongside the friendly Indians. "I had a fairly good view of the Spanish army as it yet lay in camp. With all speed, we hastened to San Antonio and reported our observations." The next day, Elizondo arrived near the Alazán Creek to the west of San Antonio and boldly took up a position in sight of the town. McLane claims the republicans were entirely surprised. "The first intelligence of the approach of an enemy was communicated by three of [the republicans'] own men, who had been captured on the 7th of June, and were sent in with a very lengthy communication from Elisondo."[26]

The royalist officer had no intention of merely serving as a scouting force for Arredondo; he wanted to take the town on his own. With arrogance and bombast, he turned to fear to get San Antonio to submit. Announcing himself as "the conqueror of the Province of Coahuila," he said he was authorized to re-conquer Texas "from the treason of its inhabitants" and "the English [sic] heretics." There would be punishment for those who had connived in "the beheading of the governors" and the "profanation of its temples." Unless the rebels submitted entirely, Elizondo made it clear that this was to be a war of annihilation:[27] "[These] have appeared to me sufficient causes for not leaving in that Province stone upon stone, beheading even the same priests that have consented to the adoration of the Idol of Baal . . . but before proceeding with this punishment, I am obliged to advise them, that if they do not separate themselves from among the heretics at this time . . . [they] will be victims of my fury without sparing life, neither to the ignorant, because . . . a rebellious town deserves it."[28]

This was his only warning, he declared, and heretics would be burned. He offered a reward for the leaders of the rebellion, "Gutiérrez, Camper [sic], Menchaca and Delgado, for whose heads I pay $1,000.00 for each one." Elizondo claimed to Arredondo that these threats had gained him as many as three hundred deserters from the city. Among these was an anonymous loyalist, who used the chaos of the moment to slip out of a cell where he was held by insurgents, condemned, he would later say, to death. "San Antonio is plunged in general distress, famine, and misery; there is nothing but desolation," he reported. "Neither flour, nor any other food is to be found there . . . you would look in vain even for a grain of salt or an article of clothing in that mournful country." The Tejano troops, he said, "are brought to despair, and the foreign adventurers who have been so blind to follow them, begin to disband."[29]

The American Samson and His Mexican Delilah

This account is colored by its author's own views; in truth, the panic was not so severe, nor the morale so low. Even though they were short about seventy Americans and a large party of Mexicans who were on a reconnaissance, the army's morale was strong. The republicans had beaten the Spanish time and time again, and many of the Anglo-Americans were contemptuous. "We had whipped them at La Bahía . . . and at Rosalis [sic]," as Beltrán reported the sentiment, "and wherever they dared come out in the open, regardless of numbers, we had sent them flying helter-skelter for their lives, and we could whip them again." Some rebels welcomed the enemy by taking an ancient Spanish twelve-pounder cannon and placing it atop the old powder house, located on the west side of San Pedro Creek, and "saluted the royalists with five shots from the gun."[30]

In fact, the Anglos had a practical reason for welcoming battle: Spanish armies marched well-stocked with supplies and potential booty. Back in the United States, their own backers had deserted or at least failed them since the executions, and the Republican Army had received no major delivery of supplies since capturing San Antonio. This, then, was a chance to replenish their stocks. "In view of former victories over the gachupines and their inclination to run away when the American rifles began to blaze, all we would have to do would be to march out, fire a few rounds, set our Indian allies after the flying wretches and gain and take possession of the spoils," Beltran wrote. "Thus reasoned the average American soldier."[31]

Ross ordered his drummers to beat the recall, and the eager Anglo-American contingent lined up in their ranks, but none of their Mexican counterparts appeared in the plaza. Ross was stunned, but soon his Mexican girlfriend, Señorita Barrera, came to him and according to Captain Gaines informed him that "the Mexicans had all determined to join the enemy and make a massacre of all the Americans." Beltrán adds more detail:[32] "The plan, as revealed by her, was this: Knowing that Elisondo's coming was to avenge the death of Herrera and his staff, it was agreed by the conspirators that they would open negotiations with the Spanish commander, put all the blame for the murder of the Spanish officers off on the Americans and that on condition that they, the conspirators, were promised immunity from further prosecution for the alleged offense, they would lead the American army into any trap the Spanish commander might propose."[33]

When the battle opened, Barrera said, the conspirators would "fall upon the American rear and not leave a man to tell the tale." There were, she added, one thousand Mexicans in San Antonio ready to take up arms. They only needed a signal from Gutiérrez. It was the same conspiracy that Ross had dismissed weeks before, but that was before the Spanish arrival changed his calculus, and having seen how fickle allegiance could be in this civil war, Ross was unsettled. The pleading of Señorita Barrera added to his worries. "She loved Ross and implored him to retreat."[34]

Her motives in doing so may have been love but possibly something else: Some sources say that she was the daughter of a Spanish officer in Elizondo's army. The Spanish officer knew of the divisions within San Antonio and may have been behind the warning. Beltrán alternatively claimed her father was a close friend of Gutiérrez. Either way, Señorita Barrera may have been the willing *or unwilling* bearer of someone else's message.[35]

Ross called his officers to a war council and told them of the plot, which he was now convinced was real, and announced that he was for abandoning the city and retreating. This they flatly and unanimously rejected. His second-in-command, Henry Perry derisively asked, "Has a Mexican Delilah shorn our American Sampson?" "They resolved they would not fly but remain & abide their fate," Captain Gaines recorded. Ross then proposed to occupy the Alamo. This too was rejected. It meant abandoning the town, and having survived a three-month siege, the Americans were no doubt loath to return to one.[36]

In this moment, Ross had become for his troops a sad mirror of Magee—the one struck down by disease, the other by love. This was not an army that could be commanded but by consent, and with their refusal to agree to his terms, Reuben Ross had lost the right to lead. Still believing he had enemies plotting to kill him, and no longer able to rely on his Anglo-Americans, Ross and one friend, John Ash, slipped out of San Antonio that night, fleeing to Natchitoches and leaving behind Señorita Barrera forever.[37]

"When his flight was made known to the men," recalled McLane, "they expressed great indignation at so pusillanimous an act by a man in whose courage they had unlimited confidence." The Republican Army of the North had lost its third commander, and the army elected a new one to replace him: Col. Henry Perry. Born in 1785 in Newtown, Connecticut, and raised in nearby Woodbury, Perry was described as "one of those heroic and chivalrous youth, whose courage springs from the noblest impulse of nature, an enthusiastic love of liberty, and a generous sympathy for all who are unfortunate subjects of despotic power."[38]

He was, in all events, one of the bravest, most respected men in the army—more tactically adept and probably better educated then Kemper, and certainly more resolute than Magee or Ross. Courageous and uncompromising to a fault, he was absolutely committed to the cause, whether it was Mexican Independence or a Burrite republic. Either way, in Perry it manifested in an extreme hostility to the gachupines. Crucially, while Ross and Magee had been quick to credit treachery from their Mexican allies, Perry, like Kemper, was inclined to trust them. But that trust had been shaken once again. The two ethnicities had vacillated between comradeship and suspicion—the former in the glow of the battlefield and the latter in periods of inactivity. The Americans were now ready to fight, but the Mexicans needed motivation. Separately, the two parties were at Elizondo's mercy, but they could match him if they could be unified. Fortunately for Perry, he had the perfect tool in his hands to do it.[39]

Elizondo had dispatched a messenger who was met outside the city by Captain Wilkinson, who conducted him into Perry's presence. The terms demanded were the immediate surrender of the city, the evacuation of all foreigners, and the immediate surrender of seventeen Mexicans, including Gutiérrez, Delgado, and Menchaca. Elizondo was trying to widen the divide between the two camps in San Antonio. His letter was addressed to the Anglo-Americans only, and in it he disparaged his own Mexican countrymen, warning that the Americans could trust them "neither for truth or courage." Elizondo cited as evidence his own experience, claiming he had returned to royalism after being betrayed by rebels in Mexico. He called on the Americans to abandon their allies and return to their country. If the Anglo-Americans complied with these orders (essentially the same terms offered by Salcedo to Magee), they could return home safely. Elizondo even offered to give them their back pay as promised by Gutiérrez.[40]

Perry now possessed direct proof that Elizondo would clearly not give the pardons he had separately promised the Mexicans. He called on his drummers to once again beat quarters, and this time, Gutiérrez and Delgado came with many of their Mexican contingent. When they arrived, Perry read Elizondo's terms to the entire army, exposing the royalist commander's deceit. Then he turned to Gutiérrez, standing among a large group of the Mexicans, and said, "What says el Señor Gutiérrez de Lara? Has he any suggestions to offer?"[41]

The Mexican was struck by the terms and was strongly emotional. "He replied," Beltrán wrote, "by reminding Colonel Perry how he and his Mexicans had fought side by side with their American comrades at La Bahía, and at Rosalis [sic], and how in every action the Mexican soldiers had proven their valor and loyalty." Gutiérrez said he could not believe Perry would betray them now into "the hands of a tyrant who would at once consign them to an ignoble death." But Perry had expected this response, and Gutiérrez's fear played into his hands. In fact, Perry had *already* sent an emissary to Elizondo with his answer: He would not accept the terms, nor would he betray Gutiérrez and his allies. "When Gutiérrez had finished speaking, Perry read aloud the reply he had sent Elisondo, and for a moment there was deep silence, the men stood in line as if transfixed, then, fully realizing the import of their grave commander's course, a cheer burst forth such as had perhaps never been heard in the old town of Béxar."[42]

Gutiérrez shook the American officer's hand. "We are more than ever convinced of the magnanimity and bravery of the American soldier," he said, then asked to lead the attack as proof of loyalty. Perry's stage management of the crisis had brilliantly reconciled the two contingents, and though he ultimately did not accept Gutiérrez's offer, he nonetheless gave the Mexicans important assignments on the army's flanks. Gaines records that both contingents marshalled on the plaza. "All were for battle ... preparations were that night made for a general assault."[43]

The first thing Perry did was increase the number of pickets outside the town, which Ross had established to cut off all communication between the Spanish and their spies. Elizondo, without this crucial input, possibly believed his effort to divide the army had been successful. But the royalists were unaware that a new commander had against all odds reunited and reinspired the Republican Army of the North. Perry had the advantage and would waste no time for spies to warn the enemy. He ordered his army to take up the march that night.[44]

The Battle of Alazán

At midnight on Sunday, June 20th, Perry roused the Republican Army and formed them up in a column of march. They made their way along the Calle Real, passing San Pedro Creek and the city cemetery (today's Milam Park) by the light of a waning moon. They carried only arms and ammunition and were ordered to maintain strict silence. "Not a whisper or tap of the drum was heard to cheer them in their solitary march," Gaines recalled. Beltrán thought that the army passing in the stillness of the summer night "had more the appearance of a host of specters than that of an army of living, determined men." The force numbered about 900, consisting of 250 Anglo-Americans (all on foot) and 500 Mexicans (200 on foot and 300 mounted). There were also about 150 Indians—Tonkawas, Towakanas, and Lipan Apaches—also mounted.[45]

The army was organized into eight companies of infantry with eight batteries of artillery interspersed. On approaching the enemy, this column—still undetected—was efficiently converted into a line, with the even companies moving out to the army's left and the odd companies moving to the right, the Mexican infantry splitting between the two wings. Perry commanded the right wing and Capt. Josiah Taylor commanded the left. The artillery, pushed forward on wheels muffled with rags, remained interspersed with the infantry. The cavalry was split on the flanks, the left being Mexicans only and the right a mixture of Mexicans and Indians, as they had been at Rosillo. Gutiérrez remained in the rear with a sizeable bodyguard. The republicans lay in the brush and waited for the dawn. Beltrán recalled:[46]

> Still preserving the utmost silence, each division took its allotted position, with orders to lie flat on the ground until the order to advance was passed down the lines. The minutes seemed like hours to us, owing, I suppose, to the intense excitement which always thrills the soldier on the eve of battle; but, in truth, we had been but a very short time in position when the first rays began to light up the eastern horizon, and a moment later we could hear the hum of voices in the Spanish camp, which gave token that the enemy was astir.[47]

The Spanish were encamped on a hill on the west side of the Alazán Creek, about a mile from the town, with a deep ravine at their front and a bastion of artillery on either side of the camp. The position on their left protected the head of the ravine, through which any attack would likely come; all of the cannon faced Béxar. Despite these well-planned dispositions, the army was relaxed. No scouts were sent out; only a narrow picket was set to their front. Elizondo was confident and indeed told his men to go to bed early that night to prepare to march to San Antonio, for he planned to meet the enemy in the morning. But the enemy was already upon him.[48]

Some of the Spanish were just stirring amid their tents, arrayed in a square on the hill, while others cooked breakfast or prepared for mass, since it was Sunday morning. The republicans, Beltrán asserts, watched as most of the Spanish army gathered around their commander's flag for the service. Although he did not see it himself, he was later told that "seemingly, every female camp follower had hastened to be among the first to be found kneeling before the altar." The republican artillerists trained their eight cannons at the best targets and waited for the order. One of these big guns, commanded by the former Neutral Ground bandit James McKimm, was trained on Elizondo's flag. The others, loaded with cannister and scrap iron, targeted additional assembled Spaniards. None of the republicans apparently ever questioned the morality of what followed next, which Beltrán relates:[49]

> While this vast host was yet kneeling, occupying a large area almost directly in front of Gutiérrez's Mexican division, and while the padre, arrayed in the habilaments of his holy office was making intercession for his people, the order "fire" rang out like the notes of a clarion and, with a detonation that

seamed to shake the very foundations of the earth, our . . . guns belched forth, sending their hurtling missiles of death crashing through the concourse of kneeling worshipers, each iron messenger leaving a swathe of blood and writhing, mangled humanity.[50]

The belching of the guns was the signal for the charge and with "loud exultant shouts and yells, every man sprang forward to the assault." The republican troops still had to cross the creek to attack the royalists. Elizondo formed up his men in a line, taking shelter in ditches to oppose the oncoming enemy. Accurate fire from republican artillery, under Dr. Samuel D. Forsyth and Capt. Walter Young, shifted to Elizondo's guns after the initial volley and dismounted one of the Spanish cannons. Indeed, despite their likely superiority in guns—twelve to the republicans' eight—there are no accounts of Spanish artillery even firing. At Rosillo, the republicans had very effectively conducted sniping of cannon crews and likely used the same tactic again, taking away a key Spanish advantage from the very outset of the battle.[51]

Elizondo attempted to flank the republican left, attacking the Mexican infantry there. Perry ordered Capt. James Kenneday to take a company from the center to reinforce Captain Taylor and stop the onrushing royalists. McLane, who was in Kenneday's company, records the moment, which for him was the most memorable of the war:[52] "In . . . the act of wheeling to the rear, your humble servant was shot in the back, the ball breaking a rib loose from the backbone, checking the force of the ball and turning it out through the side, which saved his bacon. If the ball had missed the rib the world might have been deprived of this truthful chapter of history, of a patriotic, but much slandered expedition."[53]

Less than two miles away, the people of San Antonio anxiously awaited the result of the battle. Since many townspeople had fled to join the royalists, those who remained would assuredly be treated as rebels, with little mercy to be expected. Eighteen-year-old José Antonio Navarro, who had watched Delgado return from the execution of the royalists, now climbed to the tower of the San Fernando church. "We watched the clash of flashing weapons through our field glasses and listened to the horrifying thunder of the cannons," Navarro would later recall. The young man and the other townspeople who had climbed up with him kept the vigil for four hours.[54]

Perry conferred with Menchaca, trying to determine the weakest point in the Spanish line, when an artilleryman, George Westfield from Kentucky, came up. "The bastion on our right is the weakest; before being driven out I spiked their best gun." While Taylor was fighting off the Spanish thrust on their left, Perry threw the bulk of his forces into his right wing. The bastion was taken after fierce resistance. In all of this action, Perry would later say of the Mexican troops, "The Spaniards (Patriots) were mixed in with the American companies and fought nobly."[55]

The royalists tried to rally at the other bastion, where Elizondo was pressing Taylor, but Kenneday's company was now in place to reinforce him. These, alongside the Mexicans, beat back the Spanish, and seeing this, the entire republican line now surged forward beyond their own cannon, charging across the ravine and smashing into the royalists in the ditches. A group of Spanish teamsters and other personnel "being without arms except small swords" had taken refuge there among the troops, pelting the oncoming republicans with stones that they had piled on the bank of the creek. They and the Spanish soldiers "defended with great skill and courage" before the republican forces finally drove them out. McLane claimed Gutiérrez remained in the rear, but Beltrán averred that Gutiérrez and Delgado and their Mexican troops "fought with the courage of veterans and the ferocity of demons." The Mexican rebels surged as far as Elizondo's banner but were pushed back when Captain Arreola of the Spanish staff rallied some troops.[56]

The battle surged back and forth, sometimes devolving into hand-to-hand combat. "Finally, the Spaniards gave way," Beltrán recalled, "and then began rout and slaughter such as had never been witnessed on Texas soil." The Spanish retreated pell-mell, with one large group passing through the camp to some log pens they had built for their livestock, well behind the camp. Here they tried to mount a defense.[57]

The Indian scouts who had initially discovered Elizondo's camp had identified these pens, and Perry cleverly exploited them in his strategy. He held his Indians back behind his lines for his initial attack, but once the battle opened, he ordered them to swing around his left flank, raising their terrifying war cries as they went, to drive away the mules upon which Elizondo depended. Even if the republicans failed in their attack, this would cripple his army. The Indians, led by the Apache Chief Prieto, did so. The warriors struck the corrals just as the Spanish retreated to them. The Anglo-Americans pressed the Spaniards from the center of the line as the Indians rode among the livestock. The royalists who had fled to the corrals were shot down among the pens, some while begging for quarter.[58]

As would happen at San Jacinto two decades later, the army, its blood up, pursued and hunted down the enemy relentlessly. Everyone seems to have taken part. McLane credits much slaughter to the Anglo-Americans. Beltrán claims it was mostly the Indians and the "bloodthirsty, revengeful" Mexican contingent, who "like ravenous wolves, hungry for blood, fell upon the flying Spaniards, dealing out death and destruction not sparing age, sex or even the wounded." Some of this carnage may be attributable to an order of Perry's before the battle that the Indians would be rewarded for their service based on the number of scalps they produced. Beltrán, though a friend of Chief Prieto, was horrified when this chief's men produced a copious amount of the grizzly trophies, many of which he suspected were from Spanish women.[59]

The Battle of Alazán was over in an hour or two. The brutality of the fight is evident in the casualty figures. Elizondo fled the field, leaving 350 dead, but also 82 wounded and 50 captured. The republicans lost only 29 killed and 17 wounded out of a force of 900, according to a report forwarded to Shaler. The numbers were double these in Beltrán's accounts, but he also reported the Spanish losses at over 1,000. Either way, the dead in the battle, as they had been at Rosillo, were heavily lopsided in favor of the republicans.⁶⁰

Among the rebels who perished was one of Gutiérrez's most loyal assistants—his secretary of state, Louis Massicott. José Antonio Navarro described him as "a young Frenchman, who for accomplishments, valor and personal beauty, could worthily be ranked among the noblest of Napoleon's Marshalls." The secretary, who served as Colonel Perry's aide-de-camp during the battle, fell when he was struck by a rifle ball and died on the field. "Yes, the ornament of our young republic, the young father of Spanish liberty . . . he fell covered with glory in the field of battle," Gutiérrez reported ruefully. "Texas mourns; her Massicote [sic] is no more. Enough is said, he shared the fate of war; he lived and died a good and virtuous man."⁶¹

The rebels' hopes for booty were amply fulfilled. They recovered hundreds of stands of arms with plentiful powder, which were very much needed, since large numbers of the Mexican population of San Antonio otherwise available to fight were unarmed. In addition, all of the enemy's cannon were taken. Also captured were between 1,200 and 1,500 horses and mules, wagons, carts, and much-needed clothing. There was food, too, in short supply in San Antonio: 40 mule loads of flour and 4,000 pounds of biscuits. Miscellaneous goods included saddles, liquor, coffee, cigars, and more—up to $28,000 worth. The whole bounty took two or three days to haul back to San Antonio. As some of the men were occupied in this happy task, others had the grim work of burying the bodies, friend and foe alike, in a common grave. The horses were divided among the Americans and Mexicans—nearly one for each man in the army—and the mules were given to the Indians. These latter, according to Beltrán, hated the pack animals and traded as many as ten of them for each horse awarded to the white men.⁶²

20

The Fate of Texas

"THIS EVER-MEMORABLE DAY will to the end of time continue to be dear and sacred to the memory of Spanish Patriots," Bernardo Gutiérrez crowed about the victory at Alazán. The rebel used the term "Spanish," but the real meaning was Mexican, since the revolution was now irrevocably changing the identity of the people of Texas as sure as it was for its sister provinces to the south. The war in Texas was still mostly in isolation. It was, to be sure, a part of the greater Mexican struggle, and Gutiérrez and even his Anglo allies dreamed of one day pushing south to link up with the forces of Rayón, but this was becoming more and more unlikely, and the Mexican Texans were starting to take a greater stake in their own little war. "In this victory much may be said in favor of the natives," Gutiérrez wrote, "they followed the bright example of those brave Americans who have suffered everything to relieve them from their bondage and disgrace."[1]

Indeed, the Mexican/Tejano rebels—who for the first time outnumbered the Anglo-Americans in the army—had acquitted themselves well, but Gutiérrez had not. The Americans accused him of hiding in the back of the army while Menchaca, Delgado, and other Mexicans did some of the toughest fighting. The battle had not solved Texas' political crisis. To the American volunteers, the president protector was still a murderer, not a particularly valuable soldier, and they longed for an alternative. Now they had learned from Natchitoches that there *was* just such a leader waiting in the wings: Toledo. A few crowded days in late June would determine the leadership of the Republican Army of the North and the fate of its revolution against the Spanish Empire in Texas.

Gutiérrez, his suspicions aroused by Cogswell's letter writing campaign, continued to block Toledo's advance into Texas throughout the summer. The Cuban rebel, however, had won over the American special agent, William Shaler. The New Yorker was clearly meddling now and supported Toledo in solving the impasse through propaganda. The printer Aaron Mower, aided by his apprentice Godwin Brown Cotten, had brought his small Portuguese press into Texas, and on May 13, 1813, had even set his type for the first edition of his newspaper, the *Gaceta de Texas*, before the pair were forced to actually print it in Natchitoches after the retrograde. The paper was printed bilingually under the masthead: "La Salud del Pueblo es la Suprema Ley"—*The welfare of the people is the supreme law.* As it proudly proclaimed,[2] "This is undoubtedly a glorious day in which for the first time the Press sheds its light in the State of Texas! Not only is it the first time that Texas prints in its territory, but it is also the first time in which throughout all of [the] Mexican continent, one may write freely. . . . Yes, European peoples! Mexico now also has freedom of the press; it is the strongest fortress against the violence and the tyranny of despots, and one of the most precious and sacred rights of man."[3]

This initial edition was followed by a second number on June 10th, this one renamed *El Mexicano*, reflecting a decision by Toledo to broaden his audience. It was intended to influence the power struggle for command of the Republican Army of the North and railed against Gutiérrez. "The public voice accuses the GOVERNOR AND PROTECTOR, as he styles himself, of that state as responsible for a progressive series of the most frightful calamities," the paper cried. "Since his entry, he has committed errors, weakness, and monstrous crimes that we shudder at recording."[4]

The paper continued by denouncing Gutiérrez's trampling of popular sovereignty and law, of "insolent rage of vanity and vulgar fanaticism," "presumptuous ignorance," and the "visage of disappointed avarice." It continued, "These are exactly the poisonous vipers we should combat and destroy; we should wage eternal war against these genii of hell, who under the mask of hypocrisy invoke in public the Virgin of Guadaloupe [*sic*], and making the sign of the cross conspire against the dignity and glory of the Mexican people." These bilingual papers, once printed, were shipped to Texas to stir the pot of discontent.[5]

Another way to undermine Gutiérrez was to conscript well-respected Tejanos to assist. On July 15, 1813, Shaler and Toledo were meeting at the latter's residence in Natchitoches, when Toledo spied two Spanish Texans strolling in the street outside. One of these was the thirty-year-old Béxar postmaster Erasmo Seguín. He was a key royalist official and an influential member of San Antonio society, a large landowner who had helped draw up rules establishing a public school. He was an organizer of Zambrano's counter-coup in 1811, but when the rebels had taken San Antonio, the tables were turned. Incarcerated in the Alamo jail, hearing of the murder of the royalists, Seguín was sure he would be next. "I was one of those chosen to die and was spared only by the pleadings and tears of my family," Seguín would later write.[6]

Seguín's home and even his furniture had been confiscated, and his wife Doña Josefa Becerra de Seguín, six-year-old son Juan, and three-year-old daughter María were sleeping in the living room of a friend's home. After about twenty days' incarceration, Seguín sent word to Gutiérrez "in which he manifested having recognized the justice" of Gutiérrez's cause. If he had been the rebel's adversary before, Seguín said, it was because he had been deceived. He was appointed as a secretary to Béxar

Junta leader Tomás Arocha, who was sent on a mission to New Orleans, with Seguín accompanying him.[7]

The mission was of particular importance. Evidently, Gutiérrez had secured a commitment for ten to twelve thousand pesos in goods from Pedro Girard—the free Frenchman of color whom Gutiérrez had used as his emissary to Adair and Wilkinson. Arocha and Seguín dutifully traveled to Louisiana to receive these goods and recruit more American fighters, but Shaler apparently talked Arocha out of the latter. Soon afterward, Arocha and Seguín had a bitter feud, Seguín called Arocha an "insurgent" and Arocha in turn may have insinuated a threat against Seguín's family. The angry Arocha left soon thereafter for San Antonio.[8]

Erasmo Seguín was now in an impossible situation. In a war that still could go either way, he had aroused suspicion on both sides, and his family might suffer for it. But, now, Toledo placed him even further into the vice. The Cuban, upon seeing Seguín in the street, urged him to enter his residence. Inside, Seguín noted that Toledo and Shaler both had weapons: the Cuban with a sword and the New Yorker with a silver-plated dagger at his breast. Seguín was unarmed. The pair demanded that he write five letters, to be addressed to Republican Army captain Miguel Menchaca and junta members José Francisco Ruiz, Vicente Travieso, Mariano Rodríguez, and Juan Veramendi, recommending Toledo to them. Seguín would later claim he resisted, but feared the two armed men, "for they were already speaking to him arrogantly, [and] he resolved to write," the letters.[9]

Seguín praised Toledo in the correspondence as "a general who all of you have provided a fitting destiny" and urged the Béxar junta to give the Cuban command of the army. The letters, of course, were false, but once again, he had been forced to side with the rebels to protect his young family. Along with Mower's propaganda, Seguín's letters helped pave the way for a change in leadership.[10]

Cogswell's Last Ride

It was at this point that a man rode west across Louisiana for the Sabine River, hoping to stop Toledo once and for all. Nathaniel Cogswell had followed the Cuban from the East Coast to the fringes of Texas. It was a mirror of the chase four years before between Governor Salcedo and the revolutionary Frenchman D'Alvimar in 1808, only this time the stakes were even greater. His sowing of distrust had already crippled Toledo's recruitment, and now the New Englander's passion and moral certitude brought him to ride to Texas in person, convinced that only he could save the revolution.

And he almost made it. In late June 1813, Cogswell was on the very banks of the Sabine River with five young men, all dressed in "the most elegant and fanciful uniforms," whom he had persuaded to join his crusade. On the next day, they would ride into Texas, make their way to San Antonio, put the Toledo conspiracy to rest, and join Gutiérrez and the Republican Army of the North. But it was not to be. A man rode up and delivered a letter from William Shaler. Cogswell, along with his small retinue, had ridden around Natchitoches to avoid just this sort of confrontation. Four more men arrived on horseback at his camp and informed him that they were agents of the New York captain. He was summoning the Massachusetts lawyer to a meeting at a house halfway between the American town and the border. The lawyer reluctantly agreed.[11]

The meeting took place on June 29th. Cogswell, based on the curt notice, thought he would only be meeting with Shaler, but to his surprise, the American had brought about twenty citizens of Natchitoches with him. He had also brought Toledo. For the first time since they had parted in Pittsburgh, when the Cuban had still been ignorant of his protégé's enmity, the two estranged men were once again face to face. What followed was an eleven-hour debate that would effectively decide the political leadership of Texas. The Massachusetts lawyer treated it as if he were a prosecutor, but in fact, the marathon session would prove to be a trial of himself as much as the Cuban.[12]

The men gathered in the no doubt cramped house. Shaler opened the trial by demanding proof of the allegations against Toledo. Cogswell explained that he had discovered a letter from the Marquis of Villa Franca, a leading member of the Spanish Cortes. A line written in invisible ink "plainly and fully discovered that . . . [Toledo] was acting in concert with him and the friends of Ferdinand the 7th in direct opposition to the cause of the patriots." He had forwarded the letters to Gutiérrez.[13]

Toledo then interjected. If he had such letters, he must have stolen them from his desk. Cogswell was sure the remark—an admission that the letters existed—would help make his case; indeed, one neutral observer thought it "was sufficient to condemn [Toledo] a thousand times over." But he was not in the majority, for the jury had certainly been stacked by William Shaler. No one was more hostile to Gutiérrez than the American agent who had shepherded him to the frontier and now called him "the damndest . . . villain, black as the earth." Cogswell replied that such "was not the opinion the world entertained of [Gutiérrez], that the world and myself believed [he] had done more for the cause, than ten thousand such as [Shaler] and that it was my opinion he would be very soon dismissed from his office as agent." Then the debate got *really* nasty, as Cogswell reported to Gutiérrez:[14] "[Shaler] said publicly before 20 men that your throat ought to be cut, and Toledo put in your place. I told him there was not a shadow of truth, but that Bernardo's throat would be cut if ever Toledo had the power; but that I trusted in God, that providence would protect the republicans of Mexico, and that they would be saved from being cursed by a servant [of the treasonous] Miranda; for such I positively know Toledo to be."[15]

But to this, Shaler could retort with the testimony of Cogswell's former compatriots, including printer Aaron Mower's allegation of stolen money at Pittsburgh. He described their final meeting there, where, far from warning Mower and Bullard about Toledo, the lawyer was full of praise of the Cuban. In fact, Cogswell told Mower in December, when the army was surrounded at La Bahía, that Toledo was the only man who could rescue the expedition and defeat the Spanish. Magee was "but a boy" and Gutiérrez "a man of no talents." To top off his devastating testimony, Mower said Cogswell had pledged "his most sacred honor that on his part nothing should be done which would throw any obstacles in the way of the expedition."[16]

Shaler had at this point finally divulged his mission to the powerbrokers in Natchitoches. Now that there were legitimate rebels in Texas, he was the legal representative of the government to treat with them. This gave him immense leverage. Shaler dismissed Cogswell, on the other hand, as a man of no importance. At last, the jury returned its verdict. "The result was that [Cogswell] was unanimously declared to be a base and treacherous calumniator, a declaration to that effect was drawn up and signed by fourteen gentlemen including all his own friends." The lawyer, Shaler wrote, "had seduced many young gentlemen to attend him, at whose expense he has lived, they are all majors and captains and . . . have all since joined Toledo on seeing their hopes of glory and fortune blasted under the auspices of Cogswell."[17]

The Massachusetts lawyer had been bested in the trial of his life by the New York sea captain and had seen many of his friends desert him. But even now he would not give up. He wrote to Gutiérrez that, despite Shaler's lock on the popular opinion of Natchitoches, the people of Natchez were still for the Mexican rebel. He would venture to General Adair, the long-dithering old Burrite, to at last come to Texas and join the army with his now legendary host.[18]

Toledo's Fifth Column

In addition to the propaganda campaign, Toledo had another secret weapon in his struggle against Gutiérrez: Henry Adams Bullard. The idealist and literary espouser of filibuster had remained in Nacogdoches as the rest of Toledo's band returned to Louisiana following Gutiérrez's order proscribing the Cuban. In an account of the expedition, which Bullard wrote anonymously years afterward, he related how friends of Toledo tried to reason with Gutiérrez. "[He] peremptorily refused, still persisting in charging Toledo with correspondence with the enemy."[19]

In Nacogdoches, Bullard joined forces with another new arrival: Joseph Wilkinson, the son of the infamous general, whose brother James was possibly already with the army. Their father had neither stopped, nor helped the rebel army, and was shortly to be transferred to Canada, where he would prove a failure in war. Nonetheless, Joseph Wilkinson, a lieutenant in the army, somehow obtained a furlough and joined the flock of men heading to Texas, where he would reunite with his brother in the rebel force. In early June, Bullard, Wilkinson, and a small company of reinforcements they had put together marched south to La Bahía, arriving just after news of Elizondo's appearance outside of San Antonio. Gutiérrez wrote to the men to stay with the small garrison in La Bahía, as there was rumor that Arredondo would move to attack that place while Elizondo attacked San Antonio. Following Elizondo's defeat, Gutiérrez, unaware Bullard was a Toledo acolyte and perceiving no enemy movement toward La Bahía, urged them to come on.[20]

Bullard, the young Harvard alumnus enamored with Spanish American independence a few years before, was now fully in the revolutionary business himself. The twenty-four-year-old now dramatically moved from observer to central figure by an accident. The Republican Army, as noted, had lost its secretary of state, Massicott, at the Battle of Alazán and needed a replacement. Gutiérrez had written Cogswell to ask a favor, for someone fluent in English and Spanish to replace this key aide. "Spare no pains to inform yourself where such a gentleman may be found, as it is impossible for me to do without a man possessed of these qualifications or accomplishments." Bullard, fluent in English, Spanish—and even French—was the perfect man for the job. When he heard of the vacancy while already en route to San Antonio, he could not believe his luck. As the secretary of state for Texas, he would be in the perfect position to exert influence.[21]

"I came over, immediately resolved to accept the appointment with a view of being more effectually useful to Gen. Toledo by having a better opportunity of removing . . . prejudices from the mind of Bernardo," Bullard wrote to Shaler. When he entered San Antonio, he was received "in a flattering manner by the army" and was immediately put to work by Gutiérrez on matters ranging from government administration to reform to improving the government's credit. As a rare Anglo-American able to participate in the Junta, he was listened to closely in the counsels. Bullard turned to the topic of Toledo.[22] "I . . . stated that as a friend to truth it became my duty to vindicate the character of a man who had been impugned and aspersed. I then stated the whole business of Toledo and Cogswell, their characters, the base intrigues carried on against the former and the abandoned character of the latter. It was easy to perceive that the letter of Cogswell was . . . a pretext to keep Toledo out of the country."[23]

According to Bullard, Gutiérrez responded that "blood would be shed" if Toledo came to Texas. The exchange did not sour Gutiérrez on his new, much-needed secretary, but it did confirm for Bullard that the president protector's determination was unshakable. Bullard and Wilkinson began to work their influence on the Americans, who welcomed the erudite Massachusetts youth and the general's son because they knew they had Shaler's ear. Wilkinson possessed a letter Shaler had sent to the Americans, which when spread among the officers, "is sufficient to put down the most positive [opinions] of Bernardo."[24]

Though they had formed the expedition behind the agent's back, the American volunteers increasingly saw William Shaler as a friend, a man who could legitimize the enterprise. Bullard found the Americans distrustful of Gutiérrez and filled "with the absolute necessity of Toledo's presence in the army." They immediately signed a letter inviting Toledo to join the republicans in Texas but decided to wait to gain the support of their Mexican compatriots before sending it.[25]

Meanwhile, Toledo's men in the rebel camp spied on Gutiérrez. Bullard sent unflattering reports to Shaler. "The general's whole time is employed in lolling on his sofa and catching flies," he wrote in disgust. "He does not know the number of his forces nor in fact, any part of the business." At one point a despairing Gutiérrez, seeing the power slipping away from him, confided to Bullard's compatriot Samuel Alden "that he no longer exercised the functions of governor."[26]

"The Question of Ruin or Success Is to Be Decided"

The end for the Mexican rebel leader came in late June. Though the junta had soured on Gutiérrez, the Tejanos were wary of Toledo, because they were "so much influenced by the violent opposition of Gov. Bernardo, as his aspersions against the character of our general [Toledo], and also of his not being a *good Catholic*," Joseph Wilkinson wrote. But the Americans were now threatening to abandon the army and return home if Toledo was not invited to Texas. The Tejanos knew their revolution would fail if they were forced to go it alone. A meeting of the junta was called for July 26th. To stack the deck beforehand, Bullard and Perry then paid a visit to Menchaca to get the Tejanos in the army on their side. They found him together with José Francisco Ruiz, and pressed them to join with them to invite Toledo to come to Texas. According to Wilkinson, the Tejanos, along with José Maria Guadiana, the former Nacogdoches commander, agreed to do so. These men, he told Shaler, "carry with them the voice of the people and the army."[27]

Bullard next engineered a debate on the subject in the afternoon's meeting of the junta. It was a replay, shorter and in a different setting and language, of the marathon trial of Cogswell that Shaler had conducted near Natchitoches. Now it was the Spanish-speaking Harvard lawyer who assumed the role of prosecutor. At a moment when Gutiérrez was inexplicably absent from the council he nominally chaired, Bullard sensed his moment and struck.[28]

"I went before them with all the documents, letters, etc. proving the falsity of Cogswell's assertions," Bullard recorded. "The members appeared much inclined to our side." Gutiérrez, no doubt alerted by an ally, hurried to the scene. He and Bullard argued the same points Shaler and Cogswell had debated over Toledo's letters. Gutiérrez was supported by his two remaining Frenchmen, Menapier and Germaille, but few others.[29]

Having lost the case on the basis of Cogswell's letters, Gutiérrez made the shocking allegation that Toledo had sent a courier to Elizondo. The latter, according to Gutiérrez, had delayed his attack on San Antonio merely to determine which rebel was in command of the forces. He wanted to know "whether Toledo had come and said that if so, business could soon be settled." How did he know this? Bullard enquired. Two deserters had told him, Gutiérrez responded. The answer, so nebulous and implausible, must have been met with shaking heads among the crowd. These same men had stood in the town plaza almost three months before when the rebel leader told of the mysterious ship, arrived to spirit away the Spanish commanders into an obviously fictitious exile. They had cheered then; there was no cheering now.[30]

Bullard now lashed out: "To this I answered that the man who pronounced Toledo a traitor was himself a traitor," he later wrote to Shaler. "That it might be a trick of the enemy to keep the man out of the country [Toledo], whom alone they feared, knowing that eventually under the present system they had nothing to dread." Now Gutiérrez, pressed hard, brought up Toledo's freemasonry, which he had seen on display in Philadelphia. This was an appeal to the "prejudice" in Bullard's eyes, that the Mexicans in the audience had for that society:[31] "He then observed that Toledo's religious principles were such as would excite disturbance if not civil war. Asserted that in some part of his works the general had vindicated the liberty of conscience, and that he had burnt that part of his work with his own hands. He declared that liberty of conscience would not do in this country. What, gentlemen, said I, is the value of liberty without the liberty of conscience? Would you have the body free, but keep the soul enslaved?"[32]

Now Bullard produced his ace in the hole: a letter signed by the American contingent "that unless Toledo was sent for, every man would leave the country." Colonel Perry stepped forward and confirmed the letter, asking the junta who it was who commanded the army. Had Gutiérrez "ever shown himself in the field of battle or in the hour of danger?" He answered his own question in the negative. Then he added that his American volunteers "will never fight again under the command of Bernardo." Toledo, Perry asserted—despite having never met him—was a man of integrity and talents, true to the cause, and he would fight on the field of battle. How did he know? "By the letters of Shaler." The deliberation did not last long. The Mexican officers almost to a man came down on the side of Perry. What choice did they have? While there were men of courage and skill in the Mexican ranks—such as Delgado, Menchaca, Guadiana, and Savías—the bulk of the Mexican contingent were poorly armed militia with little training or proficiency at arms, or royalist deserters of questionable commitment to the cause. Could they stand alone against Arredondo when he moved north, which now seemed a certainty? "After deliberation they determined to send for [Toledo]," Bullard announced.[33]

Gutiérrez wavered from anger to moodiness to nervously engaging in his bizarre hobby of catching flies. Samuel D. Forsyth, a former US Army surgeon's mate who had commanded the guns at Alazán, observed in a letter to Shaler, "Granny is now in the junta and is now traversing the room behind me while I write this, one minute drumming on the window glass with his fingers and the other catching flies and pinching off their heads. He has just told me he will not stay in the country that he will go to the U. S. with his family, and warns me to be on my guard against Gen. T." For the aspiring lawyer Bullard, it had been a phenomenal success. Now he urged William Shaler to action:[34]

There exists here the finest materials for an army but in a most rude state, but requires only a man of talents to organize a most formidable body of troops . . . In short, the time is now come when the question of ruin or success is to be decided. Men more hardy and brave than these Americans, the world cannot boast. They urge only ahead. If you and Toledo regard the welfare of this country, and . . . respect the feelings of us who are now impatient to see you, come on and all is well.

Yours with extreme impatience.
H. A. Bullard[35]

"The Sun of Bernardo Is Forever Set."

The Gutiérrez-Magee expedition had been commenced a year earlier with the alliance of a Mexican rebel and an American soldier. Both had since been humbled and drummed from office. Magee was dead and Gutiérrez, headed to exile. "The Sun of Bernardo is forever set," Joseph Wilkinson wrote. Ultimately, neither leader had been prepared for the difficult task they had taken up. Magee had pined for glory but withered under hardship. Gutiérrez was a man in over his head, filled with delusions of grandeur but hesitant to serve at the front lines.[36]

The rebel can rightly be praised for having a vision for the independence of Northern Mexico, but he botched the implementation of it. He wrote an unimaginative constitution for his new "State of Texas" and then followed it up with a proclamation filled with excessive self-praise, winding up to hyperbolic paroxysms of republican grandeur. But these are mere failings of ability; far worse were his moral shortcomings. He had arrogated to himself near-dictatorial powers but refused to assert them when it came to the great question of what to do with the Spanish prisoners.

The most damning indictment of the rebel leader came not from the Anglo Americans, but from the young José Antonio Navarro, who recalled the events forty years later, when he was the foremost proponent of liberty and republicanism for the Tejanos. The revolution, he said, was an era in which the men of his nation suffered from an "extreme degree of ignorance and the wild fervor of their passions," who truly did not understand ideas like "Independence and Liberty" only "a cry of death and war without quarter against the *Gachupines*."[37] "There can be no doubt that this band of so-called patriots, as Bernardo Gutiérrez has said, devoured of their own accord these fourteen victims," Navarro wrote. "Yet is the excuse of Gutiérrez so frivolous, so cowardly, so unworthy of a General. . . . He should at least have abandoned a command when he saw his cause stained with a crime more infamous than ever characterized a Vandal Chief. Gutiérrez *did* participate, though it may be indirectly, in that bloody act."[38]

The rebel from Revilla was an amateur playing at the most daring and dangerous of games—revolution—and he was winging it. To be fair, Gutiérrez was not too different from many others in this sport. Shaler, competent enough as a sea captain, was frequently seized by temerity and indecisiveness as a special agent, and though he was scrupulous to stay hands off in the run-up to the invasion, he ultimately dipped those hands in fully to promote Toledo. His colleague John Robinson had no shortage of self-confidence, but this, married to his incompetence, was nearly catastrophic. The republican commanders all had their failings: Magee and Ross suffered collapses of courage, and Kemper bore at least some negligence in the murder. The great tragedy of the Republican Army of the North was the failings of all its leaders, Mexican and Anglo alike, to meet the awesome task that they had assigned to themselves.

But despite these failings, Gutiérrez was unquestionably a dedicated patriot for Mexican independence. In a revolution in which many other men would switch sides, jockeying for personal advantage or to protect their fortunes, he remained constant to his cause, animated, in his words, by "the holy fire of patriotism." Even Bullard, who spared no insults to disparage the Mexican, had to admit, "He was ... devoted to his native country, and vindictive against its oppressors." No one sacrificed more, no one served so unflinchingly in the cause, even at the risk of their life, fortune, and honor. And he had dared to dream—when doing so was mortally dangerous—and his dream had beyond all expectations liberated Texas.[39]

Gutiérrez set out for Natchitoches on the night of August 6th, while Toledo in turn would make his way to Texas. For Nathaniel Cogswell, there was one last effort. On July 14th, he walked into the office of the *Statesman* newspaper in Natchez and handed the publishers Gutiérrez's letter about the victory at Alazán, which ran under the headline, "Another victory!!" This may have been Cogswell's last service to the Republican Army of the North. Sometime later, after returning to Rapides—where he was possibly staying at the Kemper tavern—Cogswell died from disease. The tardy and confused reports that reached New England of this wayward son's demise provide a wide range of dates of death. His family history, however, preserves possibly the correct one: August 18, 1813. If indeed correct, it was a tragic coincidence, for on that same day, the Republican Army of the North—and all of Texas—would experience the very "tears of blood" that Nathaniel Cogswell had predicted.[40]

On July 14th, William Shaler wrote to Monroe, informing him that he was at last proceeding to Texas, which, having a government, fulfilled the requirements of his orders. "The truth is that very little is wanting to ensure complete success to this revolution in the four provinces," he explained. "If that little is withheld it must as certainly fail, and independent of other considerations, involve thousands in the most frightful misery and ruin." He explained he would support Toledo "in every way in my power consistent with my satisfaction." With that note, William Shaler departed on what he believed would be his permanent mission to the Mexican Republic, no doubt dressed in the makeshift uniform for which he had purchased the gold lace. It seemed that perhaps now he might indeed equal the glory of Poinsett in Chile.[41]

Shaler's letters to the secretary were still slow in arriving, the news from Texas generally six to eight weeks old. Monroe's letters were few and far between. In fact, Shaler had not yet received a single letter from Monroe acknowledging the expedition in Texas since it had begun *ten months before*. His last guidance had been given on September 1, 1812, when the project was just a rumor in Washington. When he heard of the capture of San Antonio and the massacre of the royalists, Shaler wrote Monroe by an express rider. But even this news arrived in Washington *two months* after the events had transpired in April. This time, the secretary was jolted out of his lethargy, and replied immediately:[42]

> **Department of State June 5, 1813**
> Sir,
> I have just received your letter of the 7th of May, and am much shocked at the massacre mentioned in it. It is to be lamented that any American citizens have engaged in the contest between the two parties in Mexico.
> The president is desirous that you observe strictly your instructions, not to interfere in the affairs of those provinces, or to encourage any armaments of any kind against the existing government. The United States being at peace with Spain, wish to preserve that relation with whatever government may exist there. This is the spirit of the instructions given you at the commencement of your service, and they have never since been altered.
> Perceiving that you contemplate proceeding to St. Antonio, I have to request that you decline doing so, until you receive further instructions on the subject.
> I have the honor to be,
> Sir, Very respectfully,
> your Obt. humble Svt.
> Jas Monroe[43]

Had Monroe realized what Shaler was up to in the time that the letter was in transit, the rebuke would have been even stronger. The agent was now actively working on behalf of Toledo, as additional letters en route would show. Now, a quirk of fate was to stop Shaler, just as it had connected him to Gutiérrez a year before. He had traveled as far as Nacogdoches, where he had somehow lost his horses, or they had been stolen. The delay left him and his black servant Charles, who no doubt was traveling with him, stuck in the frontier town for several days. As he waited to procure new horses, a messenger arrived bearing Monroe's letter. Shaler's dreams of a glorious reception in San Antonio were dashed, and he immediately returned across the border. Back in Natchitoches, the chastened agent replied to the secretary of state on August 7th.[44]

"I regret exceedingly having taken a step that does not merit the approbation of the President," he wrote, "for it has ever been my endeavor to act in strict conformity to the spirit of my instructions." Shaler then entered into a lengthy justification of his conduct. His defense of Toledo was not meddling but a matter of honor: "His character was attacked and I defended it on its intrinsic merits," he said, "and also against a man [Cogswell] who had prostituted the name of the government from Pittsburgh to this place." He conveniently left out his aid in printing Toledo's propaganda or browbeating Seguín. Shaler then left what would be his final summation on the origins of the expedition. "The first adventurers in this expedition assembled on the desolate banks of the Sabine, since that time there have never been within the territory of the U. S. the least appearances of armament, or military preparation," he wrote. "The volunteers went out either singly or in small bands usually armed as hunters, and what few supplies have been procured here have gone in the common way of trade."[45]

Toledo, for his part, proceeded to the Trinity on July 24th and on to San Antonio to take full authority over the new state and of the Republican Army of the North. On his way down from Nacogdoches, he picked up fifty-six additional Mexicans, along with one hundred or so Americans who had made their way to Texas. Shaler reported of the revival of Anglo-American volunteers for the cause, "I think it probable that the American corps now amounts to about 500, and there is no doubt but that it will very much increase in the course of this summer, for every exertion will be made by Toledo to wipe away the disgrace attached to the revolution by the atrocious conduct of Bernardo, and to give it a fair character abroad."[46]

Toledo not only welcomed new recruits but wanted to open the floodgates to new immigrants, notwithstanding the junta's reticence on the subject. In a proclamation, he declared, "The government of Texas, wishing, by all the means in its power, to promote industry and the population of the country . . . invites foreigners of all nations, excepting those of Spain, to a secure asylum and paternal protection." In place of "barbarous laws of the Spanish government" that prohibited immigration and commerce, Texas now had a free government. The proclamation declared that since "liberal maxims have taken [the] place of oppression it is one of the first efforts to favor . . . the ingress of all foreigners who may bring with them any occupation or provision on which they can subsist."[47]

Toledo hoped that the offer would attract "thousands of individuals [who] would flock to this province from all parts." The language spoke of "settlers," but the real audience was potential fighters. There was indeed one important recruit to the Republican Army who arrived at this time, its former commander, Samuel Kemper, who had led the army to victory at La Bahía and Rosillo. Upon his return, Henry Perry, without a word of controversy, stepped aside and Kemper resumed his command of the army. Perry took on the job of quartermaster (Davenport's old role before he abandoned the army) and inspector general of arms. He supervised the thorough repair of all weapons and filled the Alamo with the captured stores of Alazán.[48]

Toledo Arrives

Toledo, journeying to the republicans, "will be received as their savior," Shaler predicted. Indeed, as Navarro recalled, Toledo's charisma quickly won over many of the Americans. "He was a young man of but thirty-two summers, apparently possessed of liberal principles, fluent in speech, of handsome exterior, of extreme affability and happy conceits," the Tejano wrote. "With such an assemblage of fascinating traits, he took by storm the hearts of the army, and extended his captivation to the population of San Antonio, and thus . . . assumed without opposition the command of the army."[49]

Navarro was likely not being truthful. In fact, there was a real tension among many of the key Tejano leaders, who were far less accepting of Toledo. Even before inviting the Cuban to join their army, the council had sent him a list of conditions reflecting the concerns Cogswell had raised. Toledo must be second in command in the army to the American colonel (who was presumably neutral in the internal political debates), must promise not to introduce freedom of conscience or anything that would injure "our sacred religion," not form institutions of freemasonry, and protect the property of all republicans. Toledo was authorized to bring in as many as one thousand additional American volunteers, with "no more than that being admitted because they are not necessary." Any foreigners who might come must on the conclusion of the war return to the United States and not obtain Mexican citizenship unless they could "provide sufficient proof of their abilities, talents, and love of this Mexican soil, and that they undertake some useful craft beneficial to the development of this kingdom."[50]

But even with these concessions, Toledo still faced skepticism—and outright hostility. Tejano leaders may not have loved Gutiérrez, but he had been one of them: a creole, a patriot, a Mexican. He had indeed raised some of them to prominence. Nine days after Alazán, the president protector elevated Capt. Miguel Menchaca to *colonel,* thus attaining equal rank with Perry. And while Gutiérrez did not fight in battle, he had sacrificed for the cause in other ways, like so many of them.[51]

For Tejanos like Menchaca, it was bad enough that their leader had been ousted by these foreigners who had the temerity to dictate the leadership of their cause on *Mexican* soil. What really concerned them was this stranger who would replace him. Toledo was the son of a Spanish-born official, educated in Spain. While he was technically a Creole, the locals did not see him that way, according to Beltrán. "With all Toledo's pretentions, he is after all a gachupín," Menchaca would supposedly tell Colonel Kemper, "and I have a presentiment that he will prove our undoing." He further compared Toledo to Elizondo, who had become a rebel and then betrayed the cause. "You Americans are prone to listen to the plausible tales of these gachupines, while we Mexicans have learned by long experience never to repose confidence in a Spaniard."[52]

Indeed, an anonymous account written two years later even claimed that the Tejano colonel planned a coup. When Toledo arrived, he planned an early march South to challenge Arredondo's advance. Menchaca summoned his officers "in order to form a council of war and decree the imprisonment of the general in chief of the army, on the pretext that he agreed with the enemies and that the object was the delivery of the army to the royalists." In this account, Toledo calmed the situation by arranging a fandango in the army's camp to distract the plotters. "It was the first time that the officers or ladies had seen this kind of amusement in such a place, and the novelty interested everyone." Dinner, drink, and dancing, so the account claimed, defused the scheme.[53]

The Armies Converge

When Elizondo had advanced to the fringes of San Antonio in June, his enraged commander, Arredondo, had sent a detachment of cavalry to order him to pull back, but it was too late. Following Elizondo's disastrous defeat at Alazán, he had retreated to Presidio de Rio Grande, where Arredondo chided his subordinate for "the disobedience of my repeated orders, which absolutely prohibited you not only from entering the capital of Béxar but to even come near it." Still, he did not replace Elizondo—simply ordered him to reform the remnants of his army and wait for his own forces to join them at a rendezvous called Cañada de Caballos (ravine of horses), about eighty miles south of San Antonio.[54]

Arredondo brought something almost never seen before in Texas—experienced, tested, and effective royalist troops. The armies with which Salcedo and Herrera had fought were weakened by years of neglect in training and equipment; hence the many muskets that had broken under the slightest usage in the 1809 inspection tour. Their powder was old and of poor quality. Most importantly, while some of these troops had fought Indians, they had no experience in organized combat against another army. The frontier troops who had spent their time garrisoning Nacogdoches, La Bahía, Trinidad, and Béxar were unable to match the skill of the American volunteers, and Elizondo's troops had scarcely been better. The army that General Arredondo marched with, on the other hand, was of a much higher quality. Some were Napoleonic War veterans, only recently sent to Mexico to quell the revolution there. The core of this force was the Regiment of Veracruz, with troops added in Nuevo Santander who had spent the last year honing their skills against rebels there. Arredondo had also raised a force of militiamen and spent much of the month of July training them alongside the veterans. They were good but outnumbered. To face the republicans—who had never been beaten in battle before—Arredondo needed Elizondo's men too. But when this tattered, beaten force arrived in the first week of August 1813, the sorry spectacle the general found before him was disheartening.[55]

Arredondo had a maxim: "Punish cowardice and wickedness, reward bravery and virtue." He put it into practice now. The troops who had fled at Alazán were paraded before the assembled army. Arredondo selected five men who had fought bravely in the battle and gave them commendation before the whole force. For the rest, however, particularly the "cowardly right-hand squadron," he had them stripped of their ranks and other decorations; these were replaced with white armbands with the letter "C," for *cobarde*—coward. Arredondo warned that "until they redeem themselves in action and bloodshed, they will not have their standard returned to them or their uniform, nor will the indecorous state they are in be removed."[56]

But the men needed more than just courage and gimmicks in the fight. They needed competence. Despite the urgency of his task, Arredondo halted the army for five days to train, so that he and his officers might, as he wrote, "explain and teach the most necessary and indispensable formations and maneuvers in an action or battle." Gradually, Arredondo was turning this rabble into an army.[57] "I continued my march, filled with the greatest confidence because I noticed among my troops a decided enthusiasm and bravery, a remarkable serenity of mind, and an unusual patience with which they bore the fatigue of a march so long and painful, rendered so by the unfortunate time—it being summer—in which they passed through an unsettled country so extensive as that beyond Laredo, and in a most pitiful state of nakedness."[58]

Many of his soldiers did not have shoes, some lacked proper long pants to protect them from the South Texas mesquite bushes, with their slashing thorns. Some—presumably Indian conscripts—had only breechcloths. Still, they exhibited "a most eager desire to engage, as soon as possible, the wicked rabble who had become famous on account of their cruel and unworthy deeds, and their pride resulting from the victories they had previously gained." Arredondo's combined force of 1,800 men was comparable to or slightly outnumbered the republicans, although both sides overestimated the other. Far more important than the pure numbers was the army's composition: nearly 1,000 of Arredondo's men were regulars, and two-thirds were also cavalry, though most would fight dismounted.[59]

Rebel numbers were likely similar. Reports gave a wide range, but the best estimate of the Republican Army of the North in late summer is around 1,500–1,800. The majority of the army was now Mexican, at around 1,000, with 500–800 Anglo-Americans and an unknown number of Indians. Toledo, on his arrival, proceeded to reorganize the force. While there seems to have been some mixing of the army's ranks by ethnicity before Alazán, Toledo put a stop to that.[60]

The Anglo-American forces were formed into two contingents, one under the command of Henry Perry, called the "Washington Volunteers" and the second, called the "Madison Volunteers," under Kemper, who appears to have delegated the direct command of the men in battle to Josiah Taylor while he conferred with Toledo on the broader strategy.[61]

Having learned their lesson, the rebels were more active in tracking the enemy this time. Their spies in Laredo had reported the army's movements, numbers, and artillery. Toledo's initial plan had been to march south and attack one wing of the Spanish army before Arredondo and Elizondo's forces could join together. To this end, one account claims a significant portion of the army had marched out of San Antonio on August 8th, but were short Perry's troops—since he was ill—and those of Menchaca, still hostile and skeptical of Toledo. After two days of waiting South of San Antonio, some of it in the rain, the advanced force returned to the city, in the words of the pro-Toledo account, to the "old leisure and inaction which they had been in since they occupied the capital." Nonetheless, Menchaca's bitterness aside, he and others were not, in fact idle. As the royalists pushed through South Texas, they became the victims of raids by Comanches, intent on stealing some of Arredondo's many horses. This news inspired Perry and Menchaca. They proposed to Toledo to allow Menchaca's Tejanos, who had harassed Salcedo in his retreat, to do the same to Arredondo in his advance.[62]

But Toledo, fuming no doubt over Menchaca's foot-dragging, and trained as a professional in the Spanish Navy, had nothing but disdain for such guerilla fighting. "Why should I incur unnecessary risks for a few horses?" he asked, according to Beltrán, who claimed to be present for the exchange. "One man just now is worth more than all the horses in Arredondo's army, and besides, we already have more horses than we need." Toledo, so Beltrán wrote, had a plan, had selected the ground on which he would fight, and would not waste resources in raids. On leaving Toledo's presence, Menchaca muttered under his breath, "Sus pensamientos indican perfidia!"—"His thoughts show his perfidy." Menchaca feared that Cogswell's premonitions might be true.[63]

Now the question became how to meet the enemy. Kemper or Henry Perry at one point suggested—and Toledo apparently agreed—that the army remain in the town and defend the Alamo. But the army relied on consensus and the troops themselves had a veto, which they now used. Modern readers, familiar with the 1836 battle and the somewhat exaggerated stories of disparity in casualties between attackers and defenders, might wonder why the republicans did not utilize the fortress in 1813. There are two arguments against this course. First, the fort—ruin really—of 1813 was not as stout as it would be twenty-three years later, even with the work Perry had put into it. Second, the Alamo was to the northeast, across the river from San Antonio, the opposite direction from which the invading army would come. To fortify it and bring the army within it would mean quitting the town. For the Tejanos, this meant abandoning their homes and families, something they absolutely would not do. Unlike in 1836, when they were a fraction of the defending army, in 1813, they represented the majority. To protect everything dear to them, they needed to meet the Spanish *before* the royalist forces reached the town.⁶⁴

There is a firsthand account by an unknown Tejano that describes their thinking. It shows a bravado and swagger that matched that of the Anglo contingent. One might even say that Alazán had made them cocky. "Emboldened by their past success, animated by love of their Patria, and trusting in their unsurpassed valor," the author wrote, "The forces of Independence resolved to seek out the enemy and surprise them on their route of march, against the wishes of their General."⁶⁵

This, then, was the army's decision, and Toledo, Kemper, and Perry fell in line. Despite the harassment of Comanche raids, Arredondo arrived at a camp just south of the Medina River on August 16th. He sent out scouts, who reported back that the rebel army was not in San Antonio and could not be located. McFarlan's dutiful scouts, on the other hand, had tracked the royalists.⁶⁶

The army, and indeed the whole population of San Antonio knew the importance of the battle to come. Once before, the republicans had thought their triumph complete, but had been forced to take the field again. But this time, there really was no other royalist force behind Arredondo. If the republicans could win just one more battle, Texas would remain free, possibly for all time. With the all-important lifeline to the United States opened, perhaps they could link up with the army of Rayón and complete the liberation of all Mexico. The alternative was defeat—complete, irredeemable, devastating. They knew this, for they had heard the stories of Arredondo's reign of terror in Nuevo Santander. As the Republican Army prepared to march on the morning of August 14th, Carlos Beltrán and his adoptive brother Pablo Rodríguez paid a last visit to Señora Rodríguez. She, like Menchaca, supposedly had a premonition for the coming battle, and of the Spanish-born Cuban who was leading them into it:

> Were Manchaca in command we would be safe, but who is this Gachupín? He poses as a soldier, but what do we know of his past? Has he ever won a battle? Was he ever more than a lieutenant under his Gachupín masters? ... May the holy saints protect us, but I have had awful dreams, and I fear the worst. Go and do your duty as brave soldiers, and if Toledo is defeated, as I firmly believe he will be, and if either or both of you should survive, hasten to me.⁶⁷

The Republican Army's Last March

Three years before, Spanish lieutenant José María Guadiana, the perennial second fiddle at Nacogdoches, with twenty years in service and only one promotion in all that time, had ridden through the Neutral Ground with his American counterpart, Augustus Magee, in their joint mission to clear the Neutral Ground of the banditti.

How much had changed since then! Guadiana had embraced the revolution and now, with the army grown through the influx of native Mexicans, Toledo had raised Guadiana to lieutenant colonel and acting general of the "Ejercito Republicano del Norte de México." It was he who issued the orders to march on behalf of Toledo.[68]

His superior was no mere figurehead, as Gutiérrez had been, but the general in charge of an army that had evolved much over the last year. It was a force of about 1,500–1,800 men. The Anglo-American volunteers, the core of the army for the last year, were divided into their two regiments commanded by Henry Perry (called Peres by the Mexicans), and Samuel Kemper. These contained four companies each, which in turn were led by a captain and three junior officers, a first sergeant, corporals, and fife players. The battalion had, in addition to their commander, a drum major, two surgeons, and two armorers. The artillery corps, about thirty to fifty men commanded by Capt. Thomas Hussey Luckett, was separate from this structure. The Mexican contingent organization is obscure but was arranged under Menchaca and Delgado. At the staff level, Bullard served as a translator for Toledo.[69]

The troops were supposed to be clothed "as circumstances permit with uniformity," but in practice men wore a mix of tattered Anglo hunting shirts, Mexican civilian clothes, and plundered Spanish uniforms, which after Alazán were plentiful. Those above privates did have rank insignia added to them. Colonels like Kemper, Perry, Menchaca, and Delgado wore gold epaulettes with tassels; other ranks wore fringes of colored wool, silk, or bands. Surgeons like Samuel D. Forsyth wore gold braids around their necks.[70]

The Republican Army marched out of San Antonio on August 14, 1813, amid martial music and the cheers of the women. The troops were forbidden to carry baggage, only arms. They were preceded by a force of twenty scouts, Mexicans and Americans alike. Two pieces of artillery followed, then the first company of the Washington Regiment, then the Mexican troops. Then came the bulk of the army, Mexicans and Americans in their separate contingents, with four to six pieces of artillery, ending with the Madison regiment. Behind this was the munitions train, followed by civilians—presumably cooks and other attendants of the army. At the very end of the train were the Indian allies. On the march, organization fell to a chief of the day. Perry took this role on the first day, assisted by Bullard and Lt. James Royall. On the second day, the chief spot fell to Miguel Musquíz, assisted by José Francisco Ruiz and Captain Wilkinson.[71]

On the second night, the republicans camped near the north bank of the Medina River south of San Antonio. It was in many ways a new army. Toledo had arrived barely two weeks before; he and his soldiers had never been in the field together. New troops had been added from the population of San Antonio and even some of the American volunteers were new, as fresh faces from the United States replaced others who had gone home. Kemper had been reunited with the army probably less than one week. But the core of the force had been together since the beginning. Among these men there were some who no doubt pondered the thought that it had been just over a year since they had first entered Texas. They had experienced lofty hopes, miserable want, confidence, despair, terror, exultation, fatigue, and glorious victory. But when it came to it, had not this army won all its battles before? "Never was an army more sure of victory," Beltrán would write, echoing the Tejano account. "According to reliable reports brought in by faithful scouts, the forces of the two armies were about equal, and in view of the former victories won over much larger numbers, our men felt fully assured that a still greater triumph awaited them on the morrow." But they knew the stakes, and few men slept during that tense, anxious night. On the next day, August 18, 1813, the fate of Texas would be decided.[72]

21

The Battle of Medina

THE REPUBLICAN ARMY of the North awaited the royalists in the wooded fringes of a large, open field that likely sat astride the Camino que Cortaba, a branch of the Camino Real, just beyond the Medina River south of San Antonio. Toledo commanded in the field. It was the first time that this army of the Mexican Revolution was led by a Spanish speaker, though he was still no Mexican. Toledo's colonel leading the Anglo-American volunteers was Samuel Kemper, whose brother Reuben had arrested the Cuban a few months before. But on this day the former member of the Spanish Cortes and the former tavernkeeper-turned-revolutionary were now standing as allies at the decisive battle for Texas. Alongside Kemper as the commander of the army's right wing—as he had served so successfully at Alazán—was the former US Army artillery officer Josiah Taylor.[1]

In 1806, Kemper and Taylor had taken the Mexican Association's oath "to use all lawful means to aid and assist in effecting the emancipation of Mexico and Peru." They had pledged to liberate America's neighbors but knew that success depended on the natives who joined them. Ultimately, this was a Mexican revolution, and the battle would be fought with a larger Mexican presence than in any of the Republican Army's engagements before. On the left of the army, Toledo's commander of this native contingent was Miguel Menchaca, who had skillfully led the ambush that had been the beginning of the end of the La Bahía siege and who had been wounded at Rosillo. Menchaca led a company of cavalry, while Antonio Delgado, who had executed the royalist officers, led another on the opposite wing. Between these bookends were the Mexican and American volunteer infantry contingents and from four to eight cannon.[2]

The site the army occupied on the morning of August 18 had been chosen by Kemper and Henry Adams Bullard. It was a well-planned ambuscade, hidden among "low scrubby timber" and dense brush, with one source noting large hills on the flanks, securing them. "The army was extremely satisfied with the chosen position," one account says. The force was possibly a good distance south of the Medina River, but from its position could cover the Camino Real and two to three fords across the river, which was otherwise confined in a steep bank at this point. They lay in ambush facing southward in a grove of post oak with a clearing to their front and a small creek running near the camp. The army was in jovial spirits, with the Tejano corps singing a newly composed song mocking the Spanish commander, who wore an eyepatch:[3]

> "Hay biene el tuerto Arredondo á pelear con los de Texas penzará
> que son obejas delas que trajo Elizondo."

Had the bilingual Americans like Bullard translated for their comrades, the English version would have been:

> "Here comes the one-eyed Arredondo, come to quarrel with the
> Texans. He must think that we are sheep, like the men who
> marched with Elizondo."[4]

But Arredondo was not the type of soldier to advance without having—metaphorically at least—both eyes open to the dangers before him. Lacking good intelligence on the rebel army's whereabouts, on the day before the battle he paused his army about six miles south of the Medina, camping at a place called Rancherías, near a small lake. The next morning, he sent out scouts who were instructed to ride as far as San Antonio to locate the republican force. They were unsuccessful in finding the army, but "the corporal and four soldiers found numerous traces of people on foot and on horseback," Arredondo wrote. Now knowing the republicans were out there, somewhere to his front, Arredondo on the morning of August 18th sent out Elizondo with a 180-man cavalry force to scout out ahead of the army, "directing him to proceed with the greatest caution and vigilance until he saw the enemy, and then to make, as far as possible, a careful observation of their number, but not to engage them in battle unless he thought himself strong enough to inflict an exemplary punishment upon them." Arredondo sent two of his key aides along with Elizondo to ensure compliance. He wanted no repeat of Alazán.[5]

The Battle Begins

At about 9:00 a.m., Beltrán recalled, "our scouts reported the enemy advancing in force, and presently he came in sight." One of Elizondo's men, Ensign Francisco López, became separated from the rest of the force and stumbled onto the republican left. Menchaca, fearful that the scout would reveal the ambush site, ordered his men to fire on him. This they did but failed to bring him down. López spurred his horse back to Elizondo's position. The officer dispatched a fast-riding cavalryman back to Arredondo to call for reinforcements.[6]

In the meantime, Elizondo's force came under fire and retreated out of range to reform a line. Menchaca and Kemper were eager to attack. The former approached

Toledo and asked him his plans. "Toledo remarked to him that the maneuvering was only intended as a decoy to ascertain the strength of his troops," wrote Antonio Menchaca years later. "[But] that [Miguel] Menchaca might take some of his men and engage with them but under no consideration to follow them far if they retreated, and that Arredondo merely wished to get him out of his position in order to take him at a disadvantage." Menchaca's troops, "charged vigorously on the enemy," followed soon after by the Anglo-Americans. Elizondo, still busy reforming, saw Menchaca's Mexicans closing on him. "They fired a few volleys and then resumed their retreat slowly, keeping up a desultory firing," Beltrán wrote, "until they were joined by a large body of troops." This was a relief force of 150 men and 2 cannons under the command of the republicans' old nemesis from the Casas Revolt, "Sam Brannon"— Juan Zambrano. Some rebels mistook this force for the bulk of the Spanish Army and saw in this an opportunity to inflict a severe beating on the disorganized enemy.[7]

But it was not, and the republicans' failure to realize this was a serious error. The rebels overestimated the size of this group, and possibly thought these two groups were part of a train of Spanish forces. If they had indeed caught Arredondo still on the march, then driving the vanguard back against the main body could have precipitated a devastating rout. Thoughts like these may have run through the minds of the rebels Menchaca and Kemper as they abandoned their prepared positions to pursue the disorganized enemy. Some accounts claim Toledo ordered the charge, but most insist he was opposed to it. The youth from San Antonio, Antonio Menchaca, records an even more confrontational account of his namesake rebel. After arriving at the larger body of Spanish troops, the headstrong Miguel Menchaca sent word to Toledo asking him to advance the remainder of the republican ranks, since Menchaca would not turn back. Toledo responded that such an act would be "worst than madness" and he would be defeated if he did.[8] "Upon receiving this reply, Menchaca, infuriated, himself came over to Toledo's position, where the balance of the force was, and told the troops that the fight had commenced; that under no consideration would he . . . quit until he and the men under him had either died or conquered; that if they were men, to act as men and follow him, whereupon all the forces became encouraged and moved in a body to follow Menchaca."[9]

This spirited account and others show much more agency and leadership on the part of the Mexican troops in this battle than was possible under Gutiérrez. The irony was that although the Americans and possibly some elite Mexicans preferred Toledo, he had not won the love—and consent—of the common soldier. In the heat of the battle, men followed leaders they respected, and the Mexican rebels were no different than the Americans in this matter. Menchaca, like Kemper, was *one of them,* and when he gave this order on the confused, smoky field, the Tejano effectively became the de-facto final battlefield commander of the Republican Army of the North.[10]

The rebels nearly encircled Elizondo, who now retreated as ordered. The two sides engaged in a running fight for about half an hour, Elizondo and Zambrano continually pulling back as the republicans pursued. But the Spanish were winning the race. Here their advantage in horses was telling. All of Elizondo's forces, and likely Zambrano's as well (given how quickly he arrived on the battlefield), were on horseback. The republicans had far fewer horses. The Mexican contingent was well-mounted, but the Americans, as at Alazán, were mostly on foot. This was not as complete a mismatch as it might seem. The Spanish cavalry was not well disciplined. Many were likely militia firing escopetas from horseback, as at La Bahía, with poor accuracy. They withdrew as ordered; had they not, they would otherwise have been routed.

For the rebels, the two alternatives looked one and the same. But as they pushed forward to follow up their initial "success," they came across a new enemy: topography. The area they were entering, known as El Encinal de Medina, was a region of oak trees growing in very sandy soil. This made for hard slogging for the foot-bound men, particularly those hand-rolling the cannon. Previously, the army had used oxen to draw their guns, but these had been turned out to forage the night before and had not been collected before the battle. In any event, they were too slow-moving for a battlefield. Having no draft horses, the rebels resorted to human power, slogging on in the unforgiving sands with their brutal loads. The wheels of the carriages sunk deeply, and the heavier guns had to be abandoned as the eager republican troops began to outpace the artillery. The Tejano cavalry also found their horses bogged down, as one of them put it, "sinking up to their knees" in the sand. The republicans also suffered from a severe shortage of water, and the men, parched from their arduous slog, "were so thirsty that they even drank the water in which the rods for loading the cannon were soaked." Without anything to clean and cool their barrels, the artillery would be useless after just a few shots.[11]

But amid these hardships, republican morale surged. "Seeing this [rearward enemy] movement, our men sprang forward with redoubled spirit and crowded the enemy so closely that the retreat became almost a rout," Beltrán recalled. Once again, Toledo tried to slow the advance. In addition to not knowing what truly lay before him, he was alarmed by the infantry outpacing their own artillery while still in ignorance of the whereabouts of the enemy's guns. Toledo, trying to reassert control, ordered his troops back to the original positions, but they ignored him. The excitement of the chase—and possibly lingering distrust of the Cuban—made it impossible to stop. As Gaines remembered, Kemper and Menchaca would hear none of it:[12] "These two colonels were opposed to Toledo personally, so that when he gave the order to retreat to the river, Kemper and Monchack [sic] galloped violently up & down the lines countermanding the order and swearing that there should be no retreat. Toledo was, as we have already stated, unpopular in the army, and the consequence was that Kemper and Monchack charged vigorously on the enemy, who still kept retreating but still fighting."[13]

Toledo at last rescinded his order, and the republicans pushed onward. But the retreat was ending. Elizondo and Zambranos's battered force had reached the

Spanish line. Arredondo himself had moved forward—north in this case—leaving his supply wagons behind and taking position with his 1,300-man main body in a densely wooded area adjacent to a clearing. He arranged his troops in the shape of a V, with infantry—including the Regiment of Veracruz—at the bottom and artillery at the edges, with the open side facing the onrushing enemy. It was, ironically, a trap similar to the one Toledo had originally planned for him. When Elizondo and Zambrano arrived, they passed over the Spanish lines and with their tired mounts, took a position on the flanks. Then Arredondo gave his infantry orders to hold their fire until the republicans marched within a few dozen paces. The storm would hit the republicans on three sides.[14]

"Not Hard To Die"

The republicans rushed into this trap and the Spanish "opened a most dreadful & destructive fire," which struck the rebels to their "utter astonishment." Kemper had convinced himself that the force retreating from him was the entire Spanish Army. But now that he was face-to-face with a force much larger than he expected, there was nothing else to do but press the attack. Indeed, even amid the storm, the republicans did not break, with the Anglo-Americans under Kemper and Taylor pushing forward "with determined impetuosity," against the Spanish left. For their part, the Mexicans under Menchaca fought "with equal gallantry" attacking the Spanish right. The Indians among the army, some of whom had just joined the republicans that morning, "stood by the Americans to the last and shared their fate." Toledo, in his first real battle since fighting alongside the British Army, was shocked at the violence of the engagement. Once again, he ordered a retreat, but the courier he sent to Kemper was killed before he could arrive. A messenger did get the order to Menchaca, but the headstrong Tejano—who had pressed the Spanish so closely that he was engaged in hand-to-hand combat—supposedly shouted, "Tell General Toledo I never turn my back on a gachupín!"[15] "Scarcely had he uttered these words when he fell from his horse mortally wounded. Having overheard the order to retreat, and witnessing the fall of their brave leader, the Mexican troops fell into disorder, some shouting, 'Adelante!' [go forward] others giving back until the confusion became so great that they abandoned the field, leaving Kemper's men to bear the brunt of battle."[16]

A musket ball had sliced through Menchaca's neck, taking down the leading Tejano rebel, and he was carried from the field. The troops which broke into retreat were certainly not the whole army, not even all of the Mexican rebels since Delgado's company continued their fight. They did not retreat far in any event, though observers in the chaos could easily have perceived it as such. At this point, an effort to rally them was made by Henry Adams Bullard, the republic's secretary of state. The idealist who had dreamed of revolution at Harvard was now experiencing it in all its brutal, bloody reality. The Spanish-speaking Anglo, who was probably on horseback beside Toledo, seems to have raced forward, rallied some of Menchaca's cavalrymen and attempted a left flanking maneuver to get behind the Spanish rear. Meanwhile, Kempers' men on the right flank, under Josiah Taylor, fought on amid the storm. As they had in all previous engagements, American sharpshooters targeted the Spanish artillerists and, killing these, silenced the guns. Kemper's men raced forward and seized a few of the cannon, amid a hail of fire from the Spanish infantry. Some of his men had finally brought up the republican's own guns, placing them within fifty yards of the Spanish lines. The battle, so hotly fought, seemed as if it might turn the republicans' way after all. Beltrán writes:[17] "The battleground became a veritable inferno. The loose, sandy soil had been reduced to an impalpable powder; the cloud of dust and the smoke of burned powder formed a dense mantle made lurid by the glare of flaming guns. But there was no wavering. In all that American host there was not a coward. They were the sons of Revolutionary sires; they were the bravest of the brave, and with them it was not hard to die."[18]

On the flank, the Mexican troops under Bullard plunged back into the fray but were beaten back with heavy loss. Still, this absorbed significant Spanish resources, even as the center of the Spanish line was pressed in the hardest fighting of the day. The fury of the republican assault against what should have been a perfect ambush unsettled General Arredondo, who had fought so many battles in Europe and America but had never been pressed so closely. Amid the chaos and smoke blinding him to the battlefield, the sudden silencing of his big guns was ominous, as were Bullard's movements on his right. Arredondo knew that if his flank was turned, only Elizondo and Zambrano's troops would be between the rebels and his rear. These had done nothing but flee all morning. The general, who was as clueless of the enemy strength as they were of his, feared that his ambush position could easily become encircled itself.[19]

At this crucial point, the destiny of Texas—and of all Mexico—was a turn away from several widely diverging roads. The nature of warfare in Texas in 1812–13 precluded a draw, as Rosillo and Alazán had shown. The army which broke first would be destroyed. If Arredondo won, the revolution in the north would be crushed. If the republicans could somehow steal a victory, the only competent royal commander and the only effective army in nearly all of northern Mexico would be annihilated. As one account put it, "in Monterrey and Monclova they were anxiously waiting for our army to shake off the yoke, while in Saltillo they were already preparing to receive us." Nuevo Santander, Coahuila, Tamaulipas, and a handful of other provinces would be opened to the rebels.[20]

The republicans, blistered by the hot August sun, exhausted by the running fight through the sandy soil which gave way at each step, and parched to madness for lack of water, had somehow, despite everything, come to the verge of a miracle. They had attacked into the teeth of the Spanish defenses, despite having "not fifty bayonets" in their army. Arredondo's concern was so real that he was beginning to pack up his mules for a retreat. This would have been a disaster greater than Alazán: Would his militiamen withdraw without panic? Abandoned by their general, would the *cobarde* of Elizondo's division stand and fight?

But at this very moment, two events intervened to turn the tide. The first was the arrival before Arredondo of a lone man on a horse. Col. Miguel Musquíz was the same officer who had served as the rebel's chief of the march down from San Antonio. Like many of the rebels, he was a former Spanish officer who had fought under Salcedo; he had even served in Zambrano's junta. He had joined the rebel army in San Antonio but, like many in the rebel forces, had been compelled to join—*after* the royalists had been executed. He was probably always a royalist at heart, and at this moment, he defected back to the king's army. The vital news he brought to Arredondo was that the rebels were exhausted and fainting for lack of water. Arredondo, so preoccupied with his own crisis, had not realized that his enemy's was even worse. The Spanish general regained his spirits:[21] "I ordered the music to start up and my drummer to beat the reveille. This had such an effect on my troops and reanimated them so much that it seemed as if they were going to advance. Confusion now seized upon the enemy; and they began to abandon their artillery. I therefore, ordered a detachment to advance on the right to seize it. The commander of the infantry, Don Antonio Elosua, advanced on the left with another detachment for the same purpose."[22]

Bravery on this day was not limited to the rebels. A Spanish lieutenant, Antonio Zárate, distinguished himself in this charge. Despite being wounded in his right thigh, he led his men forward. Arredondo would promote him on the battlefield to captain. Francisco de la Hoz, wounded in his left thigh, continued on foot and led his men, refusing all the while his superior's offer to evacuate him to the rear. Other Spanish officers stepped up, such as Col. Cayetano Quintero, the captain of the Nuevo Santander provincial cavalry. Don Cristóbal Domínguez, the old Nacogdoches commandant arrested during the Casas revolt, who had led one of the contingents at La Bahía, served as Arredondo's eyes and ears on the battlefield, maintaining order among the troops and transmitting his commands. Even the old republican nemesis, the blond-haired brawler, Col. Juan Manuel Zambrano was wounded in the action with a ball from an American or Mexican musket breaking his left arm. Bravery extended to common soldados too. "The valor, calmness, and intrepidity with which the troop fought is inexpressible, reaching its highest point in the infantry," Arredondo would recall. "Some of them, even when wounded by bullets, did not wish to leave the ranks; and, in fact, did not do so, until so weak from the loss of blood that they fell. Others, having as many as two bullet wounds, continued until they received another." Under such renewed and spirited officers and men, the royalists regained the momentum of the battle, pushed forward, and took the guns.[23]

Around this time, too, the failure of Bullard's flanking maneuver became apparent, or it was pushed back by the same counterattack. Now came the second calamity for the republicans. Taylor, in command of the American right wing, was seriously wounded and fell back from the line. Deprived of their leader, his men, like Menchaca's before them, were compelled to give way. It was the breaking point. Joseph Wilkinson, the young son of the American general, would later recall, "At this period, we had gained on the enemy and had taken one or two pieces more of their artillery and were fighting them on the ground they at first occupied—fifteen minutes more would have given victory entirely to our hands." It was not to be. The republican forces had penetrated far into the royalist lines, but their numbers were thin and the Spanish reserves tired but deep. The attacking rebels had been fighting for nearly four hours—including charging up gently sloping hills through sandy soil. Bodies, if not courage, had reached their limits. Soon, the wave at last crested, ebbed, and flowed back out, just as it had come in. The Republican Army of the North was retreating en masse, pressed by Spanish muskets, swords, and bayonets. Kemper, seeing the line collapsing, reportedly cried out in final despair, "Boys, save yourselves!"[24]

Beltrán had been fighting under Menchaca's command as part of the small republican cavalry. Shortly after the "gallant" Menchaca had fallen wounded, his own horse was shot from under him. "Just as I recovered my feet, a ball pierced my hip, inflicting a painful wound, but fortunately breaking no bones," he wrote decades later. "I had scarcely felt the sting of this wound before a glancing shot struck me just above the forehead, and I fell unconscious." He was awakened and helped back up by Lt. Pablo Rodríguez and Adolfo Pérez. They were slightly wounded but carried him to the rear. At the Medina River, the rebels washed and dressed the wounds as best they could, but the battle was pressing hard on them. Scarcely had Beltrán's bandages been placed on his hip wound, he recalled, when "someone dashed down the bank to where many of our wounded lay and announced the complete rout of the army." The messenger shouted that Captain Wilkinson had rallied a small force to cover the retreat, but the Spanish had cut the men to pieces.[25]

The lack of rebel horses contributed to the cataclysm, particularly among the foot-bound Anglo-Americans. Many of them had sold their horses to the Indians for mules (valuable back home, but useless in battle), at two for one. The Spanish cavalry pursued these fleeing men, slashing with their swords "in the small of their backs as far as the other side of the Medina." It was Alazán in reverse, and as at that battle, those killed in the rout almost certainly dwarfed the number killed in the battle itself.[26]

The royalist army proceeded to the Medina River crossing of the Camino Real. Here Antonio Menchaca claimed Arredondo shot 250 fleeing rebels. These included prisoners as well. Beltrán would later write that almost all of these were merely the wounded who had been unable to flee. José Antonio Navarro would recall an even more horrible fate, as he later related to Mirabeau Lamar. "Mr. Navarro tells me that nearly four hundred Americans and an equal number of Mexicans taken in that fight were hung up by the heels [in the trees] and perished that way."[27]

As for the remainder, the bloodied, exhausted, and parched men who escaped destruction struggled through the sandy soil, likely seeking refuge in the wooded areas near the Medina River. Some men bashed their rifles against trees so the enemy could not make them trophies. With scarcely a pause, they rolled back throughout the day towards San Antonio individually or in small groups. The valiant Miguel Menchaca was carried from the field by his men but died of his wounds and was buried on what later came to be called Seguín Road at a place called Menchaca Creek.[28]

The battle had lasted from three and a half to four hours, and the Spanish counted 950 cannon balls on the field at the end of the fight. The Royalists exulted in their triumph. Arredondo led his men in shouts of "Viva el Rey!" As the rebels fled back to San Antonio, the gachupín general paused on the battlefield, amid the carnage, and wrote out an urgent dispatch to the governor of Nuevo Santander. Arredondo informed him, "The ever victorious and invincible arms of our Sovereign, aided by the powerful hand of the god of war, have gained the most complete and decisive victory over the base and perfidious rabble commanded by certain vile assassins ridiculously styled a general and commanders."[29]

Arredondo claimed that with only a small force of "brave, intrepid and invincible soldiers," he had defeated 3,200 enemy troops "well-armed throughout, full of pride, well disciplined, and versed in military tactics." He would continue to exaggerate his success, at first claiming 600 enemies dead on the battlefield, along with "100 prisoners who are now being shot." He would later revise this number to 1,000, but the former number is more likely correct. This weighs against a claimed two dozen Spanish dead and 200 seriously wounded. The numbers are skewed in both directions. Arredondo's true losses were almost certainly in the hundreds, given the desperate fight; indeed, royalist officers told captured Americans their losses were 756, and confirmed that if the battle had lasted just a short time longer, the Spanish would have been defeated. The royalists also captured "seven cannons, wagons of muskets and carbine ammunition, much plain shot, grape, and lead, many firearms, banners, war chests and [a] medicine box."[30]

Arredondo in his final report cited several of his officers for their contributions on the battlefield, including two who would go on to serve as governors of Texas, Cristóbal Domínguez and Juan Ignacio Pérez, the latter being a close friend of the rebel Ruiz. He also praised some of his younger officers, including one destined to play a greater role in Texas history than even himself. "I recommend Lieutenant Don José María Hernández, *Don Antonio Santa Anna*, and Don Pedro Lemus who conducted themselves with great bravery" (emphasis added). Whatever else in his account may have been pride or exaggeration, Arredondo was absolutely right on the key fact: the Battle of Medina was the most complete and decisive victory not just of the campaign but for all of Texas history up to that date. The hard-fought battle was the apex of the war, but not the end of the killing. With the rebel army defeated and fleeing before him, the Spanish general turned his attention to San Antonio. The man who had pillaged Nuevo Santander had even worse in store for the capital of Texas.[31]

Blood across Texas

The brutality of Arredondo was on display from the first moment after the battle and never abated. In his biography of the general, historian Bradley Folsom refers to the reign that followed as "Caligula in Texas" and a more apt description of his subjugation of the province there could not be. In the aftermath of the battle, Arredondo sent Elizondo and his militia captain Cayetano Quintero, along with two hundred cavalrymen, to chase down and execute survivors. This they did ruthlessly, shooting and dismembering any they found, suspending body parts on pikes or tossing them into the branches of trees.[32]

The first news the people of San Antonio received of the battle was when a group of the republicans' Indian allies galloped through town on horseback. The Catholic priest, Father J. M. Rodríguez, recalled them shouting, in broken Spanish, "gachupino mucho, melicano nara." (Gachupínes much, Mexicans none). Panic ensued among the terrified populace. The next to arrive in San Antonio were the rebels on horseback, including the leaders like Toledo and Kemper. The Cuban confirmed news of the defeat, "throwing the city into a state of the wildest commotion." The arriving rebels did not tarry long, riding to the Alamo where they secured ammunition, powder, and fresh horses. Beltrán and his friends Rodríguez and Pérez had corralled riderless horses in the chaos at the Medina, and rode into the town late in the afternoon.[33] "When we reached the home of Señora Rodríguez, then situated a short distance southwest of the Military Plaza, we found that we had not a moment to lose. On all sides we were assailed by a wildly excited populace clamoring for news of the defeat and seeking advice as to what they should do. All we could say was that the day was lost, Elisondo was upon us and they must take care of themselves."[34]

In Beltrán's account, Señora Rodríguez' premonition of disaster had come true, and the woman, who had raised the young American almost as a mother, had prepared for the moment. She saddled two fresh horses for the boys along with food and water. "Be off at once," she begged Beltrán and Pablo Rodríguez. Knowing the Spanish would be hunting down refugees on the Nacogdoches road, she told them, "Do not think of following in the wake of the cowardly gachupín [Toledo]; go [west] to your friends, the Comanches." Beltrán and Rodríguez told her that they would not leave her and the children. "We will take you along and if the worst comes, we can but die together." But she would not hear it. She was too old for the journey and would place her faith in the Virgin Mary. Carlos and Pablo left her sadly and headed west. Just outside of town, they ran into a wounded Anglo-American, Abner Lane, who had been among Wilkinson's company. He joined them in their journey to the Comanches. As for their Tejano friend, Adolfo Pérez, at the last minute he parted with them, choosing to join another group of refugees heading up the main road. It was a fatal mistake, for he would be captured and executed.[35]

Only around two hundred of the approximately six to eight hundred Anglos engaged in the battle survived. Notably, many of those who were on horseback, including officers like Kemper, Perry, Bullard, and Taylor, as well as scouts like McFarlan, escaped the battlefield. The rank-and-file foot soldiers suffered in far greater proportions, but once clear of the immediate battlefield, their chances of escape were fair. In fleeing, the Anglos (mostly single men, with the occasional servant) were relatively unburdened. Mexican rebels, on the other hand, had wives, children, and parents to take with them in their flight. Their nightmare was just beginning.[36]

The misery and confusion in San Antonio were extreme. Rebels gathered up their families, their friends' families, even strangers, and hastily set out, taking only what they could carry and leaving everything else behind. Sixty-seven-year-old rebel Joaquín Leal and his wife Ana María gathered up their four sons and three daughters and left San Antonio in panic in the late afternoon. The Leals were from an Isleño family long suspected by the Spaniards. An Antonio Leal, possibly an uncle, had been a close friend and likely associate of Philip Nolan. In their flight, all the food they carried with them was a sack of corn from their fields. "They walked twelve days through the deserts and fields, with Jesus' name on their lips, stunned and terrified [by the catastrophe], and ever fearful that their enemies might descend upon them at any moment."[37]

The scene was far more panicked than the famous *Runaway Scrape* of the 1836 revolution. For all his brutality on the battlefield, Santa Anna did not kill women or terrorize children. Arredondo—and the vengeful Elizondo—did not have such scruples. They had killed and brutalized the defenseless before and would do so again in Texas. The Spanish general's infamy and Elizondo's threats before Alazán had preceded them, so among the terror-stricken fugitives on the Camino Real in August 1813, all knew what lay in store.[38]

Among those who fled were any Tejanos with a connection to the rebellion, which included many members of the most prominent families in the city, including the Leals, noted previously, the Arochas, Delgados, Traviesos, and others. As these civic leaders fled and chaos reigned, vigilante mobs of either loyalists or turncoat rebels (seeking to ingratiate themselves to the conquerors) turned on their neighbors. Some of the citizens reportedly captured fifty Anglo-Americans, turning them over to the Spaniards, although these were probably the sick and wounded in the army's hospital, likely including the rebel doctor Orramel Johnston. Their fates would be hard—but nowhere near as horrible as those of the natives.³⁹

La Noche Triste

Lieutenant Colonel Elizondo arrived in San Antonio, according to Beltrán, only an hour after the latter had fled it. The Spanish officer secured the town, executed some prisoners, and awaited Arredondo, who arrived with the bulk of the army in the afternoon of the next day. Using his commission to treat the city as a conquered province, Arredondo either granted his men license, or they took it on their own, knowing he would not object.⁴⁰

> Homes were invaded, and where resistance was offered, the defenders were butchered on their own threshold in the presence of their horrified families, the women and even tender girls, mere children, were outraged and in numerous instances, cruelly murdered and their nude bodies dragged into the street. Upon entering these homes, the first demand was for mescal . . . the next was for dinero . . . throughout all the long hours of the night the air was rent with the exultant yells of a drunken soldiery, the wails of little children and the screams of outraged mothers and daughters, and for many years afterwards the people of San Antonio spoke of that awful night as "La Noche Triste"—the night of sorrow.⁴¹

Elizondo's men went from house to house, arresting seven hundred Mexicans—half the town's male population—and from eight to fifteen Americans. Some were concentrated in the central courtyard of the Alamo; others were packed to overcrowding into local Catholic priests' cells. Along with the men, women accused of conspiring with the rebels (or simply related to them) were locked up in a private residence confiscated for the purpose. The Spanish, in brutal sarcasm, called it *"la Quinta"*—the term for a country manor or retreat. The building, which had been the home of the Curbelo family, was a stone and adobe structure located on a dirt alley—today's Dwyer Avenue. Only about fifty feet long and single-story, it was spacious for a home, but now as a prison was filled to overflowing. Navarro claims that five hundred women, nearly half of those in the city, were incarcerated here, although this likely may have included a courtyard adjacent.⁴²

For these women, the *Quinta* was a hellhole: they were abused, harassed, and forced to grind corn to feed the Spanish soldiers until they collapsed from exhaustion. Antonio Menchaca recalled that the women thus forced into the grueling work were required to make thirty-five thousand tortillas each day, for fifty-four straight days from 2:00 a.m. until 10:00 p.m. It was work traditionally done by the poor, and many of the "distinguished ladies in the society" of San Antonio had never done it before, tearing their delicate hands shucking the corn. Others then cooked it to make hominy. Still others hulled it with their feet while it was still hot, "until their feet and legs were raw and their toenails fell out," according to one anonymous Tejano account. One woman, named Crisanta, died at this task.[43]

Rape was used as a weapon here too. Two prisoners in *la Quinta* were Juana Leal de Tarín and her sister Concepción Leal de Garza. Juana was the sister of Vicente Tarín, a Spanish officer who had deserted to the rebels. Both women were raped by the guards. Beltrán records that his adoptive mother, Señora Rodríguez, along with her daughter, were imprisoned there and were "victims of Spanish persecution." He does not mention rape, though he may have been delicate in this case because the daughter would one day become his own wife. Navarro describes the struggle of these women and others as heroic, enduring their trial "with fortitude truly masculine" as they struggled against the "nefarious proposals of their jailers."[44]

The leader of these, a man named Acosta, was particularly brutal. In the account of the anonymous Tejano (likely Navarro), he whipped them repeatedly, resorted "to the grossest, indecent, ugly and impure words and deeds, which I cannot even bear to write on the page." Lamar, who described Acosta as a Moor, said he was "a most disgusting, audacious monster. In a state of nudity [he would] exhibit himself before the women and invite them to a comparison between himself and the whites, or Americans." Another source claims Arredondo would pick women from the prison to give to his officers. When the women tried to resist by locking arms each night to prevent one of their number being snatched, the Spanish seized the leader, tied her to a ladder atop *la Quinta*, and stripped her over the course of an hour before all the public of San Antonio.[45]

The children were not spared the misery. Initially, they appear to have been sent to the *Quinta* with their mothers, where they "cried day and night from hunger." Nursing mothers were denied a pause to feed their children, and one baby died in the hellhole. Eventually, Acosta separated the children from their mothers and ordered them out. "This measure nearly destroyed the spirits of our women and tore out their heartstrings," the anonymous Tejano wrote. "They rent their garments and went half-mad." The best they could advise their sobbing children was to beg in the street for food.[46]

These abandoned, half-starved waifs had seen their parents killed, brutalized, and arrested, and they would never forget it. One of them was five-year-old José María Carvajal, whose mother Gertrudis had been imprisoned in *la Quinta*. She and other mothers would, in between the beatings and the rapes, listen to the cries of their children calling for them from the streets, where they wandered pitifully. The young Carvajal would long remember the misery and would one day become one of the leading reformist politicians of the new Mexican Republic.[47]

Another child who endured the brutal night and the months that followed was thirteen-year-old Antonio Menchaca, who would later fight in the second Texas revolution. Antonio was not closely related to Miguel Menchaca, and his own father, Juan Mariano Menchaca had not taken part in the rebellion. Nonetheless, the father was accused of "some trifling thing," arrested in the middle of the night and dragged to a prison while his wife was sent to *la Quinta*. The young Antonio, who had befriended the former commander of Nacogdoches, Cristóbal Domínguez, now ran to this officer and sought to rouse him. Domínguez woke and told the boy to go away, but Antonio insisted, begging for the life of his father. "The officer finally relented and stepping out, he spoke to the men who had charge of [my] father, made them turn him loose," Antonio Menchaca recalled. "[I] then asked him to please have [my] mother liberated; he gave him an order for her release, which he took to the officer in command of the '*Quinta*' and got her released too."[48]

But such clemency was rare, and Arredondo's justice was swift. The general set up a military tribunal to determine the guilt or innocence of his prisoners. To be found guilty, it was not necessary to have participated in the rebellion, but merely to have *failed to oppose it*, and "the most trivial accusation that they were in favor of Mexican Independence" was good enough for guilt. The first to be judged were those who were taken in arms, and in this case the trial was merely a formality of being brought before Arredondo, pronounced guilty and then shot, so that "intermittent volleys of musketry on Military Plaza, proclaimed to the terrified inhabitants the revengeful policy of the triumphant Gachupín."[49]

When dusk brought an end to the first day's shootings, Arredondo ordered a group of three hundred known revolutionaries transferred from the Alamo courtyard to a granary off Main Plaza. Young Antonio Menchaca later recalled that a number of men were also taken from the San Fernando Church, which "was filled with poor men praying that their lives should be spared them." They too were placed in the makeshift prison, which belonged to rebel leader Francisco Arocha. This structure, which was twenty feet by forty, with twenty-foot-high walls and made of adobe, had been specifically built to be nearly perfectly airless, to keep vermin from the grain typically stored there. Arredondo's men crowded the prisoners into the standing-room-only space and locked the doors for the blistering August night. The prisoners, deprived of water and overcome by the suffocating conditions, fought among themselves for mere proximity to the small openings through which air could enter. When the doors were open the next day, eighteen of them had died. More than half of those who survived had to be carried out. Revived with fresh air and water, they were brought to Arredondo to be tried.[50]

Arredondo then ordered an officer in his army and a San Antonio native, Juan Ignacio Pérez, to name two residents to "call out such persons as were deserving of death" and also to name those they recommended to be put to hard labor. Pérez named Luis Galán and Francisco Manuel Salinas as the designated judges. Salinas, sixty and a second-generation resident, knew everyone in town, as probably also did Galán. Yet both men brazenly told Arredondo they knew of no one deserving of either punishment. "Upon hearing this, Arredondo selected forty which should be put to death, and the balance, 160, were handcuffed in pairs and sent to work upon the streets. Of the forty who were selected to die, every third day they would shoot three, opposite the Plaza House, until the entire number were disposed of." Those in the forced labor gangs were subjected to sadistic treatment. Antonio Menchaca recalled an event consistent with Arredondo's "practical joke" he had played against rebels in Nuevo Santander:[51]

> Breakfast was given them in this manner: [Spanish officer Francisco] Rívas stood in the door of the calaboose when the prisoners went out to work and asked those who came first whether they had breakfast. They answer "No Señor," and he gave them a sound beating in order that they might breakfast: when he asked those who came afterwards if they had . . . breakfast, they replied yes, fearful that he would give them a beating, and he said to them "well in order that the breakfast may agree [with you]," and he gave them another sound beating like the rest.[52]

The executions continued until the first of September, and Spanish forces scoured the countryside for more rebels. Because property of rebels was confiscated and given over to royalists—Arredondo's officers among them—there were no doubt a surplus of republicans found to meet the demand. Those captured outside of the city were brought into San Antonio, "the women sent to the '*Quinta*', the children turned upon the street to starve, and the men delivered into the hands of the executioner."[53]

Elizondo's Pursuit

Nor had Arredondo forgotten about the many refugees who had fled toward Nacogdoches. He detached Elizondo and his cavalry to ride after them as soon as he could spare the men. It was a mission that the junior officer relished, so humiliated as he had been by these same rebels at Alazán. He took with him five hundred men and pursued rapidly, reaching the Colorado River in three days—an average of thirty miles a day. There he left half his troops and the most tired horses to follow up at a slower pace and pushed on with his best horses. Two days later, shortly after dawn, he caught up with the first of the rebels: seven Anglo-American men and one Mexican. They bolted into the woods at the sight of the Spaniards, but he caught three of them.[54]

At 10:00 a.m. the same day, Elizondo arrived at the Brazos River and spied a small group of rebels on the opposite side. The wide river, however, prevented him from crossing. Elizondo chose to use deception to capture his prey, offering them a pardon if they would cross over the river and turn themselves in. While he negotiated, a small group of his men, stripped down and mounted bareback on horses, crossed some distance away, circled around, and captured seven men, six women, and three boys. Only one escaped. Elizondo promptly ordered four of the rebels executed, despite the offer of a pardon only moments before. The story is from Elizondo's own account—the officer gleefully reporting the murderous trick with his own pen. Antonio Menchaca, however, gives additional detail. The Spanish captured a number of rebels on the near side of the river and told them they would merely be returned to San Antonio and would be "charitably treated." He then asked for a recruit to take a message to those on the other side.[55]

> One of the men of those who had not crossed over agreed to go over and take the letter; in which was guaranteed to them, in the most sacred terms, a full and complete pardon if they would but give themselves up. He went; the letter was presented, and after considerable debate, the terms being so moderate and couched in such plausible language, they concluded to come over and give themselves up. They did, the Spaniards taking the precaution to tie their hands as they crossed over. All of them crossed that same evening, slept tied and next day were unmercifully slaughtered.[56]

Elizondo continued his brutal chase, leaving men and exhausted horses along the way. Even this pace was not enough, so he sent forty-five men led by 2nd Lt. Fernando Rodríguez and Tomas Saucedo racing on ahead to Trinidad. These reached the Trinity River but could not cross because it too was at flood stage. But they learned that many rebels—including Toledo himself—were in the town of Trinidad on the opposite bank. Rodríguez and Saucedo returned to join up with Elizondo, bringing their intelligence.[57]

On the way back, they stumbled into a prime catch: the rebel Capt. Antonio Delgado. It had been Delgado who had seen his father's head displayed as a gruesome trophy when the rebels entered San Antonio, and who had taken out his revenge by executing Salcedo, Herrera, and the other royalist leaders. After the defeat at Medina, he had raced to San Antonio and collected his entire family before fleeing. They had met up on the trail with others, including the same Joaquín Leal who had fled with his family and a sack of corn. The Spanish caught them two leagues (about five miles) short of Trinidad. Lieutenant Rodríguez called out, "Halt, rebels, traitors to your King! Halt or I will kill you all!"[58]

Fourteen soldiers surrounded the small group of men, women, and children, "like ravenous wolves hungry for the kill," as the anonymous Tejano account recalled. They shot Delgado down in front of his horrified mother. The account continued:[59]

> The Royalists showed no mercy even then, throwing off Delgado's wailing mother and spearing [his] corpse, despite his mother's pleas to let him live, or at the very least, to let him confess his sins! [Lieutenant Rodriguez] responded indignantly: "He can confess himself to the Devil. He and the

rest of you are all damned already!" Enraged, he flipped his lance around and began to beat [Angela Arocha de] Delgado over her pious screams. Once and for all they ripped her away from her son's corpse, stripped it, and left it for the wild animals.[60]

When these captives were brought before Elizondo and he was told who they were, he responded, "They all deserve death!" Despite their pleas for mercy, he ordered them taken away. The Tejano account recalled that three of the women in the party, Angela Arocha Delgado's daughters, Candida and María Joséfa, and their sister-in-law, Antonia Rodriguez, only escaped by leaping into the Trinity River and swimming to safety, with Candida struggling against the current while clutching her young niece.[61]

The women still in captivity were not killed, but there was no mercy for their sons and brothers, brought before a firing squad in front of them. One woman collapsed as her daughter rushed to her side, holding an image of the Black Christ of Esquipulas, a revered Central American Catholic icon, "pleading through her tears for consolation and strength for her anguished mother." The women cried through the night and in the morning found that animals had commenced eating the corpses of their family members. When they begged Elizondo to allow them to bury them, he refused.[62]

On August 26th, Elizondo was camped at the junction of the La Bahía road, which many rebels were using. He ordered forty men to cross the Trinity on cowhides at a narrow spot at William Barr's old ranch, with the intention of cutting off the rebels should they attempt to escape to Nacogdoches. Here they were thwarted, as the republicans had set an outpost manned by friendly Jaraname Indians. These fired on the Spanish while they tried to ford the river, forcing their retreat. Elizondo was able to cross the next day with a larger force. Many of the rebels, including Toledo, Kemper, Perry, as well as some prominent Tejanos, had escaped to Nacogdoches during the night, but many others were captured in the town.[63]

Hearing rumors that the former president of Gutiérrez's Béxar Junta, Francisco Arocha, fleeing with his family, was at one crossing known as "el Salto," Elizondo dispatched 2nd Lt. Manuel Chapa to the spot. Arocha's brother Tomás, also a member of the junta, had already been captured, and now the battle-wounded Francisco was brought in as well. The scene at this crossing was chaotic, and Chapa and his men were actually outnumbered by the refugees they were trying to detain. As the royalists apprehended some rebels, "others escaped in the confusion caused by the crowds."[64]

Chapa later captured "a platoon of rebels" at one ranch, who shouted at him that they would die rather than surrender. Once again, the Spaniards implemented a ruse to stall for time. As Elizondo reported, "[Chapa], forced by the inadequate size of his troop, most of whom were occupied in guarding prisoners, tried to keep the rebels distracted with conversation, while he signaled me for assistance, without the enemy's notice, and I immediately sent him 20 men." The royalists captured twenty-one men, fourteen women, and seventeen children, along with twenty-three rifles and forty horses and mules. One rebel whom the Spanish missed was José María Guadiana, who had been gravely wounded in the battle and fled north in the company of his nephew, "a mere lad," who hid him away from the Spanish patrols. Guadiana finally died of his wounds, and the young boy buried him.[65]

In possession of the important strategic point of Trinidad, Elizondo over the next week began catching more and more rebels, who may have traveled a number of side roads and cow paths, but who all had to come through the town to ford the flood-swollen river. At its banks they had to pause, search for crossings, then effect them. Elizondo perched in the town like a spider and spread out his web. Not a day passed without his gathering up rebels singly or in groups. Eyewitness accounts claim that at one hill called "Loma de Toro" west of the river, the royalists dug a large pit, over which they placed logs. The prisoners were forced to stand on the logs and were shot, falling into what would become their grave. Elizondo reported to Arredondo on September 2nd:[66] "To date I have ordered the execution of 27 soldiers, including 2 sergeants and four corporals, 2 insurgent captains, and other officers of the ringleaders; 31 [civilians], including several ringleaders; among all these, some that executed the worthy leaders of Texas. I have spared the life of 17 soldiers and 19 countrymen until they are brought before your excellency. In addition, I have gathered a large number of women, boys and girls."[67]

The total killed in his account is 58, but rebel sources place it much higher. Antonio Menchaca recorded the whole number of those killed as 279, though he may have confused rebels killed in the capital. The royalist officer captured Anglo Americans as well, and 29 of them were taken prisoner to San Antonio, including at least one noncombatant, Richard Cage, a trader from the Natchez area who was at La Bahía at the time of the battle and had fled at the first news. But others were released by Elizondo, on orders from his general.[68]

Although some of these Anglo-Americans like Kemper and Perry were subject to a standing order of execution by Arredondo, the royalist general had made a political decision to spare the lives of the rest. Killing Americans in arms against Spain in battle had been defensible. Massacring citizens of a foreign power close to that nation's border was more politically charged. Spain had enough problems without provoking the United States to declare war. Elizondo therefore took efforts to conceal his barbarities from American eyes, and as political theater, it was a masterstroke. Based solely on American testimony, the *Daily National Intelligencer* would say of the cruel Elizondo, "Too much praise cannot be bestowed on this meritorious officer, who is alike distinguished for his courage & humanity. In no instance did he exercise the least cruelty toward those whom the fortune of war had placed in his power." The paper admitted that "some executions" had taken place at the Trinity, but callously added that "they were of such a character as can attach no blame to the conqueror."[69]

So, on the banks of the Trinity River, a cruel selection of sorts was made of the rebels. To one side were sent most Anglo Americans, with one rifle for every ten men to defend themselves against Indian attacks. To the other were sent the Tejanos and their families, to death or brutality. What became of any mixed couples of Anglo men and Tejano women is unrecorded. The killings continued, with Elizondo focusing on prominent individuals from San Antonio known to have been ringleaders. Although many ordinary refugees were spared, this was only a temporary reprieve: They were to be brought back to San Antonio for trial. For those who faced Spanish justice on the Trinity, mercy was in short supply. With the royalist detachment was a priest, Padre José Manuel Camacho, who had served in San Antonio since 1809. When asked by the prisoners to give them last rites, Camacho, who had been wounded in the thigh at the Battle of Medina, replied, "You may have been the one who shot me, and if so, may the Lord have mercy on you." In one account, the priest violated his sacred oath and actually participated in the massacre of the prisoners.[70]

The flight had many other tragic stories, but also moments of camaraderie born amid terrible circumstances. One of the Anglo-Americans fleeing the fight was the twenty-year-old Henry William Munson, who had been born and raised in Bayou Sara, Spanish West Florida. He was likely connected to the town's famous residents, the Kemper brothers, his family members having participated in the 1810 West Florida revolt. At the Battle of Medina, Munson was seriously wounded and struggled to make his way along the Camino Real. He found a life-saving friend in a fellow rebel, Don Santiago Mordella, who helped the young man all the way to Louisiana. Munson would never forget Mordella's aid, and would ultimately name his son *Mordello* Stephen Munson in honor of the man who had saved his life. Ultimately, sixteen descendants of the family would bear the name Mordello, as late as the twentieth century.[71]

Vengeance, Murder, and Insanity

The Spanish colonel advanced on Nacogdoches, which he found empty except for three remaining loyalist families. Pushed by Elizondo's brutal pace, Toledo and all remaining rebels gave up their intention to stand at the town and fled Texas for Louisiana. The loyalists were ordered back to San Antonio and the town on the edge of the Spanish Empire, long a burden on Spanish imperial policy, was to be abandoned. Elizondo now turned back, his captives—many of them women—in tow. The anonymous account recalled, "Those lovely ladies, enriched with exquisite forms and sparkling black eyes, tethered together, were compelled to traverse the whole distance on foot."[72]

In his tent on his return trip, Elizondo and his officers no doubt felt satisfied with their week's work. What pitiful few rebels had escaped their grasp would hardly be enough to restart the revolution in Texas anytime soon. Elizondo had finally gained the success he desired, and the promotion he had always coveted. His soldiers who had fled the battle of Alazán, whom Arredondo had stripped of their ranks, had regained their honor and could throw away the armband of the *cobarde*. Elizondo's redemption, however, had come at a price. The slaughter of the last few days had been cruelty on a level usually reserved for savage Indian enemies of Spain. But these dead, though rebels, were the Spanish *soldados*' own countrymen. For one officer, at least, it was too much.

Capt. Miguel Serrano of the Third Mobile Company of Nuevo Santander had been the Spanish commander of the small garrison at Atascocita, where he had guarded against smuggling and the illegal entry of foreigners along the coastal road from Louisiana. Now, on September 12, 1813, this royal officer, either appalled by the slaughter of so many civilians, or possibly suspecting that he might be next, crept into Elizondo's tent to confront him. In the entry, he killed Capt. Isidrio de la Garza, an Elizondo relative who had sided with Gutiérrez and signed the Declaration of Independence before reverting to the loyalist cause. According to Elizondo's version, Serrano killed de la Garza in his sleep, but other accounts suggested the latter was killed trying to stop the enraged officer. Serrano then attacked Elizondo, and "with his saber he wounded one hand and stabbed me seriously on the right side." Elizondo survived to write Arredondo this account of the attack, but in the dusty, unhealthy conditions of the march, the wound festered. The end came ten days later, on the banks of the San Marcos River. Ignacio Elizondo, who had betrayed and captured Hidalgo, then left a bloody trail of hundreds of his countrymen up and down the Camino Real, died along that same road. As for Serrano, Menchaca records, "They tied him and brought him to San Antonio, a raving maniac."[73]

For the prisoners, however, there was no respite. According to the anonymous Tejano source, the militia colonel Quintero assumed command, and one day forced 114 women to remain on their feet all morning during an inspection. Before arriving in San Antonio, Quintero decided to confiscate all papers and money from the prisoners. After searching the men, the Spanish soldiers "made the women get down from their mounts so that they might endure the same examination in compliance with the orders of Vizier Quintero. So well and fully did they carry out their duty that not a single breast from even the most modest, decent maiden was left untouched in this perverted exercise."[74]

Driven on mercilessly, the Tejano men were deprived of their shoes and bound as they marched. Their leaders, Tomás Arocha, Fernando Veramendi, and Clemente Delgado "led by example, despite their diminished state, and half-dead from thirst, hunger, and fatigue." Quintero arrived on the outskirts of the city in the evening, but seeking to curry favor with his commander, delayed his arrival until 10:00 a.m. so he would have suitable lighting for his triumph.[75]

CHAPTER 21

Blood, Courage, and Taunts in San Antonio

If Arredondo's massacres had slackened, it was only because he was running out of rebels to kill. But when Quintero's troops arrived with their dead commander and more than one hundred freshly captured insurgents, the Spanish general decided it was time for one final act of punishment to bring the rebellion to a bloody close. It would not only be public, it would be a spectacle. Two files of soldiers led the captives between them into Military Plaza, where over a thousand people, including most of the population of the town, were gathered—or more likely ordered to gather.

The women were marched between the troops of Arredondo. According to the unknown Tejano, some of the women of the town had at some point taken up arms against the Spaniards, who now taunted them: "Aw, look how bashful the ladies are now! Where was that modesty when they were firing pistols at us?" The women could do nothing but fight back tears, staring at the ground, "denying the tyrants around them the pleasure of seeing them suffer."[76]

General Arredondo, who had mocked—even toyed with—prisoners in Nuevo Santander, was in a delightful mood now. He strutted about in his full uniform, carrying a staff. He had heard of the rebel's "One-eyed Arredondo" song and now sang it himself to the captured rebels gathered before him. "Ah, but look how the sheep have become lions," Arredondo said as he concluded. "Mirenme bien! [look at me] What do you think of me now? Am I one-eyed?"[77]

He then ordered the execution of the whole mass of rebels, which was conducted immediately. Then he turned to the shocked residents of Béxar. Joaquín de Arredondo had, in the last few weeks, killed or driven into exile between one quarter and one-third of the population of Texas. Hundreds of women standing before him were widows on his orders and victims of rape as well. He knew that he was not loved and had heard the rumors. One of them had claimed that when Arredondo was dead, she would make his stomach into a drum, and do *worse* with other parts of him, offering a $500 reward for his private parts. Now he addressed this proposal. "Whereabouts here is the woman who said she was going to eat my *huevos* [balls] roasted?" he shouted. He waited for a moment, then added, "They would do her more good raw!"[78]

No doubt a few Spanish soldiers joined him in laughter at the joke, but to the astonishment of all, a woman stepped forward to take the credit. It was Joséfa Nuñes de Arocha, descended from one of the oldest San Antonio families, which had been at the core of the revolt. She was the wife of the rebel junta leader Francisco Arocha, sister-in-law of member Tomás Arocha and relative of the Delgados—Manuel and Antonio—who had been killed by Salcedo and Elizondo respectively. She had borne seven children in Béxar. Her daughter, a fire-breathing rebel like her, had offered a five hundred–dollar reward for *her own newlywed husband* after he had defected to the royal side. Joséfa Nuñes de Arocha had seen so much suffering, but she herself was unbowed. Stepping out to the shocked eyes of the entire town gathered around her, she boldly admitted to Arredondo that it was she who had made the infamous insult against him.[79]

The general, perhaps stunned that a woman with almost no living male relatives left to protect her would admit it to his face, simply asked if it were true that she had planned to make a drum out of his skin. "Yes," she replied defiantly, "and I would have made it, had I got it." She supposedly demanded to be shot like the rebel men, but Arredondo turned to his troops and asked, "What should we do with these she-rebels?" The general answered his own question, "A la Quinta! A la Quinta! To grind hot corn for the troops of the King!"[80]

In San Antonio, the deaths went on. A man named Montes—possibly Francisco Montes de Oca—had his head placed on a pole in San Antonio. Vicente Travieso, the half brother of the leader of the Casas revolt, who was himself involved in the Zambrano coup, before finally serving as an ally of Gutiérrez, was also executed. The royalists, a note compiled years later recorded, "hung him, cut his head off & threw his body away." Many of these, and those who had fled before Elizondo's brutal sweep to the Trinity, were the cream of San Antonio society. It was a giant wound slashed into the heart of the town—and of the province. Texas would never be the same again.[81]

22

Rebels Never Quit

THE FIRST RUMORS of the defeat at Medina reached Louisiana around September 1, 1813. Confirmation came three days later with the arrival of Joseph Wilkinson, who provided John Sibley and William Shaler with a firsthand account of the battle. Most of the surviving remnants of the Republican Army of the North crossed the Sabine and entered Natchitoches on September 7th, a year and a month to the day that they had crossed it the first time. They were soon followed by waves of refugees. Governor Claiborne reported:[1] "The defeat of the revolutionists near St. Antoine, and the entire ascendancy of the royalists in the Province of Texas, have thrown upon this frontier, many distressed Spanish families. I have not been enabled to ascertain their precise number, but it is believed, at least twelve hundred persons have crossed the Sabine, most of whom are wholly destitute of the comforts & the necessaries of life."[2]

One-third of the civilian population of Texas—all of Nacogdoches and Trinidad and many from San Antonio and La Bahía—had suddenly been thrown nearly penniless and hungry on the frontier of the United States. The anonymous Tejano account recalled, "Some walked, some rode, but all suffered innumerable struggles, anguishes and hardships, not to mention the loss of everything they owned: their houses, their farms, their livestock, and all other goods they could not pack with them."[3]

The Americans of the Louisiana parishes where the refugees arrived opened their doors to them without hesitation—these were the areas where support for the filibuster had been strongest. Among the rebels who made it across the border were Toledo and a number of Tejano leaders whose escape would ensure that the cause of liberty in Texas would not be snuffed out entirely. Among these was José Francisco Ruiz. He would remain in exile in Louisiana with his family for nine years, imbibe the American concept of liberty during his stay, and remain committed to it later in life. Another Tejano exile who would play a key role in the future of Texas was Ruiz's eighteen-year-old nephew, José Antonio Navarro. "Behold here a family scattered and persecuted [by] many disasters," he wrote in his memoirs. Navarro's family stayed, probably in Bayou Pierre, for over two years.[4]

About two hundred Anglo volunteers made it across the border, but far more had been left on the battlefield. Natchez, Natchitoches, and Rapides would be communities torn by grief, as so many of the filibusters had come from them, or had passed through on the way to the war. Among the despairing was Martin Allen, a member of the expedition who had been on a recruiting trip in Louisiana at the time of Medina. From the survivors, he learned that his father Benjamin, brother Hiram, and nephew David had all been killed. Benjamin Allen was one of two veterans of the American Revolution known to have died at Medina, the other being Peter Sides. There were other Americans who had missed the battle, including those who had left after the murder of the Spanish royalists, and wounded officers like James Gaines (struck by a musket at Rosillo) and the former rebel captain Thomas Luckett. The late Augustus Magee's two friends, the lawyer William Murray and his young apprentice Warren D. C. Hall also survived. Darlington Hall, possibly a relative of Warren, was wounded in the battle, survived for a time, then died. His brother, Jack W. Hall, was among the survivors. Three former commanders of the Republican Army of the North lived on. Samuel Kemper and Henry Perry, who had been in the thick of the fight at Medina, survived, as had Reuben Ross, who had abandoned the army in July at the urging of his Tejana girlfriend. Henry Adams Bullard, the Toledo deputy and last secretary of the fledgling Mexican state of Texas, escaped as well.[5]

The Americans did not know it yet, but a number of their compatriots had been captured by the Spanish and sent to Monterrey in irons. This included Captain Gormly, who fought so doggedly at La Bahía, and John Villars. It also included the Johnston brothers, the lawyer Darius, who had been appointed counsel to the royalists at their trial, and Orramel, who had sounded a warning about the expedition before joining it alongside his brother. They had signed up, in the words of a family history, "allured by the spirit of adventure and of republican propagandism," but ultimately "expiated their mistake by long imprisonment in Spanish dungeons and cruel treatment and came home wrecked in health." They would never be the same. At only thirty-two years old, Darius died of a lung disease—probably tuberculosis—while Orramel remained an invalid. He practiced medicine for a time, but like his brother, he too succumbed to his illnesses in 1826 at age thirty-seven. Some prisoners would be released more than a year later as part of a grant of amnesty in honor of the birthday of King Ferdinand, though some were held as late as 1819.[6]

As for William Shaler, the American agent who had longed for diplomatic success, he determined after the failure at Medina that the revolution in Mexico was doomed and returned to Washington, disappointed. He likely suspected he had lost favor after Monroe's strong reprimand for his proceeding to Texas in July 1813, but such was not the case. The secretary of state, who had not known Shaler before he took office, seems to have warmed to him, and the former New York sea captain was to his surprise appointed to assist the delegation sent to negotiate the Treaty of Ghent, concluding the War of 1812. It was a heady job, and he served alongside such giants as John Quincy Adams and Henry Clay. But in Europe, Shaler found himself frozen out of negotiations by Adams, who in his memoirs accused him of "certain indiscretions of vanity in him which showed he was not well qualified for such a mission, and might do more harm than good in it."[7]

Disappointed once again, he returned to Washington just as President Madison needed someone to serve as US minister to Algiers, where he finally found the success he craved, playing a key role in a peace mission to end the Second Barbary War. His book, "Sketches of Algiers," was credited as serving "materially to ensure the success of the French Expeditionary Force," which captured that North African country and turned it into a colony. In 1829, he returned to Cuba as US Consul in Havana, where he died in a cholera epidemic on March 29, 1833.[8]

Pardons and Bounties

In October 1813, Arredondo, convinced he had crushed the rebel army once and for all, began his efforts to rebuild Texas, and issued a pardon for ordinary rebels, "to prove to all the world that just as all the enemies of our beloved king, Don Ferdinand VII, are punished with sword in hand, so also is clemency extended" to those who ask forgiveness. He exempted seven native rebel leaders: Gutiérrez, Toledo, junta member Francisco Arocha, José Francisco Ruiz, Juan Martín Veramendi, Vicente Travieso (later captured and executed), and Pedro Prado. Each of these had a price on their head of 500 pesos. Also exempt were three foreigners, for whom a price of 240 pesos was announced, including the Indian trader Samuel Davenport and two Frenchmen who had been in the Spanish service before joining the rebels, Gutiérrez's facilitator Pedro Girard, and Bernard D'Ortolant, the Nacogdoches resident who had embraced the Frenchman D'Alvimar. They were "men ungrateful for the benefits the Spanish government has bestowed upon them, who abused the good faith under which they were admitted and who were recognized as vassals of the most pious and lovable Spanish monarch." Anyone capturing these men was to be paid the bounty, plus "additional recompense." If they were foreigners, they would also be given the right to settle in Texas and be rewarded with land.[9]

When the rebels were finally defeated at Medina, Erasmo Seguín, the postmaster who had been coerced by Shaler and Toledo into signing letters of support of the rebels, was still in Natchitoches. He bravely decided to return, even though he was still suspected of being a rebel. The charges, he told Arredondo, would be best refuted "simply by coming such a great distance when I learned that Your Lordship had triumphed over our enemies." Along the way, he learned that the Spanish had his letters in their possession, and he knew what that meant. "Death would not be as painful as it is to watch my children hungry and miserable," he wrote, and continued his journey. Indeed, his family had been reduced to indigence. The trial lasted over five years, but at last, Erasmo Seguin was found innocent, restoring his place in San

Antonio, and saving his family. Among them was his six-year-old son, Juan Seguín, who would go on to be the foremost native Texan leader in the 1836 revolution.[10]

For no one did expulsion from Texas hit harder than Samuel Davenport. He quickly relocated to Louisiana and would never return to Texas. Indeed, Nacogdoches was virtually a ghost town for years. In the long term, the loss to the Spaniards from their Indian Agent's absence was far more important than the fate of one man. As soon as he had exiled Davenport, Arredondo had written to request a qualified replacement. None was ever found, and the Indian menace would hasten the colony's decline. When Stephen F. Austin first arrived in eastern Texas in 1821, he called it "a howling wilderness." It had not always been so, but he and many later Anglo settlers, ignorant of the recent history, knew no better. New settlers would even claim these "empty" lands that had once been the ranches of Tejanos, causing conflict for decades.[11]

The Battle for the Legacy of the Republican Army

The defeat of the revolutionists at the Battle of Medina had been total, but there was surprising optimism for the cause. Those who had been there were convinced they had come within mere minutes of winning the day and thought Arredondo's losses to be much worse than they appeared. In December, several American prisoners from San Antonio had arrived in Natchitoches, released by Arredondo, possibly in a bid to ease tensions with the republic to the north. They had the opposite effect. The prisoners reported Arredondo only had about eight hundred men left in San Antonio—less than half the force with which he had defeated the Republicans. A letter passing this information on to Shaler (by now in Washington) noted, "The people of St. Antonio are continually looking for the Americans and the troops of the royalists [are] in continual fear from this (which I now believe to be the true cause of the release of the American prisoners)."[12]

Immediately after the defeat, the Béxar Junta set up a government-in-exile in Natchitoches, and on September 12, 1813, issued a proclamation confirming Toledo's continued leadership in the struggle: "We, the inhabitants of the State of Texas, solemnly gathered, to rid ourselves of the yoke of the European Spaniards, to recover and come into possession of our legitimate rights and also our lost property . . . have unanimously determined to give broad powers to Gen. Don José Álvarez de Toledo, to form a new expedition against the royal army, which robs, persecutes and murders us."[13]

Toledo's army still existed, but only on paper. The Cuban issued documents under the heading "República Mexicana" and signed them as the "generál en jefe del ejército republicano del norte de Mexico." Signing alongside him was Ruiz as the secretary of the Béxar Junta. In late 1813, Toledo traveled to Nashville, where he recruited to the cause John Smith T, the old Burr conspirator and likely sponsor of the Menchaca filibuster in 1811. Smith T now offered Toledo 500 men, with rifles and bayonets "of a new invention," forged by a number of Smith T's enslaved black mechanics. But Toledo and Smith T ran into a surprising obstacle. In December 1813, the Cuban received a letter with stunning portents from his former aide, Don Juan Mariano Picornell. This Spanish revolutionary, as we have seen, had been a key member of Toledo's staff dating back to his time in Philadelphia. Toledo had left him in Louisiana while the Cuban ventured to Tennessee, and now it appeared the old Spaniard who had suffered in the royalist dungeons, had taken over leadership of the rebel army in his absence. Worse still, Picornell was in league with Jean Joseph Amable Humbert, the same former French revolutionary general who had tried to coopt the filibuster the year before.[14]

With Toledo away from the scene, the council organized themselves into a government with Picornell as president and Ruiz and Pedro Procela as *vocales* (deputies) and Pedro Fuentes as secretary. Toledo fired back a response urging restraint and warned Picornell, "I know not what may be the effect of a manifesto by a body calling itself a government, published in the jurisdiction of another foreign government, but . . . it may be thought extravagant."[15]

Unfortunately, Toledo's note was too late to prevent the old Spaniard, now styling himself "President of the Provinces of Mexico" from traveling to New Orleans with Humbert, placing a presumptuous, premature manifesto into the local papers, and meeting with the French consul. Picornell's absurd marriage with the Munchausen-esque Humbert soon fell apart. In his letter, among other shocking revelations, Picornell claimed former Republican Army commanders Kemper and Perry were on board with his and Humbert's takeover. This was easily disproved by Kemper himself, who wrote that he had heard "not a word from any of our friends in Natchitoches."[16]

Picornell and Humbert's farce stumbled on to an inglorious death—indeed, that might have been the idea. In New Orleans, the pair had raised pledges of funding for their chimerical army, tying up resources that might otherwise have gone to Toledo. On January 6th, Picornell had issued his dramatic proclamation, which no doubt focused the attention of all friends of Mexico upon him. Then, just a month later, the *Moniteur de la Louisiane* of New Orleans carried the bombshell news that Picornell was abandoning the cause and taking a Spanish pardon. The collateral damage was a depression of revolutionary sentiment in New Orleans, a collapse of recruitment for the filibuster, and a drying up of funds for the enterprise. Since Picornell is known to have flirted with a pardon and even possibly spied for royalists in San Antonio in 1813, his dramatic reversal ten months later has the appearance of being intentional.[17]

For Toledo, making his way back to the frontier from Nashville in the company of John Smith T, these disasters were perhaps recoverable, provided he and his Missouri partner had time to act. He had plans to bring 900 men to the frontier and carried with him 1,500 blank Mexican commissions. But scarcely had they seen the last of Picornell and Humbert when Toledo faced a new threat from a completely unexpected source—former US Special Agent John Robinson.[18]

During his journey into Mexico on his Quixotic quest in the midst of a war, Robinson had been approached by rebels there, and had become a passionate advocate for the cause. Failing to interest the US government in a filibuster, he launched his own. In Natchez, he secured the support of General Adair. The latter remained deeply skeptical of Toledo from the Cogswell affair. At a public meeting on January 18, 1814, Adair's group, on its own assumed authority, passed a resolution appointing *Robinson* as the head of the revolution in Texas. Two rival factions were now fighting for the legacy of the Republican Army, and though neither was prepared to take on Arredondo, the race for legitimacy nonetheless pushed them back to Texas. Getting there first became the priority.[19]

Robinson made the first move. Toledo tried everything he could to delay the American, even challenging him to a duel, a tactic straight out of Smith T's playbook, but it failed. In late March or early April 1814, Robinson entered Texas. He had no choice. He claimed to have financial backing and 3,000 men ready to enlist, but he could not organize on the American side of the border. Now that Louisiana was a state with the Sabine as its lawful boundary, there was no more lawless Neutral Ground in which to hide. Robinson now wrote to Smith T in an attempt to detach him from Toledo to form a unified force.[20] "By the authority of the friends of the cause in which we are engaged," he wrote, "I shall proceed immediately to Nacogdoches, with a view to render that a place of deposit and rendezvous, for it is evident that nothing can be done until that measure is taken. We must not think of embodying and organizing ourselves within the limits of the United States."[21]

Not to be left behind, Smith T, on behalf of Toledo, put together his own small force and camped near Robinson. The two leaders engaged in a farcical, letter-writing standoff from April 11–12, 1814. Both Robinson and Smith T claimed supremacy and suggested the other should subordinate themselves. Eventually, the hot-headed Smith T apparently attacked the rival camp and captured Robinson and one of his aides. This "violent outrage" committed by Smith T ended the effort. The Missouri rogue's force dissolved after losing support in Natchitoches. Robinson returned, but his dysfunctional little army, composed of "very low" men, eventually out of boredom perpetuated a series of robberies and murders that recalled the banditti of old, and they too were disavowed. Claiborne once again issued a proclamation declaring a filibuster illegal, and no one could pretend anymore the endeavor had secret government support.[22]

Toledo would continue to flirt with a number of alliances to regain his command. In New Orleans, in 1815, he kept a diary of his efforts to secure arms and supplies through several members of the Mexican Association. But as these final efforts came to naught, the Cuban at last gave up his dreams. In 1816, Toledo switched sides and sought a Spanish pardon, just as Nathaniel Cogswell had predicted he would. He became an advisor to Ferdinand VII, gained a pension, and served in diplomatic posts in Switzerland and Italy, dying in 1858.²³

While he abandoned the cause, his predecessor, José Bernardo Gutiérrez de Lara never did. When not engaged in efforts to filibuster into Texas, he plied his trade as a black and silversmith in Louisiana. In April 1814, he made his way to New Orleans, where he was approached by "interested persons" offering an army of two thousand men. This failing, Gutiérrez then turned to his faithful agent, Girard, to now reach out to Haitian dictator Alexandre Pétion, who was declined.²⁴

In 1815, around the same time the Mexican Association was reaching out to Toledo, the group also, under the name "New Orleans Associates," propositioned Gutiérrez as well. They promoted a scheme remarkably similar to the one they had pitched to Josiah Taylor and William Murray eleven years before. The attack was to start at the Spanish port of Pensacola in West Florida, where they believed were ample arms for an attack on Texas. They could even, it was suggested to Gutiérrez, turn around and sell the captured province to the United States for millions of dollars. There was just one catch: it depended on the US government paying a ransom for the province when it could just seize it instead. The experience in West Florida had shown this was a pipe dream, and Gutiérrez wisely turned them down.²⁵

Filibusters on Hold: The Battle of New Orleans

As 1814 dragged on, these futile attempts to regain the magic puttered on, but Americans now increasingly turned their attention to their own conflict—the War of 1812—which was coming to their shores in a very violent way. Governor Claiborne in Louisiana began gathering all the regular and militia troops he could to defend vulnerable New Orleans. For the men of the West, this was a battle for survival. With the Crescent City at stake, no one wanted to go fight in Mexico anymore. New recruits and old filibusters alike converged on the city for the expected confrontation with the British Army. This fight would be led by Maj. Gen. Andrew Jackson, who arrived in the city in the summer of 1814 and would eventually collect into his ranks many veterans of the Republican Army of the North, including all three of its living former battlefield commanders, Kemper, Ross, and Perry.

Kemper reported for duty with Jackson's army in a company of cavalry from his home Parish of Feliciana in West Florida, but the scourge of Spain, who had weathered the storm of battle from Baton Rouge to Mobile, to La Bahía and Medina, could not survive the biggest killer of soldiers in the early 1800s—disease. He contracted measles, and in early November 1814, Samuel Kemper, the Republican Army of the North's best battlefield commander, died in New Orleans.²⁶

Many more Texas veterans were absorbed into the forces converging on New Orleans for the climactic Battle of New Orleans. Josiah Stoddard Johnston, the "Colonel Johnson" who had been Adair's deputy in the organization of the Gutiérrez-Magee

Filibuster, was appointed commander of the 17th, 18th, and 19th Consolidated Regiment, consisting of militia from Avoyelles, Rapides, Natchitoches, Catahoula, and Ouachita Parishes. Fittingly, the unit became a veritable who's who of Texas veterans, with a dozen verifiable and several more probable fighters, including Ross, William Murray, Warren D. C. Hall, and others. John Durst, the illegitimate son of Samuel Davenport joined as well. When one includes other regiments at New Orleans, the bulk of the known Republican Army survivors (and likely many of the unknown ones too) served in the campaign. Standing alongside the Anglo veterans from Texas were many of their Hispanic colleagues, including both Toledo—who had not yet taken his pardon—and Gutiérrez, as well as other Mexican exiles. Among them was José Domingo Losoya, who likely fought at Alazán and Medina before fleeing to the United States. "Just as the Louisianans had helped the Mexicans in their fight for freedom," wrote historian Rie Jarratt, "the Mexicans were helping the Louisianans in their fight for freedom."[27]

With the incredible triumph for American arms and the end of the War of 1812, the Burrites' eyes turned again to Texas. In March 1815, Gutiérrez would write that two thousand men petitioned him to reform the Republican Army and march on San Antonio. "There was much difference of opinion in this assemblage of men," Gutiérrez wrote, but they would fight with "the assurance that my government would allow them some bounty after the conclusion of the war." But Gutiérrez's means being slight, he could not get the men to agree to terms, or so he said. Though these later accounts place Gutiérrez at the core of the efforts, by now he was no longer even a figurehead, and the Americans would move forward with other leaders.[28]

The Private War of Henry Perry

Though it was Kemper, Murray, and Josiah Taylor who declared their enmity to Spain in an oath, it was Kemper's aide, the Connecticut-born Henry Perry, who found it impossible to leave Medina behind him. The man who had led the Republican Army to its greatest victory at the Battle of Alazán now launched a personal crusade against Spain. At New Orleans, he had served as captain of Battery No. 5 and was mentioned by Jackson in a postbattle proclamation. Discharged on June 15, 1815, he instantly turned his focus back to Mexico, partnering with a Mexican revolutionary he had met in New Orleans, Juan Pablo Anaya.[29]

The effort was aided by sympathetic officers in the US Army, who allegedly helped Perry to steal six hundred muskets from army stores in New Orleans. In this effort, he was also working with an officer in the garrison of Natchitoches, Lieutenant Forsyth, possibly the brother of Perry's Texas comrade Samuel D. Forsyth, the Republican Army surgeon. Perry was also joined by another former commander, Reuben Ross. The latter, who had abandoned the army at the urging of his Tejana girlfriend, was back on the border, where he supplied arms and supplies to the same Comanche chief, "Captain Cordero," who had raided San Antonio during the siege of La Bahía. The aim was to stir him to attack the city again, drawing forces away from Perry, who was to enter Texas at La Bahía and from there move on to San Antonio, then link up with rebels in central Mexico.[30]

Also joining Perry in his efforts was a newcomer to the revolutionary team, John Davis Bradburn, who would one day become infamous in the run-up to the 1836 revolution in Texas. While Ross was working the Indians and Perry was raising recruits in New Orleans, Bradburn—who presumably had been in Smith T's party in 1814, now returned to the site of that schemer's battle with Robinson's force and recovered a small four-pounder bronze cannon that the Missouri miner had thrown into the Sabine River at the conclusion of the fight.[31]

Perry recruited heavily in the Crescent City for the filibuster. "The favorable moment has at length arrived for making a successful attempt in favor of the patriots of New Spain," Perry wrote in a Louisiana newspaper. "Our cause embraces the best interest of humanity—the general enlargement of an oppressed people." If those lofty motives were not enough, Perry added, "The enterprise offers an easy road to distinction, and promises a glorious reward for merit." Back in 1812, the administration had been slow to stop the filibuster on the frontier, but this time, the rebels were recruiting openly inside a major American city. The response was quick. On September 8, 1815, the president himself issued a proclamation against the Anaya/Perry filibuster.[32]

> Whereas information has been received, that sundry persons . . . are conspiring together, to begin and set on foot, provide and prepare the means for a military expedition or enterprise against the dominions of Spain . . . *I have therefore thought fit to issue this my Proclamation*, warning and enjoining all faithful citizens . . . to withdraw from the same without delay.
> JAMES MADISON[33]

The spirited revolutionary from Connecticut had raised three hundred men, including republican veterans like Warren D. C. Hall, but with the proclamation, his funds dried up. Perry pushed on despite these official attempts to suppress him. He obtained a schooner and transported a small force to Galveston Bay, where the ship struck a sandbar and sank, drowning sixty of his men.[34]

Undaunted, Perry joined a third expedition—the Mina-Aury expedition of 1817. Francisco Xavier Mina was a Spaniard who had fought against the French and then rebelled against King Ferdinand VII when he denounced the liberal constitution of 1812. Fleeing to the United States, he embraced the cause of the Mexican rebels, joining forces with a French adventurer, Louis Michel Aury. The two, with a small force, landed at Galveston, where Perry joined them with one hundred men on March 16, 1817. The expedition then moved on Mexico, sailed to the coast of Tamaulipas, and seized the town of Soto la Marina, in April. Here Henry Perry had an even more brilliant victory against Spain than that at Alazán. While pursuing Spanish infantry, he was attacked by 350 cavalry, more than three times his own force, and he successfully fought off their attacks. But a dispute with Mina followed that soured the victory. Perry was convinced that Texas was the key to the success of the Mexican Revolution, but Mina wanted to fight the war from Tamaulipas. A bitter feud split the army.[35]

"Perry was certainly an excellent officer; and one of the bravest of men," wrote Mirabeau Lamar, "but he was nevertheless a man of some eccentricities of temper." Abandoning Mina's army, Perry and a mere forty-three men invaded Texas on foot—this time from the south. He hoped to seize La Bahía, raise the standard of revolution at the fortress in which the republicans had endured a four-month siege, and bring in more filibusters from the United States. It was bold but foolhardy. A year and a half before, Perry had promised in his proclamation that La Bahía "will fall an easy sacrifice, it is badly defended, and its weakness is well known." But the Spanish were too strong for his little band, and Perry fled with his men northward. Two days later, they were surrounded by three hundred royalists and attacked. With most of his men killed or wounded, Henry Perry, the last living Anglo-American leader who had commanded the Republican Army of the North in the field, committed suicide rather than be captured.[36]

Perry was not the only republican veteran to venture into Texas in that year. The Spanish had effectively pulled back to San Antonio and bands of rebels, robbers—or both—roamed East Texas. In May 1817, "Little John" McFarlan and a man named Patterson were operating in Texas along with "a gang of Indians of about fifty men," likely on a mission similar to Ross's visit the year before. Two Tejano veterans, Vicente Tarín and another named Estradas, with ten to twelve adherents, also attempted to supply the Comanches. But these efforts were hampered by the American authorities, who promised stiff punishment for any such activities.[37]

The Long Expedition

In June 1819, the new American commander at Fort Claiborne, W. C. Beard, issued a flurry of letters about an unusual illegal venture taking place in his vicinity. "In a few days after my arrival at this place I was informed of a body of American citizens, enrolling themselves under the command of a Mr. Long at Natchez, as well as a party at this place to be under the command of Mr. Walker with a view to invade & take possession of the province of Texas," Captain Beard wrote. The force had bypassed Natchitoches and mustered on the West bank of the Sabine, and therefore outside of Beard's jurisdiction. This was the biggest effort yet in the six years since Medina. The army of three hundred men was twice the size of Augustus Magee's initial Republican Army invasion and had formed up and slipped across the border in half the time as Magee had done, catching the American officers off guard.[38]

James Long, the commander mentioned in the letter, was not a veteran of the 1812 filibuster himself but had been "invited to the enterprise by the citizens of Natchez"—the same Burrite group that had supported Robinson. "The inhabitants of this place," wrote Lamar, "animated by a noble enthusiasm in favor of the cause of Liberty, resolved to make one more effort to destroy the merciless dominion of Spain in that beautiful and outraged land." Once again, they turned to General Adair, who declined, and as Gutiérrez had done with Magee, the Natchez backers turned to Long.[39]

The new commander had worked as a merchant in Natchez alongside Republican Army veteran W. W. Walker—the same man he now made his new filibuster army's field commander. Veterans of the Republican Army of the North were at the core of the new force. Its "supreme council" was made up entirely of such men, including Walker, Gutiérrez himself (in a much diminished, advisory role), Samuel Davenport, Hamlin Cook, Joshua Child, Stephen Barker, and Horatio Biglow. The latter, who had helped Aaron Mower set the type for Toledo's *Gaceta de Tejas* edited Long's propaganda paper, the *Nacogdoches Texas Republican*.[40]

Tejano veterans also took part. The secretary of the expedition was Vicente Tarín, who had recently been supplying muskets to the Comanches. He was a committed rebel from the earliest days of the expedition. Tarín had been among the Spanish officers who defected at Nacogdoches in August 1812, and he fought in all of the early battles of the revolution. His wife, as we have seen, had been brutalized in the *Quinta* after Arredondo's victory. Another recruit for Long was Pedro Procela, the former Nacogdoches militia officer-turned-republican who was one of the few Tejano rebels exempted from pardon. Other veterans in Long's force included Warren D. C. Hall and Aylett Buckner, the burly man known as "Strap" for his physical prowess. Another veteran, Henry William Munson, signed up alongside Santiago Mordella—the Mexican rebel who had saved his life on the Camino Real in 1813.[41]

Historians have generally framed the Long Expedition as organized in response to westerners' anger at the Adams Onís Treaty, which surrendered American claims to Texas. This is doubtful. Long aside, the entire leadership of his filibuster was composed of men who had been fighting for republicanism in Texas for a decade, and had served in an army that had, in the Robinson affair, manifested extreme hostility to the idea of the United States directly seizing the territory. Whatever the treaty said about the border, the mere fact that their nation had signed *any treaty* with the hated Spaniards was what infuriated the filibuster class. This grievance united both the men who saw it as a betrayal of their fellow republicans in Mexico and those who saw Texas as fertile ground for American expansion. Indeed, Long's statements and his army's proclamations suggest a curious mixing of these two impulses in the filibuster's ideology. Republican expansion and American extension remained not at odds, but consubstantial in the ideology of the filibusters. And either motive was probably a veneer that was painted over the more common motive of gaining personal wealth in land or riches through revolution.[42]

Long's force left Natchez with about seventy-five men, which increased to three hundred along the way. Before the American commander at Fort Claiborne knew it, the little army took Nacogdoches and declared a republic. Long attempted to secure the aid of the pirate Jean Lafitte, but in this he was sabotaged by his own envoy, the Republican Army veteran and editor, Bigelow, whose drunkenness was so extreme during his visit to Galveston that even the notorious pirate was disgusted.[43]

From Rebel to Congress: Henry Adams Bullard

In an ironic twist, the onus to suppress Long's army fell to a man who had fought alongside most of its leaders: Henry Adams Bullard. The Harvard graduate, author, and Texas' revolutionary secretary of state had survived the Battle of Medina and his failed attempt to rally the Mexican rebels to flank Arredondo's forces. Fleeing along the Camino Real, Bullard reached Natchitoches within a few days of his twenty-fifth birthday, "destitute and worn down with fatigue and sickness."[44]

In June 1819, when the Long Expedition made its move on Texas, Bullard was serving as justice of the peace in Natchitoches. Colonel Beard at Fort Claiborne wrote him that "certain persons in this neighborhood are carrying on illegal practices in violation of the laws of the United States" and should be stopped. He added, "I tender the civil authority a sufficient part of the force under my command, to aid and assist in taking any party of men thus engaged and will deliver them into the hands of the proper authority."[45]

Bullard responded that he would be happy to "discharge my duty in support of the constitution," but with respect to the filibusters, "it does not seem to be within the scope of my duty" to support the commander. If Bullard needed the assistance of the military, he said, he would inform them. The Fort Claiborne Commander also appealed to the town marshal for help, but in this case, he picked someone even *more* unlikely to stop Long. The marshal was none other than John C. Carr, the former Justice of the Peace who had resigned his office rather than enforce Claiborne's order to suppress the Gutiérrez-Magee filibuster. While dubiously expressing opposition to Long's expedition, Carr responded, "I regret the want of authority to cooperate with you in the suppression of this illegal enterprise."[46]

It was neither Bullard nor Carr who would suppress Long, but the Spanish. Texas governor Antonio María Martínez moved forces aggressively to confront Long, who was not yet prepared to fight. The filibuster army ignobly fled back across the border. Long tried again the next year in a new filibuster, this time adding a key recruit, José Félix Trespalacios, a rebel militia officer from Chihuahua who had briefly been imprisoned alongside rebels from the Mina-Aury Expedition, which had collapsed after

Figure 8. Henry Adams Bullard. Image courtesy of the Louisiana Supreme Court.

Perry's departure. Escaping Spanish custody, he arrived in New Orleans where he sought the aid of city merchants for a filibuster into Texas. There influential persons connected him to Long. When this new effort failed too, Trespalacios, associating with another Anglo-American veteran of Long's expedition named Benjamin Rush Milam, would enter Mexico and continue the fight.[47]

As for Bullard, his small role in the Long affair would be his last connection to frontier filibustering. He had abandoned his whole life in Philadelphia to follow Toledo to Texas and at the end of the war had found himself stranded one thousand miles from home. Nonetheless, Bullard was to have, in his misfortune, the greatest luck of all the former rebels, for he happened to have a unique skill set that was irrelevant in Philadelphia but was a virtual license to print money in frontier Natchitoches. Bullard was a trained lawyer who wrote and spoke both Spanish and French. In the polyglot community, he found immediate success. He was appointed a district judge in 1822, elected to Congress in 1831, appointed to the Louisiana Supreme Court, served as Louisiana secretary of state, and taught as a law professor at the Law School of Louisiana (today's Tulane University Law School). He built a mansion on the bluffs of the Cane River in Natchitoches and stocked it with a large legal library. He was a rare intellectual on the frontier, who read the classics while his neighbors "much preferred to chase a prospective venison steak."[48]

The Revolutionary Life of Samuel D. Forsyth

The Republican Army of the North's veterans spread far and wide. One, bitten by the bug of republican adventurism, sailed to a much larger stage: Venezuela. Samuel D. Forsyth had served as a surgeon's mate in the US Army in the early 1800s, had joined Augustus Magee's expedition into Texas as its chief doctor, and had taken over command of the republican army's artillery at the Battle of Alazán.[49]

Forsyth returned to Rapides after the war to practice medicine but longed to get back into the fight. In 1816, he traveled to Columbia, and thence to Venezuela, where he embraced the cause of Simón Bolívar. The *Libertador* made Forsyth his physician general, and a colonel in the Venezuelan army, as well as a trusted agent overseas. When Commodore Oliver Hazard Perry visited Venezuela in 1819 and fell ill, Forsyth became the treating physician at the death of the American naval hero. In 1820, he returned to the United States in the service of Bolívar, buying arms for the revolution. Secretary of State John Quincy Adams called him "the ambidexter personage who is a sort of agent here from Venezuela," who was angling to get an appointment as US special agent to that country.[50]

As they grew older, the American veterans of the Republican Army of the North like Forsyth never gave up their passion for Spanish America. But when Mexico finally became independent in 1821, the veterans of 1812–13 transformed with the times as well. For many of them, it brought their wanderings back to the land for which they had fought, this time as settlers.

23

The Return to Texas

The Twilight of Spanish Texas

Ten days after the Battle of Medina, a solemn procession passed through San Antonio, bearing the bodies of the chief royalists executed four months before. The casket of former Texas governor Don Manuel Salcedo led the way. Also borne along by the Spanish military and civilian mourners was former Texas military commander Don Simón de Herrera. The officiating priest was José Darío Zambrano, the brother of the leader of the 1811 royalist coup against Casas. He was a committed monarchist but also a man of God. This faith had been unsettled by the brutality of the conquest of San Antonio, and in March 1814 he finally found the courage to write to Arredondo to ask for a favor. There was one last unresolved matter remaining from the general's pillage of Béxar *seven months* before:[1]

> *Most Excellent Sir,*
> For quite a while I have been wanting to point out to His Excellency my strong desire to give Christian burial to the corpses in the plaza. To begin with, it is hard for me to understand how Christian burial has been denied a group of men who were put to death for their crimes, while at the same time others are running around, guilty of the same crimes, but who have been pardoned. Why deny that mercy to the dead? Secondly, it is hard for me to watch the disdain with which the corpses are treated by children, who throw rocks at them.[2]

The end of the killing had not been the end of the suffering. In December 1813, Arredondo rotated out most of his Medina veterans, including Santa Anna, replacing them with a more permanent occupation force—the Extremadura Regiment under the command of Col. Benito de Armiñán. These troops went unpaid for long stretches of time and resorted to criminal activity to support themselves. "They did not seem to be other than devils," remembered Antonio Menchaca. "They stole and committed many things."[3]

To the misery of war and conquest was added economic collapse. The city was surrounded by hostile Indians, preventing almost all agriculture. A sack of corn sold for $3.00 and a pound of coffee $2.50. Tobacco was $1 per ounce. "The people being in such pressure, would at the risk of their lives go out in the country to kill deer, turkey, etc., and cook herbs for the support of their families," wrote Antonio Menchaca. Hostile natives were not just a danger in the countryside, but in the city itself. "There were so many Indians around the city, that one evening, while yet light, a lady while sitting at her door . . . was killed by a [Tawakoni], who walked up to her and shot her in the head." The Indians would sometimes dress themselves in the clothes of their victims "and promenade the streets at will." Such depredations continued until 1820, when the Comanches and other tribes finally made peace.[4]

The bloody events of these sorrowful years would not soon be forgotten by citizens of San Antonio. So many had died; so many old and powerful families like the Arochas, Delgados, and Traviesos had been devastated. There were many survivors of the *Quinta*, such as one woman who lived in the city as late as 1845 at the eve of US statehood, who had valiantly endured the nightmarish weeks in late 1813. "Every cruelty and torture were resorted to, but without effect; and she was hailed as the heroine of the Revolution." Neither was the horror forgotten by the children, who had cried for their mothers outside the *Quinta* or thrown rocks at bloated, rebel bodies for seven months afterward—the stench of which would have been incredible. It must be concluded that the entire populace would have suffered from what is in the twenty-first century is called post-traumatic stress disorder. The memory shaped every interaction the people of San Antonio had with outsiders, both north and south—and with each other—throughout the Mexican Republic and the Texas War for Independence. As the anonymous Tejano mournfully recalled:[5] "It isn't easy to put on paper what this town suffered or even to narrate with much certainty exactly what happened after the battle, because so many of those who could have borne true witness to those events have died and many of the rest took part in the oppression and tyranny of their own countrymen and thus will not tell the truth, and indeed, in many cases, have conspired for years to obscure it."[6]

Spanish Texas had always faced a precarious existence even before the conflict. Failed attempts to colonize the province, the expulsion of foreigners, and depredations by the Indians had combined to threaten the very survival of Texas as a Hispanic outpost. Then came the war and brutal conquest. Nacogdoches was abandoned; Trinidad de Salcedo and San Marcos were completely destroyed. Only a greatly reduced San Antonio and the always impoverished La Bahía remained. Agriculture collapsed so completely that Arredondo had reduced his army's numbers in the capital, principally to avoid starvation.[7]

Texas had lost about one-third of its civilian population, and it needed people urgently to avoid a total economic and demographic collapse. Immigrants from Mexico were out of the question with the revolution ongoing. The only source was those exiles who had fled Arredondo's purge. A pardon would serve to remedy the population problem but also tamp down rebellion. Arredondo, as we have seen, therefore offered a conditional amnesty that exempted only insurgent leaders, which was followed up by the proclamation of the Spanish consul in New Orleans of a royal pardon on October 15, 1815, in honor of the birthday of King Ferdinand. To apply, citizens had to reaffirm loyalty to the king and promise to never support revolution again. Most citizens of San Antonio accepted the pardon and returned home, including Joaquín Leal, the elderly resident who had fled with his family and nothing but a sack of corn.[8]

While the rebels' property had been stolen, much of it never to be returned, the Spanish did restore their now empty homes to them. The young Tejano José Antonio Navarro was fortunate in that a royalist relative had protected his family's home and much of their property. Still, even those who had escaped relatively unharmed had suffered in one way or another. "For this reason, my younger [brothers] and myself had lost the years of flower of our youth," Navarro wrote, "wasting years without improving ourselves, but in participating in the affliction of our forefathers." One commenter on the period said that in this decade, Texas had "advanced at an amazing rate toward ruin and destruction," and had been denuded of "everything that could sustain human life." Even Arredondo, who had now assumed the role of commandant general, formerly held by Nemesio Salcedo, now realized that only settlers from outside could revive Texas.[9]

In 1820, a foreigner arrived in San Antonio with a proposal to do just that. Moses Austin was an Anglo-American who had settled in Missouri in the 1790s, taking Spanish citizenship, becoming an American again after the Louisiana Purchase. In Missouri, Austin had been the antagonist in a war for control of mines with the same John Smith T who had launched filibuster raids against Texas. Now, the former Spanish resident proposed to bring in American settlers to Texas who, like himself, would embrace Spain as lawful residents. Arredondo gave final approval, and thus the Spanish general who had defeated the Mexican republicans set in motion a chain of events that would ultimately transform Texas into an *American* outpost.[10]

The back-and-forth Mexican Revolution, after ten years, finally triumphed when the royalist general Augustín de Iturbide joined the rebels under Vicente Guerrero and independence was secured on September 28, 1821. Three months before, however, Moses Austin had died, and his son Stephen F. Austin took up the colonization plan. One of the men who came from Texas to escort Austin into the province was Juan Martín Veramendi. One of the foremost citizens of San Antonio, he was even known to Americans in Louisiana before the revolution. He had been involved in both the Casas and Zambrano revolts and joined the rebels when the Republican Army of the North entered San Antonio. He had not fought at the Battle of Medina but was certainly implicated in rebel activity.[11]

When Arredondo's pardon was first announced, Veramendi was lumped with Ruiz as "unworthy of receiving any consideration whatever" and a 250-peso reward was offered for his head. But, by March 1814, even he had gained a pardon, then traveled to Monterrey, secured an audience with Arredondo, and won the return of his property. "Showing political skills that would later make him a governor," wrote historian Jesús F. de la Teja, "Veramendi met with the commandant general . . . and achieved total vindication."[12]

His exile in the United States had only deepened his ties to the Anglo-Americans. When Jim Bowie moved to Texas, one of the first people he called on was Veramendi, whom he had probably met in Bowie's hometown of Rapides. Veramendi sealed this cross-border alliance in the most traditional of ways: by marrying his daughter Ursula to Bowie. He then served as governor of Mexican Texas until he—and his daughter—died in 1833, of the same cholera epidemic that killed William Shaler in Cuba. Three years later, his son-in-law Bowie died at the Alamo.[13]

Mexican Independence and the Search for Pensions

With independence finally secured, the new government chose José Félix Trespalacios, the former Long filibuster leader, as the first governor of Mexican Texas. In 1822, as he rode north to take control of the province, he was accompanied by James Gaines, the former Republican Army of the North veteran known to his Indian fighters as "Captain Colorado." The Mexican troops stopped at the site of the Battle of Medina, where the bones of their republican predecessors still lay in the open, exposed, nine years after their bloody defeat. Trespalacios asked Gaines to help bury them "in doing honor to the bones of his brave countrymen," since most of the remains were those of Anglo-Americans. These men had fallen, Trespalacios said in a short eulogy, in the cause of Mexican liberty and independence, "and it is not right that their bones should lie thus unburied." Gaines was asked to give the Lord's Prayer in English, but perhaps affected by the moment, deferred to another American in their company. The bodies were buried in a common grave on the battleground, and the skulls were interred at the foot of a large pecan or oak tree with the full honors of war. Navarro recalled the inscription placed on the tree, visible for some years afterward:[14] "Here lie the braves who, imitating the immortal example of Leonidas, sacrificed their fortunes and lives contending against tyrants."[15]

The following year, the new Mexican nation officially recognized the Republican Army of the North as a legitimate entity that contributed to the independence of the country. This, along with Austin's subsequent advertisement for colonists, revived hopes among Anglo-American veterans for pensions for their service in Texas. One of those who sought to stake the claim to land that Gutiérrez had promised them was Joseph Carr of Mississippi, who was listed in *Niles' Weekly Register* as "missing" after the Battle of Medina, but who evidently escaped. His wife submitted a claim in 1825 that included several original documents he had brought back from Texas. One is a note from Gutiérrez dated June 14, 1813, offering him a league square of land. Along with this note, with the same date, is a document signed by the American commander at the time, Perry, certifying that Carr was owed a total of $426.33, "for the payment of which the State of Texas and the faith of the Mexican Republic stand pledged to the said Volunteer."[16]

Officers received notes with commendations for their service. "The Commander in chief of the Northern Mexican army and Governor of the State of Texas," one such note reads, "deeply impressed with the important services which have been rendered the patriots in their struggle for independence by the American Volunteers, conceives it his duty to grant Lieut. Robt. Doughty this Certificate as a manifesto of his brave and patriotic conduct while attached to the Republican Army."[17]

Even with such authentic documents from Gutiérrez, pursuing a claim was difficult, and most veterans had no such papers. The new republic further demanded that pension-seekers travel to Mexico personally to make their claim, then navigate the bureaucracy of a brand-new nation, all amid a language barrier. To surmount these difficulties, a group of veterans in Louisiana banded together to assemble new documents and file their claims jointly, in a petition to be presented by veteran Samuel Sexton. On December 10, 1825, they gathered in Rapides and drafted the following statement "to ask, demand & receive from the government of Mexico a warrant for the quantity of land to which we may be entitled for services as volunteers in the northern division of the Mexican Republican army during the years 1812, 1813 & 1814."[18]

The veterans even had a standard form printed on a press, which essentially replicated the lost Gutiérrez paper copies of their terms of service. At the head of it, in block letters, with no seal of any kind, were the words "THE MEXICAN REPUBLIC" (in English). It listed the months of service, the pay ($40 for privates), any other debts owed (such as two horses to William Custard) and credits they received, which for most of them was a small amount of cash ($10–25) they had received at La Bahía or elsewhere. Eventually, 44 men from the town registered a claim.[19]

Sexton submitted the documents in 1826, but neither these claims nor any others were ever honored. George Orr, a Pennsylvanian and one of the original captains in the expedition, fought all the way through, surviving the Battle of Medina, and submitted a claim but was denied. He nonetheless settled in Atascocita, Texas, where he and fellow expedition veteran Henry Munson—the man saved by Santiago Mordella on the road from Medina—served together as *alcaldes*. Other Americans who applied for pensions were Aylett Buckner, Thomas Luckett, and Reuben Ross, whose story was particularly tragic.[20]

The Return to Texas 335

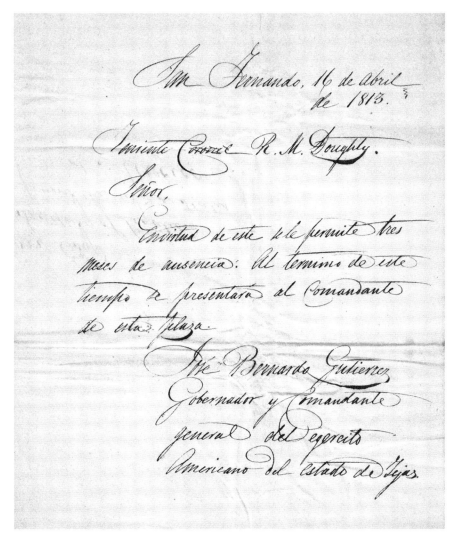

Figure 9. Testament to the service of Lt. R. M. Doughty, signed by Gutiérrez. Courtesy of US National Archives.

Having abandoned his command following the warning from his Mexican girlfriend on the eve of the Battle of Alazán, Reuben Ross returned to Virginia, but by 1816 was back in Texas to assist Perry in his filibuster. In 1821, he settled in Sparta, Tennessee. He had been thirty years old at the time of the expedition, and now, ten years later, had a family. On paper, he was wealthy, owning property and slaves, but it was a house of cards. His father was deeply in debt, and the creditors came calling on

Reuben Ross. The complex case went all the way to the Supreme Court of Tennessee and was still pending in 1828 when a desperate Ross sought salvation through his claim against the Mexican government.[21]

Ross was owed far more than other veterans. When the army was struggling in La Bahía, he had returned to the United States for additional recruits, but also supplies, for which he paid personally in cash and credit. In September 1825, he wrote to a friend in Mexico. "In the settlement of my accounts by the Junta [of] 1813 the Government was due to me some upwards of $10,000 for cash, merchandise [etc.] advanced and rendered," he wrote, arguing that the debt, contracted on behalf of Mexico, would entitle him to "some remote claim at least on the existing government." Ross ventured to Mexico to argue his case in person, and his preserved letters document the trip, his hopes for a pension, and his worries about his family, who he had left behind to face the creditors alone.[22]

Before he left for Mexico, Ross traveled through Philadelphia and there found the same Spanish rebel exile community that had encouraged Gutiérrez and Toledo thirteen years before. He became close with a member of the new Mexican provisional congress, Manuel Simón de Escudero, who was in the city on business. He described Escudero to his wife: "This gentleman was one of the first with Hidalgo to take up arms in favor of Liberty in the South American Provinces." Escudero wrote a warm letter to his friend, the secretary of state for internal relations, asking him to spare no effort to aid the former Republican Army of the North commander. The secretary was to introduce Ross to the president of the republic and consider his claims in the strongest possible way: "You will please consider Ross as Escudero, and Escudero as Ross, for Ross is my friend, and you will therefore please furnish him with any and everything that he may wish."[23]

Ross sailed from New York to Veracruz, and on April 8, 1826, wrote his wife that he was leaving from there into the interior of the country. To his surprise, he encountered a fellow veteran of the expedition, Horatio J. Offutt, also in Mexico. "This man's deposition I have taken who has a very retentive memory and has given a narrative of all the important services rendered by me during the campaigns in Texas," Ross wrote. Ross indicated his next stop was a visit to Gutiérrez, who had since returned to Mexico and was now the governor of Tamaulipas—formerly Nuevo Santander. Another expedition member who was seeking a pension at the time was Thomas Hussey Luckett, who wrote to Ross in Mexico. Luckett was in Washington and apologized that he had missed Ross when the latter passed through, "as I should have had the pleasure of embracing an old friend & fellow soldier." A mutual friend had "disclosed to me your views" on a business venture. Luckett, who had commanded the artillery at Rosillo while Ross had charged the Spanish guns opposite from him, wrote, "How would you like to associate yourself with me, in trade, with whom you have cooperated in battle?" The business venture to which Luckett referred was likely a plan to establish a steamboat line on the Rio Grande.[24]

Ross's larger plan was to monetize his grant to pay his debts, for he wanted to become an *empresario*. Aware of the contract recently obtained by Austin, Ross believed that he was owed at least as much, if not more than this newcomer who had never bled for Mexico. He gained support from Juan Antonio Padilla, the Mexican General Land Commissioner for Texas. "The aforementioned Colonel Ross, because of his valor and disposition, won victory for the Republican Army in the Battle of Rosillo," Padilla wrote Mexican officials. He added that Ross, while in San Antonio, had shown "honor, probity and fairness" to the locals.[25]

Ross signed up eight stockholders and organized his company. He briefly returned home to Nashville, but by January 1828 was back in Mexico, he told his investors, to tie up a few loose ends. Had he been successful, Ross may have become one of the great *empresarios* of Texas, but traveling across the interior of Mexico in the summer of 1828, his party was attacked by robbers. Ross, who had won a desperate sword duel with the Spanish lieutenant colonel Bernardino Montero at Rosillo, was felled by anonymous Mexican bandits nearly sixteen years later. Like his former foe, Ross ended his days in a forgotten, unmarked grave.[26]

Back in Virginia, he also left behind his long-suffering wife Frances; one son, John Randolph Ross; and a namesake nephew, Reuben Ross. Both later followed Reuben's path, and in 1836 came to Texas to fight in the second Texas revolution. Reuben Ross the younger fought at San Jacinto, and John, arriving too late for the revolution, was appointed by Republic of Texas president Sam Houston as an Indian Agent, but while traveling with the president, he died of an illness.[27]

Settling in Texas

Most American veterans did not experience the success of Henry Adams Bullard, nor could they risk the journey to certify their pensions, but the independence of Mexico offered a chance to return to the scene of their youthful adventure. As settlement was opened to Americans, they jumped at the chance. Eighteen verifiable Republican Army veterans made new homes in Texas, and they were likely joined by many anonymous comrades. Additionally, many of Texas' new settlers were recruited from communities where survivors abounded, and whose citizens were well aware of the revolutionary saga of 1811–13. This paints an interesting new image of the history of Texas colonization. In the traditional telling of the tale, the enterprising empresario and "Father of Texas," Stephen F. Austin leads wide-eyed and naïve settlers into the unexplored wilderness, where they found new Indian tribes, new lands, and strange Mexican customs. But more than a handful of his settlers would have found none of it novel.[28]

Indeed, the *very first* settler of Austin's new settlement of San Felipe de Austin was none other than John McFarlan, known to the Spanish as *Juanito*, or "Little John." He was the horse smuggler, Indian recruiter, and republican scout, who had first come to Texas in 1795, when Austin was only two years old. He returned in 1823, probably as a squatter, but was later incorporated into Austin's colony. He operated a ferry at San Felipe and died two years later in the province for which he had fought so long.[29]

Austin's famous "Old 300" settlers included other veterans like Aylett Buckner, William Parker, and Martin Allen. The latter, who had lost a father, brother, and nephew at Medina, returned to Texas in 1825 with his wife and seven children. He served in a volunteer company to defend the colony against Indian attacks, and in 1836 fought in the Texas Revolution. He presented a petition to the first congress of the Republic of Texas. "Your petitioners father and nephew ware both killed at the battle of the Medeena, 18 miles W of San Antonia on the 18th day of August 1813 where our whole army was defeted and a jenral massecree took place no quarter ware given by the enimy [sic]." He expressed indignation at the lavish grants to recent settlers that he, a Republican Army veteran, should have earned. "It is painfull [sic] for me to say that I have not been treated with equal justice with the first settlers of the country," Allen wrote.[30]

Another returnee was Edmund Quirk. He had fought in the American Revolution, settled in Texas in 1801, become by 1809 Spanish Texas' most wanted man, then the secret courier between the priest and the dueler—the "Fat Father" Huerta and John Smith T. The unlucky Quirk was imprisoned for a time in the Alamo, either escaped or was released by the Republicans when they took San Antonio, then presumably assisted the revolution in some capacity. After Medina, he was imprisoned in the Alamo again or in Monclova, where in the words of a later Mexican governor, he was "imperiled in the defense of the just cause of our mother Independence and of sacred liberty." Quirk returned to Texas and survived until 1836, dying in San Augustine, the town built on the land that had once been his ranch. A Thomas Quirk killed in the Goliad massacre was likely Edmund Quirk's son, possibly himself a Gutiérrez-Magee veteran as well.[31]

Expedition chroniclers James Gaines, William McLane, and Warren D. C. Hall returned to Texas. McLane had moved to Indiana after the war and returned to Texas in 1858, settling north of San Antonio on land that today is the community of Alamo Heights. He left his detailed notes to his son, Hiram, who wrote a novel based on the expedition.[32]

Republican veterans were well-represented in the first military units of early Anglo-Texas. When Austin established a militia on June 20, 1832, two of its members were Medina veterans, Henry Munson and Godwin Brown Cotten. The latter was also the leading journalist of the new Texas, along with Horatio Bigelow. The two had been among the printers brought by Toledo in 1813. Bigelow returned to Texas with the Long expedition in 1819 and published the *Nacogdoches Texas Advocate*. Captured by the Spanish, he eventually won his freedom and returned to northeast

Texas to publish the *Nacogdoches Mexican Advocate*. Cotten, who had aided Aaron Mower in the production of the *Gaceta de Tejas* in 1812, established (or reestablished) the *Texas Gazette* in 1829 in San Felipe.[33]

Most of Austin's colonists were initially content to be citizens of Mexico, and only a handful sought to change this state of affairs in the early years. This was even more true of the men who had once fought under Gutiérrez's banner in Texas. While American veterans of the Republican Army of the North played important roles in the filibusters against *royalist* Spain before 1821, it is worth noting that none of them played a role in the one revolt against *republican* Mexico. The Fredonian Rebellion, as this event is known, was a complicated affair that grew out of disputes between early settlers and the empresario Hayden Edwards. The latter reached out to republican veteran Aylett "Strap" Buckner, hoping to enlist him in the cause, aware that he was in the midst of a well-known feud with Austin. Buckner nonetheless put the feud aside and stayed loyal to Mexico. Along with other veterans, he signed a resolution opposing the rebels, and Edwards, lacking support, withdrew from Texas.[34]

Buckner believed at the time that American immigration and the Mexican nation were "much united and identified" in their sympathies, but six years later, he changed his tune, writing, "our rights and liberties have been much infringed. . . . We who have been born and fostered under that free and enlightened Govt. can not yield to such acts and impositions which seem to be heaped upon us." It was June 1832, and Mexican politics had devolved into a struggle between centralists and federalists that at times erupted into outright civil war. Adding to this, the Mexicans began to impose new taxes on settlers, with the prime boogeyman of the Anglo-Americans being one of their own, the Mexican customs official, John Davis Bradburn.[35]

Bradburn, who had joined Toledo's paper force after the Battle of Medina, had immersed himself in the revolution and become a committed Mexican, typically using the name "Juan." Now Buckner and a handful of firebrands, including fellow 1812–13 veterans Munson and Warren D. C. Hall, led an attack on Bradburn to "show him the blood of our colony." In the "Battle of Velasco," the rebels defeated a Mexican force, but the blood spilled was Buckner's own; he was one of the few men of either side killed in the fight. A veteran of Texas' first revolutionary struggle thus became one of the initial victims of what would become its second. At a dinner a month later, a toast was given to "A. C. Buckner, and other heroes, who fell on *freedom's side* at Fort Velasco—Such noble deeds, are as imperishable as marble."[36]

In turning revolutionary, Buckner, Hall, and Munson were the exceptions amid a generally moderate population. At a citizens' meeting after the battle, a committee including Republican Army veteran Allen disavowed the attack. Five days later, the same committee sent out a circular urging loyalty to Mexico. "Shall it be said that north Americans transplanted upon another soil . . . no longer listen to the high-minded dictates of honor and principle," the letter asked, "but that as degenerates from one clime, they in another give loose reign to unbridled passions—and illegal and unjustifiable proceedings?"[37]

Republican Veterans in the 1836 Revolution

By 1834, the crisis in Mexico was growing worse. Texas, which after the devastation of the previous revolution had become a mere political appendage to Coahuila, saw even this protection broken down. Factions in the latter state fought for control in a battle that eventually led to the dissolving of the entire state government by Antonio Lopez de Santa Anna, one of Arredondo's veterans, and now president of Mexico. Revolution would return to Texas, and veterans of the Republican Army of the North—and their children—were well-represented in the struggle. Warren D. C. Hall had been among the most active of the filibusters, fighting alongside Perry in the Mina-Aury expedition and supporting Long. He settled in Texas in 1828 with his wife Julietta near Columbia in Brazoria County and within a few years became one of the principal leaders in the nascent Texas independence movement. When independence was formally declared the following year, interim president David G. Burnet (himself a Miranda expedition veteran) chose Hall as the temporary secretary of war for the republic.[38]

Texas finally declared Independence for the *second* time on March 2, 1836, when fifty-two representatives gathered in a frigid, windowless building in the town of Washington-on-the-Brazos. Among the men inking the declaration were two veterans of the Republican Army who had been present for the signing of the first declaration: James Gaines and José Francisco Ruiz.[39]

Gaines, "Captain Colorado" of the first revolution and wounded at Rosillo, served in the Long expedition and returned to Texas after Mexican independence, as we have seen. In 1819, he bought the famous ferry of Miguel Crow, where Juan Manuel Zambrano had been briefly captured seven years before. He returned to Texas as part of Austin's old three hundred, signed the declaration, served on the committee to draft a new constitution for Texas, and was elected to the Republic of Texas Senate in 1839.[40]

Ruiz was the former Spanish quartermaster at La Bahía who had turned rebel and risen to leader of the junta-in-exile in Louisiana. As he put pen to paper on March 2, 1836, Ruiz probably did not reflect on it, but the date he signed Texas' second declaration of independence was the twenty-fifth anniversary of the date he had helped overthrow the Casas regime in San Antonio. He was one of only two native Tejano signers of the declaration, alongside his nephew, José Antonio Navarro, the young boy who had observed so many of the key events of the revolution and written them into his memoirs. Ruiz in later years joined Gaines in the Texas Senate, becoming, along with his nephew, the voice of Tejanos in the increasingly Anglo republic and state. "He became a cultural broker who lived on a physical, cultural and political frontier," said biographer Art Martinez de Vara. "He bridged the Spanish, Mexican, indigenous and Anglo American spheres, and he took center stage in many of the prominent political and military events in Texas." Ruiz, who had spent so much time in exile in America, was an advocate of Tejanos embracing the Republic of Texas. "Under no circumstance," he wrote one family member, "take sides against the Texans... for only God will return the territory of Texas to the Mexican government."[41]

Tejanos in the Second Revolution

The trauma of the conquest of Bexár devastated the generation of Tejanos who had fought for independence, and few remained of the Medina veterans twenty-five years later. One possible Tejano veteran who fought in 1836 was Ancelmo Bergara. He was the Spanish royal deserter who had gone with Luis Grande to smuggle Gutiérrez's proclamations into San Antonio. Most sources indicate Bergara was executed alongside Grande, but a man of the same name—possibly the rebel courier if he escaped, or alternatively a namesake son—survived and fought in the 1836 revolution.[42]

In the evening of March 6, 1836, Bergara was at the ranch of José María Arocha, of the clan of the most inveterate 1811–13 rebels, when a man arrived from San Antonio, bringing word that the Alamo had fallen. Bergara then rode to Texian general Sam Houston's camp, where he arrived on March 11, bearing the terrible news. He joined the volunteers and fought at the Battle of San Jacinto in the Tejano cavalry.[43]

This contingent was led by a gifted fighter, Juan Nepomuceno Seguín. He was the son of Erasmo Seguín, who had been coerced by Toledo and Shaler into supporting the revolution. Years later, Erasmo traveled with Veramendi to Louisiana to bring Stephen F. Austin to Texas and was among the first to embrace the American's plans to bring in settlers. His unpleasant experience with Shaler notwithstanding, he quickly became friendly with all of the Anglo-Americans. He served as Texas' representative to the congress that drafted the liberal 1824 constitution and was on the committee that wrote the 1824 National Colonization Law that allowed for the waves of Anglo-American immigrants which followed. It was amid this backdrop that his son, Juan, grew to manhood.[44]

Joining Seguín's Tejano troop was another likely 1813 veteran, José Domingo Losoya. Born in San Antonio in 1783, Domingo, as noted before, had likely fought at Medina, where he may have used a ford of the river—now known as Losoya's Crossing—as his escape route. After exile in the United States, in which he learned American ways and some English, Losoya returned to Texas, and applied for a land grant at the site of the ford, which may have been for sentimental reasons. When revolution again returned to Texas, Losoya joined Seguín's company, fighting at the Battles of Concepción, the Grass Fight, and the Siege of Béxar. With his knowledge of the terrain, he served as a forager for Sam Houston's army, providing much-needed foodstuffs. He also served at San Jacinto.[45]

Another youth who had endured Arredondo's conquest was Antonio Menchaca. Saved from Spanish reprisals by a sympathetic royal officer, he witnessed the last years of Spain and the early years of Mexican independence. When the 1836 revolution broke out, Menchaca first served as a courier for Jim Bowie; was briefly captured by the Mexicans; then, after being released, joined Sam Houston's forces. As one of Seguín's sergeants at San Jacinto, Menchaca, true to the legacy of his namesake Miguel from the first revolution, fought bravely. He served as a captain of a ranger company defending the frontier from Indians and lived until 1879.[46]

Heirs of the Republican Army

Many 1812–13 veterans who did not return to Texas nonetheless had family members who did. Most of these heirs of the Republican Army of the North flocked in 1836 to the land for which their fathers and uncles had fought, including Reuben Ross's son and nephew mentioned above. James McKim Jr., the son of the James McKim who had led the Neutral Ground bandits into the expedition, settled just inside the border and became a Texas Ranger.[47]

John Marie Durst, the "Paul Revere of the Texas Revolution," was the godson and likely illegitimate son of Samuel Davenport. With Mexican independence, he acquired Davenport's land titles in Texas and also a large Mexican grant. Settling in Nacogdoches, he took up a role as Indian interpreter, similar to that his father held under Spain, living in the latter's old stone house. In 1835, Durst, fluent in Spanish, served as a Texas representative in the legislature of the Mexican state of Coahuila y Tejas. He was serving in this capacity in Monclova when he learned that Martín Perfecto de Cos was marching on Texas to occupy San Antonio. Mounting his horse, Durst rode 960 miles to Texas to sound the alarm. He commanded a company in the second revolution, just as his father had commanded one in the first.[48]

American Agent William Shaler also had a tie to the 1836 revolution in William Shaler Stillwell, the son of his sister. A New Yorker like his uncle, Stillwell was a graduate of West Point, who resigned his commission in 1833 and arrived in Texas by ship on January 28, 1836, to volunteer in the revolution only a week before the fall of the Alamo. The twenty-seven-year-old fought at the Battle of San Jacinto as a lieutenant of artillery. He died the following year.[49]

Stillwell was almost certainly good friends with another "son" of the 1812–13 filibuster, for they had attended the service academy together. Albert Sydney Johnston, the most famous of these heirs of the Republican Army of the North, was actually the far younger half-brother of Darius and Orramel Johnston, and John Adair's deputy, Josiah Stoddard Johnston. Albert Sydney had been a boy of nine when his brothers had left for Texas and had seen them return broken in body after long imprisonment in Mexico.[50]

Even with their cautionary tale ringing in his mind, Albert Sidney Johnston crossed the frontier into Texas in 1836 to volunteer in the second revolution. He missed the Battle of San Jacinto but rose quickly in the Texas service, becoming adjutant general in August 1836, a year later general-in-command, and the following year secretary of war for the republic. He served as a colonel in the US Army in the Mexican–American War and as a general for the Confederate States of America in the US Civil War, where he was killed at the Battle of Shiloh on April 6, 1862.[51]

The most famous building in Texas, that crumbling mission known as the Alamo, had been a scene of much action, but no fighting, during the Texas Revolution of 1811. Restored as a fortress by the Mexican army during the years that followed, it was occupied in 1835 by Texas rebels who saw in it an opportunity for defense that their predecessors would have never considered. Three heirs to the first conflict would die there in the siege of 1836, William Phillip King, Charles Despallier, and Toribio Losoya.[52]

Republican Army of the North veteran John Gladden King had returned to Texas in 1830 and settled in Green DeWitt's Colony. When the Alamo came under siege in February 1836, recruiters near his home in Gonzales were looking for volunteers to launch a relief of the fortress and asked the republican revolutionary veteran to join. Before he could go, however, his sixteen-year-old son, William Phillip King, begged his father to go instead, and the older man agreed. Thus young William marched off with the "immortal thirty-two" for the Alamo and became the youngest defender to die there.[53]

In the fortress, King would have met another son of a Republican Army veteran, Charles Despallier. He was the son of Bernard Despallier, the key aide to Gutiérrez. Despallier's hometown of Rapides had been one of the hotbeds of recruiting for the expedition and, after the defeat at Medina, was the destination of much of the 1813 republican diaspora. It was through these veterans that a young boy from the community named James Bowie first learned about the revolution in Texas. James Bowie, only sixteen at the time, had not joined the Republican Army, but certainly knew many of its members—including possibly his own brother—and watched them return in defeat. A year later, he joined them in the local militia bound for the defense of Louisiana from the British.[54]

Bowie's connection to the revolutionists only grew as he matured. He became very close to Warren D. C. Hall, Augustus Magee's former boon companion and chronicler of the revolution. Bowie and Hall "each felt some kindred in the other." Equally close was Despallier, who aided Bowie's filing of land claims—some of them fraudulent—in the local courts. On the eve of the Texas Revolution, Bowie journeyed back to Rapides before turning once more toward San Antonio again for the final, fateful time. At his side was one of Bernardo Despallier's sons, Blaz Philipe Despallier. In Nacogdoches, Bowie wrote a friend, stating, "I am detained here today on account of the bad health of my traveling companion Mr. Dispalier who is sick with a fever."[55]

Blaz Philipe had been born in Texas in 1809, while his father was living in Trinidad, and by the 1830s, the young man showed he was cut out of the same mold as his propagandist father. He published a bilingual English/French newspaper called the *Frontier Reporter and Natchitoches & Claiborne Advertiser*. The elder Despallier had once been a propagandist for Mexico, but his son's cause was nothing less than the dismemberment of that nation. In the July 9, 1834, edition, the heir of a Republican Army veteran wrote in letters that most moderate veterans would have thought radical. "The acquisition of the beautiful and fertile territory in question [Texas] would be one of great importance," he wrote. "We have always regarded its ultimate possession by the United States as a matter of certainty."[56]

Blaz Philipe arrived in San Antonio on November 26, 1835, fought at the Siege of Béxar, and was among the first of the forces who occupied the Alamo after the battle. He became a scout for Col. William Barrett Travis, then fell gravely ill—possibly a recurrence of the symptoms he had experienced on traveling to Texas. He returned to Rapides, but that same month, his brother Charles Despallier arrived at the Presidio La Bahía in Goliad. This was the same fortress where his father had fought twenty-two years before, and in it, he joined with ninety other men of the garrison to sign a document declaring Texas once again independent. "Men of Texas," the document read, "nothing short of independence can place us on solid ground." (Signing alongside Despallier was Edmund Quirk Jr., son of the smuggler and republican spy.) After the document was affirmed, Charles ventured to San Antonio, probably unaware his brother had recently departed. He arrived in the middle of February, just ahead of the Mexican Army of Santa Anna. During the siege, Charles Despallier was cited for bravery by Col. William Barret Travis, who said he "gallantly sallied out and set fire to houses which afforded the enemy shelter, in the face of enemy fire."[57]

The Alamo's defense fell to Travis, who well knew of the parallels between his war and its predecessor. Before he became the firebrand of the second Texas Revolution, he had been a lawyer in the town of San Felipe. His law office was next door to the print shop of republican veteran Godwin Brown Cotten. It seems likely that long before Travis wrote his famous "Victory or Death" letter from the Alamo, he had heard the story of the previous revolution firsthand from his neighbor. Travis's famous letter is more poignant when one considers that he well knew the story of Medina, and the likely fate of his garrison if they were defeated.[58]

A third heir of republican forces at the Alamo was José Torribio Losoya, one of the Tejano defenders, who was the nephew of José Domingo Losoya, noted above. He had been born in the Alamo barrio just a few years before the first revolution. He grew up literally in the shadow of the fortress walls, where he married and raised three children while serving as a private in the Álamo de Parras military company under

José Francisco Ruiz, the Tejano who signed the Texas Declaration of Independence. Like his uncle Domingo, he joined the Tejano forces opposed to the centralist government of Mexico. When Mexican troops surrounded the fortress, Losoya found himself defending not only his fellow soldiers but his wife and three children, who had taken refuge in the mission chapel.[59]

On the morning of March 6, 1836, the entire garrison of the Alamo was killed by the Mexican army led by the Spanish veteran Santa Anna. One account of Jim Bowie's death indicated that the son of his old friend from Rapides was with him to the end. "Our friend Bowie, as is now understood, unable to get out of bed, shot himself as the soldiers approached it. Despalier . . . and others, when all hope was lost followed his example."[60]

That Charles Despallier would die in the fortress was supremely tragic. He was not only the son of rebel Bernard Despallier, but the grandson of Luís Grande, who was first arrested for singing incendiary songs criticizing the Spanish forty-nine years before. Grande, captured as Gutiérrez's courier of propaganda, was imprisoned, tried, and executed—almost certainly within the Alamo—in 1813. Grandfather and grandson, therefore, likely died the deaths of martyrs within a few yards of each other, twenty-three years apart. Thus the Despallier brothers, Charles and Blaz Philipe, are the only known third-generation fighters for Texas independence.

Josiah Taylor is one of the more remarkable characters in this saga. He had been the lynchpin of the Burr Conspiracy, likely faked his death, and then remade himself in Augustus Magee's invasion of Texas. He had been captured as a scout, escaped from the Alamo prison, then led the republican wings at Alazán and Medina, where his wounding precipitated the collapse of the army. Against all odds, he survived, and after returning in 1824 had five sons who fought for the Republic of Texas, including the legendary Creed Taylor, who helped defend the "Come and Take It" cannon at Gonzales, fought in the Battle of Concepción, the Grass Fight, the Siege of Béxar, and San Jacinto. Between them, father and son—Josiah and Creed Taylor—fought in every battle of *both* Texas revolutions except the Alamo and Goliad defeats.[61]

An Unlikely Reunion in an Unlikely Republic

One of the final incidents that brought together men associated with the Republican Army of the North took place not in Texas but in Mexico. In 1815, with a Spanish reward of five hundred pesos still on his head, José Bernardo Gutiérrez de Lara wrote an account for Mexican congressmen largely ignorant of the happenings in far-off Texas, which would lead to Mexico's recognition and certification of the Republican Army as a legitimate force of the revolution. In this account, Gutiérrez greatly exaggerated his own role, arrogating the victories of Magee, Kemper, and Perry to himself and generally dismissing the Anglo-Americans he had so praised two years before. He also washed his hands of culpability in the murder of the royalists.[62]

The document nonetheless helped him gain renown, which resulted—when Mexico finally won its revolution—in his being awarded the governorship of his home province of Nuevo Santander, renamed since the revolution as *Tamaulipas*. This self-serving document—propaganda disguised as history—should not be Gutiérrez's final testament. The rebel from Revilla was petulant, vain, and jealous, to be sure, but absolutely dedicated to his country's cause. For all his faults, he had remained true when men like Toledo abandoned it. He lost all of his fortune, and his family had suffered greatly. Now reborn as a provincial governor, Gutiérrez served faithfully, and in this peacetime role, avoided the delusions of grandeur and the excesses of his failed stint as a wartime governor. A more mature and thoughtful leader by this time, Bernardo Gutiérrez at last earned respect. As the legislature of the new state memorialized to the Mexican congress in 1824:[63] "The citizen Gutiérrez de Lara unites with patriotism, disinterestedness, to valor prudence, to intrepidity circumspection. . . . Decided for his country he was inflexible to the suggestions of the Spanish Government; he laughed at their intrigues: their threats did not terrify him, and he depreciated with constant firmness their pleasing seductions."[64]

In his last duty, Gutiérrez served as the commandant general of the Eastern Interior States, the republican equivalent to Nemesio Salcedo—and, later, Arredondo—in the imperial hierarchy. He struggled to protect his far-flung provinces from Indian raids and retired in 1827 to his now-rebuilt home on his family's ancestral land in Revilla. But Mexico's early history was a troubled one, and the internal struggle between centralists and federalists raged on, even after Santa Anna's defeat. Three years later, rebels in his own province seceded from Mexico to create the *Republic of the Rio Grande*. The sixty-five-year-old Gutiérrez, aged and infirm, nonetheless mounted his horse and rode to battle at the head of the loyal Mexican forces. But his army was defeated, and Gutiérrez and his men were forced to surrender.[65]

The rebel commander, Antonio Canales, sacked Gutiérrez's home and even tore the epaulets from the elderly governor's shoulders. He possibly would have killed him, but for the intervention of an officer in his own army. It was the colonel of a filibuster force from the Republic of Texas, fighting alongside the Rio Grande rebels. The commander of these "Texas Allies" was Reuben Ross, the nephew of the rebel of the same name. Twenty-six years before, the elder Ross had stood alongside Gutiérrez as commander of the Republican Army of the North. He had visited the aged Mexican rebel in his search for a pension. Now, not far from his uncle's unmarked grave, Reuben Ross the younger intervened on behalf of his uncle's former comrade, convincing Canales to spare the old Mexican revolutionary. Gutiérrez was released and died two years later, peacefully.[66]

24

Epilogue

THE TEXAS REVOLUTION of 1811 is the most important obscure event in North American history and should be dusted off and brought into the light of common knowledge, taking its rightful place as a watershed event in Texas, American, and Mexican revolutionary history. A full understanding of this conflict will shed light on many related areas and themes of history, provoking an important reassessment of existing narratives, as well as a greater appreciation of their complexity. The Mexican revolutionaries, for example, had a greater desire for American intervention than is often understood, and the failure to receive such aid was crucial in prolonging their struggle, with consequent effects on the development of Mexico as a nation. Furthermore, Texas history, generally divided into Spanish, Mexican, and Anglo periods, is in fact more seamless than typically presented, and the transition more complex. As for the American narrative, the powerful subtext of territorial expansion can be seen to be constantly evolving. While this expansion may have been destiny, its nature was not at first so clearly manifest. American frontiersmen who pushed beyond the nation's borders had complex motivations, which sometimes dovetailed with those of their government but were at other times at variance with them.

This work has said little about slavery, one of the key narratives of early American history. It was not a crucial motivating impulse in 1811–13. This is certainly not to say that the American volunteers who fought were in any way opposed to slavery's expansion. It is rather to say that the alternative to expansion—the idea that slavery might be constrained—was not even considered by them. Slavery in New Spain, by 1810 largely confined to domestic service and a peonage system for agriculture, was often milder than American slavery, but was nonetheless legal, and the volunteers took it as given that it would remain so regardless of who won the war. Slavery was hardly threatened in the United States at this time. It was still quasilegal in the northern American states, where it was being gradually abolished. New York, the home of William Shaler, still had fifteen thousand slaves in 1810. One of them was Shaler's own: his manservant Charles. Massachusetts-born Henry Adams Bullard, who would later express antislavery sentiments to the consternation of his Louisiana neighbors, did not even consider the issue in any of his early writings about filibusters.[1]

The America of 1812 was simply a different world than the one of 1836, much less 1860. The traditional narrative of American expansion, which often focuses on Southerners eager to gain new territory for slaveholding and cotton, is insufficient to explain events prior to 1820. For the War of 1812 generation, the impetus to expand was general (including efforts to conquer Canada, for instance). Cotton in 1812 was not yet king and was at best a mere prince. The sea change was the Missouri Compromise in 1820, which limited the number of new slave states that could be created. This established a new and powerful motive for expansion—*supplementing but not supplanting* the preexisting impulse. The urge to push the borders of republicanism existed before, during, and long after the period when expansion was coopted for southern political gain, with *Southern* motives merely grafted onto existing *American* ones.

"To define filibustering as an episode in American regionalism is to obscure the almost infinite variety of reasons that led young men to join expeditions," wrote historian Robert E. May. Indeed, in a filibuster in which key players were as likely to be from Massachusetts (Magee, Bullard, and Cogswell), New York (Shaler), and Connecticut (Perry) as from the South, the traditional narrative is wildly insufficient. The men who in 1812 jeered John Robinson's flag at their camp in Trinidad cared not at all for how many senators the various American regions had in Washington, DC. They wanted land and wealth for their own *personal* aggrandizement, were more inclined than not to be hostile to the US meddling in new territories they expected to win, and were far more willing to change nationalities—or create new ones—than would be later generations of Americans.[2]

Indeed, looking closer into the lives, backgrounds, and destinies of the men who invaded Texas shows that they were far more diverse than has heretofore been understood, with men of base and lofty motives serving side by side. Historian David Narrett, writing of Robinson, said he should not be considered typical "since he was more ideologically oriented and politically ambitious than the ordinary armed adventurer of the southwestern United States." True enough, but Robinson was hardly unique. Nathaniel Cogswell, Bullard, and almost all of Toledo's band of adventurers would fit this description, as would Ross, Perry, and Forsyth, as their statements show. This suggests a potentially rich source of further exploration into other filibusters, since in almost all cases, such motivations of individuals beyond merely the leader at the top are generally assumed by historians and are insufficiently studied in the detail that they deserve.[3]

Additionally, the importance of trade in the revolutionary struggle for Texas across the generations should be recognized. In the first decades of the nineteenth century, Spanish mercantilism fought against the natural impulse for trade on an impoverished frontier. The capture of Quirk, McFarlan, and the other smugglers in 1808, and the subsequent alliance between Nacogdoches rebels, Natchitoches merchants, and Burrite adventurers paved the way for rebellion in Texas. As the ferryman Crow told Spanish interrogators in 1811, "this revolution was for commercial purposes." Something similar can be seen in the early 1830s, as newly independent Mexico sought to impose taxes and import duties, leading to the Battle of Velasco and the death of Aylett Buckner. Among settlers already grown accustomed to contraband, the imposition stirred the pot of rebellion early, and gave economic incentives to revolution to firebrands and moderates alike, which were soon augmented by other grievances.[4]

The Origins of the Invasion

The Gutiérrez-Magee filibuster is frequently assumed to have been organized or condoned for purposes of American territorial expansion by the Madison administration. It was not. The case for administration support rests mainly on the supposition that Shaler, the American State Department's agent on the scene, was actively engaged in organizing the filibuster. In the beginning, he clearly was not, and though he later became a fierce meddler on behalf of Toledo, this was *on his own initiative* and in violation of his instructions.[5]

Shaler's orders were explicit that interference was not authorized, and none of the rare letters he received from Monroe contradicts them. Any secret codicil stating otherwise is also disproved: Lacking intelligence about actual revolutions, such instructions would have had to have been general and required further correspondence to adjust to changing circumstances. This need for further direction to Shaler becomes even more necessary after Robert Smith, the man who hired him, was replaced with Monroe, a man with whom Shaler had no intimacy at all. If Smith had a deal with Shaler, Monroe had to confirm it. The rocky start in their correspondence could not have given Shaler optimism that he had approval for any open-ended freelancing, and his letter to President Madison definitively disproves any side correspondence. An agent a thousand miles from home would not send such a stark complaint to the president—over the head of his superior—merely as a ruse to fool historians. He was generally concerned about his status given the lack of direction from Washington, and the letter was a cry in the wilderness from an abandoned pup. William Shaler was, for better or worse, acting *only* on his original printed and verbal instructions, which had been given to him prior to the outbreak of the Mexican revolution.[6]

Governor Claiborne, for his part, only connected Gutiérrez and Shaler in order to quickly get the former away from New Orleans and the intrigues of Claiborne's political enemies. Following their trials for treason in the Burr conspiracy, these enemies had written off—if they had ever supported—the idea of Western secession. But support of Mexico was another matter entirely, and this goal they never abandoned. Importantly, Claiborne *never perceived this distinction*. He feared this network of hostile men could threaten the fragile stability of his multiethnic territory, and somehow Gutiérrez might be a lightning rod for them. In pushing him out of New Orleans, the governor was dumping his unexpected Mexican guest on the frontier with a vague hope that he would proceed on his business without disturbing the peace in America.[7]

To what end would the government have supported a filibuster? The obvious answer would be annexation, as had been the case in West Florida. This was explicitly rejected by Smith's aide Graham in his addendum to Shaler's instructions, which pointedly deferred questions about the southwestern border to future negotiations. (Graham, it should be noted, had formerly been an aide to Claiborne, then served both Smith and Monroe, thus bridging all major policy makers.) When it came to annexation, not even Shaler was enthusiastic on the subject. In Cuba, when local elites urged it on him, Shaler's "approach to annexation was more reactionary than proactive," in the words of historian Stephen Chambers. Two years later, when Gutiérrez all but offered Texas for the price of a few troops, Shaler mocked the offer. Nor did he ever suggest it to Toledo, who was entirely reliant on Shaler for his entry into the province. Claiborne, a year after the fact, said he was still in the dark about the administration's intentions towards Texas.[8]

A final point will be made on the only possible theory of government involvement that cannot be refuted by documentary evidence. One historian has put forth the thesis that Monroe's involvement was through "unspoken words"—not through explicit action but passive non-interference. This envisions a nod-and-wink to simply let the filibuster happen once Shaler became aware of its existence. The motivation behind *inaction* is difficult to disprove, but the timeline of Shaler's letters to Monroe calls even this thesis into question. The secretary of state's office was never able to form an accurate and timely picture of events on the frontier. Monroe had received some initial warning of the recruitment of men for a filibuster not only from Shaler but also from Sibley and Claiborne. These letters were vague, and the number of men involved were almost insignificant. By the time it became clear that this filibuster was the real thing, as opposed to a rehashing of the rumors which had been circulating for six years, it was far too late to stop it. Indeed, Monroe *did* try to stop it by sending John Robinson, but by the time he arrived, he was a diplomatic Don Quixote, tilting at all the wrong windmills.[9]

If not as a proximate cause, can the "unspoken words" thesis be defensible at a broader, macro level? Narrett has argued that Thomas Jefferson, in ascribing vast boundaries to the Louisiana Purchase, made such encouragement to filibusters inevitable. "Once the president claimed territories to the Perdido (that is, a goodly portion of Spanish West Florida) and all lands southwest to the Rio Grande, he enabled many

American citizens to believe that adventurist forays into disputed Spanish territory were warranted." This could be true enough for Texas or Louisiana, but the Mexican Association oath was to liberate *all* of Spanish America, and it was administered by men hostile to, not allies of, Thomas Jefferson.[10]

In regard to Texas, the final refutation of government involvement is the existence of a compelling and consistent counternarrative that is much simpler than a fanciful, covert diplomatic scheme and, unlike it, is supported by hard evidence. This is, quite simply, that the very alliance of businessmen, merchants, disgruntled soldiers, and frontiersmen who plotted to invade New Spain alongside Burr in 1806 were the same men—individually in some cases but as a *class of men* assuredly—who implemented the same plot alongside Gutiérrez in 1812. Indeed, the evidence shows that this broad movement, evolving over time, was in some form or another a constant presence on the frontier up to and beyond 1836.[11]

The Conspiracy Behind the Filibuster

There was an organized conspiracy to invade New Spain known as the Mexican Association or Mexican Society in 1806. That it endured through 1811 is attested in Claiborne's letters. That the organization had a well-developed plan to attack West Florida first and then move on to Texas is confirmed by the three separate accounts of recruits to the cause. General Adair was chosen to be a key commander in the 1806 variant and was also selected to lead the 1812 invasion. In between, he admitted to the president that he was in the confidence of a group of men meeting the description of the organization and hostile to the United States.

Crucially, Gutiérrez, in his travels through the West *before* meeting with James Monroe, was wined, dined, and given generous offers of support in terms of men and arms by many former Burr conspirators. The offers they made to him in 1811 were not forgotten when he returned the following year. It is far more plausible that Gutiérrez embraced these siren calls to help him effect his aim than that he was a puppet in any complex scheme of government orchestration from the other end of a 1,200-mile line of communication (or noncommunication). Notably, when Toledo was procuring arms for his 1815 efforts, the men in New Orleans who were helping him were John K. West and Edward Livingston, two high-profile members of the association.[12]

While there is only one documented direct tie between the Mexican Association and the Gutiérrez Magee Expedition—the letter attributing the filibuster to Daniel Clark—the bulk of supporting circumstantial evidence points to a connection. Like the phantom that it was, the Mexican Association defies precise definition. We cannot say with certainty whether it was one conspiracy, several affiliated ones, or a series of organizations put together ad hoc. The various groups that formed the expedition contained many men who had never heard of the association. They did not need to. All they needed to know was that arms and men were flowing to the border to join them, and that a deal had been struck with Mexican rebels.

Though many Westerners shared philosophies with the Republican presidents, they were not their stooges. The fighters were independent, their backers were the merchants and their goal was to revolutionize the Spanish empire for exclusive trade purposes, which made action outside of government control a necessity. Furthermore, Texas alone was never the aim of the 1812 filibuster but was a stepping stone to Mexico and beyond. What mattered to the men of New Orleans was control of the trade with a new nation bursting with mines of gold and silver. As their mouthpiece, the *Orleans Gazette* had fantasized, New Orleans, possessing "the countless treasures of the south, and the inexhaustible fertility of the Western states . . . would soon rival and outshine the most opulent cities of the World."[13]

The connection between Burrites and the Texas Revolution of 1811 was actually well understood by people in connection with the filibusters at the time, but it is a point of which many historians have since lost sight. Henry Stewart Foote, who wrote a history of Texas while it was still a republic, asserted that after Burr had left America, "the cause to which he had so generously devoted himself was far from languishing; it was steadily advancing in the hearts and understandings of men." There were, Foote noted, "thousands who stood ready to risk their lives and fortunes in the grand conflict against Spanish dominion."[14]

As a child, Foote had actually known many of the veterans of the Republican Army of the North in Tennessee. As a boy, he was regaled with Reuben Ross's stories of the filibuster and recalled a meeting with a man he believed to be Samuel Kemper, but who was probably his elder brother Reuben (since Samuel was deceased). At the home of US attorney general William Wirt, who had been the prosecutor of Burr in his trial, young Foote nonetheless found the Burr acolyte Kemper an honored guest. "I well recollect having been forcibly struck with the marked and somewhat *deferential* courtesy exercised towards Col. K. by Mr. Wirt, and of having been constrained to render my full tribute of youthful admiration to the towering, Achilles-like" Kemper. That a man who had been involved in "an attempt to carry into execution, at least in part, the liberating project of Col. Burr, happened to find favor so far as to be invited to the house of his distinguished prosecutor is more than I can explain."[15]

Mirabeau Lamar, the president of the Republic of Texas, who conversed with Republican Army veterans and preserved many of their accounts, made it clear who was responsible for the invasion—and who was not. Gutiérrez, in "planting his banner on the banks of the Sabine, invoked the chivalry of the American people for that aid and support which he had failed to obtain from the [American] government."[16]

In the end, the support provided by these backers of the revolution fell far short, and to this circumstance we can credit Governor Claiborne's proclamation. This late effort to stop the filibuster was devastating in two ways: First, it put to lie the idea that the expedition was secretly supported by the government. This retarded recruitment and dried up potentially lucrative sources of arms, ammunition, and supplies. Had Claiborne simply said nothing, Nathaniel Cogswell might indeed have secured valuable ordnance and shipped it to the rebels, and Gen. John Adair may have marched with his vast reinforcement. By issuing his proclamation, the Orleans Territorial governor consigned the rebellion in Texas to eventual defeat—and Mexico to a ten-year war instead of a much shorter one. The fact that one of the Republican Army's leading officers, Reuben Ross, had to return to America to beg for new recruits and spend his own money to buy supplies, shows just how effective the governor's act had been. Whatever organized support the army had at the beginning, the rebels in Texas were orphans the moment Claiborne spoke out.

The Continuity of Filibusters: 1806–1836

Texas history before the 1836 revolution is frequently written in a series of discrete episodes, but when the activities, organizing impulse of former Burrites, and the commonality of men involved in all major Texas filibusters are considered, it becomes clear that these events are highly interconnected. A similar motivation can be discerned uniting the machinations along the Spanish borderlands from Phillip Nolan to Aaron Burr to Sam Houston. This was the filibuster impulse, and the driving factors were individual longing for betterment in wealth and standing, the broader community desire to expand mercantile trade, and republican idealism, genuinely embraced in some cases, but in others a veneer painted on an enterprise for moral sanction.

Edward L. Miller, in his 2004 book "New Orleans and the Texas Revolution" discerned something akin to this mercantile motive from a study focused on the end of this timeline. New Orleans capital, loans, and even men (the famous "New Orleans Greys" who died at the Alamo, for example) were the vital support network for the whole enterprise. What the history of the New Orleans mercantile community in the filibuster efforts of 1806, 1812, 1814, 1815, 1817, 1819—and, yes, 1836—shows is that this support from the Crescent City and a wider West beyond it was not an innovation. It was a Southwestern tradition, and the heart of the filibuster beat with the lust and lure of commerce. It was this commerce first, not slavery (and not *initially* annexation), which fired the imaginations of the men invading Texas, and paved common ground between Anglo-Americans and Mexicans.

Nonetheless, it would be wrong to suggest that the American passion to liberate the Spanish New World empire was purely material. America since its beginning had a special hostility to Spain, and to this latent sentiment was added the zealotry of revolution. In her superb work, *Our Sister Republics,* historian Caitlin Fitz showed how the cause of Spanish America became a cause célèbre in the 1820s, as the revolutions began to bear their first fruits. An example of this enthusiasm can be found in the case of one Aylett Buckner—not the rebel who fought in the Republican Army of the North, but a namesake cousin from Kentucky—who upon the birth of a son in 1823 chose to name his baby after a South American independence icon. *Simon Bolivar Buckner*, as the youth was called, ultimately served as a general in the army of the Confederate States of America. This was one manifestation, along with countless editorials, Fourth of July toasts, and even filibusters, showing a genuine American enthusiasm for the Spanish American revolutionary cause, even in lands where the natives were darker and more Catholic than most of the cheering white, protestant Americans would have preferred.[17]

It is crucial to note that the filibusters into Texas and northern Mexico suspended sharply with the independence of Mexico in 1821. Once republicanism and trade had seemingly triumphed in Texas under the Mexican flag, the filibusters led by men connected to the 1812 invasion ended. This is partly attributable to the removal of the implicit moral sanction provided by republican ideology, but mostly because Mexico then opened up Texas to *nonmilitary* means for Westerners to seek land and fortune. It was a peaceful alternative that many veterans took, both due to their maturity but also from a sincere effort to embrace the Mexican republic for its own sake.

The filibuster impulse from the beginning had always been a marriage between lofty idealism and naked aggression, and these would become more imbalanced over time. Even in the era of Columbian brotherhood that Fitz describes, idealist sentiments were just the dream, while the reality was becoming more sordid. As the decades went by, the idealism (or pretense) diminished and was eventually dropped, most ignobly in the case of the American William Walker, who set up two "independent" republics in northern Mexico before sailing to even greater infamy, seizing Nicaragua in 1856 and making himself president of that nation.[18]

The Settlers

Many of the Anglo-American veterans of the 1812 invasion settled in Texas after Mexican independence. Some of them, or their children, became leading players in the Texas revolutionary struggle that followed, or in the short-lived Republic of Texas. Some arrived with strong preexisting ties to their fellow republicans among the Tejano population. Historians have noted the presence of a few of them, such as Warren D. C. Hall, but the prevalence of these men in the early Anglo period of Texas history has been critically overlooked. They were practically everywhere in the young republic. When Hall suffered financial setbacks that forced him to sell his plantation in 1843, the buyer was Albert Sidney Johnston, the half-brother of two of his 1812 comrades. In the small town of Atascocita, Texas, two of the village's alcaldes were former Texas volunteers, Henry Munson and George Orr. Examples such as these are just from the names we know—which represent probably no more than one quarter of the actual Republican Army roster.[19]

These ties between the forgotten first revolution and the well-known second necessitate a reassessment of common assumptions about early Texas. To what degree are generalized assumptions about the motivations of 1820s and 1830s settlers and fighters valid when a small but influential portion of them had cast their lot with Texas in an era with generationally different political implications? Juan Mafalen (John McFarlan) and Enrique Kuerke (Henry Quirk) settled in Spanish Texas when the ink was still dry on the US Constitution and the cotton gin had not yet been invented. Can they really be lumped in with the foot soldiers of an invasion of politically motivated Southern cotton interests spurred on in the wake of the Missouri Compromise?

The Question of Annexation

Among historians, it has been taken as given that the American volunteers of 1812 supported annexation, but this is generally the result of a hindsight-induced misreading of the primary sources. Ted Schwartz, for instance, states that Sibley, in his letters "intimated that the leaders hoped for the liberation of Texas, followed by United States annexation. Shaler wrote Monroe of the same views." But a close reading of both Sibley's and Shaler's letters in this case shows this to be a false reading. Sibley merely says the plan is "deeply laid and co-extensive with the Southern and Western states." To a historian viewing backward from the perspective of 1836, this naturally sounds like annexation to support slave state interests, but seen *forward* from the more relevant Burr legacy, this is something entirely different.[20]

Moreover, in the same letter quoted previously, Sibley also states, "The leaders will say it is to aid the revolutionists in throwing off their European dependence, & establishing a government of their own, but they have more extended views, which may greatly endanger the tranquility of the U. States, *for our good they are not going to act*" (emphasis added). This suggests a Burr-like independent state, possibly a magnet for Western separatism or English intervention. Henderson Yoakum wrote that Augustus Magee had in mind "conquering Texas to the Rio Grande, and building up a republican state, with a view of ultimately adding it to the American or Mexican Union *as circumstances should admit*" (emphasis added). As West Florida had shown, annexation, if it were to come, would be at a price—one that was negotiable and which implicitly could be rejected should the ransom not be met. An independent republic, Mexican in name but beholden perhaps to Anglo warlords, was an equally possible outcome. Furthermore, the visceral reaction by the filibusters to John Robinson's mission from the United States shows a latent hostility to American authority consistent with the expedition's Burrite ancestry.[21]

Since none of the members of the expedition *at the time* made any statements on the subject, and subsequent accounts by survivors were penned decades later, these contemporary letters (and Robinson's account) are the only truly authoritative statements on the expedition's motives that one can take at face value. Contemporary voices suggesting an annexation intent, such as some American newspapers and Spanish minister Onís, were subject to assumptions to fit their authors' preconceptions. While no doubt the American volunteers had a diversity of views, and these evolved throughout the campaign, the evidence for anything remotely resembling a consensus for annexation to the United States is nonexistent.[22]

What does this all mean for later Texas? It would be an overstatement to say that 1812–13 veterans defined the wave of Anglo settlers who came to Texas during the traditional settlement period of the 1820s. They were a minority who had grown up in a far less nationalistic country, and they were swamped by newcomers of the following generation deeply tied to the nationalism of the United States and the regionalism of the South in particular. But the veterans' presence, and the implications it has on the Texas narrative, are profound. Anglo Texas was not birthed fully-grown, like Athena, from the head of Stephen F. Austin. It was the product of a continuous, evolving narrative, with threads reaching back farther into its past and more complex than previously understood.

The Texas Revolution of 1811 is *central* to this debate, though it has never been recognized as such. The destruction which it caused led directly to Arredondo's decision to open up settlement to Americans, something to which Spain had been exceedingly hostile before. There can be no doubt that the vacuum of Spanish/Mexican power on the one hand and Anglo expansionism on the other were on a collision course in any event, but absent the failure of the 1811–13 revolution, there is little reason to suppose that Spain or even Mexico would have breached their own borders by allowing in legal immigration at such levels from a neighbor.

Tejanos: The Native Drive for Liberty and Trade

Up to now, this final chapter has focused on the Anglo-American side of this story. As a part of the United States today, the key relevance of Texas in history is what it has to say about America. It is also a story skewed in this direction by the broader availability of sources on the American side. But seeing it exclusively so would be a disservice to important native participants who, rather than being mere bystanders, actively shaped their own destiny. This is a story of two impulses that came together, a marriage of convenience between a subject people dreaming of freedom and trade on the one hand, and on the other, a free people dreaming of land, specie, and markets, and willing to fight in a foreign war to get them.

The Anglo takeover of Texas after 1836, and the influx of Southerners ignorant of and dismissive of native Tejano views, has led to an enduring Texas myth. In this telling, the natives were a poor, "priest-ridden," unaspiring, and servile population who did nothing to better their station. Only with the arrival of Anglo Americans did Texas begin to emerge out of this miasma of Catholic lethargy into liberty, freedom, and ultimately, prosperity. In the twentieth century, acceptance was given to the small core of Tejano allies, but the narrative remained fundamentally the same. It was, at its heart, the old "black legend" of Spain, painted anew in Texas hues.

This is of course a flawed view of history written in both racism and ignorance. But while racism is on the wane today, the ignorance remains—even among the *Hispanic* population of Texas. These heirs to the early Tejano republican tradition seek for a relevant history, but walk blindly past this central event in their own story. Only after an effort of many years by Mexican American advocates was a small reference to José Bernardo Gutiérrez added to the *Texas Essential Knowledge and Skills*, the curriculum for Texas History in schools statewide, in 2016. Thus history books ignore a complete revolution in which more people died in each of two or possibly three battles than at San Jacinto, while belatedly representing it with a single personality (who was not even from Texas). But the story as it truly happened is much deeper and sheds arguably more light on Tejano history than it does for the history of Anglos in the Lone Star State.[23]

I call this conflict the Texas Revolution of 1811 and not that of 1812, because the story properly began with the Tejano actions, not the filibuster. Tejanos *led the way* for liberty, independence, and economic freedom in Texas. They did not wait until Anglo filibusters arrived to do so. They launched the revolution *on their own* in 1811. Only after this was defeated by Zambrano's coup was a predominately Anglo volunteer army needed to aid the republican cause and bring it to ascendancy. When this triumph was achieved in March 1813, Tejanos once again restored their liberty. They did so not as an independent republic to be manipulated by Kemper and his outsiders, but as a free state committed to a perpetual union with the nascent Mexican nation.

But they *were* a republic, and that distinction is important. The Mexican Texans' April 1813 declaration of independence and constitution were not only the first of their kind in Mexico, but they were also the *only* successful ones during the revolutionary struggle. When Mexico itself finally gained its independence in 1821, it did not do so as a republic but as a monarchy, under the viceroy-turned-emperor Augustín de Iturbide. Thus the people of Béxar, driven by the passion of Gutiérrez and the example of the Anglo volunteers—but also by their own innate struggle for self-rule—were pushing far *in advance* of Mexico proper in the drive for liberty.

American critics of Gutiérrez's constitution asserted that it was horribly flawed. But could not the same be said of the Americans' first failed charter? The Tejano failure to develop transformative leaders and institutions stemmed not from any inherent incapacity, only lack of precedent. The American Revolution was a conservative one drawing on a century of English liberal tradition. The people of Spanish Texas, equally conservative, drew likewise on their own experience, and their solution, as befitting heirs of Spanish tradition, was to focus on good government first and democratic institutions later.

Texans today of all backgrounds (and Americans and Mexicans as well) fail to appreciate the full scope of the disaster which befell this short-lived Tejano republican experiment after the Battle of Medina. It was a calamity that extinguished some of the cream of native leaders and perpetually changed those who survived, leaving them scarred, wary—even pillaged of their memories. This, the anonymous Tejano author wrote, was why Texas was not as celebrated among the Mexicans as Guadalajara, Valladolid, Zacatecas, Oaxaca, Puebla, Veracruz, and other revolutionary regions. In setting forth his account, he hoped to change that history and reclaim the lost valor of Texas.[24]

But this revival of memory, like the carefree old Tejano province of years gone by, would never materialize. The Revolution of 1811 had extinguished too many leaders, decimated too many families, and left those that remained destitute of both means and tradition. It created an economic death spiral so severe that Texas' independent status as a province was even erased, as it was subsumed into union with neighboring Coahuila. Texas would shrink ever more into the "howling wilderness" Austin discovered until the only alternative to complete collapse was the importation of foreign settlers, with the inevitable transformation of Texas from a Hispanic-dominated province to an Anglo-American one.

But for those Tejanos who had endured, and particularly those who had spent months or years in exile in Louisiana, these tragic years created among a core of surviving leaders a powerful hope to regain what had been lost. It also established a strong affinity to the American nation, its people, democratic institutions, and economy.

It is a necessity to recognize and reclaim this *lost* Tejano past. As Raúl Coronado lamented, "U. S. Latino history is often seen as beginning after some form of U. S. invasion and conquest," but actually began during these earlier struggles. The "fetishization" of the American conquest as the birth of the Latino identity, he argues, is a somewhat incomplete framing, and the lost voices of early Tejano history "have been ignored and forgotten." Reclaiming them may do much to contextualize and expand the scope of Tejano identity, both for scholars of the Latino experience and for others seeking to understand its interplay with the broader American one. As Coronado says, we should not ask, "'How were Latinos conquered and colonized?' . . . but 'How did Latinos become modern?'" In other words, what is the totality of experience that created the Latino identity we have today?[25]

For José Antonio Navarro, even while struggling with the growing marginalization of Tejanos in their own homeland after the Anglo takeover, the sacrifice was still worth it; his hopes for the future held more optimism than the dismal past of arbitrary rule, violence, and bloody revolution. He recalled how far the Tejanos had come since the pitiful widows and orphans driven by Elizondo from Trinity struggled barefoot back into Béxar at a spot that in intervening years had become a luxurious bathhouse. "Where now in voluptuous ease the ladies of San Antonio lave their graceful person, the ill-treated of their sex of a previous day were driven to moisten their delicate and care-worn limbs." The contrast between the revolutionary past and the prosperous American present was stark to eyes like his that had seen the horrors first hand:[26]

> Who would have predicted to the famous spies of Gen'l Gutiérrez . . . whom Arredondo [sic] caused to be shot at San Antonio, and their decapitated heads, enclosed in an iron grate to be elevated on a high pole—who would have predicted to those two patriot spies that where their decaying heads were once elevated on the Military Plaza as objects of terror and disgust, now proudly floats, after the lapse of thirty-three years, the flag of freedom, an emblem of dread to tyrants—a flag that the world respects?[27]

The People of the Revolution

A last word must be added about people—real people. Fundamentally, this story is about the men and women who lived, fought, triumphed, suffered, died, and endured in a short, violent, and forgotten conflict that raged across Texas two centuries ago. These people—Spanish, Anglo, Tejano, French, and Indian—were living, breathing agents of their own destiny, not just pawns of revolution or reaction. To understand this story, or any story in history, we must know who they were and learn from that what we can. It is not enough to simply judge by generalizations of type. The men who fought in Texas have been described as "nameless frontiersmen or adventurers seeking new lands" by two authors. Another wrote that "the Americans . . . seem to have been common cutthroats." Were decades-long Texas residents McFarlan and Quirk mere adventurers seeking new lands? Were elite private school graduate Augustus Magee, Harvard-trained Henry Adams Bullard, Dartmouth-educated Nathaniel Cogswell, or the well-educated Johnston brothers mere cutthroats? History often steamrolls the individual to make great sweeping declarations about an event. But no event in history happens without the individual as author or victim.[28]

The Texas Revolution of 1811 was the formative first act of modern Texas history, and it was staged by a cast of characters as noble and as weak, as heroic and as cruel, as any who have ever graced the stage of a drama. Their achievements were spectacular. "From a very small beginning, without money or arms, they had grown so formidable as to excite consternation amongst the royal party," as a newspaper of the time eulogized the Republican Army of the North. Even after a defeat in a bloody battle and the trauma of a nightmarish conquest, the curtain never fully closed on this story. The struggle between freedom and tyranny endured in Texas, playing out in minor dramas over the next decade before the final, culminating act in 1836. Even then, of course, the story of freedom in Texas was not complete, as this struggle never is. Liberty for some meant precious little to others who toiled in bondage. But it would come to these Texans too in time. Texans' liberty, from rude beginnings, progressed over the century that followed, and certainly remains imperfect to this day. This is history: It does not end. It is a permanent performance, with many twists and turns, and the curtain never closes.[29]

But, hopefully, with greater appreciation of these lost first pages to this drama, we can look back on it and see it in a new light. Most importantly, the men and women of 1811–13 can live again in our imagination: Warriors for their king like Manuel Salcedo and Juan Manuel Zambrano; crusaders for liberty like Bernardo Gutiérrez de Lara and Henry Adams Bullard; courageous fighters like Miguel Menchaca, Samuel Kemper, Henry Perry, and Juan Savías; indomitable women staring down evil eye-to-eye like Joséfa Nuñes de Arocha; and children committed to a better world than the one they were borne into like Antonio Menchaca and José María Jesús Carbajal. These were the shapers of history and the witnesses to the rebellion in Texas two hundred years ago. It is not necessary to parse who among them are the heroes and who fall short. It is enough to know that they lived.

Appendix A

List of Mexican/Tejano Rebels

The following list of Mexican/Tejano rebels is from a variety of sources, including a list compiled by the Spanish of property belonging to the insurgents who fled Béxar. This list includes some Frenchmen who were legal residents of Nacogdoches. A more detailed version, with notes on specific individuals, can be found at http://www.texhist.com/2021/11/mexicantejano-rebels-in-texas.html. Archivos del Estado de Coahuila at Saltillo. No. 663, pages 456 to 473.

Rebel Commanders:

Juan Bautista de las Casas
José Bernardo Gutiérrez de Lara
José Alvarez de Toledo

Soldiers and Rebel Civilians:

Domingo Diego Acosta
Pedro de Acosta
Francisco Arocha
Josefa Nuñez de Arocha
Josefa Paula Agapitha Arocha
Ramon de Arocha
Tomás Arocha
Antonio Baca
José Francisco Banegas
José Ignacio y Barva
Joseph de la Baume
Bernardo Benites
José Benites
Nícolas Benites
Petra Benitez
Ancelmo Bergara
Juan Blanco
Nepomuceno Bocanegra
Francisco Borrego
Jose Antonio Carbajal
Antonio Carmona
Francisco Carmona
Francisco de la Cerda
Marcelo Cervantes
Antonio Castro
Miguel Castro
Juan Cortés
Remigio Cruz
José Cuevas
José Antonio Curbelo
Juan Antonio Curbelo
Antonio Delgado

Clemente Delgado
Manuel Delgado
José Manuel Delgado
José Delgado
Joaquín Delgado
Juan Manuel Enriquez
Feliz Estrada
Tomás Examia
Jesus Falcon
Francisco Farias
José Andreas Farias
Antonio Flores
Miguel Flores
Sabas Fuentes
El Frances Galet
 ("The Frenchman Galet")
Juan Galván
José Luis Gallardo
Juan Garcia
Juana de la Garza
Ygnacio y Vicente de la Garza
Luís Grande
José María Guadiana
Francisco Hernández
Jose Andres Hernandez
Jose Antonio Hernandez
Xavier Laro
Joaquin Leal
José Leal
José Antonio de Leon
Jose Gil de Leyba
Domingo Losoya
Miguel Losoya
Antonio Martinez
Francisco Martinez
Juan Martinez
Miguel Menchaca
José Menchaca
Luciano Menchaca
José Maria Mona
Gertrudis Montes
Miguel Musquiz

Gabriel de la O
Gregorio Ortega
Manuel Pena
Ygnacio Pena
Adolfo Perez
Ambrosio Perez
Bartolo Perez
Manuel Percz
Juan de Dios Perez
Pedro Prado
Pedro Procela
Claudio Ramirez
Lorenzo Ramos
Manuel Rendon
Miguel del Rio
Mariano Rodriguez
Lt. Pablo Rodriguez
Christoval Rodriguez
Francisco Rodriguez
José Antonio Ruiz
José Francisco Ruiz
Antonio Saenz
Juan Salazar
Jose Sanchez
Manuel Sanchez
Nepomuceno San Miguel
Lieutenant Santos
Gertrudis de los Santos
José Antonio Saucedo
Juan Savías (Sava)
Vicente Tarín
Francisco Travieso
Vicente Travieso
Joaquin del Toro
Juan Antonio Urrutia
José Flores Valdes
Juan Diego Velez
Fernando Veramendi
Juan Martin Veramendi
Jose Antonio Villegas
Josefa Ynojosa (Hinojosa)

Appendix B

List of Foreign Volunteers in the Republican Army of the North

The following list of foreign volunteers in the Republican Army is from a variety of sources, including expedition accounts, Spanish sources, newspapers, genealogical works, and archival records. This list represents at most one quarter of all participants, likely fewer. A more detailed version, with notes on specific individuals, can be found at http://www.texhist.com/2021/11/list-of-foreign-volunteers-in.html.

Commanders:

Augustus Magee
Samuel Kemper
Reuben Ross
Henry Perry

Soldiers:

Samuel Alden
Benjamin Allen
David Allen
Hiram Allen
Martin Allen
William Richmond Anderson
Robert Armstrong
John Ash
J. John Baker
J. Littleton Bailey
Samuel Barber
Stephen Barker
Carlos (Charles) Beltran
Horatio Biglow
Matthew Bonnette
Peter Boone

Benjamin Bradley
Charles Brandenburg
James Brown
William Brown
Aylette C. Buckner
James Busseuil
Henry Adams Bullard
William Bullock
John G. Burnett
Joseph Burton
Richard Cage
Bernard Caillavet
Evariste Calvettes
John M. Cannon
Joseph Carr
? Caston

363

Andrew Chase
Michael Chesneu
Joshua Child(s)
Albert Cole
? Colonie
Hamlin Cook
Godwin Brown Cotten
Charles Craig
William Craig
William Custard
James A. Daniel
Samuel Davenport
? Deane
Henry Derbonne
Bernardo Despallier
George M. Dick
Peter Dillon
Pierre Dolet
Bernardo D'Ortolant
Robert M. Doughty
Anthony Dubois
William Dukes
Andrew Dumar
? Eoses
William Evans
John Ewing
William Ferguson
John Ferguson
Thomas Fetty
William Fisher
Bart Fleming
Dr. Samuel D. Forsyth
Isaac Foster
David Foster
William Francis
James Gaines
Alexander Germeuil
Henry Gilmore
Charles Gormley
[Second] Gormley
Alexis Grappe
H. Greg

Nathan M. Hale
Darlington Hall
John "Jack" W. Hall
Warren D. C. Hall
William Ham
Eli Harris
Charles A. Hickman
William Hickman
John Holly
Stephen Holstein
? Holmes
Amos Hubbard
Daniel James
George James
James Johnson
Jud Johnson
Darius Johnston
Orramel Johnston
Frank Johnstone
Blake B. Jones
David G. Jones
William Justice
James Kenneday/Kennedy
John Gladden King
Amalie Lafitte
Bernard Lafitte
Abner Lane
Charles Lauranu
Louis Latham
David Long
James Louard
Thomas Hussey Luckett Jr.
? Lutzer
John Lynch
Joel Lyon
Dan MacLean/McClean
? Madison
William Manadue
Louis Massicot(t)
A. W. McClain
John McFarlan
James McKim

William McLane
John McLannahan
Thomas McLaughlin
James McWilliams
Martin McWilliams
Francis J. Menepier
Tenoss Moinet
Aaron Samuel Mower
? Munholland
Charles Muill
Henry William Munson
William A. Murray
Jacob Myers
Samuel Noah
James O'Donnell
H. J. Offutt
George Orr
William Owens
William Parker
Anthony Parish/Pared
Alexander Patterson
Frederic Patterson
Leonard Patterson
Stephen Paul
Isaac Paul
David Phelps
W. Phierson
Joseph Phillips
Juan Mariano Picornell
George Powell
Joseph Powell
William A. Prentiss
? Prudhomme
William Price
Edmund Quirk
Michael/Miguel Quinn
William Ramage
Samuel Richards
Elisha Roberts
Andrew Robinson
Benjamin Robinson
Charles (Charley) Rollins
? Rollins
Samuel Ross
Samuel Rowe
James Royall
Lacy Rumsey
Joseph Ruth
Captain Scott
Samuel Sexton
Peter Sides
Thomas Slocum
William Slocum
Horatio Smith
Lovett Smith
Orren Smith
Patrick Smith
William Snodgrass
Benjamin Stokes
James Stone
Daniel Sullivan
Ambrose Sutton
Charles Swan
Josiah Taylor
Thomas Taylor
Chesneau Tontin
William Utridge
John Villars
W. W. Walker
Augustus Wallace
James Wallace Sr.
James Wallace Jr.
Stephen Wallace
Charles F. Walthers
Isaac Walthers
George Westfield
Osgood Whittier
Joseph Biddle Wilkinson
James Biddle Wilkinson
(Adjutant) Wilson
Samuel Winfield (Wingfield)
Michael Wolford/Wolforth
Walter Young

Notes

Introduction

1. Lamar, the second president of the Republic of Texas, was an avid historian, who collected and preserved many of the original accounts of the war. Charles Adams Gulick Jr., *The Papers of Mirabeau Buonaparte Lamar* (Austin: Pemberton Press, 1968), 2:55.

2. Based on similarities in this account and the details included in the memoirs of José Antonio Navarro, he is a likely author of this anonymous account. "Memoria de las cosas mas notables que acaesieron en Bexar el año de 13, Mandando el Tirano Arredondo." [1813] H. E. Bolton Collection, The Bancroft Library, University of California, Berkeley. Translation by Brandon Seale and Brian Alan Stauffer.

3. In choosing to call the conflict the Texas Revolution of 1811, this author recognizes the inadequacy of previous names. The "Gutiérrez-Magee Expedition" is only the *middle* phase of the war. The mostly Anglo-American force that invaded in August 1812 restarted an already existing conflict begun with the Casas Revolt of 1811. By the Battle of Medina, native-born Tejanos and Spanish deserters likely outnumbered the Anglos, a fact obscured by the Anglo-centric filibuster narrative. The "Gachupín War" references the gachupines, the Spanish-born population who dominated Mexico, at the expense of the Creoles. But this class struggle was also a just part, not the totality of the conflict.

4. Even this reference only includes mention of one person, José Bernardo Gutiérrez de Lara, and one event, the Battle of Medina. Texas Education Agency, "Texas Essential Knowledge and Skills for Social Studies, Subchapter B. Middle School," Texas Education Agency, http://ritter.tea.state.tx.us/rules/tac/chapter113/ch113b.html#113.19 (accessed June 17, 2021).

5. Raúl Coronado, *A World Not to Come: A History of Latino Writing and Print Culture*. (Cambridge, MA: Harvard University Press, 2013), 19.

6. David Narrett, *Adventurism and Empire: The Struggle for Mastery in the Louisiana-Florida Borderlands, 1762–1803* (Chapel Hill: University of North Carolina Press, 2015), 3.

7. Charles Despallier is counted twice among the Alamo victims, both under his own name and that of Carlos Espalier, the Hispanicized version of his name (D'Espallier in the original), based on two pension claims by his mother and aunt. The two men are the same. James Aalan Bernsen, "Carlos Espalier: The Alamo Defender Who Never Was," http://www.texhist.com/2021/11/carlos-espalier.html (accessed November 23, 2021).

8. Anonymous, "McFarlan, John," *Handbook of Texas Online*, published by the Texas State Historical Association, https://www.tshaonline.org/handbook/entries/mcfarlan-john (accessed July 1, 2021). Subsequently cited as *HOTO*. Anonymous, "Cotten, Godwin Brown Michael," *HOTO*, https://www.tshaonline.org/handbook/entries/cotten-godwin-brown-michael (accessed July 1, 2021).

9. Timothy Matovina and Jesús F. de la Teja, ed., *Recollections of a Tejano Life: Antonio Menchaca in Texas History* (Austin: University of Texas Press, 2013), 32.

10. The district attorney was Henry Marie Breckenridge, who wrote a history of the War of 1812, but not of the war in Texas. H. M. Breckenridge to William Shaler, December 16, 1813, William Shaler Papers, Historical Society of Pennsylvania, Philadelphia, PA.

11. Julia Kathryn Garrett, *Green Flag over Texas: The Last Years of Spain in Texas.* (Austin: Pemberton Press, 1939). Harris Gaylord Warren, *The Sword Was Their Passport: A History of American Filibustering in the Mexican Revolution* (Baton Rouge: Louisiana State University Press, 1943). Ted Schwartz and Robert Thonhoff, *Forgotten Battlefield of the First Texas Revolution* (Austin: Eakin Press, 1985). J. C. A. Stagg, *Borderlines in Borderlands: James Madison and the Spanish-American Frontier, 1776–1821* (New Haven: Yale University Press, 2009). Bradley, *We Never Retreat: Filibustering Expeditions into Spanish Texas, 1812–1822* (College Station: Texas A&M University Press, 2015).

Schwartz and Thonhoff's book is mainly a shortened reprisal of Garrett's narrative but is focused on locating the site of the Battle of Medina. Warren, Stagg, and Bradley's books cover several filibusters, but in each case, the Gutiérrez-Magee filibuster is covered across several chapters.

The articles include Kevin Brady, "Unspoken Words: James Monroe's Involvement in the Magee-Gutiérrez Filibuster," *East Texas Historical Journal* 45, no. 1 (March 2007): 58–68. Richard W. Gronet, "United States and the Invasion of Texas, 1810–1814," *The Americas* 25 (January 1969): 281–306. David Narrett, "Geopolitics and Intrigue: James Wilkinson, the Spanish Borderlands, and Mexican Independence," *William and Mary Quarterly* 69, no. 1 (January 2012), 101–46. David Narrett, "José Bernardo Gutiérrez de Lara: 'Caudillo' of the Mexican Republic in Texas," *Southwestern Historical Quarterly* 106, no. 2 (October 2002): 194–228. David Narrett, "Liberation and Conquest: John Hamilton Robinson and U. S. Adventurism Toward Mexico, 1806–1809," *Western Historical Quarterly* 40, no. 1 (Spring 2009), 23–50. David J. Pennington, "Reassessing James Madison's Ambitions in Florida and Texas, 1810–1813," *Southern Historian* 31 (April 13, 2010), 66–79. J. C. A. Stagg, "The Madison Administration and Mexico: Reinterpreting the Gutiérrez-Magee Raid of 1812–1813," *William and Mary Quarterly* 59 (April 2002): 449–80.

12. There were many other sources of which they did *not* know: the McLane account of the filibuster would not be published until the 1960s and the Robert Bruce Blake translations of the Béxar Archive—a massive feat that took thirty years to complete—had only just begun when Warren was writing. In contrast, for this book, the author had the entire collection digitized and keyword searchable. Julia Kathryn Garrett, *Green Flag over Texas: The Last Years of Spain in Texas* (Austin: Pemberton Press, 1939). Harris Gaylord Warren, *The Sword Was Their Passport: A History of American Filibustering in the Mexican Revolution* (Baton Rouge: Louisiana State University Press, 1943).

13. The only other candidates for an administration guiding hand in the expedition would be the officers of Fort Claiborne, Governor Claiborne himself, or Natchitoches Indian Agent John Sibley. Sibley is the only really plausible candidate of these, and though he had sympathy towards many of the Neutral Ground infiltrators, there is no evidence whatsoever that he played any guiding role.

14. The instruction letter resides in William Shaler's personal papers, located in the Historical Society of Pennsylvania. This is separate from the Correspondence of Special Agents folder in the US National Archives. While previous historians frequently mention the *Shaler Papers*, they generally are referencing the latter. Both Garrett and Warren do this and a detailed search of their notes indicate no documents at all from the personal folder of Shaler, indicating they missed not only the instruction letter but *all* of Shaler's personal correspon-

dence, much of it relevant. Moreover, the documents referenced from the state department files are very degraded and in many cases illegible. The Shaler Letterbooks, on the other hand, also unknown to previous writers, contain the author's pristine copies of the correspondence he sent to Washington.

15. Warren does use the term "Shaler Papers" in his notes and bibliography, but in reference to the Correspondence of Special Agents folder for Shaler, a separate collection. Nor did these writers know of the existence of the Shaler Letterbooks, which contain clean and highly legible copies of all letters Shaler wrote to the administration, whereas the State Department files of the same letters are in some cases not even legible. These two sources are hence of absolute importance for correctly interpreting the agent's actions.

16. Gutiérrez does not "immediately" plan anything. It is two weeks before his diary records any connection that appears to be connected to the filibuster. On May 15th, he writes, "Today a French gentleman came to negotiate the matter, of which I shall speak presently in a note." This was likely Bernardo Despallier, who helped Gutiérrez draft propaganda letters, which were printed ten days later. This was separate from any talk of invasion. Warren, "The Sword Was Their Passport," 22–23. Elizabeth Howard West, "Diary of José Bernardo Gutiérrez de Lara, 1811–1812. [Part 1]," *American Historical Review* 34, no. 2 (1929): 293.

17. Given Robinson's history before and after he met with the rebels, he certainly would have embraced and flattered them if such an action had implicit sanction by the administration, and it is inconceivable that Monroe wanted a filibuster while simultaneously concealing that fact from both his agents on the borders of Texas. Frank L. Owsley and Gene A. Smith, *Filibusters and Expansionists: Jeffersonian Manifest Destiny, 1800–1821* (Tuscaloosa: University of Alabama Press, 1997), ix. John Robinson to James Monroe, July 26, 1813, the Filibustering Expedition against the Spanish Government of Mexico, 1811–16, US National Archives (Henceforth CRF).

18. In discovering these names, this author had assistance from several individuals, as noted in the acknowledgments. A list of the known men and women involved in the revolution is included in the appendix of this book. Henry Walker, ed., "William McLane's Narrative of the Magee—Gutiérrez Expedition, 1812–1813," *Southwestern Historical Quarterly* 66, no. 4 (April 1963): 580–86.

19. The account is that of Carlos Beltrán, an American of obscure origin who moved to Texas in 1807, became thoroughly Mexicanized, and settled near Chihuahua in the mid-1800s. Historians have downplayed it due to its romanticized narrative. Romanticized it may be, but its facts are generally accurate and highly detailed, despite being written long before major research was conducted or published. There are numerous proof points, discussed in this work, but also in depth at James Aalan Bernsen, "The Carlos Beltrán Account," *The Texas History Blog,* http://www.texhist.com/2021/11/the-carlos-beltran-account.html (accessed November 25, 2021).

20. Julius W. Pratt, *Expansionists of 1812* (Gloucester, MA: Peter Smith, 1957), 62.

21. Shaler, after elaborating how John Adair was organizing the rebel forces, writes, "Mr. Saul of Orleans writes me that Daniel Clark is reported to be connected with Adair." Shaler to Monroe, August 18, 1812, William Shaler Letterbooks, The Gilder Lehrman Collection, The Gilder Lehrman Institute of American History, New York.

Chapter 1

1. The Summer of 1804 was already "very warm," as reported by Governor William C. C. Claiborne about three weeks prior. William C. C. Claiborne to Thomas Jefferson, May 20, 1804, in James P. McClure, ed., *The Papers of Thomas Jefferson* 43, no. 11 (Princeton: Princeton

University Press, 2017), 460–61. William C. Davis, *Rogue Republic: How Would-Be Patriots Waged the Shortest Revolution in American History* (Boston: Houghton Mifflin Harcourt, 2011), 21–22. Isaac Joslin Cox, *The West Florida Controversy, 1798–1813: A Study in American Diplomacy* (Gloucester, MA: Peter Smith, 1967), 152.

2. The quote is from Gov. William C. C. Claiborne, quoted in Cox, *West Florida Controversy*, 507. The term "West Florida" has a geographically confused history, and the name has variously been applied to all of the northern Gulf Coast between the Mississippi and the Florida Panhandle. The "West Florida Rebellion" described in this chapter generally focuses on the "Florida Parishes" of Louisiana, which were part but not all of the province as it generally is understood, and most of the events described herein pertain solely to the smaller region. Gilbert C. Din, "A Troubled Seven Years: Spanish Reactions to American Claims and Aggression in 'West Florida,' 1803–1810," *Louisiana History: The Journal of the Louisiana Historical Association* 59, no. 4 (2018): 411–12.

3. Davis, *Rogue Republic*, 22.

4. Davis, *Rogue Republic*, 22. Willis M. Kemper, *Genealogy of the Kemper Family in the United States: Descendants of John Kemper of Virginia; with a Short Historical Sketch of His Family and of the German Reformed Colony at Germanna and Germantown, Va* (Germanna, VA: G. K. Hazlett & Company, 1899), 10. Fauquier County (VA) Board of Trade, *Fauquier County, Virginia: Historical Notes* (Warrenton, VA: Fauquier County Board of Trade, 1914), 33. Francis D. Cogliano, "Failed Filibusters: The Kemper Rebellion, the Burr Conspiracy and Early American Expansion," University of Edinburgh, http://www.shca.ed.ac.uk/staff/supporting_files/fcogliano/failed-filibusters.pdf (accessed June 24, 2021).

5. Din, "A Troubled Seven Years," 416.

6. As Jefferson put it, "We should take care . . . not to press too soon on the Spaniards. These countries cannot be in better hands. My fear is that they are too feeble to hold them until our population can be sufficiently advanced to gain it from them piece-by-piece." Jefferson to Archibald Stewart, January 25, 1786, quoted in Gordon S. Brown, *Latin American Rebels and the United States, 1806–1822* (Jefferson, NC: McFarland & Company, 2015), 11. 1810 Census data from http://www.census.gov (accessed June 24, 2021).

7. Gilbert C. Din notes, "Jefferson firmly believed that Americans in Spanish territory would preserve their allegiance to the United States. But . . . he failed to perceive that many economically strapped farmers who settled on Spanish soil valued their farms that they had freely received and feared their loss in a change of national sovereignty." Din, "A Troubled Seven Years," 417. As for the British loyalists, they "had migrated to the territory specifically because it was not controlled by the Americans." Samuel C. Hyde, "Introduction: Setting a Precedent for Regional Revolution: The West Florida Revolt Considered," *The Florida Historical Quarterly* 90, no. 2 (2011): 121–32. Cody Scallions, "The Rise and Fall of the Original Lone Star State: Infant American Imperialism Ascendant in West Florida," *Florida Historical Quarterly* 90, no. 2 (Fall 2011): 195.

8. The order was approved by Carlos de Grand Pré, the governor of the Baton Rouge District. "Smith, John," Biographical Directory of the United States Congress, https://bioguide.congress.gov/search/bio/S000567 (accessed June 4, 2021). "John Smith," Ohio History Central, https://ohiohistorycentral.org/w/John_Smith (accessed June 4, 2021). Andrew McMichael, *Atlantic Loyalties: Americans in Spanish West Florida, 1785–1810* (Athens: University of Georgia Press, 2008), 83. Davis, *Rogue Republic*, 12. Cox, *West Florida Controversy*, 152.

9. Din, "A Troubled Seven Years," 433. Davis, *Rogue Republic*, 22.

10. Andro Linklater, *An Artist in Treason: The Extraordinary Double Life of General James Wilkinson* (Walker Publishing Company, New York: 2009), 77.

11. Jefferson to John C. Breckenridge, August 12, 1803, in Thomas Jefferson Randolph, ed., *Memoirs, Correspondence and Private Papers of Thomas Jefferson, Vol. 3* (London: Henry Colburn and Richard Bentley, 1829), 520.

12. Brown, *Latin American Rebels and the United States*, 19.

13. William Horace Brown, *The Glory Seekers: The Romance of Would-Be Founders of Empire in the Early Days of the Great Southwest* (Chicago: A. C. McClurg & Co., 1906), 85. Laurie Winn Carlson, *Seduced by the West: Jefferson's America and the Lure of the Land Beyond the Mississippi* (Chicago: Ivan R. Dee, 2003), 23. Frederick Jackson Turner, *The Significance of the Frontier in American History* (London: Penguin Books, 2008), 28. Samuel J. Watson, *Jackson's Sword: The Army Officer Corps on the American Frontier, 1810–1821* (Lawrence: University of Kansas Press), 29. Joyce Appleby, *Inheriting the Revolution: The First Generation of Americans* (Cambridge, MA: Belknap Press, 2001), 53. Jared Orsi, *Citizen Explorer: The Life of Zebulon Pike* (New York: Oxford University Press, 2014), 242.

14. Turner, *Significance of the Frontier in American History*, 21.

15. The Spanish had initially allowed American commerce to flow down the Mississippi through the 1795 Treaty of Madrid. The right was actually suspended several times. Walter Flavius McCaleb, *The Aaron Burr Conspiracy* (New York: Dodd, Mead and Company, 1903), 8.

16. McCaleb, *Aaron Burr Conspiracy*, 4.

17. Narrett, *Adventurism and Empire*, 3. Carlson, *Seduced by the West*, 44. Brown, *Latin American Rebels and the United States*, 17.

18. Linklater, *An Artist in Treason*, 85–90.

19. James Wilkinson to Jonathan Williams, August 11, 1805, quoted in David E. Narrett, "Geopolitics and Intrigue: James Wilkinson, the Spanish Borderlands, and Mexican Independence," *William and Mary Quarterly* 69, no. 1 (January 2012), 101. Linklater, *An Artist in Treason*, 93.

20. Brown, *The Glory Seekers*, 57.

21. Clark Jr. came to New Orleans with a namesake uncle, Daniel Clark Sr., who does not figure prominently in this account. Junius P. Rodríguez, ed., *The Louisiana Purchase: A Historical and Geographical Encyclopedia* (Santa Barbara, ABC CLIO, 2002), 71.

22. Michael S. Wohl, "A Man in the Shadow: The Life of Daniel Clark" (PhD diss., Tulane University, 1984), 19–21.

23. Wohl, "A Man in the Shadow," 19–21. Joseph F. Stoltz III, "'The Preservation of Good Order': William C. C. Claiborne and the Militia of the Louisiana Provisional Government, 1803–1805," *Louisiana History: The Journal of the Louisiana Historical Association* 54, no. 4 (Fall 2013): 426, 430.

24. Joseph Stoltz, "An Ardent Military Spirit: William C. C. Claiborne and the Creation of the Orleans Territorial Militia, 1803–1805" (master's thesis, University of New Orleans, 2009), 11. Wohl, "A Man in the Shadow," 90. Abernethy, *Burr Conspiracy*, 19.

25. Stoltz, "The Preservation of Good Order," 425–26, 430, 437–40. Peter J. Kastor, "'Motives of Peculiar Urgency': Local Diplomacy in Louisiana, 1803–1821," *The William and Mary Quarterly* 58, no. 4 (October, 2001), 822.

26. Stoltz, "The Preservation of Good Order," 425. Abernethy, *Burr Conspiracy*, 17. "The following is a letter taken from Mr. R. If's Philadelphia Gazette," *The National Intelligencer and Washington Advertiser*, November 30, 1804.

27. Claiborne to Thomas Jefferson, May 29, 1804, in Dunbar Rowland, ed., *Official Letter Books of W. C. C. Claiborne* (Jackson, MS: State Department of Archives and History, 1917), 3:176 (hereafter *CL*). Stoltz, "The Preservation of Good Order," 434.

28. Clark denied being a member of the organization but was said to be among its "leading spirits." It developed as an offshoot of the broader opposition against Claiborne, of which

he was the head. Efforts to revolutionize Mexico were likely one of Clark's many endeavors, whereas for men like James Workman and Lewis Kerr who headed the actual organization, it was their prime focus. Many sources say the group included around three hundred members. During the subsequent trials, the defense placed the number of active members at a dozen, an effort to downplay its danger to the country in the context of the charges of treason. Julien Vernet, *Strangers on Their Native Soil: Opposition to United States Governance in Louisiana's Orleans Territory, 1803–1809* (Jackson: University Press of Mississippi, 2013), 97. *The Trials of the Honb. James Workman and Col. Lewis Kerr before the United States' Court for the Orleans District on a Charge of High Misdemeanor* (New Orleans: Bradford and Anderson, 1807), transcript of proceedings, 25, 74. Andy Doolen, *Territories of Empire: U.S. Writing from the Louisiana Purchase to Mexican Independence* (Oxford: Oxford University Press, 2014), 40–42.

29. David O. Stewart, *American Emperor: Aaron Burr's Challenge to Jefferson's America* (New York: Simon and Schuster, 2011), 104–5. McCaleb, *Aaron Burr Conspiracy*, 31, 113.

30. Samuel C. Hyde Jr., "Consolidating the Revolution: Factionalism and Finesse in the West Florida Revolt, 1810," *Louisiana History: The Journal of the Louisiana Historical Association* 51, no. 3 (Summer 2010): 266.

31. Edward Randolph was later a key player in the Burr Conspiracy and was tried with Burr for High Treason on April 3, 1807. "Trial of Aaron Burr," *American Citizen*, August 10, 1807. Davis, *Rogue Republic*, 13.

32. As Andrew McMichael notes, "Spanish administration in West Florida engendered a high degree of loyalty on the part of Anglo Americans that only broke down *after* the Kemper raids" (emphasis added). It was not implicit support of the Kempers, but dismay at the Spanish authorities' inability to stop the chaos, which caused the Anglo Americans to lose faith in the Spanish government. Davis, *Rogue Republic*, 24. "Kemper Rebellion," Spanish West Florida: Archives of the Spanish Government, 1782–1816, US National Archives, vol. 8, 954–74. Andrew McMichael, "The Kemper 'Rebellion': Filibustering and Resident Anglo American Loyalty in Spanish West Florida," *Louisiana History* 43, no. 2 (April 2002), 135. Davis, *Rogue Republic*, 59.

33. US Department of State, *State Papers and Publick Documents of the United States from the Accession of George Washington to the Presidency, Exhibiting a Complete View of Our Foreign Relations at That Time* (Boston: T. B. Wait and Sons, 1817), 103–8.

34. Accounts do not mention the child, but genealogical records indicate he was born in 1802 and was living with his parents at the time. Several other men in the house—friends of the Kempers—were threatened to stay inside or they would be killed. Presumably, they protected the boy and cared for his injured mother. Davis, *Rogue Republic*, 72. US Department of State, *State Papers and Publick Documents*, 103–8.

35. U.S. Department of State, *State Papers and Publick Documents*, 105–8. *The Trials of the Honb. James Workman and Col. Lewis Kerr*, 155.

36. Cogliano, "Failed Filibusters," 7. Cox, *West Florida Controversy*, 155. Andrew McMichael, *Atlantic Loyalties*, 88.

37. Many Anglo-Americans living in West Florida were also former British loyalists, and the two groups of Americans being difficult to distinguish, the accounts rarely do so. "Daring Outrage!" *National Intelligencer and Washington Advertiser*, October 9, 1805. "Governor of the Mississippi territory to his excellency Charles de Grand Pré," *National Intelligencer and Washington Advertiser*, December 11, 1805.

38. McCaleb, *Aaron Burr Conspiracy*, 113.

39. Abernethy, *Burr Conspiracy*, 21.

40. Most accounts of the Burr expedition posit the theory of dual goals: either invasion of Mexico or severance of New Orleans from the Union. McCaleb argues that the latter

approach was only a ruse used to bait English—and even Spanish—leaders into funding the enterprise. Burr may have entertained both ideas seriously, but enthusiasm for severance of the west was declining and divisive by 1805-6. The liberation of Spanish lands, on the other hand, had near universal appeal. McCaleb, *Aaron Burr Conspiracy*, viii. James Ripley Jacobs, *Tarnished Warrior: Major General James Wilkinson* (New York: MacMillan Company, 1938), 217. Stewart, *American Emperor*, 10, 84.

41. Quoted in Narrett, "Geopolitics and Intrigue," 128.
42. Stewart, *American Emperor*, 84.
43. Stewart, *American Emperor*, 66, 103. McCaleb, *Aaron Burr Conspiracy*, 90.
44. Timothy J. Henderson, *The Mexican Wars for Independence* (New York: Hill and Wang, 2009), 19-20, McCaleb, *Aaron Burr Conspiracy*, 30. Abernethy, *Burr Conspiracy*, 81.
45. McCaleb, *Aaron Burr Conspiracy*, 30. Abernethy, *Burr Conspiracy,* 29.
46. Abernethy, *Burr Conspiracy,* 29-30.
47. The man who intercepted Kemper was Richard Raynal Keene. "Burr's Conspiracy," *Rhode Island Republican*, June 5, 1811. "From the Whig: Burr's Conspiracy," *Kline's Weekly Carlisle Gazette*, May 31, 1811.
48. *The Trials of the Honb. James Workman and Col. Lewis Kerr*, 40.
49. Workman was a local judge and member of the Orleans legislative council. Bradley, *Interim Appointment: W.C.C. Claiborne Letterbook, 1804-1805* (Baton Rouge: Louisiana State University Press, 2002), 389-93. *The Trials of the Honb. James Workman and Col. Lewis Kerr*, 40.

Kerr, like Workman, retained close ties to Britain and hoped to use that country to revolutionize New Spain. Bradley, *W.C.C. Claiborne Letterbook*, 415-17. Abernethy, *Burr Conspiracy*, 25. *The Trials of the Honb. James Workman and Col. Lewis Kerr*, 13
50. *Orleans Gazette,* May 25, 1805, quoted in McCaleb, *Aaron Burr Conspiracy*, 52. *The Trials of the Honb. James Workman and Col. Lewis Kerr*, 29.
51. The account of the Kempers' affiliation with the Mexican Association comes from a deposition made by Reuben Kemper during the fallout of the Burr affair. It was later reprinted in a newspaper article. "From the Whig: Burr's Conspiracy," *Kline's Weekly Carlisle Gazette*, May 31, 1811. The setting and description of the meeting in this account also includes likely events based on the nearly identical meetings attended by Lt. Thomas Small and William Murray, *The Trials of the Honb. James Workman and Col. Lewis Kerr,* 12-15, 25-27, 78-80.
52. Small and Murray, *Trials of the Honb. James Workman and Col. Lewis Kerr*. Burr was not mentioned, but as Ohio was to be his launching point, the efforts were clearly intended to be coordinated.
53. Small and Murray, *Trials of the Honb. James Workman and Col. Lewis Kerr.*
54. Small and Murray, *Trials of the Honb. James Workman and Col. Lewis Kerr.*
55. The unnamed Mexican was not, as Davis says in *Rogue Republic*, José Bernard Gutiérrez de Lara. The original version of the deposition was lost, possibly during the Civil War destruction of the local archives, and the only surviving account has a blank in place of a name. There is no evidence Gutiérrez had ever left Mexico before 1811. "From the Whig: Burr's Conspiracy," *Kline's Weekly Carlisle Gazette*, May 31, 1811.
56. Davis, *Rogue Republic*, 90.
57. *The Trials of the Honb. James Workman and Col. Lewis Kerr,* 25-27.
58. Gilbert C. Din, "Spain's Immigration Policy in Louisiana and the American Penetration, 1792-1803," *Southwestern Historical Quarterly* 76, no. 3 (1973): 267-68. James Wilkinson, *Burr's Conspiracy Exposed; and General Wilkinson Vindicated Against the Slanders of His Enemies on That Important Occasion* (Washington: James Wilkinson, 1811), 90-91. Abernethy, *Burr Conspiracy*, 90-91.

59. Wilkinson, *Burr's Conspiracy Exposed*, 90–91. *The Trials of the Honb. James Workman and Col. Lewis Kerr*, 27.

60. The idea of seizing the banks was also repeated in the testimony of Lieutenant Small, and an identical scheme was disclosed by Ohio Valley conspirator Harmon Blennerhassett, who was distant and likely not in contact to the Mexican Association except through Burr. Asked about this scheme at trial, Kerr and Workman dismissed it as a joke over drinks. Wilkinson, *Burr's Conspiracy Exposed*, 91. *The Trials of the Honb. James Workman and Col. Lewis Kerr*, 27, 31, 123–25.

61. Wilkinson, *Burr's Conspiracy Exposed*, 91.

62. Wilkinson, *Burr's Conspiracy Exposed*, 92.

63. The Spanish spy was Juan Cortes, who would ultimately support the republican cause in 1812. (Probably John Cortes to Samuel Davenport), November 18, 1806, *Bexar Archives*, Robert Bruce Blake Research Collection, Dolph Briscoe Center for American History, The University of Texas at Austin. Béxar Archives Supplement 5: 353. (Hereafter, Béxar Archives will be cited as BA and Robert Bruce Blake Research Collection as RBB; supplements noted by "S" before the volume number.)

64. "Cooper" and "Lt. Platt," in Small's narrative are not identified, but their full names, with associated ranks are found alongside Small in the army rolls of 1809. William Henry Powell, *List of Officers of the Army of the United States from 1779 to 1900* (New York: L. R. Hamersly & Co., 1900), 42–46. Small was also asked to recruit among his militia unit. "Deposition of Ensign Small," Walpole (N.H.) *Political Observatory*, April 3, 1807. *The Trials of the Honb. James Workman and Col. Lewis Kerr*, 13, 79, 126.

65. "Papers Relative to the Fourth Point of Inquiry," *American Citizen*, August 7, 1810. J. H. Cushing to Wilkinson, July 31, 1806, in Wilkinson, *Burr's Conspiracy Exposed*, appendix 42. Daniel Clark, *Proofs of the Corruption of Gen. James Wilkinson and of His Connexion with Aaron Burr* (1809) (reprinted Freeport, New York: Books for Libraries Press, 1970), 28. Davis, *Rogue Republic*, 92. Bradley, *W.C.C. Claiborne Letterbook*, 389–93. *The Trials of the Honb. James Workman and Col. Lewis Kerr,* 22, 82. Walter Lowrie and Walter S. Franklin, eds., *American State Papers, Class X, Miscellaneous* (Washington: Gales and Seaton, 1834), 1:312 and 2:113.

66. Harris Gaylord Warren and Jack D. L. Holmes, "Herrera, Simon de," HOTO, https://www.tshaonline.org/handbook/entries/herrera-simon-de (accessed August 1, 2021).

67. McCaleb, *Aaron Burr Conspiracy*, 106, 110. Francis Paul Prucha, *The Sword of the Republic: The United States Army on the Frontier: 1783–1846* (Bloomington: Indiana University Press, 1977), 95.

68. Linklater, *An Artist in Treason*, 244.

69. Aaron Burr, "Ciphered Letter of Aaron Burr to General James Wilkinson, July 29, 1806," Famous Trials by Professor Douglas O. Linder, https://www.famous-trials.com/burr/162-letter (accessed July 2, 2021).

70. It is unknown if Wilkinson betrayed Pike, but he probably did not. Unlike the Freeman Custis, Dunbar, and Lewis and Clark expeditions, which were organized by Jefferson, the Pike expedition was conducted on Wilkinson's own initiative, and was designed to benefit his plans, although Pike was unaware of this. Moreover, among Pike's company was Wilkinson's own son, James Biddle Wilkinson. McCaleb, *Aaron Burr Conspiracy*, 28. Dan L. Flores, "Red River Expedition," HOTO, http://www.tshaonline.org/handbook/online/articles/upr02 (accessed April 16, 2020).

71. By Río Bravo is meant the modern Rio Grande. Wilkinson to Adair, September 28, 1806, in McCaleb, *Aaron Burr Conspiracy*, 128. Linklater, *An Artist in Treason*, 244.

72. Linklater, *An Artist in Treason*, 245–51.

73. Linklater, *An Artist in Treason*, 245–51.
74. Brown, *The Glory Seekers*, 96.
75. *The Trials of the Honb. James Workman and Col. Lewis Kerr*, 100.
76. Bradley, *W.C.C. Claiborne Letterbook*, 428. "Arrived at Baltimore on Tuesday Night Last," *Alexandria Daily Advertiser*, February 21, 1807. "General Adair Released," *New York Evening Post*, February 23, 1807. McCaleb, *Aaron Burr Conspiracy*, 189–205. Henry Rightor, *Standard History of New Orleans, Louisiana* (Chicago: Lewis Publishing Company, 1900), 133. *The Trials of the Honb. James Workman and Col. Lewis Kerr*, 115–18.
77. *The Trials of the Honb. James Workman and Col. Lewis Kerr*, 62–63.
78. *The Trials of the Honb. James Workman and Col. Lewis Kerr*, 62–66, 74.
79. *The Enquirer* (Richmond, Virginia), March 1, 1808.
80. Holding Carter, *Doomed Road of Empire* (New York: McGraw-Hill, 1963), 178.

Chapter 2

1. The river noted here as the Red River is now a tributary known as the Cane River, due to shifting of the river's flow. Felix Almaráz, *Tragic Cavalier: Governor Manuel Salcedo of Texas, 1808–1813* (College Station: Texas A&M University Press, 1971), 23.

2. Such a reception would have been protocol for a visiting foreign official. One was given to a Spanish bishop who visited three years before. Powell A. Casey, *Encyclopedia of Forts, Posts, Named Camps and Other Military Installations in Louisiana, 1700–1981* (Baton Rouge: Claitor's Publishing Division, 1983), 46. Marshall Stone Miller, "The History of Fort Claiborne, Louisiana, 1804–1822" (master's thesis, Louisiana State University, 1969, 60). Casey, *Encyclopedia of Forts, Posts, Named Camps and other Military Installations in Louisiana*, 46. Miller, "The History of Fort Claiborne, Louisiana, 1804–1822," 59–60.

3. Almaráz, *Tragic Cavalier*, 23–25.

4. Manuel Salcedo had returned to Spain accompanying his elderly and sick father and attending to family matters. Nettie Lee Benson, "A Governor's Report on Texas in 1809," *Southwestern Historical Quarterly* 71, no. 4 (April 1968), 603–5. Almaráz, *Tragic Cavalier*, 23–24.

5. The Commandant General's Authority was independent of the orders of the Viceroy of New Spain until the Eastern Internal Provinces were divided into two in 1811. See María del Carmen Velásquez, *Tres Estudios Sobre las Provincias Internas de Nueva España* (Mexico City: El Colegio de México, 1979), 127–28.

6. John Sibley to Henry Dearborn, August 7, 1808, in Julia Kathryn Garrett, "Dr. John Sibley and the Louisiana-Texas Frontier, 1803–1814," *Southwestern Historical Quarterly* 46, no. 3 (January 1943), 276.

7. Colonel Herrera wrote, "Add all this to the news of the movements of the revolutionists of Burr, communicated at a same time by the Captain de Clovet from New Orleans and by the Governor Don Manuel de Salcedo, who came to this province from [Natchitoches]." "Communication of the Commander in Texas to the Commander-in-Chief," January 10, 1809. Nacogdoches Archives, RBB S15:159–60.

8. Jesus F. de la Teja, *San Antonio de Béxar: A Community on New Spain's Northern Frontier* (Albuquerque: University of New Mexico Press, 1995), 4–5. J. B. Elguézabal to commandant general, January 18, 1804, BA, RBB S4:251–2.

9. Donald E. Chipman, *Spanish Texas 1519–1821* (Austin: University of Texas Press, 1992), 230. de la Teja, *San Antonio de Béxar*, 4–5. J. B. Elguézabal to commandant general, January 18, 1804, BA, RBB S4:251–2.

10. Carlos Castañeda, *Our Catholic Heritage in Texas 1780–1810* (New York: Arno Press, 1976), 5:291.

11. Nemesio Salcedo to Don Antonio Cordero, May 27, 1808, Nacogdoches Archive, RBB S15:105–8.

12. Garrett, "Dr. John Sibley," *SWHQ* 45, no. 3 (January 1942), 286–88. G. P. Whittington, "Dr. John Sibley of Natchitoches, 1757–1837," *Louisiana Historical Quarterly* 10, no. 4 (October 1927), 467–69. Penny S. Brandt, "A Letter of Dr. John Sibley, Indian Agent," *Louisiana History: The Journal of the Louisiana Historical Association* 29, no. 4 (Autumn, 1988), 365–87.

13. David La Vere, *The Texas Indians* (College Station: Texas A&M University Press, 2004), 153–56.

14. Gov. Antonio Cordero to Nemesio Salcedo, September 11, 1805, BA, RBB S5: 73. Francisco Viana to Governor Antonio Cordero, BA, RBB April 2, 1808, S6:220. Garrett, "Dr. John Sibley," vol. 45, no. 3 (January 1942), 289.

15. John Sibley to Henry Dearborn, August 7, 1808, in Garrett, "Dr. John Sibley," vol. 46, no. 3 (January 1943), 272–76.

16. John Sibley to Henry Dearborn, August 7, 1808, in Garrett, "Dr. John Sibley," vol. 46, no. 3 (January 1943), 272–76.

17. Salcedo to Iturrigaray, September 28, 1808, quoted in McCaleb, *Aaron Burr Conspiracy*, 366. Lawrence E. L'Herisson, "The Evolution of the Texas Road and the Subsequential Settlement Occupancy of the Adjacent Strip of Northwestern Louisiana: 1528–1824" (master's thesis, Louisiana State University, 1977), 20.

18. It is likely that Salcedo met with Carr, because the governor met most important people in Natchitoches and because the latter wrote to him in Texas, sending his regards to Salcedo's wife. Salcedo also dined with Col. Constant Freeman, the commander of Fort Claiborne, while in Natchitoches. Sibley to Dearborn, August 7, 1808, in Garrett, "Dr. John Sibley" 46, no. 3 (January 1943), 276. John C. Carr to Gov. Manuel de Salcedo, May 23, 1810. BA, RBB S7:168. Almaráz, *Tragic Cavalier*, 23.

19. Manuel de Salcedo to Brigadier Don Bernardo Bonavía, Nacogdoches Archives, RBB S15:167–8.

20. Manuel de Salcedo to Brigadier Don Bernardo Bonavía, Nacogdoches Archives, RBB S15:167–170.

21. Manuel de Salcedo to Brigadier Don Bernardo Bonavía, Nacogdoches Archives, RBB S15:170–173.

22. Almaráz, *Tragic Cavalier*, 25.

23. Antonio Cordero to Nemesio Salcedo, September 16, 1808, BA, RBB S6:269.

24. Jesús F. de la Teja, "Economic Integration of a Periphery: The Cattle Industry in 18th Century Texas," *Texas Papers on Latin America* (Austin: Institute of Latin American Studies, University of Texas at Austin, 1991), 2–4.

25. The Travieso and Arocha families (and many of the elite Tejanos) were among the first residents of Texas to embrace revolution—and their fates would be tied to it. Jesús F. de la Teja, *Faces of Béxar: Early San Antonio & Texas* (College Station: Texas A&M University Press, 2016), 67. de la Teja, "Economic Integration of a Periphery," 2–4.

26. David M. Vigness, *Spanish Texas: 1519–1810* (Boston: American Press, 1983), 43. Odie Faulk, "A Description of Texas in 1803," *Southwestern Historical Quarterly* 66, no. 4 (April 1963), 513–14.

27. The population source is the governor's report to the Cortes in 1809. The total listed is 3,122, but this included 189 in Bayou Pierre, east of the Sabine, outside the modern boundaries of Texas, and not involved in the 1812–13 war except insofar as some of its residents may have joined the rebels. The name San Antonio, which originally referred to the mission (San Antonio de Valero), was applied later, mostly by Anglo-Americans, but also by some Spanish, alongside San Fernando and Béxar. All three were used interchangeably, but for the sake

of clarity, this book will use San Antonio, the modern name of the city, in most instances. Benson, "A Governor's Report on Texas in 1809," 611.

28. The town of San Marcos de Neve was abandoned shortly before the 1812 revolution. It was located about three miles southeast of the current city of San Marcos. Trinidad de Salcedo was named after the Commandant General, not his nephew the governor. Joachim A. McGraw, ed., *A Texas Legacy: The Old San Antonio Road and the Caminos Reales, a Tricentenial History, 1691-1991* (Austin: State Department of Highways and Public Transportation, 1991), xvii, 36-43. "Census of Trinidad de Salcedo," January 6, 1809, BA, RBB S6:301-14. Benson, "A Governor's Report on Texas in 1809," 611.

29. *The Social Contract* is one of the most famous philosophical tracts of republican ideology. *Cornelia Bororquia, or the Victim of the Inquisition*, is an epistolary novel attributed to a Spaniard, which harshly criticized the Inquisition and the Spanish government that promoted it. José Joaquín Ugarte to Gov, J. B. Elguézabal, February 4, 1804, BA, RBB S4:256.

The Spanish Empire was not entirely free of Enlightenment influence. It was ironically many of the more politically and socially conservative members of society, including key officials, particularly in South America, who studied economic and scientific reforms, not to overturn the system but to protect it. Arthur P. Whitaker, ed., *Latin America and the Enlightenment*, 2nd ed. (Ithaca: Cornell University Press, 1961), 11. Jay Kinsbruner, *Independence in Spanish America: Civil Wars, Revolutions, and Underdevelopment* (Albuquerque: University of New Mexico Press, 1995), 11.

30. The literacy rate throughout the Spanish Americas was only about 10 percent in the early 1800s. Coronado, *A World Not to Come*, 21. Almaráz, *Tragic Cavalier*, 20. Kinsbruner, *Independence in Spanish America*, 4-5.

31. De la Teja, "Economic Integration of a Periphery," 7-11. De la Teja, *Faces of Texas*, 80-81.

32. Almaráz, *Tragic Cavalier*, 20. José Jóaquin Ugarte to Gov. J. B. Elguézabal, August 1, 1804, BA, RBB S4:366.

33. The rationing even of paper was a severe blow to overtaxed Nacogdoches officials. Of all the correspondence in the Béxar archives after 1800, more than four-fifths of the official letters written in the entire province concerned Nacogdoches, which held only one-fifths of the population, a bureaucratic indication of its centrality for the security of all of Texas. David La Vere, "Davenport, Barr, Murphy and Smith: Traders on the Louisiana-Texas Frontier" (master's thesis, Northwestern State University of Louisiana, 1989), 20-21. Nemesio Salcedo to Governor Antonio Cordero, July 13, 1806, BA, RBB S5:329.

34. José Jóaquin Ugarte to J. B. Elguézabal, January 28, 1805, BA, RBB S5:6.

35. Mattie Austin Hatcher, *The Opening of Texas to Foreign Settlement, 1801-1821* (Philadelphia: Porcupine Press: 1971), 52-53. L'Herisson, "The Evolution of the Texas Road and the Subsequential Settlement Occupancy of the Adjacent Strip of Northwestern Louisiana," 25, 35.

36. Francisco Viana to Governor Cordero, April 1, 1808, BA, RBB S6:218.

37. In one case of smuggling by Spanish soldiers, Vicente Tarín, the sergeant of the Alamo de Parras mobile company was charged with smuggling horses to Louisiana and buying foreign goods with the proceeds, as well as allowing soldiers under his command to do the same. La Vere, "Davenport, Barr, Murphy and Smith," 76.

38. Gov. Manuel Muñoz to Manuel de Moral, June 22, 1799, BA, RBB S4:30. Pedro de Nava to Gov. J. B. Elguézabal, July 21, 1801, BA, RBB S4:132.

39. Juan Bautista Elguézabal to Nemesio Salcedo, April 25, 1804, RB S4:305. Salcedo to Elguézabal, May 22, 1804, S4:326. Salcedo to Elguézabal, June 18, 1804, RBB S4:342.

40. Governor of Texas to Pedro de Nava, January 22, 1799, BA, RBB S4:3. Nemesio Salcedo to Juan Bautista Elguézabal, May 22, 1804, and June 18, 1804, BA, RBB S4: 326, 343. McGraw, *A Texas Legacy*, 237. For more on the history of Nacogdoches smuggling, see Herbert Eugene

Bolton, *Texas in the Middle Eighteenth Century: Studies in Spanish Colonial History and Administration* (Austin: University of Texas Press, 1970), 426–31.

41. Nolan's connection to Wilkinson is well established, but the possibility that he was connected to Clark indicates the latter's very early association with Wilkinson in filibustering schemes. Nolan witnessed a contract between Wilkinson and Daniel Clark Sr. and appears to have been associated with his nephew, the Clark of this story. A Spanish interrogation of Nolan associate Jesse Cook claimed Nolan "had no other trade than with a Mr. Clark in New Orleans."

Guadiana, who led the efforts to corral Nolan, may well have been in league with him or complicit in his smuggling activities before he was ordered to do so. A Spanish official who had perhaps been bribed to allow Nolan to obtain horses wrote to a subordinate, "All this you must read and keep between yourself and our friend Guadiana." Maurine T. Wilson and Jack Jackson, *Philip Nolan and Texas: Expeditions into the Unknown Land, 1791–1801* (Waco: Texian Press, 1987), 5, 15, 79.

42. Robert Ashley later became a key player in the Burr Conspiracy and was with Burr when the former vice president the day before he was arrested on February 19, 1807. Jack Jackson, "Nolan, Philip," *HOTO*, https://www.tshaonline.org/handbook/entries/nolan-philip (accessed July 3, 2021). José Maria Guadiana to Governor Muñoz, February 27, 1799, BA, RBB S4:9. Thomas Perkins Abernethy, "Aaron Burr in Mississippi," *Journal of Southern History* 15, no. 1 (February 1949), 16. Manuel García de Texada to José Vidal, October 3, 1803, BA, RBB S4:232.

43. Little is known of Dennis, but his last name suggest he was of partial French, rather than Anglo-American ancestry. Deposition Given by Manuel Bega, October 18, 1805, BA, RBB S5:125. Castañeda, *Our Catholic Heritage in Texas*, 5:353. Expediente vs. José Antonio de Leon, September 29, 1807, BA, RBB S6:35–44.

44. The census data only lists heads of household, and among these alone, foreigners made up one-tenth of the population. See Hatcher, *The Opening of Texas*, appendix 2: "Number of Foreigners on the Texas Frontier, 1801, Census of Nacogdoches."

45. In 1809, worried about the growing numbers of foreigners in Texas, Spanish authorities undertook to interview every non-Spaniard living in the district of Nacogdoches. Although political leaders decried the class of foreigners, as individuals, all of the men declared their loyalty to Spain, and only on rare occasions did the Spanish have evidence to the contrary. Texas even had governors who were not purely Spanish. Tomás Felipe de Winthuisen (1741–43), for example, was Spanish himself, but of likely Dutch ancestry. Hugo Oconór (1767–70) was born in Ireland and had moved to Spain at age eighteen. Hatcher, *The Opening of Texas*, appendix 2: "Number of Foreigners on the Texas Frontier, 1801, Census of Nacogdoches."

46. While previous histories have accepted at face value the claim that Davenport was Irish, a Davenport genealogy was collected by Karle Wilson Baker. One letter includes the note from his great-granddaughter, Mrs. A. V. E. Johnson, that explicitly states, "Samuel Davenport was a member of a prominent Philadelphia family, of English, not Irish descent." John V. Haggard, "Barr, William," *HOTO*, http://www.tshaonline.org/handbook/online/articles/fba78 (accessed May 12, 2018). LaVere, "Davenport, Barr, Murphy and Smith," 10–11. Karle Wilson Baker Papers, Ralph W. Steen Library, Stephen F. Austin State University, Box 45, "Davenport, Samuel Corr. Re: genealogy, 1942–1945" folder. "Transcript of the Will of Samuel Davenport," in "Texas History Research, Samuel Davenport" folder, Karle Wilson Baker Papers.

47. J. Villasana Haggard, unpublished draft of dissertation, June 30, 1942, 210 (copy in Karle Wilson Baker Papers, Ralph W. Steen Library, Stephen F. Austin State University, "Texas History Research, Neutral Territory" folder).

48. Hatcher, *The Opening of Texas*, appendix 2

49. Carla Gerona, "With a Song in Their Hands: Incendiary Décimas from the Texas and Louisiana Borderlands during a Revolutionary Age," *Early American Studies* 12, no. 1 (Winter 2014): 93–95.

50. Gerona, "With a Song in Their Hands," 93–95.

51. Gerona, "With a Song in Their Hands," 98.

52. José Antonio Navarro would remember D'Alvimar's arrival in San Antonio many years later, including the exact date, September 8, 1808, and the details of his uniform (noted in the text). D'Alvimar was expelled from New Spain as a spy in 1809. Castañeda, *Our Catholic Heritage in Texas*, 5:340–43. David McDonald, *José Antonio Navarro: In Search of the American Dream in Nineteenth-Century Texas* (Denton: Texas State Historical Association, 2010), 20. "D'Alvimar, ¿espía, artista o militar?" *El Universal,* May 23, 2018, https://www.eluniversal.com.mx/cultura/dalvimar-espia-artista-o-militar-aventurero (accessed August 8, 2021). "In the Name of Napoleon, Emperor of the French," November 29, 1807, Nacogdoches Archives, RBB S15:119. Frederick C. Chabot, "Texas in 1811: The Las Casas and Sambrano Revolutions" (San Antonio: Yanaguana Society, 1941), 20.

53. "Journal of Events, Nacogdoches, June, 1805," BA, RBB S5:37–39, "Reports of the Ministers of Nacogdoches about Foreigners," BA, RBB S7:105–6, 108–9, 111. "Reports of the Governor, of the Commandant of Nacogdoches, and the Reverend ministers concerning the Foreigners Residents in that Jurisdiction," BA, RBB S7: 126–27. "Report of the Ministers of Nacogdoches about Foreigners," May 3, 1810, BA, RBB S7:105–11.

Chapter 3

1. Accounts of Bullard's history disagree on whether he actually graduated from Harvard. Some accounts say he was expelled for a prank, but this may not have been a permanent expulsion and he seems to have gotten his degrees, nonetheless. Bullard's place of birth is alternatively given as Pepperell or Groton, which are adjacent towns. J. D. B. De Bow, "The Late Henry A. Bullard," in *DeBow's Southern and Western Review*, vol. 12 (January 1852), pp. 50–56. "Memoir of Hon. Henry A. Bullard, LL. D., president of the Louisiana Historical Society, and late judge of Supreme Court of Louisiana," in B. F. French, *Historical Collections of Louisiana*, vol. 3 (New York: D. Appleton & Company, 1851), 5.

2. The best work on the history of filibusters is Robert E. May, "Manifest Destiny's Underworld: Filibustering in Antebellum America" (Charlotte: University of North Carolina Press, 2003). However, May's conclusions are generally drawn from much later filibusters, and their relevance is not absolute for earlier events, particularly on the issue of slavery, which was far more important after 1820 than it was before that year. Narrett, *Adventurism and Empire*, 5.

3. The two causes were not as separate as they appear. Even Burr and the Mexican Association spoke in terms of linking up with Miranda in Venezuela, and some of the same men who provided financial backing to Miranda also backed Burr. Abernethy, *Burr Conspiracy*, 26.

4. Lindsay Schakenbach, "Schemers, Dreamers, and a Revolutionary Foreign Policy: New York City in the Era of Second Independence, 1805–1815," *New York History* 94, no. 3–4 (Summer/Fall 2013), pp. 268.

5. Filibusters as a rule generally crossed class lines, far more so than most other activities in the nineteenth century. As Robert E. May notes, "Sons of planters, merchants, and prominent politicians joined clerks, apprentices, and immigrants in filibuster invasions. Some college students dropped out of their institutions to participate." Schakenbach, "Schemers, Dreamers, and a Revolutionary Foreign Policy," 268. Robert E. May "Young American Males

and Filibustering in the Age of Manifest Destiny: The United States Army as a Cultural Mirror," *The Journal of American History* 78, no. 3 (December 1991), p. 864. Margaret S. Henson, "Burnet, David Gouverneur," *HOTO*, https://www.tshaonline.org/handbook/entries/burnet-david-gouverneur (accessed July 3, 2021).

6. Schakenbach, "Schemers, Dreamers, and a Revolutionary Foreign Policy," 272.

7. Two sources have attributed the book to Bullard. The account claims to be a series of letters by a "gentleman who was an officer under that General, to his friend in the United States." The book was published anonymously in its first printing, then in later printings attributed to a James Biggs, who is unknown, and likely Bullard's pseudonym. Bullard never went to Venezuela personally, though he evidently interviewed a source with firsthand knowledge of the affair. Credence to Bullard's authorship is also given by the fact that he subsequently wrote additional histories, also under the cloak of anonymity. Pierce Welch Gaines, ed., *Political Works of Concealed Authorship During the Administrations of Washington, Adams, and Jefferson* (New Haven: Yale University Library, 1959), 116.

Anonymous authorship was very common in the early republic, a time when literary pursuits were typically seen as elitist and distracting from the true business of work. A man who was a "mere" writer was seen as engaging in an extravagance. As John Quincy Adams, himself a frequent writer of anonymous articles, wrote, "No small number of very worthy citizens [are] irrevocably convinced that it is impossible at once to be a man of business and a man of rhyme." Jean V. Matthews, *Toward a New Society: American Thought and Culture, 1800–1830* (Boston: Twayne Publishers, 1991), 60–61.

8. Henry Adams Bullard, *History of Don Francisco de Miranda's Attempt to Effect a Revolution in South America* (Boston: Oliver and Munroe, 1808), 4.

9. Bullard, *History of Don Francisco de Miranda*, 5.

10. Bullard, *History of Don Francisco de Miranda*, 5.

11. Bullard, *History of Don Francisco de Miranda*, 6. Narrett, *Adventurism and Empire*, 205.

12. Bullard, *History of Don Francisco de Miranda*, 7.

13. The meeting Cogswell spoke to would have been well attended, as the holiday in the early republic was the only secular holiday in the nation and held enormous significance for veterans of the revolution. Nathaniel Cogswell, *An Oration Delivered before the Republican Citizens of Newburyport in the Rev. John Giles' Meetinghouse on the Fourth of July 1808* (Newburyport: W. and J. Gilman, 1808), 4–19 (copy available at the Historical Society of Pennsylvania). For more on the early history of the July 4th celebrations, see Len Travers, *Celebrating the Fourth: Independence Day and the Rites of Nationalism in the Early Republic* (Amherst: University of Massachusetts Press, 1997).

14. E. O. Jameson, *The Cogswells in America* (Boston: Alfred Mudge & Son, 1884), 47 and 152.

15. Jameson, *The Cogswells in America*, 152. Phillips Exeter Academy, *Catalogue of the Officers and Students of Phillips Exeter Academy* (Exeter, NH: J&B Williams, 1838), 56. George T. Chapman, *Sketches of the Alumni of Dartmouth College, from the First Graduation in 1771 to the Present Time, with a Brief History of the Institution* (Cambridge: Riverside Press, 1867), 73. Everett S. Stackpole and Lucien Thompson, *History of the Town of Durham New Hampshire*, vol. 1 (publisher unknown), 279, https://archive.org/details/historyoftownofdo1stac (accessed May 5, 2020). Jameson, *The Cogswells in America*, 183.

16. "Thomas Cogswell to Thomas Jefferson, March 19, 1801," *The Thomas Jefferson Papers* at the Library of Congress, *Jefferson Papers*, https://www.loc.gov/resource/mtj1.023_0315_0316/?sp=1 (accessed May 5, 2020).

17. Cogswell, *Oration*, 3.

18. Cogswell, *Oration*, 4, 19.

19. "Fourth of July Orations," in Samuel Cooper Thacher, ed., *The Monthly Anthology, and Boston Review*, vol. V (Boston: Snelling and Simon, 1808), 452.

20. Cogswell served on the staff of Maj. Gen. James Brickett. Jameson, *The Cogswells in America*, 183. Nathaniel Cogswell to James Madison, July 11, 1808, The James Madison Papers at the Library of Congress. Microfilm Reel 10, Series 1, General Correspondence, 1723–1859.

21. George W. Cullum, *Biographical Register of the Officers and Graduates of the United States Military Academy* (Boston: Houghton, Mifflin, 1891), 92.

22. William B. Skelton, "High Army Leadership in the Era of the War of 1812: The Making and the Remaking of the Officer Corps," *William and Mary Quarterly* 51, no. 2 (April 1994), 253. Dave Richard Palmer and James W. Stryker, *Early American Wars and Military Institutions* (Wayne, NJ: Avery Publishing Group, 1986), 51.

23. Appleby, *Inheriting the Revolution*, 31. Linklater, *An Artist in Treason*, 194–96.

24. Cullum, *Biographical Register of the Officers and Graduates of the United States Military Academy*, 92.

25. Photos of the Magee family are in the collection of the Shirley-Eustis Historical Association, Boston, Massachusetts. For more of Magee's history, see James Aalan Bernsen, "Magee, Augustus William," *HOTO*, https://www.tshaonline.org/handbook/entries/magee-augustus-william (accessed November 3, 2021). William Shaler to James Monroe, August 18, 1812. Shaler Letterbooks.

26. John G. Coyle, ed., *The Journal of the American-Irish Historical Society* (New York: American-Irish Historical Society, 1918), 121. Henry Lee, "The Magee Family and the Origins of the China Trade," *Proceedings of the Massachusetts Historical Society*, vol. 81 (1969): 104.

27. Perkins's philanthropic works included the Perkins School for the Blind, which would grow into the largest of its kind in the world. Its most famous alumnus was Helen Keller. Lee, "The Magee Family and the Origins of the China Trade," 107. Thomas G. Cary, *Memoir of Thomas Handasyd Perkins* (Boston: Little, Brown and Company, 1856), 11.

28. The Shirley-Eustis House, in which Magee was raised from 1798 onward, still exists today and is a National Historic Landmark: http://www.shirleyeustishouse.org. Lee, "The Magee Family and the Origins of the China Trade," 111.

29. As one history of Perkins's empire noted, he took a paternal role for many relatives, and "just as family provided a resource for labor and capital in the Perkinses' enterprise, so too, did their business provide a resource for employing kin. Here, in this extended kinship circle, was a core of the foundation of the Perkins commercial network." Frederick C. Detwiller, "Magee Family Mariners ca. 1750–1820," 2012. (Unpublished manuscript provided by the author, of Georgetown, Massachusetts.) Rachel Tamar Van, "Free Trade and Family Values: Kinship Networks and the Culture of Early American Capitalism" (PhD diss., Columbia University, 2011), 86, 36. Lee, "The Magee Family and the Origins of the China Trade," 117. *Catalogue of the Officers and Students of Phillips Exeter Academy*, 14. Austin Coolidge and John Mansfield, *History and Description of New England, General and Local*, vol. 1 (Boston: Austin J. Coolidge, 1859), 491. Laurence M. Crosbie, *Phillips Exeter Academy, a History* (Exeter, NH: Phillips Exeter Academy, 1923), 57–58.

30. No letter of recommendation for Magee exists in the National Archive file for West Point cadets, suggesting a more personal connection secured the appointment. Perkins, a lieutenant colonel of a local Massachusetts militia company, had numerous ties to Secretary of War Henry Dearborn. Prucha, *The Sword of the Republic*, 97. Carl Seaburg and Stanley Paterson, *Merchant Prince of Boston. Col. T. H. Perkins, 1764–1854* (Cambridge: Harvard University Press, 1971), 40. US Military Academy Cadet Application Papers, 1805–1866, US National Archives, Microcopy 688, Roll 2.

31. While most previous histories of Magee assert that he was either second or third in his class, this is incorrect, since merit-based class ranks were not instituted until 1815. Prior to that date, students studied at different paces and merely graduated when they finished the coursework, which Magee did in January. His "class rank" was therefore a quirk of the calendar. Palmer and Stryker, *Early American Wars and Military Institutions*, 52; Spencer Tucker, ed., *The Encyclopedia of the War of 1812: A Political, Social and Military History* (Santa Barbara, CA: ABC-CLIO), 705–6. Lists of officer promotions, Letters Sent by the Secretary of War Relating to Military Affairs, 1800–1889, US National Archive, Microfilm M6 Roll 6 (hereafter LSSW). Cullum, *Biographical Register of the Officers and Graduates of the United States Military Academy*, 92.

32. Epperson, Jean L. *Lost Spanish Towns: Atascosito and Trinidad de Salcedo*, (Hemphill, Tx.: Dogwood Press, 1997), 51. "Declaration of the First Witness Sergeant Don Pedro de la Garza Falcón," BA, RBB 33:135. Gov. Antonio Cordero to Nemesio Salcedo, December (31), 1805, BA, RBB S5:191.

33. Declaration of Witnesses, BA, RBB 33:141, 144, 155–56.

34. The soldier José Antonio Ruiz, who captured Quirk, was a native of Béxar and the older brother of José Francisco Ruiz, who later joined the Gutiérrez-Magee Expedition, signed the Texas Declaration of Independence in 1836 and served in the Republic of Texas Senate. Frederick Chabot, *With the Makers of San Antonio* (San Antonio: privately published, 1937), 198. "Diary formed by the Distinguished Sergeant Don Pedro de la Garza Falcón," October 13–16, 1808, Declaration of Witnesses, BA, RBB 33:118–20, 135–36.

35. BA, RBB 70: 70, 112–18; RBB 46:306–8. "Government vs. Michael Quinn and John Magee," May 2, 1810, BA, RBB 70:88.

36. "Journal of Operations, etc., Nacogdoches," July 1802, January 1803, and April 1803, BA, RBB 20:52–53, 105, 137, 155. RBB S4:208–9.

37. Juan Pedro Walker was born in Spanish New Orleans to an English immigrant father and possibly French mother and raised in Natchez. He had a long record of military service to Spain and the Mexican Republic. Elizabeth A. H. John, "Walker, Juan Pedro," *HOTO*, https://www.tshaonline.org/handbook/entries/walker-juan-pedro (accessed June 16, 2021). Miguel Músquiz was the father of the future Texas jefe politico Ramón Músquiz. Miguel Musquíz to Gov. J. B. Elguézabal, July 12, 1803, BA, RBB S4:221.

38. "Diary of Expedition by José María Guadiana," March 4–6, 1808, BA, RBB S6:122–24. "Confession of the Defendant Henry Quirk," January 1809, BA, RBB 33:189. "Edmund Quirk," RBB 35:270.

39. "Diary of Expedition by José María Guadiana," March 4–6, 1808, BA, RBB S6:122–24. "Confession of the Defendant Henry Quirk," January 1809, BA, RBB 33:189. "Edmund Quirk," RBB 35:270. Francisco Viana to Governor Antonio Cordero, April 4, 1808, BA, RBB S6:221.

40. Quinn's testimony indicated he had little cash, but large assets in horses and mules. He owed a debt to Owens and had given a letter to the merchant that was to be delivered by the deceased Popejoy. "Diary, July 1808," BA, RBB S6:252. "Government vs. Michael Quinn and John Magee," May 2, October 3–4, 1810, BA RBB 70:88–103, 180–85. "Document 41: Letter that, with date of October 1, 1303, Michael Quinn wrote from Trinidad to William Owens, merchant of Natchitoches," BA, RBB 70:89–90.

41. "Communication of the Commander of Texas to that of Nacogdoches," Nacogdoches Archives, RBB S15:141–54.

42. Trinidad in the original Spanish, but to avoid confusion, this narrative will use Trinidad for the town and the modern name of the river, Trinity.

43. The family name Despallier was originally D'Espallier, and derives from the former Norman village of Les Pallieres, thirty-six miles NE of Rennes, France. Rasmus Dahlqvist, "Despallier, Bernardo Martin," *HOTO,* http://www.tshaonline.org/handbook/online/articles/fdeao (accessed May 6, 2020). Rasmus Dahlqvist, *From Martin to Despallier: The Story of A French Colonial Family* (CreateSpace, 2013), 16, 112.

44. Dahlqvist, "Despallier, Bernardo Martin," *HOTO.* Epperson, *Lost Spanish Towns,* 10.

45. Despallier to Governor of Texas in Hatcher, *The Opening of Texas,* appendix no. 6. Despallier and Brady to Governor of Texas in Hatcher, *The Opening of Texas,* appendix no. 8. Rasmus Dahlqvist, *From Martin to Despallier,* 167–77.

46. Despallier, *HOTO.* Epperson, *Lost Spanish Towns,* 10. Statement of Luis Grande to Pedro Lopez Prieto, 1806, BA, RBB S5:274.

47. "Process," BA, RBB S70:155, 163. "Government vs. Michael Quinn and John Magee," BA, RBB 70:183. José María Guadiana to Gov. Antonio Cordero, August 18, 1808, BA, RBB S6:258.

48. Dick Steward, *Frontier Swashbuckler: The Life and Legend of John Smith T* (Columbia: University of Missouri Press, 2000), 2, 6, 34–42.

49. Steward, *Frontier Swashbuckler,* 33, 42, 66, 82.

50. After a year of mild imprisonment, Pike's men had been freed, traveling first to Chihuahua and then returning through Texas before being expelled and ordered never to return. Pike's journals were not published until 1810, but long before that, news of what the young officer had seen in New Spain's northernmost territories—including the peak which would henceforth bear his name—filtered out and fed the growing interest in Spanish lands among those in the western United States. Statement and Affidavit of Timothy Kibby, July 6, 1807, in Clarence Edwin Carter, ed., *Territorial Papers of the United States* (Washington, DC: Government Printing Office, 1949), 14:133–36.

51. Steward, *Frontier Swashbuckler,* 99.

52. *Louisiana Gazette,* December 28, 1809. In Thomas James, *Three Years among the Indians and Mexicans* (Saint Louis: Missouri Historical Society, 1916), 286.

53. Brown, *Latin American Rebels and the United States,* 24.

54. Joseph McLanahan to Governor Benjamin Howard, June 12, 1812. In James, *Three Years among the Indians and Mexicans,* 289.

Chapter 4

1. Anonymous, *Biographical Sketch of General John Adair* (Washington, DC: Gales & Seaton, 1830), 3–9.

2. "Letters have been received from New Orleans," *Sentinel of Freedom,* February 10, 1807.

3. John Adair to James Madison, January 9, 1809. Manuscript/Mixed Material, James Madison Papers, 1723 to 1859: Series 1, General Correspondence, 1723 to 1859, Library of Congress. Available at https://www.loc.gov/item/mjm015214/ (accessed May 6, 2020).

4. John Adair to James Madison, January 9, 1809.

5. Adair uses the term "Democrat," but the meaning is the Republican Party of Madison, later the Democratic-Republican Party. John Adair to James Madison, January 9, 1809.

6. Din, "A Troubled Seven Years," 423–26.

7. Joseph Pulaski Kennedy has been falsely identified as a member of the Gutiérrez Magee filibuster. However, there is no evidence that Kennedy ever went west and circumstantial evidence to disprove it. Din, "A Troubled Seven Years," 423–26. Samuel Sexton File, US National Archives Record Group 76, 1839 and 1849 US-Mexico commissions, National Archives. Harry Toulmin to James Madison, July 28, 1810, *Founders Online,* National Archives,

http://founders.archives.gov/documents/Madison/03-02-02-0562. [Original source: J. C. A. Stagg, Jeanne Kerr Cross, and Susan Holbrook Perdue, ed., *The Papers of James Madison*, Presidential Series, vol. 2, *1 October 1809–2 November 1810* (Charlottesville: University Press of Virginia, 1992), pp. 447–53] (accessed May 6, 2020).

    8. The Spanish American juntas were not always revolutionary. In fact, as Raúl Coronado writes, they frequently started as a patriotic response to the Spanish mainland's own efforts to reject Napoleon. As Spanish monarchists in Cádiz formed their own junta, "the kingdoms of Spanish America and the Philippines, too, created their own regional governing councils." Jaime Rodriguez O furthermore explains that by asserting local authority, Spanish American leaders "knew that their lands were kingdoms and not colonies because they shared the same legal foundations as the kingdoms of southern Castile after they had been retaken from the Muslims." Thus the crisis necessitated local control, which could take a revolutionary form or not, and frequently began as an assertion of long-suppressed local economy and only later became a drive for independence. Cox, *West Florida Controversy*, 287. Coronado, *A World Not to Come*, 12. Jaime E. Rodríguez O., *Political Culture in Spanish America, 1800–1830* (Lincoln: University of Nebraska Press, 2017), 5.

    9. Cox, *West Florida Controversy*, 372. Hyde, "Consolidating the Revolution," 266.

    10. Din, "A Troubled Seven Years," 431–32, 449–50.

    11. Hyde, "Setting a Precedent for Regional Revolution," 125. Hyde, "Consolidating the Revolution," 265.

    12. Scallions, "The Rise and Fall of the Original Lone Star State," 210.

    13. Isaac Joslin Cox, "The American Intervention in West Florida," *American Historical Review* 17, no. 2 (January 1912), 308. "The Rise and Fall of the Original Lone Star State," 216.

    14. Mississippi Governor David Holmes came to West Florida immediately prior to the invasion to soothe the feelings of the people there. He discovered several chief complaints against the US action: (1) the debt contracted by Skipwith's government, and what would become of its creditors; (2) the lands claimed by individuals in West Florida; and (3) the status of former US Army deserters, who had joined the rebel forces under the condition that they be protected against American reprisal or trial; and (4) that if the US resumed negotiations with Spain, it was possible some territory might revert to Spain, which was unacceptable. These points are mentioned, because in a similar situation in Texas, Anglo-Americans would be even more hostile to the appearance of US agent John Robinson and cited the West Florida example. Their concerns there likely reflected those expressed to Holmes. The Governor of Mississippi Territory to the Secretary of State, in Clarence Edwin Carter, ed., *The Territorial Papers of the United States*, vol. 9 (Washington, DC: Government Printing Office, 1910), 911. Cox, "The American Intervention in West Florida," 307–8. Scallions, "The Rise and Fall of the Original Lone Star State," 217. Walter Nugent, *Habits of Empire: A History of American Expansion* (New York: Alfred A. Knopf: 2008), 107.

    15. Cox, "The American Intervention in West Florida," 307. Hyde Jr., "Consolidating the Revolution," 280.

    16. Cox, *West Florida Controversy*, 483.

    17. Din, "A Troubled Seven Years," 429. Governor Claiborne to Thomas Jefferson, December 24, 1810, in Carter, *The Territorial Papers of the United States*, 9:906. Nugent, *Habits of Empire*, 108. Scallions, "The Rise and Fall of the Original Lone Star State," 220. Hyde Jr., "Consolidating the Revolution," 282.

    18. In a last act of defiance, a group of locals rose up against the takeover in March 1811 but were silenced by a flotilla of federal gunboats that came up the Tchefuncte River. One group of citizens resurrected the old Convention flag and flew it for a day, before another group cut it down and buried it with a ceremony. The rebels "dug up the coffin as if determined not

to be in peace," one contemporary account noted. Hyde Jr., "Consolidating the Revolution," 282.

19. Salcedo to Viceroy, December 30, 1810, and August 25, 1812, Manuel Salcedo, Operaciones de Guerra, 1 Part 1, Archivo General de México, Copy in Texas State Library and Archives, Austin, Texas. Benson, "A Governor's Report on Texas in 1809," 609.

20. Cordero had approved the bulk of the immigrants from Louisiana and, despite continual complaints from Commandant General Salcedo, had remained sympathetic to them, which historian Carlos Castañeda has called "lax to the point of criminal negligence" in letting in so many who were suspicious. Castañeda, *Our Catholic Heritage in Texas*, 5:363.

21. Almaráz, *Tragic Cavalier*, 33–34; Castañeda, *Our Catholic Heritage in Texas*, 5:382–84.

22. Historian David Vigness says of Spanish policy, "A paternalist political system kept [Texas residents] always aware of the power of the King over their lives, for they were vassals living on lands which were granted to them out of his mercy—grants were, in fact, termed *mercedes* [mercies]." Manuel Salcedo to Antonio Cordero, March 23, 1809, BA, RBB S6:330. Vigness, *Spanish Texas*, 39.

23. Castañeda, *Our Catholic Heritage in Texas*, 5:388.

24. Benson, "A Governor's Report on Texas in 1809," 603–16.

25. "Journal of the New Occurrences on the Journey Made by the Sir Governor of This Province," March 1810, BA, RBB S7:42–60.

26. Castañeda, *Our Catholic Heritage in Texas*, 5: 391.

27. Gov. Manuel Salcedo to Nemesio Salcedo, March 30, 1810, BA, RBB S7:66–68.

28. Castañeda, *Our Catholic Heritage in Texas*, 5:366–67.

Chapter 5

1. In April 1804, Shaler arrived in New Orleans to report on Napoleon's preparations to invade England. On another occasion in 1809, he brought back dispatches from William Pinkney, US minister to England. "The Ship Rising States, Cap. Shaler, which arrived yesterday." *The National Intelligencer and Washington Advertiser,* April 13, 1804. "Yesterday the Spanish Frigate Cornelie," *The National Intelligencer and Washington Advertiser,* November 6, 1809. Shaler's proposal for a signaling system is contained in Shaler to Smith, November 12, 1809, William Shaler Papers, Historical Society of Pennsylvania, Philadelphia, PA. Smith to Shaler, May 24, 1810, Shaler Papers.

2. For more on the boarding house, see W. B. Bryan, "Hotels of Washington DC Prior to 1814," American History and Genealogical Project—District of Columbia, https://doc.genealogyvillage.com/hotels_of_washington_dc_prior_1814.html (accessed October 11, 2021). Office of the Historian, "Public Building West of the White House, May 1801—August 1814," US Department of State, https://history.state.gov/departmenthistory/buildings/section22 (accessed May 6, 2020).

3. Office of the Historian, "Biographies of the Secretaries of State: Robert Smith (1757–1842)," US Department of State, https://history.state.gov/departmenthistory/people/smith-robert (accessed July 3, 2021).

4. Kinsbruner, *Independence in Spanish America*, 9.

5. W. C. C. Claiborne to Robert Smith, March 9, 1809. Claiborne Letterbooks, 4:332–34.

6. There are several sources for Shaler's biography, including Andrew Alf Heggoy, *Through Foreign Eyes: Western Attitudes towards North Africa* (Lanham, MD: University Press of America: 1982), 7–8; Samuel L. Knapp, "Memoir of William Shaler," in *The New York Mirror*, May 4, 1833, 10:44; and Roy F. Nichols, "William Shaler: New England Apostle of Rational Liberty," *New England Quarterly* 9, no. 1 (March 1936), pp. 71–96.

7. Cleveland and Shaler were best friends as well as partners. Cleveland wrote extensively on Shaler and named his son, the famous landscape painter Horace William Shaler Cleveland, after him. Nichols, "William Shaler," 72–73. Hugh Golway, "The Cruise of the Lelia Byrd," *Journal of the West* 8 (July 1969), 394.

8. Nichols, "William Shaler," 73.

9. Shaler was released in Chile after he and his partner swore an oath that they were not engaged in contraband activity. A bible not being available, they swore it on a volume of Shakespeare. Presumably Shaler did not hold an oath to the bard as truly sacred, because he promptly violated it. Golway, "The Cruise of the Lelia Byrd," 394.

10. Golway, "The Cruise of the Lelia Byrd," 399. Nichols, "William Shaler," 74.

11. [William Shaler], "Journal of a Voyage between China and the North-Western Coast of America Made in 1804," in *The American Register: Or General Repository of History, Politics, and Science*, vol. 3 (1808), 137–75.

12. [Shaler], "Journal of a Voyage between China and the North-Western Coast of America"137–75.

13. William Spence Robertson, "The First Legations of the United States in Latin America," *Mississippi Valley Historical Review* 2, no. 2 (September 1915), 184–85. William Spence Robertson, "Documents Concerning the Consular Service of the United States in Latin America, with an Introductory Note," *The Mississippi Valley Historical Review* 2, no. 4 (March 1916), 562. Charles Lyon Chandler, *Inter-American Acquaintances, 2nd* ed. (Sewanee, TN: University Press, 1917), 59–61.

14. Smith to Shaler, June 18, 1810. Shaler Papers.

15. Smith to Shaler, June 18, 1810. Shaler Papers.

16. Smith to Shaler, June 18, 1810. Shaler Papers.

17. Din, "A Troubled Seven Years," 414. Smith to Shaler, June 18, 1810. Shaler Papers.

18. Smith to Shaler, June 18, 1810. Shaler Papers.

19. Shaler's instructions as consul are dated June 16th, and therefore precede by two days his instructions as agent to Cuban and Mexican revolutionaries. Quoted in Robertson, "Documents Concerning the Consular Service of the United States in Latin America," 566. The original is in the State Department Manuscripts, Bureau of Indexes and Archives, Dispatches to Consuls, 1.

20. Garrett's chapter on the beginning of the filibuster is entitled "Duplicity Succeeds." Garrett, *Green Flag over Texas*, 53. Brown, *Latin American Rebels and the United States*, 46. Graham to Shaler, June 21, 1810, Shaler Papers.

21. Watson, *Jackson's Sword*, 20. Walter Lowrie, ed., *American State Papers: Documents, Legislative and Executive of the Congress of the United States, Class V: Military Affairs*, Vol. 1 (Washington: Gales and Seaton, 1832), 252. James Ripley Jacobs, The Beginning of the US Army (Princeton: Princeton University Press, 1947), 342–352. Joseph Cross to Sec. of War, August 6, 1811, Letters Received by the Secretary of War, Registered Series, M221 Roll 35 [Hereafter, LRSWRS].

22. The presumption is made that Magee arrived in the Southwest sometime prior to October 1, 1809, when William Murray, who would be his closest friend, resigned his commission in the army. It is more likely they would have established a close relationship if they had served together. The information that he served in the Atlantic Forts comes from Cullum's register. The suggestion that Magee served in the New York forts is made based on Magee's possible connection to Lt. Col. Joseph Constant, a fellow New Englander then in command of the fortresses, who would later be reassigned to the southwestern frontier and would be

the officer who would forward Magee's letter of resignation to the secretary of war. Cullum, *Biographical Register of the Officers and Graduates of the United States Military Academy*, 92.

23. Magee had attended West Point alongside Zebulon's younger brother, George Washington Pike. G. W. Pike to Eustis, Oct. 2, 1811, LRSWRS, M221, Roll 47. Orsi, *Citizen Explorer*, 252. Watson, *Jackson's Sword*, 33.

That Magee was attached to Pike's command is clear in letters from Pike, Sibley, and Captain Wollstonecraft at Fort Claiborne. Pike's own orderly books show that he was stationed at the time at Cantonment Washington, not at Fort Adams itself, which was forty miles south, although many sources referred to both posts collectively as "Fort Adams." Orderly Books of the Adjutant, July–Nov. 1810, *Records of Units Infantry 1789–1815: Maj. Zebulon M. Pike's Consolidated Regiment, 1809–1811*. US National Archives, RG 98, NM-65, Entry 323. "A Summary View of the Regular Troops fit for Action under the Command of Brigadier General Wilkinson," [Unknown, possibly July–August 1812], LRSWRS, M221 ROLL 49.

24. Some historians have attempted to suggest Magee was a protégé of Wilkinson in the mold of Phillip Nolan. However, Magee only arrived on the frontier at the earliest in mid- to late 1809, possibly as late as 1810, and Wilkinson was recalled to Washington on December 18, 1809. If Magee ever met Wilkinson, it was only briefly, and it is unlikely a brigadier general and second lieutenant would have forged a close relationship in such a short time. James Ripley Jacobs, *The Beginning of the U. S. Army*, 351–52. Prucha, *The Sword of the Republic*, 97.

The Hampton-Cushing feud is detailed in a series of letters between the two officers, as well as in the May 14, 1812, *Louisiana Gazette*, which reported the outcome of the trial. The Freeman-Cross controversy is detailed in a series of letters between the two officers found in National Archives microfilm. Things were no more orderly on the lower side of the chain of command. Pike's record book for 1809–11 recounts almost daily courts-martial of enlisted men. "Extract from the Replication," *Louisiana Gazette*, May 14, 1812. LRSWRS, NA, M221 Rolls 35 and 45. Orderly Books of the Adjutant, [Pike's regiment] National Archives.

25. The command structure at Fort Claiborne was complex. Many prior accounts have stated that Captain Overton, an infantry officer, was the senior officer at Fort Claiborne, and he would become so in time. However, from late 1810 to August 1812, Wollstonecraft, commanding the post's small artillery detachment, held this position. Wollstonecraft himself was recalled to Fort Adams shortly after the expedition in Texas was launched, but this appears to have been a planned rotation unconnected to the filibuster. In any event, Overton assumed command after that. Crimmins, Col. M. I. "Augustus William Magee, The Second Advanced Courier of American Expansion into Texas," *West Texas Historical Association Year Book* 20 (1944), 93. Janet Todd, *Mary Wollstonecraft, A Revolutionary Life* (New York: Columbia University Press, 2002). Garrett, "Dr. John Sibley," 46, no. 3 (January 1943), 273. Miller, "The History of Fort Claiborne, Louisiana," 28–51.

26. Charles Wollstonecraft to T. H. Cushing, July 21, 1810; LRSWRS M221 Roll 35.

27. The population of the Neutral Ground was very clearly of two kinds, and a thorough reading of Spanish and American sources confirms this. Gov. Antonio Cordero to Nemesio Salcedo, September 11, 1805, RBB S5:73. Charles Wollstonecraft to T. H. Cushing, July 21, 1810; LRSWRS M221, Roll 35.

28. Cushing had not yet been relieved as part of his court-martial at the time of these letters. Wollstonecraft to Cushing, June 12, 1810; Wollstonecraft to W. Hampton, April 16, 1810; Wollstonecraft to M. Salcedo, April 16, 1810; Cushing to Wollstonecraft, April 24, 1810; and Salcedo to Wollstonecraft, July 17, 1810, LRSWRS M221 Roll 35.

29. Wollstonecraft to Cushing, June 12, 1810, LRSWRS M221 Roll 35.

30. Yoakum uses as one source the diary of James McKim, a Neutral Ground resident who joined Magee's Expedition in 1812 and later settled in Texas. The diary has since been lost. Brown, *The Glory Seekers*, 197. Henderson K. Yoakum, *The History of Texas from Its First Settlement in 1685 to Its Annexation to the United States in 1846*, vol. 1 (New York: Bedfield, 1856), 152.

31. The complexity of the Neutral Ground "banditti" is shown by the behavior of Dr. John Sibley, the US Indian Agent. He was known to be sponsoring settlers in the area, and had invested in lands himself in Bayou Pierre, technically north of the Neutral Ground, but still in dispute. Furthermore, he had some relationship with the smugglers. Michael Quinn, one of their leaders, had all of his correspondence forwarded to him through Sibley. The Spanish believed he was using his authority to stop their caravans. Yet, at the same time, he complained in his letters of the lawlessness of the area and deliberately distinguished between cutthroats and honest men. "Communication of the Commander of Texas to that of Nacogdoches," November 18, 1808, BA, RBB S15:141. L'Herisson, "The Evolution of the Texas Road and the Subsequential Settlement Occupancy of the Adjacent Strip of Northwestern Louisiana," 84. "Communication of the Commander of Texas to that of Nacogdoches," November 18, 1808, BA, RBB S15:141. Eric Hobsbawm, *Bandits* (New York: Pantheon Books, 1981), 19.

32. Wollstonecraft to Cushing, June 12, 1810, LRSWRS, M221 Roll 35.

33. Magee to Wollstonecraft, August 14, 1810, LRSWRS, M221 Roll 35; Diary of J. M. Guadiana, August 6, 1810, BA, RBB S7:228.

34. In April 1796, still only a cadet after eight years in the service, Guadiana was finally promoted to Alferez, or second lieutenant. In the early 1800s, he was raised to first lieutenant, but try as he might, he could never earn his captaincy. Gov. Manuel Muñoz to Pedro de Nava, April 25, 1796, BA, RBB S3:285.

35. Max L. Moorhead, *New Mexico's Royal Road: Trade and Travel on the Chihuahua Trail* (Norman: University of Oklahoma Press, 1954), 59.

36. Magee to Wollstonecraft, August 14, 1810, LRSWRS M221, Roll 35; Diary of J. M. Guadiana, August 6, 1810, RBB S7:228.

37. Diary of J. M. Guadiana, August 6, 1810, RBB S7:228.

38. Diary of J. M. Guadiana, August 6, 1810, RBB S7:227–38.

39. Wollstonecraft to Cushing, August 15, 1810, LRSWRS, M221, Roll 35.

Chapter 6

1. Sibley identifies the man as Jonathan Hill Platts, a native of Boxford, Massachusetts, but genealogical research confirms his appropriate middle name was Hale. Intriguingly, he was born in the same county, only seven miles from Lt. William Platt, who was a Burr conspiracy recruit (see chapter 1), suggesting a possible relationship. "Jonathan Hale Platts," Massachusetts, US, Town and Vital Records, 1620–1988, and "William Platts," in Newburyport, Essex County, Massachusetts Birth Records to 1850, http://www.ancestry.com (accessed October 10, 2021). Sibley to Eustis, November 30, 1810, in Garrett, "Dr. John Sibley," 48, no. 1 (July 1944), 69.

2. "Treason, Rebellion, Revolution," *Weekly Register*, March 28, 1812.

3. "Treason, Rebellion, Revolution," *Weekly Register*, March 28, 1812.

4. Virginia Guedea, "Autonomía e independencia en la provincia de Texas. La Junta de Gobierno de San Antonio de Béjar, 1813," in "La independencia de México y el proceso autonomista novohispano, 1808–1824" (Mexico City: Instituto de Investigaciones Históricas, 2001), 143. Orsi, *Citizen Explorer*, 230–31.

5. Herrera had an English wife and had great affinity to the United States. Also, in 1808, an informant speaking confidentially claimed that Herrera was himself engaged in smuggling and secretly admired Napoleon. De la Teja, *Faces of Béxar,* 168.

6. Castañeda, *Our Catholic Heritage in Texas,* 5:398–99.

7. Gov. Manuel Salcedo to Luís Galán, May 13, 1810; Barr and Davenport to Gov. Manuel Salcedo, June 6, 1810; and Fr. José María Huerta de Jesús to Nemesio Salcedo, July 23, 1810; RBB S7:98–99, 188, 220. Juan Cortes to John C. Carr, September 9, 1810, Texas History Research, Samuel Davenport Folder, Karle Wilson Baker Papers.

8. De la Teja, "Economic Integration of a Periphery," 12.

9. De la Teja, *San Antonio de Béxar,* 75, 78, 105.

10. Gerald E. Poyo, ed., *Tejano Journey, 1770–1850* (Austin: University of Texas Press, 1996), 1–2.

11. Juan Manuel Maldonado, Pedro Lopez Prieto to Gov. February 11, 1810, BA, RBB S7:33–35.

12. The José Antonio Menchaca mentioned here is the future Texas revolutionary, not to be confused with the José Menchaca who later figures in this narrative. Matovina and de la Teja, *Recollections of a Tejano Life,* 42–43. RBB S7:269 and James Clark Milligan, *José Bernardo Gutiérrez de Lara, Mexican Frontiersman, 1811–1841* (PhD diss., Texas Tech University, 1975), 10.

13. Castañeda, *Our Catholic Heritage in Texas,* 6:2. Laura Caldwell, "Casas Revolt," *HOTO,* http://www.tshaonline.org/handbook/online/articles/jcc02 (accessed June 2, 2018).

14. De la Teja, *Faces of Béxar,* 75–76. De la Teja, *San Antonio de Béxar,* 19–20, 36. Frederick C. Chabot, *With the Makers of San Antonio,* 163–66. The story of Don Vicente Álvarez Travieso's stand can be found in Gerald E. Poyo and Gilberto Hinojosa, ed. *Tejano Origins in Eighteenth-Century San Antonio* (Austin: University of Texas Press, 1991), 57.

15. Manuel de Salcedo, Proclamation of January 6, 1811, Béxar Archives. Chabot, *Texas in 1811,* 24. Castañeda, *Our Catholic Heritage in Texas,* 6:8.

16. Historian David McDonald suggests the choice of an outsider to lead the revolt was deliberate, and "suggests a strategy that would allow responsibility to be shifted to Casas as a scapegoat if the revolt failed. As it turned out, that is essentially what happened." McDonald, *José Antonio Navarro,* 21. The list of Casas followers comes from numerous sources, including Chabot, *Texas in 1811,* and Castañeda, *Our Catholic Heritage in Texas,* 6.

17. Chabot, *Texas in 1811,* 24. Castañeda, *Our Catholic Heritage in Texas,* 6:8–10.

18. Castañeda, *Our Catholic Heritage in Texas,* 6:8–10.

19. McDonald, *José Antonio Navarro,* 21. The quotation is the historian's, not Navarro's.

20. Coronado, *A World Not to Come,* 63.

21. Castañeda, *Our Catholic Heritage in Texas,* 6:11.

22. Garcia was actually the second in command. The nominal commander of the garrison, Don Andres Mateos, was under arrest for financial issues. Kathryn Stoner O'Connor, *The Presidio la Bahia del Espiritu Santo de Zuniga, 1721 to 1846* (Austin: Von Boeckmann-Jones Co., 1966), 85.

23. Maynes, despite being arrested, was treated with respect and ultimately joined the revolutionaries. When the revolt failed, he fled to the United States and settled in Natchitoches, where he led the Catholic congregation there. Epperson, *Lost Spanish Towns,* 53.

24. Domínguez later escaped from the troop of soldiers taking him to Béxar and fled to Natchitoches, where both royalist and republican exiles would congregate. Nemesio Salcedo to Council of Government, April 9, 1811, BA, RBB S7:316. Manuel Salcedo to Nemesio Salcedo, September 18, 1811, Salcedo, Operaciones de Guerra, AGM. José María Guadiana to Gov. Juan B. Casas, February 7, 1811, BA. RBB S7:310.

25. "Communication with details of the execution of a commission to arrest several parties," NA, RBB S15:191–193; John Sibley to William Eustis, Sec. of War, February 9, 1811, in Garrett, "Dr. John Sibley," *SWHQ*, 48, no. 4 (April 1945), pp. 547–49.

26. Sibley's letter refers to "Edward Quick," although it is certainly Edmund Quirk, either written down incorrectly through an error of Sibley's or an error of transcription by Garrett. John Sibley to William Eustis, Sec. of War, February 9, 1811, in Garrett, "Dr. John Sibley," *SWHQ* 48, no. 4 (April 1945), pp. 547–49.

27. Garrett, "Dr. John Sibley."

28. Washington *National Intelligencer,* April 9, 1811, reprinted in Chabot, *Texas in 1811,* 148.

29. Chabot, *Texas in 1811,* 77–78.

30. Sibley refers to several reluctant royalist officers shot, though other sources mention none. Certainly, there were some killed in the Casas coup, but the numbers are unknown and there is no evidence deaths were widespread. Castañeda, *Our Catholic Heritage in Texas,* 6:13. The Wichita bands involved in the raids were the Tawakoni and Taovaya. F. Todd Smith, *From Dominance to Disappearance* (Lincoln: University of Nebraska Press, 2005), 97.

31. Jesus F. de la Teja, *San Antonio de Béxar,* 157. Jesus F. de la Teja, "Review: The Mexican Wars for Independence," *Southwestern Historical Quarterly* 113, no. 4 (April 2010), 535.

32. Hugh M. Hamill Jr., "Royalist Counterinsurgency in the Mexican War for Independence: The Lessons of 1811," *Hispanic American Historical Review* 53, no. 3 (August 1973), 471.

33. Chipman, *Spanish Texas 1519–1821,* 233. Chabot, *Texas in 1811,* 24. RBB S15:197. J. Villasana Haggard, "The Counter-Revolution of Béxar, 1811," *Southwestern Historical Quarterly* 43, no. 2 (October 1939), 227.

Zambrano spelled his own name Sambrano, but the modern spelling is used in this book. S15:195–201.

34. Ignacio Pérez and Maneul Delgado to A. Cordero, December 20, 1805, BA, RBB S5:184. Haggard, "The Counter-Revolution of Béxar, 1811," 225–26.

35. Ted Schwartz and Robert Thornhoff, *Forgotten Battlefield of the First Texas Revolution* (Austin: Eakin Press, 1985), 19. Haggard, "The Counter-Revolution of Béxar, 1811," 227. Chabot, *Texas in 1811,* 25. "Notes on J. D. Zambrano," Box 48, Folder 5, Karle Wilson Baker Papers.

36. Guedea, "Autonomía e independencia en la provincia de Texas," 144. Chabot, *Texas in 1811,* 25. Castañeda, *Our Catholic Heritage in Texas,* 6:18–19. Manuel de Salcedo to Viceroy Venegas, April 19, 1811, quoted in Milligan, *José Bernardo Gutiérrez de Lara, Mexican Frontiersman,* 14. "Proclamation Relating the Revolution Which Took Place at Béxar on the 22nd January," [date unknown], NA, RBB S10:200–205.

37. "Report of the Deputies of the Province of Texas, to the Commanding General," May 4, 1811, Nacogdoches Archive, RBB 10:61.

38. "Report of the Deputies of the Province of Texas." Haggard, "The Counter-Revolution of Béxar, 1811," 229.

39. Zambrano provided a list of his associates in June 1811, and Salcedo used that as a source (with a few additions) in his proclamation announcing the success of the countercoup (RBB S10: 204). Among this list are some who were clearly republicans, both before and after, including José Francisco Ruiz, who would sign the 1836 Texas Declaration of Independence on March 2, 1836—twenty-five years to the day after he had helped overthrow the nominally republican Casas. "Answer of the Central Committee to the Communication of the General Commander," Nacogdoches Archive, RBB S15:194–202. "Proclamation Relating the Revolution Which Took Place At Béxar on the 22nd January," [date unknown], NA, RBB S10:200–205. Haggard, "The Counter-Revolution of Béxar, 1811," 229.

40. Haggard, "The Counter-Revolution of Béxar, 1811," 230.

41. Haggard, "The Counter-Revolution of Béxar, 1811," 230.

42. Guadiana was ordered to San Antonio on May 1st to answer charges. He was not imprisoned, however, and may have been spared by a general pardon given under an order from Nemesio Salcedo of the previous month. Haggard, "The Counter-Revolution of Béxar, 1811," 231. Council of Government to Nemesio Salcedo, May 1, 1811, BA, RBB S7:318–20. Nemesio Salcedo pardon order, April 20, 1811, *Béxar Archives*. [Junta] to Nemesio Salcedo, May 1, 1811, *Béxar Archives*.

43. Haggard, "The Counter-Revolution of Béxar, 1811," 231. Milligan, *José Bernardo Gutiérrez de Lara, Mexican Frontiersman*, 19. Communication to the Governor and Junta, March 2, 1811, as quoted in Castañeda, *Our Catholic Heritage in Texas*, 6:21.

44. Gulick, *The Papers of Mirabeau Buonaparte Lamar*, 5:384. Chabot, *Texas in 1811*, 97.

45. "Proclamation Relating the Revolution Which Took Place at Béxar on the 22nd January," [date unknown], NA, RBB S10:200–205.

46. Manuel Salcedo to Viceroy, June 12, 1812, Salcedo, Operaciones de Guerra. AGM.

47. Bastrop knew the governors well, for he had long experience in Texas, and indeed would continue to be a player in the province decades later as a friend and associate of Stephen F. Austin. Castañeda, *Our Catholic Heritage in Texas*, 6:26.

48. Haggard tells a slightly different story: that residents of the presidio of Rio Grande were unfavorable to the counterrevolution and forced the agents to barricade themselves in an old building. The two agents escaped and then made their way to a pro-royalist group. Chabot *With the Makers of San Antonio*,103. Castañeda, *Our Catholic Heritage in Texas*, 6:23. Haggard, "The Counter-Revolution of Béxar, 1811," 232. Castañeda, *Our Catholic Heritage in Texas*, 6:26. "Notes Taken from Menchaca and Barrera," in Gulick, *The Papers of Mirabeau Buonaparte Lamar,* 6:337–39.

49. Henderson, *The History of Texas from Its First Settlement in 1685 to Its Annexation to the United States in 1846*, 74–101. Castañeda, *Our Catholic Heritage in Texas*, 6:27–29.

50. Castañeda, *Our Catholic Heritage in Texas*, 6:30.

51. Castañeda, *Our Catholic Heritage in Texas*, 6:30.

52. Castañeda, *Our Catholic Heritage in Texas*, 6:30.

53. Castañeda, *Our Catholic Heritage in Texas*, 6:31–33.

54. Castañeda, *Our Catholic Heritage in Texas*, 6:32.

55. Haggard, "The Counter-Revolution of Béxar, 1811," 232.

56. Nemesio Salcedo to Council of Government, May 23, 1811. BA, RBB S7:320. Governing Council to Nemesio Salcedo, June 26, 1811, BA, S7:352; Chipman, *Spanish Texas 1519–1821*, 233.

Chapter 7

1. Kastor, "'Motives of Peculiar Urgency,'" 822–23.

2. Stoltz, "'The Preservation of Good Order,'" 429. "A Duel Was Fought on Monday Last," *Louisiana Gazette*, June 12, 1807; Elizabeth Urban Alexander, *Notorious Woman: The Celebrated Case of Myra Clark Gaines* (Baton Rouge: Louisiana State University Press, 2001), 117. Kastor, "'Motives of Peculiar Urgency,'" 827–28, 831.

3. Clark's investment in the project was substantial. After meeting with Burr in 1805, he took two voyages to Veracruz on business, gathering intelligence as he did. His plans were likely for the Burr enterprise, but the information was developed at his cost and initiative. Narrett, "Geopolitics and Intrigue," 127.

That the Mexican Association was still functioning as late as 1815 can be found in its support of post-Gutiérrez-Magee filibusters. See Antonio Riva Palacio López, ed., *Pliegos de la diplomacia insurgente* (Mexico City: Cámara de Senadores de la República Mexicana, 1987), 61–175. Doolen, *Territories of Empire*, 44.

4. Salcedo to Iturrigaray, September 28, 1808, quoted in McCaleb, *Aaron Burr Conspiracy*, 366.

5. Clovet to Salcedo, June 22, 1808, quoted in McCaleb, *Aaron Burr Conspiracy*, 366. Claiborne to Madison, September 7, 1808, CL, 213.

6. W. C. C. Claiborne to Col. Cushing, December 29, 1808, CL, 4:279–80. McCaleb, *Aaron Burr Conspiracy*, 30.

7. The latter refers as well to an unnamed general in league with this person, who is certainly Gen. John Adair. W. C. C. Claiborne to James Madison, September 7, 1808, CL, 4:211–13.

8. W. C. C. Claiborne to James Madison, January 1, 1809, CL, 4:282–84.

9. W. C. C. Claiborne to Don Benito Perez, July 19, 1809, CL, 5:12. Jacob y Cart to Wm. C. C. Claiborne, November 16, 1809, CL, 5:13.

10. W. C. C. Claiborne to Robert Smith, November 18, 1809, CL, 5:13–15.

11. W. C. C. Claiborne to Col. Hopkins, November 10, 1809, CL, 5:7.

12. Robert Smith to Claiborne, in Carter, *The Territorial Papers of the United States*, 9:850–52.

13. The line of questioning hints that Governor Salcedo may himself have been involved in the conspiracy. This is highly doubtful. However, his fellow governor, Simón de Herrera, had revolutionary sympathies. Newman Statement, November 24, 1809, CL, 5:18–21.

14. The strangers Claiborne refers to are American immigrants, but also a large influx of Frenchmen fleeing Haiti, and who were potential recruits to the association. W. C. C. Claiborne to Robert Smith November 5, 1809, CL, 4:420–22. W. C. C. Claiborne to Robert Smith, November 16, 1809, CL, 5:8. Newman Statement, November 24, 1809, CL, 5:18–21. Claiborne to Smith December 31, 1809, CL, 5:22.

15. "Copy of Charges exhibited against Lieut. Colonel Constant Freeman of the regiment of Artillerists," January 26, 1810, LRSWMS, M221 Roll 35.

16. [Bernardo Bonavía] to Nemesio Salcedo, January 1, 1809; José Nicolás Benítez to Bernardo Bonavía, November 11, 1809; Nemesio Salcedo to Bernardo Bonavía, November 27, 1810; Bernardo Bonavía to Manuel de Salcedo, January 4, 1810, Béxar Archives.

17. Governmental Council to Nemesio Salcedo, April 3. 1811, BA, RBB S7:314. John Sibley to William Eustis, Sec. of War, February 9, 1811, in Garrett, "Dr. John Sibley," *SWHQ* 48, no. 4 (April 1945), pp. 547–49.

18. "[Manuel Salcedo] to Pedro López Prieto," December 19, 1808; "José Agabo de Ayala to Manuel Salcedo, on Miguel Quin's escape," July 2, 1810; and "José Agabo de Ayala to Manuel de Salcedo, on the investigation of Miguel Quin's escape," July 28, 1810, Béxar Archives. Pedro Lopez Prieto, "Diary of Trinidad for July 1808," BA, RBB S6:252, Diary of Operations of Luciano Garcia to Sabine, April 8, 1810, BA, S7:72. Felipe de la Garza to Governor Manuel Salcedo, January 1, 1811, BA S7:291–92.

19. December 21, 1811, memorandum from Davenport to Salcedo. Texas History Research, Samuel Davenport Folder, Karle Wilson Baker Papers.

20. Castañeda, *Our Catholic Heritage in Texas*, 6:5. Hatcher, *The Opening of Texas*, 212. José Álvarez de Toledo, "Relación de los Oficiales Extrangeros, que baxo mis Ordenes se han distinguido en el servicio de la Republica Mexicana," February 12, 1815, Juan E. Hernández y Dávalos Manuscript Collection, Benson Latin American Collection, University of Texas at Austin.

21. James, *Three Years among the Indians and Mexicans*, 287.

22. *Louisiana Gazette*, March 14, 1811, in James, *Three Years among the Indians and Mexicans*, 287–88. Steward, *Frontier Swashbuckler*, 105.

23. A direct route to Santa Fe through Texas would have been nearly impossible, given the difficult terrain and hostle Indians between the two provinces, but Smith T. likely did not know this. Steward, *Frontier Swashbuckler*, 105–6.

24. Fort Smith was established six years later and was named for the brother of John Smith T and Reuben Smith, Thomas Adams Smith, an army officer and Wilkinson protégé who had also been a Burr conspirator before joining Wilkinson in the betrayal of the cause.

A comparison of American and Spanish sources verifies that the Spanish "Smith" was Smith T. He wrote his letter in April and the captured prisoners were interrogated in July, revealing a plot that had existed for several months. Smith T began raising his filibusters in February and March. There is no other account or even rumor of any other person on the frontier raising such men. Smith T was definitively engaged in a filibuster attempt in Texas in 1814 as well. For more on the connection between Smith T and the filibuster, see James Aalan Bernsen, "The Case of John Smith T," *Texas History Blog*, http://www.texhist.com/2021/12/the-case-of-john-smith-t.html (accessed December 4, 2021).

25. The "Captain de Ortt" mentioned by several of the witnesses as a key instigator of the conspiracy in Nacogdoches is D'Ortolant. Testimony of Thomas McKinnon, July 6, 1811, BA. RBB S7:341–44. The identification of Huerta as "the Fat Father" is in the testimony of Miguel Crow, "Expediente on Plots Against the Government," June 5, 1811, RBB S7:331–32. "4th Declaration—of José Miguel Crow," RBB S7:334.

26. Smith to Huerta, April 29, 1811, Béxar Archives. "Expediente on Plots Against the Government," June 5, 1811, BA, RBB S7:322–48.

27. Smith to Huerta, April 29, 1811, Béxar Archives.

28. Smith to Huerta, April 29, 1811, Béxar Archives.

29. Huerta actually turned over the damning letter to Spanish authorities, but this may have been a way of pretending innocence after he deemed discovery certain. The Spanish officials investigated the case under the presumption of his guilt. Another priest in the community, Father Sosa, also suspected, fled to the United States. Hatcher, *The Opening of Texas*, 213.

30. Guedea, "Autonomía e independencia en la provincia de Texas," 143. "Extraordinario," January 11, 1811 (Numero 6), *El Desperator Americano, Correo Politico Económico de Guadalajara*, http://www.cervantesvirtual.com/descargaPdf/el-despertador-americano-correo-politico-economico-de-guadalajara-6/ (accessed May 7, 2020).

31. Manuel Salcedo to Nemesio Salcedo, August 14, 1811, Salcedo, Operaciones de Guerra, AGM.

32. Testimony of Encarnacio Chirino, "Expediente on Plots Against the Government," June 5, 1811, RBB S7:325. Testimony of Thomas McKinnon, July 6, 1811, RBB S7:341–44.

33. The man supposedly killed was "a man formerly from Kentucky by the Name of John Villers," but he did not die and would join the expedition and ultimately give firsthand account to Mirabeau Lamar. McKinnon is identified in the Spanish records. Sibley refers to him in his account at "Middleton, I believe from Virginia." Captain Wollstonecraft in Natchitoches also responded, sending a force across the Arroyo Hondo, attacked the robbers, killed one and took two prisoners, dispersing the rest. *Expediente on Plots against the Government, June 5, 1811*, RBB S7:323–48. Garrett, "Dr. John Sibley," *SWHQ*, 49, no. 1 (July 1945), pp. 116–19.

34. Taylor's death date varies greatly. Cushing says July 3rd; other sources say August 20th or 27th. T. H. Cushing to Wilkinson, July 31, 1806, in Wilkinson, *Burr's Conspiracy Exposed*, appendix (Doc. No. 47), 42. "Connecticut, U.S., Hale Collection of Cemetery Inscriptions and Newspaper Notices, 1629–1934," Ancestry.com. Original data: The Charles R. Hale Collection. Hale Collection of Connecticut Cemetery Inscriptions. Hartford, Connecticut:

Connecticut State Library. "U.S., Newspaper Extractions from the Northeast, 1704–1930." Ancestry.com. Original data: Newspapers and Periodicals. American Antiquarian Society, Worcester, Massachusetts.

35. War Department to Josiah Taylor, October 12, 1802, LSSW, 1800–89, US National Archive, vol. 6, Roll 1. "Papers Relative to the Fourth Point of Inquiry," *American Citizen*, August 7, 1810. Linklater, *An Artist in Treason*, 196.

36. Daniel Clark, *Proofs of the Corruption of Gen. James Wilkinson and of His Connexion with Aaron Burr* [1809] (Reprinted Freeport, New York: Books for Libraries Press, 1970), 27.

37. Clark, *Proofs of the Corruption of Gen. James Wilkinson and of His Connexion with Aaron Burr*, 28–29.

38. *The Trials of the Honb. James Workman and Col. Lewis Kerr*, 82.

39. The Josiah Taylor who appears in the Clarke County, Georgia, marriage records in 1807 is the same Josiah Taylor who later fights in the Gutiérrez-Magee expedition. However, there is no Josiah or Joseph Taylor in Georgia in any of the 1800, 1810, or 1820 censuses. A detailed search of records for these years show eight to twelve Josiah Taylors nationwide and only four in the South, none of whom are a match, with most having established families before the marriage of the Georgia Taylor. "Georgia, U.S., Marriage Records from Select Counties, 1828–1978," Ancestry.com. Original data: County Marriage Records, 1828–1978. The Georgia Archives, Morrow, Georgia. "1800, 1810 and 1820 U.S. Federal Census," Ancestry.com. Powell, *List of Officers of the Army of the United States from 1779 to 1900*, 43.

40. Andrew Jackson Sowell, *Early Settlers and Indian Fighters of Southwest Texas* (Austin: Ben C. Jones and Co., 1900), 805.

41. Davis, *Rogue Republic*, 92.

42. Garrett, "Dr. John Sibley," *SWHQ* 49, no. 1 (July 1945): 116–19.

43. Testimony of Edmund Quirk, "Expediente on Plots Against the Government," June 5, 1811, RBB S7:326–30.

44. The notes of the interrogation were taken by Texas postmaster Erasmo Seguin, father of Juan Seguin. Assisting him was Juan Martín Veramendi, who later joined the Republican expedition, served as governor of Coahuila and Texas in 1833, and whose daughter married James Bowie. Testimony of Edmund Quirk, "Expediente on Plots against the Government," June 5, 1811, RBB S7:326–30.

45. Testimony of José Miguel Crow, *Expediente on Plots against the Government, June 5, 1811*, RBB S7:331–32.

46. Testimony of José Miguel Crow, *Expediente on Plots against the Government, June 5, 1811*, RBB S7:334–37.

47. Testimony of José Miguel Crow, *Expediente on Plots against the Government, June 5, 1811*, RBB S7:334–37.

48. John C. Carr to Claiborne, July 4, 1811, in Carter, *The Territorial Papers of the United States*, 943.

49. John Sibley to unknown [probably Secretary of War William Eustis], February 9, 1811, in Garrett, "Dr. John Sibley," 48, no. 4 (April 1945), pp. 547–49. Steward, *Frontier Swashbuckler*, 105.

Chapter 8

1. Most accounts state that Gutiérrez was a blacksmith. Henry Adams Bullard, who knew Gutiérrez well, and later wrote an anonymous account of the expedition, claimed Gutiérrez was a silversmith. It is the only account that states this, but it is possible Gutiérrez could work

with both metals. Coronado, *A World Not to Come*, 43. Milligan, *José Bernardo Gutiérrez de Lara, Mexican Frontiersman*, 4. Narrett, "José Bernardo Gutiérrez de Lara," 198. Anonymous [Henry Adams Bullard], "A Visit to Texas, Being the Journal of a Traveler, through Parts Most Interesting to American Settlers," *North American Review* 43, no. 92 (July 1836), 234. Gulick, *The Papers of Mirabeau Buonaparte Lamar*, 6:339. Milligan, *José Bernardo Gutiérrez de Lara, Mexican Frontiersman*, 4. Narrett, "José Bernardo Gutiérrez de Lara," 198.

2. Milligan, *José Bernardo Gutiérrez de Lara, Mexican Frontiersman*, 8–10.

3. Rodríguez O., *Political Culture in Spanish America*, 3–4. Narrett, "José Bernardo Gutiérrez de Lara," 198–99. Rie Jarratt, *Gutiérrez de Lara: Mexican Texan—The Story of a Creole Hero* (Austin: Creole Texana, 1949), 5. Coronado, *A World Not to Come*, 43.

4. In this account, Gutiérrez states he was for independence, but this is in hindsight. This account, written to Mexican revolutionary authorities in August 1815, after the failed expedition into Texas two years before, is a problematic source. Gutiérrez exaggerates his own role, claiming for instance a military command in the expedition which he never held. He also dismisses the Anglo leaders, never mentioning any of the four commanders by name despite the fact that they made every significant military decision. On many points, it is even at variance with his own diary of four years prior. J. B. Gutiérrez de Lara to the Mexican Congress. Account of progress of the Revolution from the Beginning, in Gulick, *The Papers of Mirabeau Buonaparte Lamar*, 1:5.

5. Milligan, *José Bernardo Gutiérrez de Lara, Mexican Frontiersman*, 10.

6. Milligan, *José Bernardo Gutiérrez de Lara, Mexican Frontiersman*, 16. José Bernardo Gutiérrez de Lara, *Breve Apologia que el Coronel D. Jose Bernardo Gutiérrez de Lara hace de las imposturas calumniosas que se le articulan en un folleto intitulado: levantamiento de un General en las Tamaulipas contra la Republica o muerto que se le aparece al gobierno en aquel estado* (Monterrey: Pedro Gonzalez, 1827), 5.

7. Gulick, *The Papers of Mirabeau Buonaparte Lamar*, 1:6.

8. Elizabeth Howard West, "Diary of José Bernardo Gutiérrez de Lara, 1811–1812 [Part 1]," *American Historical Review* 34, no. 1 (October, 1928): 57.

9. Gutiérrez de Lara to the Mexican Congress, "Account of Progress of the Revolution from the Beginning," in Gulick, *The Papers of Mirabeau Buonaparte Lamar*, 1:4–29. Testimony of John Garniere before John Sibley, September 19, 1811, LRSWRS, M221 Roll 47. Elizabeth Howard West, "Diary of José Bernardo Gutiérrez de Lara, 1811–1812 [Part 1]," *American Historical Review* 34, no. 1 (October 1928), 57.

10. The route which Gutiérrez took is unknown, but he speaks of traveling through "barbarous nations" and ultimately arrived at Bayou Pierre, in the northern extremity of the Neutral Ground, indicating his route was west and north of the Spanish settlements. That Garniere found the rebels is extraordinary, and he must have done so with the aid of friendly Indians. The possibility that he may have been a spy or was followed by the Spanish cannot be ruled out. Testimony of John Garniere before John Sibley. "Frankfort, October 18," *American Watchman and Delaware Republican*, November 9, 1811.

11. Garnier's report to the Americans also included a rumor, probably false, but perfectly tuned to American fears, that Commandant General Nemesio Salcedo was himself planning to come to Texas with a force of six thousand men, cross the Sabine, "to take possession of the Territory of Orleans and proceed on to Baton Rouge & Pensacola and punish the rascally Americans for what they had done in that quarter against his brother compatriots." At the same time, Paul Bouvet Lafitte, a resident of the Neutral Ground, recorded the account of two hundred filibusterers being organized to rescue Menchaca and Gutiérrez. These were certainly the men organized by Smith T. Lafitte included the cryptic line, "The Father has

to accompany them," which may indicate that Father Huerta had escaped to Natchitoches. West, "Diary of José Bernardo Gutiérrez de Lara, 1811–1812 [Part 1]," 58. Testimony of John Garniere before John Sibley. Paul Bouvet Lafitte to Cristóbal Dominguez, September 11, 1811, BA, RBB S7:365.

12. Cortes was a former Spanish officer who had fled due to suspicion of smuggling and worked for New Orleans businessman Benjamin Morgan, who was well-established in city society. It was in Cortes's house where the trader William Barr died. Overton, as noted, was not at this time commander of Fort Claiborne. Jarratt, *Gutiérrez de Lara: Mexican Texan*, 8. Milligan, *José Bernardo Gutiérrez de Lara, Mexican Frontiersman*, 19–20.

13. *"Extract of a Letter from a Gentleman at Natchitoches on Red River to His Friend at* Fort Columbus," *Scioto Gazette*, February 1, 1812.

14. Jarratt, *Gutiérrez de Lara: Mexican Texan*, 8. Milligan, *José Bernardo Gutiérrez de Lara, Mexican Frontiersman*, 21.

15. West, "Diary of José Bernardo Gutiérrez de Lara, 1811–1812 [Part 1]," 1:58.

16. West, "Diary of José Bernardo Gutiérrez de Lara, 1811–1812 [Part 1]," 1:58.

17. West, "Diary of José Bernardo Gutiérrez de Lara, 1811–1812 [Part 1]," 1:58–59.

18. "To James Madison from William Cocke, 28 November 1811," Founders Online, National Archives, http://founders.archives.gov/documents/Madison/03-04-02-0042 (accessed May 7, 2020). [Original source: *The Papers of James Madison, Presidential Series, vol. 4, 5, November 1811–9 July 1812 and Supplement 5 March 1809–19 October 1811*, ed. J. C. A. Stagg, Jeanne Kerr Cross, Jewel L. Spangler, Ellen J. Barber, Martha J. King, Anne Mandeville Colony, and Susan Holbrook Perdue. Charlottesville: University Press of Virginia, 1999, 38–39.] Milligan, *José Bernardo Gutiérrez de Lara, Mexican Frontiersman*, 62–63. Society of Architectural Historians, "Cragfont" https://sah-archipedia.org/buildings/TN-01-165-0022 (accessed December 2, 2020).

19. West, "Diary of José Bernardo Gutiérrez de Lara, 1811–1812 [Part 1]," 1:64.

20. West, "Diary of José Bernardo Gutiérrez de Lara, 1811–1812 [Part 1]," 1:65.

21. Jarratt, *Gutiérrez de Lara: Mexican Texan*, 10–11; West, "Diary of José Bernardo Gutiérrez de Lara, 1811–1812 [Part 1]," 1:65–66.

22. Jarratt, *Gutiérrez de Lara: Mexican Texan*, 10; Milligan, *José Bernardo Gutiérrez de Lara, Mexican Frontiersman*, 26–27, and West, "Diary of José Bernardo Gutiérrez de Lara, 1811–1812 [Part 1]," 1:68.

23. The number is close to the original force, which was to seize Nacogdoches according to the plans of Smith T., as revealed by the Spanish interrogations.

"Extract of a letter from an officer of the U. States' Army," *Alexandria Daily Gazette*, December 17, 1811. "We have been informed from a source which is respectable, that two hundred Americans have crossed the Sabine near Natchitoches," *Raleigh Register, and North-Carolina Weekly Advertiser* (Raleigh, North Carolina), Friday, December 20, 1811. Milligan, *José Bernardo Gutiérrez de Lara, Mexican Frontiersman*, 30. Gulick, *The Papers of Mirabeau Buonaparte Lamar*, 1:286. Castañeda, *Our Catholic Heritage in Texas*, 6:60.

24. *Raleigh Register, and North-Carolina Weekly Advertiser* (Raleigh, North Carolina), Friday, December 20, 1811. Gutiérrez de Lara to the Mexican Congress, "Account of Progress of the Revolution from the Beginning," in Gulick, *The Papers of Mirabeau Buonaparte Lamar*, 1:11.

25. West, "Diary of José Bernardo Gutiérrez de Lara, 1811–1812 [Part 1]," 1:70–71.

26. Pike to Eustis, October 28, 1811, LRSWRS M221 Roll 47.

27. Pike to Eustis, October 28, 1811, LRSWRS M221 Roll 47.

28. Gutiérrez's diary is the only extensive contemporary source of notes on the meetings he had in Washington, DC. The rebel envoy made efforts to show himself in a positive light. Since he was not hostile to the Americans, but wary, and since the writings were made at the time, it is reasonable to assume any distortions of the content of the meeting are relatively minor and more designed to show Gutiérrez as a clever negotiator than to disparage his American interlocutors. His subsequent writings were more jaded. West, "Diary of José Bernardo Gutiérrez de Lara, 1811–1812 [Part 1]," 1:71.

29. This is a considerably more advanced position than that provided in Shaler's instructions, which made possession of Texas a matter of minor concern to be dealt with later. This reflects either a difference in positions between war and state or an evolution at the State Department effected by the replacement of Smith with Monroe.

Eustis certainly knew Gutiérrez could not make the concession unilaterally, but was perhaps using it as leverage, or to spur future negotiations. The tactic, if that is what it was, may have actually worked. It should be noted that for all his offense in Washington, Gutiérrez when faced with a crisis at La Bahía would write to Monroe offering the same deal in exchange for an army to rescue his beleaguered forces. Narrett, "José Bernardo Gutiérrez de Lara," 204. West, "Diary of José Bernardo Gutiérrez de Lara, 1811–1812 [Part 1]," 1:72–73. Jarratt, *Gutiérrez de Lara: Mexican Texan*, 15.

30. West, "Diary of José Bernardo Gutiérrez de Lara, 1811–1812 [Part 1]," 1:73.

31. West, "Diary of José Bernardo Gutiérrez de Lara, 1811–1812 [Part 1]," 1:73.

32. Years later, in a self-serving memoir which takes great license with the truth, the Mexican revolutionary added that when the 50,000 men were offered to him, he asked to be able to command them, a proposal which was met by silence by Monroe. Milligan, *José Bernardo Gutiérrez de Lara, Mexican Frontiersman*, 35–36. West, "Diary of José Bernardo Gutiérrez de Lara, 1811–1812 [Part 1]," 1:73. Gutiérrez de Lara to the Mexican Congress, "Account of progress of the Revolution from the Beginning," in Gulick, *The Papers of Mirabeau Buonaparte Lamar*, 1:11.

33. Milligan, *José Bernardo Gutiérrez de Lara, Mexican Frontiersman*, 13, 28.

34. West, "Diary of José Bernardo Gutiérrez de Lara, 1811–1812 [Part 1]," 1:75.

35. West, "Diary of José Bernardo Gutiérrez de Lara, 1811–1812 [Part 1]," 1:76.

36. Gulick, *The Papers of Mirabeau Buonaparte Lamar*, 6: 337. West, "Diary of José Bernardo Gutiérrez de Lara, 1811–1812 [Part 1]," 1:76.

37. Nicolás Kanellos, "José Alvarez de Toledo y Dubois and the Origins of Hispanic Publishing in the Early American Republic," *Early American Literature* 43, no. 1 (2008), 91.

38. Kristin A. Dykstra, "On the Betrayal of Nations: José Alvarez de Toledo's Philadelphia *Manifesto* (1811) and *Justification* (1816)," *New Centennial Review* 4, no. 1 (Spring 2004): 278.

39. Harris Gaylord Warren, "José Álvarez de Toledo's Initiation as a Filibuster, 1811–1813," *Hispanic American Historical Review* 20, no. 1 (February 1940): 56.

40. Dykstra, "On the Betrayal of Nations," 270–71.

41. Dykstra, "On the Betrayal of Nations," 280. Kanellos, "José Alvarez de Toledo y Dubois," 88.

42. Dykstra, "On the Betrayal of Nations," 281. Kanellos, "José Alvarez de Toledo y Dubois," 88.

43. West, "Diary of José Bernardo Gutiérrez de Lara, 1811–1812 [Part 1]," 1:77.

44. Much has been made of this payment by some historians, who insinuate that Monroe was funding Gutiérrez' revolution. This is insupportable. Two hundred dollars was bare travel money, and shortly after arrival in New Orleans, even this cash ran out for the rebel.

Some intriguers on the frontier offered Gutiérrez $100,000 to agree to their schemes, so it is hardly likely that $200 by itself could have purchased his loyalty or compliance. Toledo's payment is unknown, but in his case, he ran out of this cash before even leaving Philadelphia. Kanellos, "José Alvarez de Toledo y Dubois," 84. West, "Diary of José Bernardo Gutiérrez de Lara, 1811–1812 [Part 1]," 1:77.

Chapter 9

1. The person giving this description of this city, who one day would play a major role in the history of Texas, was Lorenzo de Zavala. Andrés Reséndez, "Texas and the Spread of That Troublesome Secessionist Spirit through the Gulf of Mexico Basin," in Don H. Doyle, ed., *Secession as an International Phenomenon: From America's Civil War to Contemporary Separatist Movements* (Athens: University of Georgia Press, 2010), 193. William Shaler to James Monroe, December 27, 1811, Shaler Letterbooks.

2. *The Louisiana Gazette and Daily Advertiser*, Saturday, December 21, 1811, quoted in Dr. Otto W. Nuttli, "Contemporary Newspaper Accounts of Mississippi Valley Earthquakes of 1811–1812," St. Louis Earthquake Center (1972), http://www.eas.slu.edu/eqc/eqc_quakes/Nuttli.1973/nuttli-73-app.html (accessed August 5, 2021).

3. Shaler wrote a series of political essays both while in Cuba and upon his arrival in New Orleans. Most do not appear in the official Correspondence of Special Agents file, although some were forwarded not by Shaler, but by Governor Claiborne. William Shaler, "No. 1 'Essays on the Revolution in So. America,'" Shaler Letterbooks. For more about the essays and their relation to Shaler's views on revolution and American expansionism, see J. C. A. Stagg, ed., "The Political Essays of William Shaler," on the *William and Mary Quarterly* website, https://oieahc-cf.wm.edu/wmq/Apr02/stagg.pdf (accessed August 5, 2021).

4. Smith to Shaler, November 6, 1810, and John Graham to Nathaniel Ingraham, November 7, 1810, Shaler Papers.

5. Smith to Shaler, November 6, 1810, Shaler Papers. William Shaler to the Marqués de Someruelos, December 1810. Shaler Papers.

6. These included Cyrus Sibley, the nephew of John Sibley. The latter was certainly sympathetic with the aims of the rebels but appears to have been skeptical of the particular grouping of Americans who invaded in 1812. Joseph Carson to Governor Claiborne, February 16, 1811, in Carter, *The Territorial Papers of the United States*, 9:926.

7. It is doubtful that the Spanish knew of Shaler's secret instructions, but as soon as he arrived, they likely wrote to Onís, who could have informed them of the sea captain's history. Stephen Chambers, "No Country But Their Counting Houses," in Sven Beckert and Seth Rockman, ed., *Slavery's Capitalism: A New History of American Economic Development*, (Philadelphia: University of Pennsylvania Press, 2016), 206–7.

8. W. C. C. Claiborne to Capt. Wm. Shaler, [undated], CL 5:370–71.

9. W. C. C. Claiborne to John Graham, April 13, 1812. CL, 6:79–80.

10. Office of the Historian, "Biographies of the Secretaries of State: Robert Smith (1757–1842)," US Department of State, https://history.state.gov/departmenthistory/people/smith-robert (accessed July 3, 2021).

11. Smith Shaler, June 18, 1810. Shaler Papers. William Shaler to James Monroe, January 4, 1812, in Shaler Letterbooks.

12. Shaler to Monroe, February 16, 1812, in Shaler Letterbooks.

13. Shaler, "No. 1 'Essays on the Revolution in So. America,'" Shaler Letterbooks.

14. Shaler, "No. 1 'Essays on the Revolution in So. America.'"

15. Shaler, "No. 1 'Essays on the Revolution in So. America.'"
16. Shaler, "No. 1 'Essays on the Revolution in So. America.'"
17. William Shaler to James Madison, March 23, 1812. Shaler Letterbooks.
18. William Shaler to James Madison, March 23, 1812. Shaler Letterbooks.
19. William Shaler to James Madison, March 23, 1812. Shaler Letterbooks.
20. This is the letter that Harris Gaylord Warren misinterprets so egregiously, as noted in the introduction. Monroe was not approving Shaler in any filibustering exercises—the organization of which was still months away—he was merely approving Shaler's decision to stay nearer to Mexico to garner more information, not a particularly bold decision because Shaler's only alternative was to abandon his mission entirely and return to Washington. Monroe to Shaler, May 2, 1812, Shaler Papers.
21. Hampton to Eustis, April 1, 1812, LRSWMS, M221 Roll 45.
22. Shaler to Monroe, March 9, 1812, Shaler Letterbooks. Claiborne to John Graham, March 31, 1812, CL 6:68–69. Claiborne to Monroe, May 21, 1812, CL 6:104–5.
23. Salcedo to Wollstonecraft, June 22, 1812, LRSWRS, M221 Roll 49.
24. W. C. C. Claiborne to Carr, July 30, 1811, Claiborne to Col. Shaumberg, July 30, 1811, and Claiborne to the Officer Commanding at Fort Claiborne, CL 5: 319–21. J. C. Carr to Simón de Herrera, August 15, 1811. BA, RBB S7:354.
25. Hampton to Pike, February 6, 1812, Letters Received Secretary of War Main Series, M221 Roll 45 (hereafter LRSWMS). Hampton to Claiborne, January 23, 1812, in Carter, *The Territorial Papers of the United States*, 9:989–90. Claiborne to Monroe, April 19, 1811, CL, 5:383.
26. Claiborne to Gen. Wade Hampton, January 20, 1812, CL 6:34–35; Hampton to Pike, February 6, 1812; LRSWMS, M221 Roll 45.
27. Pike to Lt. King, February 26, 1812, Pike to Commandant at Nacogdoches, February 26, 1812, Pike to Herrera, February 26, 1812, Bernardino Montero to Commandant at Natchitoches [undated, but prior to March 27, 1812, when Captain Overton responded] LRSWMS, M221 Roll 45.
28. Lt. Elijah Montgomery is identified by Watson, *Jackson's Sword*, 49. Pike to Magee, March 3, 1812, LRSWMS, M221 Roll 45.
29. Magee to Pike, March 18, 1812, LRSWMS, M221 Roll 45.
30. Census of Trinidad de Salcedo, January 6, 1809, RBB S6:302, Felipe de la Garza to Governor Manuel Salcedo RBB S7:373, Felipe de la Garza to Salcedo, January 13, 1812, BA RBB S7:378. Magee to Pike, March 18, 1812, LRSWMS, M221 Roll 45.
31. Magee to Pike, March 18, 1812, LRSWMS, M221 Roll 45.
32. Magee to Pike, March 18, 1812, LRSWMS, M221 Roll 45.
33. Magee to Pike, March 18, 1812, LRSWMS, M221 Roll 45.
34. "General Tauro" is French Revolutionary General Louis Marie Turreau, who notoriously massacred tens of thousands of citizens of the Vendée region of France in 1793. All the bandits arrested by Magee were freed within two months except two, sentenced to seven years and one hundred lashes. The others escaped due to the "chicanery of the lawyer" in Davenport's words. John Sibley to Amos Stoddard, April 2, 1812. Sibley Family Papers, Mary E. Ambler Archives, Lindenwood University, St. Charles, Missouri. Samuel Davenport to Bernardino Montero, May 6, 1812, BA, RBB S7:403. Claiborne to Monroe, May 21, 1812, CL, 6:104.
35. Diary of Journey made by Isidro de la Garza. April 21, 1312, BA, RBB S7:388–95.
36. Gutiérrez specifically mentions a meeting with the ambassador of the emperor of Russia. Russia was at this time hostile to, and would soon be at war with, Napoleon, who was the de facto ruler of Spain; hence the ambassador's interest in revolution in Spanish America. Elizabeth Howard West, "Diary of José Bernardo Gutiérrez de Lara, 1811–1812 [Part 1]," "Diary

of José Bernardo Gutiérrez De Lara, 1811–1812. [Part 2]. Year of 1812," *American Historical Review* 34, no. 2 (1929): 283–85.

37. This conversation actually took place in New Orleans but is presented here as a vignette of the sentiment Gutiérrez saw everywhere in the United States. West, "Diary of José Bernardo Gutiérrez de Lara, 1811–1812 [Part 1]," "Diary of Gutiérrez de Lara" 2:290–91.

38. After leaving the State Department, Gutiérrez wrote to Graham three times, which writers such as Garrett have imputed to be collusion towards a filibuster, but as with Shaler, the correspondence was one-way. Graham only provided the letter of introduction to Claiborne after being asked for it by Gutiérrez. The letter still left the governor in the dark about the administration's intentions. Graham, as the only person in the department fluent in Spanish, was sympathetic to the rebel cause, but there is no evidence he supported a filibuster using Americans. In 1806, he had been one of the Jefferson administrations point people for uncovering the Burr Conspiracy and bringing its members to trial. Gutiérrez to Graham, January 20, 1812, April 28, 1812, and May 16, 1812, CRF. Claiborne to Graham, March 31, 1812, CL, 6:68. Guedea, "Autonomía e independencia en la provincia de Texas," 152. Abernethy, *Burr Conspiracy*, 86.

39. W. C. C. Claiborne to John Graham March 31, 1812, CL, 6:68–69.

40. W. C. C. Claiborne to John Graham March 31, 1812, CL, 6:68–69.

41. José Bernardo Gutiérrez de Lara, "Breve Apologia," 14. Guedea, "Autonomía e independencia en la provincia de Texas," 151–52.

42. West, "Diary of José Bernardo Gutiérrez de Lara, 1811–1812 [Part 1]," "Diary of José Bernardo Gutiérrez De Lara," 2:291. W. C. C. Claiborne to John Graham April 13, 1812, CL, 6: 78–80.

43. This quote, and other hypotheticals about US intervention, have enticed some writers to speculate that Claiborne pushed Gutiérrez to the frontier as part of a deliberate plan that ultimately became the filibuster to Texas. Nothing could be further from the truth. Claiborne was an expansionist and had bent rules in West Florida but, in doing so, was acting on clear guidance from the administration, which he did not have in regard to Texas. He wanted the Mexican to return to his country, and no doubt hoped he would restart the revolution there using native Mexicans. But he absolutely wanted to prevent a force of Americans from becoming involved in the fight, in the first place because he had no directions to the contrary from the state department, but also because any such enterprise not under official auspices would invariably be seized upon by his mortal enemies and might redound against him in the struggle for power in the Orleans Territory. W. C. C. Claiborne to John C. Carr, March 10, 1811, CL, 5:176.

44. Morgan's relation to the association is uncertain at the time but support of their aims is likely. His agent, Cortes, supported multiple filibuster attempts over the next few years. Jarratt, *Gutiérrez de Lara: Mexican Texan*, 22–23. Charles Gayarré, *History of Louisiana: The Spanish Domination*, vol. 3 (New Orleans: Armand Hawkins, 1885), 607. Michael Wohl, "Not Yet Saint Nor Sinner: A Further Note on Daniel Clark," *Louisiana History: The Journal of the Louisiana Historical Association* 24, no. 2 (Spring 1983), 195. Vernet, *Strangers on their Native Soil*, 62. Deposition of Quirk, February 12, 1816, Nacogdoches Archives, RBB S15: 219. David Head, *Privateers of the Americas: Spanish American Privateering from the United States* (Athens: University of Georgia Press, 2015), 135. Riva Palacio López, *Pliegos de la diplomacia insurgente*, 86. John Cortes to John C. Carr, September 9, 1810, Texas History Research, Samuel Davenport Folder, Karle Wilson Baker Papers. Wilson and Jackson, *Philip Nolan and Texas*, 14.

45. "The Patriots of Mexico," *Weekly Register*, August 1, 1812.

Chapter 10

1. *Louisiana Gazette*, March 14, 1811, in James, *Three Years among the Indians and Mexicans*, 287–88.

2. Reuben Smith may have had some military background and is called "Captain" Smith in some references. The biography of his brother incorrectly states that Reuben had graduated from West Point. Don Francisco Xavier de Lizana to Nemesio Salcedo, March 31, 1810, in Malcolm D. McLean, ed. *Papers Concerning Robertson's Colony in Texas, Vol. I: The Texas Association, 1788–1822.* Available at https://tshaonline.org/supsites/mclean/111.htm (accessed June 9, 2018). Steward, *Frontier Swashbuckler*, 13. Don Francisco Xavier de Lizana to Nemesio Salcedo, April 24, 1810, and the same, March 31, 1810, in Malcolm D. McLean, ed.

3. Nemesio Salcedo to Thomas Bolling Robertson, January 3, 1811, CRF. Kira Gale, *Meriwether Lewis: The Assassination of an American Hero and the Silver Mines of Mexico* (Omaha: River Junction Press, 2015), 452. Gale reports the story of Patterson witnessing the Hidalgo execution. "Famous Duellist Lived in Missouri Fifteen Men Bit the Dust Before This Conspicuous Exponent of the Code of Honor in the Early Days," *San Pedro Daily News,* November 7, 1906, https://cdnc.ucr.edu/?a=d&d=SPDN19061107&e=----en-20-1-txt-txIN----1 (accessed December 5, 2021).

4. McLanahan to Governor Howard, June 18, 1812, in James, *Three Years among the Indians and Mexicans*, 289–92.

5. McLanahan to Governor Howard, June 18, 1812, in James, *Three Years among the Indians and Mexicans*, 289–92.

6. "Observations on Robin's Travels in Louisiana, etc.," *National Intelligencer,* April 16, 1811.

7. Several secondary sources have placed the men in the expedition, but no primary source has been identified which does so. John Smith T's biographer says Reuben Smith, whose health was damaged from his ordeal, did not ever return to Texas. Steward, *Frontier Swashbuckler*, 110.

8. Shaler statement of expenses, June 1812, CSA. West, "Diary of José Bernardo Gutiérrez de Lara, 1811–1812 [Part 1]," 2:291–2.

9. Shaler to Monroe, May 2, 1812, Shaler Letterbooks, 50.

10. Castañeda and others suggested that Davenport had already converted to the republican cause, but in his May 6, 1812, letter to Nacogdoches commandant Bernardino Montero, Davenport is clearly spying on Shaler and Gutiérrez. The American "is the subject of some importance by the letters of recommendation which he brought. . . . The intention of his coming, no one up to the present is able to fathom. The public presumes that he brings some secret commission from his government." "Mexican Provinces," *Richmond Enquirer*, February 13, 1813. [Mr. Davenport], *New England Palladium*, Boston, Massachusetts, November 10, 1812. Davenport to Montero, May 6, 1812, RBB S7:403. Castañeda, *Our Catholic Heritage in Texas*, 6:79.

11. Shaler to Monroe, Natchitoches, May 2, 1812, Shaler papers.

12. West, "Diary of José Bernardo Gutiérrez de Lara, 1811–1812 [Part 1]," 2:291–2.

13. Some historians have also speculated that Claiborne had encouraged Shaler and Gutiérrez to launch a filibuster. He did not, but there are three reasons for this misinterpretation. The first are his statements in favor of the Mexican Revolution and suggesting an *official* American effort to support it. The second is based on a misreading of his actions in pushing the Mexican to the frontier, and the third is that such interpretations overlook the governor's all-pervasive fear of Clark and the Mexican Association as his motivation to send the rebel to the frontier.

14. Shaler to Monroe, May 17, 1812, Shaler Letterbooks (the National Archives copy of this letter is dated May 7). Shaler to Monroe, May 7, 1812, CSA.

15. Various letters put the earliest actual organization of a filibuster around May 3, 1812, although this was likely a mere coalescing of ongoing efforts. Linda Devereaux, "The Magee-Gutiérrez Expedition," in Barbara Comeaux Strickland, *Selected Papers of the Seventh Grand Reunion of the Descendants of the Founders of Natchitoches* (Natchitoches: Founders of Natchitoches, 1987). Joseph McLanahan to Governor Benjamin Howard, June 12, 1812, in James, *Three Years among the Indians and Mexicans*, 291–92.

16. Shaler paid the bills for Gutiérrez's boarding. The latter stayed at a boarding house run by Mary Anthony and another by Antoine Badine. Shaler Invoices, *Correspondence of Special Agents*. Sibley to Eustis, June 24, 1812, in Garrett, "Dr. John Sibley," *SWHQ* 49, no. 3 (January 1946): 407–10. Shaler to Monroe, May 17, 1812, Shaler Letterbooks.

17. Shaler to Monroe, May 17, 1812, Shaler Letterbooks.

18. Shaler to Monroe, May 17, 1812, Shaler Letterbooks.

19. Garrett, "Dr. John Sibley," *SWHQ* 49, no. 3 (January 1946), 399–431. Castañeda, *Our Catholic Heritage in Texas*, 6:71. Shaler to Monroe, May 2, 1812, Shaler Letterbooks. Nemesio Salcedo to Governor Manuel Salcedo, June 19, 1812, BA RBB S7:414–15.

20. Shaler to Monroe, August 18, 1812, and Shaler to Monroe, May 17, 1812, Shaler Letterbooks.

21. Davenport to Bernardino Montero, May 6, 1812, RBB S7:403. Salcedo to Wollstonecraft, June 22, 1812, LRSWRS, M221 Roll 49.

22. Pedro Antonio Sáenz (Saens in the original) is not the same person as the Antonio Saenz who had come to Texas as a rebel agent of Hidalgo's forces. Bernardino Montero to Governor Manuel de Salcedo, June 24, 1812, BA, RBB S7:415.

23. L'Herisson, "The Evolution of the Texas Road and the Subsequential Settlement Occupancy of the Adjacent Strip of Northwestern Louisiana," 20.

24. "Orramel Johnston to an Unidentified Correspondent, 18 May 1812 (Abstract)," *Founders Online*, National Archives, last modified April 12, 2018, http://founders.archives.gov/documents/Madison/03-04-02-0424 (original source: The Papers of James Madison). "From Orramel Johnston, 12 June 1812," The Papers of James Monroe, series 2, http://monroepapers.com/items/show/2310 (accessed May 7, 2020). Library of Congress.

25. Major Welsh is unknown, possibly Michael Walsh, who was listed as a first lieutenant three years earlier in the regiment of artillerists. See "Corps of Engineers," *The National Intelligencer and Washington Advertiser*, April 7, 1809. Captain Glass is Anthony Glass, who had led an expedition up the Red River in 1808–9 and had applied to the Spanish to settle in their territory. He was possibly also scouting for smuggling or a filibuster, though whether for a particular client or for his own purposes is unknown. Orramel Johnston to unknown correspondent, June 12, 1812, Papers of James Monroe. Miller, "The History of Fort Claiborne, Louisiana," 104.

26. Johnston, Orramel, "From Orramel Johnston, 12 June 1812," Papers of James Monroe.

27. As noted before, Wollstonecraft was senior at Natchitoches, but Overton exercised significant authority, only assuming full command when Wollstonecraft departed. Garrett mistakenly believed Wollstonecraft was sent as Overton's replacement, even though he had been at the fort since at least 1808; she also mistakenly presumed the English-American officer to be supportive of the rebels. Other writers suggest the change of command might have been an effort to put in place officers sympathetic to the filibuster. But the timing is off to suggest the replacement was part of an effort to support the enterprise. Wollstonecraft did not depart Fort Claiborne until after the filibuster commenced, and his departure was an expected rotation. It is curious that Overton was not aware of the filibuster, since William Shaler was

by this point living in his home. The likely explanation is that he was *not there*, but at Fort Adams. Orramel Johnston, "From Orramel Johnston, 12 June 1812," Papers of James Monroe.

28. Shaler places Adair as the "commander in chief" of the enterprise in late June, and in July, he was making "extensive arrangements on the Mississippi for the execution of the plans in question." Johnston, Orramel, "From Orramel Johnston, 12 June 1812," Papers of James Monroe. Shaler to Monroe, June 12, 1812; Shaler to Monroe, June 23, 1812; and Shaler to Monroe, July 12, 1812, Shaler Letterbooks.

29. Miller, "The History of Fort Claiborne, Louisiana," 13. Wollstonecraft to Wilkinson, August 2, 1812, 1812, LRSWRS, M221 Roll 49.

30. Josiah Stoddard Johnston was in later years a close ally of Henry Clay, and one of the key men behind his candidacy for president. Following the Gutiérrez-Magee Expedition, he married Eliza Sibley, the daughter of Natchitoches Indian Agent John Sibley, in 1814. Though this suggests a close connection with Sibley at the time of the filibuster, there is no evidence the Indian agent assisted in organizing the expedition. He would later be involved in such activity. He likely held back in 1812 due to personality clashes, such as his hostility to Magee. Joseph G. Tregle Jr., "The Josiah Stoddard Johnston Papers," *The Pennsylvania Magazine of History and Biography* 69, no. 4 (October 1945), 328.

31. Pedro Girard, in his letter to Gutiérrez, refers to Adair's chief deputy as "Col. Johnson" with no first name. But Wilkinson makes very clear who he is, writing, "A Col. Johnston formerly of the territorial legislature from Rapides has joined that association." Wilkinson to Eustis, August 4, 1812, LRSWRS ROLL 49, NA.

32. Shaler to James Monroe, June 12, 1812, Shaler Letterbooks.

33. Shaler to James Monroe, June 12, 1812, Shaler Letterbooks.

34. Shaler to James Monroe, June 12, 1812, Shaler Letterbooks.

35. As noted, there is no evidence the traders themselves joined the expedition. Any recruits they signed up or otherwise inspired likely came down the river independently or joined with Adair's recruits in Natchez. Shaler to James Monroe, June 12, 1812, Shaler Letterbooks.

36. Shaler to James Monroe, June 12, 1812, Shaler Letterbooks.

37. A later shipment of muskets that was intercepted by authorities were apparently government-owned weapons. Claiborne to Judge Steel, August 17, 1812, CL, 6:164. Garrett, "Dr. John Sibley," *SWHQ* 49, no. 3 (January 1946): 409. Shaler to Monroe, July 12, 1812, Shaler Letterbooks.

38. Despallier had lived in Rapides from at least 1797. As an example of how intertwined the filibuster relationships were, a child was born to Despallier shortly after his return from Texas; his godparents were Adair's aide Josiah Stoddard Johnston and his future wife, Anna Elisa Sibley, the daughter of Indian agent John Sibley. Castañeda, *Our Catholic Heritage in Texas*, 6:75. Garrett, "Green Flag," 126–27. Almaráz, *Tragic Cavalier*, 155–58. Apolinar de Masmela to Montero, in Manuel Salcedo, Operaciones de Guerra, AGM. Dahlqvist, *From Martin to Despallier,* 147, 197, 201.

39. Garrett, "Green Flag," 127. Castañeda, *Our Catholic Heritage in Texas*, 6:76–7. Dahlqvist, *From Martin to Despallier*, 215–17.

40. On May 15th, Gutiérrez noted in his diary, "Today a French gentleman came to negotiate the matter, of which I shall speak presently in a note." No note follows, but two entries later the visit to the printing office is discussed. Castañeda, *Our Catholic Heritage in Texas*, 6:77. West, "Diary of José Bernardo Gutiérrez de Lara, 1811–1812 [Part 2]," 293.

41. Apolinar de Masmela to Montero, in Salcedo, Operaciones de Guerra, AGM.

42. Montero to Salcedo, May 12, 1812, quoted in Coronado, *A World Not to Come*, 193. Apolinar de Masmela to Montero, in Salcedo, Operaciones de Guerra, AGM.

43. Garrett, "Green Flag," 128–32.

44. Castañeda, *Our Catholic Heritage in Texas*, 6:76–7.

45. Samuel Watson says of the attitude of the officer corps, "The instability and contentiousness of American politics and the immaturity of American society . . . fostered instability in the commitment and careers of the officer corps, which encouraged political irresponsibility." Nonetheless the embrace of Burr's filibuster, and the cost to those who had dabbled, was a cautionary tale and Magee, by joining the 1812 filibuster, was the exception not the rule. Watson, *Jackson's Sword*, 36–37, 54. West, "Diary of José Bernardo Gutiérrez de Lara, 1811–1812 [Part 2]," 293.

46. Shaler to Monroe, August 18, 1812. Shaler Letterbooks. West, "Diary of José Bernardo Gutiérrez de Lara, 1811–1812 [Part 2]," 293.

47. West, "Diary of José Bernardo Gutiérrez de Lara, 1811–1812 [Part 2]," 293.

48. José Alvarez de Toledo's subsequent letters show Reuben Kemper to be in league with Adair and protecting the expedition's interests in 1813. It is presumed that Reuben Kemper supported the expedition from the beginning, as his brother Samuel was a key commander. Shaler to Monroe, April 18, 1813, Shaler Letterbooks.

Adair's trip to Natchez possibly was to visit Fort Adams, where he may have sought a meeting with General Hampton, since Wilkinson had not yet returned from Washington. That Gutiérrez did not introduce Adair to Shaler, who would likely discourage the filibuster, is further evidence that the American agent was not involved in its organization but was being circumvented by Gutiérrez. Wilkinson to Eustis, August 4, 1812, LRSWRS, M221 Roll 49.

49. Pedro Girard to Gutiérrez, July 27, 1812. NA, RBB S10:209–11.

Chapter 11

1. During the American intervention and occupation of West Florida in December 1810, Claiborne brought along four hundred troops under Colonel Covington. Colonel Pike, Magee's superior officer, was in command of the reserve, meaning Magee was likely with him. Cox, *West Florida Controversy*, 493. Watson, *Jackson's Sword*, 33. Skelton, "High Army Leadership in the Era of the War of 1812," 254. Tucker, *The Encyclopedia of the War of 1812*, 970.

2. Ed Bradley, *We Never Retreat*, 36, and Wilkinson to the Secretary of War, Baton Rouge, May 6, 1811, in Garrett, *Green Flag over Texas*, 140.

3. As early as 1794, Perkins was listed as a "vote distributor" for the party, and served on the Massachusetts Federalist Central Committee. He was at the center of one of the most charged political incidents of the day, the 1806 murder of a Republican, Charles Austin, by the Federalist Thomas Selfridge. Perkins served as the foreman of the jury that found Selfridge guilty of a lesser charge of manslaughter but acquitted him of murder—a ruling that appalled Republicans. *Trial of Thomas O. Selfridge, Attorney at Law, Before the Hon. Isaac Parker, Esquire for Killing Charles Austin on the Public Exchange in Boston, August 4, 1806* (Boston: Russel, Cutler, Belcher and Armstrong, 1806), 5. Seaburg and Patterson, *Merchant Prince of Boston*, 217.

4. The Federalists' true target in this fight was new Massachusetts Republican Governor Elbridge Gerry, and Perkins continued the attack in the 1812 campaign. In this proxy war between T. H. Perkins and the president, Perkins won. *Let every Federalist do his duty, and Massachusetts will yet be saved!!! Federal republicans! Boston, April.* Boston, 1811. Broadsides, leaflets, and pamphlets from America and Europe, Portfolio 49, Folder 11, Library of Congress, https://www.loc.gov/resource/rbpe.04901100/ (accessed July 16, 2021). Brian F. Carso Jr., *"Whom Can we Trust Now?": The Meaning of Treason in the United States, from*

Revolution through the Civil War (New York: Lexington Books, 2006), 191. Cary, *Memoir of Thomas Handasyd Perkins*, 219.

5. Shaler to Monroe, August 25, 1812, Shaler Letterbooks. Orsi, *Citizen Explorer*, 101–2.

6. Burr had many friends among the wealthy planters in the vicinity of Washington, which in 1806 was the capital of the Mississippi Territory. Some of them were former army officers who had been retired when Jefferson reduced the army's strength in 1802. It was here where Burr was detained after his progress downriver had been halted, and some of the young men who had accompanied Burr settled in the area. Watson, *Jackson's Sword*, 54. Abernethy, "Aaron Burr in Mississippi," 10–11. "Christopher S. Stewart recites his version of the affair," June 1808, Spanish West Florida, Archives of the Spanish Government, 1782–1816, volumes 13–15, National Archives, Microfilm T1116, Roll 5, 14:342.

7. [Probably John Cortes] to Samuel Davenport, November 18, 1806, BA, RBB S5:353.

8. Many former officers of the frontier garrisons resigned and stayed in the community. Edward D. Turner, the officer who had established Fort Claiborne, was working as a Natchitoches lawyer two years later. Secretary of War to William Murray, January 4, 1809, LSSW, Roll 4. Powell, *List of Officers of the Army of the United States from 1779 to 1900*, 49.

"Notes furnished by W. D. C. Hall," in D. W. C. Baker, "Revolution of 1812," in *A Texas Scrap-book, Made up of the History, Biography and Miscellany of Texas and Its People* (New York: A. S. Barnes & Company, 1875), 224. The account was provided by Hall. Dueling was illegal in Orleans Territory at the time, but the law was rarely enforced. Ned Hémard, "New Orleans Nostalgia: Remembering New Orleans History, Culture and Traditions," New Orleans Bar Association, https://www.neworleansbar.org/uploads/files/Duel%20Personality_12-3.pdf (accessed, July 17, 2021).

9. Wilkinson had favored expansion west to Santa Fe to seize its riches before turning southward to Mexico proper. The Mexican Association had little interest in such a detour. Their ambition was grander and involved liberating all of Mexico and spreading the revolution to South America. They likely hoped to gain the wealth of New Spain not through expropriation, but through business monopolies with the new republic(s) thus freed. Linklater, *An Artist in Treason*, 205.

10. Lewis Kerr, the associate who had recruited the Kempers and Murray, was not involved in the 1812 effort. He had left the Orleans Territory and settled in Jamaica in around 1809. Shaler to Monroe, August 18, 1812, Shaler Letterbooks. Abernethy, *Burr Conspiracy*, 10–12. Bradley, *W.C.C. Claiborne Letterbook*, 432–33.

11. Augustus Magee to William Eustis, Baton Rouge, June 22, 1812, Letters Received by the Office of the Adjutant General, 1805–1821, M-566, Roll 13, National Archives.

12. Magee likely had served under Constant, a fellow New Englander, in the New York forts, where Constant had previously commanded. This senior officer forwarded the resignation to Washington directly. Augustus Magee to William Eustis, Baton Rouge, June 22, 1812, Letters Received by the Office of the Adjutant General. Wollstonecraft to Wilkinson, August 3, 1812, LRSWRS M221, Roll 49.

13. Yoakum, *The History of Texas*, 154. Hall account in Lamar papers, Gulick, *The Papers of Mirabeau Buonaparte Lamar*, 4(1):277.

14. The words are a paraphrase by Henderson Yoakum of a letter of US District Attorney for Louisiana John Dick. Yoakum, *The History of Texas*, 165.

15. Yoakum, *The History of Texas*, 154. Brown, *The Glory Seekers*, 203–4.

16. Wilkinson to Eustis, August 4, 1812, and Wilkinson to Eustis, August 10, 1812, LRSWRS, M221 Roll 49.

17. Gutiérrez to Wilkinson, July 16, 1812, Letters Received by the Secretary of War Unregistered Series, Roll 6 (hereafter LRSWUS).
18. Wilkinson to Eustis, August 10, 1812, LRSWRS, M221 Roll 49.
19. Wilkinson to Eustis, August 10, 1812, LRSWRS, M221 Roll 49.
20. Wilkinson to Eustis, August 10, 1812, LRSWRS, M221 Roll 49.
21. Wilkinson to Eustis, July 22, 1812, July 28, and August 10, 1812, LRSWRS, M221 Roll 49.
22. Hall account in Gulick, *The Papers of Mirabeau Buonaparte Lamar*, 4(1):277–78.
23. The account appears in the novel *Irene Viesca* by Hiram H. McLane, which is based on the actual memoirs of expedition participant William McLane. The son relied extensively on his father's account, which would not be published as a stand-alone document until decades later, with much of the fictional account being word-for-word. A novel and characters were weaved around this memoir, and the chief protagonist is clearly based on the elder McLane. It can safely be presumed that the trivia in the account preserves, or at least reflects the account handed down to the son verbally. Hiram H. McLane, *Irene Viesca: A Tale of the Magee Expedition in the Gauchupin War in Texas* (San Antonio: San Antonio Printing Company, 1886), 47–48.
24. Wollstonecraft to Unknown (probably Wilkinson), August 6, 1812, LRSWRS, M221 Roll 49. US Census, 1810, available at http://www.ancestry.com.
25. Claiborne mentions this encounter, stating, "I am sorry that the arrest of the offenders was attended with so much bloodshed—but their resistance made it indispensable and the example may, and I hope will, have a good effect." Wollstonecraft to unknown (probably Wilkinson), August 6, 1812, LRSWRS, M221 Roll 49. Claiborne to Unknown, August 18, 1812, CL 6: 166.
26. Claiborne to James Monroe, May 21, 1812. CL, 6:103.
27. Shaler used this exact same language in a letter to Claiborne a month later. Shaler to Monroe, July 12, 1812, and Shaler to Claiborne, August 27, 1812, Shaler Letterbooks.
28. Shaler to Monroe, July 12, 1812, Shaler Letterbooks. Monroe to Shaler, September 1, 1812, Shaler Papers.
29. Shaler to Monroe, July 12, 1812; Shaler to Monroe, August 18, 1812; and Shaler to Claiborne, August 27, 1812, Shaler Letterbooks.
30. Claiborne to Judge Carr, July 30, 1811, CL 5:319–21. John C. Carr to Claiborne, July 4, 1811, in Carter, *The Territorial Papers of the United States*, 9:943. Carr to Herrera, August 15, 1811, BA, RBB S7:354.
31. Shaler to Monroe, August 18, 1812, Shaler Letterbooks.
32. Overton was like most officers, sympathetic to the Mexican rebel cause, and hoped Americans could aid by "joining the cause of liberty and giving a vital stab to the old government." He took no known action to support the filibuster, but this attitude certainly played into his valuable *inaction*. Shaler to Monroe, August 18, 1812, Shaler Letterbooks. Pike to Overton, March 16, 1812, quoted in Watson, *Jackson's Sword*, 49. Letter from Captain Overton, October 21, 1811, quoted in Garrett, "Green Flag over Texas," 87.
33. The other justice of the peace appointed, William P. Cannon, is likely related to a John M. Cannon, also of Rapides Parish, who joined the expedition as well. Richard Claiborne to John Graham, November 10, 1811, in Carter, *The Territorial Papers of the United States*, 9:953, 985. For biographical information on Richard Claiborne, see "Richard Claiborne to Thomas Jefferson, 4 July 1817," Founders Online, National Archives, https://founders.archives.gov/documents/Jefferson/03-11-02-0420 (accessed May 8, 2020).
34. Watson, *Jackson's Sword*, 42.
35. Lawrence E. L'Herisson, "The Evolution of the Texas Road and the Subsequential Settlement Occupancy of the Adjacent Strip of Northwestern Louisiana: 1528–1824," 20. The Post-

master General to Benjamin Morgan and Others, March 28, 1812, in Carter, *The Territorial Papers of the United States*, 9:1013.

36. As an indication of Claiborne's scrupulousness on this point, earlier in the year, there was a lag between the expiration of his previous tenure as Orleans Territorial Governor and the start of his new commission in that same role. During this period, he had written, "I felt some delicacy in exercising any Executive Authority." It is likely he was similarly hesitant during the second disruption of the year. The governor was not the only one who reduced his vigilance during the change from territory to state, as the president of the constitutional convention wrote, "The anticipated change in the government of this territory has had a tendency to produce a considerable relaxation in some of the most important departments thereof."

Claiborne to James Monroe, June 27, 1812, Claiborne to Unknown, August 18, 1812, Claiborne to John Dawson, August 10, 1812, and Claiborne to Madison, August 2, 1812, CL 6:119, 165, 156, 138. Claiborne to the Secretary of the Treasury, January 26, 1812, and Julien Poydras to the President, January 28, 1812, in Carter, *The Territorial Papers of the United States*, 9:997–998.

37. Claiborne to Monroe, July 6, 1812, Claiborne to Paul Hamilton, July 9, 1812, CL 6:122–23, 125.

38. Claiborne to Monroe, July 6, 1812, CL 6:122–23.

39. Claiborne to Carr, July 8, 1812, CL, 6:123.

40. Claiborne to Judge Carr, August 7, 1812, CL, 6: 149.

41. William C. C. Claiborne, "A Proclamation, by William Charles Cole Claiborne, Governor of the State of Louisiana & Commander in Chief of the Militia Thereof," CL, 229.

42. Claiborne, "A Proclamation, by William Charles Cole Claiborne, Governor of the State of Louisiana & Commander in Chief of the Militia Thereof."

Chapter 12

1. There are several main sources for the campaign, and a proper telling of this story inherently involves mixing these often-contradictory accounts and harmonizing them wherever possible.

2. Sibley to Eustis, August 5, 1812, in Garrett, "Dr. John Sibley," vol. 49, no. 3.

3. Magee may also have anticipated Claiborne's proclamation, his own arrest, or other suppressive efforts after Gutiérrez tipped his hand by sending a letter via Girard. He may have thought a delay could mean government intervention. Shaler to Monroe, May 17, 1812, Shaler to Monroe, July 15, 1812, Shaler Letterbooks.

4. Account of John Villars in Gulick, *The Papers of Mirabeau Buonaparte Lamar*, 6:145. Anonymous [Henry Adams Bullard], "A Visit to Texas," 235. Watson, *Jackson's Sword*, 53.

5. Spanish soldiers who captured two of Gutiérrez's agents said the Americans were waiting for a force of from two to three thousand men but chose to invade early because of Zambrano's movements. "Declaration of the Corporal José Luís de Valle," [September 1812] RBB 70:230. Frederick Chabot, ed., *Memoirs of Antonio Menchaca* (San Antonio, Yanaguana Society, 1937). http://www.sonsofdewittcolony.org/menchacamem.htm (accessed May 8, 2020).

6. Zambrano's letter to Carr is lost, only Carr's response exists in the Bexar Archives. This is noted as being from "James C. Carr," likely an error, since no James Carr appears in any other document or census record. James C. Carr [sic] to Juan Manuel Zambrano, July 22, 1812, BA S8:3. Castañeda, *Our Catholic Heritage in Texas*, 6:83.

7. Bernardino Montero to Manuel Salcedo, July 23, 1813. "Texas History Research, Neutral Territory" Folder, Karle Wilson Baker Papers, Ralph W. Steen Library, Stephen F. Austin State University.

8. Montero lists the entire company, by names of individuals. Bernardino Montero to Gov. Manuel Salcedo, August 23, 1812. BA, RBB S8:27. Montero to Manuel Salcedo, July 23, 1813, Karle Wilson Baker Papers.

9. The Creole was Cade Lafitte. There are two Lafittes: Amalie and Bernard, who are listed in sources as being part of the expedition, and a P. B. Lafitte, who lived in the Neutral Ground and was therefore likely a close relative of Cade Lafitte. Furthermore, the Baratarian Pirates under Jean Lafitte would in later years support efforts to revolutionize Texas. However, other members of the large Lafitte clan were still loyal to Spain, such as Luis Laffite. Ermenegildo Guillen to Bernardino Montero, July 27, 1812, BA, RBB S8:4. Miguel Puga to Bernadino Montero, August 5, 1812, BA, RBB S8:9. Bernardino Montero to Manuel Salcedo, July 23, 1813, Nacogdoches Archives Vol. XVII, 39-43, copy in Karle Wilson Baker Papers.

10. Gulick, *The Papers of Mirabeau Buonaparte Lamar,* 6:145. Sibley to Eustis, August 18, 1812, Garrett, "Dr. John Sibley," SWHQ vol. 49, no. 3 (January 1946), pp. 399-431. "Declaration of the Corporal José Luís de Valle," [September 1812], BA, RBB 70:230-31.

11. The American sources all incorrectly attribute the leadership of the enemy to Zambrano, but Montero commanded. Montero to Salcedo, August 12, 1812. Karle Wilson Baker Papers. Sibley to Eustis, August 18, 1812, In Garrett, "Dr. John Sibley," vol. 49, no. 3 (January 1946), pp. 399-431. Ed Bradley, *We Never Retreat,* 40.

12. Samuel Kemper was probably the on-the-ground representative of the Mexican Association or the informal network it had spawned, as his brother Reuben was assisting in recruiting alongside General Adair.

13. Bradley, *We Never Retreat,* 40. Schwartz, *Forgotten Battlefield,* 20. Castañeda, *Our Catholic Heritage in Texas,* 6:83.

14. Galvan's inconstant conduct throughout the campaign—he deserted to the rebels, then back to the royalists—suggests he may have told a version of events that was not entirely truthful. Montero to Salcedo, August 12, 1812, Karle Wilson Baker Papers. Bradley, *We Never Retreat,* 40. Schwartz, *Forgotten Battlefield,* 20. Castañeda, *Our Catholic Heritage in Texas,* 6:83.

15. Pedro Prado to Doña María Angela Aguilera, September 1, 1812, BA, RBB S70:375.

16. Montero to Salcedo, August 12, 1812, Karle Wilson Baker Papers.

17. Montero to Salcedo, August 12, 1812, Karle Wilson Baker Papers.

18. The American sources incorrectly attribute the harangue against the citizens to Zambrano, but according to Montero's account, this officer was outside the town. Montero's letter of August 12th says he left command in the hands of Pedro Treviño, but his letter of the 15th says Pedro Procela. Treviño was a regular lieutenant and Procela a former officer who was at the time a militia commander. It was Procela who had command of the town since he wrote Montero the same day with an account of the American advance. Montero to Salcedo, August 12, 1812, Karle Wilson Baker Papers, Montero to Salcedo, August 15, 1812, (copy from the Béxar Archives), Karle Wilson Baker Papers.

19. Sibley to Eustis, August 18, 1812. In Garrett, "Dr. John Sibley," vol. 49, no. 3 (January 1946), pp. 399-431.

20. Account of James Gaines, in Gulick, *The Papers of Mirabeau Buonaparte Lamar,* 6:146. Pedro Procela to Bernardino Montero, August 11, 1812, Karle Wilson Baker papers.

21. Castañeda, *Our Catholic Heritage in Texas,* 6:83. Shaler to Monroe, August 18, 1812, Shaler Letterbooks.

22. Shaler to James Monroe, August 18, 1812, Shaler Letterbooks.

23. Shaler to James Monroe, August 18, 1812, Shaler Letterbooks.

24. Huerta to Salcedo, May 3, 1810, BA, RBB S7: 104-7. David LaVere, "Davenport, Barr, Murphy and Smith," 33, 42, 110-13. Nemesio Salcedo to Manuel Salcedo, February 22, 1809, Copy in Texas History Research, Samuel Davenport folder, Karle Wilson Baker Papers.

25. The *New England Palladium*, a Federalist paper, stated that Davenport had been arrested by Gutiérrez and only released after lending the revolution four thousand dollars. "Excellent revolutionists!" the paper remarked, sarcastically. The *Richmond Enquirer*, though a Republican paper, also reported the extorted loan, adding that Davenport, "a man very much attached to, and highly esteemed by the Spanish authorities, was dragged along with many other peaceable Spanish inhabitants by Magee and his troops of miscreants." Hatcher, *The Opening of Texas*, 215. LaVere, "Davenport, Barr, Murphy and Smith," 114–15. J. Villasana Haggard, unpublished draft of dissertation, June 30, 1942, Copy in Texas History Research, Neutral Territory folder, Karle Wilson Baker Papers, 190–91. "Mr. Davenport, a rich American Merchant," *New England Palladium*, November 10, 1812. "Mexican Provinces," *Richmond Enquirer*, February 12, 1813.

26. Shaler to Monroe, August 18, 1812, Shaler Letterbooks. Castañeda, *Our Catholic Heritage in Texas*, 6:84. Gulick, *The Papers of Mirabeau Buonaparte Lamar*, 6:146.

27. Pedro José de Aldape To Governor Manuel Salcedo, August 16, 1812, BA, RBB S8:18.

28. Pedro José de Aldape To Governor Manuel Salcedo, August 16, 1812, BA, RBB S8:20.

29. Montero to Salcedo, August 12, 1812, Karle Wilson Baker Papers.

30. Aldape writes from "Navasota" which is not the current town of that name, nor is it likely the Navasota River, since that lies below Trinidad, unless Aldape made an error. Bernardino Montero to Gov. Manuel Salcedo, August 23, 1812, Bexar Archives. Nemesio Salcedo to Governor Manuel Salcedo, June 9, 1812, BA, RBB S7:412.

31. Manuel de Salcedo to José María Tobar, August 23, 1812, RBB S8:24–25.

32. Manuel de Salcedo to José María Tobar, August 23, 1812, RBB S8:24–25.

33. Manuel de Salcedo to José María Tobar, August 23, 1812, RBB S8:24–25.

34. "Proclama anti nacional," *Correo Americano del Sur*, April 22, 1813, http://www.antorcha.net/index/hemeroteca/correo/9.pdf (accessed December 28, 2021).

35. "Proclama anti nacional," *Correo Americano del Sur*, April 22, 1813, http://www.antorcha.net/index/hemeroteca/correo/9.pdf (accessed December 28, 2021).

36. While various sources provide us with the names of participants, in most cases it is not possible to determine when those individuals joined. The expedition was a fluid thing: men were coming and going at all times over the course of the next year. The initial army at the invasion was only about 130–160 men, though there were probably 100 more already organized in Natchitoches and other towns, making their way to the frontier. Names presented here are presumed to have arrived at the beginning, though it is probable some only joined in later waves. For further biographical information on the filibusters, see James Aalan Bernsen, *The Texas History Blog*, http://www.texhist.com. Life and Activities of Antonio Dubois, July 24, 1809, BA, RBB S6:371. Life and Activities of Pierre Dolet, July 24, 1809, Bexar Archives, RBB S6:375.

37. Henry Walker, ed., "William McLane's Narrative," *SWHQ* 66, no. 4 (April 1963), 569. Biographical information on McKim provided to the author by Brian Hendrix of Houston, Texas, a McKim descendant. Gulick, *The Papers of Mirabeau Buonaparte Lamar*, 1:286.

38. The Aylett C. Buckner (sometimes spelled Aylette) who came to Texas from Kentucky is not the same Aylett C. Buckner who stayed in Kentucky, served there in the War of 1812, as a congressman in the 1840s, and was the father of Civil War general Simon Bolivar Buckner. The two were likely cousins. Don Blevins, *A Priest, a Prostitute, and Some Other Early Texans: The Lives of Fourteen Lone Star State Pioneers* (Guilford, CN: Globe Pequot Press, 2008), 26. "Descendants of Richard Buckner," Genealogy.com, http://www.genealogy.com/ftm/j/o/h/Wesley-K-Johnson-MO/GENE24-0030.html (accessed May 9, 2020). William Armstrong Crozier, ed., *The Buckners of Virginia and the Allied Families of Strother and Ashby* (New

York: Genealogical Society of New York, 1907), 63. "Buckner, Aylett C.," *HOTO*, http://www.tshaonline.org/handbook/online/articles/fbu09 (accessed July 19, 2021).

39. "Josiah Taylor," Sons of Dewitt Colony Texas, http://www.sonsofdewittcolony.org/1828census3.htm#taylorbio (accessed May 9, 2020). Dovie Tschirhart Hall, "Taylor, Creed," *HOTO*, http://www.tshaonline.org/handbook/online/articles/fta17 (accessed May 9, 2020).

40. Castañeda, *Our Catholic Heritage in Texas*, 6:78. "American Revolutionary War Patriots Buried in Texas," *Texas Society Sons of the American Revolution*, http://www.txssar.org/buried.htm (accessed May 9, 2020). "Benjamin Allen," FindAGrave.com, http://www.findagrave.com/cgi-bin/fg.cgi?page=gr&GRid=75679900 (accessed May 9, 2020). Oliver Seymour Phelps and Andrew T. Servin, *The Phelps Family in America and Their English Ancestors*, vol. 1 (Pittsfield Mass: Eagle Publishing, 1899), 402. Alcée Fortier, ed., *Louisiana: Comprising Sketches of Parishes, Towns, Events, Institutions, and Persons, Arranged in Cyclopedic Form*, vol. 1 (Madison: Century Historical Association, 1914), 174, available at https://archive.org/stream/cu31924008014007#page/n5/mode/2up (accessed June 26, 2023). For more Phelps's genealogy, see "David Phelps Born 1764 in CT Died in LA," MyTrees.com, http://www.mytrees.com/ancestry-family/le000781-1058-4642/David-Phelps-Born-1764-in-CT.html (accessed May 9, 2020). Harry Wright Newman, *The Lucketts of Portobacco* (Washington, DC: Harry Wright Newman, 1938). Available at http://www.tnfraziers.com/data/luckettpt/page3.html (accessed May 9, 2020).

41. West, "Diary of José Bernardo Gutiérrez de Lara, 1811–1812 [Part 1]," 1:59.

42. Darius's mentor in the legal profession was William T. Barry, who served in the Kentucky legislature and later rose to be US postmaster general under President Andrew Jackson. Baker, "Revolution of 1812," 224. William Preston Johnston, *The Johnstons of Salisbury* (New Orleans: L. Graham and Son, 1897), 7. See Charles P. Roland, *Albert Sydney Johnston, Soldier of Three Republics* (Lexington, KY: University Press of Kentucky, 2001), 6.

43. Carol Young Knight, *First Settlers of Catahoula Parish, Louisiana, 1808–1839* (Aledo, TX.: Self-Published by Carol Young Knight, 1985), 78–85. "Henry Dearborn to Thomas Jefferson, 23 November 1807," *Founders Online, National* Archives, http://founders.archives.gov/documents/Jefferson/99-01-02-6830 (accessed May 9, 2020). Secretary of War to Samuel D. Forsyth, April 25, 1807, January 6, 1808, and June 6, 1808, LSSW, M6, Roll 3.

44. Alan Barber, "Barber Family in Louisiana" (June 15, 1997), http://www.barberhome.com/histories/Sam_LA.pdf (accessed May 9, 2020), 3–10. Thurmond A. Williamson, *The Munsons of Texas—an American Saga* (self-published genealogical manuscript, 1987), available at http://www.munsons-of-texas.net/c7.html (accessed May 9, 2020).

45. Wilkinson to Overton, August 13, 1812, US National Archives, LRSWUS Roll 6, M222.

46. Overton to Wilkinson, August 25, 1812, LRSWUS Roll 6, M222.

47. Overton certainly knew William Shaler, for the agent at some point (it is unclear before or after the letter) moved into Overton's own home as a guest while he stayed in Natchitoches. Overton to Wilkinson, August 25, 1812, LRSWUS Roll 6, M222.

48. In Wilkinson's August 13 letter to Overton, the name of the letter bearer is left blank. However, a separate letter written the next day, also to Overton, contains the name "Mr. Seay." Not only was he to be allowed to proceed to Texas, Overton was to "equip him to follow the adventurers." Wilkinson to Overton, August 13, 1812, and August 14, 1812. LRSWUS Roll 6.

49. It is intriguing to speculate that "Mr. Seay" was one of the general's sons, Joseph or James Wilkinson Jr. The former is a confirmed member of the expedition, but he arrived months later, so the spy, if a Wilkinson, was likely James. Overton to Wilkinson, August 25, 1812, LRSWUS Roll 6, M222. Shaler to Monroe, July 14, 1813, Shaler Letterbooks.

Chapter 13

1. "Mexican News," *National Intelligencer*, October 24, 1812. Guedea, "Autonomía e independencia en la provincia de Texas," 155.

2. Shaler to Monroe, August 18, 1812, Shaler Letterbooks.

3. Shaler to Monroe, August 18, 1812, Shaler Letterbooks.

4. A report of Spanish spies suggests a ship was to be sent to Matagorda with one thousand men, muskets, and a thousand uniforms that Gutiérrez had negotiated. These never materialized. The ship story, repeated in similar form in some American accounts, may be exaggeration but may also represent an effort that was derailed by the publication of Claiborne's proclamation. Shaler to Monroe, August 18, 1812, Shaler Letterbooks. RBB 70:238.

5. The import of so much wool at this time actually created a glut in the market, with the first sales lowering the prices for subsequent ones. Overton to Wilkinson, August 25, 1812, LRSWUS. "Mexican News," *National Intelligencer*, October 24, 1812. Linnard to Mason, February 1, 1813, Letterbook of the Natchitoches-Sulfur Fork Factory, 1809–21, US National Archives, Microfilm Roll T1029 (hereafter LNSFF).

6. "Mexican Affairs," *Charleston City Gazette and Daily Advertiser*, October 30, 1812. "Extract of a Letter Dated Opelousas, September 1," *New York Herald*, October 24, 1812.

7. Gutiérrez left Natchitoches after August 10th and arrived in Nacogdoches before August 20th when James Gaines's account notes his presence. He would write an account to the Mexican congress after the fact which would inflate his command into a military one, but it was not, and at the time he never expressed any pique that he was not leading soldiers in battle.

Ancelmo Bergara, in his treason trial, notes that Magee was quartered in Davenport's house, Gutiérrez and Despallier in the home of José María Mora. Other captains were quartered in homes of men friendly to the revolution. Henry P. Walker, "William McLane's Narrative of the Magee-Gutiérrez Expedition, 1812–1813," *SWHQ* vol. 66, no. 2 (October 1962), 242–43. "Declaration with Charge of the Soldier Ancelmo Vergara," RBB 70:272. J. B. Gutiérrez de Lara to the Mexican Congress," August 1, 1815, in Gulick, *The Papers of Mirabeau Buonaparte Lamar*, 1:4–21.

8. Thomas Hussey Luckett Jr., who would ultimately command the Republican Army's artillery, was the first cousin of Samuel N. Luckett of Ohio who had been Burr's principal supply officer. "Mr. Luckett of Louisville," *Morning Chronicle*, February 4, 1807. "Letters have been received from New Orleans," *Sentinel of Freedom*, February 10, 1807. Newman, *The Lucketts of Portobacco*, 24–25. Henry P. Walker, "William McLane's Narrative," vol. 66, no. 2 (October 1962), 243. Baker, "Revolution of 1812," 224–29. Henry P. Walker, "William McLane's Narrative," *SWHQ* vol. 66, no. 2 (October 1962), 243–45. RBB 70:244.

9. Ingrid Broughton Morris and Deolece M. Parmelee, "Gaines, James Taylor," *HOTO*, http://www.tshaonline.org/handbook/online/articles/fga04 (accessed May 11, 2020).

10. Germeuil lived on a tract of land situated at Isle Beauliue in the Neutral Ground. "Neutral Ground Settlers," *Redbonenation.com*, http://redbonenation.com/history/mans-land-settlers/ (accessed May 11, 2020). Other French names among the volunteers include Michael Chesneu, Henry Derbonne, Charles Lauranu, Tenoss Moinet, Chesneau Tontin, a probable Ruscieul, and an unknown Gaulet. "American Revolutionary War Patriots Buried in Texas," Sons of the American Revolution. Available at https://www.txssar.org/buried.htm (accessed May 11, 2020). Robert Vogel, ed., "A Louisianan's View of the Mexican Revolution in 1810: Paul Bouet Lafitte's Letter to Doctor John Sibley," *North Louisiana Historical Association Journal* vol. 16 (Fall 1985), pp. 131–35. "Life and Activities of Paul Bovet Lafitte," July 24, 1809, RBB S6:382. Linda Ericson Devereaux, *Tales from the Old Stone Fort* (Nacogdoches: Linda Erickson Devereaux, 1976), 36.

11. "Revolution in Mexico," *Weekly Register,* October 17, 1812. "Proclamation of José Bernardo Gutiérrez de Lara," August 31, 1812, *The Herald Extra, Alexandria (Louisiana).* Microfilm: Beinecke Library, Yale University. http://www.sonsofdewittcolony.org//adp/archives/documents/declare.html (accessed July 19, 2021).

12. Proclamation of José Bernardo Gutiérrez de Lara, August 31, 1812.

13. Proclamation of José Bernardo Gutiérrez de Lara, August 31, 1812.

14. "From the Red River Herald," *The New York Statesman, January* 21, 1813.

15. "Not 'British Amity,'" *New England Palladium,* December 1, 1812.

16. The information, as another account in the *National Intelligencer* makes clear, comes directly from a since-lost letter of Magee himself, in which he makes it clear his plan was to continue on beyond the Rio Grande and not confine the expedition to Texas only. "A letter from Natchitoches," *Independent Chronicle,* December 31, 1812. "Multiple News Items," *National Intelligencer,* December 22, 1812. "Mexican Independence," *Daily Advertiser and Repertory,* March 20, 1813. Claiborne to Robert Smith, CL 5:15.

17. "From the Louisiana Gazette," *New England Palladium,* January 5, 1813.

18. Wilkinson to Eustis, September 7, 1812, LRSWUS Roll #6.

19. "Declaration of the Sergeant Demacio Herrera," and "Declaration of the Corporal José Luís del Valle, RBB 70:224, 237.

20. Bernardino Montero to Governor Manuel Salcedo. August 23, 1812, BA, RBB S8:15–16. "Declaration of the Sergeant Demacio Herrera," BA, RBB 70:219. Gulick, *The Papers of Mirabeau Buonaparte Lamar,* 6:337–9. Francisco Amangual to J. B. Elguezabal, January 15, 1803, RBB S4:184. "Diary of Operations for Nacogdoches," December 1806, BA, RBB 20:307. "Report of the Deputies of the Province of Texas to the Commanding General, NA, RBB S10:60. La Vere, "Davenport, Barr, Murphy and Smith," 76.

21. Additional known defectors and their new ranks included Mr. Gascon, a captain; Francisco Guerrero, a lieutenant; and Luís Procela and Andres Ruíz, as sergeants. Bernardino Montero to Governor Manuel Salcedo. August 23.1812, *Béxar Archives.* Various letters, RBB 70:280, S4:228, 426; S5:4, 417. Castañeda, *Our Catholic Heritage in Texas,* 6:87. Gulick, *The Papers of Mirabeau Buonaparte Lamar,* 6, 154. Francisco Amangual to J. B. Elguezabal, January 15, 1803, RBB S4:184.

22. The town of San Marcos de Neve, always plagued with flooding and exposure to Indian attack, had been abandoned weeks before the invasion. It was located close to the modern city of San Marcos. Castañeda writes that the garrison of Trinidad, consisting of thirty-seven men, threw down their arms and joined the rebels, though Spanish sources indicate all the troops had been pulled back to San Antonio. Shaler to Monroe, August 7, 1813, Shaler Letterbooks.

23. Both Sibley and Shaler report the experiment with "pikes," but no account shows them actually employed in battle. They were actually lances, designed to be used from horseback along with a leather shield or *adarga.* It is likely the Anglo-Americans found the weapon inscrutable and cumbersome. RBB 70:222, 235. Wilkinson to Eustis, September 7, 1812, LRSWUS Roll #6.Sibley to Eustis, August 5, 1812, in Garrett, "Dr. John Sibley," 49, no. 3 (January 1946), 413. Shaler to Monroe, November 10, 1812, Shaler Letterbooks. Jesús F. de la Teja, "Ramón de Murillo's Plan for the Reform of New Spain's Frontier Defenses," *SWHQ* 107, no. 4 (April 2004), 502–15. Wilkinson to Eustis, September 7, 1812, LRSWUS Roll #6. RBB 70:274-6. "Report of the Anglo American Companies in the Northern Mexican Army at San Antonio de Béxar, April 9th 1813," in Samuel Sexton file, US National Archives Record Group 76, specifically 1839 and 1849 US-Mexico Commission. "Orden del ciuadadaño General José Alvarez de Toledo al ciuadadaño Coronel Henry Peres, Comandante en gefe de los Voluntarios Americanos del Ejercito Republicano del Norte de México," August 5, 1813,

Arredondo, Operaciones de Guerra, Archivo General de México, Microfilm copy University of California at Santa Barbara, 4(2):193.

24. RBB S70:223, 234, 276.

25. Among those we know of was a proclamation addressed to his "Beloved, Honorable Compatriots in the Province of Texas," another entitled "To the People of Mexico," and a third was addressed "To the Officers, Soldiers and Residents of San Antonio de Béxar." Castañeda, *Our Catholic Heritage in Texas*, 6:87; Gutiérrez to Señor Don Luis Grande, September 4, 1812, Salcedo, Operaciones de Guerra, AGM.

26. "Beloved, honorable compatriots, inhabitants of the province of Texas," José Bernardo Gutiérrez de Lara, September 1, 1812, in Salcedo, Operaciones de Guerra, AGM.

27. "To the Officers, Soldiers and Residents of San Antonio de Béxar." José Bernardo Gutiérrez de Lara, September 1, 1812, in Salcedo, Operaciones de Guerra, AGM.

28. "To the People of Mexico," José Bernardo Gutiérrez de Lara, Salcedo, Operaciones de Guerra, AGM.

29. Gutiérrez to Señor Don Luis Grande, September 4, 1812, Salcedo, Operaciones de Guerra, AGM. "Declaration of the Civilian Fernando Martines, RBB 70:239, 290.

30. Gutiérrez first selected the able Miguel Menchaca with two soldiers to take the messages to San Antonio, but Menchaca and his men were met on the Camino Real by Béxar alcalde Gavino Delgado, who was coming up from the capital. Delgado warned Menchaca that the area between San Antonio and the Guadalupe River was covered with Spanish spies. Gutiérrez felt a civilian might get through easier than the well-known Menchaca. Gutiérrez to Luis Grande, September 4, 1812, BA, RBB S8:37. Rasmus Dahlqvist, "Despallier, Bernardo Martin," *HOTO*, http://www.tshaonline.org/handbook/online/articles/fdeao (accessed July 22, 2018). Schwartz, *Forgotten Battlefield*, 21. Castañeda, *Our Catholic Heritage in Texas*, 6:90. Various Depositions, RBB 70:226–7, 246, 256, 260.

31. Gutiérrez to Luis Grande, September 4, 1812, BA, RBB S8:37. Schwartz, *Forgotten Battlefield*, 21. Castañeda, *Our Catholic Heritage in Texas*, 6:90. Various Depositions, RBB 70:226–7, 246, 256, 260. Various Depositions, RBB 70:232–3, 255, 300.

32. Gerónimo Herrera was the son of Governor Simón Herrera. RBB 70:213. Manuel Salcedo to Geronimo de Herrera. October 25. 1812, RBB 70:379–88, 228. Manuel Salcedo to José María Tovar, September 22, 1812, BA, RBB S8:45.

33. A Spanish militia sergeant testified that the army had three small cannon "capable of being loaded on a mule." These would have been small pieces indeed, akin to a swivel gun for a small boat, although another Spanish soldier suggested more cannons were on the way in September. Ancelmo Bergara testified that the carts were owned by Father Francisco Maynes of the Nacogdoches Parish. The latter had served alongside the "Fat Father" Huerta, but had not previously been implicated in a conspiracy. RBB 70:222–4, 235, 278. Hall account in Lamar papers, Gulick, *The Papers of Mirabeau Buonaparte Lamar,* 4(1):279. "Declaration of the Sergeant Demacio Herrera, BA, RBB S70:224

34. Castañeda, *Our Catholic Heritage in Texas*, 6:88. Hall account in Lamar papers, Gulick, *The Papers of Mirabeau Buonaparte Lamar,* 4(1):278.

35. Monroe to Shaler, May 2, 1812, Shaler Papers. William Shaler, *Reflections on the means of restoring the political balance and preserving a general peace to the world* (Undated, probably late August 1812), Shaler Letterbooks.

36. Shaler Letterbooks.

37. Poinsett would ultimately secure a position as the nation's premier expert on Spanish-American affairs and would in due course become the permanent US ambassador to

Mexico. "Remarkable Sailing," *Daily National Intelligencer*, January 13, 1813; "Successful Privateering," *National Intelligencer*, July 13, 1813.

38. Two weeks was a typical delay in getting news from New Orleans. Recall that it had taken Shaler and Gutiérrez twenty days to make the trip encumbered with baggage.

39. Shaler to Claiborne, August 25, 1812, Shaler Letterbooks.

40. Shaler to Claiborne, August 25, 1812, Shaler Letterbooks.

41. Shaler to Claiborne, August 25, 1812, Shaler to Claiborne, August 27, 1812, Shaler Letterbooks.

42. Shaler to Monroe, August 25, 1812, Shaler Letterbooks. Monroe to Shaler, September 1, 1812, Shaler Papers.

43. Shaler to Monroe, October 5, 1812, Shaler Letterbooks.

44. "Abraham Smith's Statement Relative to the Character of Doctor John H. Robinson," July 30, 1810; "Chesley Kinney's Statement respecting the Character of Doctor John H. Robinson" (no date); and "Charles Page's statement respecting the character of Doctor John H. Robinson," September 1, 1810, in LRSWRS, Roll 35, NA.

45. Warren, *The Sword Was Their Passport*, 37. Narrett, "Liberation and Conquest," 26–27.

46. Narrett, "Liberation and Conquest," 28. Monroe to Shaler, September 1, 1812, Shaler Papers.

47. Monroe to Shaler, September 1, 1812, Shaler Papers.

48. Robinson's commission shows clearly that Monroe did not consider the banditti a filibuster-in-waiting, but simply a criminal enterprise. There was enough evidence, particularly from the pleadings of Natchitoches merchants, that the banditti were damaging American trade, and he wanted them stopped, independent of any other event. Monroe to Robinson, July 1, 1812, CRF.

49. At the time of this comment, Shaler believed a rumor that Colonel Herrera had deposed Governor Salcedo and joined the rebellion. This was incorrect. Shaler to Monroe, October 5, 1812. Shaler Letterbooks.

50. Quoted in Narrett, "Liberation and Conquest," 27.

51. Though technically not in the Neutral Ground, Bayou Pierre's status was ambiguous. Its population was Spanish and Spanish local officials still administered it, but its citizens were prohibited from visiting relatives in Nacogdoches. The Americans never protested this because it had no Spanish troops. Shaler to Gutiérrez, quoted in Shaler to Monroe, October 24, 1812, US National Archives, Correspondence of Special Agents (henceforth CSA).

52. Allegiance shifted rapidly in the revolution, but Soto appears to have been a royalist from the beginning. He was one of the early spies who reported Gutiérrez's arrival in Natchitoches to Spanish officials. Soto to Montero, Salcedo, Operaciones, AGM.

53. Shaler to Monroe, October 5, 1812, Shaler Letterbooks.

54. Gulick, *The Papers of Mirabeau Buonaparte Lamar*, 6:146. Shaler to Monroe, October 1, 1812, Shaler to Monroe, October 6, 1812, Shaler to Monroe, November 10, 1812, Shaler Letterbooks.

55. Hiram McLane, *Irene Viesca*, 49–50.

56. Robinson calls the fort "Tranquiles," but the Spanish sources reflect the more likely name. R. B. Blake, "Villa de la Santissima Trinidad de Salcedo," in RBB 46:310. Gulick, *The Papers of Mirabeau Buonaparte Lamar*, 6:146. John Robinson to James Monroe, July 26, 1813, CRF. "Declaration of the Sergeant Demacio Herrera," BA, RBB S70:223.

57. Garrett, *Green Flag Over Texas*, 168.

58. John Robinson to James Monroe, July 26, 1813, CRF.

59. John Robinson to James Monroe, July 26, 1813, CRF. Nugent, *Habits of Empire*, 108.

60. Robinson to Monroe, July 26, 1813, CRF.

61. Robinson to Monroe, July 26, 1813, CRF.
62. Robinson to Monroe, July 26, 1813, CRF.
63. Robinson to Monroe, July 26, 1813, CRF.
64. Robinson to Monroe, July 26, 1813, CRF.
65. Gov. Manuel Salcedo to Felix Ceballos, October 6. 1812, Béxar Archives. Robinson to Monroe, July 26, 1813, CRF. Castañeda, *Our Catholic Heritage in Texas*, 6:92.
66. Narrett, "Liberation and Conquest," 31. "Report of Samuel Davenport," enclosed in Shaler to Monroe, December 25, 1812, Shaler Letterbooks.
67. Robinson to Monroe, July 26, 1813, CRF.
68. "Report of Samuel Davenport," Shaler Letterbooks.
69. Report of Samuel Davenport, Shaler Letterbooks. Warren, *The Sword Was Their Passport*, 40. "Report of Samuel Davenport," enclosed in Shaler to Monroe, December 25, 1812, Shaler Letterbooks. Narrett, "Liberation and Conquest," 31.

Chapter 14

1. "Private Correspondence," *National Intelligencer,* November 26, 1812. "Multiple News Items," *National Intelligencer,* December 22, 1812.

2. The implication that Kemper was assisting Adair comes from his later intervention at that place against José Álvarez de Toledo alongside Sibley, which will be discussed in chapter 20. Sibley to William Eustis, August 5, 1812, in Garrett, "Dr. John Sibley," 49, no. 3 (January 1946), 413. Claiborne to Monroe, August 9, 1812, CL, 6:152. Shaler to Monroe, August 18, 1812, Shaler Letterbooks.

3. H. Perry, *Certificate of W. C. C. Hall's Service in the Republican Army,* June 12, 1815, in Gulick, *The Papers of Mirabeau Buonaparte Lamar,* 6:4. H. Allen Anderson and Rose Mary Fritz, "Hall, Warren D. C.," *HOTO,* http://www.tshaonline.org/handbook/online/articles/fha23 (accessed May 11, 2020).

In 1811, Noah was court-martialed for an unknown reason, with his commanding officer citing the "entire unfitness of Mr. Noah for a military command." The offense must have been minor, and his commander allowed the young officer to resign before the trial results were reported, thus quashing the court martial from Noah's record. T. H. Cushing to Eustis, March 13, 1811, LRSWRS, Roll 35. Jack D. Foner, "Jews and the American Military from the Colonial Era to the Eve of the Civil War," special supplement to *The American Jewish Archives Journal,* (January 2000), http://americanjewisharchives.org/publications/journal/PDF/2000_52_01_02_foner.pdf (accessed May 11, 2020), 84. George W. Cullum, *Biographical Register of the Officers and Graduates of the US Military Academy,* http://penelope.uchicago.edu/Thayer/E/Gazetteer/Places/America/United_States/Army/USMA/ Cullums_Register/30*.html (accessed May 11, 2020).

4. The crossing was identified by Warren D. C. Hall as just below what would later be known as Robbins's Ferry. Baker, "Revolution of 1812," 244. Shaler to Monroe, October 24, 1812, CSA. (The latter is a short letter appended to the longer letter of this date. In the Shaler Letterbooks, the date is listed as October 6, but this is inaccurate as the events described happened after this time.) Shaler to Monroe, January 10, 1813, Shaler Letterbooks. Manuel Salcedo to José María Tovar, September 22, 1812, BA, RBB S8:42–45.

5. Villars claims Nemesio Salcedo dispatched reinforcements to his nephew. The friendly Mexican is reported by Villars as a Spanish spy caught hiding in a tree, but Hall and McLane, who frequently are at odds with each other, both agree the man, though initially thought to be a spy, was friendly. Hall said that "after their arrival at La Bahía, all these statements proving true, the Mexican was released, and he subsequently fought bravely with the Americans."

Manuel Salcedo to Félix Ceballos, October 6, 1812; BA, RBB S8:47–48. Gulick, *The Papers of Mirabeau Buonaparte Lamar,* 6:146. Baker, "Revolution of 1812," 225. Walker, "McLane's Narrative," 66, no. 2 (October 1962), 246–47. The original "Report of Samuel Davenport" is enclosed in Shaler to Monroe, December 25, 1812, CSA. The quality of the document is poor, but an accurate transcription can be found in "Report of Samuel Davenport," Texas History Research, Samuel Davenport Folder. Karle Wilson Baker Papers, Ralph W. Steen Library, Stephen F. Austin State University.

6. Lamar, citing Villars, puts the number as 300/100 Anglos/Mexicans, as noted before. Warren D. C. Hall claims 300, but he does not appear to have been counting Mexicans, many of whom were poorly armed. Shaler put the number at 450/150 in September and 800/200 by November, though he himself admitted his sources were confused. Shaler gives Salcedo's numbers as ranging from a low estimate of 500 to a high estimate of 1,200. Shaler to Monroe, September 17, 1812, and Shaler to Monroe, November 10, 1812, Shaler Letterbooks. Gulick, *The Papers of Mirabeau Buonaparte Lamar,* 6:146.

7. Gulick, *The Papers of Mirabeau Buonaparte Lamar,* 6:146.

8. McLane says there were still two hundred Spanish soldiers in La Bahía who immediately joined the Republicans. Hall insists the fortress was completely empty of troops, which squares with Davenport's account, the only contemporary one. Walker, in a note to McLane's account, suggests the men in question may have been militia rather than regular soldiers, which might account for the inconsistency. "Report of Samuel Davenport," CSA. Gulick, *The Papers of Mirabeau Buonaparte Lamar,* 6:146. Walker, "McLane's Narrative," 66, no. 2 (October 1962), 247. Baker, "Revolution of 1812," 225. McGraw, *A Texas Legacy,* xvii, 36–43.

9. McLane says of the captured stores, "I eat [sic] some of the corn but did not see the houses of salt." The cash received at Goliad is noted in an extraordinary series of letters attesting to service in the army. These letters, written after the revolution to assist in claims against the new Mexican Republic, frequently list credits including cash and livestock. In several instances, they specifically claim the cash payment of ten dollars at La Bahía. The soldiers in question were all private soldiers. Mexican Republic to Benjamin Bradley, Joseph Burton, William Custard, etc., Samuel Sexton File. Walker, "McLane's Narrative," *SWHQ* 66, no. 4 (April 1963), 532–33.

10. Hall, in Baker, "Revolution of 1812," 225. Walker, "McLane Narrative," 66, no. 2 (October 1962), 248. Gulick, *The Papers of Mirabeau Buonaparte Lamar,* 6:147.

11. "Report of Samuel Davenport," CSA. Walker, "McLane Narrative," 66, no. 2 (October 1962), 247.

12. One of the "earth" bastions mentioned was probably the preexisting stone bastion. Yoakum, *The History of Texas,* 163.

13. The disposition reflected here is Villars' report in the Lamar papers, though there are other accounts that differ. Hall mentions troops at the Mission and forces east and west. The latter was probably the southern force mentioned by Villars. The east, as noted, was protected by the river, so any outpost there was probably just a small observation point. Tactically, a force South or Southwest would have trapped the rebel army sufficiently, using the river as a barrier to hem the republicans in. The description of the fortress dimensions is Magee's. The modern fortress, other than the church, is a reconstruction, but the dimensions are fairly accurate. Gulick, *The Papers of Mirabeau Buonaparte Lamar,* 6:147. Hall, in Baker, "Revolution of 1812," 225–26. Magee to Shaler, November 14, 1812, Shaler Letterbooks.

14. McLane says the royalists were ten times the rebels, which is unlikely. Hall states there were two thousand. Castañeda, estimating from Spanish records, said it was unlikely Salcedo had one thousand men, but provides no evidence for the claim, nor for his high end of the Republicans at 800. Davenport's account, the only contemporary one, claims the royalist

number was 750, but then notes it was far superior to the republicans. Given the behavior of the armies, it seems likely that the royalists had a superiority, but not the overwhelming one Hall suggests. Walker, "McLane Narrative," *SWHQ* 66, no 3 (January 1963), 458. Davenport to William Shaler, December 1812, CSA. Baker, "Revolution of 1812," 225. Castañeda, *Our Catholic Heritage in Texas*, 6:97.

15. This was the first known correspondence between Magee and Shaler. The two had met, probably at the May dinner, but Magee had made no effort to inform the American agent of his plans. A. W. Magee to William Shaler, November 14, 1812, Shaler Letterbooks. Walker, "McLane Narrative," 66, no. 2 (October 1962), 249.

16. Walker, "McLane Narrative," 66, no. 2 (October 1962), 249.

17. McLane reports that the Mexicans deserted to a man, even leaving their women and children behind in the fort. This is verifiably false, as some Mexicans such as Menchaca never switched sides. One suspects that McLane, writing in the 1850s and possibly colored by later anti-Mexican sentiments, exaggerated greatly. Gulick, *The Papers of Mirabeau Buonaparte Lamar*, 6:147. Schwartz, *Forgotten Battlefield*, 24. Walker, "McLane Narrative," 66, no. 2 (October 1962), 249.

18. "Report of Samuel Davenport," CSA.

19. Magee to Shaler, November 25, 1812, CSA.

20. "Report of Samuel Davenport," CSA. Schwartz, *Forgotten Battlefield*, 25.

21. Manuel Salcedo to Nemesio Salcedo, November 4, 1811, Salcedo, Operaciones de Guerra, A. G. M. Augustus Magee to William Eustis, Baton Rouge, June 22, 1812, Letters Received by the Office of the Adjutant General, 1805–1821, M-566, Roll 13, National Archives.

22. Schwartz, *Forgotten Battlefield*, 25.

23. The accounts of the parlay with the Spaniards vary. McLane's account suggests that Magee had agreed in writing to Salcedo to capitulate, and that a letter from Salcedo to him was read aloud by Gutiérrez to the troops, who decried the agreement. Hall, a Magee apologist, wrote "that there is not a word of truth in all this" and that no such letter, nor agreement existed. That Magee was despairing and considering a capitulation, however, is clear in the correspondence between himself and Shaler.

Gutiérrez records a very different story in later years, in which he claimed Magee promised to sell Gutiérrez to Salcedo for fifteen thousand pesos and a commission in the royalist forces. Gutiérrez's own letters at the time, however, dispute this.

Report of Samuel Davenport," CSA. Yoakum, *The History of Texas*, 164. Baker, "Revolution of 1812," 225. Gutiérrez de Lara to the Mexican Congress, "Account of Progress of the Revolution from the Beginning," in Gulick, *The Papers of Mirabeau Buonaparte Lamar*, 1:12.

24. Hall states that the cannon arrived between the 15th and the 20th, but his dates are generally a week ahead of the actual dates; there is no evidence of a major battle before the negotiations. Hall does not even mention the parlay in his account. At the time, La Bahía was situated south of the river, near the presidio, not north of it as the modern city of Goliad is today. Baker, "Revolution of 1812," 225. Gutiérrez to Shaler, November 25, 1812, Shaler Letterbooks. "Report of Samuel Davenport," CSA.

25. Baker, "Revolution of 1812," 225–27. "Report of Samuel Davenport," CSA.

26. Gutiérrez's ebullient praise of the Americans in his contemporary writings is starkly at odds with his accounts after 1815, when he minimized their performance, ignored their officers, and arrogated to himself the leadership in the field that he never exercised. This suggests enduring bitterness over his later ouster. Gutiérrez to Shaler, November 25, 1812, Shaler Letterbooks.

27. Gutiérrez to Shaler, November 25, 1812, Shaler Letterbooks.

28. Gulick, *The Papers of Mirabeau Buonaparte Lamar*, 6:148.

29. Gulick, *The Papers of Mirabeau Buonaparte Lamar*, 6:148. Pedro José de Aldape to Governor Manuel Salcedo, August 16, 1812, BA, RBB S8:18.

30. Schwartz, *Forgotten Battlefield*, 25. Gutiérrez to Shaler, November 25, 1812, and Magee to Shaler, November 25, 1812, in CSA.

31. McLane, while reporting the story of Davenport's departure almost identically (including the drum-head comment), suggests Davenport left before the parlay. The accounts written closer to the fact, including Davenport's own, give the later time period. Samuel Davenport Genealogy File, Karle Wilson Baker Papers. "Report of Samuel Davenport," and Magee to Shaler, November 25, 1812, CSA. Walker, "McLane's Narrative," 66, no. 2 (October 1962), 250.

32. "Report of Samuel Davenport," and Magee to Shaler, November 25, 1812, CSA.

33. Gutiérrez's original letter, along with Shaler's translation, was forwarded to Monroe. Gutiérrez to Shaler, November 25, 1812, CSA.

34. Gutiérrez to Shaler, November 25, 1812, CSA.

35. Not signing was Miguel Menchaca, though his leadership role in the army may have been minor at this point. Gutiérrez to Shaler, November 25, 1812, CSA.

36. Gutiérrez to Shaler, November 25, 1812, CSA.

Chapter 15

1. Warren, "José Álvarez de Toledo's Initiation as a Filibuster," 64. Julia Kathryn Garrett, "The First Newspaper of Texas: 'Gaceta de Texas,'" *Southwestern Historical Quarterly* 40, no. 3 (January 1937): 209. Warren, "José Álvarez de Toledo's Initiation as a Filibuster," 64. Charles H. Bowman Jr., "Manuel Torres, a Spanish American Patriot in Philadelphia, 1796–1822," *The Pennsylvania Magazine of History and Biography*, vol. 94, no. 1 (January 1970), 26, 30–38. [William Duane], "Death of Mr. Torres," *Aurora*, July 16, 1822, quoted in Bowman, "Manuel Torres," 33.

2. V. H. Ivy, "The Late Henry A. Bullard," *Debow's Southern and Western Review* 12 (1852): 51–52.

3. Cogswell had served a similar role on the staff of a Massachusetts major general of militia, but this merely made him the most qualified among amateurs who collected around Toledo. The elder Nathaniel Cogswell's vessel was captured in 1798 during the Quasi-War with France. "Congress of the United States" *Alexandria (VA) Gazette*, February 20, 1812; "News," *Weekly Register*, February 20, 1812. Nathaniel Cogswell to Generals Gutiérrez and Magee, December 1812, Correspondence of Special Agents. Jameson, *The Cogswells in America*, 47, 152. Brown, *Latin American Rebels and the United States*, 39.

4. Horatio Bigelow's is a possible relative of Bullard through his step-grandmother, Abigail Bullard Bigelow. From multiple sources, including http://www.geni.com and the *Bigelow Society*, http://bigelowsociety.com/rod/hor655c1.htm (accessed May 12, 2020). Gulick, *The Papers of Mirabeau Buonaparte Lamar*, 2:59.

Godwin Brown Cotten is frequently attributed to Toledo's group coming from Philadelphia. This is incorrect. In March 1812, he was living in Feliciana County, West Florida, the same county as Reuben and Samuel Kemper had lived. "Memorial to Congress from Inhabitants of Feliciana County," March 17, 1812, in Carter, *The Territorial Papers of the United States*, 9:1009.

Marilyn McAdams Sibley, *Lone Stars and State Gazettes: Texas Newspapers before the Civil War* (College Station: Texas A&M University Press, 1983), 20. Anonymous, [Henry Adams Bullard], "A Visit to Texas," 226–57. "Mexico and Texas" is a series of three related articles published together at the time of the 1836 revolution. The introductory article, "A Visit to Texas," is printed anonymously. It is attributed by multiple sources to Bullard. Bullard, Henry Adams,

1781–1851. "Mexico and Texas," AMS (unsigned); [n.p., 1836]. *North American Review*. North American Review papers, 1831–1843, MS, Houghton Library, Harvard University. Henceforth this article will be sourced by the title of the section Bullard, wrote "A Visit to Texas."

5. Harris Gaylord Warren, "The Southern Career of Don Juan Mariano Picornell," *Journal of Southern History* 8, no. 3 (August 1942), 311–12. Luis de Onís to Duke of San Carlos, Philadelphia, October 3, 1814. Quoted in Warren, "The Southern Career of Don Juan Mariano Picornell," 313.

6. Warren, "José Álvarez de Toledo's Initiation as a Filibuster," 58. Kanellos, "José Álvarez de Toledo y Dubois," 89–90.

7. Warren, "José Álvarez de Toledo's Initiation as a Filibuster," 62–64.

8. Cogswell to Gutiérrez and Magee, December 29, 1812, CSA.

9. Cogswell to Gutiérrez and Magee, December 29, 1812, CSA.

10. "South America," *The Investigator*, Charleston South Carolina, November 6, 1812.

11. "South America," *The Investigator*, Charleston South Carolina, November 6, 1812.

12. Cogswell to Gutiérrez and Magee, December 29, 1812, CSA.

13. Cogswell to Gutiérrez and Magee, December 29, 1812, CSA.

14. Cogswell to Gutiérrez and Magee, December 29, 1812, CSA. Warren, "José Álvarez de Toledo's Initiation as a Filibuster," 65.

15. The recruits were presumably Adair's and the weapons possibly those from Snyder, although this number of weapons was purely fanciful. Warren, "José Álvarez de Toledo's Initiation as a Filibuster," 65.

16. It is also possible Toledo may have intended the scheme to deter Spanish assassination attempts against him. Toledo's wife had joined him in Philadelphia, so he was particularly exposed to such intrigues. Warren, "José Álvarez de Toledo's Initiation as a Filibuster," 65.

17. "To James Madison from William Duncan, 8 October 1812," Founders Online, National Archives, http://founders.archives.gov/documents/Madison/03-05-02-0285. Original source: The Papers of James Madison, Presidential Series, vol. 5, 10 July 1812–7 February 1813, ed. J. C. A. Stagg, Martha J. King, Ellen J. Barber, Anne Mandeville Colony, Angela Kreider, and Jewel L. Spangler (Charlottesville: University of Virginia Press, 2004), 378–80.

18. [Bullard], "A Visit to Texas," 238.

19. LaTour is only identified by his last name in Bullard's account. For further background on why this author identifies him as he is identified here, see James Aalan Bernsen, "Arsène Lacarrière-Latour," *Texas History Blog*, http://www.texhist.com/2022/01/arsene-lacarriere-latour.html (accessed January 14, 2022). [Bullard], "A Visit to Texas," 238. Edwin H. Carpenter Jr., "Arsène Lacarrière Latour," *Hispanic American Historical Review* 18, no. 2 (May 1938), 222. Gene A. Smith, "Arsène Lacarrière-Latour: Immigrant, Patriot-Historian, and Foreign Agent," in Michael A. Morrison, ed., *The Human Tradition in Antebellum America* (Wilmington, DE: Scholarly Resources, 2000), 83.

20. Aaron Mower, Deposition before William Shaler, undated [probably June–July 1813], CSA.

21. Cogswell to Gutiérrez and Magee, December 1812, Correspondence of Special Agents.

22. Cogswell to Gutiérrez and Magee, December 1812, Correspondence of Special Agents.

23. Cogswell to Gutiérrez and Magee, December 1812, Correspondence of Special Agents.

24. Cogswell to Gutiérrez and Magee, December 1812, Correspondence of Special Agents.

Chapter 16

1. Shaler to Monroe, January 10, 1813, Shaler Letterbooks.

2. The mission was Mission Nuestra Señora del Rosario. McLane refers to the Legend of

Sleepy Hollow, which had not yet been published at the time, though his remembrances were penned decades later. Henry Walker, "William McLane's Narrative of the Magee- Gutiérrez Expedition," *Southwestern Historical Quarterly* 66, no. 3 (January 1963), 457.

3. Walker, "McLane's Narrative," 66, no. 2 (October 1962), 251. Hall account in Gulick, *The Papers of Mirabeau Buonaparte Lamar,* 4(1):279.

4. McLane puts this action on Christmas Day, while Hall places it on New Years' Eve, and in his account, the man was "The New Years' Gift," adding that the man eventually defected and "proved a good republican." Walker, "McLane's Narrative," 66, no. 2 (October 1962), 251. Hall account in Gulick, *The Papers of Mirabeau Buonaparte Lamar,* 4(1):279.

5. Gutiérrez in his later writings would display a deep antipathy to Magee, whom he called a "vile traitor" for talking terms with Salcedo. Baker, "Revolution of 1812," 227. Walker, "McLane's Narrative," *SWHQ* 66, no. 2 (October 1962), 458.

6. Lee, "The Magee Family and the Origins of the China Trade," 112. "A Revolutionary Irishman," PDF document, Pilgrim Hall Museum, Boston, Massachusetts, https://pilgrim hall.org/pdf/James_Magee.pdf (accessed March 12, 2020). An account of the shipwreck of James Magee's ship, the *General Arnold*, can be found at http://historicaldigression.com/2011/10/25/the-grim-fate-of-the-privateer-general-arnold/ (accessed November 15, 2021). "Latest and Authentic from the Mexican Provinces," *Alexandria Daily Gazette*, February 5, 1813. "Mexican Provinces," *Poulson's American Daily Advertiser* (Philadelphia), February 6, 1813.

7. Shaler to Magee, December 20, 1812, CSA.

8. Gaines reported a suspicion in the ranks that the colonel was "poisoned in revenge of his severe treatment" of the men of the Neutral Ground. Gutiérrez would believe this. There is no evidence for it, and the length of his illness before his ultimate death disputes it. Magee's seventeen-year-old sister Margaret had also died of tuberculosis in Boston six months before, and a growing body of medical evidence suggests a genetic predisposition to the disease. Shaler to Monroe, January 10, 1813, Shaler Letterbooks. Baker, "Revolution of 1812," 226. Margaret Eliot Magee, "Deaths Registered in the City of Boston From 1801 to 1848 Inclusive," available at http://www.ancestry.com (accessed April 29, 2021).

9. Shaler to Monroe, January 10, 1813, Shaler Letterbooks.

10. Baker, "Revolution of 1812," 227.

11. Some sources refer to this emissary as a captain named "Richard McFarland," but the evidence strongly supports the former smuggler John McFarlan as the man chosen for this particular mission. In the first place, Richard appears in no other source, whereas John is ubiquitous. He was identified as a captain and as a scout, had already slipped through Spanish lines on many occasions. Finally, while Ross was to visit tribes like the Caddo, McFarlan was sent as an emissary to the notoriously independent western Indians—including the Apaches—to recruit them to join the expedition. It seems entirely improbable that someone ignorant of Texas geography or personally unknown to such tribes could have any hope of successfully recruiting them into the war. With his history as a horse smuggler who had traveled and possibly lived among the western tribes (see chapter 3), John McFarlan almost certainly had preexisting relationships with them. Yoakum also identifies John McFarlan as an "Indian agent" for the expedition. Baker, "Revolution of 1812," 228. Yoakum, *The History of Texas,* 153–65.

12. Baker, "Revolution of 1812," 226.

13. John Warren Hunter, "San Antonio's First Great Tragedy," *Frontier Times* 3, no. 1 (October 1925), 45.

14. Hall account in Gulick, *The Papers of Mirabeau Buonaparte Lamar,* 4(1): 279.

15. Gulick, *The Papers of Mirabeau Buonaparte Lamar,* 4(1): 279.

16. Gulick, *The Papers of Mirabeau Buonaparte Lamar,* 4(1): 279.
17. Shaler to Monroe, January 10, 1812, Shaler Letterbooks.
18. LaVere, *The Texas Indians,* 159.
19. F. Todd Smith, "The Kadohadacho Indians and the Louisiana-Texas Frontier, 1803–1815," *Southwestern Historical Quarterly* 95, no. 2 (October 1991), 177–92.
20. Smith, "The Kadohadacho Indians," 200. Sibley to Eustis, October 6, 1813, in Garret, "Dr. John Sibley," 49, no. 4 (April 1946), and 49, no. 4 (April 1946), 602.
21. Sibley to Eustis, February 12, 1813, in Garret, "Dr. John Sibley," 49, no. 3 (January 1946), 422.
22. Sibley and Shaler recorded from four to six hundred Indians recruited, but this was certainly an exaggeration. The Spanish had Indian auxiliaries as well, although the numbers are unknown, and they were probably of dubious quality. Sibley to Eustis, February 12, 1813, in Garret, "Dr. John Sibley," 49, no. 3 (January 1946), 422. Baker, "Revolution of 1812," 227. Schwartz, *Forgotten Battlefield,* 28. Ingrid Broughton Morris and Deolece M. Parmelee, "Gaines, James Taylor," *HOTO,* http://www.tshaonline.org/handbook/online/articles/fga04 (accessed May 12, 2020).
23. Antonio Menchaca claims the Comanche numbers were between 1,500 to 2,000 warriors and suggests that all of them were brought to La Bahía, which is unlikely, since the event is not recorded by the rebels. If Menchaca's identification of Cordero as the leader of the Indian party is correct, it is an unusual departure from the chief's normal behavior. Cordero was a chief of the Cuchanticas band who is more generally portrayed in historical accounts as inclined toward peaceful coexistence with whites. It is also possible this stance had broken down during the stress of the revolution. Matovina and de la Teja, *Recollections of a Tejano Life,* 45n22. F. Todd Smith, *From Dominance to Disappearance,* 97.
24. Frederick Chabot, ed., *Memoirs of Antonio Menchaca* (San Antonio, Yanaguana Society, 1937), http://www.sonsofdewittcolony.org/menchacamem.htm (accessed May 12, 2020). John Warren Hunter, "San Antonio's First Great Tragedy," *Frontier Times* 3, no. 1 (October 1925), 45. Robinson to Monroe, July 26, 1813, Correspondence Relating to Filibuster.
25. Mona and Ibarbo had deserted the US Army to join the filibusters and were led into capture by Galván's defection. Upon escaping Spanish captivity in their camp, the men fled back to the United States, probably fearing they would be accused of treason if they returned to the Republican Army. "From the Natchez Papers," *Daily National Intelligencer,* May 8, 1813. Schwartz, *Forgotten Battlefield,* 27. Sibley to Eustis, March 1, 1813, in Garret, "Dr. John Sibley," 49, no. 3 (January 1946), 422. Chabot, *Menchaca.*
26. Sibley also mentions Magee's death as attributed to illness in a letter on March 7th. Hall puts the date as February 1st, while Sibley puts it as February 6th. It should be noted that Hall's chronology was recorded much later and is about a week off throughout, making the latter day more probable. Baker, "Revolution of 1812," 226. Walker, "McLane's Narrative," 66, no. 2 (October 1962), 250–51. Garret, "Dr. John Sibley," 49, no. 3 (January 1946), 423.
27. Bradley, *We Never Retreat,* 52. Extract of a letter from William Fisher, in Shaler to Monroe, March 13, 1813, CSA.
28. When Claiborne's proclamation was released, William Francis had been in New Orleans with a shipment of arms for the Republican Army. He appeared before Claiborne and claimed he had been deceived into thinking the affair was legitimate. The governor gave him a passport to travel to Natchitoches for other trade. Francis then proceeded to smuggle weapons anyway, to the governor's chagrin. Fisher (Extract), in Shaler to Monroe, March 13, 1813, CSA. Walker, "McLane's Narrative," 66, no. 3, 458 (note 84). Hall account in Gulick, *The Papers of Mirabeau Buonaparte Lamar,* 4(1):279. Claiborne to Judge Steel, August 17, 1812, CL, 6:164.

29. Fisher (Extract), in Shaler to Monroe, March 13, 1813, CSA. Hall account in Gulick, *The Papers of Mirabeau Buonaparte Lamar,* 4(1):279.

30. Bradley, *We Never Retreat*, 52. Warren, *The Sword Was Their Passport*, 45. Baker, "Revolution of 1812," 226. Walker, "McLane's Narrative," 66, no. 3 (January 1963), 458. Hall account in Gulick, *The Papers of Mirabeau Buonaparte Lamar,* 4(1): 279–80.

31. Hall account in Gulick, *The Papers of Mirabeau Buonaparte Lamar,* 4(1): 280.

32. Bradley, *We Never Retreat*, 52. Warren, *The Sword Was Their Passport*, 45. Baker, "Revolution of 1812," 226. Walker, "McLane's Narrative," 66, no. 3 (January 1963), 458. Hall account in Gulick, *The Papers of Mirabeau Buonaparte Lamar,* 4(1):280.

33. Hall account in Gulick, *The Papers of Mirabeau Buonaparte Lamar,* 4(1):280.

34. One of the dead Spanish officers was identified as "Ahzeniega," likely an Arciniega. It could have been José Miguel de Arciniega, though this would indicate that he was only wounded, not killed, as he would later serve as mayor of San Antonio.

Some estimates of Spanish losses range as high as six hundred men, but most sources reflect the lower number. Gutiérrez placed it at 150 killed and 51 prisoners. Hall says 300–400; McLane only 200. Bradley, *We Never Retreat*, 52. Fisher (Extract), in Shaler to Monroe, March 13, 1813, CSA. Gutiérrez to Ross, quoted in "From the Balt. Fed. Gaz." *Daily Advertiser and Repertory,* May 8, 1813. Walker, "McLane's Narrative," 66, no. 3 (January 1963), 458. Hall account in Gulick, *The Papers of Mirabeau Buonaparte Lamar,* 4(1):280.

35. An anonymous account in the 1850s by a resident of San Antonio, who had been eighteen years old in 1813, recalled "twenty-seven hand to hand encounters" during the siege. Presumably, he meant combat actions, not literal hand-to-hand. Anonymous account in Gulick, *The Papers of Mirabeau Buonaparte Lamar,* 4(2):6. Bradley, *We Never Retreat*, 52. Henry Walker, "William McLane's Narrative of the Magee- Gutiérrez Expedition," *Southwestern Historical Quarterly* 66, no. 3 (January 1963): 459.

36. "Mortuary Notice," *Boston Daily Advertiser,* April 16, 1813. "Elegiac Lines Inscribed to the Memory of Augustus William Magee," *Columbian Centinel,* May 19, 1813.

37. "Elegiac Lines Inscribed to the Memory of Augustus William Magee," *Columbian Centinel,* May 19, 1813.

38. Orsi, *Citizen Explorer*, 225. Pike, *The Southwestern Journals of Zebulon Pike,* 180–81. The following account is based entirely on Robinson's extensive letter to Monroe, which he wrote to extraordinary detail upon returning to the United States.

39. Robinson to Monroe, July 26, 1813, CRF.

40. Robinson to Monroe, July 26, 1813, CRF.

41. Pike, *The Southwestern Journals of Zebulon Pike,* 180–81.

42. Pike, *The Southwestern Journals of Zebulon Pike,* 180–81.

43. "Mexican Provinces," *New York Gazette & General Advertiser,* May 25, 1813.

44. Robinson to Monroe, July 26, 1813, CRF.

Chapter 17

1. It is doubtful Shaler ever met Kemper and likely formed his opinion his reputation from West Florida. Cogliano, "Failed Filibusters," 2. Shaler to Monroe, January 10, 1813, Shaler Letterbooks. Bradley, *We Never Retreat*, 64.

2. For one of the most important battles in Texas history, the final battle of the siege surprisingly has no generally accepted name. The author uses this appellation as the most logical one. Unknown to John Sibley, March 5, 1813, Correspondence of Special Agents. Gutiérrez to Ross, quoted in "From the Balt. Fed. Gaz." *Daily Advertiser and Repertory,* May 8, 1813.

3. Hall alone states that the pursuing force of mounted men, fifty in number, was led by Holmes. It is unlikely the pursuit would have been entirely led by Anglo-Americans who did not know the country, nor were many of the Americans at this time in possession of horses, while Tejanos were. It is more likely that it was the same mixed contingent that had fought under Menchaca, with Holmes replacing Francis on the Anglo-American side. Bradley, *We Never Retreat*, 64. Schwartz, *Forgotten Battlefield*, 27. Hall account in Gulick, *The Papers of Mirabeau Buonaparte Lamar*, 4(1):280. Walker, "McLane Narrative," *SWHQ* 66, no 3 (January 1963): 460. Gutiérrez to Ross, February 24, 1813, CSA. Gutiérrez to Major Reuben Ross February 24, 1813, CSA.

4. [Unknown] to John Sibley, March 5, 1813, CSA.

5. Walker, "McLane's Narrative," 66, no. 3 (January 1963), 460. Gutiérrez to Ross, February 24, 1813, CSA.

6. Simón Herrera and Manuel Salcedo to Miguel Menchaca, March 23, 1813, Gutiérrez de Lara Papers, Texas State Archives. Translation by Jesús F. de la Teja.

7. Art Martínez de Vara, *Tejano Patriot: The Revolutionary Life of José Francisco Ruiz, 1783–1840* (Austin: Texas State Historical Association Press, 2020), 21–24, 31, 40. "Diary formed by the Distinguished Sergeant Don Pedro de la Garza Falcón," October 13–16, 1808, Declaration of Witnesses, BA, RBB 33:137.

8. Martínez de Vara, *Tejano Patriot*, 40, 50.

9. Francisco Ruiz to Miguél Menchaca, March 23, 1813, Gutiérrez de Lara Papers, Texas State Library and Archives. Translation by Jesús F. de la Teja.

10. The rebel numbers noted are from Gaines's account. McLane's numbers are smaller: 270 Americans, 100 Mexicans, and 30 Coushatta Indians. Ross's reinforcements likely were not included in the latter account. Bart Fleming, possibly a soldier in the Republican Army, put the number at six hundred men, supporting Gaines. The confusion may also be connected to the term "effective men," used inconsistently by multiple authors, and not used at all by others. Baker, "Revolution of 1812," 227. Reuben Ross to William Shaler, April 15, 1813, CSA. Gulick, *The Papers of Mirabeau Buonaparte Lamar*, 5:365. Walker, "McLane's Narrative," 66, no. 3 (January 1963), 460. "1813 Letter from Bart Fleming to Levin Wailes, Esq.," June 7, 1813, in Gutiérrez de Lara collection, Eugene C. Barker Texas History Center, University of Texas at Austin, cited in I. Wayne Cox, "Field Survey and Archival Research for the Rosillo Creek Battleground Area, Southeast San Antonio, Texas," Index of Texas Archaeology: Open Access Gray Literature from the Lone Star State, vol. 1990, Article 1, available at https://scholarworks.sfasu.edu/ita/vol1990/iss1/1 (accessed August 24, 2021), 3. Jack D. Foner, "Jews and the American Military," 85.

11. Walker, "McLane's Narrative," 66, no. 3 (January 1963), 460.

12. Baker, "Revolution of 1812," 227.

13. Geologist and amateur historian Robert P. Marshall in 2015 published a study in which he identified what he believed to be the most likely location of the battle: "A gentle slope south of the present-day intersection of SE Loop 410 Expressway and South W. W. White Road." Robert P. Marshall, "Locating the Battle of Rosillo: A Newly Discovered Map Indicates the Likely Site of the 1813 Battle where the First Republic of Texas Was Born," *Southwestern Historical Quarterly* 68, no. 4 (April 2015), 398. Baker, "Revolution of 1812," 228.

McLane's account, while probably right on the republican numbers, exaggerated the host facing the rebels as "the entire male population of Texas." Hall would record it as 2,500. Ross's account, in contrast, was written days after the battle and places it at 850. Many of these, however, were likely hastily armed and conscripted citizens of San Antonio, reflecting a possible truth underlying McLane's exaggeration. Beltrán gives the total republican numbers as 1,300, but he was not present in person at the battle. Elisha Roberts, who brought news of the victory to Natchitoches, reported both sides as having 1,000 men, which is unlikely given their previous numbers, but the parity was possibly accurate. Walker, "McLane's Narrative," 66, no. 3 (January 1963), 460. "New Mexican Bulletin," *Baltimore Patriot,* June 8, 1813. Schwartz, *Forgotten Battlefield,* 29. Hall account in Gulick, *The Papers of Mirabeau Buonaparte Lamar,* 4(1):281.

14. Hall in an account years later says it was Gaines who led the attack, though contemporary sources say it was Ross. Gaines of course was in Ross's command, having joined him with the newly recruited Indians and Anglos who had come down from Nacogdoches. Reuben Ross to William Shaler, April 15, 1813, CSA. Hall account in Gulick, *The Papers of Mirabeau Buonaparte Lamar,* 4(1):281.

15. Walker, "McLane's Narrative," 66, no. 3 (January 1963), 461. Yoakum, *The History of Texas,* 167.

16. Called variously Montura, Montara, or Montano in Anglo accounts, the identification of the officer as Montero is confirmed by the testimony of Juan Antonio Padilla, who wrote a letter of recommendation for Ross in the 1820s. Hall's account says that Montero (and presumably Ross too), were mounted, though this does not seem likely from the description. "From Mexico," *Daily National Intelligencer,* July 9, 1813. For the Padilla quote, see Raúl A. Ramos, *Beyond the Alamo: Forging Mexican Ethnicity in San Antonio, 1821–1861* (self-published, 2008), 109–10. Jesús F. de la Teja, "Padilla, Juan Antonio," *HOTO,* http://www.tshaonline.org/handbook/online/articles/fpa06 (accessed May 14, 2020). Hall account in Gulick, *The Papers of Mirabeau Buonaparte Lamar,* 4(1):281.

17. Owens was the merchant who was to receive the smuggled horses of McFarlan and Quirk in October 1808. Ross to Shaler, April 15, 1813, CSA. "New Mexican Bulletin," *Baltimore Patriot,* June 8, 1813. "Document 41: Letter that, with date of October 1, 1303, Michael Quinn wrote from Trinidad to William Owens, merchant of Natchitoches," BA, RBB 70: 89–90.

18. Ross identified him as Colonel Bonega, but no officer is known of that name. It is close to the Spanish name Banegas, but the only person of that name known in Texas was a rebel courier, executed prior to this date. Walker, "McLane's Narrative," no. 3 (January 1963), 462. Bradley, *We Never Retreat,* 65–66. Schwartz, *Forgotten Battlefield,* 29. "New Mexican Bulletin," *Baltimore Patriot,* June 8, 1813. Yoakum, *The History of Texas,* 166.

19. Baker, "Revolution of 1812," 228. Bradley, *We Never Retreat,* 65–66.

20. At the time, the battle was often referred to alternatively as the Battle of Salado or Rosillo, with the latter or "Rosalis" more common. A subsequent battle during the Republic of Texas period, also along the Salado Creek, was also given the first name; historians have since ascribed the name of Rosillo to the battle in March 1813. Baker, "Revolution of 1812," 228. Walker, "McLane's Narrative," 66, no. 3 (January 1963), 462.

21. McLane and Hall agree on the Spanish casualties, but McLane also asserts the Indians did not lose a man, which Hall disputes. Bradley, *We Never Retreat,* 66–69. Schwartz, *Forgotten Battlefield,* 30. Walker, "McLane's Narrative," 66, no. 3 (January 1963), 462. Baker, "Revolution of 1812," 228. Hall account in Gulick, *The Papers of Mirabeau Buonaparte Lamar,* 4(1):281.

22. Hall account in Gulick, *The Papers of Mirabeau Buonaparte Lamar,* 4(1):281.

23. Antonio Menchaca says the letter was sent on Friday, April 3, but it seems more likely that the letter was sent immediately, rather than two days after the army's arrival outside the city. Hall says the scout was Richard McFarlan, but as noted, he previously attributed this same name to a man who was almost certainly John. Matovina and de la Teja, *Recollections of a Tejano Life,* 47. Hall account in Gulick, *The Papers of Mirabeau Buonaparte Lamar,* 4(1):281. Anonymous [Navarro] account in Gulick, *The Papers of Mirabeau Buonaparte Lamar,* 4(2):6.

24. Schwartz, *Forgotten Battlefield*, 30. "Propositions for the Capitulation of the town of San Antonio," RBB S15:203–205. "Deposition of Guillermo Saldaña," April 8, 1813, in Cox, "Field Survey and Archival Research for the Rosillo Creek," 19.

25. "Propositions for the Capitulation of the town of San Antonio," RBB S15:203–5.

26. The anonymous account, preserved by Lamar, is likely Navarro's, because the wording in parts is identical to the language preserved in his memoirs, and the age he gives in his introduction is close to Navarro's. "Propositions for the Capitulation of the town of San Antonio," RBB S15:203–205. Anonymous [Navarro] account in Gulick, *The Papers of Mirabeau Buonaparte Lamar*, 4(2):6.

27. Schwartz, *Forgotten Battlefield*, 30.

28. Beltrán's identity is mysterious, his account colorful, precise, and even romantic. For this reason, some historians have questioned its veracity. This author has validated it as at least partly authentic. It was published first in the 1920s before any of the other detailed primary accounts were generally known, and before the first published book on the subject. It aligns very well with McLane's narrative, even though his account was lost to history until the 1960s, long after Beltrán's account was written. It contains details that can be proven by information unknown at the time of its first publication, such as the identity of Oramel Johnston. For further information on Beltran and the proof of his account, see James Aalan Bernsen, "The Beltrán Account," at http://www.texhist.com/2021/11/the-carlos-beltran-account.html (accessed November 25, 2021). John Warren Hunter, "Some Early Tragedies of San Antonio," *Frontier Times* 18, no. 3 (December 1940), 115. Johnston, *The Johnstons of Salisbury*, 54. Orsi, *Citizen Explorer*, 236. McDonald, *José Antonio Navarro*, 25. "P Boon" account by Villars in Gulick, *The Papers of Mirabeau Buonaparte Lamar*, 4(1):261.

29. John Warren Hunter, "San Antonio's First Great Tragedy," *Frontier Times* 3, no. 1 (October 1925), 45.

30. No information has been discovered of Manuel Martín Delgado's trial and execution. He had been one of Zambrano's junta when the royalist recovered San Antonio, but likely was implicated in rebel activities at a later date. Gavino Delgado, who was used as an intermediary between Salcedo and Menchaca after the Battle of Rosillo, was a relative. Steve Gibson, "The Arocha Family from the Island of Palma, the 9th Family of the List of Canary Islanders taken at Quautitlan, November 8, 1730," *Béxar Genealogy*, http://Béxargenealogy.com/archives/familyfiles/arocha.rtf (accessed May 12, 2020). "The Chronicle," *Niles Weekly Register*, June 26, 1813.

31. Hunter, "San Antonio's First Great Tragedy," 45.

32. Walker, "McLane Narrative," 66, no. 3 (January 1963), 463. Castañeda, *Our Catholic Heritage in Texas*, 6:98. Anonymous [Henry Adams Bullard], "A Visit to Texas," 226–57. "Deposition of Guillermo Saldaña," April 8, 1813, in Cox, "Field Survey and Archival Research for the Rosillo Creek," 19. Hall account in Gulick, *The Papers of Mirabeau Buonaparte Lamar*, 4(1):282.

33. Martínez de Vara, *Tejano Patriot*, 29, 54. Anonymous [Navarro] account in Gulick, *The Papers of Mirabeau Buonaparte Lamar*, 4(2):6.

34. McLane claims that One of Gutiérrez's first acts upon entering San Antonio was to send an express to Nacogdoches to shut off the valve of American volunteers. This claim is disputed by other evidence but is in keeping with McLane's hostile attitude toward Mexicans. Anonymous [Navarro] account in Gulick, *The Papers of Mirabeau Buonaparte Lamar*, 4(2):6. Walker, "McLane Narrative," 66, no. 3 (January 1963), 463. "Deposition of Guillermo Saldaña," April 8, 1813; Cox, "Field Survey and Archival Research for the Rosillo Creek," 19.

35. Menchaca names Francisco, Tomás, and Ignacio Arocha, as well as Clemente, Miguel, and Manuel Delgado on the Junta. Of the latter, there seems to be some inconsistency, since

his son claimed he had been killed. This claim is repeated in all sources. Chabot, *Menchaca*. Shaler to Monroe, June 12, 1813, Shaler Letterbooks. Anonymous [Navarro] account in Gulick, *The Papers of Mirabeau Buonaparte Lamar*, 4(2):6.

36. Some historians have attempted to tie Shaler's souring with Gutiérrez to the latter's decision to write a constitution proclaiming Texas as Mexican territory, but Shaler made no statements of the kind. He simply called the constitution a farce because it was undemocratic. But this was not the beginning of Shaler's alienation from the Mexican rebel. Shaler grew skeptical of Gutiérrez even when they lived together in Natchitoches.

37. Guedea, "Autonomía e independencia en la provincia de Texas," 165.

38. "Texas' First Declaration of Independence and First Constitution," in Ernest Wallace, David M. Vigness, and George B. Ward, ed., *Documents of Texas History* (Austin: State House Press, 1994), 39.

39. "Texas' First Declaration of Independence and First Constitution."

40. "Texas' First Declaration of Independence and First Constitution."

41. Not only were the North Americans the audience, but the world of Spanish America generally, where similar revolutions were stirring. Wallace, Vigness, and Ward, *Documents of Texas History*, 40. "Republic of Mexico," July 3, 1813, *Daily National Intelligencer*.

42. "The Constitution of the State of Texas, April 17, 1813," in Wallace, Vigness, and Ward, *Documents of Texas History*, 39.

43. Castañeda, *Our Catholic Heritage in Texas*, 6:103.

44. As Coronado writes, "Historians have long dismissed these documents as mere mimicry of Anglo-American revolutionary thought. Upon closer reading, however, we see another thoroughly Catholic worldview, but one that was far more egalitarian than the royalists' vision. The political philosophy of these revolutionaries demonstrates the intellectual complexity of Catholic Hispanic thought." Coronado, *A World Not to Come*, 32.

45. Guedea, "Autonomía e independencia en la provincia de Texas," 168. Wallace, 40.

46. "Gutiérrez Proclamation," April 22, 1813, quoted in Cox, "Field Survey and Archival Research for the Rosillo Creek," 25. Gutiérrez wrote several similar proclamations.

47. "Gutiérrez Proclamation," April 22, 1813, quoted in Cox, "Field Survey and Archival Research for the Rosillo Creek," 25.

48. "Gutiérrez Proclamation," April 22, 1813, quoted in Cox, "Field Survey and Archival Research for the Rosillo Creek," 25.

49. This proclamation, continuing the trend, praised the Americans, and used them to prod or even shame Mexican rebels to join the cause. Gutiérrez asked his fellow countrymen, "Are you not encouraged to see that from the other [nation] of the North our brothers rush to your aid, abandoning their establishments and homes, and exposing their lives to all dangers for the sole interest of seeing yourselves peaceful and enjoying the happiness of independence for every man who is born with a free character?" This view of the selflessness of the Americans was probably more Pollyanna than even Gutiérrez really believed, but it is nonetheless in stark contrast to his post-1815 writings in which he diminished (it is not a stretch to say concealing) their role. "Proclamation" in Arredondo, Operaciones, AGM 4(2):6–7.

50. De la Teja, *Faces of Béxar*, 170.

51. Guedea, "Autonomía e independencia en la provincia de Texas," 171–72.

Chapter 18

1. Shaler to Monroe, June 12, 1813, Shaler Papers. Walker, "McLane Narrative," 66, no. 3 (January 1963), 464.

2. It is worth noting that the Junta did not technically exist until after the executions of the royalists, though it is presumable that an informal council of local advisors filled such a role, or accounts mentioning the Junta's role in the executions might be referencing a general feeling of vengeance against the Spaniards. Lúcas Alaman, *Historia de Méjico desde los primeros movimientos que prepararon su independencia en el año 1808 hasta la* época presente, vol. 3 (Mexico City: J. M. Lara, 1850), 484. Alaman's account is pro-Gutiérrez, and partly blames foreign, sectarian elements (presumably French sympathizers) within the San Antonio population. Bradley, *We Never Retreat*, 67. Chabot, *Texas in 1811*, 118.

3. Bradley, *We Never Retreat*, 68. Gulick, *The Papers of Mirabeau Buonaparte Lamar*, 6:280.

4. Beltrán and American sources, which are all written decades later, place the execution around April 6th or 7th, and work their timeline backward in their narratives, but contemporary Spanish sources are precise in their theirs. The Spanish soldiers Guillermo Saldāna and Guillermo Navarro fled San Antonio for Laredo, arriving on April 6th and 8th, respectively. The journey was three days, making their departure dates April 3rd and 5th. Saldaña writes in ignorance of the murders, while Navarro depicts them in detail, placing the executions on April 4th. Beltrán's timeline is adjusted here to align. Depositions of Guillermo Saldaña and Guillermo Navarro, April 8, 1813, in Cox, "Field Survey and Archival Research for the Rosillo Creek," 19–21. Bradley, *We Never Retreat*, 68. Hunter, "San Antonio's First Great Tragedy," 46.

5. Hunter, "San Antonio's First Great Tragedy," 46.

6. Hunter, "San Antonio's First Great Tragedy," 46–47. McDonald, *José Antonio Navarro*, 25. "From Mexico," *Daily National Intelligencer*, June 10, 1813.

7. Bradley, *We Never Retreat*, 68. Walker, "McLane Narrative," 66, no. 3 (January 1963), 463. Hunter, "San Antonio's First Great Tragedy," 46. Matovina and de la Teja, *Recollections of a Tejano Life*, 48.

8. Navarro said Delgado's escort was 60 men. Hunter, "San Antonio's First Great Tragedy," 47. Anonymous [Navarro] account in Gulick, *The Papers of Mirabeau Buonaparte Lamar*, 4(2):7.

9. Anonymous [Navarro] account in Gulick, *The Papers of Mirabeau Buonaparte Lamar*, 4(2):7.

10. Hunter, "San Antonio's First Great Tragedy," 47. Baker, "Revolution of 1812," 228–29. "Deposition of Guillermo Navarro," April 8, 1813, in Cox, "Field Survey and Archival Research for the Rosillo Creek," 21.

11. Salcedo's wife and daughter appear to have remained in New Orleans. It is possible they never even entered Texas. Samuel Davenport, who visited the town periodically on business, kept Salcedo informed about his family's situation. Presumably, General Herrera's family was still in Mexico. La Vere, "Davenport, Barr, Murphy and Smith," 114.

12. Harris Gaylord Warren and Jack D. L. Homes, "Herrera, Simon de," HOTO, http://www.tshaonline.org/handbook/online/articles/fhe33, accessed May 12, 2018. De la Teja, *Faces of Béxar*, 168.

13. There were fourteen royalists executed. The different sources list different names, but the correct list, taken from burial records, can be found at James Aalan Bernsen, "The Murder of the Spanish Royalists," *The Texas History Blog*, http://www.texhist.com/2021/12/the-murder-of-spanish-royalists.html (accessed December 8, 2021). Burial records from San Fernando Church Burial Book 3, 1802–1817, Archives of the Archdiocese of San Antonio, Texas. This is reprinted in Cox, "Field Survey and Archival Research for the Rosillo Creek," 27–34. Hunter, "San Antonio's First Great Tragedy," 47. Anonymous [Navarro] account

in Gulick, *The Papers of Mirabeau Buonaparte Lamar*, 4(2):8. "Deposition of Guillermo Navarro," April 8, 1813, in Cox, "Field Survey and Archival Research for the Rosillo Creek," 21. Sibley to Secretary of War, May 7, 1813, in Garrett, "Dr. John Sibley," 49, no. 3 (January 1946), 425. Chabot, *Texas in 1811*, 82.

14. Hunter, "San Antonio's First Great Tragedy," 48. "Deposition of Guillermo Navarro," April 8, 1813, in Cox, "Field Survey and Archival Research for the Rosillo Creek," 21.

15. Mexican Historian Lúcas Alaman placed the blame for the murder on Captain Pedro Prado as the commander of the execution squad, though American sources all identify Delgado as the commander of the executioners and Prado as merely a deputy. Delgado, based on other references, would have been senior. Alaman, *Historia de Méjico desde los primeros movimientos*, 484.

Hall and Beltrán both mention the one man who begged to be shot, as does Natchitoches Indian Factor Thomas Linnard. Beltrán identifies this man as Salcedo, Linnard as Herrera. Schwartz, *Forgotten Battlefield*, 31. Hunter, "San Antonio's First Great Tragedy," 48. Linnard to Mason, May 7, 1813, *Letterbook of the Natchitoches Sulphur Fork Factory*, National Archives, T1029. McDonald, *José Antonio Navarro*, 26. Anonymous [Navarro] account in Gulick, *The Papers of Mirabeau Buonaparte Lamar*, 4(2):7.

16. Anonymous [Navarro] account in Gulick, *The Papers of Mirabeau Buonaparte Lamar*, 4(2):7.

17. "Deposition of Guillermo Navarro," April 8, 1813, in Cox, "Field Survey and Archival Research for the Rosillo Creek," 21

18. Gulick, *The Papers of Mirabeau Buonaparte Lamar*, 1:280. Hunter, "San Antonio's First Great Tragedy," 47. [Bullard], "A Visit to Texas," 237.

19. John Sibley cites a second-hand source adding that Delgado's father's (or other relative's) head, after being severed in San Antonio, was "dragged by mules to Monclova and through the streets of that city." Sibley to Eustis, May 7, 1813. Garrett, "Dr. John Sibley" 49, no. 3, 425.

20. Hunter, "San Antonio's First Great Tragedy," 48.

21. "Declaration of the Corporal José Luís del Valle," BA, RBB 70:228. Gutiérrez de Lara to the Mexican Congress, "Account of Progress of the Revolution from the Beginning," in Gulick, *The Papers of Mirabeau Buonaparte Lamar*, 1:15.

22. Gulick, *The Papers of Mirabeau Buonaparte Lamar*, 1:280–1, 4(2):9.

23. Shaler to Monroe, May 14, 1813, and Shaler to Monroe, May 7, 1813, Shaler Letterbooks.

24. When the British began the invasion that would lead to the burning of Washington, Monroe would even ride out on horseback to personally scout for the army, despite holding two of the top cabinet positions in the administration simultaneously.

25. Shaler to Monroe, May 14, 1813, Shaler Letterbooks.

26. Ike Moore, "The Earliest Printing and First Newspaper in Texas." *Southwestern Historical Quarterly* 39, no. 2 (October 1935), 87. Shaler to Monroe, April 18, 1813, Shaler Letterbooks. Bradley, *We Never Retreat*, 74.

27. Shaler to Monroe, April 18, 1813, Shaler Letterbooks.

28. John C. Fredricksen, "Humbert, Jean Joseph Amable," American National Biography, https://www.anb.org/view/10.1093/anb/9780198606697.001.0001/anb-9780198606697-e-0300229 (accessed May 12, 2020).

29. Shaler to Monroe, April 18, 1813, Shaler Letterbooks.

30. Shaler to Monroe, April 18, 1813, Shaler Letterbooks.

31. Shaler to Monroe, May 2, 1813, Shaler Letterbooks. Shaler to Monroe, May 2, 1813, Shaler Letterbooks.

NOTES TO PAGES 254–259

32. "Samuel Noah," Cullum's Register, vol. 1, 79, available at http://penelope.uchicago.edu /Thayer/E/Gazetteer/Places/America/United_States/Army/USMA/Cullums_Register/30* .html (accessed May 12, 2020). Baker, "Revolution of 1812," 229. Bradley, *We Never Retreat*, 70. "From Mexico," *Daily National Intelligencer,* July 9, 1813.

33. Kemper may not have been overly dismayed at the murder of the Royalists, and left Gutiérrez on terms good enough for the latter to write to him at his home in St. Francisville. "Republic of Mexico," *Daily National Intelligencer,* July 19, 1813.

34. "From Mexico," *Daily National Intelligencer,* June 26, 1813.

35. Bradley, *We Never Retreat*, 70.

36. "Republic of Mexico," *Daily National Intelligencer,* July 19, 1813.

37. "Republic of Mexico," *Daily National Intelligencer,* July 19, 1813.

38. The tenor of Gutiérrez's comment on Kemper rings false since the former was still communicating with the latter. John Warren Hunter, "The Battle of Alazan," *Frontier Times* 3, no. 2 (November 1925): 41.

39. Hunter, "The Battle of Alazan," 41.

40. Reuben Ross Family Papers. Dolph Briscoe Center for American History, The University of Texas at Austin.

41. Gertrudis Barrera later married the Spanish commandant of La Bahía, Francisco García. Beltran alternatively identifies the woman as Francisca Ochoa. Gulick, *The Papers of Mirabeau Buonaparte Lamar,* 1:282. Shannon Selin "Presidio Commander Francisco García," in *Imagining the Bounds of History* (blog), https://shannonselin.com/2016/06/francisco-garcia / (accessed May 3, 2020). Hunter, "Some Early Tragedies of San Antonio," 128.

42. Gulick, *The Papers of Mirabeau Buonaparte Lamar,* 1:282.

43. Shaler, as the American Commissioner for Seamen, likely met Toledo's father. Shaler to Monroe, April 3, 1813, May 2, 1813, and May 7, 1813, Shaler Letterbooks.

44. Moore, "The Earliest Printing and First Newspaper in Texas," 83–99. Marilyn McAdams Sibley, *Lone Stars and State Gazettes: Texas Newspapers before the Civil War* (College Station: Texas A&M University Press, 1983), 22–23.

45. Robinson to Monroe, August 21, 1813, CRF. Bullard, "A Visit to Texas," 239.

46. Gutiérrez to Shaler, April 11, 1813, CSA.

47. Gutiérrez to Shaler, April 18, 1813, CSA.

48. Gutiérrez to Shaler, April 18, 1813, CSA.

49. Gutiérrez to Shaler, April 18, 1813, CSA.

50. Picornell may have been plotting for more than Toledo's behalf. When he later asked for a Spanish pardon, he claimed he had worked in San Antonio to undermine the revolutionary cause. He did not say if he was in league with Toledo in this work, which would validate Cogswell's fears about the Cuban's trustworthiness. Picornell may have been acting independently. That he aided the royalist cause was attested to by Father Antonio de Sedella in 1814. Warren, "The Southern Career of Don Juan Mariano Picornell," 315–16.

51. Cogswell was not the only person to sound the alarm on Toledo. In a letter written too late to reach Gutiérrez in Texas, Jorge Larvindston of Philadelphia, who had known both Gutiérrez and Toledo in that city, wrote in July 1813 about Toledo: "It had been some months since he had withdrawn himself from me and as yet I do not know the motive for his doing so. . . . His inconsistency and fickleness has not made an impression on me." Bullard, "A Visit to Texas," 239. Jorge Larvindston to José Bernardo Gutiérrez de Lara, June 5, 1812, Gutiérrez de Lara Papers. Gutiérrez to Cogswell, April 11, 1813, CSA.

52. Gutiérrez to Cogswell, April 11, 1813, CSA. Bullard, "A Visit to Texas," 239.

Chapter 19

1. Bradley Folsom, *Arredondo: Last Spanish Ruler of Texas and Northeastern New Spain* (Norman: University of Oklahoma Press, 2017), 11–40. Gulick, *The Papers of Mirabeau Buonaparte Lamar*, 6:337.
2. Folsom, *Arredondo*, 25, 28–29, 32, 35
3. Folsom, *Arredondo*, 44.
4. Folsom, *Arredondo*, 48.
5. Folsom, *Arredondo*, 60–61.
6. Folsom, *Arredondo*, 72.
7. Folsom, *Arredondo*, 72–73.
8. Folsom, *Arredondo*, 73–74.
9. Garrett, "Dr. John Sibley," 49, no. 1 (July 1945), 116–119. Folsom, 74.
10. Folsom, *Arredondo*, 74–75.
11. Folsom, *Arredondo*, 76, 79. Arredondo to Calleja, June 11, 1813, in Arredondo, Operaciones, AGM 4(2):67–68.
12. The Texas Mexican rebel command structure is poorly understood. Delgado seems to have superseded Miguel Menchaca, possibly as the latter was recovering from a wound from the Battle of Rosillo. Alternatively, the growing Mexican contingent was possibly divided, with all new recruits going to Delgado. Both men had been raised by Gutiérrez from lowly ranks. Delgado appears to have been only a militia corporal in the Spanish service. Hunter, "The Battle of Alazán," 41.
13. Hunter, "The Battle of Alazán," 42. Bullard, "A Visit to Texas," 239. Hunter, "The Battle of Alazán," 43.
14. Hunter, "The Battle of Alazán," 43.
15. Joseph Biddle Wilkinson was a known member of the expedition, but evidence suggests his brother James Biddle Wilkinson Jr. was as well. A "J. B. Wilkinson" was reported by Shaler entering *after* this date, and future correspondence from Joseph suggests it was *he* who was acquainted with Shaler, making James the most likely candidate to be with the army in July 1813. One source even claims another son, William Biddle Wilkinson, was involved. Hunter, "The Battle of Alazán," 42.

That General Wilkinson was suspected as a Spanish spy suggests that while he largely beat the charges leveled by Daniel Clark, the latter's drumbeat on the general's suspected treason had hit home for many Burrites. Hunter, "Battle of Alazán," 42. The sole source for W. B. Wilkinson is the article, "Latest from Mexico," *Daily National Intelligencer,* October 6, 1813.
16. Beltrán's account has much of the ring of truth to it, but it must be recalled that he wrote it decades after the fact, while living in Mexico as a Mexican. It was likely set to paper after the Mexican-American War, and like the Anglo writers of the same period (particularly McLane) he recasts the conflict in starker terms of ethnic conflict than the contemporary evidence seems to suggest. Hunter, "The Battle of Alazán," 42–43.
17. Hunter, "The Battle of Alazán," 42.
18. Hunter, "The Battle of Alazán," 42.
19. Hunter, "The Battle of Alazán," 42.
20. Yoakum, *History of Texas*, 1:170. Walker, "William McLane's Narrative," 66, no. 3 (January 1963), 467.
21. Robinson to Monroe, July 26, 1813, CRF.
22. Castañeda, *Our Catholic Heritage in Texas*, 6:105.
23. Republican estimates of the Spanish strength were from 1,500 to 3,000, an exaggeration and possibly a confusion from the large number of non-combatants who traveled with Elizon-

do's force. Folsom, *Arredondo*, 82–83. Hunter, "The Battle of Alazán," 45. Walker, "William McLane's Narrative," 66, no. 3 (January 1963), 469. Gutiérrez to Colonel Nathaniel Cogswell, reprinted in *The Statesman*, August 17, 1813.

24. Folsom, *Arredondo*, 82. Arredondo to Viceroy Calleja, Arredondo, Operaciones, AGM 4(2):42. Arredondo to Elizondo, Arredondo, Operaciones, AGM 4(2), 77–79.

25. Beltrán places Elizondo's ambushes the day before his arrival, which he says was June 16. Antonio Menchaca records the more probable date of June 12, and the account is adjusted accordingly. Folsom, *Arredondo*, 82–83. Robert P. Marshall, "The Battle of the Alazán: First Texas Republic Victorious," *Southwestern Historical Quarterly* 119, no. 1 (July 2015), 48. Ignacio Elizondo to Joaquín de Arredondo, June 18, 1813, quoted in Guedea, "Autonomía e independencia en la provincia de Texas," 175. Matovina and de la Teja, *Recollections of a Tejano Life*, 49.

26. Gaines says the distance to the enemy camp was four miles, McLane says 1½. The latter is the more accurate number given the distance from Alazán Creek to the town as the crow flies. Hunter, "The Battle of Alazán," 43. Walker, "William McLane's Narrative," 66, no. 3 (January 1963), 467–68.

27. "Proclamation of Elizondo," April 19, 1813, BA, RBB S15:207.

28. "Proclamation of Elizondo," April 19, 1813, BA, RBB S15:207.

29. Castañeda, *Our Catholic Heritage in Texas*, 6:107.

30. Hunter, "The Battle of Alazán," 43. Matovina and de la Teja, *Recollections of a Tejano Life*, 49. "News from Mexico," *Alexandria Gazette*, October 14, 1813.

31. Garrett, "Dr. John Sibley," 49, no. 3 (January 1946), 430. Hunter, "The Battle of Alazán," 43.

32. Gulick, *The Papers of Mirabeau Buonaparte Lamar*, 1:282.

33. As noted earlier, Beltran identifies her as Señorita Ochoa, not Barrera. Hunter, "The Battle of Alazán," 44.

34. Hunter, "The Battle of Alazán," 44. Gulick, *The Papers of Mirabeau Buonaparte Lamar*, 1: 282. Walker, "William McLane's Narrative," 66, no. 3 (January 1963), 468.

35. Walker, "William McLane's Narrative," 66, no. 3 (January 1963), 468.

36. Gulick, *The Papers of Mirabeau Buonaparte Lamar*, 1:282. Walker, "William McLane's Narrative," 66, no. 3 (January 1963), 468. Hunter, "The Battle of Alazán," 44.

37. Walker, "William McLane's Narrative," 66, no. 3 (January 1963), 469.

38. Henry Perry was the son of the Reverend Philo Perry, who had been a doctor before being ordained as an Episcopal clergyman. Young Henry trained to be a doctor and was thus, after his father and grandfather, a third-generation physician. William Cothren, *History of Ancient Woodbury, Connecticut, From the First Indian Deed in 1659 to 1854, Including the Present Towns of Washington, Southbury, Bethlehem, Roxbury, and a Part of Oxford and Middlebury* (Waterbury, Connecticut: Bronson Brothers, 1854), 454. Further genealogical information is found at http://www.geni.com, *Rev. Philo Perry Genealogy*, https://www.geni.com/people/Rev-Philo-Perry/6000000028181151909 (accessed May 13, 2020).

39. Walker, "William McLane's Narrative," 66, no. 3 (January 1963): 469.

40. While existing American accounts only mention Elizondo's letter to the Anglo-Americans (with rather mild language), and not his harsh proclamation, it is likely that the latter was addressed to the Mexican contingent and intended for them only, and this proclamation—or rumors of it, had been the cause of their failure to appear at the muster. Gulick, *The Papers of Mirabeau Buonaparte Lamar*, 1:282. Walker, "William McLane's Narrative," 66, no. 3 (January 1963), 467. Gulick, *The Papers of Mirabeau Buonaparte Lamar*, 1: 282. Walker, "William McLane's Narrative," 66, no. 3 (January 1963), 467.

41. Gulick, *The Papers of Mirabeau Buonaparte Lamar*, 1:282. Walker, "William McLane's Narrative," 66, no. 3 (January 1963), 469. Hunter, "The Battle of Alazán," 44.

42. Hunter, "The Battle of Alazán," 45.

43. The account of the confrontation between Perry and Gutiérrez is primarily from Beltrán's account. McLane provides an alternative version, in which he claims that the Mexican contingent once again did not show. Perry, according to this version, sent an ultimatum to Menchaca that if the Mexican contingent did not appear for quarters at 2:00 p.m., he would hand over the men Elizondo requested. "When parade was again called," McLane records, "the Mexicans were the first on the ground. They manifested great anxiety to be led out against the enemy." This account, like much of McLane's narrative, is more derogatory of the Mexicans, and the suggestion that Menchaca, who displayed in battle as much courage as any man in the army would be so tremulous is doubtful. Hunter, "The Battle of Alazán," 45. Walker, "William McLane's Narrative," 66, no. 3 (January 1963), 469.

44. Gaines, who maintains that Ross' girlfriend's father was a royalist, not a Mexican republican officer, reported that she had returned to her father in the Spanish camp with news of Ross's initial decision to retreat. If she or another spy had done so, Elizondo may have chosen to wait out this development in the hopes of descending on the Mexican contingent and defeating them separately. Gulick, *The Papers of Mirabeau Buonaparte Lamar,* 1:282.

45. The numbers reported by the various eyewitnesses vary greatly; however, the order of march document forwarded to William Shaler at the time of the battle lists the numbers given here, and two contemporary accounts in the *Daily National Intelligencer* match this document precisely. This number represents about 200 fewer Anglo-Americans than were shown on a similar document in April, which listed 439 Americans. Both documents can be viewed here: http://www.texhist.com/2022/01/republican-army-strength.html. This suggests the defections in the previous two months had amounted to nearly half the Anglo-American contingent. Richard Santos, "Béxar County's Forgotten Battle of Alzazán Creek," *San Antonio Express News,* Saturday, June 18, 1966. (Santos was the Bexar County Archivist.) Gulick, *The Papers of Mirabeau Buonaparte Lamar,* 1:282. Hunter, "The Battle of Alazán," 46. Bradley, *We Never Retreat,* 78. "Latest from New Spain," *Daily National Intelligencer,* August 16, 1813. "Order of March," CSA. "Report of the Anglo American Companies in the Northern Mexican Army at San Antonio de Béxar, April 9, 1813," in Samuel Sexton file, US National Archives.

46. Gaines dismisses Gutiérrez's men as not participating in the battle, though Beltrán says that according to the promise given by Perry, this contingent filled in the ranks once the battle was underway. Beltrán and McLane agree the battle was fought at dawn, but curiously, Gutiérrez in his contemporary account, states it took place at 11:00 a.m. It seems impossible the republicans could have surprised the enemy at that late hour. "Order of March," CSA. Bradley, *We Never Retreat,* 78. Hunter, "The Battle of Alazán," 46. Walker, "William McLane's Narrative," 66, no. 3 (January 1963), 470. Gutiérrez to Col. Nathaniel Cogswell, reprinted in *The Statesman,* August 17, 1813.

47. Hunter, "The Battle of Alazán," 46.

48. The battlefield has never been discovered but the generally accepted location for the center of the line with appropriate high ground is the current location of Lanier High School. Marshall (2015) a geologist and amateur historian, argues for a location slightly further to the north, placing the Spanish *across* Alazán Creek in a V-shaped spit of land with Martinez Creek on their left flank. This is a good defensive position, and that is the best argument for this location. This, however, would require the republicans to *cross* Alazán Creek (silently, with their cannon) below the V and then strike the Spanish from what effectively was their rear. This would be a bold move but would put the royalists between the republican forces and San Antonio. No account makes such a claim. The creek is not deep in any location—no

"ravine" as Beltrán states—but may also be somewhat changed due to two centuries of erosion. Marshall, "The Battle of the Alazán," 53–56.

Beltrán claims there were twelve Spanish cannons, but McLane and Gutiérrez, the latter writing contemporaneously to the battle, claimed the enemy had only two. Hunter, "The Battle of Alazán," 45–46. Walker, "William McLane's Narrative" 66, no. 3 (January 1963), 470. Gutiérrez to Col. Nathaniel Cogswell, reprinted in *The Statesman*, August 17, 1813.

49. Beltrán claims there were only four Republican cannons, but the order of march shows eight, which divided by wings when the army deployed. It is possible that Beltrán, on one of these wings, only saw its four cannons. "Order of March," CSA.

50. Hunter, "The Battle of Alazán," 46–47.

51. Contemporary news accounts place Dr. Samuel D. Forsyth in command of the artillery, which had been commanded by Thomas Luckett previously, but an account written by John Villars in 1847 placed Young in command. Based on the disposition of the artillery between the right and left wings, there could not have been only one commander for all. Gulick, *The Papers of Mirabeau Buonaparte Lamar*, 6:152. "Latest from New Spain," *Daily National Intelligencer*, August 16, 1813.

52. Most histories have assumed the unknown "Captain Kennedy" to be Joseph Pulaski Kennedy, the Mobile Filibuster and friend of the Kempers. There is no evidence he joined the army, and a "Captain James Kenneday" is shown in a list of members of the Expedition. "List of Claimants against the Mexican Republic," Samuel Sexton file. Walker, "William McLane's Narrative" 66, no. 3 (January 1963), 470.

53. Walker, "William McLane's Narrative," 66, no. 3 (January 1963), 470–71.

54. McDonald, *José Antonio Navarro*, 26.

55. Hunter, "The Battle of Alazán," 46. "Latest from New Spain," *Daily National Intelligencer*, August 16, 1813.

56. Hunter, "The Battle of Alazán," 46.

57. Hunter, "The Battle of Alazán," 46. Walker, "William McLane's Narrative," 66, no. 3 (January 1963), 471.

58. Hunter, "The Battle of Alazán," 46.

59. It is worthy of note that McLane and Beltrán, who are more partial to the Anglos and Mexicans, respectively, gave blame for the massacre to the contingent they *favored*, not to those they typically disparaged. Walker, "William McLane's Narrative," 66, no. 3 (January 1963), 471. Hunter, "The Battle of Alazán," 46.

60. Antonio Menchaca puts the casualty figures far lower, at only "forty or fifty." This is at odds with other sources, and Menchaca, who was twelve years old at the time, was not physically present as he was at other events. "Order of March," CSA. Hunter, "The Battle of Alazán," 46. Matovina and de la Teja, *Recollections of a Tejano Life*, 49. Antonio Padilla to Arredondo, in Arredondo, Operaciones, AGM 4(2):43.

61. Shaler had met Massicott in Cuba and believed him a French agent, but he may have been a Frenchman from New Orleans. Gutiérrez to Col. Nathaniel Cogswell, reprinted in *The Statesman*, August 17, 1813. Anonymous [Navarro] account in Gulick, *The Papers of Mirabeau Buonaparte Lamar*, 4(2):9.

62. It is likely that the Americans engaged liberally in this trade, for at the Battle of Medina, the army was woefully short of horses, despite the vast numbers captured two months before. Hunter, "The Battle of Alazán," 46. Santos, "Béxar County's Forgotten Battle of Alzazán Creek."

Chapter 20

1. Gutiérrez to Col. Nathaniel Cogswell, reprinted in *The Statesman*, August 17, 1813.
2. The newspaper, like many Spanish documents at the time, used the spelling *Texas*, not *Tejas*, which would be more common in the Mexican period. *Gaceta de Texas* copy in CSA. Garrett, "The First Newspaper of Texas," 200–215.
3. This claim is inaccurate, as there were other insurgent papers in other regions of Mexico. Sibley, *Lone Stars and State Gazettes*, 22–23.
4. The paper even apologized for "introducing to notice so insignificant and contemptable a character as José Bernardo Gutiérrez." *El Mexicano*, June 19, 1813. Copy in the Cammie G. Henry Research Center, Northwestern State University, Natchitoches, LA.
5. *El Mexicano*, June 19, 1813.
6. The source suggests the date of the meeting may have either been the 15th or 19th. Sumaria Ynformacion formada contra D. José Erasmo Seguín, Admor. de Correos de esta Capital acusado de Ynfidente [1814], Archivo General del Estado de Coahuila, Fondo Colonial, C35, E53. Unpublished translation by Jesús F. de la Teja.
7. In addition to Juan and María Leonidas Seguín, Erasmo had another son in between them named Tómas, who died in infancy. Jesús F. de la Teja, *A Revolution Remembered: The Memoirs and Selected Correspondence of Juan N. Seguín* (Austin: State House Press, 1991), 4.

Seguín told his fellow cellmate Bernardo Amado that he would never join the insurgent party or act against the interests of the king. Chabot, *Makers*, 118–22. Sumaria Ynformacion formada contra D. José Erasmo Seguín.

8. Shaler described Arocha as "surely so miserable a wretch was never before sent on a public mission." Of Seguín and another aide, however, he described them as "young men of promising appearance." Seguín took credit for talking Arocha out of his mission, but both Shaler and Arocha himself say it was the American agent, whom Arocha recalled (phonetically in Spanish), "Charlir."

Lt. Anselmo Pereyra, questioned on his knowledge of Seguín's loyalty, said, that Seguín supported the royalists in private, but the rebels in their presence. Sumaria Ynformacion formada contra D. José Erasmo Seguín.

9. All that is known of what followed was reported in a later trial of Seguín for treason by the royalists, and Seguín's statements must be weighed against this fact. The bulk of the evidence does support the contention that he was pushed into the rebellion against his will, and indeed, he was found not guilty by the trial. Sumaria Ynformacion formada contra D. José Erasmo Seguín.
10. Sumaria Ynformacion formada contra D. José Erasmo Seguín.
11. Cogswell's letter to Gutiérrez was not intended for Shaler to see but appears to have been copied by Dr. Samuel D. Forsyth, an American volunteer in the Republican Army with close access to Gutiérrez. Shaler to Monroe, July 10, 1813, and Cogswell to Gutiérrez, Date Unknown, CSA.
12. Cogswell to Gutiérrez, Date Unknown, CSA. Shaler to Monroe, July 10, 1813, CSA.
13. Cogswell to Gutiérrez, Date Unknown, CSA.
14. Cogswell to Gutiérrez, Date Unknown, CSA.
15. Cogswell to Gutiérrez, Date Unknown, CSA.
16. It remains unclear if Mower himself was at the "trial," though the central points of his arguments were probably represented. His deposition was apparently taken by Shaler during his very brief visit to Nacogdoches subsequent to the June 29th meeting. Aaron Mower, Deposition before William Shaler, undated (probably June–July 1813), CSA.
17. Shaler to Monroe, July 10, 1813, CSA.

18. Powell, *List of Officers of the Army of the United States from 1779 to 1900*, 64.
19. [Bullard], "A Visit to Texas."
20. While sources never explicitly state his first name, a letter written by Joseph Wilkinson to Shaler demonstrates they knew each other, and Shaler is apparently ignorant of a second Wilkinson son possibly in Texas. Bullard to Shaler, June 24, 1813, and Joseph Wilkinson to Shaler, June 25, 1813, CSA.
21. Gutiérrez to Col. Nathaniel Cogswell, reprinted in *The Statesman*, August 17, 1813.
22. Bullard to Shaler, June 24, 1813, CSA.
23. Bullard to Shaler, June 24, 1813, CSA.
24. Joseph Wilkinson to Shaler, June 25, 1813, CSA.
25. Bullard to Shaler, June 24, 1813, CSA.
26. Bullard to Shaler, June 24, 1813, CSA.
27. Joseph Wilkinson to Shaler, June 25, 1813, and Bullard to Shaler, June 24, 1813, CSA.
28. Bullard to Shaler, June 24, 1813, Correspondence of Special Agents.
29. Bullard to Shaler, June 24, 1813, Correspondence of Special Agents.
30. Bullard to Shaler, June 24, 1813, Correspondence of Special Agents.
31. Bullard to Shaler, June 24, 1813, Correspondence of Special Agents.
32. Bullard to Shaler, June 24, 1813, Correspondence of Special Agents.
33. Bullard to Shaler, June 24, 1813, Correspondence of Special Agents.
34. Samuel D. Forsyth to William Shaler, June 28, 1813, Correspondence of Special Agents.
35. Bullard to Shaler, June 24, 1813, CSA.
36. Though Beltrán claimed Gutiérrez had fought at the head of his troops at Alazán, no other sources confirm it and no other writer except Gutiérrez himself *years later* ever places him in combat in any other battle. Joseph Wilkinson to Shaler, June 25, 1813, CSA.
37. Anonymous [Navarro] account in Gulick, *The Papers of Mirabeau Buonaparte Lamar*, 4(2):8–9.
38. Anonymous [Navarro] account in Gulick, *The Papers of Mirabeau Buonaparte Lamar*, 4(2):8–9.
39. Gutiérrez de Lara to the Mexican Congress, "Account of Progress of the Revolution from the Beginning," in Gulick, *The Papers of Mirabeau Buonaparte Lamar,* 1:5, 20. Bullard, "A Visit to Texas," 234.
40. The article was prefaced by the words, "We have been politely favored with the following copy of an official letter, received at Alexandria, (Rapids of the Red River) by a gentleman who arrived in this city last evening from that place." The letter was addressed to Cogswell by Gutiérrez on the date of the battle. "Another Victory," *The Statesman,* August 17, 1813. "Died at the Rapids of the Red River," New Hampshire Patriot and State Gazette, August 2, 1814; and New England Palladium, August 5, 1814. Jameson, *The Cogswells in America*, 183.
41. Shaler to Monroe, July 14, 1813, Shaler Letterbooks.
42. Monroe to Shaler, September 1, 1812, Shaler Papers.
43. Monroe to Shaler, June 5, 1813, Shaler Papers.
44. Shaler to Monroe, July 20, 1813, and August 7, 1813, Shaler Letterbooks.
45. Shaler to Monroe, August 7, 1813, Shaler Letterbooks.
46. Shaler to Monroe, August 7, 1813, Shaler Letterbooks.
47. "Translated for the Aurora," *Daily National Intelligencer* (Washington, DC), November 15, 1813.
48. Shaler to Monroe, August 7, 1813, Shaler Letterbooks. Hunter, "The Battle of Medina," 9.
49. Shaler to Monroe, August 7, 1813, Shaler Letterbooks. Anonymous [Navarro] account in Gulick, *The Papers of Mirabeau Buonaparte Lamar*, 4(2):10.

50. "Liberty of conscience" was a sticking point between the Anglo and Mexican factions. The Mexicans insisted on Toledo opposing the idea, as they saw such a principle as an attack against the Catholic Church. Béxar Junta to Toledo, June 28, 1813, CSA. "New Mexico," *Norwich Courier*, September 1, 1813.

51. Menchaca Commission from Gutiérrez, in Warren, *The Sword Was Their Passport*.

52. Beltrán also put words in Menchaca's mouth predicting Toledo would abandon the rebels and "will yet be found holding a commission under the crown of Spain," which he in fact did hold two years later. Such a comment is plausible, but the prediction reads like hindsight, given the account was written decades after Toledo had in fact famously betrayed the rebel cause. Shaler to Monroe, August 7, 1813, Shaler Letterbooks. Gulick, *The Papers of Mirabeau Buonaparte Lamar*, 1:282. John Warren Hunter, "The Battle of the Medina," *Frontier Times* 3, no. 3 (December 1925), 9.

53. Anonymous account, Archivo General de Indias, Spanish Materials from Various Sources, Briscoe Center for American History, University of Texas at Austin. This account, a Spanish translation of a since-lost article that appeared in the Lexington Reporter in 1815, contains numerous unique details and is generally pro-Toledo. It also gives more depth and color to the controversy between Toledo and Menchaca, who was allied with Tomás de Arocha in opposing the general. It is a copy signed by Patricio Humana, Mexico City, June 30, 1815. Humana was the secretary of Viceroy Calleja, and as a royalist, he likely simply transcribed a rebel account, rather than authored it.

54. Folsom, *Arredondo*, 83–84. Arredondo to Elizondo, July 28, 1813, Arredondo, Operaciones, AGM 4(2): 77–79. Mattie Austin Hatcher, "Joaquín de Árredondo's Report of the Battle of the Medina, August 18, 1813. Translation," *Quarterly of the Texas State Historical Association* 11, no. 3 (1908): 220. http://www.jstor.org/stable/30242929 (accessed May 14, 2020).

55. Folsom, *Arredondo*, 74, 86. Bradley, *We Never Retreat*, 84.

56. Hunter, "The Battle of Medina," 11. Folsom, *Arredondo*, 84–87. Arredondo to Elizondo, July 28, 1813, Arredondo, Operaciones, AGM 4(2): 77–79.

57. Hatcher, "Joaquín de Arredondo's Report," 221.

58. Hatcher, "Joaquín de Arredondo's Report," 221.

59. Hatcher, "Joaquín de Arredondo's Report," 221.

60. The size of the army will be elaborated upon later in this chapter during the discussion of its structure. The account of Toledo changing the composition of the army is found only in a note to Lamar from Richard Royster Royall, but it contains numerous errors and cannot be verified elsewhere. Royall was a citizen of the Republic of Texas who was too young to have first-hand knowledge of the 1812–13 war. However, a possible relative, James Royall, was a member of the Republican Army. Gulick, *The Papers of Mirabeau Buonaparte Lamar*, 5:366.

61. Order of José Alvarez de Toledo to Henry Perry, August 5, 1813, quoted in Guedea, "Autonomía e independencia en la provincia de Texas," 178.

62. Folsom, *Arredondo*, 87. Gulick, *The Papers of Mirabeau Buonaparte Lamar*, 5: 366. Hunter, "The Battle of Medina," 11. Anonymous account, Archivo General de Indias.

63. Menchaca's comments were recorded by Beltrán. Hunter, "The Battle of Medina," 11–12.

64. "Minutes of the Governmental Junta of Béxar," March 6, 1811, Béxar archives. Folsom, *Arredondo*, 87. Gulick, *The Papers of Mirabeau Buonaparte Lamar*, 5:366. Hunter, "The Battle of Medina," 11.

65. "Memoria de las cosas mas notables que acaesieron en Bexar el año de 13." This account is from the Tejano, vice Toledo, perspective. Both sides tend to show their own preferred leader with the initiative and courage and the other with cowardice and temerity.

66. Folsom, *Arredondo*, 87. Gulick, *The Papers of Mirabeau Buonaparte Lamar*, 5:366. Hunter, "The Battle of Medina," 11.

67. Hunter, "The Battle of Medina," 12.
68. José Maria Guadiana, Order of March of Republican Army, August 13, 1813, Historia, Operaciones de Guerra, Arredondo, 1813–20, 4(2): 100–101.
69. Later republican sources give the following size of the army: Joseph Wilkinson, 1,200; Bullard, 1,500; and Beltrán, 1,800 (consisting of 1,000 Mexicans and 800 Americans). After the battle, Kemper and Toledo told an American newspaper editor that there were about 450 Americans and between 600–700 Mexicans, for just under 1,000 (almost certainly downplayed). The source for Kemper and Toledo's numbers is the following article: "We have no further Particulars of the affair of the 18th ult. near San Antonio," *Daily National Intelligencer*, October 18, 1813. Joseph Wilkinson to Shaler, June 25, 1813. CSA. [Bullard], "A Visit to Texas." Hunter, "The Battle of Medina," 10.

There are two documents, both captured by Arredondo, which outline the Republican Army's order of battle. The first is a letter from Guadiana to Henry Perry on August 5th and the second is Guadiana's order of march on August 13th. A detailed accounting of these sources and the estimates provided here can be found at James Aalan Bernsen, "Republican Army Strength," *The Texas History Blog*, http://www.texhist.com/2022/01/republican-army-strength.html (accessed January 14, 2022).

Orden del ciuadaño General José Alvarez de Toledo al ciuadaño Coronel Henry Peres, Comandante en gefe de los Voluntarios Americanos del Ejercito Republicano del Norte de México," August 5, 1813, Arredondo, Operaciones, AGM 4(2):193–95. José Maria Guadiana, Order of March of Republican Army, August 13, 1813, Arredondo, Operaciones, AGM 4(2):100–101. Hunter, "The Battle of Medina," 9.

70. Orden del ciuadaño General José Alvarez de Toledo al ciuadaño Coronel Henry Peres, Comandante en gefe de los Voluntarios Americanos del Ejercito Republicano del Norte de México," August 5, 1813, Arredondo, Operaciones, AGM 4(2):193–95.

71. Although Beltrán and other sources say it was only on August 17th, Guadiana's orders place it on August 14th. The anonymous account in the Archivo General de Indias also supports August 14th. José Maria Guadiana, Order of March of Republican Army, August 13, 1813, Arredondo, Operaciones, AGM 4(2):100–101. Folsom, *Arredondo*, 87–88. Walker, "William McLane's Narrative," *SWHQ* vol. 66, no. 3 (January 1963), 474. Hunter, "The Battle of Medina," 12. Anonymous account, Archivo General de Indias.

72. The army's movements are subjects of great confusion. Antonio Menchaca writes that the first night, the Republican Army camped at "Laguna de la Espada," though no historian can identify this unknown lake. An intriguing possibility is today's Mitchell Lake, Southwest of the Mission Espada, one of the few natural lakes south of the city. Although most Spanish sources give this lake a different name, Menchaca may preserve a forgotten alternate name. At about nine miles, it is consistent for a day's march. The army likely stayed there a few days before moving into its planned ambush position South of the Medina River. Matovina and de la Teja, *Recollections of a Tejano Life*, 50. Hunter, "The Battle of Medina," 12. Gulick, *The Papers of Mirabeau Buonaparte Lamar*, 5:366.

Chapter 21

1. The Camino que Cortaba is likely today's Pleasanton Road. In 1813, it was an alternative route of the Béxar to Laredo Road.

The location of the largest battle ever fought in Texas is shrouded in confusion. This version draws from five accounts claiming to be firsthand: Those of Carlos Beltrán, Henry Adams Bullard, William McLane, James Gaines, and an unnamed Tejano, as well as letters from survivors and information from additional sources, including a modern analysis by geologist

Robert Marshall. They are combined in this account, with significant variances between accounts noted as necessary. A full study of the literary and archaeological evidence is beyond the scope of this study. Beltran, "Battle of Medina," 11–13. [Bullard], "A Visit to Texas," 240–42. Walker, "McLane's Narrative," 66, no. 3 (January 1963), 474–78. Gaines's account in Gulick, *The Papers of Mirabeau Buonaparte Lamar*, 1:283. Robert P. Marshall, "Archeological Confirmation of the Site of the Battle of Medina: A Research Note," *Southwestern Historical Quarterly* 71, no. 1 [July 2017]: 57–66.

The Béxar Junta had initially made Toledo's invitation to come to Texas conditional on not serving as commander in the field. This condition was evidently removed at some point following his arrival.

2. It is unclear if Maj. William Murray, the other Burr conspirator, was still with the army. He had dined with Salcedo following the taking of San Antonio but is not mentioned in any source after the murder of the Spanish officers. Presumably, he was among those who left in protest over that act.

Navarro states there were nine cannon firing balls from four pounds to eight. Against this, the Spanish supposedly had eighteen pieces of heavy ordnance. He also says that some Mexicans from Tamaulipas and the Rio Grande (then outside the borders of Texas) had made their way to San Antonio to join the republicans.

Beltran describes the Republican Army as having a right and left wing, with artillery in the center. Bullard does not specifically break it down this way, but his account does not contradict this. McLane describes alternating Anglo and Mexican companies but does not describe how they fit into the two commands, though a plan similar to that of Alazán would have divided them equally among the two wings. Antonio Menchaca (who was not an eyewitness) in his memoirs places Delgado on the left wing and Miguel Menchaca on the right, which seems at odds with other accounts, but this may be a confusion since the republican right, seen on a map, was actually on the left as oriented north to south. The extreme flanks of the army were Mexican troops because they would have by necessity been cavalry. Hunter, "The Battle of Medina," 11–13. [Bullard], "A Visit to Texas," 240–42. Walker, "McLane's Narrative," 66, no. 3 (January 1963), 474–8. Hunter, "The Battle of Medina," 12. Antonio Menchaca, *Memoirs*, 16–17. Anonymous [Navarro] account in Gulick, *The Papers of Mirabeau Buonaparte Lamar*, 4(2):10.

3. Hunter, "The Battle of Medina," 11–13. [Bullard], "A Visit to Texas," 240–42. Walker, "McLane's Narrative," 66, no. 3 (January 1963), 474–8. Folsom, *Arredondo*, 87–88. Anonymous account, Archivo General de Indias.

4. "Memoria de las cosas mas notables que acaesieron en Bexar el año de 13."

5. The date at which these actions took place is noted as the sixteenth in some sources, but it seems unlikely Arredondo waited an entire day before reconnoitering. The scouts' failure to locate the republicans suggests the rebels were not on the main road for the ambush, or even any secondary one, unless they subsequently took up that position.

6. Castañeda, *Our Catholic Heritage in Texas*, 6:113–15. Folsom, *Arredondo*, 88. Hatcher, "Joaquín de Arredondo's Report," 223.

7. Matovina and de la Teja, *Recollections of a Tejano Life*, 51.

8. In most American accounts, it was Menchaca and Kemper who pursued beyond the prepared positions, while Beltrán claims Toledo gave the order and the Anglo-Americans protested. Beltran, it must be noted, was very hostile to Toledo, and this account is contradicted by Gaines and Antonio Menchaca, who describe the Anglos and Mexicans equally eager to attack. Folsom, in reviewing the Spanish sources, also suggests Toledo gave the order, though this may have been the much more conditional order suggested by Antonio Menchaca. An anonymous, pro-Toledo account states that several pieces of Spanish artillery

were captured, indicating Elizondo's action was a reconnaissance in force rather than a simple patrol. Folsom, *Arredondo*, 88. Hunter, "The Battle of Medina," 12. Matovina and de la Teja, *Recollections of a Tejano Life*, 51. Gulick, *The Papers of Mirabeau Buonaparte Lamar*, 1:283. Anonymous account, Archivo General de Indias.

9. Matovina and de la Teja, *Recollections of a Tejano Life*, 51.

10. Anglos contemptuous of Gutiérrez had only agreed to surrender authority to a Hispanic leader of whom they approved (Toledo). The Anglo-Americans seem to have viewed the Cuban as more like themselves. He was more refined, cosmopolitan, and certainly spoke some English. He was also a Freemason, as were likely many of the Americans. Gutiérrez, in contrast, was a provincial Catholic who spoke little English. These factors certainly made them less prejudicial against Toledo than they had been against Gutiérrez.

11. Walker, "McLane's Narrative," 66, no. 3 (January 1963), 476. [Bullard], "A Visit to Texas," 242. Matovina and de la Teja, *Recollections of a Tejano Life*, 52. "Memoria de las cosas mas notables que acaesieron en Bexar el año de 13."

12. Hunter, "The Battle of Medina," 13. [Bullard], "A Visit to Texas," 242.

13. Once again, Beltran's version is different, as he insisted that Kemper and Menchaca had opposed the advance and were the first to recognize that the attack was running into danger. Gaines, while still making Kemper and Menchaca the heroes of his version, insists that they were enthusiastic in the charge while Toledo's hesitation caused confusion and poor execution. Gaines's version suggests Kemper and Menchaca as "personally opposed" to Toledo. This was certainly true for Menchaca. As for Kemper, his Americans had demanded Toledo replace Gutiérrez only a few weeks before, but notably this happened while Kemper was on furlough, and Reuben Kemper had sought to have Toledo imprisoned in Natchez. Gulick, *The Papers of Mirabeau Buonaparte Lamar*, 1:283

14. Folsom, *Arredondo*, 90. Anonymous account, Archivo General de Indias.

15. Bradley, *We Never Retreat*, 86. Gulick, *The Papers of Mirabeau Buonaparte Lamar*, 1:283. Hunter, "The Battle of Medina," 13. Folsom, *Arredondo*, 91.

16. Hunter, "The Battle of Medina," 13.

17. Gaines claims the Mexican retreat caused the rout of the republican forces, but this clearly represents a bias against the Mexicans. There was heroism and panic aplenty in both Mexican and American contingents (and the Spanish too), reflecting just how close-run the battle was. Hunter, "The Battle of Medina," 13. Bradley, *We Never Retreat*, 86.

18. Hunter, "The Battle of Medina," 13.

19. Bradley, *We Never Retreat*, 87, 91.

20. Anonymous account, Archivo General de Indias.

21. Gulick, *The Papers of Mirabeau Buonaparte Lamar*, 1: 283. Hunter, "The Battle of Medina," 13.

22. The unknown Tejano who penned an account said of this moment, "In the confusion of the battle, [Arredondo] ordered his buglers to sound out the notes of Victory. The familiar sound animated his troops and struck fear into the Republican ranks." Hatcher, "Joaquín de Arredondo's Report," 225. "Memoria de las cosas mas notables que acaesieron en Bexar el año de 13, Mandando el Tirano Arredondo." [1813] BANC MSS P-O 811, The Bancroft Library, University of California, Berkeley.

23. Hatcher, "Joaquín de Arredondo's Report," 226–32. Chabot, *Texas in 1811*, 118.

24. J. B. Wilkinson to Shaler, [unknown, probably late August] 1813, CSA. Hunter, "The Battle of Medina," 13.

25. Arredondo claimed one of General Wilkinson's sons was found dead on the battlefield, but this is unlikely. Joseph and likely James Wilkinson escaped to Louisiana. The Spanish general incorrectly attributed to "Wilkinson's son" the position of commander of the

Anglo-American volunteers. Hunter, "The Battle of Medina," 13–14. Hatcher, "Joaquín de Arredondo's Report," 226–29. Wilkinson's Account, CSA. Gulick, *The Papers of Mirabeau Buonaparte Lamar*, 1:283. Bradly, *We Never Retreat*, 87.

26. Bradly, *We Never Retreat*, 87.

27. Account of Lamar in Gulick, *The Papers of Mirabeau Buonaparte Lamar*, 4(1):123.

28. Beltrán's description, derided as romanticized by some historians, perfectly meshes in this context with other sources, and he appears to be describing something akin to an aid station on the battlefield, likely at the republican position where they had initially planned to ambush the Spanish. McLane claims that many new enlistees in the army from among the local population switched sides to slaughter Americans, even quartering some of them to please Arredondo. No other source makes the claim, which should be viewed in light of McLane's racial animosity. Hunter, "The Battle of Medina," 13–14. Bradley, *We Never Retreat*, 87. Matovina and de la Teja, *Recollections of a Tejano Life*, 52. Anonymous [Navarro] account in Gulick, *The Papers of Mirabeau Buonaparte Lamar*, 4(2):10.

29. Folsom, *Arredondo*, 92. Hatcher, "Joaquín de Arredondo's Report," 220.

30. Although early reports claimed only one hundred Anglo-Americans survived (and this has previously been accepted by most historians), a subsequent, never-before-cited report proves this incorrect. By September 17th, American papers could report the news (almost certainly from Samuel Kemper) that "upwards of two hundred of the Americans have got in, and it is expected many more are on the way." Assuming prebattle numbers of six to eight hundred Anglo participants, then their dead would be between four and six hundred. Arredondo also wrote of the dead, "The greater part were Americans." This is likely given these numbers. Arredondo almost certainly padded his numbers, but Toledo and Kemper did as well. Speaking to an American newspaper editor a month after the battle, they downplayed the total republican losses as under two hundred. "Mexican News," *Daily National Intelligencer*, October 30, 1813. "We have No further Particulars of the affair of the 18th ult. near San Antonio," *Daily National Intelligencer*, October 18, 1813. Hatcher, "Joaquín de Arredondo's Report," 225. Matovina and de la Teja, *Recollections of a Tejano Life*, 52. "Mexican War," *Pennsylvania Gazette*, November 10, 1813.

31. Hatcher, "Joaquín de Arredondo's Report," 229.

32. Folsom, *Arredondo*, 92.

33. McDonald, *José Antonio Navarro*, 29. Hunter, "The Battle of Medina," 14.

34. Hunter, "The Battle of Medina," 14–15.

35. Of the 204 members of the expedition this author has identified, only one person other than Beltrán claimed to have escaped, "by traveling at night and hiding with friendly Indians during the day." This individual, whose story matches Beltrán's, is A. W. McClain, a native of North Carolina. The first name is unknown, but it is certainly plausible that his first name was Abner and Beltrán, writing decades later, simply assumed Lane instead of McClain. A. W. McClain is a separate individual from William McLane, who was also in the expedition and chronicled it. A. W. returned to Texas, settling in Houston County as part of Austin's Old 300. Lester G. Bugbee, "The Old Three Hundred," *Texas Historical Association Quarterly* 1 no. 2 (October 1897): 114. Schwartz, *Forgotten Battlefield*, 122. Hunter, "The Battle of Medina," 14–15.

36. "Mexican News," *Daily National Intelligencer*, October 30, 1813. "We have No further Particulars of the affair of the 18th ult. near San Antonio," *Daily National Intelligencer*, October 18, 1813.

37. José Antonio Salcedo to Governor of Texas, March 8, 1814, RBB S8:68. "Memoria de las cosas mas notables que acaesieron en Bexar el año de 13, Mandando el Tirano Arredondo."

Chabot, *With the Makers of San Antonio*, 153. John Edward Weems, *Men without Countries* (Boston: Houghton Mifflin Company, 1969), 55, 61. Wilson and Jackson, *Philip Nolan and Texas*, 79.

38. Bradley, *We Never Retreat*, 88.

39. The *Daily National Intelligencer*, citing the *Red River Herald*, reported, "there were 40 or 50 sick and disabled in the hospital at St. Antonio, have fallen into their hands." Both Darius and Orramel Johnston were captured in the battle, and would suffer greatly in their imprisonment. "We have No further Particulars of the affair of the 18th ult. near San Antonio," *Daily National Intelligencer*, October 18, 1813. Bradley, *We Never Retreat*, 89. Folsom, *Arredondo*, 93.

40. Hunter, "The Battle of Medina," 15.

41. Various sources suggest Arredondo arrived in San Antonio on the evening of the nineteenth or twentieth. Given the recovery time from the battle and the distance to march, it seems more likely that Elizondo's cavalry began the arrests and purges on the nineteenth, while Arredondo's army arrived on the twentieth. "La Noche Triste" as Beltrán describes it, was probably the first night when Elizondo held the town, although certainly the next few days merged into one horrifying memory for the survivors. Hunter, "The Battle of Medina," 15.

42. Folsom, *Arredondo*, 96. Hunter, "The Battle of Medina," 15. Chabot, *Menchaca*, 17–18.

43. Folsom, *Arredondo*, 96. Hunter, "The Battle of Medina," 15. Chabot, *Menchaca*, 17–18. "Memoria de las cosas mas notables que acaesieron en Bexar el año de 13, Mandando el Tirano Arredondo." Anonymous [Navarro] account in Gulick, *The Papers of Mirabeau Buonaparte Lamar*, 4(2):11.

44. Folsom, *Arredondo*, 97. Hunter, "The Battle of Medina," 15. Anonymous [Navarro] account in Gulick, *The Papers of Mirabeau Buonaparte Lamar*, 4(2):11.

45. Folsom, *Arredondo*, 97. Hunter, "The Battle of Medina," 15. "Memoria de las cosas mas notables que acaesieron en Bexar el año de 13, Mandando el Tirano Arredondo." Account of Lamar in Gulick, *The Papers of Mirabeau Buonaparte Lamar,* 4(1):124. (This account is also based on Navarro.)

46. "Memoria de las cosas mas notables que acaesieron en Bexar el año de 13, Mandando el Tirano Arredondo."

47. Folsom, *Arredondo*, 97.

48. Chabot, *Menchaca*, 17.

49. Hunter, "The Battle of Medina," 15. Anonymous [Navarro] account in Gulick, *The Papers of Mirabeau Buonaparte Lamar*, 4(2):10–11.

50. Menchaca places the number who died in the building at eight rather than eighteen. Hunter, "The Battle of Medina," 16. Chabot, *Menchaca*, 18.

51. Ignacio Pérez served as a royalist officer throughout the war and served as interim governor of Texas in 1816–17. Matovina and de la Teja, *Recollections of a Tejano Life*, 49, n33. Gulick, *The Papers of Mirabeau Buonaparte Lamar*, 6:340. Chabot, *Menchaca*, 17.

Chabot, *Makers of San Antonio*, 194. Chabot, *Menchaca*, 18.

52. Gulick, *The Papers of Mirabeau Buonaparte Lamar*, 6:339.

53. Hunter, "The Battle of Medina," 16.

54. The following details are from Elizondo's own account of his actions, which he sent to Arredondo, "Report of the Reduction of Trinidad de Salcedo, by Lt. Col. Ignacio Elizondo of the Royal Spanish Army, 6 September 1813," translated by independent researcher Bob Skiles, January 13, 2013, https://upload.wikimedia.org/wikipedia/commons/6/6a/Aftermath_of _Medina_4_-_destruction_of_Trinidad_de_Salcedo.pdf (accessed May 14, 2020). The original source is the *Gazette of the Government of Mexico*, November 9, 1813.

55. Arredondo, "Report of the Reduction of Trinidad."
56. Chabot, *Menchaca*, 18.
57. Schwartz, *Forgotten Battlefield,* 111.
58. "Memoria de las cosas mas notables que acaesieron en Bexar el año de 13, Mandando el Tirano Arredondo."
59. "Memoria de las cosas mas notables que acaesieron en Bexar el año de 13, Mandando el Tirano Arredondo."
60. This account of the anonymous Tejano source closely matches the memoirs of José Antonio Navarro, although the latter tells it with no names included, from the perspective of a young woman only identified as "La Bexareña." The killing of Delgado matches precisely, and the unknown woman was a niece of his, who was sent along with the surviving women, back to be imprisoned in San Antonio. "Memoria de las cosas mas notables que acaesieron en Bexar el año de 13, Mandando el Tirano Arredondo." McDonald, *José Antonio Navarro*, 30.
61. "Memoria de las cosas mas notables que acaesieron en Bexar el año de 13, Mandando el Tirano Arredondo."
62. "Memoria de las cosas mas notables que acaesieron en Bexar el año de 13, Mandando el Tirano Arredondo."
63. The Jaranama Indians, more frequently spelled Aranama, were a coastal tribe who probably spoke the Coahuilitecan language. Their numbers declined until they disappeared in the 1840s, probably merged into the Spanish-speaking population. "Report of the Reduction of Trinidad." Thomas N. Campbell, "Aranama Indians," *HOTO*, https://www.tshaonline.org/handbook/entries/aranama-indians (accessed December 11, 2021).
64. Some sources incorrectly state that Tomás de Arocha was beheaded by the Spaniards, in the presence of his wife. He was not and was later awarded a pardon. He was alive and testified in Erasmo Seguín's treason trial in January 1814. "Report of the Reduction of Trinidad."
65. "Report of the Reduction of Trinidad." Gulick, *The Papers of Mirabeau Buonaparte Lamar*, 6:153.
66. McDonald, *José Antonio Navarro*, 30. Epperson, *Lost Spanish Towns,* 60.
67. "Report of the Reduction of Trinidad."
68. Menchaca records Elizondo only captured nine Americans, who were released. However, a news article and series of letters in the United States recorded twenty-nine Americans, including Cage and John Villars, who were taken prisoner and confined in San Antonio. Villars, it is known, was subsequently transferred to Monterrey. Cage, and likely others, were still imprisoned as late as June 1819. This group of Americans was not exhaustive of all prisoners (Darius and Orramel Johnston and Peter Boone, also captured, were not on it); it was only the list known in the United States. Menchaca, *Memoirs*, 19. Jackson, Andrew, and James Cage. James Cage to Andrew Jackson. 1815. Andrew Jackson Papers: Series 1, General Correspondence and Related Items, 1775 to 1885 (15,697) US Library of Congress, Manuscript/Mixed Material, https://www.loc.gov/item/maj005852/ (accessed October 30, 2021). Schwartz, *Forgotten Battlefield*, 109. "Mr. Isler," *Mississippi Free Trader*, December 1, 1813. US Department of State, *Calendar of the Miscellaneous Letters of the Department of State from the Organization of the Government to 1820* (Washington, DC: Government Printing Office, 1897), 53.
69. The shocking claim that Elizondo committed no murders suggests something beyond gullibility on the part of Toledo and Kemper. As Elizondo had once been a rebel, it is not improbable they hoped to woo him in the future by planting such stories in the American press. To even think this was possible, however, shows that they had no true conception of his extreme of brutality at the time they gave this account. Bradley, *We Never Retreat*, 89. Folsom, *Arredondo*, 98. "Mexican News," *Daily National Intelligencer*, October 30, 1813.

NOTES TO PAGES 312–315   443

70. The account of the priest participating in the executions comes from José Antonio Navarro. This is not reported in Lamar's recording, although he likely used Navarro for his source. He also gives an alternative name for the priest: Padre Borrego, although Camacho, noted in Arredondo's letters, is more likely. Another account, also in Lamar, and certainly with Navarro as the source, says Padre Camacho gave the rebels confession, then violated his oath and informed of their participation in the rebellion to the executioners. Bradley, *We Never Retreat*, 89. Folsom, *Arredondo*, 98. Matovina and de la Teja, *Recollections of a Tejano Life*, 54n51. Account of Lamar in Gulick, *The Papers of Mirabeau Buonaparte Lamar*, 4(1):123. Anonymous [Navarro] account in Gulick, *The Papers of Mirabeau Buonaparte Lamar*, 4(2):11. Arredondo to Elizondo, Arredondo, Operaciones, AGM 4(2), 77.

71. This account is from a genealogical source on the Munson family of Texas, which speculates that Henry Munson was part of the staff at the Battle of Medina. Given his youth growing up in the same small community as Kemper, it is likely he was connected to him. The Munson history does not identify the "Mordello" in question but notes he is a relative of General José Félix Trespalacios, by which he can be properly identified as Santiago Mordella. Thurmond A. Williamson, *The Munsons of Texas—an American Saga* (self-published genealogical manuscript, 1987), http://www.munsons-of-texas.net/c7.html (accessed August 7, 2019). Mary M. Brown, *A School History of Texas, from Its Discovery in 1685 to 1893* (Dallas: Mary M. Brown, 1894), 58. Bradley, *We Never Retreat*, 195.

72. "Report of the Reduction of Trinidad." Anonymous [Navarro] account in Gulick, *The Papers of Mirabeau Buonaparte Lamar*, 4(2):12.

73. Elizondo himself suggested that the officer was "losing his marbles"—"perdiendo la chaveta"—before the encounter. Lamar, on the other hand, preserves an account that "His insanity . . . was affected to escape punishment." He did indeed escape death and was sent to the interior of Mexico to be imprisoned for insanity. Serrano on his march to Mexico "kept cursing Elisondo & others for murdering the people of the Trinity; and said that he done it [*sic*] to please his master the King, who he knew would [neve]r sanction such cruelties." Cox, "Field Survey and Archival Research for the Rosillo Creek," 25. Matovina and de la Teja, *Recollections of a Tejano Life*, 55n52–53. Nemesio Salcedo to Governor Antonio Cordero, April 4, 1808, BA, RBB S6: 223. Folsom, *Arredondo*, 99. Chabot, *Menchaca*, 19. Gulick, *The Papers of Mirabeau Buonaparte Lamar*, 6:339. Guedea, "Autonomía e independencia en la provincia de Texas," 179. Account of Lamar in Gulick, *The Papers of Mirabeau Buonaparte Lamar*, 4(1):123.

74. "Memoria de las cosas mas notables que acaesieron en Bexar el año de 13, Mandando el Tirano Arredondo."

75. "Memoria de las cosas mas notables que acaesieron en Bexar el año de 13, Mandando el Tirano Arredondo."

76. The account further suggests that women were present at the actual Battle of Medina. One Spaniard taunts them, "What did you think would happen to you, rebel whores? Riding around on saddles like men! Grasping the saddle horn for all to see!" It is the only account that suggests this. "Memoria de las cosas mas notables que acaesieron en Bexar el año de 13, Mandando el Tirano Arredondo." Folsom, *Arredondo*, 99. Chabot, *Menchaca*, 19.

77. "Memoria de las cosas mas notables que acaesieron en Bexar el año de 13, Mandando el Tirano Arredondo."

78. Folsom, *Arredondo*, 99–100.

79. Menchaca preserves a slightly different variant of the story. Arredondo called out for the "Mexican Aunt" he had heard of. "Here I am, nephew," Señora Arocha replied, stepping forward. Chabot, *Menchaca*, 19.

The daughter's name was also Josefa—Josefa Paula Agapita Arocha. Her loyalist husband was Pedro Treviño, and they were newlyweds, having been married only two weeks after the Republican Army took San Antonio. The similarity of names creates some confusion of which Josefa Arocha said which. Based on the multiple sources, this version seems most plausible. While the daughter was a descendant of the Isleño Arocha family, Doña Josefa was a descendant of an even older family, her grandfather, Miguel Nuñez Morillo, had come to Texas as a soldier in 1720. Matovina and de la Teja, *Recollections of a Tejano Life*, 56n54. Memoria de las cosas mas notables que acaesieron en Bexar el año de 13, Mandando el Tirano Arredondo." Folsom, *Arredondo*, 99–100.

80. Joséfa Nuñes de Arocha's husband was not killed, but was instead taken in chains to Monterrey, where he would be imprisoned. Folsom, *Arredondo*, 99–100. Chabot, *Menchaca*, 19.

81. Gulick, *The Papers of Mirabeau Buonaparte Lamar*, 5:383.

Chapter 22

1. Shaler to Monroe, September 5, 1813, and Shaler to Monroe, September 19, 1813, Shaler Letterbooks.

2. Claiborne to L. B. Macarty, October 6, 1813, CL, 6:272. Shaler to Monroe, September 19, 1813, and Shaler to Monroe, October 4, 1813, Shaler Letterbooks.

3. "Memoria de las cosas mas notables que acaesieron en Bexar el año de 13, Mandando el Tirano Arredondo."

4. Claiborne to L. B. Macarty, October 6, 1813, CL, 6:272. McDonald, *José Antonio Navarro*, 30.

5. As noted, most historians count fewer than one hundred survivors, but newly discovered news accounts indicate another hundred or so additional men made their escape. The Sexton files in the National Archive list more than forty survivors, most of whom claim to have served throughout 1812–13 and some into 1814. It is difficult to verify which survivors had left before the battle, but the evidence seems strong that more Americans returned than has been previously suspected.

6. The relatives of Richard H. Cage, the Natchez trader captured after Medina, continued to seek the release of him and others in captivity as late as June 10, 1819. The fate of the prisoners remains unclear, although several from their group were released at some point. John Villars remained in Mexico and married a Mexican woman. James Louard, Samuel Winfield, and Michael Wolforth returned to Mississippi, where their names appear in the Sexton list of men claiming Mexican pensions. Gulick, *The Papers of Mirabeau Buonaparte Lamar*, 6:154. Johnston, *The Johnstons of Salisbury*, 55. Jackson, Andrew, and James Cage. James Cage to Andrew Jackson. 1815. Andrew Jackson Papers. "Mr. Isler," *Mississippi Free Trader*, December 1, 1813. US Department of State, 53.

7. Heggoy, *Through Foreign Eyes*, 9.

8. Heggoy, *Through Foreign Eyes*, 9. Lewis W. Haskell, "Tablets in the English Church at Algiers Commemorative of the Deeds of American Consul General Shaler, Admiral Stephen Decatur and Commander Bainbridge," *American Foreign Service Journal* 6, no. 3 (March 1929): 97. Samuel L. Knapp, "Brief Notices of Eminent Americans—Memoir of William Shaler," *New York Mirror*, May 4, 1833. Charles Bowen, ed., *American Almanac and Repository of Useful Knowledge, for the Year 1834* (Boston: Charles Bowen), 315.

9. Some of these were pardoned the following year. Joaquín de Arredondo, "The Commandant General Expels Foreign Invaders but Pardons Mexican Insurgents, General Amnesty," October 10, 1813, in Hatcher, *Opening of Foreign Settlement, a*ppendix 25. José Antonio Saucedo to Governor of Texas, March 8, 1814, BA, RBB S8:68.

10. Sumaria Ynformacion formada contra D. José Erasmo Seguín.

11. Davenport settled in Natchitoches. His last will was signed in 1824 and there is no mention of him later than that date. One of the executors of his will was Henry Adams Bullard. "Will of Samuel Davenport," Karle Wilson Baker Papers, Ralph W. Steen Library, Stephen F. Austin State University. LaVere, "Davenport, Barr, Murphy and Smith," 117–18, 123–24.

12. Some historians treat the various filibusters into Texas and northern Mexico as discrete episodes. But the men who fought in them were invariably veterans of 1813. Accounts of these later filibusters frequently note the support of powerful merchants in New Orleans. One even mentions a "New Orleans Association," almost certainly the old Mexican Association. Daniel Clark Jr., the enemy of Governor Claiborne of Louisiana, who instigated the anti-Claiborne cabal, ironically had died in New Orleans five days before the Battle of Medina, and Lewis Kerr, another key figure, had departed for the Bahamas. But James Workman remained, as did the merchant class in general which had spawned the organization, and some form of it appears to be in operation throughout the period. Jarratt, *Gutiérrez de Lara: Mexican Texan*, 51. Bradley, *W.C.C. Claiborne Letterbook* (Workman's biography is on pages 389–413; Kerr's is on 415–37). Claiborne to L. B. Macarty, October 16, 1813, CL, 6:272-4. H. M. Brackenridge to William Shaler, December 8, 1813, Shaler Papers.

13. Texas, Habitantes de. [Autorización dada por los habitantes de Texas al general José Álvarez de Toledo para formar una nueva expedición contra el ejército realista.] Natchitoches, September 12, 1813. Unsigned. Juan E. Hernández y Dávalos Manuscript Collection, Folder HD 7–4.632. Toledo claims the original copy had 80 signatures but could not identify them.

14. One example of such a document is a statement of service document for American volunteer Thomas Luckett, issued on May 4, 1814. Thomas H. Luckett file, US National Archives Record Group 76, 1839 and 1849 US-Mexico commissions. Steward, *Frontier Swashbuckler*, 139, 190, 213. Picornell to Toledo, December 13, 1813, CSA.

15. The only known recruit into what was called the "Mexican Patriotic Army" was a James J. Johnson, enrolled in Louisiana as a first lieutenant "in a company belonging to the Montezuma Regiment of Infantry, attached to the third division of the Mexican Patriotic Army under the command of Major General De la Croix." It was a fraud. No such army existed and the general named (presumably French revolutionary General Charles-Henri Delacroix) never, so far as is known, even set foot in North America. Picornell to Toledo, December 13, 1813, CSA. Commission of James J. Johnson, December 6, 1813, CSA. Warren, "The Southern Career of Don Juan Mariano Picornell," 316.

16. Picornell to Toledo, December 13, 1813, and Toledo to Picornell, January 4, 1814, CSA. Warren, "The Southern Career of Don Juan Mariano Picornell," 317–18. Samuel Kemper to Toledo, November 26, 1813, in Correspondence Relating to Filibuster.

17. Warren, "The Southern Career of Don Juan Mariano Picornell," 317–20.

18. Harris Gaylord Warren, "Documents Relating to Pierre Laffite's Entrance into the Service of Spain," *Southwestern Historical Quarterly* 44, no. 1 (July 1940): 83.

19. Robinson also proposed filibusters to Cuba and Florida. These may have been proposed as a diversion, since the agent told the secretary of state he would remain in Pittsburgh, but very shortly thereafter left there to make his way down the Mississippi. While evidence exists to exonerate William Shaler of a conspiracy to organize a filibuster in Texas, no such definitive exculpatory evidence exists for Robinson. It is not impossible that his filibustering *was* done with the approval or acquiescence of Monroe, though at this late stage, with the War of 1812 progressing very unfavorably for the United States, it is unlikely. Robinson to Monroe, November 15, 1813, CRF.

20. Robinson to John Smith T, April 11, 1814, CRF.

21. Robinson to John Smith T, April 11, 1814, CRF.

22. No size estimates of either camp are known to exist, but the accounts suggest the two forces were evenly matched and probably numbered in the dozens. They likely included both former Republican Army volunteers—Toledo still had the chief commanders on a fictive muster list—and new volunteers, men of the same desperate sort who had been in the original banditti. The camp locations are unclear, but Robinson appears to be two miles inside Texas on the West bank and Smith on the east bank.

Steward says the two camps came to blows at this point, but the existing letters do not make this clear. They may have merely had a dispute over a boat, and no shots seem to have been fired. Robinson to Smith T, April 11, 1814, Smith T to Robinson, April 11, 1814, Robinson to Smith T, April 12, 1814, Smith T to Robinson, April 12, 1814, Robinson to Smith T (undated), Smith T to Robinson (undated), CRF. Toledo to Committee, May 10, 1814, CRF. "A Proclamation by William C. C. Claiborne," *Niles' Weekly Register*, June 4, 1814.

23. The members of the Mexican Association with whom Toledo worked included Edward Livingston, who had goaded Samuel Kemper into attacking Baton Rouge and had worked with Daniel Clark to set up the organization, as well as Abner Lawson Duncan, John K. West and (possibly) Benjamin Morgan, who had cultivated Gutiérrez in New Orleans. Riva Palacio López, *Pliegos de la diplomacia insurgente*, 62–175. "Toledo y Dubois, José Alvarez de," HOTO. Kanellos, "José Alvarez de Toledo y Dubois," 93.

24. Jarratt, *Gutiérrez de Lara: Mexican Texan*, 48–51.

25. Jarratt, *Gutiérrez de Lara: Mexican Texan*, 48–51. "Declaration of Joseph Daily to Gov. Manuel Pardo," May 7, 1817, BA, RBB S8:157.

26. US Army records show Kemper's date of death as November 7th, family records indicate November 4th. Toledo places the location as New Orleans. Bradley, *We Never Retreat*, 259. Willis M. Kemper, *Genealogy of the Kemper Family*, 65. José Álvarez de Toledo, "Relación de los Oficiales Extrangeros, que baxo mis Ordenes se han distinguido en el servicio de la Republica Mexicana," February 12, 1815, Hernández y Davalos Collection.

27. The full list is published in James Aalan Bernsen, "Republican Veterans at New Orleans," *Texas History Blog*, http://www.texhist.com/2022/01/republican-army-veterans-at-new-orleans.html (accessed January 14, 2022). The original source is US National Parks Service, Jean Lafitte National Historical Park and Preserve, *Battle of New Orleans, War of 1812 American Muster and Troop Roster List*, http://www.nps.gov/jela/learn/historyculture/upload/Battle-of-New-Orleans-Muster-Lists-final-copy-01062015.pdf (accessed May 14, 2020). William C. Davis writes that Losoya fled after Kemper's forces took San Antonio, which would make him a royalist, but other sources insist he fled Arredondo's forces, making him a rebel. Given his chosen destination, the latter explanation is more probable. William C. Davis, *Three Roads to the Alamo* (New York: Harper-Collins, 1998), 45–46. Bill and Marjorie Walraven, *The Magnificent Barbarians: Little-Told Tales of the Texas Revolution* (Austin: Eakin Press, 1993), 164. Jarratt, *Gutiérrez de Lara: Mexican Texan*, 49.

28. Gutiérrez de Lara to the Mexican Congress, "Account of Progress of the Revolution from the Beginning," in Gulick, *The Papers of Mirabeau Buonaparte Lamar*, 1:26–27.

29. There are no known reports linking the Perry/Anaya effort to the Mexican Association, but it is likely, considering its principals worked with that organization before and after. It is also possible that by this time the mercantile interests of New Orleans, while all supporting efforts to revolutionize Mexico, were disunited, supporting contending factions among the growing number of would-be-rebels seeking to take up the cause. "Address Directed by Major General Jackson," *Daily National Intelligencer*, February 27, 1815. Battle of New Orleans Sesquicentennial Celebration Commission, *Final Report to the United States Congress of the Battle of New Orleans Sesquicentennial Celebration, 1815–1965* (Washington, DC: US Government Printing Office, 1965), 118.

30. The lieutenant Forsythe mentioned is possibly J. Forsythe, a first lieutenant in 1814 or Robert M. Forsyth, who was a third lieutenant in the Corps of Artillery in 1815. Notably, Spanish sources suggest Lt. Forsythe was working with a Capt. T. McLanahan, who possibly was related to Neutral Ground resident, Santa Fe Trader and former Spanish prisoner Joseph McLanahan. Francis B. Heitman, *Historical Register and Dictionary of the United States Army, from Its Organization September 29, 1798 to March 2, 1903* (Washington, DC: Government Printing Office, 1903), 430. Powell, *List of Officers of the Army of the United States from 1779 to 1900*, 120. "Deposition of Quirk," February 12, 1816, *Nacogdoches Archives*, BA, RBB S15:219.

31. "Deposition of Quirk," February 12, 1816, *Nacogdoches Archives*, BA, RBB S15:219.

32. Margaret Swett Henson, "Perry, Henry," *HOTO*, http://www.tshaonline.org/handbook/online/articles/fpe42 (accessed May 14, 2020). Head, *Privateers of the Americas*, 142. "The President of the United States," *Raleigh Register and North-Carolina Gazette*, September 15, 1815.

33. The Madison Proclamation can be found in "Political Incendiary," *The Supporter* (Chillicothe, Ohio), Tuesday, September 19, 1815.

34. H. Perry. "Certificate of W. D. C. Hall's Service in the Republican Army," Gulick, *The Papers of Mirabeau Buonaparte Lamar*, 1:4.

35. This expedition is also linked to the "New Orleans Associates," which is likely the Mexican Association. Jarratt claims the plan was authored by them. Gutiérrez served as an agent of Aury in Natchitoches. Jarratt, *Gutiérrez de Lara: Mexican Texan*, 52.

"Perry, Henry," *HOTO*. Harris Gaylord Warren, "Mina, Francisco Xavier," *HOTO*, http://www.tshaonline.org/handbook/online/articles/fmi46 (accessed May 14, 2020). Gulick, *The Papers of Mirabeau Buonaparte Lamar*, 6:446.

36. The account, taken from Spanish dispatches intercepted by the Comanches and given to the Americans, was translated by Perry's former comrade, Henry Adams Bullard. Gulick, *The Papers of Mirabeau Buonaparte Lamar*, 6:445. "Perry, Henry," *HOTO*, Mina, Francisco Xavier, *HOTO*. "The President . . .," *Raleigh Register, and North-Carolina Gazette*, September 15, 1815.

37. There were three known Pattersons in the Republican Army of the North (see appendix B). Declaration of Joseph Daily to Gov. Manuel Pardo, May 7, 1817, BA, RBB S8:156–57.

38. W. C. Beard to Major General Ripley, June 22, 1819, LRSWMS, M221, Roll 86.

39. A David Long had served in the Republican Army. James Long was also married to Jane Wilkinson Long, niece of General James Wilkinson, but the general actually disapproved of Long's courting of his niece, and therefore it is unlikely that he influenced Long's filibuster in any way other than as the inspiration of his early efforts to infiltrate Texas. Gulick, *The Papers of Mirabeau Buonaparte Lamar*, 2:53–57. Bradley, *We Never Retreat*, 137. Jennie C. Morton, "Biographical Sketch of Governor John Adair," *Register of Kentucky State Historical Society* 2, no. 4 (January 1904): 12.

40. Lamar adds Sibley and Procela to Long's council. Sibley had previously been removed from his post as Indian Agent. Hubert Howe Bancroft, *History of the North Mexican States and Texas* in *The Works of Hubert Howe Bancroft* 16 (San Francisco: History Company, 1889), 48. "Nacogdoches Texas Republican," *HOTO*, http://www.tshaonline.org/handbook/online/articles/eenqt (accessed May 14, 2020). Gulick, *The Papers of Mirabeau Buonaparte Lamar*, 2:58.

41. Gulick, *The Papers of Mirabeau Buonaparte Lamar*, 6:154. Francisco Amangual to J. B. Elguezabal, January 15, 1803, BA, RBB S4:184. Manuel Muñoz to Pedro de Nava, June 24, 1794, BA, RBB S3:130. Miguel de Musquíz to J. B. Elguezabal, August 3, 1803; Nemesio Salcedo to J. B. Elguezabal, December 18, 1804, BA, RBB S4:228, 426. Nemesio Salcedo to Governor Antonio Cordero, April 21, 1807, BA, RBB S5:417. Bradley, *We Never Retreat*, 166.

42. Bradley, *We Never Retreat*, 166–67.

43. Bancroft, *History of the North Mexican States and Texas*, 48. (While Bancroft is an old and problematic source, he is the only one who preserves the story of Bigelow's behavior.) Gulick, *The Papers of Mirabeau Buonaparte Lamar*, 2:58–60.

44. Bullard was born September 9, 1788. Ivy, V. H. "The Late Henry A. Bullard," in *Debow's Southern and Western Review* 12 (1852): 52.

45. W. C. Beard to Bullard, June 14, 1819, LRSWMS.

46. James Gaines, in his recollection decades later, claims that Bullard was in league with the rebels. Bullard to W. C. Beard, June 18, 1819, Carr to Beard, June 18, 1819, LRSWMS. Gulick, *The Papers of Mirabeau Buonaparte Lamar*, 1: 283–4.

47. "Trespalacios, José Felix," *HOTO*, http://www.tshaonline.org/handbook/online/articles/ftr09 (accessed May 14, 2020).

48. For more of Bullard's history, see James Aalan Bernsen, "Henry Adams Bullard," *The Texas History Blog*, http://www.texhist.com/2022/01/henry-adams-bullard.html (accessed January 14, 2022). James Weldon Long, "Revolutionary Republics: US National Narratives and the Independence of Latin America, 1810–1846" (PhD diss., Louisiana State University, 2011), 88.

Bullard was not the only veteran to become a judge in Louisiana. William Murray, the early Burr recruit and friend of Augustus Magee, also became the judge of the Sixth District of Louisiana. Asbury Dickens and James C. Allen, ed. *Documents of the Congress of the United States in Relation to the Public Lands*, vol. 4 (Washington: Gales and Seaton, 1859), 510.

49. Cogswell to Gutiérrez, unknown date [probably late June 1812], CSA. H. M. Brackenridge to William Shaler, *December 8, 1813*, Shaler Papers. Brackenridge notes that Forsyth was in communication with a Johnston (presumably Adair's aide, Josiah Stoddard Johnston, since his brothers Darius and Orramel were at the time in a Spanish dungeon) in procuring documents for the history. The whereabouts of these documents is unknown. They do not appear in the Josiah Stoddard Johnston papers, located at the Historical Society of Pennsylvania.

50. "From Lisbon," *Alexandria Gazette*, January 29, 1816. "The Following Extract of a Letter of Late Date," *Daily National Intelligencer*, November 15, 1819. "From the Oronoco," *Daily National Intelligencer*, September 30, 1819. Simón Bolivar, *Escritos del Libertador* IX (n.p., 1973), 26. Capt. James R. Bloom, "Why We Vaccinate Sailors," *Military Medicine* 181 (April 2016): 297. John Quincy Adams, Diary Entry for March 30, 1820, in Charles Francis Adams, ed., *Memoirs of John Quincy Adams, Containing Portions of His Diary from 1795–1848* (Philadelphia: J. B. Lippincott & Co., 1875), 5:48. The portrait Forsyth gifted to Bolivar was by a close follower of Gilbert Stuart. "After Gilbert Stewart," *Christie's Auctions*, https://www.christies.com/lotfinder/Lot/after-gilbert-stuart-1755-1828-portrait-of-george-6125025-details.aspx (accessed May 15, 2020).

Chapter 23

1. Burial of Manuel Salcedo, August 28, 1813 (entry 539), Burial of Simon Herrera, August 28, 1813 (entry 540), San Fernando Church Burial Records, 1802–1817 Microfilm. John Ogden Leal, translator. Office of the County Clerk, Béxar County Courthouse, San Antonio, Texas. Only Salcedo and Herrera received individual burials.

2. Permission for A Christian Burial, March 9, 1814, Béxar County Archives, Microfilm reel 53, frame 0554.

3. The future president of Mexico, in his autobiography, curiously makes almost no mention of his time in Texas, merely noting that he served under Arredondo for five years and fought in the Eastern Internal Provinces. Gulick, *The Papers of Mirabeau Buonaparte Lamar*,

6:338. Ann Fears Crawford, *The Eagle: The Autobiography of Santa Anna* (Austin: State House Press, 1988), 7. Chabot, "Memoirs of Antonio Menchaca," 20.

4. Chabot, "Memoirs of Antonio Menchaca," 20.

5. Account of Lamar in Gulick, *The Papers of Mirabeau Buonaparte Lamar* 4(1):123.

6. "Memoria de las cosas mas notables que acaesieron en Bexar el año de 13, Mandando el Tirano Arredondo," [1813].

7. A precise account of casualties is impossible, but the losses to Hispanic Texas—including rebels and loyalists, alike, were substantial. Royal losses in all battles were in excess of 1,000, perhaps more than 1,500, many of whom were native to Texas. The number of Mexican rebels killed in battle may have been in the range of 400, but perhaps higher. Civilian casualties were likely similar. New Spanish soldiers were brought in, and some rebels may not have returned from exile. Even with this influx, the overall population of Texas, about four thousand troops and civilians before the war, declined to three thousand after it, and did not substantially change until Anglo immigrants were once again allowed in during the 1820s.

8. Folsom, *Arredondo*, 101. Chabot, *With the Makers of San Antonio*, 153.

9. José Antonio's sister, who had remained behind—presumably under the protection of royalist relatives, caught the eye of nineteen-year-old lieutenant Antonio Lopez de Santa Anna, her brother claimed. The young Spanish officer proposed marriage, but the Navarro family blocked it because of his reputation. McDonald, *José Antonio Navarro*, 31. McDonald, *José Antonio Navarro*, 32. F. Todd Smith, *From Dominance to Disappearance*, 101. Joaquín de Arredondo to Benito de Armiñán, April 30, 1814, BA, RBB S8:70.

10. David B. Gracy II, *Moses Austin: His Life* (San Antonio: Trinity University Press, 1987), 3–4, 102–3.

11. Eugene C. Barker, "Austin, Stephen Fuller," HOTO, http://www.tshaonline.org/hand-book/online/articles/fau14 (accessed May 18, 2020). David B. Gracy II, "AUSTIN, MOSES," HOTO, http://www.tshaonline.org/handbook/online/articles/fau12 (accessed December 27, 2019). Jesus "Frank" de la Teja, "Veramendi, Juan Martin de," HOTO, http://www.tshaonline.org/handbook/online/articles/fve06 (accessed May 18, 2020).

12. De la Teja, *Tejano Leadership*, 32–33.

13. Jesus "Frank" de la Teja, "Veramendi, Juan Martin de," HOTO, http://www.tshaonline.org/handbook/online/articles/fve06 (accessed May 18, 2020).

14. Gulick, *The Papers of Mirabeau Buonaparte Lamar*, 1:285.

15. Anonymous [Navarro] account in Gulick, *The Papers of Mirabeau Buonaparte Lamar* 4(2):12.

16. The note from Gutiérrez read: "We the governor and junta of the State of Texas in conformity to the proposals by us made to the American volunteers dated April 13, 1813 and accepted by all the commanding officers of said volunteers on the 16th of said month do hereby certify that Joseph W. Carr is entitled to one league square of land to be located on any unappropriated land in this state according to the 1st and 2nd Articles of said proposals." "Carr (Joseph W) Legal Papers," Texas State Library and Archives Commission, Austin, Texas.

17. A handwritten note similar to Carr's is preserved from Gutiérrez to William Brown with the same conditions. The Brown and Doughty documents can be found in the Samuel Sexton files, US National Archives. "Carr (Joseph W) Legal Papers."

18. This was one of several such statements. The inclusion of the year 1814 indicates that Toledo still kept his insurgents on a muster roll of some kind well into that year, which corresponds to his attempt to maintain a front of legitimacy even in exile. Samuel Sexton files.

19. Samuel Sexton files.

20. W. T. Block, *A History of Jefferson County, Texas* (Nederland, TX: Nederland Publishing, 1976), http://www.wtblock.com/wtblockjr/History%20of%20Jefferson%20County/chapter%205.htm (accessed September 25, 2016).

21. Henry Stuart Foote recalls, "With Ross I became familiarly acquainted many years ago, when a boy at school, in the town of Lexington, in the State of Virginia. Eight or ten years had then elapsed since the occurrences described above had taken place; but they were all fresh in his memory, and he delighted to detail to his friends the perilous adventures which had marked his early manhood." Henry Stuart Foote, *Texas and the Texans, or the Advance of the Anglo-Americans in the Southwest*, vol. 1 (Philadelphia: Thomas, Cowperthwait & Co., 1841), 186. *Galt v. Dibrel and others*. Nashville, December 1836, in George S. Yerger, ed., *Reports of Cases Argued and Determined in the Supreme Court of Tennessee*, vol. 10 (Louisville, KY: Fetter Law Book Company, 1903), 111–19.

22. That Ross took on such a large personal debt suggests the expedition had been abandoned financially by the outsiders who had supported it initially. These men, presumably New Orleans merchants either affiliated with the Mexican Association or independents following a similar ideology, likely began closing their wallets following Governor Claiborne's proclamation, and appear to have lost all interest by the time of the La Bahía siege. Reuben Ross to Col. Jas. C. Hays, September 11, 1825. Reuben Ross Family Papers, Dolph Briscoe Center for American History, The University of Texas at Austin.

23. Reuben Ross to Frances Ross, New York, February 5, 1826. Ross Family Papers.

24. Reuben Ross to Frances Ross, Mexico. April 8, 1826, and Thomas Luckett to Reuben Ross, Washington, March 6, 1826, Ross Family Papers.

25. Ramos, *Beyond the Alamo*, 109–10.

26. Ross briefly accepted an offer of the government to visit Nacogdoches as a commissioner to treat with the leaders of the Fredonian Rebellion, but it had been suppressed before he arrived. H. I. Offeett to Reuben Ross, Ross Family Papers. Reuben Ross to the Ross Association, Mexico, January 12, 1828, Ross Family Papers. To learn more about Ross's failed ambitions in Texas, see James Aalan Bernsen, "Reuben Ross," *The Texas History Blog*, http://www.texhist.com/2022/01/the-tragic-story-of-reuben-and-john.html (accessed January 14, 2022).

27. Ross Papers.

28. In a study conducted by this author of the names recorded in expedition accounts, half of the verifiable survivors returned to Texas. See James Bernsen, "Origins and Motivations of the Gutiérrez-Magee Filibusters" (master's thesis, Texas State University), 2016, 92. However, among the forty-four names recorded in the Sexton documents, discovered subsequently, surprisingly few did. This suggests a wide variation and geographical factors at play, since the Sexton names are almost all from Rapides. Samuel Sexton file, US National Archives.

29. "John McFarlan" *HOTO*, https://www.tshaonline.org/handbook/entries/mcfarlan-john (accessed May 25, 2021).

30. "Martin Allen" *HOTO*, https://tshaonline.org/handbook/online/articles/fal23 (accessed May 18, 2020). "Petition of Martin Allen 23 Nov, 1836," Martin Allen Legal Files Texas State Archives, Austin, Texas.

31. Thomas Quirk is mentioned in the Béxar Archives as Edmund's son and was active in the smuggling ring that included his father and uncle, Henry Quirk. He was twenty-six at the time. Genealogical sources show competing dates for Thomas Quirk's death, some supporting late March 1836, matching the Goliad massacre. Another Thomas, possibly *his* son, lived into the 1850s. "Edmund Quirk," RBB 35:86, 270.

32. Other veteran settlers included Andrew Robinson, Horatio Biglow, Godwin Brown Cotten, John Gladden King, Samuel Barber, Josiah Taylor, and John Villars. William Parker

appears in the list, but his name is common and there are no other substantiating sources such as exist for the others. There was a William Fisher in the expedition who it is possible is the same as the William S. Fisher who served in the Republic of Texas House of Representatives and was captured at Mier, but there is no clear evidence to substantiate the claim. Bugbee, "The Old Three Hundred," 108–17.

33. Gulick, *The Papers of Mirabeau Buonaparte Lamar*, 1:96. L. W. Kemp, "Bigelow, Horatio," HOTO, http://www.tshaonline.org/handbook/online/articles/fbio8 (accessed May 18, 2020).

34. "Buckner, Aylett C.," HOTO, http://www.tshaonline.org/handbook/online/articles/fbu09 (accessed May 18, 2020).

35. A. C. Buckner to J. Austin, June 20, 1832, in Gulick, *The Papers of Mirabeau Buonaparte Lamar*, 1:95.

36. Buckner is identified as Antonio—likely a Hispanicized version of his name. "List of Battle of Velasco Participants," Texas Genealogical Society, Stirpes, vol. 21, no. 3 (September 1981), 179–80. "Buckner, Aylett C.," HOTO, https://www.tshaonline.org/handbook/entries/buckner-aylett-c (accessed June 26, 2023). Gulick, *The Papers of Mirabeau Buonaparte Lamar*, 1:147.

37. Gulick, *The Papers of Mirabeau Buonaparte Lamar*, 1:120–129.

38. Hall was second in command at Anahuac in the "protest" against Juan Davis Bradburn, an Anglo-Mexican official who had joined Toledo's forces in Louisiana after the 1813 defeat, and had risen to the post of customs collector in Texas. Hall fought at Velasco, attended the Convention of 1832, and signed the early and unsuccessful Goliad Declaration of Independence in 1835. "Hall, Warren D. C.," HOTO, http://www.tshaonline.org/handbook/online/articles/fha23 (accessed May 18, 2020).

39. Sam Houston Dixon, *The Men Who Made Texas Free: The Signers of the Texas Declaration of Independence* (Houston: Texas Historical Publishing Company, 1924), 303–6.

40. Ingrid Broughton Morris and Deolece M. Parmelee, "Gaines, James Taylor," HOTO, http://www.tshaonline.org/handbook/online/articles/fga04 (accessed May 18, 2020).

41. Bernice Strong, "Ruiz, Jose Francisco," HOTO, http://www.tshaonline.org/handbook/online/articles/fru11 (accessed May 18, 2020). Martínez de Vara, *Tejano Patriot*, 1.

42. Todd Hansen, *The Alamo Reader: A Study in History* (Mechanicsburg, PA: Stackpole Books, 2003), 508–9. Index to Military Rolls of the Republic of Texas 1835–1845, available at https://tshaonline.org/supsites/military/l/florm_9l.htm (accessed May 18, 2020). (Bergara is listed in Company B, 2nd Regiment of Cavalry, Regular Texas Army.)

43. Hansen, *The Alamo Reader*, 508–9.

44. In supreme irony, Juan Seguín would share the battlefield at San Jacinto on the same side as William Shaler Stillwell, the nephew of William Shaler, the man who had threatened Erasmo Seguín in Natchitoches. It is doubtful the men met—Seguín was in the cavalry, Stillwell the artillery—much less recognized the significance.

45. Walraven, *Magnificent Barbarians*, 164. Bill Walraven, "José Domingo Losoya (1783–1869), *Corpus Christi Caller-Times*, January 13, 1986, https://www.newspapers.com/image/758318456/ (accessed March 16, 2023).

46. Matovina and de la Teja, *Recollections of a Tejano Life*, 74–78. George O. Coalson, "Menchaca, Jose Antonio [1800–79]," HOTO, http://www.tshaonline.org/handbook/online/articles/fme12 (accessed May 18, 2020).

47. Biographical information on McKim was provided to the author by Brian Hendrix of Houston, a McKim descendant.

48. Although assumed to be the son of German immigrants, Jacob and Anna Durst, John Durst was in fact the natural son of Samuel Davenport, who acknowledged him in his will

as "my natural son of which circumstance I have informed him." Davenport served as the godfather of this illegitimate son and raised him as his own son after the death of Jacob Durst. "Will of Samuel Davenport," Karle Wilson Baker Papers, Ralph W. Steen Library, Stephen F. Austin State University. Joe E. and Carolyn Reeves Ericson, "Durst, John Marie," *HOTO*, http://www.tshaonline.org/handbook/online/articles/fdu27 (accessed May 18, 2020).

49. L. W. Kemp, "Stillwell, William S.," *Veteran Biographies*, San Jacinto Museum of History, https://www.sanjacinto-museum.org/content/documents/KempSketches/SJV796.pdf (accessed May 18, 2020). "William S. Stillwell," Cullum's Register, http://penelope.uchicago.edu/Thayer/E/Gazetteer/Places/America/United_States/Army/USMA/Cullums_Register/505*.html (accessed May 18, 2020).

50. Stillwell was Class of 1827 and Albert Sydney Johnston was Class of 1826. Johnston, *The Johnstons of Salisbury*, 154.

51. Jeanette H. Flachmeier, "Johnston, Albert Sidney," *HOTO*, http://www.tshaonline.org/handbook/online/articles/fjo32 (accessed May 18, 2020).

52. In addition to Charles Despallier, lists of Alamo defenders include a "Carlos Espalier." Older historical accounts assert the men are not the same. They are, in fact, the same person. A detailed summation of the case can be found at James Aalan Bernsen, "Carlos Espalier: The Alamo Defender Who Never Was," *The Texas History Blog*, http://www.texhist.com/2021/11/carlos-espalier.html (accessed November 23, 2021). Rasmus Dahlqvist and Bill Groneman, "Espalier, Carlos," *HOTO*, http://www.tshaonline.org/handbook/online/articles/fes16 (accessed May 18, 2020). Dahlqvist, *From Martin to Despallier*, 307.

53. Russell S. Hall, "King, John Gladden," *HOTO*, https://www.tshaonline.org/handbook/entries/king-john-gladden (accessed November 25, 2020).

54. The Bowie possibly in the expedition was Rezin Bowie, although the only source for his presence in the filibuster is an article by Matilda E. Moore in *Frontier Times*, cited by William C. Davis. While such participation is certainly possible and within character, this is too thin a thread to be decisive. Davis, *Three Roads to the Alamo*, 44. Rasmus Dahlqvist, "Despallier, Charles," *HOTO*, https://www.tshaonline.org/handbook/entries/despallier-charles (accessed July 27, 2021).

55. The letter does not specify which Despallier was traveling with Bowie, and this source incorrectly assumes it was Charles Despallier, because he later died at the Alamo. Blaz Philipe is a more likely candidate, since the two effectively traded places at the fortress. Bowie to James B. Miller, June 22, 1835, quoted in Gonzales Rangers, A-E, Sons of DeWitt Colony website: http://www.sonsofdewittcolony.org/adp/history/1836/gonzales/gonzalesrangersa-e.html (accessed December 20, 2019). Dahlqvist, *From Martin to Despallier*, 237.

56. Rasmus Dahlqvist, "Despallier, Blaz Philipe I," *HOTO*, http://www.tshaonline.org/handbook/online/articles/fdeai (accessed May 18, 2020).

57. Dahlqvist, "Despallier, Blaz Philipe I."

58. The location of Cotten's print shop next to Travis' law office is marked at the Sa Felipe de Austin State Historic Site. Anonymous, "Cotten, Godwin Brown Michael," *HOTO*, https://www.tshaonline.org/handbook/entries/cotten-godwin-brown-michael (accessed July 27, 2021).

59. Walraven, *Magnificent Barbarians*, 164. Bill Walraven, "José Domingo Losoya (1783–1869), *Corpus Christi Caller-Times*, January 13, 1986, https://www.newspapers.com/image/758318456/ (accessed March 16, 2023). Randell G. Tarín, "Losoya, José Torribio," *HOTO*, https://www.tshaonline.org/handbook/entries/losoya-jose-toribio (accessed March 16, 2023).

60. A companion of Charles Despallier was Christopher Adams Parker. His father, William Parker, fought at the Battle of New Orleans and settled in Natchez, where Christopher was born. A William Parker also fought in the Texas Revolution of 1811, and as many veterans

lived in the Natchez area, there is a strong likelihood that they are the same man, but it cannot be confirmed with the information available at this time. 1820 US Census, Natchez, Mississippi, Ancestry.com.

Sam Houston to H. Raguet, March 13, 1837, quoted in Gonzales Rangers, A-E, Sons of DeWitt Colony website. Bill Groneman, *Alamo Defenders: A Genealogy: The People and Their Words* (Austin: Eakin Press, 1990), 35–36.

61. Josiah Taylor is buried in the Taylor Cemetery in Cuero, Texas, but is also honored with a headstone in the Texas State Cemetery, the only veteran of the 1812–13 Revolution so honored. "Josiah Taylor" Texas Historical Marker Texas Historical Commission, http://www.stxmaps.com/go/texas-historical-marker-josiah-taylor.html (accessed September 22, 2016). Dovie Tschirhart Hall, "Taylor, Creed," *HOTO*, http://www.tshaonline.org/handbook/online/articles/fta17 (accessed May 18, 2020).

62. Jarratt, *Gutiérrez de Lara: Mexican Texan*, 48. J. B. Gutiérrez de Lara to the Mexican Congress, "Account of Progress of the Revolution from the Beginning," in Gulick, *The Papers of Mirabeau Buonaparte Lamar*, 1:4–29.

63. [Tamaulipas] Congress, Representation to Mexican Congress Upon Services of Gutiérrez, in Gulick, *The Papers of Mirabeau Buonaparte Lamar*, 1:55.

64. Gulick, *The Papers of Mirabeau Buonaparte Lamar*, 1:55.

65. Jarratt, *Gutiérrez de Lara: Mexican Texan*, 67.

66. Reuben Ross the elder, it must be noted, did not abandon the expedition after the murder of the royalists, nor did he ever serve under Toledo, and his relationship with Gutiérrez seems to have been cordial. He was the American commander under him for about two-and-a-half months in San Antonio. Jarratt, *Gutiérrez de Lara: Mexican Texan*, 67.

Chapter 24

1. Most expedition members generally came from the Mississippi Valley states, including and south of Missouri and Kentucky, but were first-generation immigrants to these regions from across the United States. A few were slave owners, others likely aspired to that status. Several originally came from such states as New York, Massachusetts, and Connecticut.

Shaler's servant Charles is referred to in correspondence by that term, but it is clear that he was a slave. He had fathered a child by the servant of a Shaler friend, C. D. Van Oradelles, and the latter wrote to Shaler of the child in hopes of acquiring Charles. He had even entered a wager with Shaler over the outcome of the war in Mexico, which seems to indicate Charles as one of the wagers. "I acknowledge that Charles belongs to you, but I shall keep him to make a more complete servant [for] you. He will be a treasure to you in future." The father of Nathaniel Cogswell, the man who tried to stop Toledo, was also a Northern slave owner. The slave served out the rest of his life in bondage in Gilmanton, New Hampshire, under the terms of gradual emancipation. C. D. Van Oradelles to Shaler, May 5, 1813, Shaler Papers. "When Did Slavery Really End in the North?" Civil Discourse, http://www.civildiscourse-historyblog.com/blog/2017/1/3/when-did-slavery-really-end-in-the-north (accessed May 18, 2020). Jameson, *The Cogswells in America*, 92.

2. Henry Adams Bullard, for his part, was antislavery. In his 1836 article on Texas, he included an antislavery section that was redacted by the publisher. "Mexico and Texas," manuscript in North American Review Papers, 1831–43. Houghton Library, Harvard University. May, 864.

3. Narrett, "Liberation and Conquest," 26.

4. An example of this reaction is a June 4, 1835, letter citing trade restrictions in a call for a march against Anahuac. One of the signers was Republican Army Veteran Godwin Brown

Cotten. Testimony of José Miguel Crow, *Expediente on Plots Against the Government, June 5, 1811*, RBB S7:331–32. Gulick, *The Papers of Mirabeau Buonaparte Lamar*, 1:202–3.

5. As noted in this book, the interventionist narrative was incorrectly assumed by Garrett and Warren and has since been embraced without criticism by many authors. Historian Richard Gronet argued most forcefully for Madison's role in promoting the filibuster. Gronet's article was published in 1969, "during a period in which American efforts toward the containment of communism were interpreted by some as predatory rather than defensive," in the words of historian David J. Pennington. "Written during an era of bourgeoning criticism against the growing U. S. global meddlesomeness, Gronet applies what were then modern interpretations of language and international politics to suggest that Madison did in fact sponsor covert operations against Spain and its neighboring territories." Gronet, "United States and the Invasion of Texas, 1810–1814," 281–306. Stagg, "The Madison Administration and Mexico," 449–80. Pennington, "Reassessing James Madison's Ambitions," 66–79. Pratt, *Expansionists of 1812*, 85.

6. Beckert and Rockman, *Slavery's Capitalism*, 206.

7. Stagg, *Borderlines in Borderlands*, 58–59.

8. Beckert and Rockman, *Slavery's Capitalism*, 207. Watson, *Jackson's Sword*, 55–56.

9. Kevin Brady, "Unspoken Words: James Monroe's Involvement in the Magee-Gutiérrez Filibuster," *East Texas Historical Journal* 45, no. 1 (March 2007): 58–68. Available at http://scholarworks.sfasu.edu/ethj/vol45/iss1/14.

10. Narrett, "Geopolitics and Intrigue," 118.

11. For a very useful study on the relevance of the New Orleans business community to the 1836 revolution, see Edward L. Miller, *New Orleans and the Texas Revolution* (College Station: Texas A&M University Press, 2004). J. C. A. Stagg, *Borderlines in Borderlands*, 3–4.

12. José Alvarez de Toledo diary, [November?] 1815, in Riva Palacio López, *Pliegos de la diplomacia insurgente*, 62.

13. September 23, 1806, *Orleans Gazette*, quoted in McCaleb, *Aaron Burr Conspiracy*, 125–26.

14. Foote, 185–87.

15. It could not have been Samuel Kemper, for he died in late 1814. Foote, 185–7.

16. Gulick, *The Papers of Mirabeau Buonaparte Lamar*, 2:55.

17. Aylett was an allied family name that was adopted as a first name by two distant relatives. Even Southern publics and papers celebrated South American rebels who were Indian or black. While Haiti's rebellion was seen as a cautionary tale, Southerners embraced South American rebellions not because of emancipationist sentiments, but in spite of them. "Popular celebrations of Latin American independence suggests that at a gut moral level, white U. S. observers in the early nineteenth century were more open to the abstract idea of abolition and racial equality than many historians have recognized," Fitz argues. Caitlin Fitz, *Our Sister Republics: The United States in an Age of American Revolutions* (New York: Liveright Publishing, 2016), 7–12.

18. Filibusters practically exploded after the Mexican-American War. In 1855, two-thirds of the entire available ground forces of the United States was employed in California, Texas, and New Mexico to suppress filibuster efforts against Mexico. Although many of these areas overlapped with some of the most hostile Indian tribes, the fact remains that more American soldiers were employed in stopping *American Attacks against Mexico* than Indian attacks against Americans. While Americans fighting under the nominal command of native revolutionaries continued, later filibusters often included no serious native elements. Many of the American commanders who fought filibusters in the 1840s and 1850s later became general officers in the US Civil War. May, 866.

19. H. Allen Anderson and Rose Mary Fritz, "Hall, Warren D. C.," *HOTO*, http://www.tshaonline.org/handbook/online/articles/fha23 (accessed May 18, 2020). Block, *A History of Jefferson County, Texas.*

20. Schwartz, *Forgotten Battlefield,* 14.

21. "It is proper to remark here sir that much pains have been taken to spread the opinion [in Natchitoches] that the U.S. would step in and occupy that country as soon as the standard of wealth should be created there," Shaler wrote in November of 1812. But noting the hostile reception Robinson had received, he added, "I have always endeavored to contradict them and ridicule them but not always with success." Shaler to Monroe, November 10, 1812, Shaler Letterbooks. Sibley to Claiborne, July 1812, in Julia Kathryn Garrett, "Dr. John Sibley," 49, no. 3 (January 1946), 412. Yoakum, *The History of Texas,* 153.

22. Onís's views were mere speculation. His mind conceived that even the planned campaign against Canada was a false front for an effort to recruit an expedition against Mexico. His understanding of Americans failed to distinguish two key elements: the competing and even contrasting war aims of the men of the Northwest and of the Southwest and the democratic, bottom-up nature of many American efforts, in which leaders were frequently dragged forward by the people and often led by stepping before a rabble and proposing that which the rabble wanted already. Castañeda, *Our Catholic Heritage in Texas,* 6:61.

23. Texas Education Agency, "Texas Essential Knowledge and Skills for Social Studies, Subchapter B. Middle School." Texas Education Agency, http://ritter.tea.state.tx.us/rules/tac/chapter113/ch113b.html#113.19 (accessed June 17, 2021).

24. "Memoria de las cosas mas notables que acaesieron en Bexar el año de 13, Mandando el Tirano Arredondo."

25. Coronado, *A World Not to Come,* 29.

26. Anonymous [Navarro] account in Gulick, *The Papers of Mirabeau Buonaparte Lamar,* 4(2):12.

27. Gulick, *The Papers of Mirabeau Buonaparte Lamar.*

28. Owsley and Smith, *Filibusters and Expansionists,* ix. T. R. Fehrenbach, *Lone Star: A History of Texas and the Texans* (New York: Collier Books, 1968), 125.

29. "Authentic from Mexico," *Daily National Intelligencer* (Washington, DC), Monday, October 11, 1813; no. 242.

Bibliography

Primary Sources

Adams, Charles Francis, ed. *Memoirs of John Quincy Adams, Containing Portions of His Diary from 1795–1848*. Philadelphia: J. B. Lippincott & Co., 1875.
Andrew Jackson Papers, US Library of Congress.
Anonymous [Henry Adams Bullard], "A Visit to Texas, Being the Journal of a Traveler, through Parts Most Interesting to American Settlers," *North American Review* 43, no. 92 (July 1836): 226–57.
Archives of the Archdiocese of San Antonio, Texas.
Archivo General de Indias, Briscoe Center for American History, The University of Texas at Austin.
Arredondo, Joaquin, Operaciones de Guerra, Archivo General de México, Microfilm copy University of California at Santa Barbara.
Béxar Archives. General Manuscripts, Dolph Briscoe Center, University of Texas, Austin.
Béxar County Archives, San Antonio, Texas.
Bolívar, Simón, *Escritos del Libertador* 9, n.p., 1973.
Bullard, Henry Adams, 1781–1851. "Mexico and Texas." A.MS. (unsigned); [n.p., 1836]. North American Review. North American Review papers, 1831–1843, MS, Houghton Library, Harvard University.
Carter, Clarence Edwin. *The Territorial Papers of the United States*, vol. 9. Washington, DC: Government Printing Office, 1910.
———. *The Territorial Papers of the United States*, vol. 14. Washington, DC: United States Government Printing Office, 1949.
Cogswell, Nathaniel. *An Oration Delivered before the Republican Citizens of Newburyport in the Rev. John Giles' Meetinghouse on the Fourth of July 1808*. Newburyport: W. and J. Gilman, 1808. Historical Society of Pennsylvania.
Correspondence of Special Agents—William Shaler (Cuba and Mexico), US National Archives.
Correspondence Relating to the Filibustering Expedition against the Spanish Government of Mexico, 1811–1816, US National Archives.
Gulick, Charles Adams, Jr. *The Papers of Mirabeau Buonaparte Lamar*, 6 vol. Austin: Pemberton Press, 1968.
Gutiérrez de Lara, José Bernardo. "Breve Apologia que el Coronel D. José Bernardo Gutiérrez de Lara Hace de las imposturas calumniosas" (Monterrey: Pedro Gonzales, 1827).

Gutiérrez de Lara (José Bernardo) collection, Eugene C. Barker Texas History Center, The University of Texas at Austin.
Gutiérrez de Lara (José Bernardo) Papers, Texas State Library and Archives.
Gutiérrez de Lara, José Bernardo. "Proclamation of José Bernardo Gutiérrez De Lara." *The Herald of Alexandria, Louisiana*, August 31, 1812. Microfilm: Beinecke Library, Yale University.
James Madison Papers. Library of Congress.
James Monroe Papers. Library of Congress.
Joseph W. Carr Legal Papers. Texas State Library and Archives Commission, Austin, Texas.
Josiah Stoddard Johnston papers, Historical Society of Pennsylvania.
Juan E. Hernández y Dávalos Manuscript Collection, Benson Latin American Collection, University of Texas at Austin.
Karle Wilson Baker Papers, Ralph W. Steen Library, Stephen F. Austin State University.
Lowrie, Walter, and Walter S. Franklin, eds. *American State Papers: Documents, Legislative and Executive of the Congress of the United States, Class V: Military Affairs*, vol. 1 Washington, DC: Gales and Seaton, 1832.
———. *American State Papers, Class X, Miscellaneous*, vols. 1–2. Washington, DC: Gales and Seaton, 1834.
Martin Allen Legal Files, Texas State Archives, Austin, Texas.
McClure, James P., ed. *The Papers of Thomas Jefferson*, vol. 43, no. 11. Princeton: Princeton University Press, 2017.
"Memoria de las cosas mas notables que acaesieron en Bexar el año de 13, Mandando el Tirano Arredondo." [1813] H. E. Bolton Collection, The Bancroft Library, University of California, Berkeley.
Papers Concerning Robertson's Colony in Texas, Vol. I: The Texas Association, 1788–1822.
Randolph, Thomas Jefferson, ed. *Memoirs, Correspondence and Private Papers of Thomas Jefferson, vol. 3*. London: Henry Colburn and Richard Bentley, 1829.
Reuben Ross Family Papers. Dolph Briscoe Center for American History, The University of Texas at Austin.
Robert Bruce Blake Research Collection, Dolph Briscoe Center for American History, The University of Texas at Austin.
Roland, Dunbar, ed. *Official Letter Books of W. C. C. Claiborne*, 6 vol. Jackson, MS: State Department of Archives and History, 1917.
San Fernando Church Burial Records, Office of the County Clerk, Béxar County Courthouse, San Antonio, Texas.
Salcedo, Manuel. *Operaciones de Guerra*, vol. 1, part 1, Archivo General de México. Copy in Texas State Library and Archives, Austin, Texas.
[Shaler, William], "Journal of a Voyage Between China and the North-Western Coast of America Made in 1804," *The American Register: Or General Repository of History, Politics, and Science* 3 (1808): 137–75.
———. William Shaler Papers, Historical Society of Pennsylvania, Philadelphia, Pennsylvania.
———. William Shaler Letterbooks, Gilder Lehrman Institute of American History, New York Historical Society.
Shirley-Eustis Historical Association, Boston, Massachusetts.
Sibley Family Papers, Mary E. Ambler Archives, Lindenwood University, St. Charles, Missouri.
The Trials of the Honb. James Workman and Col. Lewis Kerr Before the United States' Court for the Orleans District on a Charge of High Misdemeanor, New Orleans: Bradford and Anderson, 1807. Transcript of proceedings.

BIBLIOGRAPHY

Thomas Jefferson Papers, Library of Congress.
Trial of Thomas O. Selfridge, Attorney at Law, Before the Hon. Isaac Parker, Esquire for Killing Charles Austin on the Public Exchange in Boston, August 4, 1806. Boston: Russel, Cutler, Belcher and Armstrong, 1806.
US Department of State, *Calendar of the Miscellaneous Letters of the Department of State From the Organization of the Government to 1820*. Washington, DC: Government Printing Office, 1897.
Yerger, George S., ed. *Reports of Cases Argued and Determined in the Supreme Court of Tennessee*, vol. 10. Louisville, KY: Fetter Law Book Company, 1903.

US National Archives

Letters Sent by the Secretary of War Relating to Military Affairs, 1800–1889.
Letters Received by the Secretary of War, Registered Series.
Letters Received by the Secretary of War, Unregistered Series.
Letters Received by the Secretary of War, Main Series.
Letters Received by the Office of the Adjutant General.
Letterbook of the Natchitoches-Sulfur Fork Factory, 1809–1821.
Orderly Books of the Adjutant, July–Nov. 1810, *Records of Units, Infantry 1789–1815: Maj. Zebulon M. Pike's Consolidated Regiment, 1809–1811*. US National Archives.
Samuel Sexton file, US National Archives Record Group 76, 1839 and 1849 U.S.-Mexico Commissions, National Archives.
Spanish West Florida, Archives of the Spanish Government, 1782–1816, US National Archives.
Thomas H. Luckett file, US National Archives Record Group 76, 1839 and 1849 U.S.-Mexico commissions, National Archives.
US Military Academy Cadet Application Papers, 1805–1866, US National Archives.

Books

Abernethy, Thomas Perkins. *The Burr Conspiracy*. New York: Oxford University Press, 1954.
Alaman, Lúcas. *Historia de Méjico desde los primeros movimientos que prepararon su independencia en el año 1808 hasta la época presente*, vol. 3 (Mexico City, J. M. Lara, 1850).
Alexander, Elizabeth Urban. *Notorious Woman: The Celebrated Case of Myra Clark Gaines*. Baton Rouge: Louisiana State University Press, 2001.
Almaráz, Felix. *Tragic Cavalier: Governor Manuel Salcedo of Texas, 1808–1813*. College Station: Texas A&M University Press, 1971.
Anonymous [Henry Adams Bullard]. *History of Don Francisco de Miranda's Attempt to Effect a Revolution in South America*. Boston: Oliver and Munroe, 1808.
Anonymous. *Biographical Sketch of General John Adair*. Washington, DC: Gales & Seaton, 1830.
Appleby, Joyce. *Inheriting the Revolution: The First Generation of Americans*. Cambridge, MA: Belknap Press, 2001.
Baker, D. W. C. *A Texas Scrapbook Made Up of the History, Biography and Miscellany of Texas and Its People*. New Orleans: A. S. Barnes and Company, 1875.
Bancroft, Hubert Howe. *The Works of Hubert Howe Bancroft*, vol 16. San Francisco: History Company, 1889.
Battle of New Orleans Sesquicentennial Celebration Commission. *Final Report to the United States Congress of the Battle of New Orleans Sesquicentennial Celebration, 1815–1965*. Washington, DC: Government Printing Office, 1965.

Beckert, Sven, and Seth Rockman, ed., *Slavery's Capitalism: A New History of American Economic Development*. Philadelphia: University of Pennsylvania Press, 2016.

Bernsen, James. "Origins and Motivations of the Gutiérrez-Magee Filibusters," master's thesis, Texas State University, 2016.

Blevins, Don. *A Priest, a Prostitute, and Some Other Early Texans: The Lives Of Fourteen Lone Star State Pioneers*. Guilford, CN: Globe Pequot Press, 2008.

Block, W. T. *A History of Jefferson County, Texas*. Nederland, TX: Nederland Publishing, 1976.

Bolton, Herbert Eugene. *Texas in the Middle Eighteenth Century: Studies in Spanish Colonial History and Administration*. Austin: University of Texas Press, 1970.

Bowen, Charles, ed. *American Almanac and Repository of Useful Knowledge, for the Year 1834*. Boston: Charles Bowen, 1833.

Bradley, Ed. *We Never Retreat: Filibustering Expeditions into Spanish Texas, 1812–1822*. College Station: Texas A&M University Press, 2015.

Bradley, Jared William. *Interim Appointment: W. C. C. Claiborne Letterbook, 1804–1805*. Baton Rouge: Louisiana State University Press, 2002.

Brown, Gordon S. *Latin American Rebels and the United States, 1806–1822*. Jefferson, NC: McFarland & Company, 2015.

Brown, Mary M. *A School History of Texas, from Its Discovery in 1685 to 1893*. Dallas: Mary M. Brown, 1894.

Brown, William Horace. *The Glory Seekers: The Romance of Would-Be Founders of Empire in the Early Days of the Great Southwest*. Chicago: A. C. McClurg & Co., 1906.

Carlson, Laurie Winn. *Seduced by the West: Jefferson's America and the Lure of the Land Beyond the Mississippi*. Chicago: Ivan R. Dee, 2003.

Carso, Brian F. *"Whom Can We Trust Now?": The Meaning of Treason in the United States, from Revolution through the Civil War*. New York: Lexington Books, 2006.

Carter, Holding. *Doomed Road of Empire*. New York: McGraw-Hill, 1963.

Cary, Thomas G. *Memoir of Thomas Handasyd Perkins*. Boston: Little, Brown and Company, 1856.

Casey, Powell A. *Encyclopedia of Forts, Posts, Named Camps and Other Military Installations in Louisiana, 1700–1981*. Baton Rouge: Claitor's Publishing, 1983.

Castañeda, Carlos. *Our Catholic Heritage in Texas 1780–1810*. 6 vols. New York: Arno Press, 1976.

Chabot, Frederick C., ed. *Memoirs of Antonio Menchaca*. San Antonio, Yanaguana Society, 1937.

———. *Texas in 1811: The Las Casas and Sambrano Revolutions*. San Antonio: Yanaguana Society, 1941.

———. *With the Makers of San Antonio*. San Antonio: Privately published, 1937.

Chandler, Charles Lyon. *Inter-American Acquaintances*. 2nd ed. Sewanee, TN: University Press, 1917.

Chapman, George T. *Sketches of the Alumni of Dartmouth College, from the First Graduation in 1771 to the Present Time, with a Brief History of the Institution*. Cambridge, MA: Riverside Press, 1867.

Chipman, Donald E. *Spanish Texas 1519–1821*. Austin: University of Texas Press, 1992.

Clark, Daniel. *Proofs of the Corruption of Gen. James Wilkinson and of His Connexion with Aaron Burr*. [1809] Reprinted Freeport, New York: Books for Libraries Press, 1970.

Coolidge, Austin, and John Mansfield. *History and Description of New England, General and Local*, vol. 1. Boston: Austin J. Coolidge, 1859.

Coronado, Raúl. *A World Not to Come: A History of Latino Writing and Print Culture*. Cambridge, MA: Harvard University Press, 2013.

Cothren, William. *History of Ancient Woodbury, Connecticut, from the First Indian Deed in 1659 to 1854, Including the Present Towns of Washington, Southbury, Bethlehem, Roxbury, and a Part of Oxford and Middlebury*. Waterbury, CT: Bronson Brothers, 1854.

Cox, Isaac Joslin. *The West Florida Controversy, 1798–1813: A Study in American Diplomacy*. Gloucester, MA: Peter Smith, 1967.

Crawford, Ann Fears. *The Eagle: The Autobiography of Santa Anna*. Austin: State House Press, 1988.

Crosbie, Laurence M. *Phillips Exeter Academy, a History*. Exeter, NH: Phillips Exeter Academy, 1923.

Crozier, William Armstrong, ed. *The Buckners of Virginia and the Allied Families of Strother and Ashby*. New York: The Genealogical Society of New York, 1907.

Cullum, George W. *Biographical Register of the Officers and Graduates of the United States Military Academy*. Boston: Houghton, Mifflin, 1891.

Dahlqvist, Rasmus. *From Martin to Despallier: The Story of A French Colonial Family*. n.p.: CreateSpace, 2013.

Davis, William C. *Rogue Republic: How Would-Be Patriots Waged the Shortest Revolution in American History*. Boston: Houghton Mifflin Harcourt, 2011.

———. *Three Roads to the Alamo*. New York: Harper-Collins, 1998.

De la Teja, Jesús F. *Faces of Béxar: Early San Antonio & Texas*. College Station: Texas A&M University Press, 2016.

———. *A Revolution Remembered: The Memoirs and Selected Correspondence of Juan N. Seguín*. Austin: State House Press, 1991.

———. *San Antonio de Béxar: A Community on New Spain's Northern Frontier*. Albuquerque: University of New Mexico Press, 1995.

Devereaux, Linda Ericson. *Tales from the Old Stone Fort*. Nacogdoches: Linda Erickson Devereaux, 1976.

Dickens, Asbury, and James C. Allen, ed. *Documents of the Congress of the United States in Relation to the Public Lands*, vol. 4. Washington, DC: Gales and Seaton, 1859.

Dixon, Sam Houston. *The Men Who Made Texas Free: The Signers of the Texas Declaration of Independence*. Houston: Texas Historical Publishing Company, 1924.

Doolen, Andy. *Territories of Empire: U.S. Writing from the Louisiana Purchase to Mexican Independence*. Oxford: Oxford University Press, 2014.

Doyle, Don H. ed. *Secession as an International Phenomenon: From America's Civil War to Contemporary Separatist Movements*. Athens: University of Georgia Press, 2010.

Epperson, Jean L. *Lost Spanish Towns: Atascosito and Trinidad de Salcedo*. Hemphill, TX: Dogwood Press, 1997.

Fauquier County (Va.) Board of Trade. *Fauquier County, Virginia: Historical Notes*, vol. 220. Warrenton, VA: Fauquier County Board of Trade, 1914.

Fehrenbach, T. R. *Lone Star: A History of Texas and the Texans*. New York: Collier Books, 1968.

Fitz, Caitlin. *Our Sister Republics: The United States in an Age of American Revolutions*. New York: Liveright Publishing, 2016.

Folsom, Bradley. *Arredondo: Last Spanish Ruler of Texas and Northeastern New Spain*. Norman: University of Oklahoma Press, 2017.

Foote, Henry Stuart. *Texas and the Texans, or the Advance of the Anglo-Americans in the Southwest*, vol. 1. Philadelphia: Thomas, Cowperthwait & Co., 1841.

Fortier, Alcée ed. *Louisiana: Comprising Sketches of Parishes, Towns, Events, Institutions, and Persons, Arranged in Cyclopedic Form*, vol. 1. Madison: Century Historical Association, 1914.

French, B. F. *Historical Collections of Louisiana*, vol. 3. New York: D. Appleton & Company, 1851.
Gayarré, Charles. *History of Louisiana: The Spanish Domination*, vol. 3. New Orleans: Armand Hawkins, 1885.
Gaines, Pierce Welch, ed. *Political Works of Concealed Authorship during the Administrations of Washington, Adams, and Jefferson*. New Haven: Yale University Library, 1959.
Gale, Kira. *Meriwether Lewis: The Assassination of an American Hero and the Silver Mines of Mexico*. Omaha: River Junction Press, 2015.
Garrett, Julia Kathryn. *Green Flag over Texas: The Last Years of Spain in Texas*. Austin: Pemberton Press, 1939.
Gracy, David B. *Moses Austin: His Life*. San Antonio: Trinity University Press, 1987.
Groneman, Bill. *Alamo Defenders: A Genealogy: The People and their Words*. Austin: Eakin Press, 1990.
Hansen, Todd. *The Alamo Reader: A Study in History*. Mechanicsburg, PA: Stackpole Books, 2003.
Hatcher, Mattie Austin. *The Opening of Texas to Foreign Settlement, 1801–1821*. Philadelphia: Porcupine Press, 1976.
Head, David. *Privateers of the Americas: Spanish American Privateering from the United States in the Early Republic*. Athens: University of Georgia Press, 2015.
Heggoy, Alf Andrew, ed. *Through Foreign Eyes: Western Attitudes towards North Africa*. Boston: University Press of America, 1982.
Heitman, Francis B. *Historical Register and Dictionary of the United States Army, from Its Organization September 29, 1798 to March 2, 1903*. Washington, DC: Government Printing Office, 1903.
Henderson, Timothy J. *The Mexican Wars for Independence*. New York: Hill and Wang, 2009.
Hobsbawm, Eric. *Bandits*. New York: Pantheon Books, 1981.
Jacobs, James Ripley. *Tarnished Warrior: Major General James Wilkinson*. New York: MacMillan Company, 1938.
———. *The Beginning of the U. S. Army*. Princeton: Princeton University Press, 1947.
James, Thomas. *Three Years among the Indians and Mexicans*. Saint Louis: Missouri Historical Society, 1916.
Jameson, E. O. *The Cogswells in America*. Boston: Alfred Mudge & Son, 1884.
Jarratt, Rie. *Gutiérrez de Lara: Mexican Texan—The Story of a Creole Hero*. Austin: Creole Texana, 1949.
Johnston, William Preston. *The Johnstons of Salisbury*. New Orleans: L. Graham and Son, 1897.
Kemper, Willis M. *Genealogy of the Kemper Family in the United States: Descendants of John Kemper of Virginia; with a Short Historical Sketch of His Family and of the German Reformed Colony at Germanna and Germantown, Va*. Chicago: G. K. Hazlett & Company, 1899.
Kinsbruner, Jay. *Independence in Spanish America: Civil Wars, Revolutions, and Underdevelopment*. Albuquerque: University of New Mexico Press, 1995.
Knight, Carol Young. *First Settlers of Catahoula Parish, Louisiana, 1808–1839*. Aledo, TX: Carol Young Knight, 1985.
La Vere, David. "Davenport, Barr, Murphy and Smith: Traders on the Louisiana-Texas Frontier," master's thesis, Northwestern State University of Louisiana, 1989.
———. *The Texas Indians*. College Station: Texas A&M University Press, 2004.

L'Herisson, Lawrence E. "The Evolution of the Texas Road and the Subsequential Settlement Occupancy of the Adjacent Strip of Northwestern Louisiana: 1528–1824," master's thesis, Louisiana State University, 1977.

Linklater, Andro. *An Artist in Treason: The Extraordinary Double Life of General James Wilkinson.* New York: Walker Publishing, 2009.

Long, James Weldon. "Revolutionary Republics: U. S. National Narratives and the Independence of Latin America, 1810–1846." PhD diss., Louisiana State University, 2011.

Martínez De Vara, Art. *Tejano Patriot: The Revolutionary Life of José Francisco Ruiz, 1783–1840.* Austin: Texas State Historical Association Press, 2020.

Matthews, Jean V. *Toward a New Society: American Thought and Culture, 1800–1830.* Boston: Twayne Publishers, 1991.

Matovina, Timothy, and Jesús F. de la Teja, ed. *Recollections of a Tejano Life: Antonio Menchaca in Texas History.* Austin: University of Texas Press, 2013.

May, Robert E. *Manifest Destiny's Underworld: Filibustering in Antebellum America.* Charlotte: University of North Carolina Press, 2003.

McCaleb, Walter Flavius. *The Aaron Burr Conspiracy.* New York: Dodd, Mead and Company, 1903.

McDonald, David. *José Antonio Navarro: In Search of the American Dream in Nineteenth-Century Texas.* Denton: Texas State Historical Association, 2010.

McGraw, Joachim, ed. *A Texas Legacy: The Old San Antonio Road and the Caminos Reales, a Tricentennial History, 1691–1991.* Austin: State Department of Highways and Public Transportation, 1991.

McMichael, Andrew. *Atlantic Loyalties: Americans in Spanish West Florida, 1785–1810.* Athens: University of Georgia Press, 2008.

McLane, Hiram H. *Irene Viesca, A Tale of the Magee Expedition in the Gauchupin War in Texas.* San Antonio: San Antonio Printing, 1886.

Miller, Marshall Stone. "The History of Fort Claiborne, Louisiana, 1804–1822," master's thesis, Louisiana State University, 1969.

Miller, Edward L. *New Orleans and the Texas Revolution.* College Station: Texas A&M University Press, 2004.

Milligan, James Clark. "José Bernardo Gutiérrez de Lara, Mexican Frontiersman, 1811–1841." PhD diss., Texas Tech University, 1975.

Moorhead, Max L. *New Mexico's Royal Road: Trade and Travel on the Chihuahua Trail.* Norman: University of Oklahoma Press, 1954.

Morrison, Michael A., ed. *The Human Tradition in Antebellum America.* Wilmington, DE: Scholarly Resources, 2000.

Narrett, David. *Adventurism and Empire: The Struggle for Mastery in the Louisiana-Florida Borderlands, 1762–1803.* Chapel Hill: University of North Carolina Press, 2015.

Newman, Harry Wright. *The Lucketts of Portobacco.* Washington, DC: Harry Wright Newman, 1938.

Nugent, Walter. *Habits of Empire: A History of American Expansion.* New York: Alfred A. Knopf, 2008.

O'Connor, Kathryn Stoner. *The Presidio la Bahia del Espiritu Santo de Zuniga, 1721 to 1846.* Austin: Von Boeckmann-Jones Co., 1966.

Orsi, Jared. *Citizen Explorer: The Life of Zebulon Pike.* New York: Oxford University Press, 2014.

Owsley, Frank L., and Gene A. Smith. *Filibusters and Expansionists: Jeffersonian Manifest Destiny, 1800–1821*. Tuscaloosa: University of Alabama Press, 1997.
Palmer, Dave Richard, and James W. Stryker. *Early American Wars and Military Institutions*. Wayne, NJ: Avery Publishing, 1986.
Phelps, Oliver Seymour, and Andrew T. Servin. *The Phelps Family in America and Their English Ancestors*, vol. 1. Pittsfield, MA: Eagle Publishing, 1899.
Phillips Exeter Academy. *Catalogue of the Officers and Students of Phillips Exeter Academy*. Exeter, NH: J&B Williams, 1838.
Powell, William Henry. *List of Officers of the Army of the United States from 1779 to 1900*. New York: L. R. Hamersly & Co., 1900.
Poyo, Gerald E., ed. *Tejano Journey, 1770–1850*. Austin: University of Texas Press, 1996.
Poyo, Gerald E., and Gilberto Hinojosa, ed. *Tejano Origins in Eighteenth-Century San Antonio*. Austin: University of Texas Press, 1991.
Pratt, Julius W. *Expansionists of 1812*. Gloucester, MA: Peter Smith, 1957.
Prucha, Francis Paul. *The Sword of the Republic: The United States Army on the Frontier: 1783–1846*. Bloomington: Indiana University Press, 1977.
Ramos, Raúl A. *Beyond the Alamo: Forging Mexican Ethnicity in San Antonio, 1821–1861*. Chapel Hill: University of North Carolina Press, 2008.
Rightor, Henry. *Standard History of New Orleans, Louisiana*. Chicago: Lewis Publishing, 1900.
Riva Palacio López, Antonio, ed. *Pliegos de la diplomacia insurgente*. Mexico City: Cámara de Senadores de la República Mexicana, 1987.
Rodríguez O., Jaime E. *Political Culture in Spanish America, 1800–1830*. Lincoln: University of Nebraska Press, 2017.
Rodríguez, Junius P., ed. *The Louisiana Purchase: A Historical and Geographical Encyclopedia*. Santa Barbara: ABC-CLIO, 2002.
Roland, Charles P. *Albert Sydney Johnston, Soldier of Three Republics*. Lexington, KY: University Press of Kentucky, 2001.
Schwartz, Ted, and Robert Thonhoff. *Forgotten Battlefield of the First Texas Revolution*. Austin: Eakin Press, 1985.
Seaburg, Carl, and Stanley Paterson. *Merchant Prince of Boston: Col. T. H. Perkins, 1764–1854*. Cambridge: Harvard University Press, 1971.
Sibley, Marilyn McAdams. *Lone Stars and State Gazettes: Texas Newspapers before the Civil War*. College Station: Texas A&M University Press, 1983.
Smith, F. Todd. *From Dominance to Disappearance*. Lincoln: University of Nebraska Press, 2005.
Sowell, Andrew Jackson. *Early Settlers and Indian Fighters of Southwest Texas*. Austin: Ben C. Jones and Co., 1900.
Stackpole, Everett S., and Lucien Thompson. *History of the Town of Durham New Hampshire*, vol. 1. Publisher unknown.
Stagg, J. C. A. *Borderlines in Borderlands: James Madison and the Spanish-American Frontier, 1776–1821*. New Haven: Yale University Press, 2009.
Steward, Dick. *Frontier Swashbuckler: The Life and Legend of John Smith T*. Columbia: University of Missouri Press, 2000.
Stewart, David O. *American Emperor: Aaron Burr's Challenge to Jefferson's America*. New York: Simon and Schuster, 2011.
Stoltz, Joseph. "An Ardent Military Spirit: William C. C. Claiborne and the Creation of the Orleans Territorial Militia, 1803–1805," master's thesis, University of New Orleans, 2009.

Strickland, Barbara Comeaux. *Selected Papers of the Seventh Grand Reunion of the Descendants of the Founders of Natchitoches.* Natchitoches: Founders of Natchitoches, 1987.
Thacher, Samuel Cooper, ed. *The Monthly Anthology, and Boston Review*, vol. 5. Boston: Snelling and Simon, 1808.
Todd, Janet. *Mary Wollstonecraft, A Revolutionary Life.* New York: Columbia University Press, 2002.
Travers, Len. *Celebrating the Fourth: Independence Day and the Rites of Nationalism in the Early Republic.* Amherst: University of Massachusetts Press, 1997.
Tucker, Spencer, ed. *The Encyclopedia of the War of 1812, a Political, Social, and Military History*, vol. 1. Santa Barbara: ABC-CLIO, 2012.
Turner, Frederick Jackson. *The Significance of the Frontier in American History.* London: Penguin Books, 2008.
Tyng, Charles. *Before the Wind: The Memoir of an American Sea Captain, 1808–1833*, ed. Susan Fels. New York: Penguin, 1999.
US Department of State. *State Papers and Publick Documents of the United States from the Accession of George Washington to the Presidency, Exhibiting a Complete View of Our Foreign Relations at That Time.* Boston: T. B. Wait and Sons, 1817.
Van, Rachel Tamar. "Free Trade and Family Values: Kinship Networks and the Culture of Early American Capitalism." PhD diss., Columbia University, 2011.
Vernet, Julien. *Strangers on Their Native Soil: Opposition to United States Governance in Louisiana's Orleans Territory, 1803–1809.* Jackson: University Press of Mississippi, 2013.
Velásquez, María del Carmen. *Tres Estudios Sobre las Provincias Internas de Nueva España.* Mexico City: El Colegio de México, 1979.
Vigness, David M. *Spanish Texas: 1519–1810.* Boston: American Press, 1983.
Wallace, Ernest, David M. Vigness, and George B. Ward, ed. *Documents of Texas History.* Austin: State House Press, 1994.
Walraven, Bill, and Marjorie. *The Magnificent Barbarians: Little-Told Tales of the Texas Revolution.* Austin: Eakin Press, 1993.
Warren, Harris Gaylord. *The Sword Was Their Passport: A History of American Filibustering in the Mexican Revolution.* Baton Rouge: Louisiana State University Press, 1943.
Watson, Samuel J. *Jackson's Sword: The Army Officer Corps on the American Frontier, 1810–1821.* Lawrence: University Press of Kansas, 2012.
Weems, John Edward. *Men without Countries.* Boston: Houghton Mifflin Company, 1969.
Whitaker, Arthur P., ed. *Latin America and the Enlightenment*, 2nd ed. Ithaca: Cornell University Press, 1961.
Wilkinson, James. *Burr's Conspiracy Exposed; and General Wilkinson Vindicated against the Slanders of His Enemies on That Important Occasion.* Washington, DC: James Wilkinson, 1811.
Wilson, Maurine T., and Jack Jackson. *Philip Nolan and Texas: Expeditions into the Unknown Land, 1791–1801.* Waco: Texian Press, 1987.
Wohl, Michael S. "A Man in the Shadow: The Life of Daniel Clark." PhD diss., Tulane University, 1984.
Wolf, Simon, and Louis Edward Levy. *The American Jew as Patriot, Soldier and Citizen.* Philadelphia: The Levytype Company, 1895.
Yoakum, Henderson K. *The History of Texas from Its First Settlement in 1685 to Its Annexation to the United States in 1846*, vol. 1. New York: Bedfield, 1856.

Journals/Articles

Abernethy, Thomas Perkins. "Aaron Burr in Mississippi." *Journal of Southern History* 15, no. 1 (February 1949): 9–21.

Aslakson, Kenneth. "Immigrant Lawyers and Slavery in Territorial New Orleans." *Tulane European and Civil Law Forum* 31/32 (2017): 33–77.

Benson, Nettie Lee. "A Governor's Report on Texas in 1809." *Southwestern Historical Quarterly* 71, no. 4 (April 1968): 603–15.

Bloom, Capt. James R. "Why We Vaccinate Sailors." *Military Medicine* 181, (April 2016).

Bowman, Charles H., Jr. "Manuel Torres, a Spanish American Patriot in Philadelphia, 1796–1822." *Pennsylvania Magazine of History and Biography* 94, no. 1 (January 1970): 26–53.

Brady, Kevin. "Unspoken Words: James Monroe's Involvement in the Magee-Gutiérrez Filibuster." *East Texas Historical Journal* 45, no. 1 (March 2007): 58–68.

Brandt, Penny S. "A Letter of Dr. John Sibley, Indian Agent." *Louisiana History: The Journal of the Louisiana Historical Association* 29, no. 4 (Autumn 1988): 365–87.

Bugbee, Lester G. "The Old Three Hundred." Quarterly of the Texas State Historical Association 1, no. 2 (October 1897): 108–17.

Carpenter, Edwin H., Jr. "Arsène Lacarrière Latour." *Hispanic American Historical Review* 18, no. 2 (May 1938): 221–27.

Crimmins, Col. M. I. "Augustus William Magee, the Second Advanced Courier of American Expansion into Texas." *West Texas Historical Association Year Book* 20 (1944): 92.

Cox, Isaac Joslin. "The American Intervention in West Florida." *American Historical Review* 17, no. 2 (January 1912): 290–311.

Coyle, John G., ed. *The Journal of the American-Irish Historical Society*. New York: American-Irish Historical Society, 1918.

DeBow, J. B. B. *DeBow's Southern and Western Review* 12 (January 1852): 50–56.

De la Teja, Jesús F., "Economic Integration of a Periphery: The Cattle Industry in 18th Century Texas." *Texas Papers on Latin America*. Austin: Institute of Latin American Studies, University of Texas at Austin, 1991.

———. "Ramón de Murillo's Plan for the Reform of New Spain's Frontier Defenses." *Southwestern Historical Quarterly* 107, no. 4 (April 2004): 502–15.

———. "Review: The Mexican Wars for Independence." *Southwestern Historical Quarterly* 113, no. 4 (April 2010): 535–36.

Din, Gilbert C. "A Troubled Seven Years: Spanish Reactions to American Claims and Aggression in 'West Florida,' 1803–1810." *Louisiana History: Journal of the Louisiana Historical Association* 59, no. 4 (2018): 409–52.

———. "Spain's Immigration Policy in Louisiana and the American Penetration, 1792–1803." *Southwestern Historical Quarterly* 76, no. 3 (1973): 267–68.

Dykstra, Kristin A. "On the Betrayal of Nations: José Alvarez de Toledo's Philadelphia Manifesto (1811) and Justification (1816)." *New Centennial Review* 4, no. 1 (Spring 2004): 267–305.

Faulk, Odie. "A Description of Texas in 1803." *Southwestern Historical Quarterly* 66, no. 4 (April 1963): 513–15.

Garrett, Julia Kathryn. "The First Newspaper of Texas: 'Gaceta de Texas.'" *Southwestern Historical Quarterly* 40, no. 3 (January 1937).

———. "Dr. John Sibley and the Louisiana-Texas Frontier, 1803–1814." *Southwestern Historical Quarterly* 45. no. 3 (January 1942): 286–301. (Series of articles over several volumes.)

———. "Dr. John Sibley." *SWHQ* 46, no. 3 (January 1943): 272–77.
———. "Dr. John Sibley." *SWHQ* 48, no. 1 (July 1944): 67–71.
———. "Dr. John Sibley." *SWHQ* 48, no. 4 (April 1945): 547–49.
———. "Dr. John Sibley." *SWHQ* 49, no. 1 (July 1945): 116–19.
———. "Dr. John Sibley." *SWHQ* 49, no. 3 (January 1946): 399–431.
———. "Dr. John Sibley." *SWHQ* 49, no. 4 (April 1946): 599–614.
Gerona, Carla. "With a Song in Their Hands: Incendiary Décimas from the Texas and Louisiana Borderlands during a Revolutionary Age." *Early American Studies* 12, no. 1 (Winter 2014): 93–142.
Golway, Hugh. "The Cruise of the Lelia Byrd." *Journal of the West* 8 (July 1969): 390–401.
Gronet, Richard W. "United States and the Invasion of Texas, 1810–1814." *The Americas* 25 (January 1969): 281–306.
Guedea, Virginia. "Autonomía e independencia en la provincia de Texas. La Junta de Gobierno de San Antonio de Béjar, 1813." In *La independencia de México y el proceso autonomista novohispano, 1808–1824*. Mexico City: Instituto de Investigaciones Históricas, 2001, pp. 135–84.
Haggard, J. Villasana. "The Counter-Revolution of Béxar, 1811." *Southwestern Historical Quarterly* 43, no. 2 (October 1939): 222–35.
Hamill, Hugh M., Jr. "Royalist Counterinsurgency in the Mexican War for Independence: The Lessons of 1811." *Hispanic American Historical Review* 53, no. 3 (August 1973): 470–89.
Haskell, Lewis W. "Tablets in the English Church at Algiers Commemorative of the Deeds of American Consul General Shaler, Admiral Stephen Decatur and Commander Bainbridge." *American Foreign Service Journal* 4, no. 3 (March 1929): 97–100.
Hatcher, Mattie Austin. "Joaquín de Arredondo's Report of the Battle of the Medina, August 18, 1813. Translation." *Quarterly of the Texas State Historical Association* 11, no. 3 (1908): 220–236.
Hernandez, Jorge A. "Merchants and Mercenaries: Anglo-Americans in Mexico's Northeast." *New Mexico Historical Review* 75, no. 1 (January 2000).
Hunter, John Warren. "San Antonio's First Great Tragedy." *Frontier Times* 3, no. 1 (October 1925), 41–48.
———. "The Battle of Alazan." *Frontier Times* 3 no. 2 (November 1925): 41–48.
———. "The Battle of the Medina." *Frontier Times* 3 no. 3 (December 1925): 9–16.
———. "Some Early Tragedies of San Antonio." *Frontier Times* 18, no. 3 (December 1940): 115–41.
Hyde, Samuel C. "Introduction: Setting a Precedent for Regional Revolution: The West Florida Revolt Considered." *Florida Historical Quarterly* 90, no. 2 (2011): 121–32.
———. "Consolidating the Revolution: Factionalism and Finesse in the West Florida Revolt, 1810." *Louisiana History: Journal of the Louisiana Historical Association* 51, no. 3 (Summer 2010): 261–83.
Kanellos, Nicolás. "José Alvarez de Toledo y Dubois and the Origins of Hispanic Publishing in the Early American Republic." *Early American Literature* 43, no. 1 (2008), 83–100.
Karachuk, Robert Feikema. "A Workman's Tools: The Law Library of Henry Adams Bullard." *American Journal of Legal History* 42, no. 2 (April 1998): 160–89.
Kastor, Peter J. "'Motives of Peculiar Urgency': Local Diplomacy in Louisiana, 1803–1821." *The William and Mary Quarterly* 58, no. 4 (October 2001): 819–48.
Lee, Henry. "The Magee Family and the Origins of the China Trade." *Proceedings of the Massachusetts Historical Society* 81 (1969), 104–18.

Marshall, Robert P. "Archeological Confirmation of the Site of the Battle of Medina: A Research Note." *Southwestern Historical Quarterly* 71, no. 1 (July 2017): 57–66.

———. "The Battle of the Alazán: First Texas Republic Victorious." *Southwestern Historical Quarterly* 119, no. 1 (July 2015): 44–56.

———. "Locating the Battle of Rosillo: A Newly Discovered Map Indicates the Likely Site of the 1813 Battle Where the First Republic of Texas Was Born." *Southwestern Historical Quarterly* 68, no. 4 (April 2015): 395–403.

May, Robert E. "Young American Males and Filibustering in the Age of Manifest Destiny: The United States Army as a Cultural Mirror." *Journal of American History* 78, no. 3 (December 1991): 857–86.

McMichael, Andrew. "The Kemper 'Rebellion': Filibustering and Resident Anglo American Loyalty in Spanish West Florida." *Louisiana History* 43, no. 2 (April 2002): 133–65.

Moore, Ike. "The Earliest Printing and First Newspaper in Texas." *Southwestern Historical Quarterly* 39, no. 2 (October 1935): 83–89.

Morton, Jennie C. "Biographical Sketch of Governor John Adair." *Register of Kentucky State Historical Society* 2, no. 4 (January 1904): 7–13.

Narrett, David. "Geopolitics and Intrigue: James Wilkinson, the Spanish Borderlands, and Mexican Independence." *William and Mary Quarterly* 69, no. 1 (January 2012): 101–46.

———. "José Bernardo Gutiérrez de Lara: 'Caudillo' of the Mexican Republic in Texas." *Southwestern Historical Quarterly* 106, no. 2 (October 2002): 194–228.

———. "Liberation and Conquest: John Hamilton Robinson and U. S. Adventurism toward Mexico, 1806–1809." *Western Historical Quarterly* 40, no. 1 (Spring 2009): 23–50.

Nichols, Roy F. "William Shaler: New England Apostle of Rational Liberty." *New England Quarterly* 9, no. 1 (March 1936): 71–96.

Pennington, David J. "Reassessing James Madison's Ambitions in Florida and Texas, 1810–1813." *Southern Historian* 31 (April 13, 2010): 66–79.

Robertson, William Spence. "The First Legations of the United States in Latin America." *The Mississippi Valley Historical Review* 2, no. 2 (September 1915): 183–212.

———. "Documents Concerning the Consular Service of the United States in Latin America, with an Introductory Note." *Mississippi Valley Historical Review* 2, no. 4 (March 1916): 561–68.

Scallions, Cody. "The Rise and Fall of the Original Lone Star State: Infant American Imperialism Ascendant in West Florida." *Florida Historical Quarterly* 90, no. 2 (Fall 2011): 193–220.

Schakenbach, Lindsay. "Schemers, Dreamers, and a Revolutionary Foreign Policy: New York City in the Era of Second Independence, 1805–1815." *New York History* 94, no. 3–4 (Summer/Fall 2013): 267–82.

Skelton, William B. "High Army Leadership in the Era of the War of 1812: The Making and the Remaking of the Officer Corps." *William and Mary Quarterly* 51, no. 2 (April 1994): 253–74.

Smith, F. Todd. "The Kadohadacho Indians and the Louisiana-Texas Frontier, 1803–1815." *Southwestern Historical Quarterly* 95, no. 2 (October 1991): 177–204.

Stagg, J. C. A. "The Madison Administration and Mexico: Reinterpreting the Gutiérrez-Magee Raid of 1812–1813." *William and Mary Quarterly* 59 (April 2002): 449–80.

Stoltz, Joseph F. III. "'The Preservation of Good Order': William C. C. Claiborne and the Militia of the Louisiana Provisional Government, 1803–1805." *Louisiana History: The Journal of the Louisiana Historical Association* 54, no. 4 (Fall 2013): 424–47.

The Texas Genealogical Society. "List of Battle of Velasco Participants." *Stirpes* 21, no. 3 (September 1981): 179–80.

Tregle, Joseph G., Jr. "The Josiah Stoddard Johnston Papers." *Pennsylvania Magazine of History and Biography* 69, no. 4 (October 1945): 326–29.

Vogel, Robert, ed. "A Louisianan's View of the Mexican Revolution in 1810: Paul Bouet Laffite's Letter to Doctor John Sibley." *North Louisiana Historical Association Journal* 16 (Fall 1985): 131–35.

Walker, Henry, ed. "William McLane's Narrative of the Magee-Gutiérrez Expedition, 1812–1813." *Southwestern Historical Quarterly* 66, no. 2 (October 1962): 234–51

———. "William McLane's Narrative of the Magee-Gutiérrez Expedition," *Southwestern Historical Quarterly* 66, no. 3 (January 1963): 457–79.

———. "William McLane's Narrative of the Magee-Gutiérrez Expedition, 1812–1813." *Southwestern Historical Quarterly* 66, no. 4 (April 1963): 569–88.

Warren, Harris Gaylord. "Documents Relating to Pierre Laffite's Entrance into the Service of Spain." *Southwestern Historical Quarterly* 44, no. 1 (July 1940): 76–87.

———. "José Álvarez de Toledo's Initiation as a Filibuster, 1811–1813." *The Hispanic American Historical Review* 20, no. 1 (February 1940): 56–82.

———. "The Southern Career of Don Juan Mariano Picornell." *Journal of Southern History* 8, no. 3 (August 1942): 311–33.

West, Elizabeth Howard. "Diary of José Bernardo Gutiérrez de Lara, 1811–1812. [Part 1]." *American Historical Review* 34, no. 1 (October 1928): 55–77.

———. "Diary of José Bernardo Gutiérrez De Lara, 1811–1812. [Part 2]. Year of 1812." *The American Historical Review* 34, no. 2 (1929): 281–94.

Whittington, G. P. "Dr. John Sibley of Natchitoches, 1757–1837." *Louisiana Historical Quarterly* 10, no. 4 (October 1927): 467–73.

Wohl, Michael. "Not Yet Saint Nor Sinner: A Further Note on Daniel Clark." *Louisiana History: Journal of the Louisiana Historical Association* 24, no. 2 (Spring 1983): 195–205.

Unpublished Sources

Detwiller, Frederick C. "Magee Family Mariners ca. 1750–1820." 2012. (Unpublished manuscript, provided by the author, of Georgetown, Massachusetts.)

"Sumaria Ynformacion formada contra D. José Erasmo Seguín, Admor. de Correos de esta Capital acusado de Ynfidente [1814]," Archivo General del Estado de Coahuila, Fondo Colonial, C35, E53. Unpublished translation by Jesús F. de la Teja.

Web Resources

"A Revolutionary Irishman" PDF document, Pilgrim Hall Museum, Boston, Massachusetts, available at https://pilgrimhall.org/pdf/James_Magee.pdf.

Bernsen, James Aalan, *The Texas History Blog*, http://www.texhist.com.

Cogliano, Francis D. *Failed Filibusters: The Kemper Rebellion, the Burr Conspiracy and Early American Expansion*. University of Edinburgh, available at http://www.shca.ed.ac.uk/staff/supporting_files/fcogliano/failed-filibusters.pdf.

Cox, I. Waynne. "Field Survey and Archival Research for the Rosillo Creek Battleground Area, Southeast San Antonio, Texas." Index of Texas Archaeology: Open Access Gray Literature from the Lone Star State, vol. 1990, article 1, available at https://scholarworks.sfasu.edu/ita/vol1990/iss1/1.

Gibson, Steve. "The Arocha Family from the Island of Palma, the 9th Family of the List of Canary Islanders taken at Quautitlan, November 8, 1730," *Béxar Genealogy Home Page*, 2002, available at http://Béxargenealogy.com/archives/familyfiles/arocha.rtf.

Selin, Shannon. "Presidio Commander Francisco García." In *Imagining the Bounds of History* (blog), available at https://shannonselin.com/2016/06/francisco-garcia/.

Sons of DeWitt Colony, available at http://www.sonsofdewittcolony.org.

Stagg, J. C. A., ed. "The Political Essays of William Shaler." *William and Mary Quarterly* website, https://oieahc-cf.wm.edu/wmq/Apr02/stagg.pdf.

Texas Education Agency. *Texas Essential Knowledge and Skills for Social Studies, Subchapter B. Middle School.* Available at http://ritter.tea.state.tx.us/rules/tac/chapter113/ch113b.html#113.19.

Texas State Historical Association. *Handbook of Texas Online.* https://tshaonline.org/handbook.

Williamson, Thurmond A. *The Munsons of Texas—an American Saga* (self-published genealogical manuscript, 1987), http://www.munsons-of-texas.net/c7.html.

US National Parks Service, Jean Lafitte National Historical Park and Preserve. *Battle of New Orleans, War of 1812 American Muster and Troop Roster List* (accessed May 14, 2020), available at http://www.nps.gov/jela/learn/historyculture/upload/Battle-of-New-Orleans-Muster-Lists-final-copy-01062015.pdf.

Index

Acosta (rapist), 306
Adair, John, 72, 145, 162–63; Burr Conspiracy, 11, 22, 29–31; efforts after 1813, 321–22, 326, 342, 351, 353; organizing of the expedition, 149, 151–53, 157–58, 165, 170, 172–74, 176, 183, 199, 204, 219–20, 241, 253, 259, 277, 279, 369n21, 403n28, 403n31, 403n35, 403n38, 404n48, 408n12, 415n2, 419n15; warning to the president 65–66
Adams, Francisco, 44
Adams, John, 17, 49, 50, 52
Adams, John Quincy, 318, 329, 380n7
Adams Onís Treaty, 326
African Americans, 20, 29, 225
agents to Spanish Empire: French, 64, 67, 89, 98, 131, 148, 241, 253, 433n61; US, 6–9, 74–79, 95. *See also* Lowry, Robert K.; Poinsett, Joel Roberts; Robinson, John Hamilton; Shaler, William
agriculture, 41, 90, 331, 347, 148; cotton, 38, 66, 348, 355; stock raising, 38, 40, 91, 98; wool, 174, 179, 187, 411n5
Aguallo, Nuevo Santander, 121
Alabama, 12
Alamo, 3, 39, 93, 103, 206, 236, 248, 268, 290, 303; 1836 siege and battle of, 2, 4–5, 333, 341, 342–45, 353, 367n7; as prison 91–92, 207, 239, 247, 276, 305, 307, 338, 345; as rebel headquarters, 240, 287
Alamo de Parras company, 38, 190–91, 344, 377n37
Alazán Creek, 266, 271, 432n48. *See also* Battle of Alazán

Aldama, Ignacio, 98–100, 103, 114, 121, 262
Aldama, Juan, 98, 102, 121
Aldape, Pedro José de, 180, 212
Alden, Samuel, 216, 220, 281, 363
Alexandria Daily Gazette, 223
Allen, Benjamin, 183, 317, 363
Allen, Martin, 4, 317, 338–39, 363
Allende, Ignacio, 102
American flag, 9, 32–33, 35, 201–02, 348, 359
American Revolution, 13, 16, 22, 57, 65, 83, 96, 125, 182–83, 223, 317, 338, 357
Anaya, Juan Pablo, 323–24, 446n29
Angelina River, 55
annexation sentiment: Cuba, 350; Florida, 67–69; Texas, 162, 214, 350, 353, 355–56
Apache Indians, 28, 86, 232, 237, 249, 420n11; Chief Cordero, 109, 227, 324, 421n23; Chief Prieto, 245, 273; Lipan, 38, 92, 227, 235, 262, 270
Arcos, Miguel, 14, 249
Arkansas, 66, 81, 111, 132
Armiñán, Benito de, 330
Arocha, Francisco (rebel), 94, 307, 310, 314, 318, 361, 425n35, 434n8
Arocha, Francisco José de, 38
Arocha, José María, 341
Arocha, Joséfa Nuñes de, 2, 314, 360, 361
Arocha, Tomás, 227, 310, 313, 314, 361, 425n30, 425n35, 442n64
Arredondo, Joaquín de, 2, 321–22, 327, 346, 356, 359; Battle of Medina, 295–96, 298, 300–303; campaign in Northern Mexico, 121–22, 149, 260–61; conquest of Texas,

471

303–305, 307–08, 311, 313–15, 318–19; planning for Texas, 262, 264–67, 280, 282, 288–91; post-revolution, 330–33, 340, 342
Arredondo, Nicolás, 260
Arroyo Hondo, 28, 83, 123, 393
Arroyo las Borregas, 175
artillery, 218, 324, 432n48; advantages of American, 37; rebel, 149, 154, 175, 183, 188, 194, 200, 206–07, 212, 225, 236, 240, 266–67, 270–73, 292, 294, 297, 300, 329, 336, 411n8, 413n33, 417n24, 433n51, 438n2; Republic of Texas, 342, 345; Spanish, 73, 103, 173, 205, 207, 211, 228–30, 236–39, 262, 271–74, 290, 296–99, 301–302, 433n51, 438–9n8; US army, 82–83, 151–52, 162, 387n25, 447n30
Ashley, Robert, 43, 378n42
Atascocita (later town), 313, 334, 354
Atascocito (Spanish fort), 180
Atlantic Coast Forts, 55, 82
Attoyac, 176
Aurora, 130
Aury, Louis Michel, 324
Aury-Mina Expedition, 324, 327, 340
Austin, Moses, 60, 332
Austin, Stephen F., 4, 44, 319, 332–33, 337–41, 356, 358
Ayala, Agabo de, 94
Ayala, Tadeo Ortiz de, 141

Baltimore, 5, 30, 59, 141, 182, 204, 218, 237
banditti. *See* Neutral Ground
Banegas, José Francisco, 156, 361
Barr and Davenport, 44–45, 84–85, 123
Barr, William, 40, 44–45, 84, 89–90, 143, 146, 179, 310
Barrera, Gertrudis, 256, 268, 429n41
Bastrop, Baron de, 101–102, 391
Bastrop, Texas, 205
Baton Rouge, 12, 82, 106, 137, 150, 167, 202, 322, 395n11, 446n446; target of filibusters, 15, 19–20, 24, 26–27, 66–69, 160, 176
Battle of Alazán, 270–73, 275, 280, 284, 287–89, 291–92
Battle of Calderon Bridge, 102, 121
Battle of La Bahía. *See* La Bahía
Battle of Medina, 2–4, 294–303, 309, 312, 316, 317–19, 358, 433n62; aftermath, 322–23, 325, 330, 333–34; veterans of, 327, 334, 338–39, 341, 343–45
Battle of Rosillo, 2, 235–238, 240, 244, 424n20; aftermath, 246–47, 254, 265, 271, 272, 274, 294, 299; veterans of, 256, 286, 317, 336–37, 340
Battle of San Jacinto, 2, 273, 337, 341–43, 345, 357, 451n44
Battle of Trafalgar, 33–34
Battle of the White Cow, 224–26
Bayou Piedra, 85
Bayou Pierre, 28, 41, 199, 241, 316, 376n27, 388n31, 395n10, 414n51
Bayou Sara, 12, 14, 19, 312
Beard, W.C., 325, 327
Bedlow Island, 82
Beltrán, Carlos, 266–71, 287, 290–91, 293, 363; background and veracity, 239–40, 369n19, 425n28; Battle of Medina and aftermath, 295–97, 299, 301, 303, 305–306; executions and aftermath, 247–49, 251, 266–71, 427n4; service in Republican Army, 263–64, 273–74
Bergara, Ancelmo, 193–94, 249, 251, 341, 361, 411n7, 413n33
Béxar (town). *See* San Antonio
Béxar Junta: in exile, 319, 336; under Gutiérrez, 241, 243–44, 246, 252, 255, 277, 280–82; under Toledo, 286, 310, 314, 318, 319; under Zambrano, 99–100, 300
Bidais Indians, 194
Bigelow, Horatio, 216, 327, 338, 418
Binns, John, 217–18
bishop of Monterrey, 262
bishop of New Orleans, 22
Black Christ of Esquipulas, 310
Blennerhassett, Harman, 253
blockade, 34, 85, 110, 114, 150
Blount, William, 16–18, 21, 65, 125
Bolivar, Simón, 5, 329, 354
Bonaparte, Joseph, 34–35, 64, 94
Bonaparte, Napoleon, 13, 49, 65, 88, 106, 141, 204, 209, 216, 385n1, 389n5; takeover of Spain and efforts to coopt empire, 33–36, 46, 62, 67, 76, 100, 110, 113, 384n8
Bonavía, Bernardo, 70–72, 84, 89
Boone, Daniel, 44
Boone, Peter, 363, 442n68

INDEX

border dispute, Texas-Louisiana, 13, 27–29, 39, 81, 83, 137–38, 321, 350
Bowie, James, 5, 224, 333, 342–45
Bowie, Rezin, 452n54
Bradburn, John Davis, 324, 339, 451n38
Bradford, J.M., 24
Brady, John, 59
Breckenridge, Henry Marie, 253, 368n10
Brenton, Joseph, 56, 84, 93
Britain, 1, 16, 55, 83, 131, 148, 153–54, 158–59, 217, 226, 244, 373n49, 385n1; and Napoleonic Wars, 33–34, 64, 75–76, 195; US fear of intervention by, 36, 64, 106, 128, 198, 204, 257; War of 1812, 164, 166, 170–71, 174, 219
Brown, James, 116
Buckner, Aylett (of Kentucky), 354, 409n38
Buckner, Aylett (of Texas), 4, 140, 182, 326, 334, 338, 339, 349, 363, 409n38
Buckner, Simon Bolivar, 354, 409n38
Bullard, Henry Adams, 359, 360, 363; aiding Toledo, 215–16, 218, 220–21, 257, 259, 278–284; Battle of Medina, 292, 294–95, 298–99, 301, 304; 317; college and early writing, 48–53, 148, 379n1, 380n7; subsequent career, 327–29, 337, 347–48
Burgess, Harriet, 56
Burnet, David G., 49, 340
Burr, Aaron, 10, 21–23, 25, 27–31, 33, 49, 150, 219, 253, 263, 349, 352, 405n6
Burr Conspiracy, 378n42, 388n1; efforts of 1805–1806, 10–11, 21–31, 34, 36–37, 48, 391n3; after 1806, 60–62, 65–66, 71, 81, 84, 89, 105–110; connection to filibuster, 113–16, 117, 157–58, 166, 176, 184, 345
Burrites, 11, 162–63, 176, 181, 183, 188, 225, 229, 239, 253, 269, 279, 319, 323, 326, 349–55; sentiment, 15–16, 19, 24–25, 71, 124, 125, 145, 151–52, 156, 160, 173, 201, 240, 263–64, 351

Caddo Indians, 35, 37, 226, 420n11
Cádiz, 34, 40, 129; junta, 64, 75, 129, 216, 243, 384n8
Cage, Richard, 311, 363, 444n6
Caintucks, 67
California, 78, 454n18
Calle Real, 270

Calleja, Félix María, 260–61
Camacho, José Manuel, 312
Camino que Cortaba, 294
Camino Real, 39, 41, 58, 71, 94, 194, 202, 232, 294, 295, 327, 413n30; massacres along, 301, 304, 312, 313, 326; rebel advance along, 205–206
Camp Tranquitas, 200
Campeche, 107
Canada, 9, 49, 64, 128, 168, 173, 185, 204, 217, 279, 348, 455
Cañada de Caballos, 288
Canadian River, 111
Canales, Antonio, 346
Canary Islands, 72; islanders, 90, 92, 97, 216; Tenerife, 33, 92, 216
Cane River, 329
cannon. *See* artillery
Cantonment Washington, 82, 387n23
Caracas, Venezuela, 79, 218, 221
"Cariolanus," 15, 18
Carr, John C., 36, 118–19, 143, 174, 327, 334, 376n18; failure to stop filibuster, 137–40, 168–71, 187, 196, 199
Carr, Joseph, 183, 334, 363
Carvajal, José María, 306
Casa Calvo, Marques de, 116
Casa de Contración, 40
Casas, Juan Bautista de las, 92–100; 101–104, 156, 192, 240, 246, 262, 330, 390n39
Casas Revolt, 92–104, 179, 192, 207, 228, 235, 241, 248, 296, 300, 315, 318, 332, 340, 361, 390n30; aftermath, 109, 111, 114, 117–18, 121, 137, 139, 146, 158, 168; impact on Spanish policy, 260; pardon of rebels, 177
castas, 37
Catholic Church, 35, 39, 42, 59, 91, 96–98, 121, 129, 155, 179, 239, 281, 310; American attitudes toward, 15, 22, 174, 256, 354, 356, 439n10; impact on Tejano governance, 242–43; rebel appeals to, 193; refugees from Louisiana, 44–45; Spanish appeals to, 181, 203, 262, 267
Catholic clergy, 41, 45, 59, 94, 96, 249, 303, 305, 338, 393n29; role in filibusters and revolution, 21–22, 88–89, 91, 103, 111, 113–114, 121; in royalist service, 312, 330

cattle, 19, 32, 38, 40–41, 86, 87, 90–91, 98, 192, 212, 225–226
cavalry, 35, 94, 97, 127, 192, 208, 211, 235, 248, 258, 266, 271, 288–89, 249, 295, 297, 299–301, 303, 308, 322, 325, 341, 438n2, 441n41
Charles (Shaler's servant), 285, 347, 453n1
Charles IV of Spain, 34
Chickasaw Indians, 35
Chihuahua, 27, 42, 63, 86, 114, 149, 153, 197, 231–32, 254, 327, 369n19, 383n50
China, 54, 78
Choctaw Indians, 35, 59, 226–27
Citizen Genêt, 17
Claiborne, Richard, 143, 169
Claiborne, William C. C., 36, 104, 126, 204, 214, 241, 316, 322, 327, 350–51, 353, 368n13; background, 18–19, 105; Burr Conspiracy, 29–31, 116; connection to Shaler and Gutiérrez, 133–34, 141–43, 349; Florida, 68–70, 79; opposition to filibusters, 105–109, 115–16, 118, 137–38, 146–48, 150, 156, 167–72, 190; proclamations, 171, 174, 184, 187–88, 196, 200, 217, 219, 263, 321, 352; sympathy for Mexican Revolution, 75–76
Clark, Daniel, 36, 43, 118, 149, 170, 371n28, 378n41, 401n13, 430n15; aftermath of Burr Conspiracy, 31, 62, 115–16; background, 17–18; Gutiérrez-Magee filibuster, 142–43, 163, 351, 369n21; Mexican Association and Burr Conspiracy, 11, 19, 21–24, 26–29, 105–107, 351, 371–72n28
Clark, George Rogers, 182
Clay, Henry, 15, 126, 318, 403n30
Cleveland, Richard J., 76, 78, 386n7
Coahuila, 34, 70, 94, 181, 261, 265–66, 340, 342, 358, 394n44; revolution in, 100–103, 121, 299
cobarde, 289, 300, 313
Cogswell, Nathaniel, 55, 284, 286–87, 290, 321, 348, 353, 359, 380n13, 453n1; aide to Toledo, 216–218; anti-Toledo crusade, 220–221, 259, 275; oration, 51–53; trial, 277–81
Colorado River, 194, 205, 308
Columbia, Texas, 340

Comanche Indians, 28, 232, 237, 249, 303–304, 447n36; coordinating with later filibusters, 323, 325–26; intervention in revolution, 227–28, 245, 290–91, 421n23; threat to San Antonio, 33, 38, 92, 96, 331
Commandant General of the Internal Provinces. *See* Salcedo, Nemesio de
commerce. *See* trade
compadrazgo, 235
Congress: Mexican, 124, 336, 341, 345, 346, 411n7; Orleans Territorial representative, 26, 31, 105; preparations for war, 55, 128, 164; Republic of Texas, 338, 340; republican veteran elected to, 327; US, 20, 37, 66, 72, 137–38, 144, 147, 168, 170, 252, 329
Connecticut, 51, 76, 269, 323–24, 348; Newburyport, 51–52, 216, 380n13; Newtown, 269
Constant, Joseph, 163–64, 386n22, 405n12
Constitution: Mexican, 341; Spanish, 324; Texas (1813), 2, 206, 243–45, 252, 283, 357, 426n36; Texas (1836), 340; US, 78, 131, 181, 327, 355
contraband. *See* smuggling
Cook, Jesse, 378
Cooper, William, 27
Cordero, Manuel Antonio, 59, 70–71, 89, 121, 181
Correa, Diego, 216–17
Correo Americano del Sur, 181, 186
Cortes (Spanish Parliament), 128–30, 218, 278, 294
Cortés, Juan, 90, 123, 143, 257, 361
Cotten, Godwin Brown, 4, 216, 275, 338, 339, 344, 364, 418n4, 450n32, 452n58
cotton, 38, 66, 348, 355
court martial, 82–83, 87, 107, 164, 170, 184, 250, 387n24, 387n28, 415n3
Coushatta Indians, 59, 139, 226–27, 236, 254, 256, 423n10
Cragfont, 125
Crow, Miguel, 44, 86–87, 91, 115, 117–19, 140, 164, 175, 340, 349
Cuba, 7, 9, 75, 79–81, 95, 128–29, 147, 167, 195; filibuster designs on, 106, 445n19; and Florida, 66, 69, 133; proposed exile of Texas leaders, 247, 249; revolutionary

plans for 128–31; Shaler returns as consul, 318, 333; William Shaler in, 95, 132–34, 136, 142, 350, 398n3, 433n61
Cunningham, James, 86
Curate Sosa, 123
Cushing, Thomas, 82, 84, 115, 162, 170, 387n24, 387n28, 393n34

D'Alvimar, Octaviano, 35–36, 46–47, 64, 89, 98, 111, 188, 248, 277, 318, 379n52
Dartmouth College, 52, 359
Davenport, Samuel, 123, 286, 364, 374n63, 378n46, 399n34, 401n10, 416n8, 416–17n14, 427n11, 445n11, 451–52n48; Casas Revolt, 95; efforts to counter rebels, 146, 148, 150, 155, 174; Neutral Ground patrols, 85, 87, 140; possible coercion, 409n25; post-rebellion, 318–19, 323, 326, 342; return to Nacogdoches, 223–24, 257; role in filibuster, 179, 187–88, 190, 192–93, 202, 205–206, 208–209, 211–13, 411n7; target of banditti, 58, 83–84, 110, 115; trading firm, 44–45, 90
Davenport and Barr. *See* Barr and Davenport
Dearborn, Henry, 36, 381n30
décima, 45, 47
Declaration of Independence: American, 78, 113; Texas (1813), 2, 4, 242, 313, 340, 357; Texas (1836), 340, 345, 382n34, 390n39
Dehahuit (Caddo Chief), 35, 226–27
Delassus, Charles DeHault, 67
Delaware, 130, 216
Delgado, Antonio, 361, 427n8, 428n15, 428n19, 438n2, 442n60; capture and death, 309–310, 314; executions and trial, 248–51; rumored conspiracy, 264; service in later campaign, 267, 269, 272–73, 275, 282, 292, 294, 298; service with republicans, 228, 233, 240, 246
Delgado, Clemente, 313, 362, 425n35
Delgado, Gavino, 94, 96, 192, 234, 413, 425n30
Delgado, Manuel Martín, 240, 249, 314, 425n30, 425n35
democratic ideology, 8, 15, 47, 88, 357
Department of State, 8, 10, 75, 79, 81, 126, 132–34, 213, 231, 349

deserters: Florida, 68–69; Mexican republican, 102, 145, 212, 224, 267; Spanish, 37, 156, 173, 178, 180, 193–94, 222, 228, 230, 233–34, 238, 254, 261, 281–82, 341, 367n3; US, 37, 44, 164, 384n14
Despallier, Bernard Martin, 2, 4, 70, 369n16, 383n43, 403n38, 411n7; background, 58–59; in the filibuster, 178, 180–82, 188, 190, 192–93, 205, 212, 232; joining with Gutiérrez, 154–56; legacy, 343–45, 364
Despallier, Blaz Philipe, 344–45, 452n55
Despallier, Charles, 4, 343–45, 367n7, 452n52, 452n55, 452n60
Detroit, 204
Dolores, 88
Domínguez, Cristóbal, 94–95, 100, 114–15, 118, 207, 300, 302, 307, 389n24
D'Ortolant, Bernard, 46, 111, 188, 318, 364, 393n25
Doughty, Robert, 334–35, 364
Drake, Francis, 48
Duane, William, 130, 215, 216
duels, 10, 18, 21, 60, 105, 162, 211, 217, 237, 256, 321, 337, 338
Dunbar Expedition, 374n70
Duncan, Abner Lawson, 446n23
Duncan, William, 219–20
Durango, 70
Durst, John, 323, 342, 451n48

East Texas, 4, 59, 70, 71, 182, 200, 225, 234, 325
Edwards, Hayden, 339
El Encinal de Medina, 297
El Mexicano, 276
El Sordo (Kotsoteka chief), 96, 227
Elguézabel, Juan Bautista de, 33–34, 38, 70
Elizondo, Ignacio: Battle of Alazán, 270–73, 279–81, 431n25, 431n40, 432nn43–44, 438–39n9; Battle of Medina, 288–90, 295–300; chasing survivors and death, 303–305, 308–315, 358, 441n41, 441n54, 442nn68–69, 443n73; defection to royalists, 101–103, 245; invading Texas, 265–70
Ellis, John, 160
Ellis Island, 82

Elosua, Antonio, 300
Embargo Act of 1807, 55, 62, 66
Empire of Liberty, 48–49
England. *See* Britain
Enlightenment, 39, 121, 377n29
Erskine, David M., 75
Escamilla, Francisco Ignacio, 91, 94
Escandón, José de, 120
escopeta, 208, 297
Escudero, Manuel Simón de, 336
Escuela Naval de Cádiz, 129
Espalier, Carlos. *See* Despallier, Charles
Essex Junto, 53
European Spaniards, 34, 88, 129, 319; *peninsulares*, 90, 97
Eustis, William, 84, 124, 126–27, 159–60, 397n29
expansionism, 9, 13, 18, 49, 83, 217, 257, 326, 347–49, 356, 405n9
exploratory expeditions into New Spain, 29, 61–62, 85, 110, 113, 116, 231, 279, 374n70
expulsion of foreigners from Texas, 72–73, 84, 139, 182, 319, 331
Extremadura Regiment, 330

Falcón, Pedro de la Garza, 56–57, 60, 92, 103
fandango, 256, 288
Faneuil Hall, 160
Farjon, Madame Theresa de St. Xavier. *See* St. Xavier Farjon, Madame Theresa de
"Fat Father." *See* Huerta, José María
Federalist Party, 17, 52–54, 66, 82, 99, 147, 159–60, 189, 190, 201, 404nn3–4, 409n25
Ferdinand VII, 129, 217, 278; imprisoned by Napoleon, 34–35, 64; rebellions for and against, 68, 75, 88, 91, 98, 100, 106, 324; restoration and pardons, 317–18, 322
Fisher, William, 230, 364, 450–51n32
Florida, 9, 15, 21, 50, 55, 60, 64–65, 79, 106, 110, 125, 159–60, 162, 164, 176, 184, 198, 200, 201, 224, 233, 242–43, 254, 312, 322, 350–51, 355, 370n2, 372n32, 372n37; 1810 revolt, 66–69; Burr Conspiracy, 19, 23, 66, 133; convention, 67–70, 384n18; Kemper Revolt, 12–13, 114; Pensacola, 24, 49, 322, 395n11
Folch, Vicente, 19, 66, 69, 198
foreign settlers in Spanish Texas, 4, 13, 89–90, 179, 378nn44–45; connection to filibuster, 148, 180, 318; connection to smuggling, 56–58, 60; expulsion of, 72–73, 84, 139, 331; in Nacogdoches, 44–45, 47
Forsyth, Samuel D., 163, 169, 348, 433n51, 434n11, 448nn49–50; in Bolívar's service, 329; in Republican Army, 183, 187, 237, 272, 282, 292, 323;
Forsythe, (US Army Lieutenant), 323, 447n30
Fort Adams, 26, 55, 69, 82, 139, 150, 159, 163, 183, 205, 387n23, 387n25, 402–3n27, 404n48; filibuster sentiment, 160–61, 402n27; patrols to stop filibuster, 167
Fort Claiborne, 32, 42, 82–83, 123, 156, 162, 163, 228, 258, 327, 368n13, 387n23, 387n25; filibuster sentiment, 107, 109, 160; efforts against banditti and filibusters, 138–39, 151–52, 169, 184, 325
Fort McHenry, 30
Fort San Carlos, 68
Fort Smith, Arkansas, 111, 393n24
Fort Stoddart, 82
Fort St. Philip, 190
France, 59, 195, 220, 253, 260, 262, 383n43, 399n34; impact on Spanish Texas, 33, 242; impact on US domestic politics, 16–17, 65, 75, 76; Normandy, 58
free trade, 17, 49, 62, 71, 76, 78, 95, 103, 182, 217
Freeman, Constant, 82, 87, 108, 115, 376n18
Freeman Custis Expedition, 29, 374n70
freemasonry, 26, 59, 129, 282, 287, 439n10
French creoles, 18, 32, 46, 58, 60, 70, 111, 154–55, 175, 182, 184, 188
French Revolution, 46, 140, 220, 248, 253, 320, 399n34, 445n15
Frio River, 265–66
Frontier Reporter and Natchitoches & Claiborne Advertiser, 344

Gaceta de Texas, 20, 326, 339
gachupín, 96, 181, 260, 267, 298, 302–303, 307; Creole hostility to, 90, 101, 120, 245, 251, 269, 283, 287–88, 291; rebel actions against, 94, 240; war, 2, 367n3
Gaines, Edmund Pendleton, 188, 214
Gaines, James Taylor, 4, 182, 224, 225, 268, 270, 297, 317, 364, 439n13, 439n17; on

executions of royalists, 247, 251, 263; postwar, 333, 338, 340; in republican service, 188, 194, 226, 227, 424n14
Galán, Luis, 100–101, 307
Gallatin, Albert, 75
Galván, Juan, 176, 208, 212–13, 223, 362, 408n14, 421n25
Galveston, 59, 324, 327
Gálvez, Bernardo, 232, 249
Garbolán, Antonio. *See* Correa, Diego
Garcia, Luciano, 94
Garniere, John, 122, 395n10
Garrett, Julia Kathryn, 6–10, 368n11, 368n14, 386n20, 402n27, 454n5
Garza, Concepción Leal de, 306, 345
Garza, Felipe de la, 139
Garza, Isidrio de la, 140, 244, 313
Genêt. *See* Citizen Genêt
Georgia, 115, 117, 394n39; Clarke County, 116
Gilmanton, New Hampshire, 52, 453n1
Girard, Pedro, 157–58, 165–66, 186, 241, 277, 318, 322, 403n31, 407n3
Glass, Anthony, 151, 402n25
gold, 78, 102–103, 122, 128, 189; and US perceptions of New Spain, 22, 89, 111, 135, 181, 217, 243, 258, 263, 352
Goliad, 231, 338, 344, 345, 416n9, 450n31, 451n38
Gonzales, Vicente, 176, 192
Gonzales, Texas, 343, 345
good government, 96–97, 129, 357
Gormley (Captain), 229–30, 364
Governor of Orleans Territory. *See* Claiborne, William C. C.
Graham, John, 81, 126, 127–28, 134, 141–42, 148, 350, 400n38
Grand Pré, Carlos de, 370n8
Grande, Luís, 4, 45–46, 59, 193–94, 242, 249, 251, 341, 345, 362
Greenup, Christopher, 33, 71
Grito, 88, 90–91, 101, 120, 194
Guadalupe River, 38, 92, 202, 205–206, 413n30
Guadiana, José María, 109, 362, 388n34, 391n42, 437n69, 437n71; capturing D'Alvimar, 46; confronting smugglers, 42–43, 45, 56–57, 60, 378n41; investigating foreigners, 72–73, joint patrol, 86–87, in rebellion, 95, 100, 103–104, 111, 114, 118, 139, 143; in Republican Army, 163, 178, 188, 190, 194, 227, 244, 281–82, 291–92, 311
Guanajuato, 98, 101
Guaymas, 78
Guerrero, Francisco, 214, 412n21
Guerrero, Vicente, 332
gunsmith, 144, 212, 239
Gutiérrez de Lara, José Antonio, 120–21, 149
Gutiérrez de Lara, José Bernardo, 7–8, 11, 91, 120–25, 215; after departure, 310, 313, 315, 318; declaration of independence and constitution, 242–44; entering Texas, 180–81, 183, 186, 196–97, 200, 202–203; falling out with Toledo, 216, 217–18, 221, 226; at La Bahía, 206, 211–14, 223–24, 230, 233–35; in Natchitoches, 146–47; organizing filibuster, 148–54, 156–58, 163, 165–67, 172–74; post-revolution, 322–23, 326–27, 333–36, 345–46, 359, 360, 361, 369n16; proclamations and propaganda, 155–56, 177, 187–89, 193–94, 244–45, 255, 341; replacement by Toledo, 257–59, 275–84, 285, 287, 292, 296; Republic of Rio Grande, 345–46; at San Antonio, 238–41, 253–56, 262–71, 273–74; trial and execution of royalists, 246–52; in Washington and New Orleans, 126–131, 141–143
Gutiérrez-Magee Expedition, 2, 6, 10–11, 157, 172, 261, 349–52, 357, 367n3, 368n11

Harvard University, 48–50, 55, 280–81, 298, 327, 359, 379n1
Havana, 79, 81, 129, 131–33, 135, 241, 253, 318
Hernández, José María, 302
Herrera, Geronimo, 249–50
Herrera, Pedro de, 101
Herrera, Simón de, 70, 148, 268, 288, 309, 330; arrival and creation of Neutral Ground, 28–29, 37–38, 83, 139; Casas revolt and imprisonment, 93–94, 96, 101–102; execution, 246, 248–49, 256, 262, 448n1; La Bahía siege, 207, 210–11, 227–29; partnership with Salcedo, 89, 91; possible sympathy with rebels, 89; return

to San Antonio and Battle of Rosillo, 232, 234, 236–38, 245; return to Texas, 138, 168, 197, 202–203
Hidalgo, Miguel, 3, 113, 121, 137, 200, 246, 251, 336, 402n22; background of revolution, 88–89, 92, 95–96, 101; capture and execution, 102–103,121, 144, 265, 313, 401n3; desire for American assistance, 135
Holmes, David, 384n3
Hopkins, Henry, 107
horses, 23, 110, 175, 177, 180, 208, 224, 227, 232–34, 238, 245, 248–49, 263, 266, 274, 285, 288, 290, 297, 301, 303, 308–309, 311, 334, 382, 423; trade and smuggling, 23, 38, 43, 45, 47, 55–58, 90, 98, 109, 189, 192, 200, 377, 378, 424, 433
Howard, Benjamin, 62
Hudson River, 53
Huerta, José María, 111–13, 117–18, 143, 145, 177, 178, 338, 393n29, 395–96n11, 413n33
Humbert, Jean Joseph Amable, 253, 320–21

Ibarbo, Antonio Gil, 42
Independent Chronicle, 189
Indians. *See* Native Americans
Ingraham, Nathaniel, 133
Ingraham, Phoenix and Nixsen, 76
Inquisition, 39, 216, 377n29
Internal Provinces of New Spain, 27, 33, 106, 126, 146, 198, 375n5, 448n3
Interventionist interpretation, 6–7, 10–11, 454n5
Ireland, 24, 44, 54, 56, 253, 378n45
Irene Viesca, 406n23
Irish, 17–18, 21, 24, 26, 40, 44, 54, 57–58, 90, 105, 113, 138, 171, 200, 263, 265, 378n46
Isleños. *See* Canary Islands, islanders
Iturbe, Manuel de, 120
Iturbide, Augustín de, 322, 357

Jamaica, 134, 405n10
Jaraname Indians, 310
Jefferson, Thomas, 17–18, 39, 74–75, 105, 115, 159; Embargo Act, 55; relation to filibusters, 19–20, 25, 29, 48–50, 69, 350–51, 400n38; response to Spanish Imperial crisis, 64, 66, 370n6; skepticism of military, 52–54, 405n6; vision of Western expansion, 13–14, 370n7
Jesuits, 22–23
Jiménez, José Mariano, 114, 120–21
Johnston, Albert Sydney, 4, 342–43, 354, 452
Johnston, Darius, 152, 179, 184, 246, 317, 342, 359, 364, 448n49
Johnston, Josiah Stoddard, 157, 322, 342, 403, 448n49
Johnston, Orramel, 150–52, 157, 179, 184, 249, 305, 317, 342, 359, 364, 448
junta, 67, 75, 384n8. *See also* Béxar; Cádiz

Kadohadacho Indians. *See* Caddo
Kemper, Nathan, 20, 67
Kemper, Reuben, 106, 352, 404n48, 415n2, 433n52; confrontation with Toledo, 253, 259; recruitment for Texas, 152–53, 163, 17; Florida revolt, 12–13, 19–20
Kemper, Samuel, 2, 256, 269, 345, 352, 357, 360, 363, 422n1, 429n33, 437n69, 438n8, 440n30, 442n69, 443n71, 446n23, 446n26–27, 454n15; Battle of Medina, 294–99, 301, 303–304, 310–11; command of Republican Army, 224, 228–30, 233–35, 238–43, 246–50, 253–54; escape and death, 317, 320, 322–23; filibuster in Texas, 163, 176, 183, 187, 200–201, 204, 208; Florida revolt, 13–14, 20, 68, 70; recruitment to Burr Conspiracy, 23–26, 67, 117; return to command, 286–87, 290–92
Kemper Brothers, 110, 157, 284, 312, 352, 373n51, 408n12, 418n4, 439n13; recruitment to Burr Conspiracy, 23–28, 30–31, 115, 162, 373, 405n10; Florida revolt, 12, 14, 19–21, 23, 50, 66–68, 114, 160, 184, 372n32
Kennedy, Joseph Pulaski, 66, 68, 364, 383n7, 433n52
Kentucky, 13, 26, 37, 57, 163, 192, 354, 410n42; filibuster sentiment, 15, 19, 22, 24, 29, 33, 65, 72, 118, 124, 149–50, 165; origin of 1812 filibusters, 183, 263, 272, 393n33, 409n38, 453n1
Kerr, Lewis, 24–28, 30–31, 107, 116, 161–62, 224, 371–72n28, 373n49, 374n60, 405n10, 445n12
Kimball, Frederick, 69

INDEX 479

King, John Gladden, 343, 364, 450n32
King, William Phillip, 343

La Bahía, 235, 236, 238, 240, 244, 249, 256, 261, 263, 267, 269, 286, 288, 294, 297, 300, 317, 322, 340; after republican defeat, 316, 331, 334; background, 39, 44, 73, 86; battle, 228–230, 232–34; in Casas Revolt, 94, 96; in later filibusters, 324–25; presidio, 213, 344; road, 310; Siege, 206–209, 213, 225–228, 246, 336, 415n5, 416nn8–9, 421n23, 450n22; under republican control, 247–248, 279–80, 311
La Bororquia, 377
La Lanterne Magique, 107
La Quinta, 305–308, 315, 326, 331
Lafitte, Jean, 327, 408n9
Laguna de la Espada, 437n72
Laguna de las Ánimas, 98
lances, 192–93, 255, 266, 412n23
Lane, Abner, 304, 364, 440n35
Laredo, 250, 262, 265–66, 289–90, 427n4, 437n1
Latham, Louis, 86, 182
Latour, Arsène Lacarrière, 220–21, 253–54, 419n19
Leal, Antonio, 304
Leal, Joaquín, 304, 309, 332, 362
Legion d'honneur, 100
Lelia Bird, 78
Lemus, Pedro, 302
limpieza de sangre, 260
Lipan Apache. See Apache Indians
livestock, 38, 46, 56–58, 86, 90, 96, 98, 101, 240, 262, 265, 310, 319, 338, 341; rancherías, 295; Rancho de las Botija, 45
Livingston, Edward, 351, 446n23
Lizana, Francisco Xavier de, 144
Logia de los Caballeros Racionales, 129
Lone Star flag, 19, 69, 114, 200
Long, James, 325–28, 333, 338, 340, 447nn39–40
Los Adaes, 45, 83–84, 109, 139
Losoya, José Domingo, 323, 341, 344, 362, 446n27
Losoya, Toribio, 343–45
Louisiana: Alexandria, 59, 186; Rapides, 59, 117, 119, 137, 146, 150–53, 155, 157–58, 169–70, 176, 183, 204, 253–54, 284, 317, 323, 329, 333–34, 343–45, 403n31, 403n38, 406n33, 450n28; St. Francisville, 69; Upper, 21, 60, 66, 81, 116, 153
Louisiana Gazette, 62, 111, 132, 144, 387n24
Louisiana Purchase, 13, 17–18, 27, 61, 134, 188, 214, 332; effect on Spanish Texas, 39, 45, 58; relation to Florida, 66, 69; US claims to Texas from, 71, 81, 127, 350
Lowry, Robert K., 79
Luckett, Thomas Hussey, 183, 188, 267, 254, 292, 317, 334, 336, 364, 411n8, 433n51, 445n14

Madison, James, 7, 49, 53, 64–65, 106, 108, 150–52, 219, 290, 292, 318; alleged role in filibuster, 6, 9, 214, 258, 349, 454n5; domestic politics, 159–60, 201, 204, 383n5; foreign policy, 74–76, 78–79; Shaler's letter to, 136, 147; Statements and policy towards Spain, 81, 95, 124, 126–27, 148, 168, 324; Florida, 68–69, 133–34
Madrid, 59, 126, 132
Magee, Augustus William, 11, 233, 236, 241, 243, 246, 249, 252, 261, 265, 268–69, 279, 283, 284, 291, 317, 325–26, 329, 343, 345, 348, 355, 359, 363, 381nn28–30, 382n31, 386n22, 387nn23–24, 404n, 407n3, 409n25; denied promotion, 159–64, 166, 170; early history, 54–55, 82–87, 95, 139–141, 150, 157, 158; at La Bahía, 207–213, 221, 223–24, 228, 230–31, 416n13, 417n15, 417n23; launching expedition, 174–76, 178–83, 186–87, 189–90, 196–97, 411n7, 412n16; training the army, 192–94; in Trinidad, 199–201, 203–206
Magee, James, 54–55
Magee, Joseph, 56, 58–60, 71, 93, 103, 110
Manifest Destiny, 3, 11, 14, 69, 130
Manifesto or Satisfaction in a Point of Honor, 130
Marqués de Someruelos, 133
Marquis of Villa Franca, 278
Martinez, Antonio María, 327
Masmela, Apolinaris de, 150, 155–56, 174
masonry. See freemasonry
Massachusetts, 94, 209–210, 220, 278–79, 280, 348, 381n25, 381n30, 388n1, 404nn3–4, 418n3; Bedford, 33; Boston,

48, 51, 53–55, 159, 160, 163, 189, 216, 231; Pepperell, 48, 379; Roxbury, 54
Massicott, Louis, 188, 241, 259, 274, 280, 364, 433n61
Matagorda Bay, 35, 71, 234, 247, 249, 411n4
Mauritius, 76
Maynes, Francisco, 94, 389n23, 413n33
McClain, A. W., 4, 364, 440n35
McFarlan, John, 4, 93, 238, 355, 359, 364; joining expedition, 167, 182, 205; post-revolution, 325, 337; recruiting Indians, 225–27, 420n11; scouting, 207, 222–23, 234, 265, 291, 424n23; smuggler, 56–58, 84, 349
McKim, James (Jr.), 342
McKim, James (Sr.), 182, 207, 236, 271, 342, 364, 388n30, 409n37
McKinnon, Thomas, 110, 115, 393n25, 393n33
McLanahan, Joseph A., 60, 62, 85–86, 110, 144–45, 148, 447n30
McLane, Hiram H., 200, 338, 406n23
McLane, William, 338, 365, 415n5, 437n1, 438n2; Alazán to Medina, 268, 272–73, 423n10, 423–24n13, 424n21, 425n28, 425n34, 430n16, 431n26, 432n43, 432n46, 432–33n48, 433n59, 440n28, 440n35; La Bahía, 208, 222–23, 228, 230, 416nn8–9, 416–17n14, 417n17, 417n23, 418n31, 419–420n2, 422n34; narrative, 9, 187–88, 368n12, 406; Rosillo to San Antonio, 236, 238, 247, 254, 266
Medina River, 291, 292, 294, 295, 301–302, 303
Menchaca, José (rebel), 122, 124, 126, 131, 138, 143, 145–46, 157, 191, 251, 320, 362, 389n12, 395n11
Menchaca, José Antonio (chronicler), 91, 301, 305–09, 311, 313, 331, 342, 360, 389n12, 421n23, 424n23, 431n25, 433n60, 437n72, 438n8, 441n50, 442n68, 443n79
Menchaca, Juan Mariano, 307
Menchaca, Miguel, 2, 191, 307, 342, 360, 362, 413n30, 425n30, 425n35, 430n12, 432n43; Gutiérrez/Toledo feud, 277, 281–82, 287–88, 436nn52–53; La Bahía to Alazán, 229–30, 232–35, 237–38, 240, 247, 251, 264, 267, 269, 272, 275, 417n17,

418n35, 423n3; Medina, 290–92, 294–299, 301–302, 438n2, 439n13
mercantilism, 40, 47, 59, 62, 71, 76, 163, 206, 242, 348
mestizos, 127
Mexican-American War, 3–4, 343, 430n16, 454n18
Mexican Association, 11, 401n13, 405n9, 445n12, 446n23, 446n29, 447n35, 450n22; after 1813, 321–22, 391n3; Burr Conspiracy, 18, 22–23, 26–27, 30–31, 62, 373n51, 374n60, 379n3; Gutiérrez-Magee Expedition, 183, 224, 241, 294, 351, 408n12; Florida to Texas, 66, 89, 105–106, 116, 142–43, 149, 153–54, 161–64
Mexican revolutionaries, 1, 3, 91, 327, 386n19, 395n4, 426n36, 426n49; conspiring with Americans, 118, 138, 148, 324, 352; interior Mexico, 168, 198, 254; Need for American aid, 10–11, 89, 114, 347; in Republican Army, 199, 204–205, 212, 246, 266, 272–73, 296, 298, 304, 449n7; South American, 26, 49, 329, 354, 454n18
Mexican Revolutionary Army. See Republican Army of the North
Mexican War of Independence, 3, 101, 110, 127, 186–87, 241, 243, 256, 294, 325, 332, 349
Mexico: Mexico City, 103, 122, 125, 204; Oaxaca, 181, 358; Revilla, 120, 122, 142, 153, 194, 212, 239, 262, 284, 346; San Blas, 78; Xalapa, 135; Yucatan Peninsula, 107. *See also* New Spain
Miami Indians, 65
Micheli, Vicente, 45
Midway, Texas, 205
Milam, Benjamin Rush, 328
Milam, Texas, 175
militia, 21, 30, 69, 110, 145, 154, 189, 204, 205, 212, 219, 282, 327, 338, 343, 381n30, 418n3; Kentucky, 22, 29, 149; Orleans Territory, 17, 19, 27, 107, 138, 143, 151, 163, 167, 169–70, 322–23, 374n64; Spanish, 12, 20, 41, 46, 59, 72, 92, 97–98, 100, 175, 177–78, 180, 190, 192, 234–35, 240, 244, 265, 288, 297, 300, 303, 313, 326, 408n18, 413n33, 416n8, 430n12

INDEX

Mina, Francisco Xavier, 324–25
Mina-Aury Expedition, 324–25, 327, 340
mining, 15, 22, 60–62, 85, 109–110, 144, 189, 332, 352
Miranda, Francisco de, 26, 49–51, 75, 113, 130, 147–48, 215–16
Miró, Esteban Rodríguez, 17
missions, 33, 38–39, 46, 59, 90–91, 222, 343–45, 376n27, 416n13; Concepción, 98, 238, 306; Espada, 238, 437n72; Espiritu Santo, 207; Nuestra Señora del Rosario, 234; San Antonio de Valero (*see* Alamo)
Mississippi River, 12, 14–16, 20, 30, 33, 82, 106, 141, 164, 165, 167, 171, 196, 220, 253, 263, 370n2, 371n15, 403n28, 453n1
Mississippi Territory, 12, 14, 18–21, 25, 55, 65–66, 68, 82, 105–106, 124, 150, 153, 183, 188, 204–205, 334, 384n14, 405n6, 444n6, 445n19
Missouri, 60–61, 66, 81, 85–86, 110–11, 144–45, 148, 152–53, 197, 258, 320–21, 324, 332, 453n1; compromise, 348, 355; St. Genevieve, 62
Mobile, 24, 27, 66, 68–69, 82, 176, 322, 433n52; Society, 66, 162
Monclova, 100–102, 174, 202, 231, 263, 299, 338, 342, 428n19
Moniteur de la Louisiane, 320
Monroe, James, 6–9, 170, 204, 258, 369n17, 414n48, 428n24; John Hamilton Robinson, 195, 197–99, 254, 350; relations with Gutiérrez, 124, 128, 131, 141, 147, 149, 165, 213–14, 351, 397n29, 397n32, 397n44; relations with Shaler, 134–38, 146–47, 149–51, 153–54, 167–68, 186, 199, 252, 284–85, 317, 349–51, 355, 399n20; relations with Toledo, 219
Montero, Bernardino, 139, 155–56, 174–78, 180, 190, 192, 237, 256, 337, 408n8, 408n11, 408n18, 424n16
Monterrey, 97, 232, 262, 299, 317, 333, 442n68, 444n80
Montevideo, 64, 76
Monthly Anthology and Boston Review, 52
Mora, José María, 193, 411n7
Mordella, Santiago, 312, 326, 334, 443n71
Morelos, José María, 146, 242

Morgan, Benjamin, 143, 396n12, 400n44, 446n23
Mower, Aaron, 216, 220, 257, 275, 277–79, 326, 339, 365, 434n16
Munson, Henry William, 184, 312, 326, 334, 338–39, 354, 365, 443n71
Murray, William, 11, 322–23, 365, 386n22, 405n10, 438n2, 448n48; Burr recruitment, 26–28, 30–31, 115, 117; recruitment of Magee, 161–62; Republican Army, 163–64, 183, 188, 210–11, 223, 229–30, 246, 317
Músquiz, Miguel, 57, 292, 300, 362, 382n37

Nacogdoches, 35, 62, 72, 83, 84, 86, 200, 205–206, 212–13, 234, 237, 244, 281, 288, 291, 300, 307, 316, 318, 331, 377n33, 377n40, 378nn44–45, 393, 396, 401, 414, 425; background and economics, 39–47, 55–57; capture by Republican Army, 173–82, 185–90, 192–93, 411; early phase of rebellion, 88–90, 94–97, 100, 103–104, 111, 114–15, 118–19, 126, 138, 145–46, 150, 155–56, 163, 167–68, 349, 413; foreigners and settlement plans, 44–47, 70, 71; as hub for rebel forces, 194, 226, 257–58, 264, 279, 285–86; later filibusters and settlement, 321, 327, 342, 344, 450; after Battle of Medina, 303, 308, 310, 312, 319; *Nacogdoches Texas Advocate*, 338–39; *Nacogdoches Texas Republican*, 326; stone house, 95, 137, 187, 342
Nacogdochito Indians, 194
Napoleon. *See* Bonaparte, Napoleon
Napoleonic Wars, 3, 5, 11, 52, 76, 288; conquest of Spain, 34, 62, 64, 67
Natchez, 33, 82, 124, 132, 311, 317, 321, 382n37, 403n35, 444n6, 452n60; *Chronicle*, 143; connection to Burr Conspiracy, 36, 106; connection to Gutiérrez-Magee Expedition, 150, 152–54, 157–58, 163, 167, 169–70, 187, 199–200, 204, 220–21, 253, 257, 279, 404n48, 439n13; later filibusters, 325–327; *Natchez Statesman*, 284; Natchez and Texas Trail, 36, 170; Natchez Trace, 188
Natchitoches, 8, 28, 33, 90, 134, 142–5, 318–19, 349, 376n18, 389nn23–24, 395–6n11,

396n23, 403n30, 405n8, 410n47, 414n48, 414n52, 421n28, 423–24n13, 428n15, 445n11, 451n44, 455n21; background and relation to Nacogdoches, 32, 35–36, 39–42, 44, 46, 57–58, 73; banditti and early filibuster efforts, 109, 111, 113–15, 117–18, 123–25, 137–38; early period of revolution, 178–79, 182, 186–87, 192, 195, 197–199, 205, 223, 226, 411n7; later filibusters; organization of filibuster, 146–57, 162, 164–65, 167–68, 170–71, 173–74, 320–21, 323, 325, 327, 329, 409n36; later period of revolution, 232, 241, 248, 252–53, 257, 264, 268, 275–76, 278–79, 281, 284–85, 316–17; and US military, 82–84, 87, 138, 140, 402–3n27

National Gazette, 128

National Intelligencer, 20, 88, 95, 186, 204, 243, 252, 311, 412n16, 441n39

nationalism, 13, 44, 48, 243, 356

Native Americans, 1, 15, 32, 34, 37, 39, 71, 101, 125, 170, 263, 338, 342, 346, 359, 395n10, 442n63, 454nn17–18; relations with republicans, 122, 155–56, 189, 194, 206, 225–27, 235–37, 254, 256, 266–67, 270–71, 273–74, 289, 292, 298, 301, 303, 310, 312, 324–25, 333, 337, 421n22, 423n10, 424n14, 424n21, 440n35; relations with Spanish, 34–35, 38, 40–41, 44–46, 57–59, 85, 90, 92–93, 96, 102, 110, 114, 127, 155, 227, 232, 262, 288, 289, 313, 319, 331, 421n23; relations with US, 29, 35, 65, 81, 139, 185, 226. *See also individual tribes*

Navarro, Ángel, 97

Navarro, Guillermo, 427n4

Navarro, José Antonio, 93, 99, 239, 249, 250, 272, 274, 283, 287, 302, 305–306, 316, 332, 333, 340, 358, 367n2, 379n52, 425n26, 427n8, 443n70, 449n9

Neches River, 56, 206

negro. *See* African Americans

Neutral Ground, 37, 41, 95, 158, 163, 166–67, 172–73, 188, 388n30, 395nn10–11, 408n9, 411n10, 447n30; agreement, 29, 70, 83, 249, banditti, 11, 58, 60, 62, 83–85, 87, 109–10, 114–18, 124, 138–41, 146, 148, 150, 152–53, 159, 162, 164, 168–69, 177, 179, 182, 198, 231, 271, 291, 321, 342, 368n13, 387n27, 388n31, 414n51, 420n8, 446n22; expeditions to clear, 85–87, 137–141, 150

Neutrality Act of 1794, 16, 31, 49, 138, 148, 168

New Braunfels, 205

New England, 51, 87, 201, 277, 284, 386, 405n12; *New England Palladium*, 189, 409n25. *See also individual states*

New Grenada. *See* Columbia, Texas

New Jersey, 49

New Madrid, 132

New Mexico, 24, 34, 61–63, 85, 106, 109, 144, 454n18

New Orleans, 7, 45, 55, 60, 75, 81, 89, 118, 123–24, 127, 131, 154, 167, 184, 190, 217, 219, 224, 253, 328, 332, 349–50, 371n21, 372–73n40, 385n1, 396n12, 398n3, 400n37, 414n38, 427n11, 433n61, 450n22, 452n60, 454n11; filibuster organizing in, 21–27, 29–31, 106–108, 115–16, 148–49, 164, 166, 173, 277, 421n28; importance to the West, 9–12, 15–16; post-1812 filibusters, 320–24, 351–52, 353, 445n12, 446nn26–27, 446n29, 447n35; Shaler and Gutiérrez in, 132, 134–37, 141–43, 397n44; War of 1812, 171, 220, 257, 322

New Spain, 9, 36, 39–40, 59, 81, 86, 101, 134, 135, 154, 197–98, 201, 204, 241–42, 254, 258, 347, 373n49, 375n5, 379n52, 383n50, 405n9, 412n23; filibuster designs on, 17–19, 21–22, 28, 83, 109, 145, 148, 199, 324, 351; revolution in, 94, 260–61; Spanish defense plans, 33–35, 70–71; US government designs on, 128

New York, 33, 49, 59, 74, 76–77, 82, 131, 142, 186, 275, 277–79, 317, 336, 342, 347–48, 386n22, 453n1

Newburgh Address, 51–52

Newman, Francis, 107–109, 115, 156, 160

Nicaragua, 354

Niles, Hezikiah, 88

Niles' Weekly Register, 88, 334

Noah, Samuel, 205, 235, 254, 365, 415n3

Nolan, Phillip, 16, 43, 56, 86, 95, 143, 304, 353, 378n41, 387n24

Noroña, Miguel Cabral de, 216

North Carolina, 182, 440n35
Northern Provinces. *See* Internal Provinces of New Spain
Nueces River, 207, 214, 265
Nuevo León, 28, 70, 100–101, 190, 248
Nuevo Santander, 91–92, 120–21, 155–56, 190, 212, 260–61, 288, 291, 299–300, 302–303, 308, 313–14, 336, 346

Ochoa, Francisca, 429
O'Fallon, John, 16–18
Ogden, Peter V., 30
Ohio, 13, 23–24, 37, 35, 72, 373n52, 374n60, 411n8; river, 17, 33, 106, 220–221, 253
"Old 300", 4, 338, 440n35
Onís, Luis de, 64, 75, 130–31, 216–21, 356, 398n7, 455n22
Opelousas Parish, 119, 150–52, 187
Orcoquisac, 59
Orleans Gazette, 24, 107, 352
Orleans Territory, 7, 12, 17–18, 21, 27, 31–32, 34, 65–66, 68–69, 81, 105, 126, 133, 149, 152, 164–66, 168, 170, 196, 369n21, 373n49, 395n11, 400n43, 405n8, 405n10, 407n36
Orr, George, 234, 334, 354, 365
Overton, Thomas, 123, 125
Overton, Walter H., 123, 148, 151–52, 156, 166, 169–70, 184–85, 187, 199, 387n25, 396n12, 402n27, 406n32, 410nn47–19
Owens, William, 58, 182, 237, 365, 382n40, 424n17

Padilla, Juan Antonio, 337, 424n16
Paillet, Jean Jacques, 148, 155, 253–54
Parker, William, 338, 365, 450–51n32, 452–52n60
Patterson, James, 62, 86, 111, 144–45, 401n3
Peñelas, José, 192
Pennsylvania, 44, 74, 187, 334, 368n10; Philadelphia, 16, 33, 35, 53, 110, 128–29, 131, 141, 155, 215, 218–19, 282, 320, 328–29, 336, 378n46, 397–98n44, 418n4, 419n16, 429n51; Pittsburgh, 33, 220, 253, 278, 286, 445n19
Pennsylvania Democratic Press, 217
Peres, Nieves, 41, 47
Pérez, Adolfo, 301, 303–304, 362

Pérez, Benito, 107
Pérez, José Ignacio, 235, 240
Pérez, Juan Ignacio, 302, 307
Perkins, Thomas Handasyd, 54–55, 159–60, 163, 189, 201, 381n27, 381nn29–30, 404nn3–4
Perry, Henry, 183, 187, 237, 268, 320, 328, 345, 348, 360, 363, 431n38; Battle of Medina, 289–92, 304, 310–11, 317, 437n69; later filibuster, 322–25, 334–35, 340, 446n29, 447n36; Republican commander, 269–74, 281–82, 286–87, 432n43, 432n46
Perry, Oliver Hazard, 329
Pétion, Alexandre, 322
Phelps, David, 183, 365, 410n40
Phillips Exeter Academy, 52, 55, 160
Picornell, Juan Mariano, 216, 220–21, 259, 320–21, 365, 429n50
Pike, Zebulon, 29, 62–63, 82, 89, 126–27, 138–40, 145, 159–60, 169, 197, 199, 202, 205, 231, 279, 374n70, 383n50, 387nn23–24, 404n1
Platt, William, 27, 374n64, 388n1
Poinsett, Joel Roberts, 79, 195–96, 257, 284, 413n37
Popejoy, Edward, 56, 58, 110, 382n40
Portugal, 260
Prado, Pedro, 177, 318, 362, 428 n15
Presidio de Rio Grande. *See* Rio Grande
Presidio La Bahía. *See* La Bahía
Prevost, John, 24
priests. *See* Catholic clergy
printing press, 216, 257, 276, 334
prisoners, 101, 140; of republicans, 207, 234, 238–39, 246–51, 283, 433n62; of Spanish, 56, 103, 117, 133, 178, 234, 239, 261, 301–302, 305–308, 310–14, 317, 319, 393n24, 393n33, 442n68, 444n6
privateers, 54, 159, 196, 223
Procela, Pedro, 177, 192, 199, 214, 320, 326, 362, 408n18, 447n40
propaganda, 4, 8, 91, 130, 149, 156–58, 177, 181, 193–94, 203, 209, 257, 262, 264, 275, 277, 279, 286, 326, 345–46, 369n16
Protestantism, 22, 39, 45, 64, 181, 354
Puerto del Salado, 266

Quasi-War, 17, 76, 418n3
Quinn, Miguel, 58, 110, 114, 116, 118, 124, 140, 143, 153, 176, 182, 365, 382n40, 388n31
Quinta. *See* la Quinta
Quintero, Cayetano, 300, 303, 313–14
Quirk, Edmund (Sr.), 4, 57–59, 95, 110–11, 113, 117, 143, 145, 153, 173, 176–77, 182, 338, 365, 390n26
Quirk, Henry, 56–58, 60, 62, 71, 84, 93, 103, 110, 182, 235, 349, 355, 359, 382n34

ranching. *See* livestock
Rayón, Ignacio López, 141, 146, 149, 153–54, 173, 186, 204, 275, 291
rebels, Mexican. *See* Mexican revolutionaries
Red River, 26, 32, 35, 152, 189, 375n1, 402n25, 435n40
Regiment of Veracruz, 288, 298
Republic of Texas, 4, 49, 93, 337–41, 345–46, 352, 354, 367n1, 382n34, 423n10, 423n13, 424n20, 436n60, 450–51n32
Republic of the Rio Grande, 346
Republican Army of the North, 1, 173–75, 194, 205–207, 214–16, 218–19, 226–29, 232–34, 239, 241, 254–55, 265, 268, 275–78, 280, 284, 286, 291–94, 296, 301, 316–17, 319–23, 346, 359, 411n8, 443–44n79, 447n37, 447n39; composition and organization, 183, 187–93, 199, 212, 227, 230, 286, 289, 423n10, 432nn43–46, 423n48, 437n69, 437nn71–72, 438n2; ethnic tensions within, 247, 256, 264, 266–67, 269–70; ideology, 200–201, 263–64; logistics, 200, 204, 266, 353, 421n23, 421n28; veterans, 4–5, 322–29, 332–45, 352, 354, 446n27, 453n61
Republican Party (Jeffersonian), 17, 52, 150, 383n5
republicanism, 5, 22, 34, 51, 53, 76, 77, 142, 216, 348; conflation with American expansion, 48, 186; French, 39, 49; in New Spain and Texas, 94, 120, 244, 249, 283, 326, 354
Reverend Giles' Meeting House, 51, 52
Revolutionary War. *See* American Revolution
Rio Frio. *See* Frio River

Rio Grande: river, 29, 120–22, 163, 173, 189–90, 241, 246, 262, 265, 336, 412n16; as potential border, 81, 165, 350, 355, Presidio, 101, 288, 391n48; valley, 91–92, 124, 156, 438n2
Rio Hondo. *See* Arroyo Hondo
Rio Trinidad. *See* Trinity River
Robinson, John Hamilton, 9, 249, 254, 258, 265, 284, 348, 350, 355, 445n19, 446n22; arrival in San Antonio, 202–203; background and mission, 197–99, 414n48; impact on royalist morale, 205, 209; later filibuster, 321, 324, 326; mission to Chihuahua, 231–32; reception by Republican Army, 201–202, 243, 369n17, 384n14
Rodríguez, (Señora), 291, 303, 306
Rodríguez, José de Jesús, 202, 205
Rodríguez, Mariano, 98, 235, 241, 277, 362
Rodríguez, Pablo, 247, 291, 301, 303, 362
Rollins, Charles, 227, 236
Rosillo. *See* Battle of Rosillo
Rosillo Creek, 236
Ross, Reuben (Jr.), 337, 342, 346
Ross, Reuben (Sr.), 2, 183, 187, 222, 240, 246, 248, 250, 284, 317, 348, 352–53, 363, 420n11, 432n44, 450nn21–22, 450n26, 453n66; Battle of Rosillo, 234–38; command of Republican Army, 256, 262, 264, 267–70; efforts to obtain Mexican pension, 334–37, 424n14, 423nn16–18; later filibusters, 322–25; recruiting for republicans, 225–27, 423n10, 423n13
Rousseau, Jean Jacques, 39, 47, 77
Royal Academy of Ocaña, 33
Royal Guard, 260
Royal Navy, 80
Royal Seminary of Nobles, 33
Royall, James, 292, 365
Ruiz, José Antonio, 362, 382n34
Ruiz, José Francisco, 4–5, 97, 234–35, 240, 277, 281, 292, 302, 316, 318–20, 333, 340–41, 345, 362, 382n34, 390n39
Ruiz, José Manuel, 234
Runaway Scrape, 304

Sabine River, 44–45, 57, 122, 126, 146, 182, 255, 259, 277, 286, 376, 395n27,

INDEX

396n23; banditti and their suppression, 85–86, 109, 117–18, 139–40; beginning of filibuster, 149, 154, 167, 174–77, 187, 196, 199; border dispute, 28, 83, 138; after Battle of Medina, 316, 321, 324–25, 352
Sáenz, Antonio, 91, 92, 94–97, 362, 402n22
Sáiz, Teodoro, 180
Salado Creek, 236, 249, 424n20
Salazar, Juan, 98–99, 103, 262, 362
Salcedo, Manuel, 41, 43, 48, 55, 96, 97, 108, 122, 170, 177, 179, 251–52, 256, 261–62, 269, 277, 288, 290, 300, 309, 314, 330, 360, 375n4, 375n7, 376n18, 392n13, 425n30, 427n11, 428n15, 438n2; background and journey to Texas, 32–38; besieging rebels, 207, 209–211, 213, 219, 223, 227–30, 417n23; dealings with banditti, 58, 83–84, 150; defeat and execution, 232, 234–35, 238–40, 242, 245–46, 248–49; filibuster invasion, 156, 175, 180–81, 189, 202–203, 205–206, 414n49, 416–17n14; four governors, 70–72; Hidalgo and Casas Revolts, 89, 91–94, 99–106, 114, 390n39
Salcedo, Nemesio de, 27, 33, 41–42, 57–59, 63, 77, 83, 89, 149, 179–80, 197–98, 231, 254, 332, 346, 385n20, 391n42, 395n11; appeal from Texas governors, 70–71, 73
Salinas, Francisco Manuel, 307
Salitre Prairie, 176, 208
Saltillo, 40, 101–102, 121, 299
"Sam Brannon," *See* Zambrano, Juan José Manuel
San Antonio, 5, 33, 34, 38–40, 45–46, 72–73, 84, 86, 101, 103, 121–22, 126, 191, 319, 376n27, 379n52; after Battle of Medina, 302–309, 311–16; filibuster, 149, 174–75, 177–78, 180, 181, 192–94, 202–203, 205–207, 209, 211, 225, 227, 230–236, 238–39, 413n25, 413n30, 422nn34–35, 423n13, 425n30, 438n2, 443–44n79, 446n27; Indian raids, 227, 324; post-revolution, 323–25, 330–33, 337–38, 340–44, 356, 359; rebel activity and sentiment in, 90–100, 111, 156, 241; river, 2, 206–207, 230, 238, 249; smuggling and foreigners, 43–44, 88; under Republicans, 241, 244–45, 247, 249–50, 252, 254, 256, 258–59, 262, 265–69, 271–72, 274, 276–77, 279–81, 285–88, 290–92, 294–96, 300
San Antonio de Valero. *See* Alamo
San Diego, 78
San Felipe de Austin, 337–39, 344
San Fernando Church, 99, 272, 307, 376n27
San Fernando de Béxar. *See* San Antonio
San Jacinto. *See* Battle of San Jacinto
San Luis Potosí, 120, 258
San Marcos de Neve, 39, 331, 377n28, 412n22
San Marcos River, 206, 313
San Pedro Creek, 267, 270
Sánchez, José, 247–48, 362
Santa Anna, Antonio Lopez de, 5, 260, 302, 304, 330, 340, 344–46, 449n9
Santa Fe, 29, 61, 82, 85, 111, 118, 393n23, 405n9; trading expedition, 62–63, 79, 86, 110, 113, 144, 152–53, 173, 197, 447n30
Santa Rosa, Coahuila, 101
Savías, Juan, 2, 180, 212, 222, 233, 255, 282, 360, 362
Scott (Captain), 205, 208, 365
Scott, Winfield, 53, 205
Seay ("Mr. Seay"), 185, 410n48–49
secession, 15, 31, 65, 106, 125, 201
secretary of state: 6–8, 49, 53, 64, 68, 74–75, 106, 108, 124, 128, 134, 136, 142, 151–52, 195, 197–98, 204, 252, 285, 317, 350, 445n19; Louisiana, 329; Texas, 274, 280, 298, 327. *See also*, Adams, John Quincy; Monroe, James; Smith, Robert
secretary of the navy, 74
secretary of war: Republic of Texas, 340, 343; US, 21, 36, 84, 95, 123, 126, 159, 160, 165, 210, 252, 381n30, 382n31
Seguín, Erasmo, 276–77, 286, 318, 341, 394n44, 434nn6–9, 442n64
Seguín, Juan, 2, 276, 319, 341–42, 451n44
Serrano, Miguel, 313, 443n73
Sexton, Samuel, 334, 365, 444nn5–6, 450n28
Shaler, William, 6, 74–78, 126, 256, 316–19, 333, 342, 347–48, 355, 368–69nn14–15, 369n21, 385n1, 386n7, 386n9, 386n19, 402n16, 403n28, 406n27, 412n23, 414n38, 414n49, 414n51, 415–16nn5–6, 418n33, 421n22, 453n1, 455n21; in Cuba, 95, 131, 429n43; efforts to replace Gutiérrez,

253, 257–59, 275–82, 426n36, 434n11; instructions, 8–9, 79–81, 349–50, 397n29, 398n7, 399n20; in Natchitoches, 146–49, 151, 153–54, 157, 160, 163, 165, 167–70, 178–79, 182, 186–88, 190, 192, 195–200, 204, 208–209, 213–14, 223, 233, 236, 241, 244, 252–53, 284–87; in New Orleans, 132–37, 142–43, 273; relation to filibuster, 45, 118, 350, 401n13, 402n27 417n23, 422n1, 430n15, 433n61, 434n8, 434n16, 435n20

Shaumberg (Colonel), 138, 143, 169–70

Shays's Rebellion, 14, 18

Shirley, William, 54

Sibley, Cyrus, 398n6

Sibley, John, 35, 44, 72, 88, 95, 104, 115, 117, 119, 123, 138, 140, 143, 149, 167, 169, 171, 173, 204, 227–28, 233–34, 248, 316, 350, 368n13, 388n31, 390n26, 390n30, 393n33; revolutionary sympathies, 36, 126, 147, 226, 355, 398n6; support for Neutral Ground settlement, 83–84, 87, 109

Sides, Peter, 183, 317, 365

silver, 19, 78, 89, 98, 102–103, 114, 121–22, 135, 163, 179, 181, 217, 243, 256, 262; mines, 15, 22, 109, 189, 352

Skipwith, Fulwar, 67–69, 243, 384n14

slaves, 3, 17–21, 32, 95, 113, 125, 130–31, 144, 157, 160, 197, 225, 233, 242, 262, 264, 320, 335, 348, 353, 355, 379n2, 453nn1–2; in filibuster schemes, 19, 25; runaways to Texas, 37, 56, 183; in Spanish Texas, 46, 98, 193, 347

Slocum, Thomas, 187, 208, 365

Small, Thomas W., 27, 30, 115, 162, 373n51, 374n60, 374n64

Smith, Reuben, 62, 86, 110–11, 144–45, 401n2, 401n7

Smith, Robert, 7, 68, 74–76, 78, 81, 108, 128, 133–34, 195, 349–50

Smith, Thomas Adams, 393n24

Smith, William Stephens, 49–50, 147

Smith T, John, 60–62, 85, 110–14, 116, 118–19, 126, 144, 152–53, 164, 319–21, 324, 332, 338, 349, 393n23–24, 395–96n11, 396n23

smuggling, 41–43, 45, 85–86, 89, 95, 103, 140, 143, 176, 192, 205, 235, 237, 242, 313,

337, 344, 377n37, 377n40, 378n41, 386n9, 388n31, 389n5, 396n12, 402n25, 420n11, 421n28; Quirk, McFarlan and Brenton band, 56–58, 60, 71–73, 78–79, 84, 93, 110, 167, 182, 349, 424n17, 450n31

Snyder, Simon, 218–19, 419n15

Society of the Cincinnati, 51, 183

Sonora, 78

Soto la Marina, 324

South America, 13, 49–50, 62, 77, 249, 260, 336, 354, 377n29, 405n9, 454n17; Argentina, 75; Buenos Aires, 34, 64, 76, 79; Patagonia, 132; Peru, 27, 76, 164, 294; Río de la Plata, 260; Tierra del Fuego, 34; Venezuela, 5, 26, 49, 62, 75, 218, 329, 379n3, 380n7

South Carolina, 22

Spanish government, 12, 19, 29, 37, 107, 109, 179, 198, 242, 311, 318, 346, 384n8; defense of Texas, 70–71, 109; immigration policy, 13, 34, 45, 58, 182, 286, 332, 356; imperial crisis and rebellions, 66–67, 75–76, 133, 135; Napoleonic War, 33–34, 64, 76; trade policy, 17, 40, 62, 187; US hostility towards, 15, 22–24, 28, 34, 72, 144, 232, 326, 339, 353, 357

spies, 24, 31, 41, 44, 102–103, 110, 144, 155, 175, 190, 194, 203, 229, 260, 266, 270, 290, 359, 411n4, 413n30, 414n52

St. Xavier Farjon, Madame Theresa de, 23

State Department. *See* Department of State

Stillwell, William Shaler, 342

Stirling, Alexander, 12, 14, 67

Strait of Magellan, 13, 37

Swan, William, 115, 152, 154

Swartwout, Samuel, 28

Tarín, Juanal Leal de, 21, 306

Tarín, Vicente, 92, 191, 306, 325, 326, 362, 377n37

Tawakoni Indians, 331, 390n30

Taylor, Creed, 345

Taylor, Josiah, 152, 322–323, 345, 365; in Burr Conspiracy, 25–27, 31, 162; in Republican Army, 161, 163, 183, 188, 193, 207, 225, 238–39, 271–72, 290, 294, 298–99, 301, 304; suspicious "death," 115–117, 393n34, 394n39

INDEX 487

teamsters, 192–93, 265, 273
Tejanos, 1, 3–5, 38, 40, 56–59, 356–59, 437n1, 439n22; postwar, 319, 325–26, 331–32, 340–41, 344–45, 354; refugees and exile, 304, 306, 309–10, 312–14, 316, 442n60; in Republican Army, 191, 193, 229, 232, 235, 241–43, 245–47, 250–51, 254, 266–67, 275–76, 281, 283, 287–88, 290–91, 293, 296–98, 361, 367n3, 423n3; as revolutionaries, 10–11, 91–104, 111, 118, 122, 155, 157, 173, 178, 376n25
Tennessee, 16, 24, 37, 60, 65, 72, 105, 123–25, 150, 154, 165, 256, 263, 320, 335–36, 352; Knoxville, 125–26, 157; Nashville, 30, 125, 319–20, 337
tertulias, 131
Texas Essential Knowledge and Skills, 2, 357, 367n4
Toledo, José Álvarez de, 328, 336, 346, 348–50, 404n48, 415n2, 418nn3–4, 419nn15–16, 429n43, 429nn50–51, 436n50, 436nn52–53, 436n60, 436n65, 437n69, 439n10, 439n13, 440n30, 442n69, 453nn66–1; coming to Texas, 215–222, 252–54, 257–59, 275–286, 338, 341, 438n8; later activities, 319–23, 326, 339, 351, 445nn13–16, 446nn22–23, 449n18, 451n38; in Philadelphia and Washington, 129–31, 155, 397–98n44; as Republican commander, 287–92, 294, 296–99, 303, 309–10, 312, 316–18, 361, 437–438n1
Tonkawa Indians, 227, 270
trade, 13, 15–17, 48, 54–55, 75–76, 81, 115, 146, 311, 322, 414n48, 421n28; American, 31, 43, 49, 62–63, 66–67, 78–79, 126, 142, 144, 162, 187, 217, 336, 352–54, 453n4; Indians, 32, 40, 44–45, 110–11, 226, 274, 433n62; Spanish-Texan, 1, 5, 33, 35, 38, 40–41, 43, 47, 57–59, 63, 71, 78–79, 85, 89, 95, 100, 103–104, 118, 145, 156, 181–82, 206, 242, 247, 348, 356. *See also* smuggling
Travieso, Francisco, 92–97, 104, 362
Travieso, Vicente, 277, 315, 318
Travieso, Vicente Alvarez, 38, 92
Travis, William Barret, 2, 4, 344, 452n58
Treaty of Ghent, 317
Trespalacios, José Félix, 327–28, 333, 443n71
Trujillo y Torres, Manuel de, 215
Trinidad de Salcedo, 56, 72–73, 94, 139, 155, 180, 192, 194, 199, 224, 288, 344, 348, 377n28, 409n30; background, 39, 58; connection to smuggling, 59, 110; captured by Republican Army, 200, 208, 213, 412n22; refugees and, 309, 311, 316, 331
Trinity River, 39, 58, 202–203, 205, 227, 286, 309–12, 315, 358, 382n42
tuberculosis, 224, 317, 420n8
Turner, Frederick Jackson, 15, 371n13

US Army, 81–82, 183, 343; connections to filibuster, 25, 109, 115–16, 160, 237, 282, 294, 323, 329, 384n14, 421n25; efforts to stop filibuster, 150–152, 164–67, 184–85; policing the neutral ground, 83–87, 137–38
US House of Representatives, 105, 126
US Military Academy, 53, 55, 82, 159, 205, 210, 235, 254, 342, 381n21–4, 386–87n22, 401n2
US Senate, 7, 65, 125, 129
US Supreme Court, 129
Ugalde, Juan de, 86
Ursuline Convent of New Orleans, 23

Valparaiso, Chile, 78
Vanegas, Francisco, 261
Veracruz, 7–9, 33, 40, 95, 122, 134, 137, 144, 198, 336, 358, 391n3; regiment of, 260, 265, 288, 298
Veramendi, Juan Martín, 97, 238–39, 277, 318, 322, 333, 341, 362, 394n44
Viana, Francisco, 41–42, 58
viceroy of New Spain, 38, 59, 91, 181, 230, 260–262, 266, 357, 375n5
Villa de Croix, 92
Villars, John, 212, 317, 365, 415n5, 416n6, 416n13, 433n51, 442n68, 444n6
Virgin of Guadalupe, 193–94, 200
Virginia: Fauquier County, 13; Washington County, 225, 256
volunteer, 5, 25, 49–50, 126, 151–153, 188–189, 224, 334, 341–343; American, 111, 181–184, 192–193, 234, 240–244, 256, 286–294, 347, 354–357; list of, 363–365

Walker, Juan Pedro, 57, 382n37
Walker, W. W., 325–26, 365
War of 1812, 3, 75, 171, 219, 241, 257, 317, 322–23, 348, 368n10, 409n38, 445n19
War of Independence. *See* American Revolution
War of Spanish Independence, 64
War of the Pyrenees, 260
Warren, Harris Gaylord, 6–9, 368n11–12, 368n14, 369nn15–16, 399n20
Washington, D.C., 17, 26, 30, 74, 81–82, 105, 131, 135, 137, 141, 143, 148, 151, 153–54, 162–64, 166–67, 170, 172, 186, 189, 197–98, 243, 285, 317–19, 336, 348–49, 369n14, 387n24, 397nn28–29, 404n48, 428n24; Gutiérrez and Toledo in, 123–26, 128–29
Washington, George, 14, 16–17, 24, 28, 51–52
Washington, Mississippi, 21, 82, 405n6; Cantonment, 82, 387n23
Washington-on-the-Brazos, 340
Washita, 106
Watkins, John, 18, 31
Wells of Baján, 102, 121, 248
West, John K., 351, 446n23
West Florida. *See* Florida
West Point. *See* US Military Academy
westerners; 31, 69, 106–107, 128, 151, 263, 322, 326, 348, 349, 351–55, 373n58, 383n50; background, 9–10, 13–22; reception of Gutiérrez, 124–26, 157; revolutionary and filibuster sentiment, 33, 36, 49, 65–66, 72, 83, 106, 113–14, 130–131, 173; support of Texas filibuster, 143, 145
Whiskey Rebellion, 14, 18, 169

White Hall Plantation, 65
Wichita Indians, 35, 96, 227, 390n30
Wilkinson, James (Jr.), 269, 292, 301, 304, 365, 410n49, 430n15, 439n25
Wilkinson, James (Sr.), 37, 55, 60, 66, 81–83, 107, 119, 139, 145, 151, 157, 159, 163, 197, 249, 374nn59–62, 374n65, 374nn69–71, 378n41, 387n23, 403n31, 404n48, 404n2, 430n15, 439n25, 447n39; background and Spanish service, 16–18, 43; Burr Conspiracy, 21–22, 23, 26, 28–31, 61–62, 65, 110, 115–17, 393n24, 393n34, 405n9, 405n12; Gutiérrez-Magee Expedition, 164–66, 171, 184–86, 190, 214, 263, 277, 410nn45–49
Wilkinson, Joseph, 279–81, 283, 301, 316, 365, 410, 430n15, 435n20, 439–40n25
Williams, Robert, 21
Winchester, James, 125
Winthuisen, Tomás Felipe de, 378n45
Wirt, William, 352
Wollstonecraft, Charles, 83–85, 87, 109, 137–38, 150–52, 156, 163, 167, 185, 258, 387nn23–29, 393n33, 402n27
wool, 174, 179, 187, 292, 411n5
Workman, James, 19, 24–28, 30–31, 116, 371–72n28, 372n35, 373nn48–54, 373n57

Zambrano, José Darío, 330
Zambrano, Juan José Manuel, 111, 122, 137, 140, 192, 234–35, 240, 251, 276, 360, 390n33, 390n39, 407n6; capture of, 114–15, 117–18, 164; coup, 96–103, 241, 340, 357; escape to Coahuila, 246; filibuster beginning, 173–180, 187; 296–98, 300, 315, 408n11, 408n18; return with Arredondo, 265